84   6995
                                      65B

The Ethics of Romanticism

Publication of this work has been supported in part by a grant from the Abraham and Rebecca Stein Faculty Publications Fund of New York University, Department of English.

The Ethics of Romanticism

LAURENCE S. LOCKRIDGE

Department of English, New York University

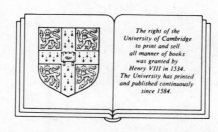

The right of the
University of Cambridge
to print and sell
all manner of books
was granted by
Henry VIII in 1534.
The University has printed
and published continuously
since 1584.

CAMBRIDGE UNIVERSITY PRESS

Cambridge

New York   Port Chester

Melbourne   Sydney

Published by the Press Syndicate of the University of Cambridge
The Pitt Building, Trumpington Street, Cambridge CB2 1RP
40 West 20th Street, New York, NY 10011, USA
10 Stamford Road, Oakleigh, Melbourne 3166, Australia

© Cambridge University Press 1989

First published 1989

Printed in Great Britain by the
University Press, Cambridge

British Library cataloguing in publication data
Lockridge, Laurence S.
The ethics of Romanticism.
1. English literature, 1745–1837.
Romanticism – Critical studies
I. Title
820.9'145

Library of Congress cataloguing in publication data
Lockridge, Laurence S.
The ethics of romanticism / Laurence S. Lockridge.
p.   cm.
Bibliography.
Includes index.
ISBN 0–521–35256–8
1. Romanticism.   2. Ethics.   I. Title.
PN603.L63   1989
809'.9145–dc19   88–31180   CIP

ISBN 0 521 35256 8

to my mother
VERNICE LOCKRIDGE NOYES

Contents

Acknowledgments

In one of those rare instances when duty merges wholly with inclination, I would like to thank the many people who have assisted in the writing of this book.

From its inception, Susan Fox has given it a good measure of her energy and intellect, reading and re-reading the manuscript with a warm commitment to its aims. For a critique that generously blended scrutiny with reassurance, I thank Marilyn Gaull. Aileen Ward and Paul Magnuson, colleagues and fellow Romanticists, have been responsive well beyond the call of collegiality.

Several distinguished scholars, critics, and writers have been helpful in small ways and large: M. H. Abrams, J. Robert Barth, Walter Jackson Bate, Frederick L. Beaty, John Beer, Charles Bell, Harold Bloom, Jerome Hamilton Buckley, Walter Crawford, Donald Davie, Anthony Dawson, Erika Duncan, Sheila Emerson, Norman Fruman, Christine Gallant, Frederick Garber, Michael Goldman, Jean Hagstrum, Anthony J. Harding, Richard Haven, John Holloway, Carren Kaston, William Keach, John Kleinig, Kenneth Lewes, Thomas McFarland, Martin Mueller, David Perkins, Donald Reiman, Mark Roberts, Max Schultz, Richard Scowcroft, Stuart Sperry, Anya Taylor, George Thompson, Carl Woodring, Jonathan Wordsworth, and Laurence Wylie.

Many colleagues at New York University have read portions of this book or have helped in other ways: Jess Bessinger, William Buckler, Joseph Byrnes, Una Chaudhuri, Christopher Collins, Roger Deakins, Denis Donoghue, Carol Flynn, Ernest Gilman, Dustin Griffin, Richard Harrier, Josephine Hendin, David Hoover, Daniel Javitch, Frederick Karl, Galway Kinnell, John Kuehl, Ilse Lind, Anthony Low, Perry Meisel, Roger Oliver, Robert Raymo, M. L. Rosenthal, Philip Schultz, Kenneth Silverman, Jeffrey Spear, and Donald Stone. James Tuttleton and John Maynard, who have served as Chairs of the Department of

English during the writing of this book, have been consistently supportive. Mary Tedeschi, Secretary to the Graduate Program in English, has been as heroic in her patience as sane in her wit.

I would like to thank Kathleen Coburn, H. J. Jackson, J. R. de J. Jackson, and Bart Winer, authorities in Coleridge studies, for their expert assistance with some previously unpublished Coleridge texts.

Several graduate students at New York University, all of them by now experienced teachers and critics, have helped me formulate ideas and have commented on this study at various stages: Charles De Paolo, Doucet Fischer, Kathleen Fowler, Thomas Goldpaugh, Panayotis Kayalis, Lilach Lachman, and Phyllis Frus McCord. I profited from colloquies with the late Peter Snyder.

For a miscellany of remembered acts of kindness and of love, I thank my siblings Ernest Lockridge, Jeanne Lockridge, and Ross Lockridge; also Tulle Hazelrigg, Kay Lockridge, Ann Murray, Laurel Richardson, Cynthia Ross, Stephanie Tevonian, Valerie Wise, and the late Clona Nicholson. I regret that Russell Noyes, inspiration to so many in Romantics studies, did not live to see publication of this book.

For his editorial expertise, I am grateful to Andrew Brown of Cambridge University Press; also to Kevin Taylor. For copy-editing a manuscript that none would wish longer, I thank Rosemary Morris. I have profited from intelligent commentary by Press readers.

I am grateful to the National Endowment for the Humanities and to the John Simon Guggenheim Memorial Foundation for financial support; the latter funded a study of ethics and modern criticism, the first fruits of which appear in Chapters 1 and 10.

I would acknowledge the cooperation and assistance of trustees and librarians at the Henry W. and Albert A. Berg Collection of the New York Public Library, the Bobst Library and the Fales Library of New York University, the British Library, the Henry E. Huntington Library, the Houghton and Widener Libraries of Harvard University, the Lilly Library of Indiana University, and the Victoria University Library.

For permission to quote from as yet unpublished Coleridge manuscripts and from Volume IV of the Coleridge *Notebooks*, I thank Princeton University Press.

Marcia Scanlon, sculptor and painter, has lived with this book as I have. Her uncommon understanding of the life of writing and her generous spirit have guided, supported, and cheered me to the end.

Editions and abbreviations

William Blake

PWB   *The Poetry and Prose of William Blake*, rev. edn. Edited by David V. Erdman. Berkeley: University of California Press, 1981. All texts, including letters, cited from this edition.

AL   "Annotations to Lavater"

BU   *The Book of Urizen*

DC   *A Descriptive Catalogue of Pictures, Poetical and Historical Inventions*

EP   *Europe a Prophecy*

FZ   *The Four Zoas: The Torments of Love & Jealousy in the Death and Judgement of Albion the Ancient Man*

J   *Jerusalem: The Emanation of the Giant Albion*

M   *Milton: A Poem in Two Books*

MHH   *The Marriage of Heaven and Hell*

VDA   *Visions of the Daughters of Albion*

VLJ   *A Vision of the Last Judgment*

Lord Byron

The Works of Lord Byron: Poetry. Edited by Ernest Hartley Coleridge. 7 vols. London: John Murray, 1898–1904. Hereafter, *Works*.

The Complete Poetical Works. Edited by Jerome J. McGann. Oxford: Clarendon Press, 1980– .

LJ   *Byron's Letters and Journals*. Edited by Leslie A. Marchand. 11 vols. Cambridge, Mass.: Harvard University Press, 1973–81.

xi

LJP	*The Works of Lord Byron: Letters and Journals*. Edited by Rowland E. Prothero. 6 vols. London: John Murray, 1898–1901.
CN	*Cain: A Mystery*, vol. V in *Works*.
CH	*Childe Harold's Pilgrimage*, vol. II in *Works*.
DJ	*Don Juan*, vol. VI in *Works*.
MF	*Manfred: A Dramatic Poem*, vol. IV in *Works*.

Samuel Taylor Coleridge

The Collected Works of Samuel Taylor Coleridge. Kathleen Coburn, General Editor. Bollingen Series 75. Princeton: Princeton University Press, 1969– . Hereafter *The Collected Coleridge*.

The Complete Poetical Works of Samuel Taylor Coleridge. Edited by Ernest Hartley Coleridge. 2 vols. Oxford: Clarendon Press, 1912.

AR	*Aids to Reflection*. London: Taylor and Hessey, 1825.
BL	*Biographia Literaria*. Edited by James Engell and W. Jackson Bate, 1983. Vol. VII in *The Collected Coleridge*.
CL	*Collected Letters of Samuel Taylor Coleridge*. Edited by Earl Leslie Griggs. 6 vols. Oxford: Clarendon Press, 1956–71.

On the Constitution of the Church and State. Edited by John Colmer, 1976. Vol. X in *The Collected Coleridge*.

EOT	*Essays on His Times in The Morning Post and The Courier*. Edited by David Erdman. 3 vols., 1978. Vol. III in *The Collected Coleridge*.
F	*The Friend*. Edited by Barbara E. Rooke. 2 vols., 1969. Vol. II in *The Collected Coleridge*.
IS	*Inquiring Spirit*. Edited by Kathleen Coburn. London: Routledge & Kegan Paul, 1951.

Lectures 1795: On Politics and Religion. Edited by Lewis Patton and Peter Mann, 1971. Vol. I in *The Collected Coleridge*.

M	*Marginalia*. Edited by George Whalley. 2 vols., 1980– . Vol. XII in *The Collected Coleridge*.
N	*The Notebooks of Samuel Taylor Coleridge*. Edited by Kathleen Coburn. Bollingen Series 50. 4 vols. New York: Pantheon, 1957, 1961; Princeton: Princeton University Press, 1973– .
NB	Unpublished Notebooks. Berg Collection, British Library, Huntington Library, Victoria University Library.

OM   Opus Maximum MS. 3 vols. Victoria University Library, Toronto.

PL   *The Philosophical Lectures of Samuel Taylor Coleridge.* Edited by Kathleen Coburn. London: Pilot Press, 1949.

SM   *The Statesman's Manual,* in *Lay Sermons.* Edited by R. J. White, 1972. Vol. VI in *The Collected Coleridge.*

TT   *Table Talk.* Edited by Henry Nelson Coleridge. Vol. VI in *The Complete Works of Samuel Taylor Coleridge.* Edited by W. G. T. Shedd. 7 vols. New York: Harper, 1853.

Thomas De Quincey

The Works of Thomas De Quincey. Edited by David Masson. 14 vols. Edinburgh: Adam and Charles Black, 1890. Hereafter *Works.*

A   *Autobiography,* vols. I, II in *Works.*

CEO   *Confessions of an English Opium-eater* (1856 version), vol. III in *Works.*

EM   *The English Mail Coach,* vol. XIII in *Works.*

SP   *Suspiria de Profundis.* Edited by Aileen Ward, in *Confessions of an English Opium-eater and Other Writings.* New York: New American Library, 1966.

William Hazlitt

The Complete Works of William Hazlitt. 21 vols. Edited by P. P. Howe. London: J. M. Dent. Cited by volume and page numbers.

Essay   *An Essay on the Principles of Human Action.* 1805; rpt., Gainesville, Florida: Scholars' Facsimiles & Reprints, 1969.

LWH   *The Letters of William Hazlitt.* Edited by Herschel Sikes, assisted by Willard Bonner and Gerald Lahey. New York: New York University Press, 1978.

LA   *Liber Amoris: Or, The New Pygmalion.* Edited by Gerald Lahey. New York: New York University Press, 1980.

John Keats

The Poems of John Keats. Edited by Jack Stillinger. Cambridge, Mass.: Harvard University Press, 1978.

ED	*Endymion*
FH	*The Fall of Hyperion: A Dream*
H	*Hyperion*
	The Keats Circle: Letters and Papers, 1816–1878, 2 vols., rev. edn. Edited by Hyder Rollins. Cambridge, Mass.: Harvard University Press, 1965.
L	*The Letters of John Keats.* Edited by Hyder Rollins. 2 vols. Cambridge, Mass.: Harvard University Press, 1958.

Percy Bysshe Shelley

SPP	*Shelley's Poetry and Prose.* Edited by Donald E. Reiman and Sharon Powers. New York: W. W. Norton, 1977.
SPR	*Shelley's Prose.* Edited by David Lee Clark. Albuquerque: University of New Mexico Press, 1954, rev. edn. 1966.
	The Complete Works of Percy Bysshe Shelley. Edited by Neville Rogers. Oxford: Clarendon Press, 1972– .
C	*The Cenci*, in *SPP*.
DP	*A Defence of Poetry*, in *SPP*.
E	*Epipsychidion*, in *SPP*.
JM	*Julian and Maddalo*, in *SPP*.
LPS	*The Letters of Percy Bysshe Shelley.* Edited by Frederick L. Jones. 2 vols. Oxford: Clarendon Press, 1964.
PU	*Prometheus Unbound*, in *SPP*.
PVR	*A Philosophical View of Reform*, in *SPR*.
SM	"Speculations on Morals," in *SPR* as *Treatise on Morals*.
TL	*The Triumph of Life*, in *SPP*.

William Wordsworth

	The Poetical Works of William Wordsworth, 2nd edn. Edited by Ernest de Selincourt. 5 vols. Oxford: Clarendon Press, 1952–9.
B	*The Borderers.* Edited by Robert Osborn. Ithaca: Cornell University Press, 1982.
EX	*The Excursion*, vol. V in *Works*.
HG	*Home at Grasmere.* Edited by Beth Darlington. Ithaca: Cornell University Press, 1977.

LWD   *The Letters of William and Dorothy Wordsworth*. Edited by Ernest de Selincourt; 2nd edn. rev. Chester Shaver, Mary Moorman, and Alan Hill. Oxford: Clarendon Press, 1967– .

P   *The Prelude: or, Growth of a Poet's Mind*. Text of 1805. Edited by Ernest de Selincourt. London: Oxford University Press, 1933, rev. edn. 1960.

PD   *The Pedlar*. Edited by James Butler. Ithaca: Cornell University Press, 1979.

PLB   Preface to *Lyrical Ballads* (1800), in *PRW*, vol. I.

PRW   *The Prose Works of William Wordsworth*. Edited by W. J. B. Owen and Jane Worthington Smyser. 3 vols. Oxford: Clarendon Press, 1974.

RC   *The Ruined Cottage*. Edited by James Butler. Ithaca: Cornell University Press, 1979.

       The Salisbury Plain Poems. Edited by Stephen Gill. Ithaca: Cornell University Press, 1975.

TPP   *The Prelude, 1798–1799*. (The Two-Part *Prelude*.) Edited by Stephen Parrish. Ithaca: Cornell University Press, 1977.

Introduction

The British Romantics are rarely accused of immoderate virtue. From their day to ours, the attention they have commanded has been tinged with fascinated disapproval. Coleridge's and De Quincey's opium-eating and intellectual thefts, Byron's sexual plasticity and Hazlitt's crazed courtship of his landlord's daughter, and Shelley's implication in scandal and death, come to mind so readily as to inform our larger concepts of each, despite our abstention from easy and irrelevant censure. Even the better behaved among them invite the kind of gossip we customarily relegate to the borders of literary criticism. Wordsworth's love affair with Annette Vallon and attachment to his sister Dorothy subtly sexualize the poetry in our minds. We may have been disappointed to learn, in recently discovered correspondence, that passion for his wife exceeded passion for his sister. Biographers debate which one Keats was more likely to have had – syphilis or gonorrhea – reminding us in a literal pathogenetic way of the painful fusion of disease and desire in his art. This leaves only Blake – in his poetry the most vigorous immoralist, and regarded by some of his contemporaries as mad and seditious – leading a virtuous life of modest means, marital fidelity, and hard work.

No other group of authors in British literature has been so subjected to moral adjudication. From their contemporaries in the reviews to the Victorians to the New Humanists and beyond, their critics have invoked moral criteria in judging them delinquent or exemplary, shallow or profound. I believe this pattern is in good measure the result of the Romantics' own strenuous engagement with the ethical. For better or worse, they have perennially put their readership in mind of such questions through what Tolstoy would term a process of infection.

Matthew Arnold's judgment that the Romantics "did not know enough" is well known, but he nonetheless ranks Wordsworth highest

1

in the language since Shakespeare and Milton in offering us a "criticism of life" and the means of dealing with the puzzle of "how to live." Great literature is the application of "moral ideas" to life, writes Arnold, and a "poetry of revolt against moral ideas is a poetry of revolt against *life*; a poetry of indifference towards moral ideas is a poetry of indifference toward *life*."[1] I will follow the Arnoldian attention to moral ideas – if with different terms and methods – and will attempt to change whatever impression we may retain that Romantic authors except for Wordsworth are lacking in knowledge commensurate with the concerns of human action and moral value they address. They are somewhat wiser than Arnold imagines. Their very failures in wisdom, often self-announced, occasion in us a diagnostic seeking that seems textually legislated. The Romantics confirm the common reader's intuition, as well as Aristotle's and Arnold's, that human action and moral value are stubbornly linked to the grounds of literary art – an intuition routinely regarded as ingenuous in modern criticism.

An occupational hazard of working with Coleridge is that he provides a "path of transit" to other authors, disciplines, or specialized topics. Someone inducted into Coleridge studies by the Ancient Mariner may discover the morrow morn that he or she is investigating the history of scrofula. While working with Coleridge's moral thought, I found that other British Romantics had, like Coleridge in his Opus Maximum manuscript, attempted formal essays on ethics.[2] These writers are often overtly propositional in matters ethical, writing treatises when they are not advising us, like the Mariner, to love all things great and small. But their concern with moral ideas more pervasively informs their writings. In this interdisciplinary and comparative reading of the eight major British Romantic authors, I evaluate the earnest disquisitions but seek as well an underlying moral orientation in poems, plays, familiar essays, autobiographical and other writings. And I explore how thematic concerns relate to the ethics of composition, concepts of language, the sense of audience, and the life of writing.

In the wake of deconstructive unravelments, for a critic to set about rehumanizing the Romantics with a sober display of what is affirmative about them would be as futile as it is unnecessary. They themselves lament the vulnerability of value to the subversions of skepticism, nihilism, conventionalism, and subjectivism. They attack

---

[1] "The Function of Criticism at the Present Time," *Essays in Criticism*, First Series, III (New York: AMS Press, 1970), 7; "Wordsworth," *Essays in Criticism*, Second Series, IV (New York: AMS Press, 1970), 105–6.

[2] See my *Coleridge the Moralist* (Ithaca, N. Y.: Cornell University Press, 1977).

their own glittering structures so pointedly that they need few lessons in demolition from modern critics. But I do find in them an ethical play of mind more directed to articulation of values than to their subversion. The textual evidence for this is presented throughout. It is not a matter of seeing whether affirmations outweigh denials, rather of seeing how the Romantics articulate values in relation to their potential negation, and how their will to value is the more intense for it. Belief in radical evil desentimentalizes humanism in Coleridge instead of arraigning it in Calvinist denial. Blake emerges as a larger mind than the flower-child reading of him because the values he urges are attained only by arduous mental fight, and not by a laid-back apprenticeship in virtue. For both, the will to value is expressed through embattled dialectic.

In Part One of this book I describe the dominant ethical tendency of Romanticism relative to other post-Renaissance views. I begin by sketching a set of related observations, mostly in the affirmative mode, that forms a regulative structure against which patterns of departure in individual authors can be gauged. This regulative structure I term "Romantic humanism," and I find it most fully developed in Blake, Coleridge, and Shelley. All eight authors are to varying degrees revisionists of it, but it persists, at least implicitly, as the nucleus around which the Romantics engage a play of perspectives on ethical questions. This larger play of perspectives I call "the ethics of Romanticism." It owes much to the Romantics' awareness of European moral traditions, Continental as well as British. Not an exercise in intellectual background, Part One lays out the argument of the study as a whole by placing the British Romantics within European intellectual history. It closes with a discussion of the ethics of Romanticism in light of modern metaethics and ethical terms. Contextualizing the British Romantics within the broader discourse of European philosophy would facilitate the extension of most of my conclusions to other Romantic literatures, German, French, and American, in which as in Great Britain the ethical would emerge, I believe, as a principle of continuity amidst the many differences in politics, religion, and literary practice.

What I call a "will to value" is the dominant ethical tendency in Romantic writers; it is their response to a moment in history when concepts of value are seen to be reduced or denuded. It has notable affinities with what is termed "ideal utilitarianism," in contrast to "hedonistic utilitarianism." The Romantic will to value coordinates awkwardly with concepts of action, however. The question of what is to be done – registered in, for instance, their tendency to avoid resolute narration and representations of completed action on their own terms

– problematizes language, structure, and purpose in literary art. Far from signalling literary failure, this questioning the grounds of action, combined with an intense will to value, is a distinguishing mark of Romantic literature, constitutive of literary value in its own way.

In Part Two I consider three authors – Blake, Wordsworth, and De Quincey – by means of whom we can delineate within Romanticism a scale of power that descends from strong to weak humanism. Whatever the anguished and violent nature of human mind in its sub-Edenic condition, Blake like Coleridge locates power more in the human agent than in scene and circumstance. All human acts as acts are lovely, the imagination can obliterate the material world, and we can drive our carts over the bones of the dead – if only we aspire beyond mere wishing to willing. Freedom for Blake comes when human mind achieves the self-empowerment that frees itself from circumstance, the past, and its own "mind-forg'd manacles." He castigates Wordsworth for overvaluing nature and memory. If Blake is the poet of freedom and empowerment, Wordsworth is the poet of necessity and tragic limitation. He inverts a Blakean–Coleridgean ratio by locating power more in scene and circumstance than in the moral agent – to use the terminology of Kenneth Burke.[3] Moving down the scale of power, we come to De Quincey, who transforms Wordsworth's tragic vision into absurdism. Where Wordsworth sees a necessity at the heart of things, De Quincey sees the world as improvidentially contingent.

In all three authors, however, we find a preoccupation with how the self in its isolation can still seek values or objects of veneration at a moment when collective ascriptions of value have weakened. And we find the related problem of coordinating value with act. In Blake there is a conflict between the qualitative character of the acts he urges upon us and the values we should embody in the perfected human form; in Wordsworth a retreat from the imperatives of action when these brutalize consciousness; and in De Quincey an overwhelming sense that the unpredictable relationship of act and consequence invalidates in advance our best-intentioned gestures.

In Part Three I turn to the "second generation" of Romantic poets and to Hazlitt, who offer correctives to the first generation, and who respond persistently to what Charles Lamb and Wallace Stevens both term "the pressure of reality." Shelley addresses key problems in Blake and Coleridge – the discontinuity between "right" and "good" in Blake and the discontinuity between ethics and politics in the later

---

[3] *A Grammar of Motives* (1945; rpt. Cleveland: World Publishing, 1962), pp. xvii–xxv, 3–20.

Coleridge. Reversing the drift toward psychology and the self, he directs ethical imperatives outward toward social and political reform and calls for a "poetry of life." Unlike Wordsworth and De Quincey, he affirms the possibility of altering human and natural circumstances through will and imagination, provided the historical moment does not exert too great a drag. Not given to Shelley's mode of prophetic urging but equally concerned with the perils of self-reflexive idealism, Hazlitt, Keats, and Byron bring to this discussion various perspectives of moral realism. In their meditations on time, history, circumstance, and passion, they place limits on the dialectical ethics of Blake, Coleridge, and Shelley. This is not to say that the latter have consistently evaded reality or overwhelmed it with suspect private vision. But Hazlitt, Byron, and Keats pull back from a legislative poetics and are more emphatic about how visionary desire, for the sake of sanity, must make its accommodation with the light of common day.

Hazlitt is a dissenter who expresses a moral and political indignation similar to Shelley's, and who, like the poets of the second generation, is angry at the political "apostasy" of Coleridge, Wordsworth, and Southey – radicals in their youth, Tories in their dubious maturity. But entertaining faint hopes for historical progress and individual redemption, Hazlitt is not much of a reformer. And ironically he finds in sympathetic imagination – which he, Shelley, Keats, and others place near the center of the moral life – a potentially depraved power, the source of error, lust, and horror. Sanity is recovered when one can calmly say that what is, is – a view reluctantly voiced by Byron also.

The affinity between Byron and Keats is greater than usually observed: their skepticism, their questioning of dialectical progression, their fits of exuberance and *tedium vitae*, and their doubts as to whether the life of writing is the life of action. Keats brings together Wordsworth's tragic vision and Hazlitt's concern with identity in his version of what becomes the "self-realizationism" of the later nineteenth century (he calls it "Soul-making"). Dialectic is purged of the cheat of transcendence as Keats works towards an ethics of immanence. Byron, who derides the "Lakers" and any idolatry of the imagination, is too intimately linked with the Romantics to distance himself wholly. In his call for an "ethical poetry," he answers to Shelley's call for a "poetry of life" (a phrase he uses also), as Shelley was aware when he pronounced *Don Juan* a masterpiece. Byron's heroes and narrators do not quietly acquiesce in the reality principle. Byron bequeaths to the later nineteenth century much of its notion of the Romantic will; his heroes challenge the titans of history, whole continents, even the cosmos. He has his own ethics of composition and his own expansive sense of value, which belie the notion that he is a nihilist. His relationship with the visionary company is more dialogic than dismissive, and it is fitting that with the clearing sanity of *Don Juan* he should have the last word.

This book employs many concepts and some terminology of ethics, classical and modern, that some students of literature may find indigestible. Such a term as "universal act utilitarianism" may seem to have taken us far afield of the author of *The Cenci*. Students of ethics know that ethical terminology cannot be dismissed as "labeling" in their own discipline; it is an interpretive agency without which ethical discussion makes little progress in large issues or small. The praxis of a poet will not tidily conform, let us hope, to the precise definitions of the ethicist. But the literary critic aware of a broad range of ethical terms and concepts can discern and make sense of this very untidiness, which often has functional implications. Blake's conflict between the right and the good, Hazlitt's uncertainty as to whether passion *ought* to be or *is* the "chief ingredient in moral truth," Shelley's unannounced shift from value monism to value pluralism, Coleridge's ambivalence with regard to a deontological ethics – all have deep implications for our total reading of them. Moral philosophy is only ancillary to the moral interpretation of literature – and much of what I say about the Romantics is only indirectly indebted to it – but it has been under-utilized in modern criticism.

I have considered textual evidence of all kinds, whether literary texts or prose disquisitions or letters. My bias is literary: a poem or play gives more compelling evidence of significant moral viewpoint or sensibility than does a prose disquisition. *The Cenci* takes precedence over Shelley's "Speculations on Morals." The same brain originated both texts, however, and a non-literary text can gloss a literary in a variety of ways – corroborating a value structure, suggesting a moral intentionality, making explicit what may be only implicit in the literary text. In the case of these two Shelley texts, the play provides a format in which his own ethical preconceptions can be tested, revised, or even countermanded.

I situate these writers within ethical discussion of their time and do not mediate them with any single modern critical lens, whether Nietzschean, Marxist, Freudian, Wittgensteinian, or Derridean. Nor do I think they are in need of a wealth of modern analogues to lend them intellectual respectability and keep our attention. Wordsworth does not strictly need Heidegger any more than Keats needs Phillipa Foot. As much as possible I let their own terms prevail while I make linkages among disparate texts and seek structures that go some distance in announcing themselves. Jerome J. McGann has warned against explaining Romanticism in terms of its own ideology, arguing that a more compelling investigation requires the critical distance found, for instance, in Heine and Marx.[4] I cannot rehearse the historicist debate here but would simply state my own methodological commitments. An important step in historical understanding is to become familiar with the interpretive structures that obtained in a particular period – to know what a people or group understood by their own discourse, how they regarded their institutions, how they conceived of themselves as speakers and writers. As Coleridge says, we should attempt to understand someone else's understanding; and where McGann would use Heine, I use Coleridge as someone of the period who attempts to speak for as well as to it. But one can only approximate to such understanding, and for the sake of it one cannot and should not remain entirely within the terms and structures of an episode in intellectual and cultural history close to two centuries past. One *can* not because, as Heidegger and Gadamer remind us, we will always to some degree interpret through our own prejudicial horizon, our own moment in history, and our own value judgments. My readings may be partially skewed, for instance, by modern liberal humanism, however much I attempt also to be critical of it. One *should* not because objectivity does require a distancing and contextualizing – the invoking of some perspective not wholly contained in the matter of observation.

But instead of a strongly willed single grammar of interpretation such as one finds in Freud or Marx or Wittgenstein, I deliberately employ a weak one: the terms of modern moral philosophy that attempt to provide in "weak" neutrality a grammar of the entire range of possible ethical positions. They are tools that would ideally facilitate a neutral, objective discovery procedure. One can assume that they are themselves not value free, and that they will in time prove to have been partially time-bound, prejudicial, and strong – symptomatic perhaps of academic power structures within the field of twentieth-century moral philosophy. It becomes a matter of degree, therefore, but I think it probable that the set of descriptive terms I employ is less prejudicial than a system of interpretation with its own built-in ethical commitments would be. With a subject like mine, an evidentiary standard of evaluation is fitting; minimally, this means finding and citing the texts where the Romantics say what I say they say. With writers as complex as Blake, Coleridge, and Shelley, the critic's most humane *modus*

[4] *The Romantic Ideology: A Critical Investigation* (Chicago: University of Chicago Press, 1983).

operandi with respect to the reader is to attempt to de-problematize them – sorting them out as much as possible on their own ground – and to think twice before compounding their esoterism with his own. We are at that moment in the profession of letters when a slight relaxation of critical will might prove gainful.

The Romantics have left a fair amount of their own willful theoretical discourse in the field of ethics. They write "metaethical" commentary that goes beyond normative recommendation to questions concerning the nature and justification of moral statements and the meaning of moral terms. There has recently been a shift in moral philosophy back to the more practical issues of normative ethics, but twentieth-century moral philosophy has been predominantly metaethical, much to the exasperation of undergraduates entering ethics courses in hope of finding a creditable path through life. The Romantics indulge metaethical talk for its possible elucidation of normative wisdom. Their practical bent is clear in Coleridge's remark that "Ethics are not Morals – any more than the Science of Geometry is the Art of Carpentry or Architecture. We make maps by strait lines, and celestial observations, determining distances as the Crow would fly; but we must travel by Roads" (NB 49, f. 36ᵛ).

Normative moral topics fall under two traditional headings – matters of obligation and matters of value. The first includes such questions as what acts are right or wrong? what is one's duty and how does one know it? what principles or maxims should one follow? should one shoot an albatross, abscond from Manchester Grammar School, sleep with one's half sister, make love to a coy woman by means of a proxy, or bring down the state? The second includes such questions as what things are morally good or bad? what is the nature of happiness? what kind of character traits or virtues and what kind of self should one develop? Is it better to be Coleridge dissatisfied than Robert Southey satisfied?

The first category pertains largely to action or doing; the second to states of consciousness and of being. Though the two categories are often closely related – benevolence can be both a moral principle and a virtue – they are distinguishable. Moral philosophers earlier in this century struggled over whether "right" can be derived from "good," or vice versa. Teleologists believe those actions are right that are directed toward or actually result in good, whether good be conceived as moral values of justice, the good will, and various virtues or as non-moral values of culture, health, and physical pleasure. They contrast with deontologists, who believe that certain acts are intrinsically right, or at least right with regard to some factors other than consequences.

Frequently I use the phrase "the ethical dimension of literature" to signify the plane of organization of all that pertains to obligation and value. Its axes cut through and link the textually represented world of plot, character, thought, and image, the authorial act of bringing the text into being, and the relatedness of the text to a readership. It embraces rather a lot, but this is my point. It is very difficult for the writer of poems, plays, and novels *not* to impinge on moral categories, *not* to reveal a moral orientation. The ethical includes an enormous range of literary phenomena, and we are the poorer if we de-emphasize it or take it for granted. The pervasiveness of the ethical dimension will be demonstrated if, as I believe, my study could serve in passing as an advanced introduction to each of the eight writers discussed at length. This focus takes us to their dominant concerns and provides an ordering principle for their work as a whole.

Instead of the "is" of naturalistic observation and description, the ethical dimension of literature concerns the "ought": what ought to be done, what ought to be valued? I will argue throughout and in closing that it provides internal resistance to a reduction of the literary text to purely textual status. It makes its own reality claims on us, transcending textual self-reference by dint of its powers of reference and of bearing.

There has been a tendency in modern criticism, only recently changing, to overlook the ethical dimension, demote it to manifest content or theme best regarded as a displacement of "real" compositional motives, reduce it to single dynamics such as "desire" or "pleasure," tie it to a moribund humanism, or outflank it by the presumed larger concepts of sociology, politics, and religion. But an interest in human action and moral value has characterized critical theory and practical criticism from Plato and Aristotle to the earlier decades of this century. The ethical should remain a privileged issue in modern criticism as well. In noting its pervasiveness and in urging its legitimacy as ironically a new direction for critics and theorists, I would help redress what seems to many the by turns portentous and trivial ways of modern criticism. To take another look at the ethical dimension will not return us to schools of naive mimesis or naive pragmatics. It remains pertinent even to those advanced critical schools that treat it as if it were neither here nor there.[5]

[5] Among the many introductions to the discipline of ethics, I recommend William K. Frankena, *Ethics* (Englewood Cliffs, N. J.: Prentice-Hall, 1963); Richard T. Garner and Bernard Rosen, *Moral Philosophy: A Systematic Introduction to Normative Ethics and Metaethics* (New York: Macmillan, 1967); W. D. Hudson, *Modern Moral Philosophy* (New York: Anchor, 1970); and Richard Norman, *The Moral Philosophers: An Introduction to Ethics* (Oxford: Clarendon Press, 1983). For more advanced readings, see the Select Bibliography.

PART ONE

The Will to Value

1

In pursuit of the ethical

The best metaphysical road

Among the earlier works of Blake, Wordsworth, Hazlitt, and Shelley are explicit treatments of ethics: Blake's "Annotations to Lavater" (probably written in 1788 or early 1789), Wordsworth's "Essay on Morals" (1798–9), Hazlitt's *Essay on the Principles of Human Action* (1805), and Shelley's Notes to *Queen Mab* (1813) and his "Speculations on Morals" (1817, 1821). In *Biographia Literaria* (1817) Coleridge recalls that he "retired [on December 31, 1796) to a cottage in Somersetshire at the foot of Quantock, and devoted my thoughts and studies to the foundations of religion and morals" (*BL* I 200; cf. *BL* I 187). His most extensive ethical treatise is written years later as part of the still unpublished Opus Maximum, but his concern with ethics as a discipline appears in his earliest essays, letters, and notebook entries. Keats, too, plans in April, 1818, to retire from the world and take on wisdom, after finding out from Hazlitt "the best metaphysical road I can take." He probably has in his possession a copy of Hazlitt's *Essay*. And one day before his twentieth birthday, Byron gives in a letter his most pointed exposition of an ethical orientation, a qualified Epicureanism.

More often than not, "philosophy" or even "metaphysics" means moral philosophy for the Romantics. Their youthful interest in the subject argues in itself its importance to them. We are dealing not with the sober reflections of octogenarians who have taken up ethics for want of better occupation, rather with interested writings on the meaning and conduct of life that gloss an oeuvre very much still in the making. Blake's account of act and evil in his "Annotations to Lavater" is a key to the puzzling nature of action in the major prophecies. Wordsworth's assertions in his "Essay on Morals" that moral philosophy and discursive reason have no influence on a person's behavior, that language must speak to the affections, and that action is secondary, connect him with the British morality of the sentiments and take us to some central issues in *The Prelude*. At age eighteen, Coleridge writes two short essays for his schoolmaster that dwell on "remorse," "diseased fancy," "darkness, and haunts obscene and frightful," and on habits that destroy freedom – prophetic of his Mariner and his own life as a drug addict. Hazlitt's account of the sympathetic imagination in his *Essay* points to recurring themes in his later writings. Shelley's discussion of necessity in his Notes to *Queen Mab* proves useful in our reading of *Prometheus Unbound*, and his discussion of benevolence and justice in "Speculations on Morals" explains the needed continuity of ethics and politics, the principal corrective he offers the politically apostate Lake poets, Wordsworth, Southey, and Coleridge. The young Romantic authors arm themselves with an ethics before assaulting Parnassus.

The greatest British moralist of the period, and perhaps the greatest that Britain has ever produced, is Coleridge, who is unmatched in acuity of moral observation and creative speculation. He writes that Godwin has demonstrated the "most important of all important Truths, that Morality might be built up on its own foundation, like a Castle built *from* the rock & *on* the rock" (*CL* III 313–14). He admires this type of structure in Kant also, but he has no knack for emulating either philosopher in it. None of the British Romantics achieves anything like a structured, propositional system – nor, of course, do we wish this of them. Perhaps the most overt attempt is Hazlitt's early *Essay*, but its flatulent exposition makes plain that he and we are better off in the less ambitious pieces. Hazlitt is the figure most recognizably a moralist because so many of his writings, like those of Samuel Johnson, are addressed specifically to moral topics. But it is up to the interpreter to find partial system in what Hazlitt has left as a prodigal and unsorted mass of moral commentary. And it is often up to the interpreter to see connections between these ruminations and the interests of literature.

The Romantic humanists

Irving Babbitt, best known of the conservative "New Humanists" of the twenties and thirties, gives an unequivocal assessment of the ethics of Romanticism worth bearing in mind. As he puts it in *Rousseau and Romanticism* (1919), "There is no such thing as romantic morality."[1] The phrase is for him an oxymoron. His polemic, which blames Romanticism on the one hand and science on the other for a decline in

---

[1] *Rousseau and Romanticism* (Boston: Houghton Mifflin, 1930), 217.

modern life, is a compendium of views that still surface, not only in blue books. But an undergraduate today is likely to find Romanticism congenial for the very reasons Babbitt finds it distasteful. Babbitt's notion of Romantic morality takes its cue from Rousseau's brag: "I am made unlike any one I have ever met; I will even venture to say that I am like no one in the whole world. I may be no better, but at least I am different."[2] Babbitt thinks such stuff and nonsense is an undisciplined individualism that heeds no decorum, inner or outer; it is a policy of self-expansionism. Invoking his own dualistic concept of a higher self that observes the rule of reason, and an unruly, self-seeking lower or natural self, he complains that Rousseau and all who follow in his wake have upset this inner economy. The Romantics' idolatry of emotion and energy leads to chaos of personality and indeterminacy of desire. Schiller's *schöne Seele* – the beautiful soul for whom duty is identical with inclination – is a sentimental ideal that, in doing away with inner resistance, does away with morality as well. The "civil war in the cave" of the psyche makes necessary an "inner check" on natural inclination and emotion.

The Romantics' radical inversion of value begins earlier than Rousseau, Babbitt observes, in the British moral philosophers, the Earl of Shaftesbury and Francis Hutcheson, for whom conscience, no longer conceived of as reason acting on the will, is redefined as "sentiment" or "feeling." Shaftesbury's absorption of ethics into aesthetics destroys ethics by replacing normative judgment with subjectivity, preparing the way for the Romantics' view of morality as sentimental egoism. Pity and sympathy are absurdly overvalued by Wordsworth and Hugo. Rousseau's life bears witness to the fact that sympathy alone is not a moral principle: Rousseau "abandoned his five children one after the other, but had we are told an unspeakable affection for his dog" (p. 143). Though Romanticism and science flank "humanism" on opposite sides and reveal themselves in different ways – Romanticism glorifying the self and science the world of things – they agree in "making of man a mere stop on which Nature may play what tune she will." Since both "are prone to look upon man as being made by natural forces and not as making himself" (p. 163), the passive eolian harp is a fitting symbol for the period.

Babbitt thus indicts Romantic morality for its emotionalism, sentimentality, primitivism, anti-intellectualism, self-indulgent individualism, passivity, and repudiation of the reality principle in an undisciplined riot of the imagination – not to mention its carnality and

---

[2] *The Confessions*, trans. J. M. Cohen (New York: Penguin, 1953), 17.

libertinism as practiced by such nympholepts as Byron and Chateaubriand.

Babbitt's clear and distinct misrepresentation of the ethics of Romanticism still has some currency, despite his own near-total critical eclipse long ago. Individualism, emotionalism, and subjectivism remain staples of period characterization, and they *are* half-truths. His misrepresentation serves as one foil against which the Romantics' complex vision can be articulated, and which will be most pointedly undercut by Shelley. To his credit, Babbitt is one of surprisingly few critics or historians to single out "Romantic morality" as a topic per se. Another who does is Yvor Winters. Though disliking the latent mysticism of Babbitt's "inner check," he attacks Romanticism for most of the same reasons, practicing what he calls "moralistic" criticism and perpetuating the notion that the moral and the Romantic are heartfelt foes: the Romantics "offer a fallacious and dangerous view of the nature both of literature and of man. The Romantic theory assumes that literature is mainly or even purely an emotional experience, that man is naturally good, that man's impulses are trustworthy, that the rational faculty is unreliable to the point of being dangerous or possibly evil."[3] My study has as its ironic backdrop the fact that the emergence of ethical criticism in this century is largely associated with anti-Romantic reaction. To write of "the ethics of Romanticism" is an ultimate act of critical rehabilitation.

Some generalizations concerning "Romantic humanism" will set forth a standard against which to gauge patterns of departure in each author. The ethics of Romanticism, as the larger play of ideas concerning moral questions in Romantic literature and philosophy, will prove to be more critical and compelling than the imperiled humanism which grounds it.

(1) More than most other literary figures, the Romantics expressly concern themselves with ethics and assert its primacy in their own enterprise. I do not imply that British Romantic literature is more ethical than other literature, only that it more adamantly underscores its own ethical concerns.

(2) Despite their abhorrence of "didactic poetry" (Byron excepted), the Romantics, even more than Renaissance and Neoclassical theorists, hold to the moral improvement of audience as a primary end of poetry and develop a poetics closely aligned with ethics. Invariably their views can be termed interactionism, but they represent a spectrum of opinion on how and to what degree poetry takes on ethical

[3] *In Defense of Reason* (Denver: University of Denver Press, 1947), 7.

16

content and purpose. Blake seems to banish morality from poetry only to reinstate it more profoundly, the blight of "moral virtue" eradicated by imagination. Wordsworth's Preface to *Lyrical Ballads* is hedonistic: the "end of Poetry is to produce excitement in coexistence with an overbalance of pleasure" (*PLB* 146). (Is it not sometimes overlooked that both Horatian ends of poetry – teaching and delighting – are moral?) By means of the pleasures of poetry, and not by precept or example, the reader's feelings are "rectified." As Coleridge puts it, "the communication of pleasure is the introductory means by which alone the poet must expect to moralize his readers" (*BL* II 131). Shelley's poet manages to be a "legislator of the world" only if he refrains from didactic poetry. Ironically, it is Byron who presumes on his own "canonical credentials" in touting "didactic" or "ethical poetry."

(3) Contrary to Babbitt's opinion, the Romantic imagination is unabashedly moral. For Coleridge, imagination functions in two ostensibly contrary ways, both of them moral in implication. On the one hand it is the unifying or shaping power, and it unifies the poet and reader as well as the poem, indeed activating the "whole soul." The poet "diffuses a tone, and spirit of unity, that blends, and (as it were) *fuses*, each [faculty] into each, by that synthetic and magical power, to which we have exclusively appropriated the name of imagination" (*BL* II 15–16). Poesis is a moral act because it profoundly implicates personality, indistinguishably poet's and reader's. As the "modifying & fusing" power, imagination fosters unity of self corresponding to unity of the poem, and is egoistic in the sense of augmenting the self's value and establishing internal order according to a scale of values. It is involved in self-fashioning – the way we choose to present ourselves, the way we choose to lead our lives. Coleridge's definition of "secondary imagination" (*BL* I 304) implies egoism: not accepting the world as given, imagination "dissolves, diffuses, dissipates, in order to re-create" according to its own lights and the "conscious will." This is its fictional, visionary, image-making power. Imagination creates our sense of integral identity and attempts mentally to shape the world as conforming to our desire of it.

This egoistic function is countered by another: imagination as sympathetic identification. In Coleridge's conversation poems, particularly "This Lime-tree Bower My Prison" (1797) and "Frost at Midnight" (1798), the poet is mentally joined to another through the willed imaging of another's experience of landscape. In the Opus Maximum and elsewhere, he described good conscience as the imaginative identification of I with Thou, the recognition of the reality and worth of the other. Sympathetic imagination occasions a spectrum of feelings, from love to quiet sympathy to outrage. Protesting the slave trade, Coleridge argues that to shield oneself from another's pain is damnable: one must imagine the feel of the rotting slave ship.

The evidence of this book weighs against one aspect of the current tendency to see affinities (where before there had appeared to be disjunctions) between Romanticism and Modernism. Both are sometimes said to have emphasized a retreat into the isolated image in a forsaking of the poet's social role.[4] But the Romantics bring both private poetic consciousness and the sense of the poet's moral and social responsibilities to a new and heightened pitch. An extremism at both these poles accounts for the unsettled dramatic energy that attends their engagement in moral questions.

A wealth of modern thinkers from behaviorists to Marxists to post-structuralists have dubbed the self obsolete. This tendency is often part of a more general attack on liberal bourgeois ideology, wherein self-ownership and ownership of property are related forms of false consciousness. One difference between the Romantics and modern critics is that Blake, Coleridge, and Keats believe moral and social participation entails increased self-definition, whereas Jameson, Foucault, and Derrida see such participation or other recognitions as leading to the subversion of the self, and to the end of valorizing self as a standard. But the Romantics are not naive students of self; for them the self should through sympathetic imagination de-center itself and become what is more than a self – a moral agent.

The sympathetic imagination is emphasized in the British moral tradition, the organic, fictional, self-augmenting imagination in the German; and Coleridge's joining of these traditions makes him a pivotal figure. The Romantics dramatize moral dangers corresponding to both traditions.

(4) Far from ignoring internal discipline or letting corporeal vapors tyrannize upper levels, the Romantics seek a creative structuring of the self. Instead of Babbitt's reading of this structure as simple inversion in valuation of lower and higher self, they enlist a complex psychology with new ways of valuation. Traditional dualisms of mind and body, reason and passion are questioned. An interdependency of mental powers in the unity psychology of Blake and Coleridge challenges any formulaic division between "higher self" and "lower self," although hierarchical structures are not completely abandoned. The psyche becomes a force field instead of a group of independent faculties. They

---

[4] Frank Kermode gives the most influential statement of this view in *Romantic Image* (New York: Macmillan, 1957).

do value energy, emotion, and libido to an unprecedented degree, but the Romantics seek new forms of internal discipline. Blake conceives the fall of humankind as failed discipline: the four powers of reason, emotion, sense, and imagination lose definition and fall into anarchy. Regeneration comes through a new ordering analogous to the defining line of the engraver. Shelley writes that the heart, corrupted by the mutiny of natural passion, must be "tempered" to its object.

(5) Suffering, loss, and failure can be redressed through active human willing. Since human beings can exercise control over situation, act, and even consequences, Romantic humanism tends to be non-tragic in character.

This tenet will be seriously questioned, however, within the larger scope of Romantic ethics. Blake, Coleridge, and Shelley subscribe to it in different ways, but Wordsworth and Keats in their acknowledgment of circumstantial limitation and natural process express a tragic sensibility. De Quincey, Hazlitt, and Byron, if not possessed of this, still do not consider human will to be the equal of circumstance. A distinction must be made, also, between the Coleridgean view of will, which makes large claims for human powers at the same time that it admits to an ineradicable human depravity, and the Blakean view, which treats evil as a "hindering" of will, the free expression of which is always good. The Romantics vary interestingly in the extent to which they think human beings empowered to script their own lives.

(6) Whether perceived as a natural setting or a larger materiality, nature is a "non-ego," as Fichte says, that can be made to yield to ego. The British Romantics conceive of imagination as the component of ego most directed to altering the face of things; it has the power of humanizing nature. Unlike the mastery of environment through science and technology, humanization is psychologistic – a heightening of perception that invests ordinary objects with color, warmth, light, wonder, and even language. "Where man is not[,] nature is barren," writes Blake. The humanization of nature is prescribed by imperatives less determinate than the imperative to improve man's dark estate. Pragmatists, social workers, and environmentalists would find this aspect of Romanticism quiescent and merely aesthetic. The imperative informing Romantic nature poetry is to alter one's vision, to cleanse the doors of perception; the face of nature brightens and takes on a more human form. But the relationship of a valorized landscape to ethical demand is strained, as we learn in Blake and Wordsworth.

(7) The Romantics see social and political value structures as emanating from individual moral consciousness. None of them would accept

the Marxist insight that this process is reversed. Their views of the relationship of ethics and politics vary, however. An older Coleridge thinks the literal extension of individual ethics to the political affairs of nations is the subversive error of the Jacobins. But Shelley thinks politics should be the morality of a nation. The Romantics in either case tend toward a liberal ethics, whether they are politically on the left, like the younger Wordsworth and Coleridge, Hazlitt, Byron, Shelley, Keats, or on the right, like the older Wordsworth and Coleridge, and De Quincey.

This liberalism is manifested in the extent to which individualism persists even in Romantic authors with a strong social orientation, such as Coleridge and Shelley. It is found in still higher measure in the self-reliance doctrines of the American transcendentalists, Emerson and Thoreau. Thoreau's individualism is the ethical corollary of his political anarchism, that ironically would subvert the bourgeois value system commonly supposed to have given rise to individualism in the first place. In Great Britain the romance of the self is often less absolute than its American counterpart, but it too underlies varying degrees of anarchistic sentiment – not only in Shelley and Hazlitt but also in a writer, De Quincey, whose overt politics are early on aligned with reaction. The Romantics are not precisely anarchists, of course, but many of their writings, literary and otherwise, imply a sympathy with anarchism that makes Shelley's attachment to the philosophical anarchism of William Godwin not wholly anomalous.

(8) I accept the view that the thrust of British Romanticism is secular, and indebted to the very Enlightenment against which in other ways it revolts. But only the "thrust," because the status of religion among leading writers of the period is deeply contradictory. Many European Romantics participate in a post-Enlightenment Christian revival. The young Rousseau is for a time a convert to Catholicism, if for strategic motives, and later advances a forbidding conception of state religion; Chateaubriand, Lamartine, and the young Hugo are Catholics. In Germany Novalis is a Christian mystic, whose reactionary *Christendom or Europe* (*Die Christenheit oder Europa*, 1799) urges a return to a pre-Reformation church in a new confederation of Christendom. Brentano and Friedrich Schlegel are Catholics, and in Italy so is Manzoni. In England, Coleridge and Wordsworth become Anglicans, while De Quincey is one from the beginning. Byron questions Christianity but never totally disowns it, and Shelley, who does, seems recidivist in some of his later works, and is always sympathetic to Jesus's ethics. Blake's *Jerusalem* compromises the radical anthropocentrism of *The Marriage of Heaven and Hell*, and not even Keats, who condemns

Christianity as a "vulgar superstition," seems wholly innocent of a belief in the soul. Obviously there is conflict and contradiction in this matter – their secularism is always alloyed.

The evidence of this book does confirm their basic secularism, but with the important qualification that they resist any naive division of sacred and secular.[5] The imagination – as a privileged light that, Blake says, is the "Eternal Body of Man" in which "All Things Exist" – effects the continuation of religion by non-doctrinal means and does not spawn either a pure naturalism or a pure humanism. The Romantics do not normally argue the autonomy of ethics from all supernatural sanctions (Byron's Lucifer advances this argument), but they do assent to the power and privilege of individuals to develop according to their own lights. Oothoon, in Blake's *Visions of the Daughters of Albion*, does not derive her insight from an "allegorical abode" elsewhere but from her own resistant and fully human imagination.

The deepest motive for the eighteenth-century absorption in moral philosophy is the growing anxiety about the legitimacy of theological sanctions. The Romantics are heirs to the Enlightenment in continuing this pursuit of the ethical as a counter-measure to the waning of faith. They are drawn to the idea that "Morality might be built up on its own foundation" as a kind of contingency measure. Moral agents, even if bereft of a deity watching over them and providing an ultimate context for all human acts, would not inhabit a valueless universe, would not be rudderless and alone on a wide wide sea of moral indifference. The commonly assumed status of ethics as a subcategory of religion is belied by the historical evolution of ethical thinking parallel to the evolution of religious doubt, and by the gradual relocation of conscience within secular consciousness.

(9) Although some of them – notably Wordsworth, Byron, and De Quincey – echo primitivist notions of prelinguistic virtue, the Romantics are more likely to conceive of human mind in a prelinguistic condition as chaotic and in need of language as an expressive and cognitive agency which orders the very passion that gives birth to it. And despite a belief in the incarnational properties of the "symbol," they are not so inclined to overvalue the "sign" as some critics think, nor do they mistake the sign for the thing. Signifiers become unhinged from signifieds, and the sign from reality; the usual problematics obtain here, even more so. The moral implications of language use are related to these problematics. Dysfunctional language can confuse us,

[5] In this matter, my study supports the argument of M. H. Abrams in *Natural Supernaturalism: Tradition and Revolution in Romantic Literature* (New York: W. W. Norton, 1971).

shield us from reality, and even poison us. Language properly commits us to the world, and poetic language does this to a greater degree. Shelley values the "science of things" over the "science of words," and attempts in prefaces and letters to draw attention away from linguistic and formal properties of his own poems and plays. Eschewing any fetishistic overvaluation of signs in themselves, he stresses the performative force of language, both in his theoretical writings and in such a poem as "Ode to the West Wind." For all their interest in language, the Romantics would be puzzled by the hegemony of linguistics in modern criticism and psychology. The idea that the self is a linguistic construct, for instance, would seem to them counter-intuitive and diminishing.

(10) Relative to the great moral traditions, British and Continental, the Romantics are erratic and eclectic in their reading but critical in what they absorb. Other dominant ethical tendencies are perceived as limited, anaemic, or divisive. They may be based on too exclusive a notion of value, as in hedonistic utilitarianism, or on too divisive a concept of duty, as in Kantian formalism, or on too mild a concept of virtue, as in Christian ethics, or on too taxonomic an account of human psychology, as in the British moral sense school. Instead, they synthesize aspects of many schools in developing an ethics notable for its value pluralism, which, relative to other ethical possibilities, has a precise, not nebulous, meaning. To replenish values in a world that seems to have lost its hold on them is the imperative that most typifies their ethical enterprise. The augmentation of self is but one dynamic of this will to value. European moral schools betray an impoverishment of values. But the Romantics disagree on the qualitative properties of acts that might lead to replenishment. "Will to value" is my own coinage. The phrase does not denominate yet another reified faculty but a prominent collective tendency in these authors as I read them. It is useful in contrasting with the darker Hobbesian–Nietzschean "will to power" and with any ethics that foregrounds the imperatives of action.

Ethics, politics, and modern criticism

The uncertain status of ethical criticism is one legacy of anti-Romantic critics such as Irving Babbitt and Yvor Winters. Whatever their strengths – and they are strong critics – they have left the impression that ethical criticism risks the embarrassment of *ex cathedra* pronouncements on human values and that it too readily assumes a direct linkage between moral judgment and literary value. Of greater continuing influence in modern letters is F. R. Leavis, who eschews blanket characterizations of Romantic authors – and who finds much to praise in Wordsworth and Keats – but who does perpetuate many prevailing views of the anti-Romantic critics. "Shelley's poetry is repetitive, vaporous, monotonously self-regarding and often emotionally cheap, and so, in no very long run, boring." In the same breath that he disapproves of any "general description," he says of the Romantics:

What they have in common is that they belong to the same age; and in belonging to the same age they have in common something negative: the absence of anything to replace the very positive tradition (literary, and more than literary – hence its strength) that had prevailed till towards the end of the eighteenth century.

One aim of my study is to refute this estimate with respect to Leavis's primary criterion, a writer's ethical engagements.

Known for the value judgments that have done much to reorder the literary hierarchy, Leavis militantly refuses to elevate his criteria to the level of theory. He speaks of the great author's "full engagement in life" that challenges readers into a "radical pondering" of "our most important determinations and choices"; we readers make value judgments out of our "personal living"; the "responsible critic" is one who helps form and define "the contemporary sensibility." But when René Wellek – who Leavis thinks has misread his *Revaluation* (1936) as an attack on the Romantics – argues that Leavis should have made his "assumptions more explicitly and defended them systematically," he replies that philosophy and criticism should remain independent one of the other to avoid the "consequences of queering one discipline with the habits of another."[6] The critic can decide ethical questions in literature through "completeness of possession" and "fullness of response" alone.

Many schools of twentieth-century criticism have tended to marginalize ethical criticism and theory, when they are not directly hostile. Formalist critics disallow the critical significance of audience response, moral or otherwise, and do not welcome literary questions more related to content than to form; or with Northrop Frye they fold the ethical dimension into the formal.[7] Structuralists are not greatly respectful of referential thematics and see such ethical phenomena as self, character, act, and purpose as fueling naive interpretive strategies that focus on semantics to the exclusion of the verbal conventions that

[6] *The Common Pursuit* (London: Chatto & Windus, 1952), 221, 185, 213.
[7] *Anatomy of Criticism* (Princeton: Princeton University Press, 1957), 113–15. This view is qualified in Frye's later writings.

constitute literary texts.[8] Sociological critics see such phenomena as secondary to larger social issues concerning class, production, and reception.[9] Psychological critics subsume ethics into psychology as one psychological phenomenon among others, characteristically treated as a defensive reaction formation initiated by the superego against the imagination's power, whether one is speaking of poet, critic, reader, or fictional representations.[10] Marxist critics think a focus on ethics is evidence of bourgeois "individualistic categories" and urge a broader critical horizon. Deconstructionists eviscerate the moral concept of play as expounded by Schiller, and dissolve into textuality the determinants of agent, act, and purpose. And so on. (I will single out these last two views shortly.)

Even so, some modern critics have long acknowledged the claims of ethics: Lionel Trilling speaks of literary texts as expressions of authorial moral will, and Kenneth Burke provides a grammar of human motives applicable to literary texts. Paul Ricoeur asks whether a presumed "ethical neutrality of the artist" may "suppress one of the oldest functions of art, that it constitutes an ethical laboratory where the artist pursues through the mode of fiction experimentation with values."[11] In the past four or five years a relatively small group of critics has begun to refocus our attention on the ethical.[12]

[8] Jonathan Culler summarizes the fate of novelistic "character," for instance, in the hands of structuralists: "the general ethos of structuralism runs counter to the notions of individuality and rich psychological coherence which are often applied to the novel. Stress on the interpersonal and conventional systems which traverse the individual, which make him a space in which forces and events meet rather than an individuated essence, leads to a rejection of a prevalent conception of character in the novel: that the most successful and 'living' characters are richly delineated autonomous wholes, clearly distinguished from others by physical and psychological characteristics. This notion of character, structuralists would say, is a myth." *Structuralist Poetics: Structuralism, Linguistics and the Study of Literature* (London: Routledge & Kegan Paul, 1975), 230.

[9] Jeffrey Sammons discusses this limitation in sociological criticism throughout *Literary Sociology and Practical Criticism* (Bloomington: Indiana University Press, 1977), with emphasis on modern German criticism.

[10] Harold Bloom, to be sure considerably more than a "psychological critic," argues that the "only guilt that matters to a poet" is "the guilt of indebtedness" to precursors; moral criticism is a reduction of the poem to a conceptualization, and reductionism is the main enemy of a true "antithetical criticism." *The Anxiety of Influence* (New York, Oxford University Press, 1973), 94, 117.

[11] *Time and Narrative*, trans. Kathleen McLaughlin and David Pellauer (Chicago: The University of Chicago Press, 1984), I, 59.

[12] To mention a few: Charles Altieri, Warner Berthoff, Gerald Bruns, Stanley Cavell, Christopher Clausen, Geoffrey Harpham, Jean-François Lyotard, and Tobin Siebers. An issue of *New Literary History*, 15 (1983) is devoted to "Literature and/as Moral

The moral emphasis of these critics is forthright enough, but there are many others whom I would term crypto-ethical. In speaking so insistently of "pleasure," "desire," and "self," modern critics with a broad range of orientations have evaded the embarrassment that attaches to such baldly moral topics as right and wrong, good and bad, virtue and vice, praise and blame. But "pleasure" is an ethical category and to speak of "the pleasures of the text" raises the spectre of ethical criticism. So too with "desire," whether one is extending the criticism of Nietzsche or Frye. The word "self" suggests a proud amorality that secures the critic from preacherly normative ethics. "Self-realization-ism" is itself a branch of normative ethics, however. The literary criticism indebted to it covertly urges that we be in possession of resilient, prolific, sensitive, liberal, playful, sexual, experimental, suffering, and existential selves.

The most conspicuous school in American criticism of the sixties and early seventies was crypto-ethical: ethical criticism that dared not speak its name, as if for fear that its mildly subversive edge would be blunted by admission of its normative character. American criticism of the "self" is particularly relevant to my undertaking, since it is a latter-day recapitulation of the moral concerns of the Romantics. To judge by book titles alone, this entity – the self – is central, conceived, corporeal, created, divided, elusive, evolutionary, examined, emergent, imagined, imperial, individuated, journeying, mutable, opposing, observant, open, performing, poetic, protean, sexual, social, solitary, split, transparent, unexplored, and universal, not to mention disowned and buried. Obsession with the self, evident in hundreds of critical studies where it does not usurp even the title, never did lead to an analytic confrontation with its own moral premises. Contemporary Marxist critics, structuralists, and sociologists have targeted these modern versions of "self" criticism rather than the more complex versions of the late eighteenth and early nineteenth centuries, with which I will be concerned in part.

Twentieth-century "self" criticism broadly recapitulates the Romantics' own position relative to empiricism and science. As I have mentioned, modern psychologists of empiricist or behaviorist schools, not to mention sociologists, have cast doubt on the existence of the self. Until recently, students of literature have tended to promote it as both entity and value, taking in literary studies the position taken by post-

Philosophy." Contributors include Mary Ann Caws, Cora Diamond, Patrick Gardiner, Murray Krieger, Richard Kuhns, Angel Medina, Maurice Natanson, Martha Craven Nussbaum, Hilary Putnam, D. D. Raphael, Nathan A. Scott, David Sidorsky, and Richard Wollheim.

25

Freudian self theorists and ego therapists in psychological studies. A self-realizationist ethics lurks in these studies. What Quentin Anderson calls the "imperial self" of Emerson and Whitman is in keeping with Babbitt's description of the self of romantic expansionism; and like Babbitt, if for different reasons, Anderson is wary of it. But most modern critics of the self have treated the strong "sense of self" – whether authorial or fictional – as an intrinsic value.

The Romantics similarly look on the threatening "mechanico-corpuscular" tradition of Hobbes, Locke, Newton, and Hartley, that seems to deny human freedom and dignity in making consciousness epiphenomenal. In response, they attempt to shore up the integrity of the self. Hobbesian psychological egoism is repellent to them, and yet they wish to retain an egoism of their own within a more comprehensive view of human personality. Many of them – Blake, Coleridge, and Keats – voice one or another form of self-realizationism, but more than the moderns they are at the same time committed to the self and the other as opposing terms of an arduous dialectic. Modern literary discussion of the self wore thin well before it attained the complexity of such discussion by poets, critics, and philosophers of the Romantic period.

Critics of the self are indebted to the tradition of liberal humanism to which the Romantics made a profound contribution – the liberal humanism loathsome to New Humanist conservatives. But, as I have indicated, "Romantic morality" is not so blatantly seductive as Babbitt makes it out to be, and its liberalism gives way by turns to greater strictures and to more aggressive insurrectional energies. Nor is the ethics of Romanticism so vulnerable as its modern liberal counterpart to assertions by Marxist critics that its bourgeois, individualistic categories betray the arrested development, personal and social, that is characteristic of liberal humanism. It is instead a critical posture, subversive of its own categories and often dialectical; and in its time it was in opposition to prevailing ideologies. By contrast, modern liberalism, which is much indebted to it as well as to Enlightenment formulations, assumes in literary criticism a congenial but often ineffectual character through the very familiarity of its bland pronouncements. Through its eyes, Blake is watered down into sentimental platitudes about the fully realized personality and human potential.

In these various approaches to the relationship of ethics and literature, the question of politics often arises and calls for more comment here. I will be describing later on the Romantics' emphatic views on the intersection of ethics and politics; they serve as a test case for the legitimacy of ethical criticism and imply strong correctives to those who would displace it by perspectives deemed broader or more fundamental.

What is the relationship of ethics and politics in literary texts? Reversing the Marxist argument, one *could* subsume politics into ethics simply by defining the former, classically, as "a branch of ethics concerned with the state or social organism as a whole rather than the individual person: a division of moral philosophy dealing with the ethical relations and duties of governments or other social organizations" (Webster's Third). But I will adhere to the usual understanding that ethics deals with obligation and moral value as they pertain to individuals in their relatedness to themselves and to others; politics deals with larger groups or governments wherein expediency may or may not – depending on which politics is invoked – properly override moral objections.

At least on a manifest level the ethical dimension dominates over the political in literary texts. Well before the onslaught of bourgeois individualism, narrative and drama foreground individuals in their moral relatedness to others. This is true even of overt allegories where a figure may represent a class of persons or a single moral trait, or of texts where a fictional character does not have the "subjectivity" or self-consciousness of modern counterparts. This seems such an obvious point that one might ask, so what? Is not its level of generality such that the ethical is useless as an interpretive tool? But obviousness or even uselessness is not in itself disqualifying: the true and the obvious, let us hope, frequently intersect, and it is doubtful that literature exists for the sake of interpretation. It is this very obviousness of the ethical that those who look beyond it for the "real" meaning must labor to undermine. Historical or overtly political fictions – e.g., the novels of Sir Walter Scott or Tolstoy – must utilize moral interaction even where fictional characters are representative of classes or are caught up in larger economic, historical, and political forces. A hermeneutics that reads moral action as political allegory must somehow negotiate the ethical as perhaps the most stubborn of literal levels.

One common error in thinking about the ethical dimension of literature is to align it monolithically with a particular ethics or politics. Though representing different politics and approaches to literature, the American critics John Gardner, Fredric Jameson, and J. Hillis Miller err in this way, it seems to me. In his diatribe against trivialization and cynicism in modern literature, *On Moral Fiction*, Gardner, well-known novelist as well as critic and scholar, argues that the ethical is not what it is often taken to be – a negative – but is instead whatever "affirms life" and whatever is "unselfish, helpful, kind, and noble-hearted."

Most modern literature gives us "escapist models or else moral evasiveness, or, worse, cynical attacks on traditional values such as honesty, love of country, marital fidelity, work, and moral courage." Included in his indictment are Mailer, Heller, Albee, Stoppard, Beckett, Grass, Bellow, Doctorow, and Genêt. For Gardner, "moral fiction" affirms a set of culturally reactionary values – good old-fashioned New England values, he calls them – or it is not moral at all. His argument culminates in the assertion that "art is in one sense fascistic: it claims, on good authority, that some things are healthy for individuals and society and some things are not. Unlike the fascist in uniform, the artist never forces anyone to anything. He merely makes his case, the strongest case possible."[13] The conservative tendency of much great literature is clear enough, but Gardner's assumption that a morally engaged literature promotes conservative values unnecessarily limits the kinds of moral commitment a writer can make, and indulges some question-begging as to what values should prevail in literature as in life.

Although Jameson, with greater sophistication, is arguing from a different cultural and political position, he too unnecessarily limits the range of ethical possibilities by equating the totality of ethics with one of its categories. I will dwell on his argument for a moment, since it is the most direct and influential critique of ethical criticism to have appeared in recent years. In attempting to refute it, I will invoke the breadth and diversity of those elements in literature we must denominate as ethical, and I will suggest how difficult it is – in theory, however sophisticated – to outflank the ethical. Jameson's argument in *The Political Unconscious* derives from the Marxist position stated most clearly by Engels in *Anti-Dühring* (1878). (There is a spare amount of writing by Marx and Engels directed towards ethics per se.) Morality has always been class morality – the ruling classes' rationalized code of conduct and value imposed on the producing classes to perpetuate their hegemony. In a classless society morality as such will wither away, to be replaced by what Engels calls a "really human morality" but which he does not directly describe. "In a society in which all motives for stealing have been done away with . . . how the preacher of morals would be laughed at who tried solemnly to proclaim the eternal truth: Thou shalt not steal!"[14] This historicizing of ethical positions with reference to economic base means that claims to universality or permanent truth in ethics have always been a rationalization of class interests.

[13] *On Moral Fiction* (New York: Basic Books, 1978), 101.
[14] *Anti-Dühring* (Moscow: Progress Publishers, 1947), 114.

Jameson argues in turn that critics might well repudiate ethical criticism for what it is: a fraudulent search in literary texts for universal, non-historicized human truths and a bourgeois centering of the self or subject as the standard. Literary critics have not yet learned the wisdom of Nietzsche, who understood that ethics is based on an exclusivist, non-dialectical binary of good and evil, where evil is simply "whatever is radically different from me" and therefore threatens my existence. Good and evil are positional terms, historically and economically derived, that lock us up in a stagnant individualism. The remedy is the dialectic:

if we grasp the problem as one of escaping from the purely individualizing categories of ethics, of transcending the categories into which our existence as individual subjects necessarily locks us and opening up the radically distinct transindividual perspectives of collective life or historical process, then the conclusion seems unavoidable that we already have the ideal of a thinking able to go beyond good and evil, namely the dialectic itself.[15]

Jameson acknowledges the great difficulty of transcending ethical categories: even Marx and Engels have enough residual humanism that their classic texts are to a degree moralized (pp. 116–17), especially Marx's *Economic and Philosophic Manuscripts of 1844*. Literary texts have inscribed in them the contradictions of class conflict even when overt moral themes may obscure them. A political "unconscious" can be exhumed from them. Joseph Conrad's *Lord Jim* (1900) may seem to be about the existential crunch of choosing between good and evil, about courage and cowardice – but Jameson argues that this theme must not be taken at face value, just as dreams are not. Demonstrating how this novel is actually about "nineteenth-century rationalism and reification," "the texture of ideology," and "the ruling class of the British Empire" will require, he says, a "complex argument" spread over a very long chapter. The manifest ethical theme will then be demonstrated to be merely "diversionary." The notable intricacy of his exposition may stand as evidence in itself of the great effort required to dislodge the ethical dimension from its seeming predominance. Near the end of his analysis Jameson writes, "But if this is what *Lord Jim* is really all about, then it only remains to ask why nobody thinks so, least of all Conrad" (p. 265).

I do not wish to expound or comment on his argument concerning this particular novel or to deny that ethical categories can be translated into socio-economic ones. I am even willing to grant for the sake of

---

[15] *The Political Unconscious: Narrative as a Socially Symbolic Act* (Ithaca, N. Y.: Cornell University Press, 1981), 116.

argument that the political dimension may in some sense be an "ultimate" critical horizon, assuming for now it is not itself flanked by, say, the astrophysical. In passing I would suggest that one could agree that *Lord Jim* is on one level about "the texture of ideology" but still reject Jameson's characterization of the ethical level as merely "diversionary." Critical devaluations of a text's manifest meaning tend to be willful; one is tempted by way of refutation simply to kick a Johnsonian stone – here, the many passages of hefty reflection in Conrad's novel on moral themes of choice, courage, act, and guilt. I would comment more substantially, however, on a few assumptions that permit Jameson to devalue the ethical so neatly.

The most questionable of these is that all ethical systems emerging from within a bourgeois capitalistic system are necessarily egoistic or individualistic. This assumption is subsumed into one even more grandiose – that ethics, simply because it foregrounds the individual, must be egoistic in its so-called "purely individualizing categories." This is tantamount to saying that an ethics is rarely an ethics, since in many ethical systems egoism is the very problem purportedly addressed. Much moral philosophy of the later seventeenth century to the present (the period of emergent capitalism) is an attempt to answer Hobbesian psychological egoism and to locate a bump of benevolence somewhere on our moral craniums. Are these theorists – from Shaftesbury and Butler to Hutcheson and Rousseau to Coleridge, Hazlitt, and Shelley – doing something altogether different from what they think they are doing? Are they merely providing a code that will justify private property and the continued subjugation of the producing classes? Perhaps they do not fully de-center the subject or self, but are they not at least trying? Jameson seems to deny the social dynamic of all those modern ethical systems that are not overtly egoistic.

His argument is contradicted by other Marxist theorists. David Levin, for example, argues that one *can* properly speak of a Marxist ethics. In a period of revolutionary change, it is an oppositional, working-class ethics that seeks, like other moralities, its own class interests, not some universal human interest or abstract truth. It is superior to a bourgeois property ethics, however, because it knows its own non-universal, relativistic character. Its fundamental imperative is, in Marx's words, "From each according to his ability, to each according to his need." Such an ethics would not be individualistic but collective, and it would not wither away upon the arrival of a classless society: "To think otherwise would be to dream that people will someday altogether lose all drive to meet their interests at the cost of others."[16] Levin thus tempers utopian expectation where Jameson does not. Levin observes that one should not expect to win a member of one class over to the ethics of another, however. A determinism persists in his account, as it does in Jameson's. So bound are we to the economic mode of production and to our particular class that we would not subscribe to an ethics that opposes the values of our own class.

One wonders whether this rigidity of ethical commitment is not belied by ancient Greek philosophy alone, where so many ethical positions are articulated by a small population in a brief timespan. Western post-feudal bourgeois society has somehow managed to give expression to systems as varied as egoism, hedonism, utilitarianism, formalism, self-realizationism, relativism – not to mention the various metaethical positions from cognitivistic non-definism to non-cognitivistic definism and other horrors. Can such a diversity of ethical positions be always correlated with class structure? Granted that the history of philosophy has such correlations, is philosophic intellect to be granted no independence to range and make its own commitments? Borges may overstate the case for philosophy as a branch of fantastic literature, but should we not make some allowance for the philosophic *imagination* as something other than a leaden conduit of ideology? Marxists themselves term "vulgar Marxism" any mechanical wholesale determination of thought and culture by economic base, but it strikes me that Jameson and Levin come close to making such an assumption in this matter of ethics.

The ethico-political nature of the imagination, which will be a concern of this study, has long been a subject of controversy. Plato's fear of the poet issues from the imagination's subversive character, but Plato knew poets could be enlisted in the service of the state. Schiller will argue that imaginative play is the source of human freedom; Blake and Shelley that imagination is a revolutionary faculty. But Hazlitt, also on the political left, thinks poets tend to end up Tories, and that imagination is attracted to the glamorous trappings of political power. One can partially reconcile these views in arguing that imagination (or, if this smacks of hypostatizing a function, the writer imagining) has no formal commitment to a particular politics – this is the ground of its freedom, attested to by Hazlitt himself in his early treatise on the "disinterestedness" of imagination – but that materially or after the fact it will commit itself to one or another politics. Such a view has several implications: first, it nominally accounts for the great diversity

[16] "The Moral Relativism of Marxism," *The Philosophical Forum*, 15 (1984), 249–79.

of ethico-political views in literary texts (imagination *can* take up residence in an Ezra Pound); second, it does not deny that imagination is influenced by socio-economic circumstance; and third, the formal non-alignment of the imagination provides the ground on which writers may question or repudiate the ideological components of their class and even their own earlier work. If the imagination is granted a degree of autonomy from class conditioning – and many Marxist theorists from Lenin, Trotsky, and Lukács to Goldmann, Fischer, and Sartre will grant it this – a wedge of reflexive questioning can be driven through ideology.

The experience of the Romantics attests to this likelihood and to the importance of moral recognition as a condition of political awakening. When a young and politically complacent William Wordsworth resides in France in 1791–2 he engages in political discussion with people sympathetic to the Revolution, but he does not perceive the insufficiency of sentimental pastoralism until he is struck with the blatant fact of human misery and exploitation – a hunger-bitten girl spiritlessly leading a heifer along a country road. "'Tis against *that /* Which we are fighting," says his mentor, the French republican Michel Beaupuy. Political consciousness begins here in moral witness and outrage, the imagination extending the strongly registered *image* of injustice. Whatever its own ultimate insufficiency (and Wordsworth does end up a Tory), moral recognition as a prelude to political consciousness is a pattern evident in the lives, literature, and speculations of many Romantic writers, from Blake and Shelley to Byron and Keats. Moral outrage at poverty, injustice, crime, and war educates the imagination toward personal dissociation, if only partial, from class ideology.

This ethically induced dissociation is found in the Romantics' own attack on bipolar ethics. Well before Nietzsche, Blake targets the delimiting binary of the ethical in *The Marriage of Heaven and Hell*, written near the beginning of the very historical and cultural period regarded as the progenitor of individualistic categories and modern capitalism. He, Coleridge, and Shelley give us a dialectical ethics, even as other Romantic writers – Hazlitt and Byron – correct its inherent utopianism.

An important point here is that ethics can itself be dialectical, despite Jameson's blanket characterization of it as binary and exclusivist. Those who urge a transvaluation of good and evil envision a qualitatively different ethics wherein concepts of good and evil are redefined or renamed; but acts of moral valuing still obtain. Blake and Nietzsche give us an ethics. I am not championing a dialectical ethics here but correcting the notion that the ethical need be reduced to restrictive polarizing formats. The question of *which* ethics cannot be begged.

Whether one argues for the priority of the ethical to the political (with the Romantics) or the reverse (with the Marxists), one can acknowledge that imaginative literature tends to foreground the ethical, which proves difficult to dislodge in theory or practice. Critical theorists from Aristotle on have assumed that the primary object of literary representation is human action and character, to which considerations of right and wrong, good and bad, are hardly deemed irrelevant in the *Poetics*. Jameson argues that tragic drama already transcends the double bind of the ethical binary of good and evil. To my mind Iago remains evil. If Jameson says the trouble is with my mind, I reply that while a larger fate may override moral distinctions in *Othello*, the play's overt working out is by means of human agents caught up in ethical dynamics of willing, moral (mis)-judgment, and passion.

Perhaps we cannot conceive of the literature of a classless society because of our present position in an as yet unfulfilled dialectical struggle; we reveal ourselves to be bourgeois critics with an inadequate sense of utopian possibility. Such a surmise is strictly unanswerable, of course, because one is then arguing against an untestable, absent eventuality which by its nature resists both verification and falsification. In the abstract the literature of a classless society might be said to transcend the double bind of the ethical, but I wonder. Can we not assume that literary texts of whatever genre or politics must voice, narrate, or dramatize some type of resistance, some dilemma – even in the name of a continuing dialectic or permanent revolution – to retain what in an emphatic sense we call *interest*? Would not this projected classless literature necessarily fall into ethical categories? Are we not otherwise assuming a featureless, antiseptic utopia, a cold heaven? Someone's backsliding into ethical ways of thinking – with a dialectical resolution in his or her rescue from false consciousness – might become a narrative paradigm, for all I know. And would not a classless literature still have to fictionalize individuals in their relatedness to others, not producing tales of groups or classes alone? And would not such representations of individuals moralize the text, even if they were somehow "transindividuals"? I pursue this rather literal line of thought on behalf of what I take to be the stubbornness of the ethical dimension in the face even of theoretical dislodgments.

I conclude that advanced criticism need not propose a "transcendence of the ethical" at all. Even dialectical transvaluation in

Blake, Shelley, Marx, and Nietzsche yields yet other ethics – other ways of judging the obligations and moral values that obtain in the relatedness of individuals to themselves and to other people. The ethical can perhaps be contextualized by a broader critical horizon, but it need not and should not be transcended, condescended to, or made to wither away. We might otherwise suspect either weak authorial vision or consciously willed exclusionary acts on the part of a writer or critic. The repression of a perennial source of the writer's practical equipment for writing would surely prevent literature from becoming what Kenneth Burke has called "equipment for living."

A defense of ethical criticism has recently come from an unexpected quarter, deconstruction, with J. Hillis Miller's *The Ethics of Reading*. Miller says he pursued the ethics of reading rather than the "politics of interpretation" because the latter "is likely to be vague and speculative, often unhelpfully polemical," whereas the former deals with the "concrete" situation of reader confronting page. One might have thought deconstruction forever inimical to ethical criticism, surely logocentric in its pursuit of themes and significance. One would have thought the ethical cast of characters – self, agent, obligation, act, purpose, principle, value, necessity – routed by that roving band of unruly signifiers. In what has struck some as a supreme critical chutzpah, Miller now writes that we readers must have the same respect for a text that Kant says we must have for persons and the moral law. The text imposes its law, but the "law" turns out to be the undecidability of language, which rightly overcomes the reader's inclination to decide among interpretations. His example of the ultimate ethical reader is Paul de Man: "I would even dare to promise that the millennium would come if all men and women became good readers in de Man's sense."[17]

The consistency of Miller's argument with the usual practice of deconstruction can be debated elsewhere. I would only note that we encounter again the question-begging of what kind of ethics obtains in ethical analysis of literary texts. For Miller and de Man, it turns out to be the ethics of deconstruction, which I take to be one rendering of a familiar face in modern ethics – non-cognitivism. Miller says that in "the case of ethics it is a necessity to make judgments, commands, and promises about right and wrong which have no verifiable basis in anything outside language" (p. 50). Likewise, non-cognitivists hold that moral judgments are not objectively true but are kinds of utterances we use for various purposes – praising, expressing feelings, making promises, altering the attitudes of others, facilitating social

[17] *The Ethics of Reading* (New York: Columbia University Press, 1987), 58.

intercourse through linguistic conventions, etc. The sentence "Murdering people is wrong" is neither true nor false; it means the speaker disapproves of murdering people and rather hopes we will refrain from doing so. Following de Man, Miller argues that "ethics is a form of allegory, one form of those apparently referential stories we tell to ourselves and to those around us" – "apparently," because they believe ethics a category wholly apart from "truth." "For de Man the categories of truth and falsehood can never be reconciled with the categories of right and wrong, and yet both are values, in the sense of making an unconditional demand for their preservation" (p. 49). There exists a break between epistemology and ethics, between fact and moral value.

This version of the "ethics of reading" applies to the act of reading any and all texts, it seems, whatever the particular ethical commitments of particular authors. Separated from truth, ethics is but one mode of discourse among others; it is inaugurated for the sake of order in civil society, just as the social contract, says de Man, is a socially pragmatic fiction. From this premise, Miller draws some conclusions balanced on the trope of paradox: to make a promise is a performative speech act that is necessarily a lie, since it cannot be ultimately grounded; its seeming "referentiality" is an "error." The "true ethics of reading" is found in our acknowledgment of lying as a universal principle. We show our "respect" for a text by seeing how it betrays itself into lying, how it is "true to the obligation to lie" (p. 53). Miller attempts to show how Kant in his *Groundwork of the Metaphysics of Morals* cannot tell us what the moral law is, and must resort to narrative (story-telling, lying) to bridge the gap (abyss) between the universal moral law and the particular maxims we might propose to cover concrete moral situations. Miller thinks he has rescued deconstruction from the charge of nihilism and indeterminacy because readers must necessarily read the text in accordance with "the implacable law of language," which means paradoxically that they fail to read the text, reenacting the text's own failure to read itself.

Miller's theory therefore aspires beyond the reach of formal refutation, because it announces its self-contradictory premises upfront: the ethics of reading is blithely based on the presumed linguistic necessity of lying, contradiction, and undecidability. One cannot refute such an argument by appealing to the law of contradiction, since this very law and even the concept of refutation are disallowed in advance. But one could still complain that, in altering beyond recognition the *use* of the word "ethics," Miller has given us a theory that is neither true nor false but definitionally meaningless.

Beyond this, deconstruction in its bearing on the ethical dimension of literature makes some questionable assumptions. First, it assumes that all ethical themes as overtly announced in literary texts are displacements. De Man announces that "Everything in [Proust's] novel signifies something other than what it represents, be it love, consciousness, politics, art, sodomy, or gastronomy: it is always something else that is intended."[18] And Miller writes that the "thematic dramatizations of ethical topics in narratives are the oblique allegorization of [a] linguistic necessity" (p. 3), thereby restricting ethics in literature to "linguistic transactions involved in the act of reading." In all cases ethics is "doing things with words." Deconstruction thus echoes the conventional formalist embarrassment at the thematic. Second, without having gone through a rigorous philosophical deduction, the deconstructor privileges a single ethical theory among many – non-cognitivism – as applicable to all texts, thus impoverishing the range of ethical possibilities. (It must be added that Miller's ethics of lying ultimately contradicts the non-cognitivist assumptions that ground his ethics of reading; non-cognitivism retains the notion that ethical language has determinate, translatable *meaning*, even when meaning becomes identified with use.) Such a procedure is at best premature; the burden of proof would lie on the deconstructors, whose presentation of evidence, judged by standards of inferential logic, is strictly anecdotal.

Tobin Siebers has recently argued that modern critics have adopted pluralism and skepticism as ways of defusing the element of violence thought to be inherent in critical discourse.[19] Though modern critics rarely use the word "ethical," they are practicing an ethics, argues Siebers, insofar as they attempt to refrain from the violence Foucault, Lévi-Strauss, Kristeva, Derrida, de Man, and Miller associate with exclusionary, judgmental interpretation and with the very nature of language. These critics, and many others including Frye, are practicing what Siebers terms "Romantic ethics," because in their wish to avoid totalitarian critical modes they sympathize with the discourse of marginality developed in the Romantic tradition, whose great progenitor is Rousseau. As proponent of individualism and equality, Rousseau lends sympathy to the victim in his *Discourses*, and in *The Confessions* writes of his own exclusion from humanity. But Siebers strongly argues that the ethical tendency of modern criticism is self-contradictory. In supplanting "human" with linguistic constructs – in

---

[18] *Allegories of Reading* (New Haven: Yale University Press, 1979), 77; quoted by Miller, p. 47.

[19] *The Ethics of Criticism* (Ithaca, N. Y.: Cornell University Press, 1988).

an effort to deny the logocentric and totalitarian coercions of the older humanistic discourse – modern critics have committed their own act of violence. The denial of the human or the self is a strictly self-defeating act of aggression which leaves us with reified language where before we had reified self. Moreover, the discourse of marginality becomes a system, as in the institutional triumph of deconstruction; and the "victimary rhetoric" of critical martyrdom acquires "the magnitude of a movement," as in de Man (p. 99). Siebers thinks the full ethical development of criticism, as of literature, will come when the bogus freedom *from* choice – as in critical indeterminacy and pluralism – is replaced by active choosing, and when the value of human community is acknowledged by critics over willful marginality.

Whether or not Siebers and others have overdramatized the violence inherent in critical discourse – and therefore the power and restraining conscience of critics – one notes that his concepts of "ethics" and "Romantic ethics" are tailored to the special contexts of his argument. Ethics is not wholly contained in the intuitive formula of refraining from violence to others, with its corollaries of equality and human community – albeit this formula is a strong component of any normative ethics that would have a hold on us today. More the issue here, the Romantics do create a discourse that begins in marginality and subversion, but I argue that they move toward revolutionary synthesis. They are critical of their own victimary rhetoric, and attempt gigantically to close the distance between self and other. Their very failures here are a purposeful witnessing to the need of moving beyond marginality. What I call the Romantic ethics of Blake and Keats has little in common with the "Romantic ethics" of Derrida, de Man, and Miller. Siebers thinks the Romantics begin the foregrounding of language over critical choice and action that has eventuated in linguistic pluralism. It will be my argument that their *ethical* pluralism – which to be sure contains a degree of indeterminacy – is grounded in a militant humanism precise in its refusal to let language gain ascendency over the human. Though I will cite some striking passages in Coleridge where the self and language are said to be analogous or even homologous, language remains for the Romantics chiefly an expressive agency of human will and intellect.

I am not saying that "humanism" necessarily prevails in literature or ought to, because to say this would be again to beg the question of what kind of ethics. Writers need not seek permanent human truth or wisdom and can instead embrace moral relativism or indeterminacy – and still find that the ethical so conceived feeds the act of composition. Critics might take their cue from the particular ethical interests and

37

modes of composition of particular writers before they impose, "violently," a uniformity principle. John Gardner, E. L. Doctorow, Nadine Gordimer, Saul Bellow, Cynthia Ozick, and Octavio Paz are among the contemporary writers of diverse politics and ethics who have recently spoken of the centrality of the ethical dimension in any literature with a claim on us. Writers, if not necessarily theorists, acknowledge the perennial force of the ethical. I offer the enormous engagement of the Romantics with ethics as evidence of one direction our critical energies might fruitfully take in future years.

2

British Romanticism, Coleridge, and European moral traditions

General observations

Though it is not the first thing on their minds when they sit down to write *The Prelude, Prometheus Unbound*, or even the Opus Maximum, the British Romantics conceive an ethics powerfully situated relative to major post-Renaissance moral schools. Linked by common vocabulary, sources, concerns, and varying degrees of awareness one of another, they respond to other traditions, contradicting, assimilating, supplementing, and transforming them in distinguishable patterns. No figure speaks consistently for the whole group – not even its biggest talker, Coleridge – but striking generalizations can still be made. The Romantics are knowledgeable about these schools – egoism, rationalism, sentimentalism, formalism, idealism, and utilitarianism – if not always profoundly so. Whenever they do not directly comment on these various "isms," an implicit relationship can be discerned. What emerges is a strong ethical tendency identifiably their own. I argue that these literary figures take over issues usually handled by philosophers designated as such in our histories. I am not concerned here with laying out an intellectual "background," but will describe the *relatedness* of the Romantics to these thinkers and will make reference only to those aspects of Hobbes, Shaftesbury, Kant, Schelling, Hegel, Godwin, *et alii*, that have bearing on the moral situation of Romanticism.

My reason for undertaking this discussion is that, despite the attention routinely paid Romanticism as a pivotal moment in cultural and intellectual history, no critic has yet systematically explored its ethical determinants within the larger discourse of European moral traditions. It seems important to do so, if only because the sensibility we term "Romantic" has so informed concepts of value, action, and self in modern Western culture. We now take this for granted but tend to assume that the ethical legacy was a vague cluster of notions and

39

mythologies. And though we do not often acknowledge it, our casual assessments of Romanticism tend to remain vaguely ethical, well past the days of Irving Babbitt. What more precisely were the ethical grounds of Romanticism before these were taken up into various interested discourses – ethical, aesthetic, political, religious – where they occasioned misreading, reduction, vilification, and sometimes praise? What ethical problems were addressed, what problems only compounded? Here I marshall evidence for the large claims I make with regard to the intellectual substance – if not truth – of the ethics of Romanticism. Some of this requires the patient labors of the currently unfashionable doxographer. Recovery of texts and doxographic commentary are required, first, to demonstrate what would otherwise be only asserted, and second, to position these writers with respect to other texts and other thought. The ethics of Romanticism is both revolutionary and synthetic. Its own terms cannot be understood without reference to those it borrows, rejects, redirects. It differs from all competing ethical systems, and this difference is a measure of its assimilative powers. Ironically, it is because it tends toward synthesis that it becomes vulnerable to reductive misreading by schools known more for intellectual exclusivity.

In the great age of British moral philosophy – beginning in 1650 and 1651 with Thomas Hobbes's *Human Nature, or The Fundamental Elements of Policy* and *Leviathan* and continuing to 1789, with Jeremy Bentham's *Introduction to the Principles of Morals and Legislation* – one can distinguish readily enough between the moral philosophers, who gain admittance into histories of philosophy, and what I will call the literary moralists, who by and large do not. The philosophers – Hobbes, Richard Cumberland, Ralph Cudworth, John Locke, the Earl of Shaftesbury, Samuel Clarke, Bernard Mandeville, William Wollaston, Francis Hutcheson, Joseph Butler, John Balguy, John Gay (the Reverend, not the dramatist), David Hume, David Hartley, Richard Price, Adam Smith, William Paley, Thomas Reid, and Jeremy Bentham – do of course figure in histories and anthologies of literature.[1] To varying degrees they adopt quasi-literary formats and embody literary

---

[1] I take the list from *British Moralists: 1650–1800*, ed. D. D. Raphael, 2 vols. (Oxford: Clarendon Press, 1969). The argument of this chapter is my own, but it has been informed by several major studies in intellectual history, including: M. H. Abrams, *Natural Supernaturalism*; Walter Jackson Bate, *From Classic to Romantic: Premises of Taste in Eighteenth-Century England* (Cambridge, Mass.: Harvard University Press, 1946); Ernst Cassirer, *The Philosophy of the Enlightenment*, trans. Fritz Koeller and James Pettegrove (Princeton: Princeton University Press, 1951); *The Platonic Renaissance in England*, trans. James Pettegrove (Edinburgh: Nelson, 1953); Frederick Copleston, S. J.,

values.[2] Shaftesbury, Berkeley, and Hume write dialogues, and Bernard Mandeville writes of psychological egoism in tetrameter couplets. His Latin verse autobiography and translations of Homer aside, Hobbes is a good writer by any standard. We could grant "philosophical writing" some place in a classification of literary genres. But we think of these figures more as philosophers than as writers per se.

The literary moralists – Sir Thomas Browne, John Dryden, John Bunyan, John Milton, Samuel Butler, Jonathan Swift, Joseph Addison, Richard Steele, Alexander Pope, Samuel Johnson, James Boswell, Henry Fielding, Laurence Sterne, Edmund Burke – address serious questions of normative ethics but do not treat ethics in the language and spirit of philosophical inquiry. Nor do they cross the divide between moral recommendation, as a function of normative ethics, and discussion *about* ethics, or metaethics. Indeed a deep distrust of philosophical thinking runs through this tradition. Philosophers tend to be objects of derision in Swift, Johnson, and Sterne. A philosophical poem such as Pope's *Essay on Man* is not an inquiry but a brilliant compendium of traditional thinking on moral and metaphysical questions. Even Milton goes without mention in histories of philosophy. I am not pointing out a deficiency, only a pattern that has already been tacitly acknowledged by historians of philosophy and of literature.

The British Romantics merge these categories: they are literary moralists – in poems, plays, and essays they speak to the great issues of normative ethics – and they also attempt in the spirit of inquiry to extend our thinking about ethics. They enter into what today we would call the discourse of philosophy. I have said that they write essays on the subject and attempt to define their position relative to

A History of Philosophy, vols. V–VII (Garden City: Doubleday, 1959–66); James Engell, *The Creative Imagination: Enlightenment to Romanticism* (Cambridge, Mass.: Harvard University Press, 1981); Lilian Furst, *Romanticism in Perspective: A Comparative Study of Aspects of the Romantic Movements in England, France and Germany* (New York: St. Martin's Press, 1969); Peter Gay, *The Enlightenment: An Interpretation: The Rise of Modern Paganism* (New York: Random House, 1966); John Herman Randall, Jnr., *The Career of Philosophy: From the Middle Ages to the Enlightenment* (Vol. I) and *From the Enlightenment to the Age of Darwin* (Vol. II) (New York: Columbia University Press, 1962, 1965); Leslie Stephen, *A History of English Thought in the Eighteenth Century* (London: John Murray, 1902); Peter Thorslev, *Romantic Contraries: Freedom versus Destiny* (New Haven: Yale University Press, 1984); Hayden White, *The Emergence of Liberal Humanism: An Intellectual History of Western Europe* (New York: McGraw-Hill, 1966–70); Basil Willey, *The English Moralists* (London: Chatto & Windus, 1946).

[2] See John J. Richetti, *Philosophical Writing: Locke, Berkeley, Hume* (Cambridge, Mass.: Harvard University Press, 1983).

various moral philosophers. This interest extends into their literary productions as well. In merging the discourses of literature and philosophy, they find their counterparts more readily in the Continental than in the British tradition. Pascal, Diderot, Voltaire, Rousseau, Goethe, and Schiller are certainly literary moralists but they also occupy more or less prominent places in histories, anthologies, and encyclopedias of philosophy. Similarly, the British Romantics could rightly fill a chapter in the history of moral thought, occupying what would otherwise have been a lacuna between the major late eighteenth-century British figures, Bentham and Godwin, on the one hand, and mid- to late nineteenth-century figures, John Stuart Mill and Herbert Spencer, on the other (a lacuna that Dugald Stewart does not fill single-handed). To be sure, an imponderable like "moral thought" is never carried on solely by the titans of philosophy; the whole of a culture contributes. But beyond this non-specific eligibility for inclusion in a moral history, the Romantics make such conspicuous leaps into the "quick silver mines of metaphysic depths." They are a literary school that has incorporated the concerns, vocabulary, and speculative curiosity of moral philosophy.

The larger argument of this chapter is rather simple. Each of the major European moral schools defends certain mental powers, states of mind, values, and principles over others in arguments that develop oppositionally. Taking Hobbes to be the first stage in this development (he stands in opposition to his own predecessors and contemporaries, such as Descartes and John Bramhall), we can see how various moral schools are subsequently united in opposition to him but on grounds that are themselves opposed. Philosophers of the natural affections and sensibility, such as Shaftesbury and Hutcheson, think that human behavior emanates from a natural inclination of higher value than Hobbesian appetite and fear of death. This natural inclination to the good is reified as the "moral sense." Seventeenth- and eighteenth-century rationalists – William Wollaston, Samuel Clarke, and John Balguy – argue that the moral faculty is not a sense or feeling but a rational intuition. Richard Price, the most sophisticated of the rationalists, accuses the moral sense school of downgrading the moral faculty to "an affair of taste." Later in the eighteenth century, Kantian formalism and British utilitarianism both oppose Hobbesian egoism but differ radically as deontological and teleological ethics respectively, the former valuing acts based on rational respect for categorical moral law and the latter valuing acts that in their consequences yield the greatest amount of pleasure and happiness. Kantianism values intrinsic qualities of an act as they relate to the motive of the agent;

utilitarianism values an act's consequences as registered in a social group.

The British Romantics create a literature informed by an ethics that unites aspects of these and other schools of thought. My principal observation is that the oppositional character of European moral schools as they develop historically is inscribed internally in the Romantics' augmented conception of human personality, action, and moral value. Romantic moral psychology recapitulates structurally the historical dialogue of European ethics that has preceded it. The diachrony of philosophical debate becomes the synchrony of the self's mental theatre.

As I have said, the ethics of Romanticism is impelled by a will to value in the face of a prevailing reduction of value. Rather than assign value by means of exclusionary modes of argument – whereby one might value reason over passion or mental predisposition of the agent over consequences of the act – the Romantics assign value inclusively and make judgments that mingle consequentialist and formalist perspectives. We will see that their tendency toward synthesis (never fully achieved) arises from discriminating dialectic rather than from a weakly interpretive eclecticism. My argument is quasi-Hegelian but more directly Schilleresque: the Romantics preserve aspects of the traditions they are reacting against and attempting to transcend. The will to value is hardly omnivorous but it tends toward acts of inclusion, whether these acts be conceived as conceptual, linguistic, imagined, or literal.

With respect to Hobbes, the Romantics see the force of the argument for psychological egoism, and they see much that does not delight them in the paragon of animals. But they value an egoism freed of moral narrowness – one that fuels the self's integrity and power, an ethical egoism that acknowledges some degree of truth in the Hobbesian perspective. With respect to Shaftesbury, Hutcheson, and Hume, they see happy evidence of natural affections but doubt their sufficiency, either as motive spring or as sanction. Some of the heart's affections are hideous, not holy, and must be chastened. With respect to the eighteenth-century rationalists, they value discursive and intuitive reason more than is often assumed. In the spirit of the Enlightenment, Shelley preserves reason's skeptical, clearing, prophylactic function when he questions the grounds of religious doctrine and social institutions. But like the later Coleridge, who speaks of "Reason" as an agency of noumenal apprehension, Shelley thinks human mind possessed of suprarational consciousness – the imagination in its wide range of functions.

43

As connoisseurs of consciousness, the Romantics, with Kant, value the quality of the agent's motivation; but with the utilitarians they see human action in terms of ends and consequences. They are prophets with a hunger for futurity. Kantian formalism and Fichtean idealism are as deficient in psychology as they are austere in moral absolutism. Coleridge objects, finding in Schiller and Schelling some answers to his more than formal need for a view of human mind grounded in both opposition and synthesis.

This synthetic personality proves a forbidding ideal, however, and much of my commentary treats of strains and fissures. We rarely find portrayed in Romantic literature a harmonious democracy of mental powers. It is an ideal that spawns its own imperatives, often uncomfortably indeterminate, and its own thankless offspring of guilt and bad temper.

Not all this discussion will be centered around "faculties" or human "powers," but one must acknowledge the extent to which the Romantics continued a faculty psychology while reordering its terms and priorities. This reordering can be formulated with attention to changing concepts of the moral faculty, several of which are prominent in British ethics leading up to the Romantics: the "reason" of the Cambridge Platonist Ralph Cudworth and the school of rational morality, Richard Cumberland, John Locke, Samuel Clarke, William Wollaston, John Balguy, and Richard Price; the "conscience" of Joseph Butler, which is an innate monitor; the empirical "moral sense" of Shaftesbury, Hutcheson, and Hume, which is an inherent faculty but activated by moral experience (Adam Smith's "sympathy" is a modification of this concept); and the associationist "moral sense" of Gay and Hartley, which is acquired experientially through instruction, rewards, punishments, and the sunny recognition that virtue is more pleasurable than vice.[3] For these thinkers the major question is the relatively specialized one of how we come by our notions of right and wrong, good and evil. What moral faculty permits us to know what we already know and agree on? Normative issues – what is in fact right and wrong as it applies to particular acts, situations, personalities – are seldom raised. The moral sense schools, whether empirical or associationist, may be concerned with moral psychology but they remain weak on questions of motivation and action. Even weaker in this respect is the school of rational morality, which in its extreme forms

---

[3] See James Bonar, *Moral Sense* (London: Allen & Unwin, 1930); D. D. Raphael, *The Moral Sense* (London: Oxford University Press, 1947); and W. D. Hudson, *Reason and Right: A Critical Examination of Richard Price's Moral Philosophy* (London: Macmillan, 1970).

converts moral psychology into a species of geometry. The individual agent who confronts moral dilemma and is something other than the sum of the faculties is missing in the formulations of these schools.

The Romantic imagination is so extended in its range of function that it effectively supplants moral sense, reason, and conscience as the principal moral faculty. Beyond its power of "sympathy," a concept well developed in eighteenth-century ethics, imagination is a productive power through which self-definition emerges, whether it empower love, work, poetry, or action. Imagination, writes Shelley, is a valuing faculty which is itself valued above reason and other faculties in his psychological reordering. In Blake, Shelley, Keats, and the others, we do not find an egalitarian society of faculties; there are more and less valuable functions to be performed. But their deep interdependency and ceaseless dynamics still militate against the rather static hierarchical taxonomy of faculties that dominates eighteenth-century moral psychology. It becomes more appropriate in Romantic literature and philosophy to speak of the psyche as a force field that extends to the body. In the mythic grammar of Blake and Shelley, the psyche is portrayed in the giant forms engaged in the mental fight of *The Four Zoas* and *Prometheus Unbound*. Coleridge gives witness to this reordering of the psyche less in a disquisition on faculties such as is found in the Appendix to *The Stateman's Manual* than in the tormented play of mind in its concreteness that he communicates in letters, notebook entries, and the major poetry.

Egoism and natural affections

It is characteristic of their synthesizing temper that the Romantics should take Hobbesian thought seriously. They sense that merely notional refutations, as in the eighteenth-century balancing act of "self-love" and "benevolence," are inadequate in a world where depravity reigns from China to Peru. Hazlitt acknowledges that Thomas Hobbes is the father of "modern philosophy," a philosophy he disapproves of and which he labors over years to refute. For Hobbes, the two ruling principles that govern human life – desire or will to power and fear of death – are both egoistic. Fear of death has its use, however, in putting limits to egoistic expansionism; we fear lethal retaliation by our neighbors on whose lawns we would otherwise dump garbage. The Romantics recognize the motive power of both desire and fear of death. They recognize also that the self's vitality requires some components of egoism. Their complaint with Hobbes is that these principles do not come close to providing a sufficient description of human nature; there are other principles as well.

Affinities with Hobbes are easily found. Hazlitt gives a comprehensive portrait of human desire, the perversity of which is often Hobbesian in spirit. Beyond ruthless physical appetencies of hunger and sex, desire is seen in our will to power over others and in envy, the suppressed desire to exterminate one's betters or the better off. His *Liber Amoris* (1823) is a casebook of the physical and mental imbalance induced by implacable desire. Elsewhere, he quotes Hobbes's *Human Nature* approvingly on the self-defeating nature of desire: "Seeing all delight is appetite, and desire of something further, there can be no contentment but in proceeding," but no object of desire, once obtained, satisfies it. As Hazlitt elaborates, "[O]ur desires are kindled by their own heat," and require obstacles. "Thus an object, to which we were almost indifferent while we thought it in our power, often excites the most ardent pursuit or the most painful regret, as soon as it is placed out of our reach" (XX 49–50). Similarly, the life Coleridge gives us in poems, notebooks, and letters is solitary, poor, nasty, brutish, and hardly short enough. The dark moralistic economy of desire dictates that one pays for what one does not get. He senses envy in his relationship with Wordsworth: his frustrated will to power as poet occasions an envy directly proportional to Wordsworth's justifiable but insufferable pride. Even John Keats, the kindliest and most generous of the visionary company, is not wholly out of step with Hobbes: "Very few men have ever arrived at a complete disinterestedness of Mind: very few have been influenced by a pure desire of the benefit of others —" (L II 79).

If anything, Hazlitt and Coleridge exceed Hobbes in their estimate of human depravity. For Hobbes the anarchic tendency of human desire is our natural inheritance, and as he says in a passage quoted in part by Hazlitt (II 145), anyone who locks his doors at night recognizes its pernicious quality. "But neither of us accuse man's nature in it. The Desires, and other passions of man, are in themselves no sin. No more are the actions, that proceed from those passions, till they know a law that forbids them."[4] Laws that forbid have no essential rightness but only a conventional one, as is the case with all human institutions aimed at bettering our dark estate. Hobbes's conventionalist position – that good and evil are defined by the will of the sovereign – disclaims any radical sin in human nature; judgment of our motives and acts has no essential justification. What human beings are by nature cannot, in

[4] *Leviathan*, in *The English Works of Thomas Hobbes*, ed. Sir William Molesworth, III (London: John Bohn, 1839), 114.

any event, be a matter of praise or blame. But as an essentialist, Hazlitt sees human fault as a cheat on an original inheritance of benevolence, a culpable falling away from the better half of our nature: "I believe in the theoretical benevolence, and the practical malignity of man" (XX 343). Coleridge goes further than either Hobbes or Hazlitt in defining a radical depravity. In a profound sense, all willing, as aboriginal and existential desire, recapitulates the pride of Satan.

Hobbes's important treatise, "Of Liberty and Necessity" (1640), directly influences Hazlitt and, indirectly, Shelley (by way of Locke and Hume); it may even influence Blake. Here their revision of Hobbes gives the human being greater power for both good and evil. Hobbes defines liberty as "the absence of all the impediments to action that are not contained in the nature and intrinsical quality of the agent." So defined, liberty can co-exist with necessity or strict causation, and also with the agent's incapacity. If he lacks the intrinsic power to move, he is still free, in the absence of external impediments, to do so:

> As for example, the water is said to descend *freely*, or to have *liberty* to descend by the channel of the river, because there is no impediment that way, but not across, because the banks are impediments. And though the water cannot ascend, yet men never say it wants the *liberty* to ascend, but the *faculty* or *power*, because the impediment is in the nature of the water, and intrinsical. So also we say, he that is tied wants the *liberty* to go, because the impediment is not in him, but in his bands, whereas we say not so of him that is sick or lame, because the impediment is in himself.[5]

Hobbes frequently speaks of humanly imposed external restraints as "*hindering*" liberty.[6] Likewise, Blake, who I speculate may directly or indirectly get the vocabulary from Hobbes, speaks of infringements on liberty both as crimes and as hindering: "Murder is Hindering Another," "Theft is Hindering Another" (*AL* 601).

Blake and Hazlitt part company with Hobbes on the nature of freedom, however, and it is a major revision toward augmentation of

---

[5] "Of Liberty and Necessity," in *The English Works*, IV, 273–4.

[6] E.g.: "To *lay down* a mans *right* to any thing, is to *divest* himself of the *liberty*, of hindring another of the benefit of his own right to the same. For he that renounceth, or passeth away his right, giveth not to any other man a right which he had not before; because there is nothing to which every man had not right by nature: but only standeth out of his way, that he may enjoy his own original right, without hindrance from him; not without hindrance from another"; "Fear and liberty are consistent; as when a man throweth his goods into the sea for *fear* the ship should sink, he doth it nevertheless very willingly, and may refuse to do it if he will: It is therefore the action of one that was *free*: so a man sometimes pays his debt, only for *fear* of imprisonment, which because nobody hindered him from detaining, was the action of a man at *liberty*" (*Leviathan*, in *The English Works*, III, 118, 197).

human power and responsibility. Liberty or freedom for the Romantics is not only the absence of external restraints on personal will, whether from other persons or from forces of nature. To this negative criterion they add a positive one: empowerment. Blake affirms that the "Staminal Virtues of Humanity" free one from the constraints of "Causes & Consequences," as one is empowered to exercise "Individual propensity." After praising Hobbes's argument and adopting, as Blake does not, the doctrine of necessity, Hazlitt writes (somewhat misconstruing Hobbes):

> My notion of a free agent, I confess, is not that represented by Mr. Hobbes, namely, one that when all things necessary to produce the effect are present can nevertheless not produce it; but I believe a free agent of whatever kind, is one which where all things necessary to produce the effect are present, can produce it . . .   (II 255)

The Romantics tend to think of "liberty" or "freedom" as requiring both the absence of external restraints, natural or human, and the internal power to obtain objects of the will. Someone mentally or physically debilitated is not free, even if permitted by all to do whatever he pleases. Ultimately, freedom requires the full development and exercise of distinctly human capabilities. Whether, like Blake and Coleridge, they believe in "origination" that can free one from "Causes & Consequences," or whether, like Hazlitt and Shelley, they believe in theory that all acts are caused and therefore necessitated, the Romantics see freedom as empowerment. The human being is a more capable creature than Hobbes's natural machine, in which will is simply the last "appetite" in the mechanically necessitated string of deliberations.

Hobbes thinks psychological egoism – the theory that the only motive by which we can ever act is self-interest – an inescapable and dismal truth. "*Pity* is *imagination* or *fiction* of *future* calamity to *ourselves*, proceeding from the sense of *another* man's calamity."[7] The authoritarian Commonwealth militates against egoism, channeling individual inclination into protective institutions. The Romantics agree with Hobbes that the "Natural Man" can be piggishly selfish. They think, too, that there are empirically verifiable dimensions of human personality – imagination, benevolence, reason – that disprove psychological egoism. Hobbes himself speaks of the "natural affections of parents to their children" and other virtues that would seem not to collapse into egoism. But he still treats man "as not a moral but only a frightenable Being," complains Coleridge (N III 3548). With

---

[7] *Human Nature*, in *The English Works*, IV, 44.

reference to *Leviathan*, De Quincey mocks Hobbes's own legendary fear of being murdered. Hobbes would have no right even to resist murder "since, according to himself, irresistible power creates the very highest species of right, so that it is rebellion of the blackest dye to refuse to be murdered when a competent force appears to murder you. However, gentlemen, though he was not murdered, I am happy to assure you that (by his own account) he was three times very near being murdered, – which is consolatory."[8]

In their extensive arguments against narrow psychological egoism, Coleridge employs his metaphysics of will and Hazlitt his psychology of feeling and imagination. The "mechanico-corpuscular philosophers" – Coleridge's term for what Hazlitt calls "modern philosophers" – hypothesize that mind is only matter in motion, whereas both deduction and observation point to the contrary. Coleridge notes that if we were as subject to the mechanical whims of motives and impulses as these philosophers assert, we would suffer a chaotic unpredictability of character, going to bed benign and waking up vicious (OM B_2 ff. 56–9). Instead, an abiding identity, anchored in individual will, originates and gives a total pattern to psychological process and human behavior; it empowers us to continue freely in our own being. This is a higher-order egoism. Coleridge also employs Joseph Butler's argument against Hobbes that the end of a desire is the simple gratification of that desire, not a larger principle of self-interest.[9] In his *Essay* Hazlitt argues that the self cannot in theory even be the object of selfish interest, because the imagination, which projects objects of desire in futurity, cannot directly posit the self as object. At any one moment one's "present" self is not identical with one's "future" self, and therefore cannot be a greedy recipient of the imagination's labors.

Hobbes's cheerless view of human nature finds, then, a degree of reluctant accord among the Romantics, some of whom go even further than he in their estimate of human depravity. But they see redemptive powers as well in the human beast without resort to Leviathan. Hobbes's negative conception of desire – as a self-perpetuating, mechanical, egoistic, appetitive, and futile pursuit of self-preservation and power – is supplanted by a conception of desire as vitality, self-empowerment, and the will to value. And Hobbes's famous definition

---

[8] "On Murder Considered as One of the Fine arts,' in *Works*, XIII, 29.

[9] For a fuller treatment of Coleridge's arguments against psychological egoism, see my *Coleridge the Moralist*, 232–42. For his appreciation of the difficulty of refuting Hobbesian psychology, see his *Marginalia*, II, 635–6, where he argues that Fichte has failed to refute Hobbes.

of imagination as *"decaying sense"* yields to a considerably nobler paradigm.

In their view of the uses of desire and passion, the Romantics differ from a figure who also argues against Hobbes and who is often considered (as in Babbitt) their forerunner, Anthony Ashley Cooper, third Earl of Shaftesbury. He has an affinity with – if not direct influence on – the Romantics in his repudiation of psychological egoism and in his concept of nature as a vast "system." Similar things by nature cohere one with another to promote cosmic harmony and health. Concerning the "Parts and Proportions of *the mind*, their mutual Relation and Dependency," Shaftesbury thinks that "the Order or Symmetry of this *inward Part* is, in it-self, no less real and exact, than that of the Body," and that to violate one part of our mental "anatomy" damages the entirety of our *"inward Constitution."* It is a matter of observable fact that in addition to "self-affections" there are "public affections" or "natural affections": "'Tis impossible to suppose a mere sensible Creature originally so ill-constituted, and unnatural, as that from the moment he comes to be try'd by sensible Objects, he shou'd have no one good Passion towards his Kind, no Foundation either of Pity, Love, Kindness, or social Affection."[10] His vision is of systems within systems, smaller ones willingly sacrificing self-interest for the interest of larger ones.

Shaftesbury's ideas of "social affections" and the internal harmony of self have counterparts in Romantic thought, but with significant differences. Harmony for Shaftesbury is in the nature of things, and whatever disturbs it is to that degree vicious. In many disturbances there is the pleasing truth that, as in the pain of teething or of one "planetary System or *Vortex*" swallowing up another, a larger system may profit from the destruction of a smaller. For the Romantics, harmony is much more problematic – an ideal rather than a fact of nature, if an ideal that has a tie with nature. The notion of the Fall, whether in Blake, Coleridge, Shelley, or Keats, implies fragmentation of self and separation from others, beyond which the opportunity may exist for reintegration, but only through struggle. The unified, healthy psyche in Blake is a rather turbulent affair, with faculties dialectically interrelated and conversing in "thunderous majesty." Shaftesbury, who begins the irksome vogue of "calm" self-love, advances a more tranquil ideal. For him, the affections, social and self-directed, "balance" each other by nature. They can get out of line; even kindness or love, "if it be immoderate and beyond a certain degree . . . is

10 "An Inquiry Concerning Virtue, or Merit," in *Characteristics of Men, Manners, Opinions, Times*, II (rpt. Greggs International, 1968), 43.

undoubtedly vitious" (p. 27). But imbalance justly entails personal unhappiness of the vicious party and tends to be self-corrective. Shaftesbury's concept of moral beauty underlies more an aesthetics than an ethics of the self.

Next to the Romantics' conception of desire and the affections, Shaftesbury's is therefore rather tame. Though the seat of the moral life for him is the "heart" – a word used obsessively by Wordsworth and Shelley – Shaftesbury would be dismissive of Keats's talk of the "holiness of the Heart's affections" or "fine intensity." The affections and passions have as their end social harmony, and are of instrumental, not intrinsic, value. But the Romantics see a splendid heightening of being in the very exercise of the affections. They value a much higher energy level within the self than the eighteenth-century moralists would condone. Coleridge complains that Shaftesbury's idea of "virtue" is merely "notional," devoid of the "*manly energy*" that etymologically it is entitled to (*AR* 7, 188). Shaftesbury speaks eloquently on the harmony and beauty of the cosmos in his philosophical dialogue, *The Moralists: A Philosophical Rhapsody* (*Characteristics*, vol. II), but this is more the enthusiasm of the art critic moving amid masterpieces than of the moralist urging that we get greater passion into our lives.

One finds little in *Characteristics* on questions of action, moral dilemma, choosing, or the moral agent. Shaftesbury concerns himself with the qualities of a moral judge, not agent.[11] In setting the tone for much of British ethics, he asks how we come by our notions of approbation and disapprobation, how we perceive character or situations or acts. The virtuous person is one who can clearly perceive and has a "taste" for the morally beautiful. The Romantics reverse a pronounced tendency in British ethics to avoid questions of moral action, commitment, and participation. Virtue is more than how we mentally register the world; it is more than moral psychology. It includes also how we express moral sensibility in the world through gesture, decision, and act. Withdrawal into psychological states of being is a debilitating temptation away from the imperatives of doing. It is ironically their very fascination with action and consequences that underlies the common observation that the Romantics cannot portray action, whether in narrative or drama. Such portrayal, in conventional structures, is inhibited by a heady interpretive consciousness and by a frank uncertainty as to what is to be done.

Romantic texts often have as their focus the nature and conse-

---

[11] See Randall, *From the Middle Ages to the Enlightenment*, 744–5.

quences of a single transforming act. The *locus classicus* is *The Rime of the Ancient Mariner* (1798), in which a single act, mysterious in its origins and intent, generates narrative as extended consequence but with uncertain causality. Blake's *Visions of the Daughters of Albion* (1793) anatomizes the nature and consequences of a violent rape, and his *Milton* (1804–10) those of a galvanic descent from Eden. Shelley's *The Cenci* (1819) has at its center the act of incestuous rape, and his *Prometheus Unbound* (1819) the retraction of a curse. De Quincey's *Confessions of an English Opium-eater* (1822, 1856) follows out the consequences of his escape from Manchester Grammar School. The connection between acts, consequences, and interpretive reading of these is rarely obvious. Both consciousness and action have been questioned well beyond anything dreamt of in Shaftesbury's philosophy.

The Romantics look to action with fascination, envy, and guilt, for many of them see their lives and careers as studies in inactivity. Byron prefers "the talents of *action*" to those of poetry, and finally sets off to Greece to prove it. Coleridge's preoccupation with duty, Shelley's with reform and revolution, Hazlitt's admiration of Napoleon (the supreme actor of the age), Wordsworth's resolve to leave the safety of private consciousness to become a "moral agent . . . who was to *act*" – all these betray varieties of performance anxiety. Hence the presence of alter egos capable of acting where they themselves cannot act. Blake thinks that all acts insofar as they are *acts* are good: "Accident is the omission of act in self & the hindering of act in another, This is Vice but all Act [from Individual propensity] is Virtue" (AL 600). But others see acts springing from the deepest sources of personality, where both love and hate are found. Shelley, commenting on Wordsworth's lines in "Tintern Abbey" – "Those little, nameless, unremembered acts / Of kindness and of love" – observes that these acts "as well as those deadly outrages which are inflicted by a look, a word – or less – the very refraining from some faint and most evanescent expression of countenance; these flow from a profounder source than the series of our habitual conduct, which . . . derives its origin from without" (SM 192). This "profounder source" Coleridge identifies with the personal will, the exercise of which always risks evil and makes problematic, if not useless, all imperatives governing action.

If this alignment of act with evil would seem unduly worrisome to Shaftesbury, it would seem perverse to Joseph Butler, who thinks human beings possessed of a power – conscience – that scrupulously attends to such matters. Butler is immensely influential in British ethics and was required reading in British schools up into the twentieth century. I have mentioned that Coleridge pays his respects in this quarter by incorporating Butler's still-admired refutation of Hobbesian psychological egoism into his Opus Maximum. Hazlitt quotes him at length on self-love in his *Lectures on English Philosophy* (II 224–5). Butler's portrait of the self and its faculties is more highly structured than Shaftesbury's. He complains that Shaftesbury has omitted from the "system" of human nature an account of "conscience," which presides over the "principles" of self-love and benevolence, as well as over the various passions, appetites, and affections. The stoic imperative to "follow nature" still holds, he says, if we recognize, contrary to Hobbes, that our "nature" includes higher intuitive faculties as well as lower desiring ones. The interplay of faculties has its parallels in Blake and Coleridge. Passions and appetites are not summarily devalued: they seek particular concrete objects necessary to the system as a whole but not necessarily answering to selfish motives. "Cool self-love" works in concert with conscience to arbitrate among passions and appetites, deciding which objects of desire best answer to true self-interest, identified with our higher nature.

Relative to Romantic psychology, Butler's system of human nature is simplistic. His view of conscience, for instance, is all too mellow. It exists as an innate faculty and the evidence for it is everywhere: "it cannot possibly be denied that there is this principle of reflection or conscience in human nature." Though his concept of conscience as regulator of the faculties is innovative, he declines to describe its nature. It is enough that it exists, "whether called conscience, moral reason, moral sense, or divine reason; whether considered as a sentiment of the understanding, or as a perception of the heart, or, which seems the truth, as including both."[12] Butler fails to acknowledge the tyranny conscience can impose. In Blake's *The Book of Urizen* (1794), conscience produces a grotesque skeletal simulacrum of a human being and is the negation of imagination. Butler's reconciliation of self-love and benevolence is too easy, academic, and notional for the Romantic temper; these are instead true and often brutal contraries. Coleridge debates the claims of inclination and duty and sees their ideal reconciliation, but he also testifies to their dreadful existential conflict. Like Shaftesbury, Butler does not see that the civil war in the cave can be this intense.

Sensibility, associationism, and language

The reply to Hobbesian psychological egoism, after Shaftesbury and Butler, continues doggedly into the Age of Sensibility. Francis

---

[12] *British Moralists*, I, 342, 397.

Hutcheson elaborates an entire system upon Shaftesbury's "moral sense" – an inherent power exercised variously as approbation or disapprobation, sympathy, and the urge to act benevolently. Conjoined with the moral sense are the affections, passions, and sentiments that assist it in its good work. In the ethical systems of Hutcheson, Adam Smith, and Hume, we find the philosophical analogue of the literary vogue of the Man of Feeling. In these philosophers there is less emphasis on "system," "harmony," and the "constitution" of human nature than one sees in Shaftesbury and Butler. Instead, we find a complex taxonomy of psychology which expounds, sometimes drearily, the mechanics of affective response. David Hartley answers Hobbes within the framework of Lockean epistemology in propounding an experientially acquired moral sense. With reference to a different psychology from Hutcheson's, he too thinks a network of social affections insures benevolence, even if the benevolent person is an automaton of sorts.

As Hutcheson develops the concept, moral sense is both cognitive and volitional: it is a direct, non-rational intuition and judgment of moral experience which also impels the agent to act morally. Unlike conscience, traditionally linked to fault, guilt, and pain, the moral sense leads to a pleasurable state of mind – the pleasure of moral recognition and of being virtuous. Hartley goes so far as to call "scrupulosity" or guilt a "Degeneration of the Moral Sense."[13] This faculty registers concrete moral experience as "uneasiness" – for Locke the primary motivational principle – if that experience is disharmonious. But its natural tendency is toward enhancement of pleasurable states of feeling, of qualitatively higher and higher moral pleasures. This optimism is greatest in Hartley, for whom, as Basil Willey puts it, the human being "may be regarded as a sort of refinery in which the loftiest spirituality is being mechanically distilled out of sense."[14] In its pleasurable response to harmonious experience, the moral sense retains the aesthetic function Shaftesbury assigns it in discussing moral beauty.

The British moral rationalists will criticize the concept of moral sense because it seems to degrade moral awareness by making it analogous to subjective sensory response. The most blatant anti-rationalist

---

[13] *Observations on Man*, 2 pts. (London: Leake and Frederick, 1749), I, 498.

[14] *The Eighteenth-Century Background* (London: Chatto & Windus, 1940), 144. Ironically, Hartley's optimistic psychology derives from Locke's chapter, "Of the Association of Ideas," in the fourth edition of *An Essay Concerning Human Understanding*, in which association is the unnatural, idiosyncratic connection of ideas occasioned by "chance or custom," often manifested in unreasonable (we might say neurotic) antipathies dating from accidental associations in our youth. See Locke's *Essay*, ed. Peter H. Nidditch (Oxford: Clarendon Press, 1975, 1979), Bk. II, 394–401.

defense of "moral sentiment" is found in Hume. Arguing that his is an empirically derived and non-metaphysical view, he writes, "The hypothesis which we embrace is plain. It maintains that morality is determined by sentiment. It defines virtue to be *whatever mental action or quality gives to a spectator the pleasing sentiment of approbation;* and vice the contrary."[15] Hume makes the fact/value dichotomy absolute, and declares the province of reason to be solely the assessment of facts and their interrelatedness. Value judgments are occasioned by feelings alone, and only these directly motivate action. The cognitive moral sense of Hutcheson is revised by Hume in the direction of non-cognitivism. As a philosophic *provocateur,* he writes: "Nothing can oppose or retard the impulse of passion, but a contrary impulse . . . Reason is, and ought only to be the slave of the passions, and can never pretend to any other office than to serve and obey them . . . It is not contrary to reason to prefer the destruction of the whole world to the scratching of my finger."[16]

Wordsworth, Lamb, De Quincey and others sometimes casually use the term "moral sense," which by the early nineteenth century has lost its affiliation with one or another ethical system and is no longer at the center of ethical debate. Rather than dismiss the term out of hand, Coleridge and Hazlitt are more analytic and redeploy the term as a species of the sympathetic imagination, supremely cognitive in function. In a lengthy philosophical disquisition of 1825 entitled "SENSE," Coleridge describes sense as the capacity to "subjectivize" the world of objects in such a way as to know the grounds of our relatedness to them. The object world includes natural objects, other persons, and our personal object world of body, language, and, through reflexivity, our own mind. The perception of ourselves as simultaneously object and subject can be extended to the larger object world: we can subjectivize it through the inferential and comparative power of "sense." It permits us to know our way in the world, to attain "some practical purpose." If we have "*sound* Sense," we know how to direct our will toward objects "on which those powers may be exercised, and in or by means of which those Wishes and Aims may be realized—." Being-in-the-world requires sense as a pragmatic cognitive power. It becomes "*Moral* Sense" insofar as it joins the interests of other persons with our own in a common subjectivity:

In short, Knowing for the sake of Knowing is Science: Knowing for the sake of Being is Sense. If in exclusive reference to the responsibility of *personal* Being, it

---

[15] *An Inquiry Concerning the Principles of Morals,* ed. Charles W. Hendel (New York: Liberal Arts, 1957), 107.
[16] *A Treatise of Human Nature,* in *British Moralists,* II, 5–6.

is the *Moral* Sense—to the peculiar interests of the Individual, it is what we call good Natural Sense—The perfection of human Nature arises where the first is allowed to be an end but yet in subordination to the second, as the alone *ultimate* end, and where this second existing in combination with the third elevates & takes it up into its own class by the habit of contemplating both the common & the peculiar Interests of *all* Individuals, as far as they be within his sphere of influence, as his own individual Interest—Here we have the Man of practical Rectitude, with right Principle prescribing the Rule, Discretion determining the Objects, and Judgement guiding the application. He seeks his own happiness, and he seeks the happiness of his Neighbors, & he seeks both in such a way and by such means as enables him to find each in the other.

(N IV 5280).

Moral sense goes beyond personal to a collective subjectivity.

The affinity between this concept of moral sense and imagination is seen in Coleridge's illustration of sense in action. He speaks of how a "youthful Poet" might respond to Sir Francis Chantrey's marble bust of Wordsworth (rediscovered by Russell Noyes and now in the Lilly Library). The sculpture would cease to be an object as the "material gives way & hides itself," the surface becoming a mirror that shows the poet his own deepest "Nature & Humanity." "A lovely Child contemplates his form in the mirror & believes it another—& even so thro' Love & Self-oblivious Admiration of Excellence without, we have sought the existence of the excellence in ourselves." Sense permits a mutual transparency of self to world and world to self. Just as the stone becomes a mirror, so the "surrounding Shell of [the poet's] accidental individuality becomes transparent" (*N* IV 5280). As the power of subjectivizing the object world, the moral sense is distinguishable from sympathetic imagination only in that Coleridge thinks the personal self not lost in projection, but discovered, serviced, enhanced. Coleridgean bad conscience is conspicuous in its absence from these formulations.

Hazlitt challenges Helvetius's scurrilous brand of enlightened psychological egoism. The French philosopher finds the English laughable for being so enamoured of "moral sense," which he declares non-existent if only because it cannot be ascribed to any of the five senses that make up the "physical sensibility." Hazlitt finds it "strange" that Helvetius and other Continental writers

choose to insult the English writers for daring to wear the plain, homely, useful, national garb of philosophy, while their most glossy and most fashionable suits are made up of the shreds and patches stolen from our countryman Hobbes, disguised with a few spangles, tinselled lace, and tagged points of their own.

(II 222−3).

Hazlitt thinks the question of

> whether there is a moral sense, is reducible to this: whether the mind can understand or conceive, or be affected by, any thing beyond its own physical or mechanical feelings. It if can, then there is something in man besides his five senses and the organs which compose them, for these can give him no thought, conception, or sympathy with any thing beyond himself. Or even with himself beyond the present moment. (II 220)

The "something," as he argues ad nauseam in *Essay on the Principles of Human Action* and elsewhere, is the imagination.

It is easy to see why the Romantics express no hostility to the term "moral sense." They enter their own brief against the rationalists, do not denigrate sense experience or analogies based on it, and conceive an interaction of the ethical and the aesthetic. For them "moral sense," like "moral beauty," is no oxymoron. But the term "moral sense" is rendered largely obsolete by "imagination," which has, like the moral sense, a valuing power: "Reason is the enumeration of quantities already known; imagination is the perception of the value of those quantities, both separately and as a whole" (*DP* 480). Shelley's formulation echoes Hume's distinction between the functions of reason and moral sentiment. Imagination is also, like moral sense, a motivational power: "The great instrument of moral good is the imagination . . . Poetry strengthens that faculty [imagination] which is the organ of the moral nature of man, in the same manner as exercise strengthens a limb." The spectator of Greek drama imaginatively sympathizes with that "ideal perfection and energy which every one feels to be the internal type of all that he loves, admires, and would become. The imagination is enlarged by a sympathy with pains and passions so mighty, that they distend in their conception the capacity of that by which they are conceived . . ." (*DP* 488, 490). And though Shelley, more than Hartley, is aware of the "pains of the imagination," he speaks of the pleasure that originates in perception of harmony, rhythm, and order.

The Romantic imagination's claim to truth as well as beauty and goodness counters the non-cognitivism of Humean moral sentiment and the subjectivism of moral sense as usually described. Imagination appropriates the powers that the moral rationalists ascribe to reason and judgment. As Shelley implies, the fact/value dichotomy defines the modern temper and must be overcome: "We want the creative faculty to imagine that which we know." Although the Romantics are often taken to be subjectivists, it is noteworthy that none of them is an

57

ethical relativist. Their stubborn belief in intuition wards off the relativistic implications of moral sense.

On the Continent a figure more powerful than Shaftesbury, Hutcheson, or Hartley challenges Hobbes on the supposedly protective influence of human institutions, arguing instead that they corrupt an original innocence. Rousseau's *Julie: ou La Nouvelle Héloïse* (1761) contributes greatly to the cult of sensibility, the close monitoring of the heart's responses. In Germany of the *Sturm und Drang*, such works as Goethe's *The Sorrows of Young Werther* (*Die Leiden des Jungen Werthers*, 1774) and Schiller's *The Robbers* (*Die Räuber*, 1781) help create the commonplace, which as M. H. Abrams notes would have seemed strange to earlier generations, that the worth of the human being is gauged by the quality and intensity of affective response. Complex currents, literary and philosophical, blend to produce this idea, which has much impact on the Romantics. They come to it rather late in the day and, Babbitt's view notwithstanding, subject it to a severe testing. In a post-revolutionary era, they cannot be innocent readers of Werther, Saint-Preux, René, or – within their own tradition – of Ossian, the Vicar of Wakefield, and Uncle Toby.

It is helpful to make a distinction with respect to how various British Romantics view the role of the affections. Those who at least entertain the idea that moral worth depends on the quality and intensity of affective responses include Wordsworth and De Quincey, Hazlitt and Keats. (They are hardly uncritical of the idea.) Arguing from the beginning the radical insufficiency of the affective life are Blake and Coleridge, Shelley and Byron.

This division roughly corresponds to two schools of thought within the poetics of Romantic expressivism – the school of Longinus and the school of Plotinus.[17] The former, which I call emotive expressivism, tends to valorize emotion, spontaneity, intensity, and sensibility; it includes such figures as John Dennis, Wordsworth, Hazlitt, Keats, and John Stuart Mill. These critics and poets are far from assuming that an equivalence necessarily exists between the poet's affective intentionality and the poem. The poet must discover what language is commensurate to inner life, what language is "the echo of a great soul." To this end, Longinus gives an inventory of rhetorical figures and Wordsworth warns against stale rhetorical conventions.

The school of Plotinus, which I call organic expressivism, includes such figures as Edward Young, Schiller, Schelling, Blake, Coleridge,

---

[17] This discussion builds on M. H. Abrams's seminal study, *The Mirror and the Lamp* (1953; rpt. New York: W. W. Norton, 1958).

Shelley, Carlyle, and Emerson (but not Byron). For them emotion is but one component of the creative mind's total emanation, whether the context is literature or life. Coleridge writes that poetry is a "mode of composition that calls into action & gratifies the largest number of the human Faculties in Harmony with each other, & in just proportion" (*N* III 3827) – a formula more grandiose than Wordsworth's that poetry is the "spontaneous overflow of powerful feelings" taking "its origin from emotion recollected in tranquillity."

But even those Romantic authors who center human values in the "Heart's affections" give us more an analytical than a panegyrical view of them. Wordsworth – who has been the subject of a lengthy comparison with Rousseau and who echoes some of the conventions of late eighteenth-century sentimentalism – makes frequent use of the standard vocabulary of sensibility and associationist psychology.[18] In his familiar lyrics that set up conventional antagonisms between heart and head, he favors an ethics of feeling. The language of the affections, sentiments, and passions remains a constant in his work, even though he may be shifting, in other respects, from empiricism to organicism or from liberalism to conservatism. Matthew, Michael, and the Pedlar are morally good in their resoluteness and the continuity of their attachments. Up to a point, "feeling comes in aid / Of feeling."

Though the increased value given the affections has a precedent in the ethics of feeling from Shaftesbury to Hume, there is little in this philosophical tradition to prepare one for Wordsworth. For one thing, there is a wishful assumption in Hutcheson, Hartley, and others that the increase of sensibility entails an increase in happiness. But Wordsworth, like Rousseau, knows human beings are in love and love what vanishes. For another, with the exception of Hume who discounts the integral "self" altogether, the British philosophers do not portray the supplement of consciousness, the apperception of beings who perceive their own functioning minds and bodies in a wealth of circumstance, human and material. This observation points not so much to the greater power of literary over philosophical texts as to a limitation in the British moral tradition itself. Its philosophers expound so doggedly their taxonomy of moral psychology that they neglect either to reconstruct mental parts into a functional totality or to describe the experiencing consciousness. Even more than Rousseau, Wordsworth attempts to perceive the feeling and constructing mind

---

[18] See Margery Sabin, *English Romanticism and the French Tradition* (Cambridge, Mass.: Harvard University Press, 1976), 3–124, on Wordsworth and Rousseau; and James Averill, *Wordsworth and the Poetry of Human Suffering* (Ithaca, N. Y.: Cornell University Press, 1980), 21–54, on Wordsworth and the sentimental background.

from within, to discover the self's continuity amid radical change in circumstance. De Quincey too attempts to communicate this inwardness, the feel of feeling, the perception of perception. For him, "the true internal *acts* of moral man are his thoughts, his yearnings, his aspirations, his sympathies or repulsions of heart" (XI 180). States of feeling, as in Wordsworth, are linked to the deepest layers of memory and will. De Quincey exceeds the philosophers of sensibility in the depth of context he envisages for human feeling.

In rejecting Godwinian rationalism, Hazlitt writes that "passion . . . is the essence, the chief ingredient in moral truth" (XII 46). But in many respects he is critical of passion, which in itself sets no standard. In *Remarks on the Systems of Hartley and Helvétius* (only a micron more stimulating than his *Essay*, to which it is an appendix), he objects to Hartley's treatment of the passions. Sympathy for another's pain is felt, says Hartley, whenever we are reminded through association of our own pain in some previous moment. Noting that this is "the doctrine of sympathy advanced by Adam Smith" as well, Hazlitt complains that Hartley's concept of feeling is "in fact neither self-love nor benevolence, neither fear nor compassion, nor voluntary attachment to any thing, but an unmeaning game of battledore and shuttlecock kept up between the nerves and muscles" (I 80). If there is to be human freedom, one must be capable of fastening feeling to object with some discrimination, irrespective of random association (I 72).

The seminal influence on Hazlitt with respect to the passions is, I think, Rousseau, and not the British moralists of the sentiments. He spent "two whole years in reading [*Julie* and *The Confessions*]; and (gentle reader, it was when we were young) in shedding tears over them. 'As fast as the Arabian trees / Their medicinal gums.' They were the happiest years of [my] life." Rousseau's

passions never went down, the pulse that agitated his heart never ceased to beat. It was this strong feeling of interest, accumulating in his mind, which overpowers and absorbs the feelings of his readers. He owed all his power to sentiment. The writer who most nearly resembles him in our own times is the author of the *Lyrical Ballads*. (IV 91–2)

Hazlitt himself more closely resembles Rousseau in such matters as individualism and arrogance, and in the erotic character of his autobiographical *Liber Amoris*. In *The Confessions* Rousseau writes, "I may omit or transpose facts, or make mistakes in dates; but I cannot go wrong about what I have felt, or about what my feelings have led me to do [ni sur ce que mes sentiments m'ont fait faire]; and these are the chief subjects of my story."[19] *Liber Amoris* is similarly an account of what Hazlitt's feelings *have led him to do*. The phrase implies that feelings can dangerously overpower the larger self, that one can take some pride in them even when dreadful, and that they do not fully constitute identity. Hazlitt often controverts any simple correspondence of a scale of value with a scale of intensity.

Influenced by Hazlitt's writings on sympathy and intensity, Keats expresses an ethics of feeling: "I have the same Idea of all our Passions as of Love they are all in their sublime, creative of essential Beauty—" (*L* I 184). What may resemble a Shaftesburyian optimism about the affections promoting beauty and harmony is soon dropped for a stormier view; it is "breathing human passion" that "leaves a heart high-sorrowful and cloyed, / A burning forehead, and a parching tongue." Keats's "yearning Passion . . . for the beautiful" (*L* I 404) is just that – a yearning, or *Sehnsucht*, subject to the contradictions that beset strong desire.

In Blake and Coleridge, Shelley and Byron, we will find a more direct critique of an ethics of feeling and sensibility. Of these Coleridge is most explicit and my focus here. He attacks Laurence Sterne "and his imitators" as more pernicious than Hobbes:

The vilest appetites and the most remorseless inconstancy towards their objects, acquired the titles of *the Heart, the irresistible Feelings, the too tender Sensibility*: and if the Frosts of Prudence, the icy chains of Human Law thawed and vanished at the genial warmth of Human *Nature*, who *could help it*? It was an amiable Weakness!

(*AR* 53–4)

Feelings are not self-vindicating; they must be appropriate to context and compatible with "Universal Reason." Sensibility is "no sure pledge of a Good Heart." If undisciplined, a seemingly good emotion, such as pity, can "co-operate to deprave us" (*CL* II 711). Sensitive to the ironies and duplicities of sentimentality, Coleridge cites the lady who weeps while reading *Werther* and sipping a "beverage sweetened with human blood" – sweetened with sugar produced through the slave trade. Though he laments the desiccation of spirit brought on by loss of the "Natural Man" in him, Coleridge thinks the overvaluation of passions is degenerate.

Passions and feelings do of course have value, both instrumental and intrinsic, and Coleridge situates them in human psychology and the scale of values. In a letter to Southey of 1803 he offers an offhand revision of associationism, which he thinks

---

[19] *The Confessions*, trans. J. M. Cohen (New York: Penguin, 1953), 262.

61

depends in a much greater degree on the recurrence of resembling states of Feeling, than on Trains of Idea / . . . Believe me, Southey! a metaphysical Solution, that does not instantly *tell* for something in the Heart, is grievously to be suspected as apocryphal. I almost think, that Ideas *never* recall Ideas, as far as they are Ideas—any more than Leaves in a forest create each other's motion—The Breeze it is that runs thro' them / it is the Soul, the state of Feeling—.

(CL II 961)

By this time Coleridge has already rejected associationism on the grounds of its insufficiency as a model of mind; now he attacks it within the narrower psychological compass where it might have retained some validity.

With respect to Locke and Hartley there is a blur in this oft-quoted passage in Coleridge's use of "Ideas," since for these thinkers feelings are themselves ideas. Hartley writes that "our Passions or Affections can be no more than Aggregates of simple Ideas united by Association." The strength of these passions derives from the fact that they combine the "Traces of the sensible Pleasures and Pains" that always accompany our experience and that singly might not exert such force.[20] He is building on Locke, who thinks that the "internal sensations" of pain and pleasure "form to ourselves the ideas of our passions . . . Thus any one reflecting upon the thought he has of the Delight, which any present, or absent thing is apt to produce in him, has the *Idea* we call *Love*."[21] Desire and will for both thinkers undergo a comparable reduction. For Locke desire is "an *uneasiness* of the Mind for want of some absent good." Uneasiness alone determines the will, which is the power to think one thing rather than another and "to prefer the motion of any part of the body to its rest."[22] For Hartley the will is "that Desire or Aversion, which is strongest for the then present Time . . . Since therefore all Love and Hatred, all Desire and Aversion, are factitious, and generated by Association; *i.e.* mechanically; it follows that the Will is mechanical also."[23]

It would be unlike Coleridge himself to make any strict separation of "ideas" (Lockean or otherwise) and "feelings." And in the letter to Southey he is not valuing feelings over concepts. Rather, he is objecting to the notion that human mind is as mechanical and heartless as all that; he seeks a more vital principle.

In *Biographia Literaria* he expounds at length (with not a little quiet

[20] *Observations on Man*, I, 368.
[21] *An Essay Concerning Human Understanding*, Bk. II, 230.
[22] *Essay*, Bk. II, 250–8.
[23] *Observations on Man*, I, 371.

assistance from J. G. E. Maass's *Essay Concerning the Imagination* [*Versuch über die Einbildungskraft*, 1792, 1797]) his objections to Hartley, whose model of mind would entail an uncontrollable "delirium" of impressions because of the "absence of all interference of the will, reason, and judgment" (*BL* I 111). The passivity of mind in Hartley's scheme places all mental phenomena on the same level, and in explaining everything associationism explains nothing. Human will, reason, judgment, "instead of being the determining causes of association, must needs be represented as its *creatures*, and among its mechanical *effects*," which reduces will to the chance union of an indefinite number of mental currents (*BL* I 110). In reducing human mind to the "mere notion of my muscles and nerves," the associationist denies the very possibility of a moral agent, now supplanted by "blind causes, the only true artists." Human feelings lose any necessary connection with value. "We only *fancy*, that we act from rational resolves, or prudent motives, or from impulses of anger, love, or generosity. In all cases the real agent is a *something–nothing–everything*, which does all of which we know, and knows nothing of all that itself does" (*BL* I 120).

For Coleridge the place of the affective life is to mediate the physical and the intellectual. He opposes Cartesian dualism, with its wholesale separation of physiology from psychology. But he also opposes the reduction of psychology to physiology, a tendency he traces from Hobbes to Locke to Hartley. In what he calls his "Psychosomatic Ology," emotion is an intermediate state; passion is described as "a state of emotion, which tho' it may have its pre-disposing cause in the Body, and its occasion in the external Incidents or Appearances, is yet not *immediately* produced by the incidents themselves, but by the person's Thoughts and Reflections concerning them." In a rather stern spirit he speaks of "the right Discipline of the Passions, whether by control, or prevention, or suppression" (*IS* 66–7). Coleridge has thus put feelings in their place. The impulse to do so is shared by many of these authors, often said to be passion's slaves.

The heart must be educated, then, in keeping with its mediating role, but it must also be listened to. Coleridge complains of the "conscientious persecutors" of the Inquisition, who believed that they were acting "on fixed principles." There is a danger in "the substitution of principles or motives for the good heart." What he calls the "temperamental *pro*-virtues . . . are not built to stand the storms of strong temptation; yet on the whole they carry on the benignant scheme of social nature" (NB 29, f. 112). The sins of passion are less culpable than those of intellect.

The British Romantics echo some primitivist assumptions concerning the origins of language in natural passion, but they are doubtful of an outright correspondence of the natural and the virtuous. Passion is again in need of supplement and control before it takes on moral value. In his *Essay on the Origin of Languages* (*Essai sur l'origine des langues*, 1755, published 1781), Rousseau had written that natural pity or compassion is activated by imagination, giving rise to language. As the first social institution and ground of all others, language degenerates the farther it descends in time from its source in spontaneous natural passion. In his Preface to *Lyrical Ballads*, Wordsworth observes that in "low and rustic life" "the essential passions of the heart find a better soil in which they can attain their maturity, are less under restraint, and speak a plainer and more emphatic language" (*PRW* I 124). The paradox one finds in Rousseau – that the very linguistic ability distinguishing us as human, in its first use signals a decline from natural virtue – is seen in Wordsworth, whose search for a speech originating in natural passion tends to situate human virtue in prelinguistic states of being. The history of English poetry gives evidence of the more general decline of language abstracted from its vital roots in passion. The poet attempts to overcome the conventional aspect of language by means of language itself, repossessing its passional origin and approximating a natural language.[24] (Those modern linguists who insist on the arbitrary nature of the sign would brand the effort strictly futile.)

Among the other major figures, Byron most frequently indulges primitivist nostalgia and the view of language as a tarnishing of original innocence. When Don Juan and Haidee encounter one another on a Greek isle, they do not share a verbal language, but "they *thought* a language":

> And all the burning tongues the Passions teach
>   Found in one sigh the best interpreter
> Of Nature's oracle—first love,—that all
> Which Eve has left her daughters since her fall.   (*DJ* II 189)

This is prelinguistic communication engendered by passion. If Haidee were to have spoken of "scruples," or made or demanded vows, or spoken of constancy – if she had committed any speech act at all – she would have stained her "pure Ignorance," and jeopardized the innocence and intensity of their love. In its most conventional development, language serves the interests of cant, an institutionalized discrepancy

---

[24] For a contrary reading of Wordsworth on this issue, see James McKusick, *Coleridge's Philosophy of Language* (New Haven: Yale University Press, 1986), 110–18.

between signs and social reality that Byron derides. De Quincey, in the Ann of Oxford Street episode of his *Confessions*, testifies that no amount of impassioned prose can ever approximate the impact of a simple, loving, non-verbal gesture – for instance, a teenage London prostitute's giving a down-and-out, expiring youth a glass of hot wine without his asking.

But the assumption of prelinguistic virtue is not all that common in the writings of the British Romantics. More so is the assumption of an original chaos in human personality that is partly disciplined through verbal expression. This pattern reverses the values primitivism assigns to the nature/culture antinomy. Blake speaks of "English, the rough basement. / Los built the stubborn structure of the Language, acting against / Albions melancholy, who must else have been a Dumb despair" (*J* 36: 58–60). Linguistic structure, a product of imagination, grounds and permeates other mental processes. In speech one ex-presses negative passion. Language for Blake is a primary agency of "awakening" to full, original, Edenic humanity. Similarly, Shelley depicts speech as a gift of Prometheus to alleviate man's dark estate (*PU* II iv 72); and language is ideally "a perpetual Orphic song" which "rules with Daedal harmony a throng / Of thoughts and forms, which else senseless and shapeless were" (*PU* IV 415–17). Language controls the mutiny within of natural passion. In *Childe Harold's Pilgrimage*, Byron speaks of the teeming muddle of interior feeling and sensation that he would focus in a single word, with the Longinian power of "lightning"; but he confesses to ultimate linguistic impotence. Self-destructive passion persists beyond his ability to express and purge it (III 97). The greatest compliment Hazlitt gives Coleridge is to say that this brilliant underachiever had given him a language, without which Hazlitt's own understanding would have remained "dumb and brutish" (XVII 107). His larger writing career is a series of cathartic speech acts, a torrent of passion purged, and *Liber Amoris* an ultimate attempt to purge and discipline through writing. In *The Eve of St. Agnes* Keats speaks of the pain Madeline feels from amorous passion:

> No uttered syllable, or, woe betide!
> But to her heart, her heart was voluble,
> Paining with eloquence her balmy side;
> As though a tongueless nightingale should swell
> Her throat in vain, and die, heart-stifled, in her dell.　(203–7)

No facile partisans of the passional self, the Romantics tend to see language originating in passion for the sake of expressing and ordering it. One speaks in order not to be ill.

Coleridge is most advanced in his speculations on language, mind, and passion. Language is for him an active agency of mind that expresses human will and culture. He questions Locke's theory of the arbitrariness of the linguistic sign and the linguist Horne Tooke's extensions of the empirical view of language.[25] William Godwin should not "cease to appear as a *bold* moral thinker," writes Coleridge, and should therefore

> write a book on the power of words, and the processes by which human feelings form affinities with them— . . . 'Is Logic the *Essence* of thinking?' in other words—Is 'arbitrary' a misnomer? Are not words &c parts & germinations of the Plant? And what is the Law of their Growth?—In something of this order I would endeavor to destroy the old antithesis of *Words* & *Things*, elevating, as it were, words into Things, & living Things too. (*CL* I 625–6)

Active thinking is impossible without a natural or "living" language not identified with logic.

Coleridge is not arguing that words are intrinsically expressive of the things to which they refer. It is a fundamental error to say that "words and their syntax are the immediate representatives of *Things*, or that they correspond to *Things*. Words correspond to Thoughts" (*CL* VI 630). But he is arguing that words are themselves things in a special sense. He adapts an etymology from Tooke, in which the words "think" and "thing" are said to have a common origin, and he turns it against Tooke's passive, mechanistic concept of mind and language: "Thought is the participle past of Thing – a thing acts on me but not on me as purely passive, which is the case in all *affection* affectus, but res agit in co-agentum [the thing acts upon the co-agent] – in the first, I am *thinged*, in the latter I thing or think—" (*N* III 3587). It is by means of language that we deny ourselves as passive things, and instead "*thingify*," or read and substantiate, the world according to our thought of it. Through the order of words, itself an empowering structure of things generated by mind, we retain power over the order of things.

> But above all do not let me forget, that Language is the medium of all Thoughts to *ourselves*[,] of all Feelings to others, & partly to ourselves—now a . . . thing

---

[25] Locke writes: "Thus we may conceive how *Words*, which were by Nature so well adapted to that purpose [of human communication], come to be made use of by Men, as *the Signs* of their *Ideas*; not by any natural connexion, that there is between particular articulate Sounds and certain *Ideas*, for then there would be but one Language amongst all Men; but by a voluntary Imposition, whereby such a Word is made arbitrarily the Mark of such an *Idea*" (*Essay*, Bk. III, 405). My discussion is indebted to McKusick, *Coleridge's Philosophy of Language*, 41–52.

cannot be a medium in the living continuity of nature but by essentially partaking of the nature of the two things mediated. Hence our native Language, by the incessant process of unification without loss of distinction . . . becomes indeed επεα Ζωοντα—*living* words. (*N* III 4237)

As the medium of expressing our feelings and thoughts to others and to ourselves, language permits us to read our selves and to prevent the passions from rendering us passive.

Ideally language retains the imprint of its origin in passion and puts us intimately in touch with its referred world. As Coleridge says, in agreement with Descartes, "Words act upon us immediately, exciting a mild current of Passion & Feeling without the regular intermediation of Images" (*CL* II 698). But the Romantics are sophisticates with respect to questions regarding a metaphysics or linguistics of presence. To be sure, Wordsworth writes that language should be an "incarnation" of thought, not simply its clothing; and Coleridge, in a theological context, speaks of how the symbol is "consubstantial" with what it represents. But no poet is more obsessed than Wordsworth with the fact that the memorials we erect in landscape or poems give us traces instead of presence. He dramatizes both the need for presence and sad perplexity at limits to repossession. Coleridge speaks of the symbol's "outness," which promises more substance than it yields – the central predicament in love relationships:

All minds must think by some *symbols*— the strongest minds possess the most vivid Symbols in the Imagination— yet this ingenerates a *want*, ποθον, *desiderium*, for vividness of Symbol: which something that is *without*, that has the property of *Outness* (a word which Berk[e]ley preferred to "Externality") can alone fully gratify/even that indeed not fully—for the utmost is only an approximation to that absolute *Union*, which the soul sensible of its imperfection in itself, of its *Halfness*, yearns after. (*N* III 3325)

He notes that a "focal word" may combine a large number of personal associations in an exponential increase of power, just as many separate rays of light may combine to create an image as powerful "as if a solid flesh and blood reality were there" – when in fact it is absent. "The focal word has acquired a *feeling of reality*—it heats and burns, makes itself be felt. If we do not grasp it, it seems to grasp us, as with a hand of flesh and blood, and completely counterfeits an immediate presence, an intuitive knowledge" (*IS* 101). The focal word *counterfeits* an immediate presence; language may be most treacherous when most alive with the imprint of its passional origin. For De Quincey, who quotes Wordsworth's comments on language as incarnation approvingly, it is nevertheless because language fails to communicate the presence of one mind to another that verbal communication, spoken or written, chronically miscarries. Few people in De Quincey's voluble autobiographical writings ever grasp what anybody else is talking about. We carry with us the "burden of the incommunicable." And Hazlitt writes that "no language, no description . . . can strictly come up to the truth and force of reality" (XII 45).

The moral dangers of language issue from these problematics. For Wordsworth, a chief danger is abstraction, or the use of "lifeless words" to distance us from "those feelings which are the pure emanations of nature." For Coleridge a correlative danger is language's shielding power; William Pitt's vacuous generalities distance him from human suffering (*EOT* II 319–29). A demagogue's language, indistinct and fetishized, can in turn incite fanaticism, a debased form of the sublime. The young Shelley, influenced by Locke, announces that words "are merely signs of ideas"; one moral danger of too early an education in words is that one will attach improper ideas to them, especially the moral vocabulary of "honor, virtue, duty, goodness." These comments apply to poetic language as well. Rather disarmingly, Shelley says in his Preface to *Laon and Cythna* (1817) that he does not wish "any system relating to mere words to divert the attention of the reader," and that he has used "the most obvious and appropriate language" throughout. The poet should not deliberately problematize language. Concerning some of his poems sent in a letter, Keats says, "they will explain themselves—as all poeems [sic] should do without any comment" (*L* II 21).

Whatever their affinities with skepticism, increasingly emphasized in modern criticism, and whatever their degree of assent to the notion that language derives from passion, the Romantics view language as an instrument of cognition, even its precondition: Prometheus "gave man speech, and speech created thought / Which is the measure of the Universe (*PU* II iv 72–3). The misuse of language – the misappropriation of signifier to signified and of sign to referent – is what Shelley terms an "education in error." The philosopher performs a useful task in demonstrating error, even if it leaves a "vacancy," because this vacancy "reduces the mind to that freedom in which it would have acted but for the misuse of words and signs, the instrument of its own creation" (*SPR* 173). Blake and Shelley both term moral truth "self-evident," but for Blake the "doors of perception" must still be cleansed and for Shelley the errors in our language must still be rooted out. Coleridge is a philosopher of language refining the language we use; and at the same time he believes the way we use language tells us much of the nature of moral truth. His method of "desynonymizing" –

discriminating between words popularly taken to be synonymous – addresses such moral pairs as prudence/morality, conscience/consciousness, maxims/principles, power/strength, ethics/morals, and pleasure/good. Intellectual failure has moral consequences, he thinks, and conflation of these terms can give false sanctions to conduct – as when we mistakenly consider self-serving prudence a substitute for principled action, or when we tell ourselves that maximizing our own pleasure is a moral end in itself. We need more logomachy, not less, to prevent these errors. We are not helplessly controlled by the language we inherit from our culture, but can actively alter and direct language to cultural ends. Beyond believing in language's origins in passion and its semantic coherency, Romantic authors seek to understand and harness its performative power, and to move beyond the dialogue of the mind itself.

Rationalism and Enlightenment

The partial truth of oversimplification must be granted to the conventional view that the Romantics are hostile to Enlightenment reason. Blake's Urizen *is* most often the villain of the piece; Wordsworth does write against that "false secondary power by which / In weakness we create distinctions"; Coleridge does downgrade "understanding" to the level of "mere." Usually their complaint is not with reason per se but with its usurpation of other powers, the very complaint made, in turn, about the tyranny of feeling. Reason in various senses is everywhere rehabilitated by these same authors. Blake's Urizen in his regenerate form is wisdom and "sweet science"; Wordsworth speaks of imagination as "reason in her most exalted mood" (P XIII 170); Coleridge's "Reason," a higher intuitional faculty, supersedes imagination in his later writings. For Shelley and Byron, reason is prophylactic and subversive, warding off dogma and cant before they deaden other powers. Discursive reason, wielded passionately in his prose writings on government, religion, and culture, has for Shelley the same subversive function that anarchic energy has for Blake. Byron speaks of reason as the supreme faculty, next to which imagination is the possession of any inspired drunkard.

The British moral rationalists have little direct influence on the Romantics but the implicit relationship of the two helps us to place the Romantics in the history of ethics. The seventeenth-century Cambridge Platonists have some influence on Coleridge, if more so in epistemology than in ethics. The title of Ralph Cudworth's *Treatise*

69

concerning Eternal and Immutable Morality (1731; written sometime before 1688) suggests much of its drift. As opposed to the Hobbesian view that right and wrong are relative to the person who makes moral judgments and, in the commonwealth, are conventions reflecting the will of the sovereign, Cudworth thinks they are inherent in the nature of things. "Natural justice" commands certain actions because they are right; actions are not right simply because they are commanded. The essence of good and evil can be grasped by reason, "that higher station of the mind," which surpasses individual sense experience and is independent of personal will.

British rationalists agree that morality is fixed in the nature of things but differ as to whether moral knowledge is sufficient to impel us to the good. Cudworth and Henry More, in keeping with Christianized "right reason," think the right moving of the will requires something more than intellectual recognition of right and wrong. More's "boniform faculty" is a special inclination one has toward the good. Cudworth and More admit the testimony of the passional self more than eighteenth-century Newtonian rationalists do, and their reason or "nous" is attractive to Coleridge. Theirs is a rather poetic rationality, and their view of nature as a vast "plastic" universe is more in keeping with Romantic sensibility than the eighteenth-century rationalists' dry moral geometry. One finds scant references among the Romantics to William Wollaston, Samuel Clarke, John Balguy, and Richard Price (the latter the most sophisticated and a figure much discussed among modern theorists). Clarke and Wollaston think moral judgments can be made with the same confidence as mathematical or geometrical truths. Right can be distinguished from wrong with the same certainty as a straight line from a crooked. (Locke makes a similar argument, but more on conventionalist than on intuitionist grounds.) Someone who acts contrary to morality acts incorrectly in the same way one might miscalculate an algebraic equation.

The Romantics in effect synthesize aspects of the competing rationalist and moral sense schools. Eighteenth-century rationalists accuse the moral sense theorists of subjectivism and relativism: how can a moral *sense* be assumed to have an intersubjective, universal character? Does it not conflate moral judgment with personal whim? How does it answer the relativism of Hobbes? We have seen the moral sense theorists argue, in turn, that reason is powerless to explain motivation and value judgments. The Romantics do not pointedly arbitrate what has become by their time a moldy dispute on the nature of the moral faculty, but the belief of many of them in an interdependency of the subjective and objective, of mind and nature, makes their position evident. The imagination is not an exclusively subjective power; its sympathy leads the self toward the world. Its ultimate moral function, beyond benevolence, is love, described by Coleridge and Shelley as an intense kind of knowing. The healthy affective state for the Romantics is a transitive one – affections have attached to objects decidedly there, as constituted in our minds by the imagination. Self-involuted feeling is one of their great themes, but it is treated as a pathology. While avoiding the potential subjectivism and relativism of moral sense, they of course retain will and feeling as essential components of morality, well beyond what any of the rationalists would allow. Relative to the eighteenth-century moral debates, it takes some gumption for the Romantics to assert what may now seem an inert commonplace – that the moral life requires equal donations of reason and sentiment.

Of greater direct impact on the ethics of Romanticism is the more public-spirited, historical, and skeptical rationalism of the Enlightenment. Romanticism is often said to be a reaction against the Enlightenment, a reinstatement of myth and religion after the modern pagans have done their best to undermine superstition, and a rejection of the sane and practical reason of Enlightenment thinkers. Not to deny it an element of truth, one can qualify this view with reference to Shelley, whose continuity with Enlightenment figures is marked, and, in different ways, to Blake, Coleridge, Hazlitt, Keats, and Byron.

The Romantics, both individually and as a group, express ambivalence toward the Enlightenment. Wordsworth's infamous denunciation in *The Excursion* of Voltaire's *Candide* (1759) ("that dull product of a scoffer's pen") is in turn denounced by Hazlitt, who agrees that it is indeed the product of a scoffer, "but after reading the Excursion, few people will think it *dull*" (V 14). Coleridge sometimes speaks of Locke, Gibbon, Hume, Holbach, Condillac, and Voltaire as if they are a consolidation of error equal to the Anti-Christ, but the "giant's hand" of Kant emerges from the late Enlightenment to take hold of him. Blake sees Newton as a false prophet of materialism, whose efforts to blow the trumpet of apocalypse bring in a harvest of dead leaves. But Wordsworth speaks of Newton's statue at Cambridge as "the marble index of a mind for ever / Voyaging through strange seas of Thought, alone" (*P* [1850] III 62–3). Byron is markedly ambivalent toward Voltaire and Gibbon: the former was "historian, bard, philosopher," whose wit and ridicule made "all things prone,— / Now to o'erthrow a fool, and now to shake a throne" (*CH* III 106); the latter was "lord of irony" who "shaped his weapon with an edge severe," bringing down upon him the wrath of zealots. But Byron, who identifies with the anti-establishment energies of these figures,

71

cannot decide what judgment to bring to bear: "Yet peace be with their ashes,—for by them, / If merited, the penalty is paid; / It is not ours to judge,—far less condemn" (*CH* III 107, 108). The Romantics' disagreement about the Enlightenment stems partly from their different political and religious sympathies – Coleridge's dislike and Shelley's admiration, for example, are based on the same threat the Enlightenment poses to Christian orthodoxy.

For Shelley the moral contribution of the Enlightenment is its skeptical treatment of received systems. His writings against tyrannies of church and state and in favor of atheism, meliorism, vegetarianism, necessity, materialism, divorce, and popular sovereignty owe much to Locke, Hume, Rousseau, Condillac, Holbach, Paine, Condorcet, and Godwin. He too maintains a critical view of Enlightenment figures, however. The French Revolution "was occasioned by the literary labors of the Encyclopaedists," he writes in 1812. It was a revolution that promised the overthrow of centuries of tyranny in France. That it itself became tyrannical was owing to the fact that its progenitors – Voltaire, Rousseau, Helvétius, and Condorcet – were inconsistent. They were great forces in the evolution of liberty, but "Voltaire was the flatterer of kings, though in his heart he despised them – so far has he been instrumental in the present slavery of his country. Rousseau gave license by his writings to passions that only incapacitate and contract the human heart." That we can now perceive this inconsistency in itself vindicates for Shelley the Enlightenment truth, enunciated by Condorcet, that "we are in a state of continually progressive improvement" (*SPR* 67–8).

In his later *A Defence of Poetry* (1821) Shelley points to the limitation of reason in contrast to the moral power of imagination:

The exertions of Locke, Hume, Gibbon, Voltaire, Rousseau, and their disciples, in favour of oppressed and deluded humanity, are entitled to the gratitude of mankind. Yet it is easy to calculate the degree of moral and intellectual improvement which the world would have exhibited, had they never lived. A little more nonsense would have been talked for a century or two; and perhaps a few more men, women, and children, burnt as heretics. We might not at this moment have been congratulating each other on the abolition of the Inquisition in Spain. But it exceeds all imagination to conceive what would have been the moral condition of the world if neither Dante, Petrarch, Boccaccio, Chaucer, Shakespeare, Calderon, Lord Bacon, nor Milton, had ever existed; if Raphael and Michael Angelo had never been born; if the Hebrew poetry had never been translated. (*DP* 502)

He adds a note to this passage, significantly exempting Rousseau from the list since he was "essentially a poet. The others, even Voltaire, were mere reasoners." In the visionary pageant of *The Triumph of Life* (1822), Voltaire, Frederick the Great, Kant and others of the Enlightenment are said by the guide, Rousseau, already to have been judged obsolete by the world.

If he lacks Shelley's sympathies with them, even Blake grants Enlightenment figures a place in progressive mental fight. He attacks them on the grounds of hypocrisy: "Voltaire Rousseau Gibbon Hume. charge the Spiritually Religious with Hypocrisy!" (*J* 52), but are guilty of overrating their own virtue. Their belief in "Natural Morality" or Deism, a morality conducted in light of reason alone, is responsible for "All the Destruction . . . in Christian Europe." Urizen is the architect of a "stupendous Building on the Plain of Salisbury," made of "Reasonings: of unhewn Demonstrations." "The Building is Natural Religion & its Altars Natural Morality / A building of eternal death" (*J* 66: 2–3, 8–9). Urizen is thus contrarily associated both with the censorious ethic of the Decalogue and with an ethic that praises the "Virtues of the Human Heart" (*J* 52). The former arises in too low an estimate of human nature, the latter in too high. But for Blake the error of the Enlightenment is less profound than that of Puritanism; Natural Morality is less repressive than Moral Law. Urizen's participation in Deism is a stage in human development leading toward regeneration. Blake's attitudes toward Voltaire reveal this: he is a hypocritical Deist as intolerant as an Inquisitor, a materialist who understands nothing except what is before his eyes; yet he is still prophet of the French Revolution whose soul shines over the head of Lafayette.[26] In both his original and his regenerate condition, as the "first born Son of Light," Urizen is the wise guide of Albion. He is "Faith & Certainty" instead of rationalist doubt. Originally he occupied "sweet fields of bliss / Where liberty was justice & eternal science was mercy" (*FZ* 39: 10–11). This final vision sounds very much like a program for the Enlightenment itself, even though Blake has his own notions of dark religions (they include the Enlightenment religion, Deism) and of science (it excludes what he takes to be "Newton's sleep"). Blake adopts a meliorism based on progress of human intellect and defeat of religious superstition, a meliorism that has the form but not the content of Enlightenment vision.

The Romantics have a more highly wrought vision of human possibility than is found in the public-minded liberalism of the Enlightenment. The human will – insurrectionary in Blake, productive in Coleridge, legislative in Shelley – outstrips *phronesis* (the practical,

[26] See the entry on Voltaire in S. Foster Damon's *A Blake Dictionary: The Ideas and Symbols of William Blake* (Providence: Brown University Press, 1965).

socially oriented reason of the Enlightenment) in its drive to moral transcendence. Enlightenment thinkers value not self-transcendence, which would seem a vain and empty metaphysics, but the social consciousness that permits us to lead a clear-headed life unimpeded by superstition and vanity. Coleridge and Hazlitt criticize Locke for underrating the mind's productive shaping power.[27] They give imagination – a second-order faculty in the Enlightenment – a pivotal role in the moral life. The power they ascribe to it is more psychologistic than pragmatic, however, and their metaphysics of consciousness undercuts the Enlightenment emphasis on praxis. If, as Peter Gay remarks, "the philosophes' manner of philosophizing increased man's power [over nature] by mitigating his claims" to an omnipotence of thought, the Romantics make some new claims for human mind at the risk, I think, of decreasing man's literal power in the world – in their wariness of science, industry, and economics.[28] Coleridge is a Hamlet figure in his overwrought consciousness and hesitancy, and Blake's unfallen Urizen remains a far remove from that Enlightenment legacy to the nineteenth century, the social worker. Coleridge and Hazlitt also repudiate the principal ethical filiation of the Enlightenment – utilitarianism – because of its limited conception of human need.

This sketch – to be fleshed out in discussions that follow of Kant, Romantic social criticism, utilitarianism, Godwin, and Wollstonecraft – has suggested a pattern of selective, not wholesale, repudiation of Enlightenment moral thought by Romantic writers. Shelley's indebtedness to Enlightenment texts is only the most pronounced evidence of a degree of assimilative sympathy they have with their formidable predecessors.

Kantian formalism

Kant's profound critique of eighteenth-century thought is compelling to Coleridge. Though he alone among the major British Romantics discusses Kantian ethics at any length, his responses to this figure of the late Enlightenment – who yet provides rich perspectives on it – illustrate many premises of the larger group. In his concepts of practical reason and freedom, Kant seems to offer an escape from the necessitarianism adopted by figures as diverse as Spinoza, Hobbes, Hume, Priestley, and Hartley. His elevation of morality above

---

[27] See Coleridge's letters to Josiah Wedgwood, *CL*, II, 677–703; and Hazlitt's *Lectures on English Philosophy*, in *The Complete Works*, II, 146–215.
[28] *The Enlightenment: An Interpretation*, I, 186.

prudence informs Coleridge's indictment of the spirit of the age. Kant, like Coleridge, arraigns the ethics of egoism, sensibility, hedonism, and utilitarianism. Yet more positively he inquires into the nature and meaning of will and motive – questions skirted by the British Newtonian rationalists. Kantian rationalism rises above the various reductive readings of human nature and purpose seen in other ethical schools, rationalist or otherwise. Coleridge repudiates a large portion of Kantian ethics as he conceives of it, but even its rigorism is seductive at times. His ambivalence toward Kantian ethics illustrates the general ambivalence we have seen in the Romantic response to Enlightenment figures.

Some of Coleridge's attitudes toward Kantian ethics can be traced to his own idiosyncratic psychology. The categorical imperative – as translated by him, "So act that thou mayest be able, without involving any contradiction, to will that the maxim of thy conduct should be the law of all intelligent Beings—" (*F* I 194) – offers the errant opium-eater a seemingly sturdy guide to the moral life. It has an authority on the level of idea that is analogous to what he seeks in other people – from his upright older brother George, to the reliable Thomas Poole, to the rigid and rather cold Southey, to the purposeful and wise Wordsworth. In 1795 a young Coleridge stands on a platform in Bristol urging that human conduct and affairs of government be based on "fixed principles." When in 1803 he discovers Kant's imperative, this early search for principle finds a precise formula. He admires the last words of John Wordsworth (William's brother), as he prepares to sink during his first try as captain: "Let us do our duty!" All profound systems of ethics, he thinks, have been austere, counseling degrees of self-denial (*CL* II 768; *N* II 2537).

In contrast to the stern side of Kant, however, there is another, which takes its point of departure from the third formulation of the categorical imperative: "So act as to treat humanity, whether in thine own person or in that of any other, in every case as an end withal, never as means only." A closely related distinction is made between "persons" and "things." This formulation, far from being austere, expresses a liberal ethics that promotes disinterested respect and justice. Coleridge reiterates the persons/things distinction frequently. It is the "principle indeed, which is the *ground-work* of all law and justice, that a person can never become a thing, nor be treated as such without wrong" (*F* I 190).

But from his first reading of *Groundwork of the Metaphysic of Morals* (*Grundlegung zur Metaphysik der Sitten*, 1785) in 1803, Coleridge is disturbed by Kant's refusal to grant moral value to affective components of motivation (*N* I 1705, 1710). We are meritorious to the degree we obey the categorical imperative from rational respect (*Achtung*) for the imperative. Our personal inclinations, emanating from the "pathological" side of our nature, have no bearing on the act's moral value. We are all the more praiseworthy for obeying the moral law despite a strong disinclination. But Coleridge, with his passion for unity, hopes anxiously that Kant is wrong, that a unity of duty and inclination might be achieved, and that we would be judged the worthier for it. "The Feelings, that oppose a right act, must be wrong Feelings" (*AR* 91–2). He questions whether "respect" for the moral law can be considered wholly rational anyway. As an "imposed Necessity," it would be "fear or an Analogon of Fear," but as a "Necessity imposed on us by our Will it is a species of Inclination" (*N* I 1710). And he wonders whether Kant has unnecessarily restricted his conception of action as it relates to duty and feeling: "Will not a pure will generate a feeling of Sympathy / Does even the sense of Duty rest satisfied with mere *Actions*, in the vulgar sense, does it not demand, & therefore may produce, Sympathy itself as an Action?/—This I think very important/ —" (*N* I 1705). Kant, he suspects, is a "wretched Psychologist." In 1817 he writes:

I reject Kant's *stoic* principle, as false, unnatural, and even immoral, where in his Critik der Practischen Vernun[f]t he treats the affections as indifferent (ἀδιάφορα) in ethics, and would persuade us that a man who disliking, and without any feeling of Love for, Virtue yet *acted* virtuously, because and only because it was his *Duty*, is more worthy of our esteem, than the man whose *affections* were aidant to, and congruous with, his Conscience. (*CL* IV 791–2)

The Kantian conscience, described in the later *Metaphysic of Morals* (*Metaphysik der Sitten*, 1797), is a censorious monitor, within mind yet separable from it to the degree that it can sit in judgment. Since the perfect "holy will" – in which no discrepancy exists between duty and inclination – is but a hypothetical construct, conscience must always cry foul. Coleridge could claim that in this particular he conforms to the Kantian ethic: his is the most lavish of bad consciences. The court of conscience properly judges not the "criminal *Deed*" but the "sinful *Act*." A deed is characterized by its "singleness, its detachability for the imagination, its particularity, and, above all, its pastness." We may attempt in bad faith to conflate an evil act with a mere deed, and regard it as no longer pertaining to our own will. But conscience forces us to confess to the "continuing and abiding *presentness*" of our own acts.[29]

---

[29] Written in Southey's copy of *Aids to Reflection* (1825). Bound transcript, Victoria University Library.

Like his Mariner, Coleridge feels the weight of his own sinful acts, but finds little about it that impels him to the good. If it never relinquishes its habit of self-incrimination, conscience proves disabling. The more he feels the weight of duty – which for him acts more as a "narcotic" than a "stimulant" – the more he is disinclined to perform it (*N* I 1833, *CL* III 489).

Coleridge thus objects to what he takes to be a fracturing in Kant's ethics. The argument for rational freedom in *Critique of Practical Reason* (*Kritik der praktischen Vernunft*, 1788) seems to reinstate dualisms of rationality and sensibility, mind and body, noumenal and phenomenal. Seeking interrelationships of mind and nature or body, most Romantic authors would not warmly receive a Kantian ethics. The fracturing of phenomenal and noumenal, and our inability to have direct knowledge of the latter, give freedom of the will the status of an hypothesis, as Coleridge notes (*CL* IV 863). Like other post-Kantian idealists, he hopes for a more direct intuition of the truth of human freedom.

Coleridge is not alone in his uneasiness at ethical austerity. Objecting to stoicism, De Quincey seeks an ethics that would "condescend more to the infirm condition of an opium eater." In Blake's mythology the harmony of duty and inclination is expressed as the reconciliation of Urizen and Luvah, whose antagonism generates the initial fall of Albion. Censorious conscience is repudiated by Shelley in *Prometheus Unbound*, where Prometheus in remembering and undoing his curse against Jupiter frees himself from "self-contempt" and makes possible a larger apocalyptic consciousness. In "Ode to Duty" (1804) Wordsworth debates the duty/inclination problem, and in a stanza omitted in a later version describes how his "submissiveness" to duty is ideally his own "wish" and "choice." Otherwise he reveals a new austerity here: he will rid himself of the "weight of chance desires" and submit to duty in a "spirit of self-sacrifice." Sensing sour grapes in this, Coleridge thinks of responding with an "Ode to Pleasure" (*N* II 2091).

Another aspect of Kantian ethics limits its cogency for the Romantic temper. As a formalist, Kant argues – according to most readings of him and according to Coleridge – that the rightness or wrongness of an act is determined solely by its congruity with the categorical imperative without regard to consequences. He opposes teleological theories such as egoism or utilitarianism, in which an act's rightness or wrongness is a function of whether it promotes an end – usually, the pleasure or happiness of individuals or society. But the Romantics are inveterate teleologists: their poets are visionaries, their mythology images new heaven and new earth, their ethics, I will argue, is partly utilitarian and partly self-realizationist. The relationship of act and consequences haunts their narratives.

There is an urgency in their anticipatory stance and moral sensibility that deeply informs their view of the relationship of ethics and aesthetics – a view radically differing from Kant's. In their aggressive merging of these categories, they go some distance in undoing the *Critique of Judgment* (*Kritik der Urteilskraft*, 1790), which expounds aesthetic judgment – the faculty of judgment applied to matters of taste – so as to delimit it relative to cognition and ethics. For Kant, imagination (*Einbildungskraft*) is an active cognitive faculty that connects sensibility with understanding. But with regard to aesthetic experience (the subjective feeling of pleasure in response to beauty), imagination and understanding, working in harmony, operate *as if* they were yielding knowledge, when actually they are not. Kant insists from the beginning that aesthetic judgments "do not of themselves contribute a whit to the knowledge of things."[30] Instead, the imagination and understanding are engaged in "free play," productive of the pleasure that comes from awareness of the purposiveness of form. This purposiveness is felt in response to works of art or beautiful natural objects. But intrinsic purpose cannot be attributed in fact to either: the sense is aesthetic, and in this way practical and hypothetical. Kant thus does not divorce the aesthetic judgment from the activity of cognition, but insofar as we regard a work of art in a purely aesthetic way, we can say nothing about it as object. Our judgment of taste relates solely to our subjective feelings of pleasure or displeasure taken in aesthetic representation.[31]

As for the relationship of aesthetic judgment to ethics, suggested in the quasi-duty of valid aesthetic judgment, Kant again attempts to establish both boundaries and linkages. The aesthetic judgment is "disinterested" in the sense that it expresses no desire for the literal existence of its object or for its possession; it is only the object's appearance that engages the free play of imagination and understanding. But the ethical sphere is defined by desire. The moral will – the practical reason or faculty of desire – attempts to bring into being a world governed by respect for the categorical imperative.[32] (As a moral

---

[30] *The Critique of Judgement*, trans. James Creed Meredith (Oxford: Clarendon Press, 1952), 5.

[31] Kant nonetheless argues for the validity of aesthetic judgments, in which we may all be assumed to have the same cognitive faculties and in which we are not swayed by personal interest. There is an intersubjective standard of taste such that one can request another's assent to the statement "This is beautiful" as if it were a duty.

[32] Having established this essential difference between the aesthetic and the ethical, Kant still sees significant linkages. Some are only contingent, such as the fact that

agent one still acts disinterestedly, in the sense of fairly and according to rational respect for the moral law, and not for the sake of self-interested consequences.)

I will be arguing that the Romantics go well beyond Kantian claims for the mediating linkage of the aesthetic with the cognitive on the one hand and with the ethical on the other. For them the imagination has a hold on that highest of cognitive claims, "truth." It is something more than a cognitive accessory to understanding. And more than sanctioning an "analogy" to the moral life, as in Kant, imagination is a productive power that creates a *homology* of art and ethics because it is the source of both. The Romantics insist on a deeper association of the aesthetic and the ethical than Kant permits – or for that matter than most other theorists or poets permit.

Shaftesbury had merged ethical and aesthetic categories beyond the analogical in his writings on moral beauty, but moral sense, unlike the Romantic imagination, is more a witnessing than a productive faculty. Genetic mutuality is argued by Shelley, for whom "the great instrument of moral good is the imagination." Often assuming an impingement of imagination onto areas where the aesthete would say it has no business, the Romantics resist the tendency of Kantian aesthetics to keep imagination in its place. Babbitt has said that to absorb ethics into aesthetics deprives ethics of all force. They say quite the opposite: to

---

someone who responds spontaneously to the sublimity of nature is likely also to possess a good will. More crucial linkages are propounded in discussions of the sublime and of beauty. Our experience of the sublime – a term applied to subjective experience and not to an intrinsic property of nature or art – puts us in mind of practical reason or morality because it too makes us aware of a "supersensible" existence. Outstripping by its indefiniteness or infinitude the imagination's power of ordering or combining, a sublime landscape can make us aware of the supersensible world of freedom not bound by the phenomenal world. We participate morally in this supersensible world through the faculty of practical reason, though that participation is but a necessary hypothesis for living. The imagination, by virtue of being overwhelmed or even "outraged" by sublime experience, puts us in mind of our desire to overcome sense experience. Beauty in turn is said to be a "symbol" of morality because it prompts us to see analogies between itself and the moral world. Kant is speaking here of the projective, humanizing function of imagination that, as he says, prompts us to "call buildings or trees majestic and stately, or plains laughing and gay." These "excite sensations containing something analogous to the consciousness of the state of mind produced by moral judgements" (p. 205). Beauty reminds us by analogy of the highest elements in human nature. This ultimate linkage, however, arises by means of analogy only; Kant does not intend to blur the distinctions he has labored to make. I simply disagree with the heavily moralized reading a few critics now give the *Critique of Judgment*. Tobin Siebers's interesting account in *The Ethics of Criticism* (pp. 24–9), for instance, strikes me as more applicable to Schiller than to Kant.

ground both in the productive imagination is to strengthen the one in exercising the other.

We will see more of this later, especially in Shelley, but a notable exception is Charles Lamb, whose delightful essay "On the Artificial Comedy of the Last Century" (1823) makes a seductive case for leaving the "coxcombical moral sense" at home, at least when viewing Restoration comedy. On the non-metaphysical level of the British familiar essay, Lamb approximates to the Kantian position. The British do not know how to enjoy Congreve and Wycherley:

We do not go thither, like our ancestors, to escape from the pressure of reality, so much as to confirm our experience of it; to make assurance double, and take a bond of fate. We must live our toilsome lives twice over, as it was the mournful privilege of Ulysses to descend twice to the shades. All that neutral ground of character, which stood between vice and virtue; or which in fact was indifferent to neither, where neither properly was called in question; that happy breathing-place from the burthen of a perpetual moral questioning – the sanctuary and quiet Alsatia of hunted casuistry – is broken up and disfranchised, as injurious to the interests of society . . . In our anxiety that our morality should not take cold, we wrap it up in a great blanket surtout of precaution against the breeze and sunshine.[33]

Lamb would prefer "to take an airing beyond the diocese of the strict conscience" at these theatrical productions, thus escaping "the pressure of reality" (a phrase Wallace Stevens may derive from this essay). He makes several interesting claims in passing: that there is lasting therapeutic value in a temporary escape from moral categories ("I wear my shackles more contentedly for having respired the breath of an imaginary freedom"); that the value of Restoration drama resides in its power to create a feeling of "indifference" toward moral values; and that it is inappropriate to transfer dramatic characters from the contexts of the stage to the contexts of what he calls "real life." With our heavy-duty moral sense, we lack "the courage to imagine a state of things for which there is neither reward nor punishment. We cling to the painful necessities of shame and blame. We would indict our very dreams" (p. 144). Congreve and Wycherley give us "sports of a witty fancy" that become "a world of themselves almost as much as fairyland."

Lamb does not say outright that this argument could serve as the first principle of a poetics; he even seems to regard Restoration comedy as a special case, quite unlike "a modern play," where "I am to judge of the right and the wrong." But one senses that it informs much of his

---

[33] *The Essays of Elia*, in *The Works of Charles and Mary Lamb*, II (London: Methuen, 1903), 142.

larger sensibility and that he is to be distinguished from his more conscience-shackled peers. He, rather than Byron or Keats, is the major exception among the British Romantics to an aesthetic sensibility defined by a good dose of that "detestable coxcombry of moral judgment upon every thing." Keats in his letter on the poetical character disencumbers the poet of moral anxiety, but tacitly rejects this position in *The Fall of Hyperion*. For Coleridge, De Quincey, Wordsworth, and Keats, it is precisely in dreams where responsibilities begin. The imagination, far from offering an escape from moral recognitions, is the source of them.

Post-Kantian idealism: Schiller, Fichte, and Schelling

Much of the force of post-Kantian idealism for Coleridge is its attacks on Kant's splitting of duty and inclination, on his epistemological dualism, on his restricting the truth claims of poetry and art, and on the non-teleological character of his ethics. Idealism both supplements Kant and rescues the young English poet-philosopher from the "Procrustean Bed of Kantean Formalism." (Fichte, however, would attempt in some ways to throw him back on it.) Once again it is only Coleridge among the major British Romantics who follows German idealism closely; De Quincey places a distant second. Later in the century Carlyle will prove a close student but will appropriate it to his own poetically conceived "Natural Supernaturalism." The ethical concepts of German idealism are strongly interpretive of British Romantic literature, in any event.

I will be discussing four figures – Schiller, Fichte, Schelling, and Hegel – but the list could have been extended to include Jacobi, Schleiermacher, Friedrich Schlegel, and eventually, Heine, Marx, and Nietzsche – any one of whom could be used as an interpretive key to British Romanticism (and why not add Fries, Bouterwek, and Krug?). Many of these figures have been so used recently.[34] I have preferred to use Coleridge, since he himself appropriates German idealism, and directs it toward intellectual and cultural concerns of the British tradition. Through his mediation, one can avoid reliance on analogy alone, or on *Weltanschauung* as methodological justification. I will restrict myself to clear parallels on ethical questions, many of them

[34] E.g. Tilottama Rajan, *Dark Interpreter: The Discourse of Romanticism* (Ithaca, N. Y.: Cornell University Press, 1980), Nietzsche; Thomas McFarland, *Coleridge and the Pantheist Tradition* (Oxford: Clarendon Press, 1969), Jacobi and others; Anne K. Mellor, *English Romantic Irony* (Cambridge, Mass.: Harvard University Press, 1980), Friedrich Schlegel; Jerome J. McGann, *The Romantic Ideology*, Heine and Marx; and David Punter, *Blake, Hegel, and Dialectic* (Amsterdam: Rodopi, 1982).

involving Coleridge. In Schiller, whom he reads, translates, and plans a biography of probably before his first reading of Kant, he finds an answer to the duty/inclination problem. In Fichte, despite what he sometimes terms a gross egoism, he finds a dialectical drama of self and not-self. In Schelling, he finds a concept of will as source of both evil and life's intensity. These and other ethical concerns suggest lines of influence via Coleridge between German idealism and British Romanticism, as well as arresting analogues.

Kenneth Burke remarks that in the era of philosophical idealism, we should expect greatest emphasis on the agent, as distinguished from other elements of his pentad for a grammar of motives – agency, act, purpose, and scene.[35] The "self" of the British Romantics is not exactly the non-psychological intersubjective ego of German philosophical idealism. Their grounding of self in literary texts and contexts gives the impression of a more psychologically plausible habitat. We remain aware of particularities of place and history as they confront the individualized moral agent possessed of a particular past and specific psychological traits. The same can be said of German Romantic literature relative to strictly philosophical texts of German idealism. But the foregrounding of moral self-consciousness in Romantic lyric, drama, and narrative suggests an affinity that makes interrelationships of Romantic literature and idealist philosophical texts meaningful. And the British Romantics – Coleridge, but also Wordsworth, De Quincey, Hazlitt, Shelley, and Carlyle – write disquisitions that imply knowledge of philosophical idealism, German or otherwise.

In *On Grace and Dignity* (*Über Anmut und Würde*, 1793) Schiller attacks Kant's separation of duty and inclination, and he proposes the ideal of beautiful soul (*schöne Seele*), which Babbitt says is morally disastrous. Since human nature is both sensuous and rational, Schiller thinks it contradicts the human inheritance to develop one aspect at the expense of the other. In a typically triadic resolution he merges these polarities into a higher state of being – rationality enlivened by sensibility, sensibility given form by rationality. Coleridge was probably familiar with this essay when he first read Kant's *Groundwork of the Metaphysic of Morals*. In his essay *On Naive and Sentimental Poetry* (*Über naive und sentimentalische Dichtung*, 1795), Schiller makes clear that psychological harmony is not so easily achieved as this geometrical coalescence of polarities implies. Someone who lives in a state of nature, such as the ancient Greek or the child, has a harmony of faculties: "He functions as an undivided sensuous unity and as a

---

[35] *A Grammar of Motives*, 171–5, 460.

unifying whole. Sense and reason, passive and active faculties, are not separated in their activities, still less do they stand in conflict with one another."[36] For those of us who are post-pubescent and not living in Ancient Greece, "sensuous harmony" exists only in idea as object of desire. Instead of possessing natural unity, we aspire to unity, and this quality of aspiration makes ours a "*moral* unity." Adapting the Enlightenment idea of progress to the human personality, Schiller denies, with Rousseau, that fully realized humanity is found in returning to original innocence. To have fallen from innocence is lamentable, but it makes real the possibility of progress, gives human action a telos, and vindicates culture as the means of achieving reintegrated moral harmony. Such moral unity in culture is "infinitely superior" to sensuous unity in a state of nature. At the same time, the moral telos of a higher order of unity recedes forever. The "ideal is an infinitude to which [one] never attains" (pp. 112–13).

Schiller's great essay thus defines the predicament of modern life as desire: our longing for nature and childhood reflects a sense of having lost an original inheritance. Prospectively, the moral telos induces the state of striving for the unattainable. The condition of desire, once innocence is lost, can never undo itself. Schiller's vision is teleological and self-realizationist: we should strive for a harmony of faculties greater in kind than innocent harmony. But it is a harmony that will forever elude us. If Kant's ethics is austere, Schiller's is decidedly fatiguing.

Analogues between Schiller's essay and British Romantic literature, not to mention German Romantic, come so readily to mind as to convince that we are dealing with a dominant structural principle. Wordsworth's *The Prelude* associates nature with childhood, is structured by repeated oppositions of nature and culture, is pervaded by a sense of loss and striving, and narrates the yearning of fallen sensibility for the "calm" of nature. Nature lures us, Schiller writes, with a "character of calm necessity" that makes our own free will feel like a curse. His essay as a gloss on *The Prelude* makes partially regressive the poet's return from the world's great stage to his original nourishing landscape. The "calm" that nature induces can never be fully curative, for original harmony and innocence cannot be repossessed. Dialectical evolution must instead come through moral confrontation with culture.

Blake's innocence/experience dialectic of the early Lambeth books combines the categories of the naive (possession of innocence) and the

---

[36] *Naive and Sentimental Poetry*, trans. Julius Elias (New York: Frederick Ungar, 1966), 111.

sentimental (longing for innocence). The speakers of some of the *Songs of Innocence* (1789) are harmoniously one with scene and manifest the naive perspective of childhood. The reader necessarily provides the sentimental perspective as longing for a condition in itself limited and illusory. The clash of these perspectives is fundamental irony. Struggle toward *"moral* unity" in *Visions of the Daughters of Albion* (1793) is seen in the progress of the heroine, Oothoon, from pastoral unity to the disunity of guilt and masochism (after having been raped by Bromion, representative of fallen culture and social oppression) to a state of desire for a harmony with landscape and her would-be lover, Theotormon. Such harmony eludes them, fixed as Theotormon is in sentimental desire for Oothoon's lost innocence, fixed as Oothoon is in sentimental desire for a future that will elude her.

In *Letters on the Aesthetic Education of Man* (*Briefe über die ästhetische Erziehung des Menschen*, 1795), Schiller defines the "drive" or "impulse" that would move rationality and sensuousness toward a dialectical new emergent, the "sublimest humanity." No direct external evidence, but some internal, exists that Coleridge read the essay. Whether he did or not, it too is a powerful interpretive analogue for our understanding of the ethics of Romanticism, British and Continental. With his habit of inclusiveness and dialectical synthesis, Schiller attempts to embrace what is true in the rival moral schools of sensibility and rationalism. Neither perspective is all-encompassing and neither should be permitted dominion over the other. The "two opposing forces" of sense and reason are termed drives "since they drive us to the realization of their object." These drives, the sensuous (*Stofftrieb*) and the formal or rational (*Formtrieb*), are not necessarily destructive one of the other. If they become "negatives" instead of true "contraries" in the Blakean sense, the one will indeed be asserted over the other. If rationality prevails over sensuousness, "only uniformity can result, never harmony, and man goes on forever being divided. Subordination there must, of course, be; but it must be reciprocal."[37] In *Maria Stuart* (1800) Schiller dramatizes the conflict of the formal and sensuous drives in the persons of Queen Elizabeth and Mary Stuart, when at that historical moment no reciprocity can be achieved.

A third drive, which permits a reciprocal relationship through mediation, is the play drive (*Spieltrieb*), Schiller's extension of creative imagination beyond specialized faculty to generalized drive. Just as the end of the sensuous drive is to augment life, and the end of the formal drive is to augment form, so the end of the play drive, combining

[37] *On the Aesthetic Education of Man, in a Series of Letters*, trans. E. M. Wilkinson and L. A. Willoughby (Oxford: Clarendon Press, 1967), 85n.

these, is "living form: a concept serving to designate all the aesthetic qualities of phenomena and, in a word, what in the widest sense of the term we call beauty" (p. 101). Schiller adapts the argument of *Critique of Judgment* in noting that the play drive does not pursue a particular moral or intellectual result; it does not tell us what to do or what to believe. But he goes well beyond Kant's delimited conception of imagination. This drive enables one "by the grace of Nature to make of himself what he will – that the freedom to be what he ought to be is completely restored to him" (p. 147). Rather than dictate a particular course of action, it gives us the "power of becoming human, leaving the use and practice of that power to our own free will and decision" (p. 149). As the instrument of progressive culture, the play drive intuits our freedom to pursue the idea of sublime humanity, which exists as a teleological "symbol" of indeterminate and therefore "infinite" meaning. It gives rise to "the whole edifice of the art of the beautiful, and of the still more difficult art of living." The sensuous drive and the formal drive, independent one of the other, intersect harmoniously by means of play drive, beyond which they emerge as art and the moral life, homologously related. Both art and the moral life retain, therefore, components of the sensuous and the formal brought into new unity.

Several texts of Coleridge that extend imagination's sphere beyond poetry to broader modalities of culture and the moral life reveal either Schiller's influence or close affinity. Schiller complains in *Letters* that in fragmented individuals and societies, spontaneous forms of participation are inhibited; the "dead letter takes the place of living understanding, and a good memory is a safer guide than imagination and feeling" (p. 35). Similarly, Coleridge writes that when the lower faculties of fancy and understanding prevail over imagination and reason, there is an overvaluation of body as "shape" instead of "forma efformans," which, as Kathleen Coburn points out, is close in meaning to Schiller's *lebendige Gestalt*, or living form. "Life may be *inferred*, even as intelligence is from black marks on white paper – but the black marks themselves *are truly 'the dead letter'*." He plans to "deduce the worth & dignity of poetic Imagination, of the fusing power, that fixing unfixes & while it melts & bedims the Image, still leaves in the Soul its living meaning—" (*N* III 4066). Imagination as a "fusing power, that fixing unfixes" parallels Schiller's view that the play drive disciplines both sensuous and formal drives with a restraint that paradoxically cancels all restraints. In his single most Schilleresque passage, Coleridge writes: "The poet, described in ideal perfection, brings the whole soul of man into activity, with the subordination of its faculties to each other [recall Schiller's "reciprocal subordination"], according to their relative worth and dignity." As he continues in this familiar passage, the imagination "reveals itself in the balance or reconciliation of opposite or discordant qualities." The examples he gives of these oppositions are manifestations of the sensuous versus the formal drive: difference/sameness, concrete/general, individual/representative, emotion/order, enthusiasm/judgment, nature/art, matter/manner. He somewhat favors the sensuous over the formal element of poetry – nature over art, matter over manner – whereas Schiller somewhat favors the formal.[38]

But for both writers, imaginative activity predicates the larger moral life, and this life is conceived of as a totality of being and doing. Schiller writes, "The destiny of man is not to accomplish isolated moral acts, but to be a moral being," because ideally "it is not this or that particular action, it is the entire character which is moral."[39] For Coleridge, it is "the Totality, the whole articulated Series of Single Acts, taken as a Unity," that represents the good will. "Is it in this or that limb, or not rather in the whole body, the entire Organismus, that the law of life reflects itself? Much less then can the Law of the Spirit work in fragments" (AR 289–90). During his stay in Göttingen of 1798–9, Coleridge may have become more familiar with Schiller's philosophical writings than has been assumed. His later work, in any event,

---

[38] Keats's famous complaint about Coleridge – that he lacks the "Negative Capability" of Shakespeare, described as the capability "of being in uncertainties, Mysteries, doubts, without any irritable reaching after fact & reason – Coleridge, for instance, would let go by a fine isolated verisimilitude caught from the Penetralium of mystery, from being incapable of remaining content with half knowledge" (L I 193–4) – finds a parallel in Schiller's discussion of how the formal drive, if undisciplined by the play drive, may exhibit a "premature hankering after harmony." If we approach the richness of immediate experience with our sense organs "innocent and wide open," subduing the "impatient anticipations of our reason," then we may be astonished at how much more we see. The "violent usurping of authority by ratiocination in a field where its right to give orders is by no means unconditional" (p. 89) can be redressed by the play drive, which, as Keats in effect says, is content with half-knowledge, and does not repress the sensuous image for an intellectual construct. The play drive is a liberal mediator, because it neither pushes toward an intellectual conclusion nor coerces with a dogmatic moral principle. Rather, it drives us to the larger telos of living form, and thus yields a more comprehensive intellectual conclusion and a more humane moral principle. The play drive is instrumental in the progress of science, also impeded by an irritable reaching after fact and reason. (Coleridge, for once, should not have to cry *mea culpa!*, since his own tendency to defer intellectual conclusions is notorious, and his great forte is precisely the "fine isolated verisimilitude caught from the Penetralium of Mystery.")

[39] *On Grace and Dignity*, trans. anon (New York: Harvard Publishing, 1895), 206.

shows a marked debt to Schiller, as Kathleen Coburn has been demonstrating.[40]

These parallel texts illustrate that Schiller gives us, in the German tradition, the most comprehensive exposition of the ethics of Romanticism. My argument that antagonistic ethical schools, as they have developed in modern European intellectual history, are merged in Romanticism and inscribed in Romantic moral psychology is explicitly enunciated by Schiller in texts from *Philosophical Letters* (*Philosophische Briefe*, 1780–8) to *On Grace and Dignity* to *Letters on Aesthetic Education*. The Romantics' challenge to various dualisms – the sensuous and the rational, inclination and duty, the determined and the free – is aggressively argued by Schiller in his reaction to Kant. And just as the Romantics in their hyperbolizing of the imagination resist by implication the Kantian delimiting of aesthetics, so Schiller sees the play drive as most instrumental in the development of humanity and culture. More than the philosopher, the poet fulfills the will to value, creating symbolic forms that make a human context within a universe not fully accessible or accommodating to human mind.

We find in British Romanticism no single document on the relationship of ethics and aesthetics with the clarity and force of the three Schiller essays just discussed. Coleridge's philosophical writings are more scattered, less formal, but often more imagistic than Schiller's, more vivid in linking theory with facts of daily perception. Coleridge gives the sense of a more skeptical, more tentative, less categorical probing, one more sensitive to psychological nuance, and more conscious of the linguistic properties of metaphysical speculation. This contrast obtains even more with the other great post-Kantian idealists, Fichte, Schelling, and Hegel.

Coleridge willfully misreads Fichte, conflating the intersubjective ego with the individual ego, and accusing Fichte of a monstrous egoism bordering on solipsism. His "burlesque on the Fichtean Egoismus" in *Biographia Literaria*, a dithyrambic ode by one Querkopf Von Klubstick, runs in part:

> The form and the substance, the what and the why,
> The when and the where, and the low and the high,
> The inside and outside, the earth and the sky,
> I, you, and he, and he, you and I,
> All souls and all bodies are I itself I!
>> All I itself I!

[40] See, especially, Notes to the *Notebooks*, vol. III.

> (Fools! a truce with this starting!)
> All my I! all my I!
> He's a heretic dog who but adds Betty Martin!   (*BL* I 159n)

But Fichte himself would add Betty Martin, since his "ego" is a transindividual one. Coleridge elsewhere refers to the "monkish-Cell of Fichtean pan-egoistic Idealism" (NB 29, f. 121^v). The use of "pan-egoistic" hints that he knows the Fichtean egoismus is not subjectivist, but here and elsewhere (e.g. *M* II 596, 615, 622) he delights in parodic reduction.

Coleridge is skeptical of his own metaphysical speculations: "O Lord! What thousands of Threads in how large a Web may not a Metaphysical Spider spin out of the Dirt of his own Guts / but alas! it is a net for his own super-ingenious Spidership alone!" (*N* II 2784). Fichte would be a prime target for this satiric thrust. He "overbuilt" his metaphysical system "with a heavy mass of mere notions, and psychological acts of arbitrary reflection" (*BL* I 158). But Coleridge praises Fichte for "having prepared the ground for, and laid the first stone of, the *Dynamic* philosophy by the substitution of Act for Thing" (*CL* IV 792). And condensing Fichte's argument in *The Science of Ethics* (*Das System der Sittenlehre*, 1798), he works out a transcendental deduction (*N* III 4186), evidently valuing it as something more than cobwebby discourse. The "I" or "Self" or "Spirit" is a subject which is its own object, which knows itself immediately through pure intuition of its own activity, and which defines itself through limitation or immersion in the not-self, or objective world. The self is to a degree productive of its own world and grows through voluntary striving against limitation.

From the same text Coleridge translates a passage describing the empirical moral life, which is said to begin when the individual discovers that he lives in a world of limitation, a "definite sphere or circumscription." The moral goal is "the absolute emancipation from all limitation or circumscription of resistance (to be free even for the sake of being free)," and the means is a Fichtean version of the categorical imperative: "Treat every thing according to its nature, as revealed to thee by thy conscience" (*N* III 3673). Fichte conceives the moral life as continuous striving toward self-realization through active vocation in the world, a striving that sacrifices merely private pleasure. Coleridge may derive some notions of conscience from Fichte, who in *The Vocation of Man* (*Die Bestimmung des Menschen*, 1800) argues that conscience, an inherent power within consciousness, forces us to reject solipsism and assent to the reality of other selves.[41]

There is a joylessness in much of this, and Coleridge has the same objection to Fichtean ethics that he has to Kantian, only more so. He has enough latent hedonism, and sympathy with the impulses of the "natural man," to make Fichtean formalism seem only to intensify everything he initially dislikes about Kant as psychologist. Fichte "in his moral system is but a caricature of Kant: or rather he is a Zeno with the Cowl, Rope, and Sackcloth of a Carthusian Monk" (*CL* IV 792). His ethics consists of "an ascetic, and almost monkish, mortification of the natural passions and desires" (*BL* I 160). Coleridge is right to see a forbidding single-mindedness in Fichte's conception of duty – which Fichte practiced as the world's most unpopular school administrator – that makes his system too rigorous for an opium-eater. To Fichte's uncongenial "If I ought, I can," enforced to the point that no circumstances could ever condone telling a lie, Coleridge might reply that his own experience strongly implies, "If I ought, I cannot." Where Fichte finds evil in relaxation of moral will, Coleridge cries that his have been *only* sins of omission; the sin of lax will is less heinous than positive acts of will expressing aggression and pride. The stern Fichtean ethic finds a more receptive ear later in Carlyle. Whatever Coleridge's hostility to Fichte, this forerunner of existentialism (insufficiency acknowledged as such), with his themes of alienation and solitude, strife and nature, act and duty, self-realization and conscience, describes many aspects of the Coleridgean predicament and could provide his own gloss to *The Rime of the Ancient Mariner*.

I think the closer parallel to Fichte in the British tradition is Blake. Fichte's friendship with the German Swiss physiognomist, moralist, and poet Johann Kaspar Lavater (1741–1801) creates a tangential but suggestive Blake–Fichte linkage, since the marginalia to Lavater's *Aphorisms on Man* (1788) are the most succinct expression of Blake's moral views (*AL* 583–601). As a friend of Herder and collaborator of Goethe, Lavater is associated with the *Sturm und Drang*. Like Blake, he takes human form to be the pattern of truth, values emotion as at least the equal of reason, is hostile to abstraction, and exalts creative genius, friendship, subjectivity, imagination, spiritualism, and even magic. His *Aphorisms on Man* is widely praised as an antidote to the misanthropy of La Rochefoucauld and Chesterfield, as R. J. Shroyer notes, and Blake relishes its spirited generosity. Lavater's "Keep him at least three paces distant who hates bread, music, and the laugh of a child" (Aphorism 328) earns Blake's comment, "the best in the book" (*AL* 590).[42]

---

[41] Coleridge is, to be sure, overtly hostile to this work. See *M*, II, 600–15.

[42] Fichte first became acquainted with Lavater in Zurich in 1788 at age 26, a few months after Lavater had published his two-volume *Vermischte unphysiognomische Regeln zur Selbst- und Menschenkenntnis* (1787, 1788). On these volumes, Blake's artist friend

Fichte, Lavater, and Blake are united in a voluntarism anchored in stubborn humanism. For all three, religion is an offspring of human consciousness. Lavater's anthropocentrism is echoed in Blake's announcement that all deities reside in the human breast; and Fichte believes conscience to be the source of religious conviction. They therefore place the burden of redemption on personal will. Blake writes "Admirable!" next to Lavater's remark, Fichtean in character, that he who "has many wishes has generally but little will." Also Fichtean is Lavater's comment, "If you ask me which is the real hereditary sin of human nature, do you imagine I shall answer pride? or luxury? or ambition? or egotism? no; I shall say indolence – who conquers indolence will conquer all the rest" (Aphorism 487), beneath

J. H. Fuseli based his translation, with its frontispiece engraved by Blake after Fuseli's design. The older man was already famous throughout Europe for his *Physiognomische Fragmente* (1775–8), which in four illustrated volumes purports to demonstrate the interrelationship of personality and physiognomy. Lavater introduced Fichte to intelligentsia of Zurich and helped him in many ways professionally. Fichte's fiercely non- or even anti-naturalistic approach to ethics, as developed later, contradicts the idea that our character is correlative to our looks, but Lavater's "*un*physiognomische Regeln," which he most likely read before his career had been decided for philosophy, assert a voluntarist ethics not tied to bodily appearance.

Blake tends to disagree with those aphorisms where Lavater, like Fichte, praises duty at the expense of pleasure and passion. And he objects to others that smack of Christian piety, the virtues of forgiveness and patience. What Blake takes to be Lavater's limited conception of act, where he does not push his exuberant voluntarism far enough, prompts Blake's most provocative moral inquiry, as we will see. Soon after publication of Lavater's "aphorisms" or "Regeln," both Blake and Fichte are writing their own: Blake's "Proverbs of Hell" and Fichte's "Aphorisms on Religion and Deism" ("Einige Aphorismen über Religion und Deismus," 1790). But whereas Fichte continues to conceive of ethics in terms of rules, in the manner of a rule-deontologist like Kant, Blake repudiates rules as the heart of the moral life. His "Proverbs of Hell" are a subversion of their own format. And the Devil says, "I tell you, no virtue can exist without breaking these ten commandments. Jesus was all virtue, and acted from impulse, not from rules."

For a bibliographical and critical discussion of Lavater's *Aphorisms on Man*, see R. J. Shroyer's Introduction to the facsimile reproduction of Blake's copy of the first English edition (Scholars' Facsimiles & Reprints, Delmar, New York, 1980), which I cite here. For discussions of the Lavater–Fichte relationship, see Ernst Gelpcke, *Fichte und die Gedankenwelt des Sturm und Drang* (Leipzig: Felix Meiner, 1928), 36–43, 79–81, 141–3; and Christian Janentzky, *J. C. Lavaters Sturm und Drang im Zusammenhang seines religiösen Bewusstseins* (Hall a. S.: Max Niemeyer, 1916), 332–8. The substantial correspondence between Fichte and Lavater covers the period from spring of 1789 to August, 1800, and is contained in Johann Gottlieb Fichte, *Briefwechsel*, ed. Reinhard Lauth, Hans Jacob, and Hans Gliwitsky (Stuttgart–Bad Cannstatt: Friedrich Frommann, 1970–). See especially IV, 187–93, 208. On the Lavater–Fuseli–Blake relationship, see Leonard M. Trawick, "William Blake's German Connection," *Colby Library Quarterly*, 13 (1970), 229–45.

which Blake notes that "abundance of Idleness" (in addition to pride and too much bread) "was the sin of Sodom." Lavater, like Blake, thinks the great personality exhibits "energy," "exuberance," and "ferment," and that these accompany great acts. Like Fichte, who places "act" at the beginning of his system, Blake says that "all Act is Virtue," and that one's duty is to express the self through acts. He underlines Lavater's assertion that "Who can act or perform as if each work or action were the first, the last, and only one in his life is great" (Aphorism 272). These three figures, if in different ways, urge an ethical voluntarism as strenuous as it is visionary.

The mediation of Lavater apart, one finds a Fichte–Blake correlation in that each expresses the most non-naturalistic ethic within his particular tradition. For Fichte nature is the not-I that the I overcomes through striving, a process defined by alienation (*Entäusserung*). For Blake, where man is not, nature is barren, and to be situated within the menacing contours of unredeemed nature, in a world without human qualities, is the broadest characterization of moral fault. Moral truth is a category of human mind in no way preexistent in nature.

For these two advocates of the French Revolution, ethics means activism in overcoming the resistance of unredeemed society as well as nature. But the great ontological and ethical burden they place on the ego threatens, both formally and practically, a collapse into subjectivism, ideality, and egoism – a collapse away from transindividual moral dialectic. In terms of his own ethic, each might indict the other of such a collapse: Blake with Coleridge might accuse Fichte of encouraging a debilitating false consciousness through the stranglehold of inflexible duty and conscience; Fichte might accuse Blake of capitulation to nature in overvaluation of the body.

Schelling is less preoccupied with ethics than are Schiller and Fichte, and what he does say on the subject frequently has precedent in these philosophers. In works prior to *The Nature of Human Freedom* (*Das Wesen der menschlichen Freiheit*, 1809), he describes a somewhat less strenuous voluntarism, but it too asserts, in effect, that where nature is, there ego shall be. Unlike Fichte, who starts with ego and then deduces the non-ego or nature, Schelling begins with a philosophy of nature, assenting to the reality of nature as a first principle, while at the same time adopting a Fichtean transcendental idealism as a complementary deduction. Like Herder and Goethe, Schelling revises Spinoza's nature in vitalistic terms. These figures see nature as imbued with life, power, and purpose, instead of with Spinoza's unchanging, purposeless "substance." Schelling's complementary deductions of *Naturphilosophie* and idealism lead to the notion of interpenetration of ego

91

and world. Nature is a teleological system that seeks to realize itself in the absolute pattern of the organism, and that becomes conscious of itself through human ego. Ego, in turn, seeks to maximize its freedom by actualizing its will in the objective world.

But instead of focusing, like Fichte, on moral action per se, Schelling says, with echoes of Schiller, that it is in aesthetic intuition and artistic creation that the ego most perfectly manifests itself in the world. The artist's work is a supreme act of self-realizing will, a supreme imposition of the ideal on the real, yet an imposition which fulfills nature as the supreme expression of its own telos. On these grounds, Schelling argues the interpenetration of ethics and aesthetics, well beyond the sanction of Kant's *Critique of Judgment*.

Coleridge is sufficiently taken by the argument in Schelling's *On the Relation of the Plastic Arts to Nature* (*Über das Verhältnis der bildenden Künste zu der Natur*, 1807) to paraphrase and sometimes translate (or, as some would say, cop) portions of it in a lengthy notebook entry prepared for a lecture (*N* III 4397), published with many alterations after his death as the essay "On Poesy or Art." Schelling's treatise has analogues in Blake, Wordsworth, and Shelley. Revising the concept of mimesis, Schelling says the artist must first withdraw from nature, or as Coleridge puts it, *"eloign* himself in order to return to her with full effect." The consciousness of the artist, like all human beings, "has the same ground with Nature," and to look within instead of being slavishly fixed on the object as object is to produce living form instead of mechanical reproduction. The artist recapitulates in his or her own creative act the creative activity of nature, but in so doing achieves in consciousness what is unconscious in nature. Thus, mimesis is a productive, not reproductive, activity that submits life's energies to the "anguish of form." "Art demands a certain fullness," writes Schelling, and therefore "prefers to grasp immediately at the highest and most developed, the human form."[43] Art, like nature itself, is directed teleologically toward the human form.

Blake's "human form divine" comes to mind, but an even more Blakean idea in Schelling's essay is that "passion should be moderated by beauty itself," instead of repressed by negative form. Negative form results from "reflection," which separates mind from nature, form from feeling. One should instead "oppose to passion a positive force. For as virtue consists, not in the absence of passions but in the mastery of the spirit over them, so beauty is preserved, not by their removal or abatement, but by the mastery of beauty over them" (p. 452). One of

[43] *On the Relation of the Plastic Arts to Nature*, trans. J. E. Cabot, in *Critical Theory Since Plato*, ed. Hazard Adams (New York: Harcourt Brace Jovanovich, 1971), 450.

the major dynamics of Blake's prophecies is stated here: the passional aspect of the psyche, Orc–Luvah, is ultimately given form less by Urizen, or reason, than by Los–Urthona, the power of imagination and art. "The Treasures of Heaven are not Negations of Passion but Realities of Intellect [for Blake, imaginative vision] from which All the Passions Emanate Uncurbed in their Eternal Glory" (*VLJ* 564). Coleridge is somewhat more suspicious of these passions than either Schelling or Blake, and conceives the process as a conquering; "To the idea of Life[,] Victory or Strife is necessary – As Virtue not in the absence of vicious Impulses but in the overcoming of them / so Beauty not in the absence of the Passions, but on the contrary—it is heightened by the sight of what is conquered—" (*N* III 4397). "Determinateness of form is in nature never a negation, but ever an affirmation," writes Schelling, who describes individuality and particularity as a "creative energy" that has submitted to form: "no particular exists by means of its limitation, but through the indwelling force with which it maintains itself as a particular whole, in distinction from the universe" (p. 449). Blake's "minute particulars" are instances of this synecdochic concentration: precise focal points through which eternity may be seen. As in the work of art, so in the human personality: for the Romantics, individuality develops through interpenetration of energy and form.

Schelling is quick to dissociate this process from narrow egoism. The form that expresses natural energy is said to transcend its own hard delimitation through Schilleresque "grace" (*Anmut*). "Rigid outlines" of repressive form disappear in both the work of art and the human personality. As "the medium of connection between moral goodness and sensuous appearance," grace results in an imperturbable gentleness of demeanor and a sense of interconnectedness that Schelling, echoing the *Symposium*, identifies with love. Thus, self-realizationism is freed of narrow egoism: "The soul in man, therefore, is not the principle of individuality, but that whereby he raises himself above all egoism, whereby he becomes capable of self-sacrifice, of disinterested love, and (which is the highest) of the contemplation and knowledge of the essence of things, and thus of art" (p. 453). But Blake insists on "outline," and his vision of the unified self is more highly charged than Schelling's; the state of mental strife persists even in Eden, where contraries resound with ever greater force. The impulse toward egoism is stronger in Blake than in the gentler Schelling and Schiller, aligning him, once again, more with Fichtean sensibility.

Analogues to Schelling abound in Wordsworth, who speaks of a shared "ground" between mind and matter, "That sense of dim similitude which links / Our moral feelings with external forms" (*TPP* II 164–5). With Schelling he believes the breach between mind and nature has been the result of "reflection." The tripartite structure of aesthetic experience – artists must "eloign" themselves from nature in order to return to it "only in the final perfection" – informs the larger structure of *The Prelude*. In the Mount Snowdon episode and subsequent meditation, Wordsworth, like Schelling, describes imagination as engaged in production, not reproduction: poets become *like* nature in their own great creating power, not simply re-presenting nature.

Schelling's account of nature's intrinsic worth and consoling beauty parallels Wordsworthian lyricism, but Fichte's more severe account of nature's alienating facticity parallels the severities of Wordsworthian narrative. The more traditional reading of Wordsworth emphasizes the idea of reciprocity of mind and scene, and analogues with Schelling (not direct influences) have been set forth at length by E. D. Hirsch.[44] But other critics – especially David Ferry and Geoffrey Hartman – have emphasized on varying grounds the opposition of nature and mind. This school of criticism thus represents a shift in analogue, I think, from Schelling to Fichte. But either analogue is partial. With Schelling, Wordsworth does dwell on the "sympathies" we have with the natural world; to repress them is to lose the self's power. Nature has intrinsic value and is more than the non-ego that diminishes human ego to empirical status. But the great narratives are driven, more in the manner of Fichte, by strenuous imperatives in a world of striving and suffering. The poet feels he must leave the nourishing landscape to become a "moral agent." We withdraw from nature not to "ascend into the realm of pure ideas," as Schelling says, but to discover our vocation in an unjust world. We return to nature only after a period of trial and self-alienation. To combine the analogues of Schelling and Fichte as an interpretive key to Wordsworth would yield a more comprehensive reading of this great poet.

Schelling provides equally striking analogues to Shelley, who explores the union of energy and form that defines both human personality and art. The imagery pattern of *Prometheus Unbound* is of indefinite, veiled, and shadowy things taking on clarifying form and light. Shelley's vision in this work is reminiscent of Schelling's in its gentleness. Instead of the firm outline of the militant Blake, Shelley's characters become "gentle, radiant forms" who embody what Schelling and Schiller mean by grace. As the twin threats of repression and

[44] *Wordsworth and Schelling: A Typological Study of Romanticism* (New Haven: Yale University Press, 1960).

chaos recede, they step forth transfigured. Schelling's comment on grace (*Anmut*) echoes the imagery and tonality of *Prometheus Unbound* from Act III iii to the conclusion of Act IV:

By a gentle morning blush stealing over the whole form, the coming soul announces itself; it is not yet present, but everything prepares for its reception by the delicate play of gentle movements; the rigid outlines melt and temper themselves into flexibility; a lovely essence, neither sensuous nor spiritual, but which cannot be grasped, diffuses itself over the form, and entwines itself with every outline, every vibration of the frame.[45]

A state of grace exists when the beauty of living form is expressed as love. Form no longer delimits, as individuality or egoism delimits, but softens, becomes gentle and mild, permitting a total radiating of person into scene. In terms of this visionary if unscientific dialectic, the ego's energies become one with love.

Schelling's writings after his intensive reading of Boehme – *Philosophy and Religion* (*Philosophie und Religion*, 1804) and *The Nature of Human Freedom* (1809), both of which Coleridge read and annotated – are theological in emphasis. The latter, Schelling's most imaginative and portentous work, supplements the ethical perspectives just outlined. Schelling, like Boehme, visualizes human evil as a centrifugal movement of the many away from the one, a fall from Godhead into particularity. The finite human will recapitulates the fall in leaving the "center" of acquiescence to God's will, and moving toward the "circumference" that is self-will. Human beings have an unconscious will, an abyss of energy and appetite, which moves them to be "free as a creature." Human will is the source of evil and freedom, as one moves toward a prideful individualism. But Schelling does not counsel lifeless acquiescence, for "activated selfhood is necessary for life's intensity."[46] To be fully human is to recapitulate the satanic project. In mitigation, there exists also a conscious or rational will, in God and potentially in man, manifested as love and developed through strife and error, as the darkness of unconscious will is gradually sublimated into light. But human personality originates in unconscious will and continues to have its motive spring there. Powers of love and wisdom are acquired experientially. Schelling's text anticipates, contradictorily, both the psychological determinism of the Freudian unconscious and the Sartrean imperative of living freely beyond one's essence.

[45] *On the Relation of the Plastic Arts to Nature*, 452–3.
[46] *Of Human Freedom*, trans. James Gutmann (Chicago: Open Court, 1936), pp. 40, 78–80.

Despite some hostile marginalia to *The Nature of Human Freedom*,[47] Coleridge speaks in a similar way when he writes that exercise of will is "the condition of all moral good while it is latent, and hidden, as it were, in the center; but the essential cause of fiendish guilt, when it makes itself existential and peripheric – si quando in circumferentiam erumpat" (F I 425–6n; "whenever it erupts into the circumference"). The will for Coleridge is *causa sui*, the source of our individual being, ideally anchored in the Universal Will of God. He calls it "the dark and hidden radical of the bodily life" (NB 29, f. 89^r) as of our spiritual life, a force beneath consciousness both godly and demonic. He sees in it an inherent tendency to fall away in satanic selfhood from its union with Universal Will. It is the ground of the Mariner's satanic act of individuation in shooting the Albatross, just as it is the ground of his spontaneous blessing of the creatures. Many of Coleridge's late writings on the will show the influence of Schelling's argument, which illuminates his poetry and life from the Ancient Mariner to the Sage of Highgate. In a despairing moment, he cries that his soul is "infinite in the depth of darkness, an infinite craving, an infinite capacity of pain and weakness, and excellent only as being passively capacious of the light from above" (CL III 463). But to resign the will, and not to foster life's intensity – Coleridge's personal affliction – risks dissolution of personality.

Throughout Romantic literature there is the sense that to augment life's intensity is to risk the psychological backlash of guilt. Broadly speaking, Romantic humanism conflicts with decorous acquiescence to social, political, and religious structures. It is most literally displayed in Byron, whose Manfred defies all taboos and sanctions, whose Childe Harold is a proud outlaw carrying with him a secret sin, whose Cain has an "instinct of life" that makes him resist God's tyrannical law and "form an inner world / In [his] own bosom (II ii 463–4). Other prideful and defiant figures of the period – Oothoon, Rivers, the Ancient Mariner, René, Prometheus – are punished for the will's exertion and for making themselves objects of fascination. To varying degrees they feel guilt and are guilty, but each of them manifests a compelling surplus of "creature-will." That Byron can make us sympathize with Cain reveals how much the Romantics' sympathies are with the Devil – for, ironically, it is Lucifer who teaches us how to be human. The dilemma propounded by Schelling and Coleridge – to resign the will is boredom and underdevelopment, but to activate

---

[47] The marginalia are published as an appendix to *Biographia Literaria*, ed. Henry Nelson Coleridge and Sara Coleridge, in *The Complete Works of Samuel Taylor Coleridge*, ed. Shedd, III, 691–9.

it is satanic pride – expresses much of the Romantic sensibility of guilt.

Post-Kantian idealism: Hegel

The most important of the post-Kantian idealists, Hegel, is least known to Coleridge, who takes Schelling to be the main figure of this school.[48] In Great Britain, Hegel was not generally recognized in the intellectual community until J. H. Stirling's *The Secret of Hegel* was published in 1865; and he did not have a pervasive influence until the British neo-Hegelianism of T. H. Green, Bernard Bosanquet, and to a lesser degree F. H. Bradley, in the 1880s and 1890s. Influence apart, most of the analogues so far noted between British Romantics and German idealists could be broached by means of Hegel alone, since his is arguably the most comprehensive philosophical exposition not only of the German idealists but of any school since the Academy.

Hegel may be a product of German idealism and the larger sensibility of Romanticism, but he attempts a philosophy of philosophies that sets Romanticism as one of many stages in the evolutionary process leading toward the realization in history of Geist, or Spirit. Later in the century, Marx resists this devouring Hegelianism by arguing Hegel's own historical determinants, contradictions, and limitations in terms of the economic base that makes even this encompassing master-spirit an interested apologist for parochial social conventions of early nineteenth-century Prussia. Though Hegel does offer a powerful critique of many moral ideas popularly deemed Romantic, I suggest, first, that the Romantics, British and Continental, have sufficient disengagement from these ideas to position them in their own way, whether in commentary or literary art; and second, that the Romantics, if certainly not outflanking Hegel, contrast with him on key moral issues in such a way that their own unwritten critique of Hegel can be surmised.

The most important ethical distinction in Hegel – one that takes us to the heart of his quarrel with Romanticism – is between *Moralität*, or morality as an internal matter of individual conscience, and *Sittlichkeit*, variously translated as "social morality" or "the ethical life."[49] Hegel

---

[48] See *Marginalia*, II, 988–97, for Coleridge's comments on Hegel's *Wissenschaft der Logik* (1812, 1813, 1816); and G. N. G. Orsini, *Coleridge and German Idealism* (Carbondale and Edwardsville, Ill.: Southern Illinois University Press, 1969), 242–5, for Coleridge's slight and slighting commentary on Hegel.

[49] This distinction is developed in *The Phenomenology of Mind* (*Phänomenologie des Geistes*, 1807), the *Encyclopedia of the Philosophical Sciences in Outline* (*Encyklopädie der philosophis-*

indicts a morality that does not transcend subjective will and conscience, or what he takes to be the *Moralität* of Kant's purely formal and abstract ethics. In Hegel we encounter the paradox that this seemingly most abstract, and certainly most difficult, of philosophers declares himself an antagonist of abstraction who seeks to describe ethics as a concrete manifestation of Geist. *Moralität* is ethics restricted to the individual subject as it experiences its own subjective identity and freedom. "The subjective will, directly aware of itself, and distinguished from the principle of [universal] will . . . is therefore abstract, restricted, and formal."[50] Because the individual will in its subjectivity is not yet identical with universal will, it experiences the moral point of view as "relation, of ought-to-be, or demand." The subjective wills of others are at this stage recognized only in their difference from the individual subject, and are therefore part of an objectivity not yet subsumed by the subject. Hegel's general argument is that only when "subjectivity and objectivity are [no longer] distinct from one another, or united only by their mutual contradiction," only when the individual subject is in total agreement with the larger universal will, does it become both concrete and infinite – a "concrete universal." It is in particularity uninformed by the larger totality that we find "abstraction" and the merely formal. Realizing the moral self is the gradual process of identifying the subject with the larger social universe, the "objective mind" most fully embodied in the state. Beyond objective mind is the "absolute mind" of art, religion, and philosophy (in that order).

The individual subject's sense of certainty with regard to pursuit of the good is what is meant by "conscience" (*das Gewissen*), but it is in conscience itself that Hegel extraordinarily locates the possibility of evil:

> To have a conscience, if conscience is only formal subjectivity, is simply to be on the verge of slipping into evil; in independent self-certainty, with its independence of knowledge and decision, both morality and evil have their common root. (PR 139: 92)

By contrast, Kant had written that "an *erring* conscience" is "a logical impossibility," a contradiction in terms, and that "if someone is aware that he has acted with the approval of his conscience, then so far as

chen Wissenschaften im Grundrisse, 1817), and especially *Elements of the Philosophy of Right* (*Grundlinien der Philosophie des Rechtes*, 1821, 1833).

50 *Philosophy of Right*, trans. T. M. Knox (Oxford: Clarendon Press, 1942), no. 108, p. 76. Hereafter cited in the text as *PR* 108: 76.

guilt or innocence is concerned nothing more can be required of him."[51] Conscience is an inherent power, the practical reason holding up our duty before us; conscience does not err but we err in not listening to it.

It is this kind of commentary that Hegel finds "formal" and "abstract," as well as narrowly censorious. It may seem strange that Kant could also be accused of an ethics of subjectivity, since he is better known for giving ethics a categorical or universal standard rising above whim and inclination. But Hegel thinks his very formalism collapses into subjectivity. In not lending ethics a content, Kant leaves it up to each person to provide one. Uninformed by the concrete totality of universal will, the personal conscience "can draw its content only from the determinate content of the natural will, from desire, impulse, inclination, &c" (*PR* 139: 93). And since the Kantian internal monitor always finds the person in the condition of fault, "morality itself is incomplete." Kantian ethics promotes the unhealthy subjectivity associated with endless struggle, guilt, and yearning: "chill duty is the final undigested lump left within the stomach," and "no thought is given to a system of the self-realizing spirit" in which the universal would have been attained.[52]

For Hegel, then, the post-Kantian idealists err not so much in repudiating Kant as in repeating and augmenting his errors of formalism and subjectivity. Kant had written at the beginning of *Groundwork of the Metaphysic of Morals* that there is nothing in the world "within the power of human conception that can without qualification or limit be regarded as good, save the Good Will alone" (Coleridge's translation, OM B$_2$ f. 63). Hegel thinks the post-Kantians and others of Romantic persuasion have sentimentalized this idea dangerously:

if a good heart, a good intention, a subjective conviction are set forth as the sources from which conduct derives its worth, then there is no longer any hypocrisy or immorality at all; for whatever a man does, he can always justify by the reflection on it of good intentions and motives, and by the influence of that conviction it is good.

(*PR* 140: 99)

In his *Lectures on the History of Philosophy* (*Vorlesungen über die Geschichte der Philosophie*, 1805–1830, 1836), he faults the subjectivity of Fichte, Friedrich Schlegel, Schleiermacher, and Novalis. Only Schelling has in

---

[51] *The Doctrine of Virtue*: Pt. II of *The Metaphysic of Morals*, trans. Mary J. Gregor (Philadelphia: University of Pennsylvania Press, 1964), 61.
[52] *Lectures on the History of Philosophy*, trans. E. S. Haldane and Frances H. Simson (London: Routledge & Kegan Paul, 1955), III, 461.

part succeeded in escaping it, but in a formulaic, non-dialectical way. For all his talk of a "non-ego," Fichte errs in a total subjectivity wherein everything empirical is excluded from transcendental deduction (III 486). The ego and the non-ego it posits are not united in true dialectic but merely oscillate in endless contradiction, recapitulating the effects of Kantian dualism. "Everything determinate which the ego possesses it has through its own positing; I even make a coat or a boot because I put them on," Hegel says derisively. "There remains only the empty repulsive force, and that is the Kantian Thing-in-itself, beyond which even Fichte cannot get, even though the theoretic reason continues its determination into infinitude" (III 495). This infinitude is what Hegel considers a false infinite, such as we have seen in Schiller. Ethically, "the activity of the ego is a yearning or striving," falsely valued in itself. Hegel is most opposed to the fragmentation or radical incompleteness that Thomas McFarland has argued is a first principle of Romanticism.[53] The Fichtean ego can never attain a "unity of thought," and instead of "life" and "spirit" we find in him "absence of spirituality," "woodenness," and indeed "utter foolishness" (III 506).

Friedrich Schlegel, Schleiermacher, and Novalis, seen by Hegel to be followers of Fichte, urge different forms of limited subjectivity. Schlegel champions "irony," the simultaneous creation and de-creation of our own visions – a concept which Anne Mellor has recently used as a paradigm of English Romantic literature, especially Byron, Keats, and Carlyle.[54] Irony, says Hegel, "knows itself to be the master of every possible content; it is serious about nothing, but plays with all forms" (III 507). But he notes that in Schlegel ironic subjectivity, as a form of skepticism, gives way to "religious subjectivity":

The utter despair in respect of thought, of truth, and absolute objectivity, as also the incapacity to give oneself any settled basis or spontaneity of action, induced the noble soul to abandon itself to feeling and to seek in Religion something fixed and steadfast. (III 508)

Schlegel, for all his irony and sense of play – or even because of them – converts to Catholicism, which Hegel takes to be a religion of sentiment, feeling, superstition, and the miraculous. Schleiermacher, like Jacobi, sentimentalizes religion by placing "absolute reality above Knowledge," and giving it over to the trivializing subjectivity of "the

---

[53] *Romanticism and the Forms of Ruin: Wordsworth, Coleridge, and the Modalities of Fragmentation* (Princeton: Princeton University Press, 1981).
[54] *English Romantic Irony*, 3–30.

heart" (III 508–10), while in Novalis this subjectivity is so extravagant that it passes into madness.

The Hegelian attack on subjectivity has centered on *Moralität*, which, if it does not lead to *Sittlichkeit* and thereafter to still higher manifestations of mind, stagnates into various vanities. In a positive sense, as the "right of subjective freedom," *Moralität* assumes the form of "love, romanticism, the quest for the eternal salvation of the individual, &c" (*PR* 124: 84), but these require a larger social contextualization if they are not themselves to become vanities.

This book will show that the British Romantics conceive of the problem in similar terms. Hegel underestimates the degree to which the German Romantic tradition, philosophical and literary, treats subjectivity as a problem instead of a solution; and in England one finds everywhere this questioning of subjectivity and *Moralität*. We have seen that Coleridge has his own quarrel with conscience if it serves as a severe internal monitor rather than as our self-defining consciousness of others. Like Hegel he sees (if inconsistently) the malignity of conscience uninformed by a larger social consciousness: an "Inquisitor's conscience prompts first to torture and then burn alive hundreds of women and children for mere words without meaning—."[55] From a Hegelian point of view, such figures as Werther, René, the narrator of *The Prelude*, the Ancient Mariner, Childe Harold, and the Poet in *Alastor* are cases of arrested development; they have not progressed beyond inwardness to a recognition of their station and social duties, their responsibility to the whole in the ethical life. But it does not require Hegelian dialectic so to position them; the literary texts do this obviously enough on their own terms. The Romantics will not go so far as Hegel in renouncing subjectivity, but they do not exactly worship at the inner shrine of the self.

Hegel's concept of *Sittlichkeit* proved his undoing in the eyes of both Marx and modern liberals. The concrete social embodiment of the idea of freedom, as expounded in *The Philosophy of Right*, has seemed to many to be circumstantially descriptive of the Prussian social institutions of Hegel's day.[56] Marx complains of this text that "Hegel is not to be blamed for depicting the nature of the modern state as it is, but rather for presenting what is as the essence of the state. The claim that

---

[55] Bound Transcript, Notes on Lord Lyttleton, *The History of the Life of Henry the Second, 1767–1771*, Victoria University Library, Toronto.

[56] See Charles Taylor's refutation of such a reading as based on a "lamentable historical ignorance" of the Prussian state in 1821, which was in many respects underdeveloped relative to the state Hegel describes in *The Philosophy of Right*: in *Hegel* (Cambridge: Cambridge University Press, 1975), 452–4.

the rational is actual is contradicted precisely by an irrational actuality, which everywhere is the contrary of what it asserts and asserts the contrary of what is."[57] In *The Phenomenology of Mind* Hegel defines *Sittlichkeit* as "the real objective ethical order" and "the totality of customs and laws of a particular people, a specifically determinate ethical substance";[58] and in *The Philosophy of Right*, he describes it in a determinate way indeed. The family, with its responsibilities divided according to gender, has the "husband as its head" serving an active life of learning, labor, and struggle, while the woman "has her substantive destiny in the family, and to be imbued with family piety is her ethical frame of mind" (*PR* 166: 114). The husband controls and administers the "family capital"; property is passed on strictly according to primogeniture; within civil society, where man is said to be the "burgher or *bourgeois*," the nature of capital necessitates that there be class divisions. Hegel makes his way through the court of justice, the police, the corporation, and finally to the state as a "constitutional monarchy," about which he writes that "this final end has supreme right against the individual, whose supreme duty is to be a member of the state" (*PR* 258: 155). *Sittlichkeit* is for him the opposite of alienation.

Apologists for Hegel claim that he is not saying what he may seem to be saying. His larger argument is that individuals in fact realize their powers only as social creatures, from the language they speak to the position they occupy in the larger society. He is not saying that whatever is, is right (as Bertrand Russell complains), or that one should follow the dictates of the state, no matter what. He was writing before the Third Reich, and however mistaken he might have been, he thought Prussian society was evolving toward a realization of Geist in history. It can be argued that Hegel demands total allegiance only insofar as the state is already assumed to be worthy of it. Within that state, individuals are rational and autonomous in the sense that the state expresses the law of their highest nature.[59]

---

[57] *Critique of Hegel's 'Philosophy of Right'*, ed. Joseph O'Malley (Cambridge: Cambridge University Press, 1970), 64.

[58] *The Phenomenology of Mind*, trans. J. B. Baillie (New York: Harper & Row, 1967), 378.

[59] See Taylor, *Hegel*, 377–88, for a reading of Hegel along these lines. It seems to me this approach does not altogether do away with the authoritarian implications of Hegel's treatment of *Sittlichkeit*, given that the society he describes is authoritarian and the actualization of an ideal, even if it is not the final dialectical resultant. One does not have to suffer from what Taylor calls liberal "atomistic prejudices" to balk at Hegel's apologia for war as the proper and necessary means that different societies, acting as individuals, use to settle their conflicts (albeit his hatred of the French Revolution makes him protest against violent overthrow within a state); or his comment that the

102

My intent is not to settle this controversy concerning Hegel but to raise the question of *Sittlichkeit* as it relates to Romantic writers. As we will see repeatedly, they do not sanction a retreat into ego, whatever their concern with private consciousness. But they part company from the Hegel of *The Philosophy of Right*, at least as Marx reads it, in attempting vigorously to extrapolate, from the way things are, the way things should be. Analogous to Part III of this work are the English cantos of *Don Juan*, where, however, Byron has his own way of turning Hegel upside down. Here we find a description of a particular people's social customs at the present historical moment, but they are targeted for satire. Hegel discusses hypocrisy under the heading of *Moralität*; it is one's consciousness of a conflict between private volition and the true universal (*PR* 140: 94). And he discusses the "vacuousness" of "rhetorical eloquence" as the discourse of an empty abstract individualism that imagines its own high ideals to be in conflict with "the course of the world," itself ultimately good.[60] Byron targets rather the way hypocrisy can be institutionalized in the language and customs of a people, or of a subgroup such as the ruling class. This institutionalized hypocrisy he calls "cant," and he affirms the occasional triumph over it by individuals acting according to their private inclinations. It is only an enlightened individual who can see a collective hypocrisy, the false ideals and empty rhetoric of a social class.

Byron thus joins the other British Romantics in reversing the Hegelian ratio: *Moralität* remains privileged as the perspective from which *Sittlichkeit* is judged. It is the private conscience that sees through the sham, that insists on the continuity of ethics and politics, that lends sympathy to the producing classes and the oppressed. Social consciousness must be developed but in accordance with the intuitional powers of the individual. When Coleridge speaks of conscience as the development of a sense of "I" by means of "Thou," he argues their reciprocal relationship. Ego is not so radically diffused into social contexts as it is in Hegel, nor is it wholly determined by economic base. Coleridge and the visionary company remain "Romantics"

"personal majesty of the monarch," whose legitimacy is properly based on rights of birth and inheritance, "as the final *subjectivity* of decision, is above all answerability for acts of government" (*PR* 284: 187). At least Hegel is dangerously ambivalent on the key issue of whether the individual is or is not permitted to resist the status quo, or for that matter whether individual willing has any influence on history. The very fact of readings as contrary as Marx's and Russell's on the one hand, and Taylor's on the other, gives evidence of this ambivalence.

[60] *The Phenomenology of Mind*, 408–10.

insofar as the "I" ideally retains its power of reciprocity and origination.[61]

It remains to ask what *Sittlichkeit*, as the concretization of moral consciousness in social institutions of family, civil society, and the state, is or would be for the Romantics. As we will see throughout, there is no uniform vision among our eight authors, but on three levels – descriptions of contemporary social life, utopian visions, and reform proposals – *Sittlichkeit* is a matter for exhortation, not acquiescence, even when one is dealing with such "Tory" documents as *The Excursion* (1814) and *On the Constitution of the Church and State* (1830).

In the descriptive mode, Blake's *Songs of Innocence and of Experience* and other early works depict the contamination of family life by replication of authoritarian structures found in the larger society. Fathers tell their children what not to do, economic principles of trade dictate the selling even of one's children. In the Lambeth books, Blake describes a society in which work is exploitation, marriage legalized prostitution, the law a code imposed by the ruling classes on the producing. The city ("London") is the local unit of oppression. Since its manacles are said to be "mind-forg'd," Blake leaves ambiguous the degree of responsibility individuals must bear for their own entrapment, but at least with respect to children he preserves the distinction between villains and victims. In broad terms, social morality is a conventional code that exists for the sake of repressing libido, personal and collective. Blake's is the most sustained attack on the *Sittlichkeit* of late eighteenth-century England, but others target it as well. Words-

[61] In *Fear and Trembling* (1843) Kierkegaard criticizes Hegel's *Philosophy of Right* for not admitting of the paradox of faith, which is that the particular individual may be required to "suspend the ethical" or "universal" in obeying the will of the "absolute." In so doing, the individual rises above the universal. Thus, Abraham in his willingness to sacrifice his son, Isaac, goes against all ethical (universal) principles, and from a Hegelian standpoint ought to be condemned. But Kierkegaard argues that to obey the will of God is a higher duty than the merely ethical; the ethical is here the temptation not to kill one's son. The conflict of the ethical with the absolute is the absurd: one cannot understand Abraham but must admire him. Kierkegaard's irrationalism is frightening in its implications. He himself asks (but does not answer except through a line of circular reasoning), "How then does the individual assure himself that he is justified?" (*Fear and Trembling* and *The Sickness unto Death*, trans. Walter Lowrie, Princeton: Princeton University Press, 1941, 72.) This presumption of the subjective or, as Kierkegaard calls it, this "teleological suspension of the ethical," is mostly guarded against by the British Romantics. Blake and Coleridge both position the ethical relative to other modalities. Blake urges that we transcend mere "moral virtue" through energy and imagination; he thereby attacks a small-minded ethics with a more comprehensive one. Coleridge urges that we not indulge the Socinian reduction of religion to ethics, but he thinks any religion that offends our sense of morality is shoddy religion.

worth's *Lyrical Ballads*, *Salisbury Plain* poems, *The Ruined Cottage*, *Michael*, and other poems portray the consequences of economic and social dislocation, the Continental wars, the plight of the peasant, the brutality of the city. Shelley's *Queen Mab* describes the rampant miseducation emanating from the ruling classes that sends poison "through the bloodless veins / Of desolate society." He questions laissez-faire capitalism and social conventions from paper money and meat-eating to conscription, sexual politics, and those largest social organizations, church and state. Recognition of the conventional, not natural, origins of social life and corruption is the ground of Romantic social criticism. Judgment of social ills by means of an intuitional ethics (*Moralität*) reproves a pragmatic historicism, such as Edmund Burke's, or a laissez-faire economics, such as Adam Smith's or Malthus's.

The utopianism of the Romantics builds on such recognitions and is markedly anarchistic, whatever the politics each ultimately professes. Key utopian texts can be found in each of the eight major figures, correlative both to their diagnosis of social ills and to the more practical proposals they elsewhere make, as if in concession to the limits of day-dreaming. Blake's mythic form, Jerusalem, in the poem of that title, is the "city of peace" and "Liberty" that fulfills on the social level the ethical imperatives of the "Annotations to Lavater." An ideal human community is one where all "hindering" of one person by another ceases. Coleridge's Pantisocracy entails a small society of intimates in a self-sufficient economy, where all conditions that lead to evil have been removed and where all would reap equally the fruits of non-exploitative labor. His conversation poems subsequently retain the idea of a group of intimates bound not by conventional ties of social class or work or sometimes even family, but simply by friendship – a "natural" bonding. And the social context is reduced from the city to the village to the cottage or farmhouse, in a disclaiming of a larger social network. Even "Fears in Solitude" (1798) – which treats civil society as "one scheme of perjury" where "Courts, Committees, Institutions, / Associations and Societies" engulf and corrupt "individual dignity and power," and which discusses the larger scene of warfare between England and France – opens and closes in a country cottage suitable for "solitary musings" and domestic affections. Wordsworth's *Home at Grasmere* describes the poet's retreat from social and political upheaval, the industrial revolution, and sordid capitalism, to a pastoral village, where the bonding principle is the shared sympathy of a small group of intimates. In absconding from Manchester Grammar School, De Quincey becomes for a time the anarchist he nourishes within; he seeks out Wordsworth and even joins him in Grasmere.

105

The anarchistic principle that personal power and freedom can and ought to be found in semi-autonomous local groups with shared interests takes different forms in the others. The Haidee episode in *Don Juan*, during which the piratical father is temporarily out to sea and the lovers and other inhabitants of the Cycladic island can follow their inclinations in classless celebration, unites literal anarchism (i.e. being without a leader), innocence, the passions of the natural heart, and escape from language, which is the social convention that in itself assures one's eviction from Eden. Keats's lovers in *The Eve of St. Agnes* escape into a self-created exclusionary world of total intimacy, where sinister, trivializing, and chilling claims of family, society, and religion do not obtain. In *Prometheus Unbound* Prometheus and Asia retire to a cave where art and human culture can be created, preparatory to the regeneration of time and human history announced by the Spirit of the Hour. This retirement into intimacy and creativity initiates a larger anarchistic social regeneration, when humankind will be "sceptreless" and "free," not to mention "Equal, unclassed, tribeless, and nationless." And finally, Hazlitt's "Project for a New Theory of Civil and Criminal Legislation" urges a minimum of governmental interference and a maximum of individual rights.

These utopian texts are predicated on a negative, non-Hegelian judgment of the prevailing *Sittlichkeit*. When individuals are alienated from the conventional values of the larger social structure, social morality is properly reconstituted on the basis of personal intuitional ethics. The free association of intimates in non-exploitative creative labor becomes paradigmatic of whatever society the author wishes to project – from Coleridge's cottage to Shelley's world.

Most of them acknowledge the utopian status of this vision: Don Juan must leave the dying Haidee, Dove Cottage proves drafty and sooty and subject to crashing by opium-eaters, De Quincey is soon down and out in London, the Spirit of the Hour acknowledges such remaining "clogs" as "chance and death and mutability." They therefore write non-utopian texts as counterparts to utopian, in concession to all that thwarts their will to value. These focus on reform and practical issues or acknowledge a larger social structure already in place – a structure which, short of the millennium, will not deconstruct. They then commonly write in accordance with an organic, instead of an anarchistic, paradigm.

In *A Philosophic View of Reform* Shelley is reformist, not revolutionary. He urges such practical measures as abolishing the national debt, disbanding the standing army, doing away with tithes and sinecures, making all religions equal in the eyes of the law, and ending exorbitant taxation of workers. He stops short of universal suffrage (the women are not quite ready) and does not disown some national pride. Coleridge's *On the Constitution of the Church and State* – the culmination of writings on practical social and political issues in *The Watchman*, *The Morning Post*, *The Courier*, *The Friend*, and *Lay Sermons* – might seem to be more purely descriptive of the prevailing makeup of civil society, thus recapitulating what Marx complains of in Hegel's *The Philosophy of Right*. Coleridge describes the state in organic, quasi-dialectical terms: the polar forces are the principle of "permanence," embodied in landowners big and small, and the principle of "progression," embodied in professional, producing, manufacturing classes. But he introduces also the "Clerisy," a mediating class engaged in "producing and re-producing, in preserving, continuing and perfecting, the necessary sources and conditions of national civilization."[62] The Clerisy includes teachers, scholars, clergymen, and presumably writers and artists. Coleridge thinks the Church of England has historically served this function in large part, but he does not identify the Clerisy altogether with the Church and says that this third class requires its own independent economic base, its own national endowment. He is presenting the "Idea" of the Clerisy, not the "existing state of things," and thereby steps beyond descriptive history and sociology to recommendation. Elsewhere, Coleridge leaves a vast commentary on current social issues: the education of women, child labor, slavery, commerce, poverty, the role of parental authority in marriage, and so forth. His position is usually rather liberal, despite his opposition to the 1832 Reform Bill. (Hegel's final essay is a repudiation of this Reform Bill.)

In non-utopian texts from "The Old Cumberland Beggar" (1798) to *The Excursion* (1814) to *Two Letters on the Kendal and Windermere Railway* (1844), Wordsworth retains a version of modern pastoral but drops the call for any elitist utopian intimacy. He speaks of a society of modest means and wants that is bound instead by the sense of neighborhood and virtues of charity, industry, patience, and piety. He hopes that "Statesmen" will have a sufficiently large conception of national interest to permit this way of life to continue. De Quincey sees in the fall of Napoleon and "Recovered Christendom" a vindication of class society based on Tory principles. These ultimate matters settled, he can write a practical treatise on casuistry that deals with finer points of social life, such as usury, dueling, and writing letters of recommendation for servants. Keats's *The Fall of Hyperion* is an anti-utopian text that points to the social role of the poet; it is an implicit rejection of the poet

[62] *On the Constitution of the Church and State*, 53

as "recluse," whether Wordsworthian or Coleridgean, in favor of an activist role.[63] And it is also Keats's rejection of his own poetic past. The private utopia of dreamers is a self-indulgence. The case of Blake is more problematic, but one can find a sub-utopian treatment of *Sittlichkeit* in his city of Golgonooza, which is constructed by means of the social virtues (*J* 12: 30–7). Though it ultimately takes on a utopian perfection, it is built laboriously and imperfectly through human industry over vast periods of time.

Whether they are describing the present state of social morality or urging utopian vision and/or practical reform, we can conclude that the Romantics are critical rather than accepting. They recognize a need to transcend subjectivity for participation in the ethical life. But when they most vigorously extrapolate from individual conscience to social vision, they are apt, in a non-Hegelian way, to project it in anarchistic terms as a small society of intimates who eschew conventional or institutional alignments for natural or self-generated ones, such as friendship, sibling bonding (a natural bond, unlike marriage, which is institutional), affinity of sensibility, passionate attraction, a living arrangement in which human enterprise is insulated by an agreeable and profitable natural environment, and an unwritten small-scale constitution that regulates potential conflicts of interest, divides the fruits of labor, and defines common goals.

Whenever individual conscience is less projective, the Romantics make their accommodation with large-scale social institutions, and readmit the organic view of the state, while maintaining conscience as a corrective principle of social reform. The movement away from conscience as sanction finally undergoes a break, seen most clearly in *The Friend*, where Coleridge confusedly argues that the affairs of state must be regulated by prudence, not individual morality. Yet, despite what some see as a manifest contradiction, he attempts to speak as a *moral* critic of society.[64] Hegelian dialectic itself retains earlier stages in later, but the Romantics are more insistent on the ontological priority of the moral to the social, on the duty of the private citizen to be critical of convention and institutions and to retain the sanctity of private conscience. Coleridge may sound at times like a ruthless apologist for *Realpolitik*, but he also insists that we should "Reverence the Individuality" of our friends, regarding social life as having many centers, not only one's own – a "close neighborhood of centres" in which "room is

---

[63] See Marilyn Butler, *Romantics, Rebels and Reactionaries: English Literature and its Background, 1760–1830* (New York: Oxford University Press, 1982), 151–4.
[64] John Colmer describes this problem in *Coleridge: Critic of Society* (Oxford: Clarendon Press, 1959), 99–103.

allowed for every point to have a small circumference of its own" (*IS* 308–11).

Turning to the question of dialectic in general, we recall that Hegel is but one of many dialectical minds in the period. From Blake's "contraries" without which there is no progression, to Coleridge's "Tetractys" (a dialectical account of the Trinity and nature), to Shelley's Jupiter–Prometheus–Asia triad (Demogorgon is the power that impels dialectical movement as a whole), dialectic is a staple of British Romanticism. In Germany dialectic is well established irrespective of Hegel, in Kant's antinomies and categories, Schiller's formal drive, sensuous drive, and play drive, Fichte's (not Hegel's) thesis, antithesis, synthesis, Schelling's polarities and his synthesis of mind and matter in the Organism. I will be using the word "dialectic" in the sense which lies deeper than the marginally different conceptions of it among the figures just named: dialectic is progressive movement resulting from oppositional forces. As such, it can be a feature both of "thought" and of "reality," whether the reality of nature, or of history, or of personal history – the dialectic of the moral life.

The eight major British Romantics can be scaled according to the extent they employ dialectical structures. Blake and Coleridge are both markedly dialectical; and I propose a descending scale thereafter of Shelley, Keats, Wordsworth, De Quincey, Hazlitt, and Byron. (In Hazlitt and Byron – and occasionally the others – the word "dialogic" is more appropriate, as suggesting a play of contraries or voices that does not aim at merger.) Fuller justification for this scale will emerge in discussion of individual authors. In general terms, Blake, Coleridge, Shelley, and in some respects Keats and Wordsworth tend to image contrary forces, rhetorically foregrounded as such, that precipitate a teleological process of transformation beyond simple "change." This transformation (reconciliation, synthesis, revelation, or new emergent) may or may not occur; frustrated dialectic, as in Coleridge and Keats, is still dialectic. This structure can be embedded in everything from lyrical poems to plays to letters to essays to novels. Its principal mode is narrative, whatever the actual genre. Dialectical process is manifested as a chain of phenomena (whether events, happenings, acts, moods, qualities, words, images, or ideas). These phenomena, causally linked along a temporal axis, give the impression of leading to an ending but without a full consciousness, at any point, of precisely what that ending will be or of the stages of its fulfillment. Fichte's dialectical model – thesis, antithesis, synthesis – is more immediately descriptive of British Romantic dialectic than is Hegel's. Hegel speaks rather of the inherent contradictions or limitations at any particular stage of the development of consciousness (Geist), partial awareness of which necessitates a transformation to a higher stage. But Hegel has a deeper bearing than Fichte on writers who so often struggle to resolve psychic pain and imbalance by bringing their own contradictions into full consciousness – writers who yearn to leave off yearning.

The dialectical imagination – obviously at work in such texts as "The Tyger," *The Marriage of Heaven and Hell, The Four Zoas,* "Kubla Khan," *Biographia Literaria, Theory of Life, Julian and Maddalo,* "Ode to the West Wind," and *Prometheus Unbound* – treats moral problems as necessary stages in a developmental process. An implicit imperative in them all is that moral oppositions must not permanently structure moral reality: the oppositions of reason and passion (duty and inclination), self and nature, self and other, self and society. We become hermeneutically locked into these binary structures, which might yield to a more encompassing reading of human possibility. Blake, Coleridge, and Shelley project, with varying degrees of visionary presumption, a fruitful dialectical engagement of these oppositions. In Blake, warring psychological faculties eventually unite in Night the Ninth of *The Four Zoas,* thus awakening human consciousness and redeeming history and nature. In Coleridge the mysterious dialectic of will and reason (the unconscious and consciousness) brings about the evolution of the self. Sexual opposition is at the heart of love, in which each person strives to be the other and "both together make up one whole" (TT 348). In Shelley's *Prometheus Unbound* an initial mental fragmentation is healed by desire, and the resulting human freedom reinvigorates all of nature, which becomes a warm "Necessity." After this social regeneration, "men walked / One with the other even as spirits do."

The other British Romantics are more cautious in dialectical vision. We have seen analogues in Schiller, Schelling, and Fichte to Wordsworthian texts, but I will argue for tragic vision in Wordsworth. Cyclical naturalism routinely limits dialectical movement. In his "Vale of Soul-making" letter, Keats gives overt expression to a dialectical view of human identity, and his Odes are dialectically structured. But like Wordsworth he takes a more modest view of human willing, is even more cautious about powers of prophecy, does not foresee any "reconciliation" of the various ethical dualisms, and embraces a tragic naturalism that halts the "march of passion and endeavour."

De Quincey, Hazlitt, and Byron are in turn basically anti-dialectical. De Quincey's absurdist view of human action and character, his astonishment at the contingency of things, his fearful sense of conse-

110

quences running amok, and his lament that what is lost is lost forever, even in our dreams – all pit him against a belief in dialectical transcendence. For Hazlitt and Byron, dualisms remain dualisms, the idea of progress in history is at best tenuous. Movement is governed more by the trope of repetition than of progression: people will remain true to their fixed internal bias and they will go on being rascals. Hazlitt's hostility to German idealism registers his anti-dialectical point of view. Byron's heroic fictions (*Childe Harold's Pilgrimage, Manfred*) are deliberately regressive, while *Don Juan* could, as he says, go on for another fifty cantos; self-transcendence is hardly the point. And as we will see, *Don Juan* shares with the rest of Byron's corpus a tendency to portray human values in patterns of mutual exclusion, of permanent irreconcilability. The narrators in De Quincey, Hazlitt, and Byron give us bracing dialogue, not presumptuous dialectic.

Hegel, who thought even Schelling inadequately dialectical, might have said the same of the British Romantics, from Blake to Byron. His ability to make such a judgment arises from his extreme metaphysical presumption, which exceeds all the Romantics, British and Continental. Though Schelling, for one, presumes much about the ability of human mind to apprehend the infinite, he has some skepticism too, as consciousness is permanently excluded from the dark abyss or ground of reality. Similarly, it is excluded from the abyss of our own unconscious will. Schelling leaves room for the unknowable. But Hegel, who sees history as higher and higher manifestations of Geist, believes there is no limit to what can ultimately be manifested as real to consciousness (granted that there is some question as to whether Geist as absolute self-consciousness is for Hegel a *human* consciousness). Hegel takes skepticism to be but one stage – though an important one – in the emergence of Geist in history: "In Skepticism consciousness gets, in truth, to know itself as a consciousness containing contradiction within itself."[65]

It seems fitting that Great Britain's foremost dialectical idealist, Coleridge, is incapable of putting together that grand system he promises, that magnum opus which, even if written, would do no more than Hegel actually achieves. The British philosophical tradition – most pointedly in the Scottish School of Common Sense – resists system-building, and the British Romantics follow suit. That audacious visionary Shelley has been for many years discussed in terms of the skeptical tradition, and though I argue against this reading as

[65] *The Phenomenology of Mind*, 250. In *Romantic Contraries* (76–8), Peter L. Thorslev, Jnr., describes some dangers in dialectical thinking, including its denial of the law of contradiction, its blurring of distinctions, and its anti-intellectualism.

the master-key, it is easy to agree that he sets limits to human knowing.[66]

The post-Kantian German idealists, then, propound colossal mental structures that make the efforts of the British Romantics look chaotic and fragmentary. While Coleridge is receptive to their lead, others remain proudly hostile. Hazlitt, who says he has no theory to maintain, brands Kant's system "the most wilful and monstrous absurdity that was ever invented" (XVI 123). There is a gulf between the intellectual sensibilities of British writers and the more rarefied German idealist tradition, from Leibniz to Kant to Hegel, that makes the likes of Hobbes, Locke, Hartley, and Godwin seem level-headed and almost companionable. Still, the Germans provide interpretive models for our reading of British Romanticism and make explicit many ideas left at the level of hint or implication by the British.

In addition, the influences and analogues I have noticed supplement the British moral tradition in ways congenial to the Romantics. With some exceptions on both sides, the Germans are more concerned than the British moralists with conative issues: willing, acting, the ego striving in the world. As a psychological corollary to their concern with action, they give a more searching anatomy of desire. Schiller's discussion of "sentimental" yearning, Fichte's of the ego expressing itself as pure act, Hegel's of consciousness unfolding toward a telos of the Absolute: all these find in desire the psychological basis of the impulse toward "capacities of greater perfection," the fully realized personality. In contrast, the British moralists from Shaftesbury to Adam Smith have emphasized "virtues," and affective more than

[66] The degree to which Blake is out of keeping with the skepticism and resistance to system-building of the other British Romantics is debatable. David Punter has recently argued the affinities of Blake and Hegel, an argument based on readings of both that differ from my own (*Blake, Hegel and Dialectic*). Blake scholars cannot agree on whether Blake is a Hegelian, a Marxist, or a Maoist. I suspect he is none of these. His very obscurity makes him the more pliable to critical will. To my mind, he portrays reason as obscuring vision until the final moments of its rehabilitation, when it once again becomes "Faith & Certainty." The progressive recognitions of the Hegelian Geist in its historical emergence and its greater and greater degrees of self-consciousness are even reversed by Blake, whose Urizen as reason works through history toward greater and greater opacity, until a consolidation of error before his final apotheosis. With regard to the Hegelian *Aufheben*, Leopold Damrosch, Jnr. writes that "the developed Blakean myth has no place for the upward spiral that absorbs each preceding stage, emphasizing instead that the spectral or Satanic must be expelled utterly" (*Symbol and Truth in Blake's Myth*, Princeton: Princeton University Press, 1980, 179). As for "system," Blake's is the construction not of the author but of his critics, a construction that has required to date several decades of inferen-

conative psychology – the internal affective apparatus of the self and the connection between affective response and moral judgment. Something so portentous as how the self realizes itself in the world is hardly their concern.

It should be added that neither school is much concerned with concrete issues of act and obligation, of what kinds of moral decisions must be made in specific moral situations, of how one chooses among rival goods or lesser evils, of what it is like to be a moral agent making such choices, and of how one brings moral theory to bear on the practical issues of the day. Fichte and Hegel agree that moralists should supplement the formal character of Kant's system. The British Romantics will give their own supplement, both through the opportunity of imaginative literature to make vivid what the philosopher is likely to present as hypothetical and abstract, and through much of their ethical writing itself.

Self-realizationism

In preceding discussions of post-Kantian idealism from Schiller to Hegel, the implicit ethics has been self-realizationism. I will now focus on this position and bring Coleridge to the fore as one of its most searching expounders. Self-realizationism is not the final formulation of the ethics of Romanticism but itself becomes, as we will see, a tenet within a more encompassing moral view.

Although further inquiry into the "self" has been condemned by some post-structuralist critics, Coleridge's writings on this entity beg a reprieve. They offer anticipations of the insights, constructions, and doubts of later nineteenth- and twentieth-century discussion, as well as much that is of intrinsic interest. In engaging the concept of self where autobiographical, linguistic, and ethical discourses intersect, Coleridge is at his most inventive and vivid, all the more so because often diagnosing a pathology. I will first retrieve the more striking of these texts and construct their argument. (Coleridge will often do the thinking for us, if we scout through the corpus for missing links to a particular train of thought he has set in motion.)[67] Then I will expound what I take to be the principles of a self-realizationist ethics, with a view to situating Coleridge and other Romantics writers relative to this

tial interpretation. Whatever his own obscurity, Hegel, who may be all things but is still not exactly a poet, attempts to provide the scaffolding of his own thought.

[67] See my "Explaining Coleridge's Explanation: Toward a Practical Methodology for Coleridge Studies," in *Reading Coleridge: Approaches and Applications*, ed. Walter B. Crawford (Ithaca, N. Y.: Cornell University Press, 1979), 23–55.

now unfashionable ethical position. He shares many of its principles, but confronts its inadequacies and contradictions, and even advances some refinements.

Coleridge's son Hartley haunts him as would a parodic *Doppelgänger*. In his listlessness and lack of discipline, Hartley does not display "Self-will," which might have given Coleridge greater hope. Rather, it is "the absence of a Self, it is the want or torpor of Will, that is the mortal Sickness of Hartley's Being, and has been, for good & evil, his character – his moral *Idiocy* – from his earliest Childhood." Hartley displays no "narrow proud Egotism," but lacking also in "manly self-love," he has become the

relationless, unconjugated, and intransitive Verb Impersonal with neither Subject nor Object, neither governed or governing,   (*CL* V 228–33)

If Hartley

could but promise himself to be a *Self* and to construct a circle by the circumvolving line—.   (*CL* VI 551)

These two remarks taken together imply that the self-definition of the circumvolving line comes only in relatedness to other circles, other selves.

Coleridge feels he too lacks self-definition. He is "whirled about without a center – as in a nightmare – no gravity – a vortex without a center" (*N* III 3999). Dogged by the "haunting sense" that he is "an herbaceous Plant, as large as a large Tree, with a Trunk of the same Girth, & Branches as large & shadowing—but with *pith within* the Trunk, not heart of Wood," he is an "involuntary Imposter," and nothing in himself. His face "expresses great Sloth, & great, indeed almost ideotic, good nature. 'Tis a mere carcase of a face: fat, flabby, & expressive chiefly of inexpression" (*CL* I 259). Coleridge speaks of this demeaning self-image as a "representative image" that, if it usurps self-consciousness, induces "a sort of unnatural outwardness," the interior self farmed out to an impoverished public image (*IS* 68–9; OM B$_2$ ff. 48–51).

There is that within us which resists this flabbiness, imprecision, and vacancy of self. We can observe as "the inseparable Adjunct of our individuality and *personal* Nature, and flowing from the same source as Language does, the instinct and necessity in each man of *declaring* his particular existence and thus of *singling* or singularizing himself" (NB 29 f. 110^v).[68] Self-assertion is spoken of as if it were a speech act, a

---

[68] The passage appears with variants (e.g. no emphases) in *Omniana, or Horae Otosiores*, ed. Robert Gittings (Carbondale, Ill.: Southern Illinois University Press, 1969), 353.

"declaring" that comes from the "same source as Language." (Here Coleridge briefly goes beyond linguistic analogy to homology, but he leaves the suggestion unexplained.) Just as the language we speak is grounded in "difference," so the self we declare implies differentiating ourselves from others in the system of social life. Saussure calls language a relational structure, "a system of inter-dependent terms in which the value of each term results solely from the simultaneous presence of the others." The strict moral analogy is that the self, as moral term, is nothing in itself, which recognition Coleridge pursues in a wealth of writings.

In speaking of "the Dynamic Construction of Grammar," he writes: "I make a duplicate of I, and combining it with It or Not-I—I have the notion of a Spirit He, or She—Then I again modify it by I—and I have Thou—" (*N* III 4426). In this deduction "I is a perpetual, i.e. ever recurring Thesis," the object known as subject and vice versa, by means of which other pronominal relations are generated. But the I requires a Thou. "Not for myself but for my conscience—i.e. my affections & duties toward others, I should have no Self—for Self is Definition; but all Boundary implies Neighbourhood—& is knowable only by Neighbourhood, or Relations" (*N* II 3231). "Without a *Thou* there could be no opposite, and of course no distinct or conscious sense of the term *I*." He goes so far as to define conscience as the "equation of *Thou* with *I* by means of a free act by which we negative the sameness [see that I and Thou are not identical] in order to establish the equality [see that I and Thou are equally real and valuable]" (OM B$_2$ ff. 143–6). Instead of a divisive faculty of self-incrimination as in Kant, conscience should become a means of self-definition.

Coleridge is, as it were, a structuralist of the self, but the self should have properties analogous to those of a natural language of social interconnectedness; it should not be an arbitrary, autonomous language system with no necessary connection with the world. And we must be more than pronouns – we must be verbs. He agrees with Fichte that "Will" is "the Being itself, the absolute I or Self, not a modification or faculty" (*N* II 2382), and that in the "Dynamic Philosophy" one substitutes "Act for Thing" (*CL* IV 792). We must become like strong transitive verbs to avoid Hartley's fate, the "relationless, unconjugated, and intransitive Verb Impersonal."

Imagination has a crucial role in "declaring the self" in its relatedness to others. The "desire of Distinction," which expresses "a wish to remain the same and yet to be something else and something more," transcends the egoism that impels it ("the poor ghost of Narcissus now pining for the absent Echo," as Coleridge writes in a deleted passage).

By it one is

impelled and almost compelled to pass out of himself in Imagination, and to survey himself at a sufficing distance, in order to judge what figure he is likely to make in the eyes of his fellow men. But in thus taking his station as at the apex of a Triangle, while the Self is at the one angle of the Base, he makes it possible at least that the Image of his Neighbor may appear at the other . . . for the purposes of the comparison, and so both be contemplated at equal distance. But this is the first step toward disinterestedness.

(NB 29 ff. 110^v–111^r)

As a passing out of oneself, imagination extends the range of conscience, the "testifying state" of our relatedness to others, and is not necessarily its antagonist, as "This Lime-tree Bower" and "Frost at Midnight" movingly demonstrate in their own way.

   Coleridge has a passion for both well-defined unity and expansiveness, and in the figure of the organism he hopes to find both. Confronted by the lack of a center and by indeterminacy within himself, he finds a therapy in it; in Yeats's words, "By the help of an image / I call to my own opposite." Education is the "educing" of latent powers, and Plato knew that it should not "fill, bucket by bucket, the leaden cistern" but should awaken the "principle and *method* of self-development." It is not information stored in the passive mind, "as if the human soul were a mere repository or banqueting-room." Rather, education must place the mind "in such relations of circumstance as should gradually excite the germinal power that craves no knowledge but what it can take up into itself, what it can appropriate, and reproduce in fruits of its own" (F I 472–3). "Method" he describes as a "path of transit" from one stage of development to another, a disciplined focus of the will on its interests and vocation. If his method is at best the method of Hamlet, ostensibly mad, Wordsworth has the more conventional, admirable kind: he knows

that we can do but one thing well, & that therefore we must make a choice—he has made that choice from his early youth, has pursued & is pursuing it—and certainly no small part of his happiness is owing to this Unity of Interest, & that Homogeneity of character which is the natural consequence of it—.

(CL II 1033)

But the self is not for this reason defined by deficiency or limitation. Otherwise,

the wiser a man became, [and] the greater his power of self determination, with so much less propriety could he be spoken of as a person; and vice versâ the more exclusive the limits & the smaller the sphere enclosed, in short the less will he possessed, the more a person, till at length his personality would be

116

at its maximum when he bordered on the mere animal or the ideot i.e. when according to all use of language he ceased to be a *person* at all. (OM B₃ ff. 173–4)

The ultimate educing of the self's "germinal power" is experienced in love. The loved one must be "one who is & is not myself – not myself, & yet so much more my Sense of Being . . . Self in me derives its sense of Being from having this one absolute Object" (*N* II 3148). To love another without a component of egoism is to lose oneself, to suffer a "Self emptied," as he says of his relationship with Sara Hutchinson (*CL* V 250).[69]

What is the "self" for Coleridge? In light of these and other texts, we can deduce that it is determinate, unified, relational, transformational, functional, and conscious – most of which characteristics are for him mutually implicating. It easily fulfills Piaget's well-known criteria for a structure: wholeness (Coleridge, like Piaget, distinguishes an integral whole or unity from a mere "aggregate"); the power of transformation (as a function as well as entity, the self can remain the same and yet absorb new information and experience, producing, as Coleridge says, "fruits of its own"); and self-regulation.[70] With regard to this last criterion, Coleridge does not separate the self from the larger social structure of selves. But in his discussion of "method," "Unity of Interest," and "will," he acknowledges a qualitative autonomy, identifying the self with the power of self-origination as well as of self-government. "The necessity for external government to man is in an inverse ratio to the vigor of his self-government" (*TT* 458). In its perfection the self is like an active transitive verb governing its objects and miraculously aware of itself.

The supplement of consciousness distinguishes the self from any other structure, including living organisms such as plants and animals. Just as the degree and quality of consciousness vary greatly, so do the degree and quality of the self, from the comprehensiveness of "myriad-minded Shakespeare" to the vanishing point of the idiot and animals. Rather than "allow Self-consciousness to animals," which he regards as somnambulists, he would either "find another term for 'Self' or another term for 'Consciousness' " (NB 29 f. 129). One develops a self over time:

The moment, when the Soul begins to be sufficiently self-conscious, to ask

---

[69] For a fuller treatment of self, method, and love, see my *Coleridge the Moralist*, 146–98. See also Stephen Bygrave, *Coleridge and the Self: Romantic Egoism* (New York: St. Martin's Press, 1986).

[70] Jean Piaget, *Structuralism*, trans. Chaninah Maschler (London: Routledge & Kegan Paul, 1971), 5–16.

concerning itself, & its relations, is the first moment of its *intellectual* arrival into the World – Its *Being* – enigmatic as it must seem – is posterior to its *Existence*. Suppose the shipwrecked man stunned, & for many weeks in a state of Ideotcy or utter loss of Thought & Memory – & then gradually awakened/. (*N* III 3593)

Unlike the existentialist, Coleridge assumes a full potentiality that must be educed; we do not fashion our self *ex nihilo*. But in this text and elsewhere he does give the impression that we are thrown into a world in a disastrously ill-prepared condition even so, and must spend a lifetime gaining power over it, finding a hospitable home for a consciousness inclined to dread, imbalance, fragmentation, and in need of convalescence. As in Wordsworth, the growth of consciousness comes through alienation, the Ancient Mariner having narrated the darkest scenario of a universal predicament. It is more the ministry of dread than of fear that "fosters" us.

Coleridge thinks the self that has achieved full "Being" is more than a fictional paradigm projected to haunt us in our condition of radical fault. The self can achieve power over circumstance by an intuition of its own radiating centrality. Though *"bethinged"* by the "Circumstances & Inclosure" of infancy, by "the larger Hedge-girdle of the State," and by the "ring-fence" and "circummurations" of nature, one can see that

this conspiration of influences is no mere outward nor contingent Thing, that rather this necessity *is* himself, that that without which or divided from which his Being can not be even *thought*, must therefore in all its directions and labyrinthine folds belong to his Being, and evolve out of his essences.

(*N* III 4109)

In this matter he is close to Blake: if we can gain a full intuition of the mind's centrality, we can cast aside the "mind-forg'd manacles" that we had mistaken for constraints of circumstance. Coleridge says full consciousness of the possibility of reversing our way of thinking empowers us "to beget each in himself a new man." No longer enclosed by circumstance, one begins to "construct a circle by the circumvolving line" – to "be a *Self*" – embracing the experiential world through power of consciousness instead of "forming narrower circles, till at every Gyre [the Soul's] wings beat against the *personal Self*" (*N* II 2531).

In a notebook entry watermarked 1828, Coleridge with some assistance from his amanuensis and disciple Joseph Henry Green draws a literal circle, entitled "a *Schema* of the *total Man* as a whole," around and within which he charts "the Faculties, Acts, Functions, Products, & States of Man's nature as an Intelligent Will under the condition of finite existence."[71] He describes man as "a finient being, an intelligence, which by power of his Will dat sibi finem [gives himself a boundary], *determines* the relations of his own being & of that being to Nature . . . The Ground of Man's Nature is the Will in a form of Reason. It is this which gives the Totality, One-ness." Coleridge speaks as usual of a dialectical interdependency of faculties, and in so doing preserves a hierarchical scale of being and value within a force field imaged as the circle of the self. In any human act or stage of development there may be "a preponderance" of one faculty over another, but each "may be modified by one or all," and "all may act in each." He goes on to make intriguing correlations of "Reason" with the "Symbolic Imagination" and of "Will" with the "Ideal Imagination," in an ascending scale of being – the ontology of self.

One implication of this scale of being is that the will, which is the ground of self-origination and which brings the "whole soul of man into activity" without mediation, is higher in function than the symbolic imagination, which works through mediated structures. The moral life is a direct, unmediated product of "Ideal Imagination," the direct incorporation of ideal form into our own lives. The full evolution of self ("I=Self=Spirit") from sensate awareness to individuality to integrity to a full self-declaring in the spiritual "I Am" supersedes in value even our highest mediated construct, the system of symbols that is the poem. Poetry itself insists that we subordinate "art to nature; the manner to the matter" (*BL* II 17). The interdependency of such powers and values entails our choosing both, however. Coleridge is a far remove from the aesthete, since imagination necessarily functions as a moral force. As he writes elsewhere, the "imaginative power" is a "multiform power, which acting with its permeative modifying unifying might on the Thought and Images specificates the Poet"; it exercises "the same power in moral intuitions and the representations of worth or baseness in action," and is consequently "the essential constituent of what is called *a Good Heart*" (*PL* 452n).

In these and other writings Coleridge ponders questions addressed in the ethics of "self-realization." I believe he probably introduced the

---

[71] Egerton MS 2801, ff. 77ʳ–77ᵛ, British Library. I am grateful to Professors Bart Winer, H. J. Jackson, and J. R. de J. Jackson. The latter advised me on the date of this undated text, the hand, and transcription. I am publishing the full text with commentary in "Coleridge and the Perils of 'Self-Realization'," in *Coleridge's Theory of the Imagination Today*, ed. Christine Gallant (AMS Press, 1989), 257–73.

term into English.[72] In a discussion of the Romantic movement, Bertrand Russell concludes that "Man is not a solitary animal, and so long as social life survives, self-realization cannot be the supreme principle of ethics."[73] Yet many who propound such an ethics are quick to say that it ought not be confused with strict egoism. We have seen how Schiller, Fichte, Schelling, and Coleridge manage this paradox. Similarly, self-realization for Hegel means broadening the self's context beyond the particular to the universal. That it does not necessarily reduce to narrow egoism lends it a degree of respectability in some quarters, but other problems remain. There has been tacit agreement as to who can be grouped among the self-realizationists. Its basic tenets have not been sufficiently clarified, however.[74]

In view of the fact that Plato and Aristotle are often said to have spawned the concept, self-realizationism has had a sporadic history in Western philosophy (a history yet to be told in any detail). The term is rarely applied again before the Romantic period. One can argue its applicability to the post-Kantian idealists, to the British Romantics, to the American Romantics Emerson, Thoreau, and Whitman, and to the later nineteenth-century British idealists, T. H. Green, Bernard Bosanquet, and F. H. Bradley. The latter uses the term as his organizing principle. These British idealists are indebted to Hegel, as is the younger Marx, whose *Economic and Philosophic Manuscripts of 1844* has a pronounced element of self-realizationism. Nietzsche most aggressively states the position later in the century. In the twentieth century it has been absorbed into psychology, especially the post-Freudian ego psychology associated with such figures as Alfred Adler, Carl Jung,

---

[72] The *OED* gives the first use to F. H. Bradley in 1876. But Coleridge uses the term in an interpretive paraphrase of Fichte's *Das System der Sittenlehre* (1798) in a notebook entry of 1813–15: "However, we yet do distinguish our Self from the Object, tho' not in the primary Intuition—Visio visa—now this is impossible without an act of abstraction—we abstract from our own product—the Spirit snatches itself loose from its own self-immersion, and self-actualizing distinguishes itself from its Self-realization—But this is absolutely impossible otherwise than by a free Act—" (*N* III 4186). I have seen its various forms in the Opus Maximum manuscript: e.g. "If then personeity, by which term I mean the source of personality, be necessarily contained in the idea of the perfect Will, how is it possible that personality should not be an essential attribute of this Will, contemplated as self-realized" (B_3 f. 243); also in the Huntington Library MS "On the Divine Ideas," f. 73, and in SM 9. Coleridge does not use the term as the kingpin of an ethical system, however, and the context in these passages is sometimes more theological than ethical.

[73] *A History of Western Philosophy* (New York: Simon and Schuster, 1945), 684.

[74] Two recent critiques make good progress toward clarification: Kai Nielsen, "Alienation and Self-realization," *Philosophy*, 48 (1973), 21–33; and Isaac Franck, "Self-realization as Ethical Norm: A Critique," *The Philosophical Forum*, 9 (1977), 1–25.

A. H. Maslow, Carl Rogers, Karen Horney, G. W. Allport, Erik Erikson, Otto Rank, and Erich Fromm, who looks back to the younger Marx.

That such a seemingly heterogeneous group – from Ancient Greeks to European and American Romantics to the neighborhood self-therapist – could be crowded under this umbrella suggests both the breadth of the concept and its weakness as a tool of specification. But it is a cluster concept of some use, even so. The major tenets, several of which have been seen in Coleridge, are these:

(1) Good is conceived teleologically as a projected version of the self, which as "future" or "ideal" self differs in kind and degree from "present" self; yet

(2) there is a continuity and sameness of present and ideal self, the movement from potential to actual or from unconscious to conscious not constituting a quantum leap. Nietzsche says you must become what you are.

(3) The ideal or "healthy" self is a complex structure of faculties that is metaphorized in terms of "harmony," "organic unity," and even vegetative life. Shaftesbury, with his delight in harmony of faculties, is a predecessor of Romantic self-realizationists. Coleridge has described the method of "educing" the self from the "germ."

(4) Pleasure or happiness is not in itself the moral goal, but either may accompany pursuit of the good. Coleridge gives an elaborate critique of hedonism.[75]

(5) Moral progress is gauged by the development of "virtues" or "excellence" or "skills." These have both instrumental and intrinsic value, as they make up part of the ideal self toward which they are directed. The structure of the *Nicomachean Ethics* implies that these virtues or skills are both moral and non-moral (intellectual), but even intellectual skills are moralized insofar as they educe the self. Coleridge writes that all knowledge which "enlightens and liberalizes, is a form and a means of Self-knowle[d]ge, whether it be grammar, or geometry, logical or classical" (*CL* VI 630).

(6) The theory is teleological but not in the ordinary sense consequentialist. Acts are not judged in terms of how much value they promote in the world at large. Coleridge severely criticizes William Paley's consequentialist ethics. Instead, the valued consequence is an altered condition of the agent. This means a coalescence (or, less generously, a conflation) of efficient and final causes.

(7) The self is realized in both acts and "activity," both pivotal

---

[75] See my *Coleridge the Moralist*, 224–34.

decisions and the daily pursuit of goals. Acts and activity ex-press the self in the sense of leading it out of potentiality; this is an expressivist ethics.

(8) Freedom and necessity become synonyms in that freedom is said to be one with acting according to one's proper destiny, or, in more prosaic terms, finding one's vocation.

The cluster concept of self-realizationism becomes inelegant when we consider additional tenets, about which there is disagreement.

(1) The realized self is basically social; this ethic is improperly labelled egoistic. Those agreeing are Aristotle (for whom, as Alasdair MacIntyre reminds us, the virtues are social virtues),[76] Coleridge, Hegel, Marx, F. H. Bradley, and Fromm. Those who tend, after all is said and done, to foreground the ego include – in my reading of them – Blake, Emerson, Nietzsche, and many modern-day ego psychologists.

(2) Concepts of obligation are secondary to concepts of value. Strict rule-bound notions of duty are seen as destructive of value; and obligation tends to be displaced by "opportunity." Praise and blame take on an aesthetic component, since one judges another according to criteria of harmony and health. This tendency begins with Aristotle, who writes extensively on the virtues, relatively little on praise and blame, and still less on moral rules and duty. Schiller, Blake, Coleridge, and Nietzsche imagine a self more generously proportioned than one stunted by the crunch of conscience. Some ego psychologists and self therapists have notoriously included in their protocol the eradication of guilt, whatever crimes we might have indulged in. But others – Fichte, Thoreau, and Bradley – insist on the centrality of duty, just as Coleridge is unable attitudinally to displace it. And although Nietzsche denigrates Christian bad conscience, he urges an imperative productive of guilt in his own way – that we should continually "overcome" ourselves.

(3) Self-realization is a dialectical process, one that entails deep oppositional suffering. It is based on a psychology of the will; human nature is a striving in which such forces as the Hobbesian will to power and Lockean "uneasiness" are taken to be evidence of a mental asymmetry that leads to dialectical movement instead of to a restless repetitiveness ending only in death. This ideal is paramount in German and British idealism, in Schiller, Fichte, Hegel, and Nietzsche, and in Blake, Coleridge, and Bradley. Aristotle is not dialectical in this

---

[76] *After Virtue: A Study in Moral Theory* (Notre Dame, Ind.: University of Notre Dame Press, 1981), 137–53.

sense; virtues may be "means" between extremes, but they are not dialectical emergents. Many of the ego psychologists, in turn, have a sunnier version of self-realization, often as a corrective to Freudian gloom concerning neurosis, pleasure, and freedom.

(4) Self-realizationism is a naturalistic ethical theory. The preoccupation with naturalism, which turns almost obsessional in ethicists of the first half of this century, begins with G. E. Moore. Few ethical thinkers, let alone poets, before the present day neatly conform to either a naturalistic or a non-naturalistic ethics.[77] Aristotle is naturalistic in the sense that he bases ethics on what he takes to be a verifiable fact of human nature – that human beings by nature desire the good or desirable. MacIntyre and others have argued that such a premise does not necessarily commit a "naturalistic fallacy" (derive "ought" statements from "is" statements); rather, it asserts a fact regarding our biological makeup, from which ethical investigation can properly take its start. The German idealists and British Romantics are difficult to sort out on this issue. Schelling tends toward naturalism, Fichte toward non-naturalism. Blake and Coleridge tend to think of ethics as a non-naturalistic category of human understanding, a special category not solely derived from – though certainly indebted to – facts of human psychology or external nature. Wordsworth tends toward naturalism. Modern ego psychologists, aspiring to science and subordinating ethics to psychology, are often downright sentimental in their naturalism: if only we would heed what our basic nature inclines us to do, we would be whole and healthy.

The difficulty in making a hard and fast determination about naturalism with respect to the larger minds of the tradition is seen in Nietzsche. Walter Kaufman concludes that he

is consistently naturalistic, insofar as he insists that man need not break completely with his own animal nature to do the good and create the beautiful. When he adds, however, that man should transfigure his *physis*, perfect himself, and aid nature, one must ask whether that, too, is naturalism – and Nietzsche fails to answer that question.[78]

[77] The "naturalist" believes moral judgments pertain to natural properties observable in the world or in human nature. Moral terms – "good," "right," "honorable" – can be replaced by non-moral terms from the language of psychology, sociology, or politics – such as "tending to promote pleasure," or "tending to promote the well-being of a group of people," or "tending to extend one's skills, powers, and well-being." The "non-naturalist" thinks moral judgments and terms are their own category and cannot be verified through observation in the same way that scientific judgments can be verified.

[78] *Nietzsche: Philosopher, Psychologist, Antichrist* (New York: Vintage, 1968), 176–7.

Enough has been said to suggest that self-realization is a rather ungainly theory, and unlikely to appeal to empirical, positivistic, or analytic traditions.[79] Self-realizationists may be more muddled than deep, but they are clear in their opposition to hedonistic utilitarianism, the fact/value dichotomy, and the overthrow of personality by sociology. Self-realizationism is one component of the Romantic will to value.

The theory as embodied in Romanticism and elsewhere creates its own problems with value. One of these is suggested by Kant, who writes that human beings have "capacities of greater perfection" that if ignored would "perhaps be consistent with the *maintenance* of humanity as an end in itself, but not with the *advancement* of this end."[80] To develop these capacities is only a "meritorious" or "lax" duty, however, because we could *conceive* a world in which nobody develops such capacities, even though we could not rationally *will* such a world. One could go beyond Kant in this matter and remove self-realization (thought of here as simply the development of one's talents) from the realm of obligation altogether, and give it to the realm of mere recommendation. To treat recommendation as if it were obligation imposes on the conscience an anxiety it need not accept. Why should we feel *guilty* for not becoming what we might become? If what we might have become is a local T.V. anchorman, should we feel guilty for having become only a college professor? Dissatisfaction, yes, but why guilt? The Romantics are not the only ones to blur these categories.

There is another problem with the theory, which assumes the self is germinally latent and simply in need of being led out of potentiality. An implicit metaphor beyond that of "germ" is at work: we must find the "real" self, the homunculus who is the core of personality and whom we may cheat on or misrepresent in our words, gestures, and acts. This view reverses the existentialist predicament. As an essentialism, it says that one must bring into existence what is already somehow there in essence. The organic metaphors of vegetative growth seem counter to concepts of human freedom and conscious choosing. Does not this fixed essence imply that one can properly unfold in only one way? Or, if one assumes the organism does not consciously and inevitably unfold according to its own inner law, how

---

[79] See Ruth Wylie, "The Present Status of Self Theory," in *Handbook of Personality Theory and Research*, ed. Edgar Borgatta and William Lambert (New York: Rand McNally, 1968), 728–87.

[80] *Fundamental Principles of the Metaphysic of Morals*, trans. Thomas Abbott (New York: Liberal Arts, 1949), 47.

is one to discover *which* way? If one feels miscast, how shake off what Wordsworth calls "that burthen of my own unnatural self"? How calm the anxiety that one is cheating on the essential self, since no evidentiary standard can be brought to bear? A more formal but related complaint, voiced by Hastings Rashdall, is that self-realizationism is a tautology. Everything that we do actualizes some potential, or we could not do it – from sitting still to going to sleep. The "precious formula" that "Self-realization is the end of life," as found in F. H. Bradley, gives us "just no information at all" and "leaves out the whole differentia of Morality; and it is a differentia presumably which we are in search of when we ask, 'What is Morality?' and are solemnly told, 'It is doing or being something which you are capable of doing or being.' "[81]

Finally, the emphasis on "wholeness," a seemingly benign strategy, leads to some vexatious questions. We might well say that a particular individual should develop this or that propensity, and we might universalize this as the principle that everyone should seek some expertise or other. But, as Isaac Frank notes, it is more cumbersome to make wholeness of personality the object of moral will. Particular moral goals for particular persons can be prescribed, such as learning to love our children or ceasing to drink laudanum at breakfast. Many goals might also be non-moral: piano-playing, gardening, knowing how to take a business trip. But how do we prescribe activity for the entire personality? And what about murdering infants in their cradles, if this expresses one aspect of the whole self seeking realization? If we are not sentimentalists with regard to human nature, we would wish only some capacities, and not others, to be developed. Do we not have to invoke other ethical systems to decide what should become the realized content of the self – whether love or artistry or a strong sense of duty, and preferably not the fine art of murder? An ethics other than self-realizationism must supersede it to settle such a question.

We can sum up these objections by saying that the theory imposes a sense of obligation, inappropriately, at the same time as it gives no specific directions and no sanctions. Its inadequacy is felt, experientially, as empty brooding and anxious movement toward an end always seen as a blur – of our own image projected and somehow transformed in time, and yet discovered to have been our essence all along. The organic metaphors informing self-realizationism might seem to legislate an unconscious, deterministic educing of the self according to a personal destiny. But ironically, if we make self-

[81] *The Theory of Good and Evil*, 2 vols. (London: Oxford University Press, 1907, 1924), II, 62.

realization our maxim, we are consigned to a state of indeterminate ethical desire.[82]

Where does Coleridge stand relative to the objections that can be raised against the theory? On the issue of indeterminacy he has spoken vigorously: to become a self is to draw an expansive but containing circle, to set limits, to differentiate the self from others in the very act of increasing one's awareness of them. Where we might have expected him to say that man is potentially infinite, he has written that "Man is a finient being," self-determining and shaping. ("Finient," from the Latin *finio*, "set limits," is not in *OED*.) Imagination is the shaping "co-adunating" power of the self, at the same time that it is the power of passing beyond the self to the other. The "*method* of self-development" requires discipline and awareness of structure. Coleridge resists the deconstruction of the self precisely because he suffers and monitors it – as a kind of walking aporia which transcribes the *self*-contradiction not as cognitive possibility alone but as a daily torment in which little resembling deconstructive play may be found. His brilliant analogy of self with language is intended to illustrate the ways of structuring the self, not of deconstructing it.

The objection that the "germ" of self, hardly indeterminate, has a *pre*determined essence that can healthily grow in only one way is resolved, in theory, by equating the germ itself with freedom. Coleridge says that a true liberal "education" is an "educing" and a "training up": it is "that which *draws* forth, and trains up the germ of free-agency – Educatio, qui *liberum* facit: and the man, who has mastered all the conditions of *freedom*, is *Homo Liberalis*—" (*CL* VI 629). The germ can be inhibited, the plant stunted. Of a young boy who exhibits a "great deficiency of *initiative* power, of *setting* himself off on the skaits," he speculates that what is lacking is a "*specific* sensibility, having it's seat and source in some special energy of the organic and organific Life." Coleridge wonders if it might have arisen "from a fault in the Germ" or "from some nipping Frost or Blight in early Spring" (*CL* V 517–18). William Pitt the Younger, under the influence of his father Lord Chatham, "was cast, rather than grew," with the result that "that, which he *might have been*, was compelled into that, which he *was to be*" (*EOT* II 319–29). Educing the germ of free-agency is perilous

---

[82] From a Hegelian point of view, these objections could be faulted for their non-dialectical literalism. It is in the nature of dialectical movement that consciousness does not fully know itself or its own goals – and is to that degree indeterminate; the larger movement is away from contradiction, abstraction, to the full concreteness of the universal. But to assent to this is to assent to the entire Hegelian baggage, which hangs on a monumental paradox, the concrete universal.

and hardly inevitable; its growth can be inhibited, blighted, coerced. But Coleridge denies that growth can take only one predetermined form. Human beings are distinguished from vegetables and animals in that their organic being is guided by consciousness and will – ultimately by the "Ideal Imagination." We are potentially self-trans-forming, self-regulating, self-defining organisms, who too frequently revert to the mental sleep of animals and vegetables. "But what the plant *is*, by an act not its own and unconsciously – *that* must thou *make* thyself to *become!*" (*SM* 71), wherein we find Coleridge's implicit answer to Rashdall's charge of "tautology." "The nurture and evolu-tion of humanity is the final aim" (*F* I 508), and just as we can declare our own language and even assist its historical development – invent-ing, correcting, desynonymizing it – so we can imagine a better self, construing it in our fashion. Peter Thorslev, Jnr., rightly notes the difficulty of deriving an ethics of freedom from organicism, with its built-in concepts of unconscious development and immanent destiny, but Coleridge (like many nineteenth-century idealists) believes that organicism admits of the evolution of consciousness and intelligent choosing.[83]

As for the need of other ethical modalities to supplement or super-sede self-realizationism, it can be said that for Coleridge it *is* but one major ethical tendency. Other views uneasily co-exist with and chasten it: a conventional Christian ethics and, I will suggest shortly, a Romantic version of "ideal utilitarianism."

The other objections to self-realizationism are displayed more than answered in the Coleridgean situation. The philosophically unsound merger of the categories of obligation and opportunity underwrites his entire life. He is in a continuous state of guilt for not having fully exercized his "capacities of greater perfection." As for the problem of prescribing activity to the entire personality, one must concede that Coleridge writes himself one of the world's longest prescriptions. He wishes to know it all, to be an encyclopedist who would write a magnum opus uniting the various branches of knowledge into a single massive "Tree of Knowledge" (*CL* VI 628). Though he knows he is not "a sapless *Stick*" like specialized professionals who do not possess the vital trunk of knowledge, he feels weak and overextended, like that overgrown herbaceous plant which clumsily branches out in too many directions, his own drive toward unity frustrated by the multitude of initiatives he makes. But Coleridge's very failures in recking his own rede, so prominently self-displayed, seem now heuristic to us, and

[83] *Romantic Contraries*, 86, 111–12.

revelatory of that self and those notions he tried so unremittingly to declare.

Beyond its place in the life of Coleridge, self-realizationism as a philosophical idea is an operative force in Romantic literature. It is not exactly that bad philosophy makes great literature, but that literary texts, which rarely grant protagonists a complete wisdom or uncluttered life, can demonstrate its badness. The noble affliction, indeterminate ethical desire, tempts dark gods throughout European Romantic literature. The more we are caught by a strong desiring state founded in egoism, and directed toward some vague self-projection, the more the imagination will fail us, setting up trivial objects of desire, as if to mock our grandiosity. Desire then manifests its underside of dissolution and death. The Lord issues the imperative that a human being should be "active," and Faust – who fastens variously onto knowledge, power, sensual experience, and Gretchen – affirms active striving for its own sake: "It is restless action makes the man" (l. 1759). But Mephistopheles insists that "You are in the end . . . what you are . . . You remain forever what you are" (ll. 1806, 1809).[84] Faust and Mephistopheles offer false alternatives, the one affirming the state of desire over and beyond particular goals, the other calmly denying the possibility of transcendence. In *Faust Part Two* the hero recognizes states of being and doing beyond both undisciplined self-realization and acquiescence of will.

Chateaubriand's René, suffering a bad case of Weltschmerz akin to the strain Childe Harold is to catch a few years later, says his wanderings are impelled by an "excess of life" that drives him "in search of some unknown good, whose intuition pursues [him] relentlessly." Excess of life as desire is founded in "the vast emptiness of [his] existence," and converts into its contrary, an "aversion for life." Desire for an unknown good is strictly meaningless; he is trapped in a narrative that makes no sense, and recognition of this drives him, like Faust, to consider suicide. Ironically, a sense of strong attachment brought about by the death of his sister cures him of all this: "Now that my sorrows were real, I no longer wished to die."[85] In a curious homeopathy, grief acts as cure of despair. An unhappy indeterminacy is redressed by the overdetermination of death, because grief is a wholly determinate desire – or as Coleridge says, a "craving" – for someone in particular. More generally, the pains of self-realization are

---

[84] Johann Wolfgang von Goethe, *Faust Part I*, trans. Louis MacNeice (London: Faber & Faber, 1951).

[85] François René de Chateaubriand, *René*, trans. Irving Putter (Berkeley: University of California Press, 1952), 109.

alleviated by a sturdier sense of self-definition that comes with a more precise focusing of human will and affection.

We find such patterns in texts as diverse as Goethe's *Die Leiden des jungen Werthers* (1744), Rousseau's *Les Rêveries du promeneur solitaire* (1782), Brentano's *Godwi* (1801), Novalis's *Heinrich von Ofterdingen* (1802), Senancour's *Obermann* (1804), Constant's *Adolphe* (1807), Chamisso's *Peter Schlemihls wundersame Geschichte* (1814), Lamartine's *Méditations poétiques* (1820), Balzac's *La Peau de chagrin* (1831), Sainte-Beuve's *Volupté* (1834), Musset's *La Confession d'un enfant du siècle* (1836), and Hugo's *Les Contemplations* (1856). The desire for self-realization is frustrated by an indeterminacy that plagues the concept. In drawing the determinate circle of self, Coleridge responds to this problem with a metaphor, but translating metaphor into the daily practice of life leaves the problem where it was, as Romantic literary texts illustrate. Far from glorifying the personal will, European writers offer an analytic of it in the cautionary mode. Using a phrase similar to the one I employ, Babbitt speaks in *Rousseau and Romanticism* of "infinite indeterminate desire" (p. 307) and indicts Romantic literature for exhibiting it. But indeterminate ethical desire has demonstrably lent itself to powerful literary art. And Babbitt could be consoled that it is a desire more frequently punished than rewarded in Romantic literature.

In Great Britain we find the problem of ethical indeterminacy consciously confronted in works as various as Blake's "Ah Sunflower," *The Book of Thel*, and *Visions of the Daughters of Albion*, Wordsworth's *The Prelude*, Byron's *Childe Harold's Pilgrimage*, Shelley's *Alastor* and *Lines Written Among the Euganean Hills*, and Keats's *Endymion*. The object of desire may sometimes seem to be, like the blue flower of the German Romantic cult, determinate; Blake's sun and Shelley's "two eyes" seem determinate enough. But such images ironically serve as symbols of the state of indeterminate desire itself. They do not announce their meaning but remind us only of our desire that our desire were for a known good as vivid as these. We seek something as vivid as the sun, but are left wondering still what it is we seek. As has often been noted, Romantic narrative has a quest structure but lacks the iconographical resoluteness of medieval narrative. Many of these texts are cautionary tales, and the Romantics – though continuing to value the quest for enhanced identity – invoke other moral structures as correctives. The wise sachem in *René* offers the most practical of these: "Happiness can be found only in the common paths." This sentiment would unceremoniously put our self-realizing heroes in their place, but of course it has rarely been happiness that they seek.

Hedonistic utilitarianism

To turn from the deeps of German idealism and its closely related self-realizationism to the shallows of British utilitarianism begs a period of acclimatization beforehand, but there does exist a principle of continuity: they are both teleological. Moral principles and acts are judged in terms of some valued end – characteristically, the fully evolved person in the former, the happiness of society in the latter. Both contrast with Kantian formalism, which decides rightness or wrongness with respect to the quality of the agent's will and an act's intrinsic properties relative to the categorical imperative, irrespective of consequences. Utilitarians concern themselves with the overt ethical life, asking what acts or principles will be most beneficent to society as a whole. One dilemma of the self-realizationist – how does one direct egoistic impulses into a concern for Betty Martin? – is skirted by the utilitarian, who worries about the beneficence of acts, not the quality of motivation. The teleological, progressive character of utilitarianism has some allure for the Romantics, especially Shelley, who does not valorize psychological states of being to the extent the others do.

Utilitarianism in Great Britain has mostly been of the "hedonistic universalistic" variety – one should promote those acts or favor those moral rules that would result in the greatest happiness for the largest number of people, a formula first enunciated by Hutcheson and then canonized by Bentham. The unitary value that acts and rules should promote is pleasure and/or "happiness," a broader hedonic term. The Romantics are wise enough to know that pleasure or happiness is a value. Their quarrel with utilitarianism is over its insistence that hedonic value is or ought to be the sole end of human action and that it can be measured in quantitative ways alone.

Coleridge's impressive critique of hedonism is based on the way we use language. If one assumes a total equivalence of "good" to "pleasure," then the word "good" could be replaced by "pleasure" in all contexts without altering meaning. But Coleridge thinks it not tautological to say, "Pleasure is a good and pain an evil"; it is not equivalent to saying "black is black & white is white." Even the hedonist does not say that there is "no pleasure but pleasure and no pain but pain" (OM B₂ ff. 61–2). Pleasure is therefore only a good, not *the* good. Coleridge's argument from trivialization closely anticipates G. E. Moore's "open-question" argument against the definability of "good" in terms of a naturalistic property such as "pleasure."[86] The

---

[86] When people "say 'Pleasure is good,' " writes Moore, "we cannot believe that they merely mean 'Pleasure is pleasure' and nothing more than that." No predicate can

hedonist, moreover, conflates "is" with "ought" in telling us that the "desired" is the "desirable." He improperly assumes that *"Good* is nothing more than a reflex idea of the mind after a survey and calculation of agreeable or delightful sensations included within any given time, the whole of our life for instance." Coleridge, whose opium addiction may provide the subtext for these subtleties, replies that it is an error to "call that good which I feel I desire, instead of endeavouring to desire that only which I know to be *good"* (*PL* 153).

Having argued that pleasure or happiness is not the sole or even principal value of a coherent ethics, Coleridge still deems it an important value, and designates four hedonic levels (*N* III 3558, 4422). These are all accompaniments, ideally, of virtuous acts and not ends toward which acts are or should be directed.

(1) The quantitative hedonist like Bentham is correct about only one level, the physical or *hedone*; here the only question to ask is, how much? not what kind. *"How much on the whole*? the contrary, *i.e.* the painful and disagreeable having been subtracted. The quality is a matter of *taste*: et de *gustibus* non est disputandum" (*AR* 41). Coleridge objects to the leap the psychological hedonist makes to ethical hedonism. One cannot assume that because people do desire certain pleasures that they *ought* to. "*What* happiness? That is the question." If I assert that I "delight in Milton and Shakespeare more than turtle or venison," the psychological hedonist replies, "That is not my case. For myself, I think a good dish of turtle and a good bottle of port afterwards give me much more delight than I receive from Milton and Shakespeare" (*PL* 142). We need more discriminating criteria than the psychological hedonist offers to settle such disputes, and Coleridge offers three levels on which questions of kind rightly enter in.

(2) "Happiness" itself, or *eutuchia*, is the sense of general well-being, of "good hap," the "aggregate of fortunate chances" or "circumstances" ("whatever *stands round* us"), a level in which Coleridge feels himself particularly deficient.

(3) Intellectual pleasure, or *eunoia*, is described, in terms reminiscent of Spinoza, as the result of passing from confused to distinct conceptions. It is "the immediate consequent or accompaniment of the intellectual energies," felt for example when we cry "Eureka" (*PL* 141).

(4) Moral pleasure, or *eupraxia*, results from having acted virtuously for virtue's sake. If instead we act well for the sake of pleasure – as

be found to substitute for "good" about which one could not intelligently ask the question, "Is that good?". *Principia Ethica* (Cambridge: Cambridge University Press, 1903), 1–21.

Mandeville thinks we must – then the pleasure is necessarily corrupted, a "counterfeit." "Bliss, not Happiness, is the true Summum Bonum, [Socrates] asserted: but Bliss, or perfect Well-*being* is one and the same with Well-*doing*, and Eupraxia accurately expresses this identity" (*PL* 409 n34).

Coleridge's critique of hedonism is largely formal, but it emanates from the torments of his own life. "Joy" is his word for a fruitful union of the sensuous and the intellectual, the highest expression of life's intensity. When his capacity for joy diminishes, he doubts the continuance of life. He describes himself as "a genuine Tantalus," whose nature is "made for Joy – impelling me to Joyance – & I never, never can yield to it" (*N* I 1609).

Among other Romantic authors, pleasure is an acknowledged value of the first order. For Wordsworth, the production of pleasure is not a "degradation of the Poet's art," because "we have no sympathy but what is propagated by pleasure" (*PLB* 140). "Lines Written in Early Spring" (1798) speaks of pleasure at the heart of the poet's faith in nature: "'tis my faith that every flower / Enjoys the air it breathes." The hedonistic element in Romanticism has, if anything, been underappreciated. But pleasure remains only a value, not a principle of conduct. The deliberate pursuit of pleasure, as Byron knows, reaps a hangover.

Coleridge and Hazlitt criticize utilitarianism from complementary perspectives, formal and cultural. Bentham is subjected by Coleridge to reductio ad absurdum: "The American savage, in scalping his fallen enemy, pursues *his* happiness naturally and adequately. A Chickasaw or Pawnee Bentham . . . would necessarily hope for the most frequent opportunities possible of scalping the greatest possible number of savages, for the longest possible time" (*TT* 369). Ethnic slur and historical error apart, this piece of cleverness mistakes Bentham's universalistic hedonistic utilitarianism for hedonistic egoism – but there is no record in the *Table Talk* that anyone sitting at the table called him on this.

Coleridge's critique of the smaller mind, William Paley, is more sophisticated. Paley's theory of "general consequences" is an early example of rule-utilitarianism: one ought to act in accordance with those moral rules that, if followed by everyone in the community, would bring about the greatest good for members of that community. Coleridge has several objections, most of which express the larger objection that this is ironically a more impractical method than the time-honored one of conscience. It is "no less *ideal*" than other systems because "the agent's mind is compelled to go out of itself in order to bring back conjectures" about what the "general consequences *would* be, all other things remaining the same, if all men were to act as he is about to act" (*F* I 318). Nobody is this accurate a prophet. If we understand the basic act well enough to subject it to multiplication, have we not already answered all questions about its nature? Coleridge objects to utilitarianism's false claim of concreteness. To consider the outward properties of an act – the body in motion, or the resulting changes in circumstance that heighten or lessen pleasure – is to divorce the agent from the act, with ironically a lessening of its tangibility. The act becomes an abstraction, out there, disjoined from the agent's interior life. Conscience "knits us to earth," while expediency "makes man a thing of generalities and ideal abstractions, Shadows in which no life is, no power" (*N* III 3875).

Hazlitt's objections to utilitarianism on cultural grounds set forth the terms of a major debate for the remainder of the nineteenth century. The brutal criterion of usefulness and the lack of clear discernment among qualitatively different pleasures explain why the utilitarians "would pull down Stonehenge to build pig-sties, and would convert Westminster Abbey into a central House of Correction" (XII 248–9). Literature and the arts may not be strictly useful, but they are not therefore without value. Hazlitt sees in the theory the same justification for banality of spirit that Matthew Arnold will call philistinism and that Ruskin will call Mammonism. Just as sinister in its implications is the fact that utilitarianism justifies a tyranny of the majority: banal pleasures of the majority can morally take precedence over refined pleasures of a minority.

An exception to this censure of hedonistic utilitarianism is Shelley, who adopts utilitarian elements of Helvétius, Hume, and Godwin. In his note on Necessity in *Queen Mab* (1813), he writes that "utility is morality; that which is incapable of producing happiness is useless" (*SPR* 111), and in his "Speculations on Morals," in a portion written probably in 1817, he writes summarily that that is "called good which produces pleasure; that is called evil which produces pain" (SM 187). But it is an error, on the basis of a few such passages, to term the author of *Prometheus Unbound* a hedonistic utilitarian. The bulk of his poetry and certainly a later prose work like *A Defence of Poetry* (1821) support the view that he too is a value pluralist. The appeal of utilitarianism to Shelley is its focus on social contexts and, in theory, its progressive view of reform.

It is not Bentham but William Godwin who is the seminal utilitarian mind for the British Romantics. To a greater degree than they acknowledge, he stimulates their moral inquiry, sometimes as a result of their misreadings of him.[87] We have already noted Coleridge's admiration of Godwin for showing that "Morality might be built up on it's own foundation, like a Castle built *from* the rock & *on* the rock." It is Godwin more than Bentham who introduces Wordsworth, Coleridge, Hazlitt, and Shelley to hedonistic utilitarianism, and of a kind that differs from Bentham's in certain respects. Godwin and Bentham agree insofar as they are "act-utilitarians": they judge a particular act in terms of its consequences – its promotion of pleasure and happiness – and do not, like Paley and other rule-utilitarians, judge in terms of whether an act conforms to a rule, the general adoption of which by a larger society

[87] Blake's connection with Godwin is tangential, as far as we know. In 1791, well before Godwin's marriage to Mary Wollstonecraft in 1797, Blake designed and engraved illustrations for her *Elements of Morality* (1791; translation of a text by C. G. Salzmann) and *Original Stories from Real Life* (1791, 1796). Blake and Godwin dined in each other's company with the radical publisher, Joseph Johnson, at least once (4 April 1797), and shared acquaintances. Blake's early biographer, Alexander Gilchrist, writes that Blake "got on ill" with Godwin, however. Whatever the reason for this, if true, Blake's revolutionary stance differs markedly from Godwinian gradualism, and any deeper relationship between the two remains a matter of inference. More direct relationships can be charted for the other Romantics. Godwin's *Enquiry Concerning Political Justice* (1793, 1796, 1798), the first edition of which was read at least in part by Southey in November 1793, provides a model for Pantisocracy, the never-realized community of rational equality Southey and Coleridge plan for the banks of the Susquehanna. Godwin claims to have converted Wordsworth in 1795 from an ethics of self-love to an ethics of benevolence. Although their Godwinian period is brief, Godwin exerts continuing influence on Wordsworth and Coleridge, as an adversary. They both undertake formal disquisitions on ethics largely to refute him. Coleridge's *Lectures 1795: On Politics and Religion*, his periodical *The Watchman* (1796), and an unpublished sermon of 1799 (Literary Transcript 29, Victoria University Library) contain such refutations. A projected "Reply to Godwin" never appeared. Wordsworth's fragmentary "Essay on Morals" (1798) is directed against Godwinian rationalism. In *The Prelude*, X (1805) he tells of a bleak period, probably spring of 1796, when he "yielded up moral questions in despair." A period of adherence to Godwinism had probably preceded this dark moment. More positively, Godwin helped persuade Joseph Johnson to publish Hazlitt's first and in some ways single most important work, *Essay on the Principles of Human Action* (1805). De Quincey hates Godwin's novel, *Caleb Williams* (1794), disparages the second edition of *Political Justice* as a "travesty of the first" (the "Titan slinger" against government having become appalled by his own treatise), and says in 1837 that "Most people felt of Mr Godwin with the same alienation and horror as of a ghoul, or a bloodless vampire, or the monster created by Frankenstein." But Hazlitt, Shelley, Byron, and Keats all admire Godwin, for one reason or another, and are united in their admiration of his gothic novel, *St. Leon* (1799). Shelley's relationship with Godwin is legend, even if critics have gone too far in saying that *Prometheus Unbound* is Godwin's finest work. (For one thing, Godwin found it unreadable.) For a summary of the influence of *Political Justice* on the Romantics, see F. E. L. Priestley's Introduction to his edition of *Enquiry Concerning Political Justice*, 3 vols. (Toronto: University of Toronto Press, 1946), III, 100–14. This edition is cited below.

has such and such consequences. Godwin in fact shifts from a marked tendency to rule-utilitarianism in the first edition of *Political Justice*. In 1793 he argues on behalf of the rule that one should never tell a lie, but in 1796 he writes: "General principles of morality are so far valuable, as they truly delineate the means of utility, pleasure, or happiness. But every action of any human being, has its appropriate result; and, the more closely it is examined, the more truly will that result appear. General rules and theories are not infallible" (I 345). (Ironically, Hazlitt, who agrees with this estimate of general rules and theories, turns it against that young Godwinian, Shelley, whom he dubiously brands a fanatic of moral absolutes.) The end of moral action for Godwin is happiness: "Morality is nothing else but that system, which teaches us to contribute upon all occasions, to the extent of our power, to the well-being and happiness of every intellectual and sensitive existence" (I 159).

Unlike Bentham and most hedonistic utilitarians, Godwin adds our state of mind as agents to the moral calculus. Only if we act from feelings of disinterested benevolence can we be considered virtuous, even if we have increased the fund of happiness. "I would define virtue to be any action or actions of an intelligent being, proceeding from kind and benevolent intention, and having a tendency to contribute to general happiness" (I 149; cf. III 251). (Strictly speaking, this inclusion of the agent's intention makes him more an "act-deontologist" than a utilitarian.) Godwin devotes whole chapters and appendices to "sincerity," a value which becomes increasingly fashionable in the period and which "would necessarily bring every other virtue in its train" (I 331). Coleridge's complaint that the utilitarians consider only the outer act and its consequences cannot be directed against him.[88]

Godwin differs from Bentham also in proposing a qualitative, instead of merely quantitative, assessment of pleasure and happiness. In the second edition of *Political Justice* he gives a qualitative "scale of happiness" roughly correspondent to the four-fold scale in Coleridge, though only Godwin links the scale with social class. Laborers, debauchees, men of taste and leisure, and those so virtuous they rise above "the mechanical ideas of barter and exchange" feel different kinds of pleasure. He distinguishes among physical, intellectual, circumstantial, and moral pleasures, the last seen in the "man of benevolence," who "ascends to the highest of human pleasures, the

---

[88] Godwin's novel, *Caleb Williams*, concerns the problematics of moral judgment on this point. The protagonist, Falkland, is said to be possessed of benevolence but nonetheless commits murder. We must try to sort out a total moral judgment of him with regard to a gulf between character and deed.

pleasures of disinterestedness" (I 444–8). Perhaps such affinities permit Godwin and Coleridge to remain friends, with some bumpy intervals, over many years. In his way, Godwin resists the reduction of value the Romantics find so menacing in utilitarianism and other ethical schools.

Political Justice is nonetheless objectionable to Coleridge and his contemporaries on other grounds. One of the perverse pleasures of this text is found in the way Godwin soberly denounces marriage, parenting, domestic affections, and gratitude. Justice entails the promotion of happiness for all people equally. Domestic affections play favorites, however, and we are likely by their sway to favor the happiness of our own household over a more general happiness. We might even refuse to lend a stranger money that he needs more than we, thus violating the principle of justice. (Whenever Godwin finds himself impecunious, this principle comes in handy.) In a famous illustration that puts the domestic affections in their place, he says that, if one must choose, one should of course rescue Fénelon from a burning building instead of his chambermaid, even if she happens to be one's own wife or mother. Why? because Abbe Fénelon – Archbishop of Cambrai and author of the prose epic, *Télémaque* (1699), much read in Dissenting academies – would be more likely to increase the happiness of the human race than would one's wife or mother, especially were she "a fool or a prostitute, malicious, lying or dishonest" (I 126–8). Godwin is simply being true to his act-utilitarianism here, but Hazlitt, Coleridge, and hundreds of others are sickened. Their panegyrics on filial devotion rather miss the point and fail to refute the argument. Coleridge announces that the "intensity of private attachments encourages, not prevents, universal Benevolence."[89] Disappointingly, Godwin backs away from his outrageous depreciation of the affections in the later editions of *Political Justice*, and in his Preface to *St. Leon* announces that his novel is based on the principle that "domestic and private affections" are "inseparable from the nature of man, and from what may be styled the culture of the heart." They are "not incompatible with a profound and active sense of justice in the mind of him that cherishes them."

In addition to changing his mind about the domestic affections Godwin backs away from strict rationalism. After 1798 he no longer believes the perception of truth in itself provides a sufficient motivational spring for a just act. But in 1793 he argued that we desire what we judge to be desirable, and act accordingly. The very distinction

[89] *Lectures 1795: On Politics and Religion*, 164.

between desire and judgment is bogus. Sentimentalists like Hume exaggerate the power of passion over our actions. If in the midst of the "progressive voluptuousness" of love-making someone is told that his father is dead or that his horse is missing, his ardour will droop – thus illustrating, says Godwin, the power of belief over passion (I 73). He is not arguing an arid rationalism but is saying that our perception of the way things are determines what we desire and how we act. Since we are capable of perceiving truth if it is properly presented, and since justice is most desirable and productive of happiness, the human race will gradually approach perfection.[90] The core of his argument is that "Every truth that is capable of being communicated, is capable of being brought home to the conviction of the mind. Every principle which can be brought home to the conviction of the mind, will infallibly produce a correspondent effect upon the conduct" (I 93). By "perfectible" he insists he has meant only "the faculty of being continually made better and receiving perpetual improvement," not "the capacity of being brought to perfection," but there is an optimism that survives even so through the third edition of *Political Justice*.[91]

The teleological thrust of Godwin's writings – their socio-political optimism – is attractive and consoling to a generation of disappointed radical liberals, who have had to confront the significance of the Reign of Terror. His rationalism is based on Lockean empiricism: the fact that there are no innate ideas has the liberal corollary that human beings become what they are through education, environment, and experience. There *is* an innate capacity, reason, that impels human beings toward perfection; it works by means of experience toward greater and greater clarity. We have seen that the Romantics can conceive of the rehabilitation of reason where they do not, like Byron, honor it outright. Godwin's own brand of perfectionism is quite different from self-realizationism, but he answers for a brief time to the Romantics' need for a politics of change, despite the sober undercutting of early revolutionary hope.

---

[90] See Don Locke, *A Fantasy of Reason: The Life and Thought of William Godwin* (London: Routledge & Kegan Paul, 1980), 96–9.

[91] His optimism does not survive for long thereafter. In a memorandum of September 1798, and in his "Reply to Parr" of 1801, he blatantly retreats from the idea that reason supplies a sufficient motivational spring for just acts. Partly as a result of his short, tragic relationship with Mary Wollstonecraft and partly as a result of the historical thwarting of progressive hopes, he learns the instrumental force of feelings and passions, and now thinks, sadly, that the "voluntary actions of men are under the direction of their feelings." We could call this retreat the romanticizing of William Godwin. It is the rationalist Godwin, in any event, who most engages the Romantics.

Godwin is best known in the history of political science as the father of philosophical anarchism. Any institution that does not promote happiness and function on the basis of reason must be based on prejudice and false authority. With this criterion he pronounces most human institutions corrupt. It is one's duty to ward off the prejudicial notions these institutions enforce and to resist encroachments on personal freedom. In *Political Justice* he follows out the implications doggedly: many cooperative institutions restrict the freedom of individuals to follow the dictates of reason, such as marriage, family, church, city, law, nation, and – not least – orchestras! Perhaps surprisingly, Godwin dismisses Paine's talk of natural rights as redundant and dangerous: if an act is just, then we have the duty to perform it; and if it is unjust, then we should not be given the right to perform it. Natural rights are invoked by many as sanction for the selfish hindering of others. Godwin's politics are distinguished above all by his refusal to separate politics from ethics. The ethical determinants of the individual are projected onto the larger scene of political relationships, with few concessions to the conventions of prudential cooperation. His utilitarianism differs from Bentham's also in not condoning majority rule, a bullying encroachment on human freedom. The continuity of ethics and politics proves attractive to Shelley, just as it proves frightening to the older Coleridge. Godwin is, however, a gradualist: he writes chapters – "Of Resistance," "Of Revolutions," and "Of Tyrannicide" – that advise against violent overthrow, and he tells Shelley not to support political associations in Ireland, since they adopt too revolutionary a program.

It is precisely because institutions are based on "prejudice" that Edmund Burke finds them honorable and necessary. In moving from the Godwinian left to the Burkean right, Wordsworth, Coleridge, and Southey reveal an attachment to the tradition-bound feeling that informs the institutions Godwin attacks. (Godwin himself, in some respects, moves similarly, as if in acknowledgment of the hold that Burke had on him in the years preceding *Political Justice*.) But as I have said in discussing Hegel, an anarchistic tendency, based on the priority of ethics to politics, survives in Blake, Hazlitt, Shelley, and Keats, whether or not derived from Godwin. And even in admitted Tories this tendency exists in contravention of their professed politics. Coleridge and Wordsworth look back with nostalgia to their days in Racedown, Alfoxden, and Nether Stowey, when they could talk treason if they chose (oblivious of government spies), when the imagination could range anarchistically, when they first "Together wantoned in wild Poesy." The subversive power of imagination –

138

supplanting received structures with its own – is acknowledged in their very retreat from it in later years. The Ancient Mariner had been an anarchist of sorts, walking alone on the social periphery and interrupting public ceremonies.

Mention of Coleridge's greatest poem reminds us, however, of Godwin's limitations relative to the Romantics. These are, once again, grounded in Godwin's ultimately limited sense of value and human possibility. Coleridge, who spends much of his life pondering the nature of evil, can have little patience with someone who opines that this "is one of the plainest subjects upon which the human mind can be engaged" (I 439). Though many of them see the force of arguments for "necessity," they would have little patience with someone who says that "Man is in reality a passive, and not an active being" (I 389). Godwin's philosophical anarchism does not provide for a mutuality based on love, a human function higher than disinterested bene-volence and one that Shelley conceives as productive of cosmic harmony. Love's source is a human power Godwin equates with prejudice: the imagination. Though never announcing it, Shelley will break with his master, for reasons beyond Godwin's incessant dun-ning of him for more cash.

Modern terms and Romantic metaethics

Categorizing moral philosophers of the past with today's portentous vocabulary is frustrating business. Was Aristotle an act-utilitarian cognitivist non-definist, or something worse? It is not agreed that Kant was what we thought he was – a rule-deontologist of the formalist variety.[92] Even greater is the difficulty of so categorizing writers of literature, who by nature of their craft resist encapsulation in single ethical points of view, and who usually present moral belief in something other than direct propositional formats. The ancient quarrel between poets and philosophers is played out in the very enterprise of a philosophical reading of literary texts. Many of the Romantics them-selves adopt philosophical formats, however, and these constitute an aid to this kind of reading.

My purpose here is to see if modern ethical terms can be useful in sorting out the major dynamics of the ethics of Romanticism, thereby placing it more precisely in the development of modern thought. None

---

[92] John Rawls, for instance, says that *no* serious ethical theory, even Kant's, completely disregards consequences. See *A Theory of Justice* (Cambridge, Mass.: Harvard University Press, 1971), 30, 251–7. Our use of the word "formalist" would need to be qualified.

of these writers is wholly consistent with any ethical term, nor is any writer wholly consistent with any other writer, nor are these terms themselves rigid and above controversy. Still, I will show how the vocabulary and definitions of modern ethics are useful in distinguishing the ethical tendencies of this literary movement. The result will be a formal, not thematic, grounding for the discussion of individual authors that follows and is, in a strict sense, preliminary. Since literary figures are not often discussed in this way, my discussion is experimental. The terms are abstract, but I set them forth as conflictual, not as inertly taxonomic. They will acquire even a certain pathos when played out in the mental life of individual writers.

We have seen the affinity the Romantics have with teleological thought. Both influence and analogue can be discovered in British utilitarianism (Godwinian, not Benthamite) and post-Kantian idealism. To varying degrees, the Romantics impose on us their concern with futurity in a humanized eschatology. But strictly speaking none of them is a teleologist, who in ethics is often defined as someone who regards *only* consequences as determining the rightness or wrongness of acts. The moment one mixes in any other criteria – for example, the motivational disposition of the agent or the intrinsic rightness or wrongness of certain acts – one becomes by some accounts a deontologist, whatever one's resistance to this metamorphosis. I have mentioned that Godwin ceases to be a teleologist, and therefore a utilitarian, by this strict standard, and the same can be said of Shelley. From the beginning we confront a quandary as to the propriety of terms. Aspects of two major kinds of teleological theory – ethical egoism and utilitarianism – remain embedded in Romanticism and it is counter-intuitive to define them away.

Modern philosophers have begun to see the wisdom of merging teleological and deontological positions. Robert Nozick, for example, comments:

Writers tend to plunk for one of these forms, deontological or teleological, and quickly "refute" the other, perhaps with the aid of a few artfully chosen examples. However, this procedure ignores the powerful and deep intuitive force of the rejected alternative, a force which is not merely to be explained away as the result of a simple mistake or illusion. Can deontology and teleology somehow be harmonized in an ethical view that preserves the insights of each?[93]

In making claims for both camps, the Romantics are registering the intuitive force of each.

[93] *Philosophical Explanations* (Cambridge, Mass.: Harvard University Press, 1981), 494.

Perfectionism, a broader term for self-realizationist theories, is itself one of the more interesting forms of ethical egoism – the view that one has the right (or even the duty) to act in one's own interest. We have already seen practical and theoretical problems in perfectionism and have said that its very ambiguities make it a powerful structuring concept in literature, especially in Romantic narrative, where the hero may long for a finer version of himself, often with disastrous personal results.

Turning first to the matter of teleological ethics, I propose a continuity between the Romantic version of perfectionism and one form of utilitarianism – "ideal utilitarianism." We have seen Romantic hostility to hedonistic utilitarianism, with its monistic concept of good as pleasure or happiness. But there is another form of utilitarianism, expounded in this century principally by Hastings Rashdall and G. E. Moore. An ideal utilitarian is defined as someone who has a teleological view of ethics but who thinks a plurality of values – and not pleasure or happiness alone – should be the object of moral striving.[94]

Since teleologists argue backwards from concepts of good to concepts of right (the rightness of an act is decided by a prior determination of what results are good), we should explore the Romantics' concept of good. Coleridge is emphatic about the need to challenge the reduction of good to pleasure alone:

The sum total of Moral philosphy is found in this one question—Is "good" a superfluous word?—or lazy synonime for the pleasurable, and its causes? at least, a mere modification to express degree & comparative duration of pleasure?—/—Therefore we may more unanswerably state the question—Is "good" superfluous as a word exponent of a *kind*?—If it be, then moral philosophy is but a subdivision of physics? If not, then the writings of Paley & all his Predecessors & Disciples are false & *most* pernicious.   (N III 3938)

There is no more pointed evidence, within their formal ethical discourse, for the Romantic will to value than Coleridge's reflections on the use and meaning of "good" in relation to "pleasure." In the previous section we saw his objections to substituting "pleasure" for "good," which is proved untenable by common language use. Focusing on the use and meaning of "good" in itself, he tells us that, unlike pleasure, "good" denotes the *"genus generalissimum* of whatever is desirable for our nature" (*PL* 152). The hedonist, in reducing the

[94] *The Theory of Good and Evil*, I, 184–221; *Principia Ethica*, 183–225.

meaning of "good" to "pleasure," uses pleasure as "a mere lazy synonym, whereas it is the business of the philosopher to desynonymize words originally equivalent." But our common use of the word "good" demonstrates that it is a more inclusive term than "pleasure": "This medicine is exceedingly unpleasant, but it is very good for me." If asked what "this good is which determines what is desirable, instead of deriving its meaning from it," Coleridge relies on the argument from intuition: "*I know—intuitively know*," and admits that the precise nature of "good" "passeth all *understanding*." As Moore will argue a century later, "good" resists strict definition. One may describe, if not define, "good" as the most general term for what, as Coleridge says, is desirable for and even constitutive of human nature (*PL* 152–3). Monistic reductions of value, seen in hedonism and hedonistic utilitarianism – as well as in other competing ethical schools – must be rejected in favor of what is called in ethics "value pluralism."

Filling out the prescription for "good" is the task of the individual writers under consideration here, and will be a primary concern in subsequent chapters. Although there will be no uniformity principle, certain patterns will emerge as the Romantics ponder the "*genus generalissimum* of whatever is desirable for our nature."

In focusing on the question of value, we approach a deep truth about Romanticism relative to other major cultural movements: it consciously attempts to revalue a world where value has seemed to be displaced. Keats's Odes, rhetorically structured as acts of veneration, are paradigmatic of the larger movement. What can be found that is desirable for our nature? In the career of Shelley, we see a gradual rejection of hedonistic utilitarianism for value-rich perspectives. Hazlitt's attack on hedonistic utilitarianism is likewise on its absurdly limited conception of "good." Other major schools – psychological egoism, rationalism, sentimentalism, hedonistic utilitarianism, Kantian formalism – seem more symptomatic of the reduction of value than remedies for it. This intuition has governed the Romantics' larger response to European moral schools.

In their visions of what is good, the Romantics challenge the distinction between moral and non-moral value, which has plagued ethicists, who do not agree on the criteria for either. William Frankena believes moral values pertain to "persons, groups of persons, traits of character, dispositions, emotions, motives, and intentions – in short, persons, groups of persons, and elements of personality. All sorts of things, on the one hand, may be non-morally good or bad, for example: physical objects like cars and paintings; experiences like pleasure, pain, knowledge, and freedom; and forms of government like democracy."[95] But other philosophers would call these experiences and forms of government moral values. They might also argue that in judgments of decisions and acts the distinction is of little or no use.

With respect to the Romantics, the breaking down of the distinction is symptomatic of their intense moralization of things in general. The most emphatically non-moral of values is the physical world – nature and natural or human-made objects. But a moment's reflection on Wordsworth – for whom landscape, with a quasi-consciousness of its own, takes on properties of a moral agent, and for whom the experience of nature leads to moral development – suggests his appropriation of non-moral by moral value. We have seen the Romantics' tacit repudiation of the Kantian distinction between the aesthetic and the ethical. For Hazlitt a painting, with its "character of power" that "obtrudes" on the eye, has moral value; it too shows what he calls "the moral uses of the imagination." For Coleridge *all* knowledge "that enlightens and liberalizes, is a form and a means of Self-knowle[d]ge, whether it be grammar, or geometry, logical or classical" (*CL* VI 630); non-moral knowledge is a contradiction in terms.

The Romantics' conceptions of what is good and what constitutes the good life vary with each author. They formally share an embattled will to value against the perceived backdrop of an attenuation of value. The precise content of their various value structures will become more vivid in their differences one from another. A few generalizations can be made, however. (1) As I have said, moral values tend to subsume non-moral values, in keeping with their radical humanizing of things in general. For Blake, all deities reside within the human breast. A corollary is their fierce opposition to the utilitarian and bourgeois commodification of value, which converts moral to non-moral quantification, and conflates the value of persons with the value of things. (2) It is a familiar tenet of intellectual history – true but in need of many refinements – that the Romantics value certain human attributes, particularly imagination, feeling, and the body, and devalue others, particularly discursive reason with its spawn of dispassionate virtues such as prudence, common sense, and restriction of the emotions. (3) Hedonic values of pleasure and happiness are positive "contributory" values – the rewards of virtue that enhance the good life – but are not to be pursued for their own sake. They are scaled qualitatively. (4) Social values of love, friendship, and justice are often portrayed as contraries

[95] *Ethics* (Englewood Cliffs, N. J.: Prentice-Hall, 1963), 47–8. In his introductory but influential discussion, Frankena goes on to make distinctions among types of non-moral value.

of individual values of self-love, self-government, and personal freedom – but in reconciliation there is ideally a mutual intensification of each set. The Romantics are enthusiasts for both self-love and benevolence. (5) Prescriptions for the good life vary greatly, but the Romantics share certain emphases that distinguish their set of values from a predictable, non-heroic affirmation of friendship, love, justice, happiness, etc.

On this last point, I would single out self-empowerment and meaning. The former, seen pervasively in the lives and the work, is underwritten by the Romantic myth of the Fall as fragmentation and devitalization, and redemption as a matter of renewed unity and intensity. Self-empowerment as value is seen in the need for Blake's Albion to awaken from the Rock of Ages; for Coleridge to break the force of accursed habit by exertion of the self's "radical," identified with will; for Shelley to burn with the intensity of visionary commitment to "reforming the world"; for Wordsworth to write the poem that Milton has not already written; for Hazlitt to make his way into an art gallery after hours ("where there's a will, there's a way"); for Keats's Porphyro to shape events so as to obtain Madeline in a triumph of desire; for Byron to seek freedom in exile and to write *Don Juan* as he damn well pleases. The Romantics are not blind worshippers of will – and Wordsworth and De Quincey see larger forces controlling it – but self-empowerment is for them a primary value both intrinsic, as displaying the excellence of the self, and extrinsic, as the means by which will translates into gesture, act, and sympathetic engagement with the world. In this value as in most others, the Romantics are guided by a standard of intensification, not moderation. "More! More! is the cry of a mistaken soul, less than All cannot satisfy Man," writes Blake.

"Meaning" is a value for the Romantic conception of the good life because of their heavily self-imposed hermeneutics. Meaning becomes a constituent of the good life, not simply a consequence of it or a redundancy. Lives attain to meaning in symbolic and mythic enhancements of the literal and ordinary. A life not enhanced by the symbolic is impoverished. In Blake's apocalyptic narration, minute particulars and pulses of the artery contain eternity, and petty professional dealings with an art patron are transposed into a mythic narrative featuring Satan. We can see meaning as value also in Wordsworth's romance of the everyday, in Keats's reading of his own life in terms of purposeful professional activity leading to a goal conceived of in absolutist terms (whether the ascent up Parnassus or the sacrificial suffering of the poet as humanist-physician), in De Quincey's Dark Interpreter, which enhances meaning through the hermeneutics of the sublime. Enhanced meaning of whatever tenor – even the horrific experience of the Mariner – is a positive value relative to the reduction of value seen in literalists, the unimaginative whom Shelley calls the "morally dead" and whom Arnold will call "Philistines." Carlyle complains that his age can no longer believe even in the Devil. With a more self-consciously constructed hermeneutics Carlyle continues the will to value of his Romantic predecessors. The good life is one that generates as it goes a continuously enhanced significance. Even sufferers like the Ancient Mariner, Childe Harold, Cain, and the Poet of *Alastor* see the symbolic significance of their life narratives – a necessary if obviously insufficient condition of the good life. The loss of a sense of radiating significance – painfully seen in Keats on his deathbed but not, in my reading of it, fully confronted in Romantic literature itself – is the descent beneath the literal to the nihilistic. But even the inhabitants of Blake's Ulro – the mental realm of value negation – can read their way out of it.

The value pluralism of ideal utilitarianism is descriptive of the Romantics. Rashdall notes that ideal utilitarianism has been sub-scribed to throughout the history of philosophy, from Plato and Aristotle to the Cambridge Platonists to Hegel; it is the implicit ethics also of late nineteenth- and early twentieth-century thinkers such as Rudolf Lotze, Eduard von Hartmann, Friedrich Paulsen, and John McTaggart.[96] As a perennial philosophy, the ideal utilitarianism of the Romantics is differentiated from other episodes by the contexts that call it forth at its historical moment and by its embodiment in a radiant imaginative literature. It is for them a crisis ethics brought about by the impoverishment and imminent collapse of collective value structures: the French Revolution with its vast international scenario of upheaval, promise, and betrayal; the acceleration of the Industrial Revolution with its commodification of value; the Enlightenment revaluation of Christianity, seen now as a somewhat shopworn myth among other myths; the seemingly reductive character of competing secular systems of value enunciated in the various moral philosophies of the day – late Enlightenment rationalism and Kantian formalism, British utilitarianism, scientism, common sense philosophy, moral sense and sensibility. The Romantics attempt to replenish values in fierce reac-tion against this consolidation of error. *The Prelude* is, as Carl Woodring says, written in response to Coleridge's encouraging Wordsworth to write "the great philosophical poem, doctrinal to a nation, that Words-

---

[96] *The Theory of Good and Evil*, II, 216–18.

worth alone could write, in order to eradicate the general disillusionment that had followed the French Revolution."[97] We will multiply
instances where a plurality of values is perceived against a backdrop of
negation.

I am not arguing that the Romantics ought to be termed "ideal
utilitarians," which would suggest an unwarranted formulaic consistency and an identification of the whole with one of its parts. Rather,
ideal utilitarianism comes closest, among the perennial ethical views,
to describing the dominant tendency of their writings. It is an aid to
situating them within what is otherwise an undifferentiated mass of
ethical possibilities. The designation becomes the more vivid to the
extent we have grasped the ethical views from which it is differentiated. But vividness will be achieved only in degrees. The lack of
tidiness, inherent in the concept, as to precisely what values are to be
pursued guarantees that the Romantics have not been pinned to the
wall with a formulated phrase.

One basic difference between ideal utilitarianism and perfectionism
is that the former conceives of a plurality of values with reference to a
collective of persons, and "right" is determined by what acts produce
the greatest possible amount of good on the whole; whereas perfectionism or self-realizationism, with its proximity to ethical egoism,
asks this question with reference primarily to individuals. Could the
Romantics, those students of self-consciousness, be said to subscribe
to both? The answer is yes, if we understand their own dissatisfaction
with perfectionism as egoism and their attempt to compound it with
social sympathy. The perfection of character implies acting well in the
world; it is not a self-enclosed reservoir filled with quiescent moral
virtue.

I propose, therefore, that ideal utilitarianism is the larger perspective
that encompasses Romantic perfectionism, correcting egoism yet
accepting as one portion of its own plurality of values a concern with
self, motive, consciousness, and inwardness. The values associated
with perfectionism or self-realizationism are themselves plural, as we
have seen, even to the point of indeterminacy. How are we to know
what it is we should become? Coleridge's circle of self and description
of man as ideally a "finient being," not an amorphous "infinite" one,
are his acknowledgment of the need for determinacy. The more
socially oriented imperatives of ideal utilitarianism correct in theory
the deficiency of perfectionism on this point. As Coleridge has said, it

[97] "Shaping Life in *The Prelude*," in *Nineteenth-Century Lives*, ed. Laurence S. Lockridge,
John Maynard, and Donald Stone (Cambridge: Cambridge University Press, 1989),
12.

is through neighborhood and awareness of others that the self is "educed" and achieves self-definition. Shelley is even more resolute about directing the energies of the self to social and political reform. In moving from hedonistic to ideal utilitarianism, he expands beyond both pleasure and self-realization the ends of the will to value.

A plurality of values makes it more difficult to set up a single standard for right acts that might bring about all this good. As John Rawls says, "In a teleological theory any vagueness or ambiguity in the conception of the good is transferred to that of the right. Hence if the good of individuals is something that, so to speak, is just up to them to decide as individuals, so likewise within certain limits is that which is right."[98] With the Romantics it is not so much vagueness or ambiguity as richness in their sense of the good that problematizes action. Sensing a plurality of values that ought to be realized, both in the self and in the world, they are all the more anxious about what is to be done. The will to value ironically makes more problematic a philosophy of right.

We will see anxieties and contradictions enough in literary representation of action and in Romantic autobiography. Contradictions on the level of theory, however, are illustrative not so much of the Romantics' moral confusion as of the inadequacies of rigidly exclusivist theories to contain complex ethical vision. If, for example, the purported teleologist admits any criteria other than consequences in deciding right and wrong, he or she becomes, by some accounts, a deontologist of non-formalist persuasion: "the rightness (wrongness, obligatoriness, and so on) of an action or the correctness of a rule is a function of many factors, some of which are or may be the consequences of that action or rule."[99] The act-deontologist believes that each act must be judged according to its particular circumstances; general rules can but need not be invoked. Such a judgment, often derived intuitively, is independent of whether an act promotes the general good.

Coleridge states the clearest case for an act-deontologist position so understood. We have seen him argue against Paley's rule-utilitarianism, which is based solely on evaluation of consequences in light of general rules. But Coleridge does not therefore banish consequences from his moral calculus. This is a person who claims to have fallen into the deepest immorality – opium addiction – because of a lack of prudence. Prudential calculation of consequences surely has some place in the moral life: "For if the Law be barren of all consequences, what is it but words? To obey the Law for its own sake is really a mere

[98] *A Theory of Justice*, 559.

[99] Richard T. Garner and Bernard Rosen, *Moral Philosophy*, 83–4.

sophism in any other sense: you might as well put abracadabra in its place" (*IS* 142). He thus dispatches strict formalism.

Coleridge proposes instead a mixture of criteria – the intrinsic character of a particular act, the worthiness of the agent, the general rule, the circumstances, the consequences – as all having bearing on the judgment of right. Neither the general rule nor the consequences alone suffice. Even assassination might in some cases be right: such an exception to a general rule prohibiting murder "supposes and implies a complexity and concurrence of peculiar circumstances, each single instance being itself a species, to be tried on its own grounds, and resting its whole pretences for acquittal or mitigation of censure on its *peculiarity*." We must make a total judgment of the agent before we summarily judge the act. With a worthy assassin like Brutus we judge according to "the *man*, the sum-total of his known moral being, collated with the customs and creeds of his age and country" (*EOT* II 209–10). (He subscribes here to the historicizing of moral judgment.) We make such determinations not by mechanical deductions from universal principles but "by the effect produced on our *feelings* by the sum total of all the data and circumstances of the particular case." These feelings are prompted "by *realities* only, by the contemplation of actual individual cases with all the many and nice circumstances that individualized them, and not by those meagre and shadowy generalities which may serve to elucidate a general law" (*EOT* II 212). A late letter sums it up: "A morality of consequences I, you well know, reprobate – but to exclude the necessary *effect* of an action is to take away all meaning from the word, action – to strike Duty with Blindness." A case must be decided in its "*particulars*, personal and circumstantial, with it's Antecedents and *involved* (N.b. not it's contingent or apprehended) Consequents" (*CL* V 177–8, 182). It is a pity that the Ancient Mariner could not have arranged for such counsel on the high seas.

Coleridge's point about the "*particulars*, personal and circumstantial," upon which moral judgments must be decided is characteristic of the Romantics. An eye to moral particularity is a first criterion for Blake, whose poems of outrage reflect precise witnessing of "minute particulars"; for Wordsworth, who is converted to the revolutionary cause in France by direct confrontation with poverty; for Hazlitt, who says the common failing of reformers is that they substitute theory for fact; and for Shelley, who speculates, in an extreme instance, that "no one action has, when considered in its whole extent, an essential resemblance with any other" (*SPR* 192).

Like act-deontologists, the Romantics admit the importance of consequences but deny them absolute force. Arguing against the tyrannical implications of a utilitarian commitment to "good on the whole" – it can justify the slave trade by reminding us of the benefits to the white majority – Hazlitt says the slave trade offends our sense of justice and the slave traders themselves are brutalized. "In a word, the sympathy of the individual with the consequences of his own act is to be attended to (no less than the consequences themselves) in every sound system of morality; and this must be determined by certain natural laws of the human mind, and not by rules of logic or arithmetic" (XII 50). Shelley, a professed utilitarian, is often offended by moral judgment in terms of consequences alone. Paley's inducement to virtue – the prospect of a heavenly reward – makes him livid, and he goes so far as to agree with Jesus "that virtue is its own reward." Perhaps most winning in his treatment of act and consequences is De Quincey, who says that, confronted as we are by a vast Hercynian forest of possible consequences that extend we know not where, we might understandably hesitate to act at all. The Romantics take a broad view of what ultimately enters into moral judgment and action, and step from ideal utilitarian to act-deontological positions and back again, without letting on to any embarrassment.

The principal tendency of Romantic ethics remains, I think, teleological. These authors hope to re-value a world whose older value systems have become vitiated and whose new ones are either illiberal or banal. To this end they envisage as intrinsic values a more replete personality (Blake and Coleridge) and a society based on a more irradiating and encompassing sympathy (Shelley). Within these larger goals, their moral inquiry often broaches deontological questions – the intrinsic rightness or wrongness of acts and the mental state of the agent. One possible way (among others) of reconciling the two orientations is stated by Nozick: it

would be to try to transcend the distinction between teleological and deontological, to see each alternative as saying something correct about the ethics of a partially developed person, whereas a fully developed person would face no conflict between these modes, perhaps because a truly good teleological aim (of the sort he would have) simply could not be achieved by any deontologically impermissible means.[100]

Without saying why, Nozick thinks this solution is false, but true or false it suggestively glosses Romantic practice. I will be arguing that in Blake the partially developed but dialectical personality is

[100] *Philosophical Explanations*, 496.

characterized by a cleavage of the deontological and the teleological, which translates in this case into a temporarily needful conflict between the right and the good; and that in Shelley this conflict can and should be overcome even at early stages on the road to redemption.

Turning from normative to metaethical considerations– the nature, meaning, and justification of moral statements – we can once again place the visionary company on a theoretical grid, with some help, as usual, from Coleridge. He views ethics as a unique cognitive category and says that "the usage of all languages" confirms that "ought" is categorically distinct from "is." In the Opus Maximum he argues this closely (OM B₂ ff. 1–14), and attempts to define the nature and status of moral judgments. Rationalists like Clarke, Cumberland, and Wollaston err in likening these to mathematical or geometrical proofs, which we cannot contest without proving ourselves absurd. But Coleridge says that in refusing assent to a moral judgment – e.g. that we should give aid to an ailing parent – we are not acting absurdly. Rather, we are simply acting against what he calls a "postulate of humanity," which is an intuited assumption of what it means to be human, and which requires, on our part, an act of assent. An act of assent is not required to see truth in the proposition that a straight line is the shortest distance between two points. Shelley agrees with Coleridge, arguing that we cannot demand "a mathematical or metaphysical reason for a moral action" any more than we can demand "a moral reason for a mathematical or metaphysical fact" (SPR 173).

On the other hand, moralists who describe moral judgments in terms of empirical or psychological evidence – "naturalists" such as Bentham and Paley, who describe "good" as the psychological experience of pleasure or happiness – err in giving too much weight and dignity to hypothetical assertion. All empirical evidence, including our experience of pleasure and happiness, is based on "fact," and fact is by nature hypothetical, or "nothing more than an assertion respecting particulars or individuals." Although the factual basis of empiricism and psychology is hardly dismissed by Coleridge, empirical propositions are different in kind from moral ones in that they can always be contradicted or revised by other assessments of the evidence. But moral judgments, assuming they have the intuitional force of "postulates of humanity," can be denied only by an "act of mind" that separates us from the entire grammar of morality. Coleridge admits to the circular nature of his argument: it is a primary intuition that "I *ought* because I ought i.e. because I see the act in question, inclusively in that law of conscience, by which this *ought* is the contradistinguishing

150

ground & predicate of my humanity—" (OM B$_2$ ff. 131, 133).[101]

These arguments place Coleridge squarely in the metaethical school of cognitivist non-definism, and since he urges more logomachy, not less, he can hardly protest.[102] Some later philosophers of this school include W. D. Ross, G. E. Moore, Henry Sidgwick, H. A. Prichard; but Aristotle is sometimes claimed for it. Someone of this school, often called intuitionism, believes we have moral knowledge, usually direct intuitional knowledge, and that – contrary to the naturalists' theories – moral judgments cannot be translated into expressions having the same meaning yet containing no moral terms. Statements of what morally "ought" to be cannot be translated into "is" statements derived from nature, science, social science, or psychology. As Coleridge says, you ought because you ought. Cognitivist non-definists are apt to speak of special moral faculties of knowing, such as "moral sense" or "conscience," or "imagination."

Other Romantic authors agree with Coleridge as to the intuitional character of moral judgments, a fact that should qualify the current passion to find a skeptic in every Romantic bush. Keats is the only one who speaks of moral truths as undecidable, and only Wordsworth is emphatically a "naturalist," translating moral judgments into the non-moral language of psychology and natural observation. Otherwise,

---

[101] Some people are indeed separated from the grammar of morality. During an unhappy period late in 1806, when in love with Sara Hutchinson and confirmed in opium addiction, he laments: "I have been more and more convinced, tho' I pretend not to *understand* much less *explain* the fact, that our *moral nature* is a power of itself; and not a mere modification of our common Intellect / so that a man may have wit, prudence, sense, &c &c & yet be utterly destitute of a true *moral* sense. And when I observe the impotence of this moral sense, however highly possessed, unassisted by something still higher, &, if I may so express myself, still more extra-natural, I own, it seems to me, as if the goodness of God had occasionally *added* it to our nature, as an intermediate or connecting Link between that nature and a state of Grace" (*CL* II 1203).

[102] Other metaethical candidates are no more appetizing on first glance. Cognitivist definism or "naturalism" claims that moral judgments can be objectively true and, as we have seen, that they can be translated into other expressions having the same meaning but containing no moral terms. The fact/value dichotomy is disallowed, because values are implicit statements of fact. The moral judgment "Thulloh is a good man" might mean "Thulloh has traits that are in fact desired by many people," or "Thulloh gives pleasure to people in his dealings with them, owing to his winning ways." Non-cognitivist theories deny that moral judgments are capable of being objectively true but agree that moral terms can be translated into non-moral ones. Thus, "Thulloh is a good Man" might mean "I like Thulloh." Moral judgments are expressions of approval or disapproval with no cognitive content. See Garner and Rosen, *Moral Philosophy*, chs. 10, 11, and 12, for lucid exposition of the metaethical options.

ethical judgment is one area where some certainty can be found, even if its incorporation into life and poetry is neither simple nor direct. "Video meliora proboque, / Deteriora sequor – was the motto of my Life," says Coleridge, quoting Ovid (*CL* IV 626; "I see and approve of the better, but I follow the worse"). Blake growls that the "Man who pretends to be a modest enquirer into the truth of a self evident thing is a Knave The truth & certainty of Virtue & Honesty i.e. Inspiration needs no one to prove it it is Evident as the Sun & Moon" (*PWB* 613). The young Shelley announces that "Virtue is self evident" (*LPS* I 109). Hazlitt speaks of values as existing independently of mind; objects "affect our minds in a certain manner because they are essentially good or evil" (*Essay* 52). For Hazlitt, whatever else he may complain of, there is both moral reality and moral knowledge. Even Byron's Lucifer in the drama *Cain* believes in intrinsic value: "Evil and Good are things in their own essence, / And not made good or evil by the Giver" (II ii 452–3). In his letter on "Ethical Poetry," Byron equates ethics with reality and truth. Any truth worth knowing is available to unmetaphysical intellect or common sense. Wordsworth attacks rationalist moral philosophy as "powerless in regulating our judgments concerning the value of men & things," and proposes instead that we become aware of moral truth through images or pictures of human life impressed upon us through habitual associations and registered in our feelings. But this too constitutes moral knowledge. De Quincey thinks all the essential moral truths are directly known by feeling, not reasoning, and that they can be found in Christianity. The problem is one of application – either of applying them to one's own predicament (where all may be obscure) or of using casuistical reasoning to see how the general truth may fit the particular case. Only Keats goes so far as an out-and-out moral skepticism, complaining that the "lore of good and ill" can never be his. "Things cannot to the will / Be settled, but they tease us out of thought," he writes in a verse epistle. And yet his Urn will speak of "truth."

We have seen that the Romantics tend to conceive of imagination as a moral power that takes over functions ordinarily ascribed to conscience or moral sense, and that – far from a beauty-making power alone – imagination is an intuitional power that puts us in touch with truth and goodness. An important consequence is that the Romantics finesse any contradiction between value as created or projected and value as discovered. This becomes a false opposition insofar as the imagination is both the "perception" of value, as Shelley says, and the productive agency of value. In an imaginative universe the productive and perceptual functions of imagination would be identical. This is not to argue, by means of a few quotes, some drabber than others, that the vast struggles and moral confusions of Romantic literature are not there, or are simply finessed by the ontology of the imagination. It is a fallen, not an imaginative, universe these poets confront. They are in constant doubt as to whether they personally possess an imagination strong enough to ward off illusion and self-deception. It is to say, rather, that for all their dark sublimity and moral paralysis, they entertain the hope of an emergence into clarity, the mind freed of prejudice, fear, envy, political and ecclesiastical power, and all other negations of the values they strenuously and anxiously imagine as the deepest truth of things. Keats is not alone in knowing that the dreamer may awaken to a cold hill side.

To have situated the Romantics on what we have seen in this section is a rather fluid grid of formal classification – with boundaries hardly settled by professional ethicists – is a preliminary to a fuller description of their moral commitments and sensibilities. Coleridge has been the leading voice here, but we will see that he has not spoken in isolation from the others. The terms of modern ethics – strikingly anticipated in the overt formulations of Romantic writers – help articulate the formal more than thematic grounds of their major ethical tendencies and of their relatedness one to another. These terms, rooted in centuries of ethical debate, also help us see how competing moral schools leading up to and contemporaneous with the Romantics have erred or proved insufficient.

The heuristic for the chapters that follow is that the Romantics represent an ethical tendency characterized by value pluralism within an ethical framework that most resembles ideal (not hedonistic) utilitarianism. Although they help develop an ethics centered on the self (self-realizationism or perfectionism), they are extremists with respect to the polarity of self and other; individual consciousness is self-defining only in its capacity to intuit the reality and worth of the other. Hence self-realizationism is jeopardized as a discrete ethical position; in the dynamics of literary texts it must yield to a more comprehensive ethical modality. Within the context of late European intellectual history, this Romantic will to value is predicated on crisis, since these writers confront what they perceive to be an unprecedented reduction of value, evident in rival ethical points of view, in cynical social and economic philosophies, and in the general sense of value deflation following the early optimism – indeed the ethico-political millennialism – of the French Revolution. As ethical intuitionists, they feel sufficiently possessed of moral knowledge to speak strongly on what the good is, on what constitutes human possibility in the highest sense. But we will see time and again that their concepts of value coordinate awkwardly with concepts of action and obligation, and that, writing well before Marx and Shaw, they often lack a firm sense of praxis. Shelley comes closest to providing it, but even he disrupts conventional expectations in the representation of action. Within the contexts of literary art, this problematic becomes a compositional and structural dynamic. To say – and it is often said – that the Romantics fail to represent action is not in itself to have rendered a literary value judgment.

Turning now to individual authors beyond Coleridge, we will watch them explore how, given so large a range of values, the moral agent may begin to answer what it is that one ought to do, and what become. Not ideally an isolated creature with a superfluity of useless consciousness, the self pursues its vocation in the world, its plan of life, with a passion for values personal and social. But how does indeterminate ethical desire become determinate? Like Coleridge with his circle of self, none of these authors gives a final resolute answer to this imponderable, but in engaging it they agree that we must transcend the prison of private consciousness, which may be the source of all valuing acts but which also cooperates, as Coleridge would say, in depraving us.

These and other questions are taken up by the Romantics in one of the most vigorous collective engagements with moral issues of modern times.

PART TWO

Agent, Power, Scene

3

Blake: the poetry of violence

Despite Blake's paradigmatic status, he is not a Platonic primary to whom all other Romantics are only footnotes. Shelley, for one, implicitly redresses a contradiction in Blake's poetry between the "right" and the "good," and Coleridge, Hazlitt, and others revise and supplement him in basic ways. In constructing Blake's ethics, I will place him relative to other moral possibilities, and will suggest limits in his thought which must be seen, in keeping with his own attitude toward delineative outline, as both restricting and enabling. My aim is not to diminish a large and strange vision but to pursue the implications of his own moral dialectic to conclusions unsettling beyond the offense one hopes he still gives to the moral proprieties.[1]

I accept the view that Blake is in a strict sense the leading Romantic "optimist." For him, evil is accidental, not essential; imagination can

---

[1] The following studies have most influenced my thinking: John Beer, *Blake's Humanism* (Manchester: Manchester University Press, 1968) and *Blake's Visionary Universe* (Manchester: Manchester University Press, 1969); Harold Bloom, *Blake's Apocalypse: A Study in Poetic Argument* (Garden City: Doubleday, 1963); Stuart Curran and Joseph Anthony Wittreich, Jnr., eds., *Blake's Sublime Allegory: Essays on The Four Zoas, Milton, Jerusalem* (Madison: University of Wisconsin Press, 1973); S. Foster Damon, *A Blake Dictionary*; Leopold Damrosch, Jnr., *Symbol and Truth in Blake's Myth*; David Erdman, *Blake: Prophet Against Empire*, 2nd rev. edn. (Princeton: Princeton University Press, 1969); Susan Fox, *Poetic Form in Blake's Milton* (Princeton: Princeton University Press, 1976); Thomas R. Frosch, *The Awakening of Albion: The Renovation of the Body in the Poetry of William Blake* (Ithaca, N. Y.: Cornell University Press, 1974); Northrop Frye, *Fearful Symmetry: A Study of William Blake* (Princeton: Princeton University Press, 1947): Jean Hagstrum, *William Blake, Poet and Painter: An Introduction to the Illuminated Verse* (Chicago: University of Chicago Press, 1964, 1978); Eric Donald Hirsch, *Innocence and Experience: An Introduction to Blake*, 2nd edn. (Chicago: University of Chicago Press, 1975); W. J. T. Mitchell, *Blake's Composite Art: A Study of the Illuminated Poetry* (Princeton: Princeton University Press, 1978); Morton Paley, *Energy and Imagination: A Study of the Development of Blake's Thought* (Oxford: Clarendon Press, 1970); Mark Schorer, *William Blake: The Politics of Vision* (New York: Henry Holt, 1946).

ultimately triumph over negation and human freedom over constraint; history can be redeemed through apocalyptic release from cycles of repression and revolt. Blake's is the highest estimate of human power to be found in the period. But he images the quest for Edenic vision as so arduous, the end so frustratingly deferred, that in a deeply practical sense he does not distance himself so far from an ethics of radical fault after all. Although he calls good all human acts springing from virtuous energy of the self, he so rarely portrays a complete act – and when he does, it is of such complexity – that he ironically underscores the great obstacles to acting unhindered, whether the hindering comes from within or without. His rigorous ethical voluntarism is in its way as forbidding as Fichte's, as I have suggested in Chapter 2. Imperfection extends into the Edenic condition itself.

I believe there is a ruthlessness in his moral view, manifested in the fact that "right" – as acts that should be done – and "good" – as qualities that should be valued – function in marked asymmetry. Throughout the corpus, acts leading to higher and more virtuous states of being are violent and qualitatively out of keeping with the end proposed. Blake declaims against "Corporeal War" and in favor of "Mental Fight" (M 1, 31: 23–5), but this is hardly to temper the violent action and imagery of the bulk of his prophetic verse. Mental fight proves to be every bit as violent as physical, if not even more so. And in any event there is no naive division between the mental and the physical in Blake. Violent dialectic is the mechanism of historical change – of class conflict and exported revolution – and also of personal life, from sexuality to friendship to vocation and art.

There is ruthlessness also in the imperialism of imagination, a common Romantic imbalance but most advanced in Blake. The organic, egalitarian balance of human powers (reason, feeling, sense, imagination), often assumed to be the Blakean norm, conflicts with new hierarchical orderings. In The Four Zoas an alliance of imagination and sense (bodily instinct) prevails over the dialectical struggle of reason and feeling. The warfare among these four basic powers makes this work, in its narrative and imagistic unfolding, the most violent poem in the English language. The subordination of reason to imagination and the senses entails a hostility to nature and the natural sciences except as they are "redeemed" by imagination; it entails also a hostility to wise or prudential calculation in human affairs. The subordination of feeling in turn denies love any claims to moral sufficiency; pity or sympathy becomes for Blake a potentially dangerous acquiescence. He projects the poet's situation to cosmic proportions, Los calling "his sons to the strife of blood" in unceasing mental fight. Imagination does not so much oppose morality as subsume it: the artist delineates the human form and tinctures it with "blushing love."

Blake propounds an ego-emanation structure of the psyche that, by weight of its own metaphor, does not grant full reality to others. The emanation, said to be the agency of social awareness, is reclaimed by the ego when ego is fully realized. The reality of the external world and of other selves is questioned in a drift toward a mentalism that, in works following *The Four Zoas*, may eclipse the generative body as well. The individualism of the "Annotations to Lavater" implies an anarchistic politics, but Blake never fleshes out socio-political structures on the other side of successful insurrection. His myth is not hospitable to structures made up of a plurality of persons.

Finally, there is ruthlessness in Blake's valuing clarity and intuition and declaiming against doubt. His hostility to skepticism is illiberal in its treatment of honest hesitancy in human affairs and intellectual commitments. He differs here from all the major Romantic writers who follow him.

I am speaking of tendencies, not doctrines, in this great and powerful writer, and will be citing many counter-examples. There is a state of ethical calm called Beulah; and there is tenderness in the *Songs of Innocence and of Experience*, and even in *Milton* and *Jerusalem*. To the extent Blake sees there are victims in the world, he acknowledges we do not bring all suffering on ourselves with our "mind-forg'd manacles"; to this extent, he believes in the reality of others. In the visionary domain of Eden, the contradiction between "right" and "good" would disappear. But there is too frequently in Blake criticism a tendency to "read back" notionally from a presumed Edenic perspective of normative sanity, in the assumption that Blake must ex post facto have redressed violence, psychological imbalance or tyranny, illiberality, and the dispiriting deferment of ends. I will direct attention instead to the moral sensibility expressed in the larger arc of his mythic narrative and, line by line, in the bulk of his poetry and prose. That such conflict is not resolved in his poems until their final lines is hardly a unique narrative ploy. What is unique here is the sensibility that narrates the ways and means of our journey toward Eden, and the disquieting contradictions – which go far beyond any formulaic concept of "contraries" – in the value structure that sensibility embraces. We often hear of the Blake who said he was delighted to be in good company. But we must also take stock of the cantankerous Blake, so prone to brand anyone an idiot who intellectually parted company from him. To confront these darker qualities can increase our sense of his poetic power, which to my mind is diminished by partisan efforts to render him palatable, congenial, and sane in all matters.

Poetry and ethics

Blake distinguishes with some vehemence between the domains of poetry and ethics. "Cunning & Morality are not Poetry but Philosophy." Like other poets of the period, notably Shelley, he thinks moral didacticism obscures vision and limits energy. Though he may appear to urge a total transvaluation of good and evil in poetry (and life), he tells us that imagination must subsume doctrine into poetic form, that poetry is a means of portraying moral dialectic leading to a higher good through the "purgation" of "vice" – not to something beyond "good" altogether – and that the whited sepulcher "Moral Virtue" is no morality at all. We can simultaneously acknowledge Blake's antinomian energies and the fact that his is a philosophical poetry fairly steeped in the ethical.

Other Romantic authors acknowledge what Plato called the "ancient quarrel between philosophy and poetry." Supporting in theory a fruitful interchange between them, Coleridge knows it is a dangerous liaison. He blames his own poetic decline on having delved into the "unwholesome quicksilver mines of metaphysic depths" (*BL* I 17). Philosophical abstruseness and depth are qualities the poet, whose nurture is found in "the cultivated surface," may find noxious. Wordsworth's depression of 1796 is aggravated by intractable problems of moral philosophy. In yielding up "moral questions in despair," he takes a first step toward recovery. Despite the contrariety of poetry and philosophy, and despite Wordsworth's own disavowal of moral philosophy in particular, Coleridge thinks his friend could succeed, where he himself has failed, in uniting the two enterprises: Wordsworth could write the "FIRST GENUINE PHILOSOPHIC POEM" (*BL* II 156). Poetry and philosophy are contraries that could be powerfully reconciled. Wordsworth's *The Excursion*, published in 1814, attempts to fulfill this imperative three years before Coleridge articulates it in *Biographia Literaria* (1817). To most readers *The Excursion* confirms how dangerous such a liaison can be. Coleridge awaits a philosophic poem of a different character.

For Blake, philosophy does not degrade poetry if it is properly subservient. Describing his engraving of Chaucer's pilgrims, he says of the Clerk of Oxenford:

This character varies from that of Chaucer, as the contemplative philosopher varies from the poetical genius. There are always these two classes of learned

160

sages, the poetical and the philosophical. The painter has put them side by side, as if the youthful clerk had put himself under the tuition of the mature poet. Let the Philosopher always be the servant and scholar of inspiration and all will be happy.

(DC 537)

But Blake acknowledges the ready quarrel between the poetical and the philosophical; the latter often fails to be subservient. When Henry Boyd, a nineteenth-century translator of Dante, argues that a reader cannot sympathize with morally remiss characters ("We cannot sympathise with Achilles for the loss of his Mistress, when we feel that he gained her by the massacre of her family"), Blake replies in a marginal note that "nobody considers these things when they read Homer or Shakespear or Dante." Boyd observes that we prefer "in point of sentiment" the *Odyssey* to the *Iliad* because Odysseus is morally preferable to Achilles. Blake replies that if Homer's merit were to be found in moral sentiments, "he would be no better than Clarissa." Boyd makes one comment with which any other Romantic poet would concur:

Antecedent to and independent of all laws, a man may learn to argue on the nature of moral obligation, and the duty of universal benevolence, from Cumberland, Wollaston, Shaftesbury, Hutcheson; but would he feel what vice is in itself . . . let him enter into the passions of Lear, when he feels the ingratitude of his children . . . and he will know the difference of right and wrong much more clearly than from all the moralists that ever wrote.

By this point in Boyd's commentary, Blake is rankled to the point of issuing one of his crotchety antinomianisms:

The grandest Poetry is Immoral the Grandest characters Wicked. Very Satan. Capanius   Othello a murderer. Prometheus. Jupiter. Jehovah, Jesus a wine bibber
Cunning & Morality are not Poetry but Philosophy the Poet is Independent & Wicked the Philosopher is Dependent & Good
Poetry is to excuse Vice & shew its reason & necessary purgation[.]

PWB 633–4)

So the poet is independent and wicked, the philosopher banally dependent and good – a formulation similar to the ironic inversions of *The Marriage of Heaven and Hell* (1790–3). But note that the poet does not elude moral categories. His very wickedness implicates him as moral agent: he will purge "Vice" by portraying it as Shakespeare does in Othello. He will "shew its reason," making it comprehensible and thus eradicable.

The thrust of Blake's hyperbole is rather to free poetry from inap-

161

propriate moral censure. Poets should be judged on *how well* they portray human character. Alluding to Aristotle's *Poetics* II, he writes:

Aristotle says Characters are either Good or Bad: now Goodness or Badness has nothing to do with Character. an Apple tree a Pear tree a Horse a Lion, are Characters but a Good Apple tree or a Bad, is an Apple tree still: a Horse is not more a Lion for being a Bad Horse. that is its Character; its Goodness or Badness is another consideration.   (*PWB* 269)

He reminds us that the value of Shakespeare's portrayal of Iago, for instance, is distinct from a literal assessment of his badness. Such literalism is seen also in interpretive reductions of poems to moral formulas. But we should no more seek a unitary "Moral of a whole Poem" than we should judge a work in terms of the "Moral Goodness of its parts." Morality is a "secondary consideration" that belongs "to Philosophy & not to Poetry, to Exception & not to Rule, to Accident & not to Substance. the Ancients calld it eating of the tree of good & evil" (*PWB* 269–70).

A rehabilitated morality remains one of the purposes of art. Blake's quarrel is not with morality per se but with a certain conception of it – the restrictive, banal, pusillanimous morality of respectability, or the guilt-ridden submissiveness he equates with Mosaic law. He will invest his mythic figure Urizen with this fallen sensibility so that it might be understood and purged. He has in fact an enlarged notion of the moral and political power of poetry: "Poetry Fetter'd, Fetters the Human Race!" (*J* 3). When the Rev. Dr. Trusler, author of *Hogarth Moralized* (1768), complains of his obscurity, Blake answers: "You say that I want somebody to Elucidate my Ideas. But you ought to know that What is Grand is necessarily obscure to Weak men. That which can be made Explicit to the Idiot is not worth my care. The wisest of the Ancients considerd what is not too Explicit as the fittest for Instruction because it rouzes the faculties to act. I name Moses Solomon Esop Homer Plato" (*PWB* 702). Rousing the faculties to act denotes in a single phrase the pragmatics of poetry. However poetry achieves this, Blake knows it is not through the soporific of a pious morality poeticized.

To the questions of what impels the poet to create, what the purpose of poetry is, and what its content, the "antinomian" Blake replies as a moralist to all three. He creates because it is his "duty," not his delight or pastime: "it is a part of our duty to God & man to take due care of his Gifts," and "I cannot live without doing my duty to lay up treasures in heaven." His patron William Hayley, in forcing him to do hack work, hinders performance of duty: "Why this [determination to do my duty] should be made an objection to Me, while Drunkenness Lewdness Gluttony & even Idleness itself does not hurt other men let Satan himself Explain" (*PWB* 723–4). The famous vow, "I must Create a System, or be enslav'd by another Mans" (*J* 10: 20), reveals that Blake feels duty-bound to free himself. But poetry's ultimate purpose is not self-directed. Blake wishes to display his giant forms "To the Public," and as prophet of a new revelation he seeks to unfetter the human race.

The ideal relationship of art and morality is more intimate than even the homology spoken of in Chapter 2; it approaches identity:

> The great and golden rule of art, as well as of life, is this: That the more distinct, sharp, and wiry the bounding line, the more perfect the work of art; and the less keen and sharp, the greater is the evidence of weak imitation, plagiarism, and bungling . . . What is it that distinguishes honesty from knavery, but the hard and wiry line of rectitude and certainty in the actions and intentions. Leave out this line and you leave out life itself; all is chaos again, and the line of the almighty must be drawn out upon it before man or beast can exist. (*DC* 550)

Every line written by the poet or drawn by the artist is a moral act. As the giant form of imagination, Los labors for human regeneration and civilization. For eons he attempts to put human flesh on the skeletal Urizen, usually a figure of censoriousness and debased reason. Though his attempts to fashion the human figure in *The Book of Urizen* (1794), *The Four Zoas* (1797), and *Milton* (1804–10) often produce grotesque parodies – infected as he is by the sensibility of his mighty opposite – Los dares to frame the perfect human form. And it is with moral vision that he builds Golgonooza, the city of art and manufacture: "The blow of his Hammer is Justice. the swing of his Hammer: Mercy. / The force of Los's Hammer is eternal Forgiveness" (*J* 88: 49–50).

Blake's pronouncements on the "great and golden rule of art" have contradicted a common tenet in writings on the sublime that power is enhanced by indefiniteness, obscurity, and chiaroscuro. He may seem to contradict his own dictum that the "not too explicit" rouses the faculties to act. But he thinks his prophecies have a visionary lucidity beyond what Coleridge calls the level of the understanding. They are radiant and clear in outline to those who share a visionary reality; they are obscure to idiots (to which category their complexity consigns most professional students of literature).

While Los goes about building Golgonooza, the Zoas – the four "living creatures" beheld by Ezekiel and used by Blake to signify the basic human powers of emotion (Luvah), reason (Urizen), the senses and bodily instincts (Tharmas), and imagination (Los) – cry:

Let all Indefinites be thrown into Demonstrations
To be pounded to dust & melted in the Furnaces of Affliction:
He who would do good to another, must do it in Minute Particulars
General Good is the plea of the scoundrel hypocrite & flatterer:
For Art & Science cannot exist but in minutely organized Particulars
And not in generalizing Demonstrations of the Rational Power.
The Infinite alone resides in Definite & Determinate Identity
Establishment of Truth depends on destruction of Falshood continually.

(J 55: 58–65)

Blake eschews the abstract "General Good" as a sanction. Just as the artist draws the "minute particulars" of human form instead of generalized nature, so the moral agent registers the particulars of moral situations, the uniqueness of the other.

Blake is contemptuous of moral doubt. Wherever it appears, doubt is the dark shadow, the illusion, the reasoning spectre or "idiot Questioner," which must be dispelled as prelude to vision. In ethical questions Blake is an uncommonly belligerent cognitivist; he assumes we can all attain moral knowledge and that such knowledge is directly intuitable:

The Man who pretends to be a modest enquirer into the truth of a self evident thing is a Knave The truth & certainty of Virtue & Honesty i.e. Inspiration needs no one to prove it it is Evident as the Sun & Moon [What doubt is virtuous even Honest that depends upon Examination] He who stands doubting of what he intends whether it is Virtuous or Vicious knows not what Virtue means. no man can do a Vicious action & think it to be Virtuous. no man can take darkness for light. he may pretend to do so & may pretend to be a modest Enquirer. but he is a Knave. (PWB 613–14)

Significantly, Blake deletes his own saving clause, printed here in brackets, that there may be honest, virtuous doubt. He subscribes to Lavater's admonition that the "moral enthusiast, who in the maze of his refinements loses or despises the plain paths of honesty and duty, is on the brink of crimes" (AL 600).

Moral doubt is thus a weakening of self-definition. The human personality should have the determinate clarity of a Blake engraving. Blake might scoff at Coleridge's complaint about the "slippery and protean nature of all self-inquisition." The fully realized personality has broken through obscurity, doubt, and indefiniteness to perfect human form, and ceases to be opaque to itself.

Clarity, self-definition, and unambiguous action contradict, to say the least, the perplexities of Blake's psychic drama. But these qualities are desired *ends*, approached only through the most arduous mental fight. It is not until Night the Seventh that Los articulates the artist's

164

desire "to fabricate embodied semblances in which the dead / May live before us in our palaces & in our gardens of labour." Thereupon he and Enitharmon begin to shape a visionary cosmos suffused with moral value:

> And first he drew a line upon the walls of shining heaven
> And Enitharmon tinctured it with beams of blushing love
> It remaind permanent a lovely form inspir'd divinely human
> Dividing into just proportions Los unwearied labourd
> The immortal lines upon the heavens. (FZ 90: 9–10; 35–9)

Los continues his gigantic labors, which range from drawing the human form to creating human civilization. Building the city of Golgonooza, like drawing the human form divine, requires acts of conversion. Los converts places associated with horror and death, such as Tyburn and Calvary, into buildings of "pity and compassion." Here is a homey inventory of Golgonooza moralized:

> The stones are pity, and the bricks, well wrought affections:
> Enameld with love & kindness, & the tiles engraven gold
> Labour of merciful hands: the beams & rafters are forgiveness:
> The mortar & cement of the work, tears of honesty: the nails,
> And the screws & iron braces, are well wrought blandishments,
> And well contrived words, firm fixing, never forgotten,
> Always comforting the remembrance: the floors, humility,
> The cielings, devotion: the hearths, thanksgiving. (J 12: 30–7)

The development of art – in its fullest sense, every imaginative, delineated human expression, whether in painting, poetry, architecture, or manufacture – is a casting out of error. Going against the tendency of eighteenth-century thinkers from Shaftesbury to Addison to Burke to Hume to Reynolds to Kant, Blake removes art from the category of taste and places it with morality and truth. His poetics is a repudiation of aesthetics and, by implication, of Kant's *Critique of Judgment*:

No man can Embrace True Art till he has Explord & cast out False Art such is the Nature of Mortal Things or he will be himself cast out by those who have Already Embraced True Art Thus My Picture [of the Last Judgment] is a History of Art & Science the Foundation of Society Which is Humanity itself. What are all the Gifts of the Spirit but Mental Gifts whenever any Individual Rejects Error & Embraces Truth a Last Judgment passes upon that Individual.

(VLJ 562)

Though Blake may appear to have divorced poetry from ethics, a close look reveals an extraordinary joining of the two. The poet must have freedom to create his own system, but this is no entitlement to a retreat from the ethical, nor a relegation of it to an unlovely byway called philosophy. Like Shelley, Blake extends the power of imagination to all creative activity, whether poetry, "sweet science," or human acts. He severely compromises poetry's autonomy in merging it with the full range of life's activities – a merging that will shamelessly characterize poetic theory and practice of the period.

Act and energy

In his Annotations to Lavater's *Aphorisms on Man* (1788), Blake responds directly to moral discourse.[2] Unlike many authors subjected to his marginal inquisition, Lavater is treated respectfully: "the name Lavater. is the amulet of those who purify the heart of man." But he finds Lavater's concept of action faulty:

He makes every thing originate in its accident he makes the vicious propensity not only a leading feature of the man but the Stamina on which all his virtues grow. But as I understand Vice it is a Negative— . . .
  Every mans leading propensity ought to be calld his leading Virtue & his good Angel But the Philosophy of Causes & Consequences misled Lavater as it has all his cotemporaries. Each thing is its own cause & its own effect Accident is the omission of act in self & the hindering of act in another, This is Vice but all Act [from Individual propensity] is Virtue. To hinder another is not an act it is the contrary it is a restrain on action both in ourselves & in the person hinderd for he who hinders another omits his own duty. at the time
  Murder is Hindering Another
  Theft is Hindering Another
  Backbiting. Undermining Circumventing & whatever is Negative is Vice.
(AL 600–1)

This key statement, which has bearing on Blake's poetry, sets forth the optimistic pole of Romantic humanism.

  The main points are these: (1) "Virtue" is defined as strength or "propensity." In this matter Blake is close to Coleridge, who defines "virtue," with the Latin root in mind, as "*manly* energy." "Virtue" commonly implies the suppression of energy and inclination, as in conventional Christian ethics; and in Blake's satanic lexicon "Moral Virtue" does signify a baleful suppression. But in the "Annotations to Lavater" he argues that "we who are philosophers ought not to call the Staminal Virtues of Humanity by the same name that we call the omissions of intellect springing from poverty" (AL 601). By "leading"

[2] For a discussion of the Lavater–Fichte–Blake connection, see above pp. 89–91.

or "Individual propensity" Blake means something close to what we would call the personal will. (2) All acts emanating from individual propensity are good, and in this sense human nature is good. (3) Individualism, the virtuous assertion of this propensity relative to others, is the moral norm. All persons have a "duty," not only a right, to act according to their propensity. All such acts are self-defining because they destroy the accidental and enrich the essence of the self, its "Staminal Virtues."[3] (4) Evil – as accident, not essence, as negation, not positivity – is a failure in self-definition, a "restraint on action . . . in ourselves." Our vice hinders others, preventing their own expression of "act in self" by, for example, murdering them. Blake's use of "hindering" contains a wealth of implication: all the points I am itemizing here, plus the recognition that evil can come from without. Our own "mind-forg'd manacles" may not be entirely to blame for what ails us. (5) Freedom need not be hindered by nature, or "Causes & Consequences," because human beings have the power of self-origination. All acts to be defined as acts must originate freely in the self, not in circumstances, and all self-empowered acts are virtuous. Blake grants the human will sufficient power to originate its own acts, a view challenged with considerable sophistication by Hobbes, among others. (6) No social or political structure for mediating among conflicting wills is envisaged here; Blake's political position is anarchistic.

Coleridge contrasts with Blake interestingly on these points. Accepting the first – that human excellence is expression, not repression, of energy – he rejects the second, believing instead in radical evil, conceived of as the very act of self-origination Blake praises. Satan's fall is the prideful act of finding in self alone an independent base. Though Blake makes clear in the prophecies that the process is neither inevitable nor easy, Coleridge does not think evil eradicable by virtuous acts. The author of *The Rime of the Ancient Mariner* fears the essence of humans *is* evil, yet he remains a humanist in urging the development of humane and liberal consciousness from out the mainspring of personal will itself. His complex posture is to maintain a liberal ethics even because of the potential for human depravity, which traditional Christianity is not alone in countering with an ethics of self-restraint or mortification. Coleridge's *Rime* and the conversation poems taken together declare this empowering paradox.

The moral sensibility of the conversation poems is grounded in an

---

[3] Blake deleted the phrase, printed in brackets above, that all act "from Individual propensity" is virtue. Perhaps he acknowledges a redundancy in it, just as, strictly speaking, the phrase "virtuous act" or "free act" is redundant.

intense but gentle mutuality quite unBlakean in character. To be sure, Blake's moral monster is the "selfhood," a debased form of egoism; and in *Milton* and especially *Jerusalem*, we lose sight of the strong individualism of the early prophecies and "Annotations to Lavater." But Blake could never have written a conversation poem, both because it employs a rhetoric alien to apocalyptic urgency and mental fight and because Coleridgean vicariousness in a Blakean scheme of things would invite heteronomy.

Finally, whereas Blake's view of "act in self" implies anarchism – if each person were to follow individual propensity, there would be a mutual increase in happiness – Coleridge's view of personal will seems, after his early period of liberal politics, to require strong constitutional controls.

The "Annotations to Lavater" assert that whenever an "act in self" is "hindered," it fails to express the self and shares the imperfection and passivity of "vice." I suggest that the number of free and complete acts represented as such is extremely small in Blake's poetry. Strictly, there are only two: the descent of Milton from Eden into the Ulro and the awakening of Albion. All other acts are partially or totally hindered, despite the preponderance of active verbs and participles that lends Blake's poems so great a sense of activity.

The Book of Thel (1789) portrays a frustrated rite of passage from innocence to experience, an incomplete act. Caught in a pastoral limbo where she has not found a "use," the virgin Thel exists a second remove from the real. Faintly present to herself she is only "like" a set of phenomena themselves evanescent and not fully real: dreams of infants, parting clouds, reflections in a mirror. Her interlocutors – personified Lilly, Cloud, and Clod of Clay – offer scripts for a life narrative suitable to themselves within the cycles of nature but not to a questing human who seeks a use answering to her own unrealized propensity. A voice from a grave speaks of the senses as inlets of pain: "Why cannot the Ear be closed to its own destruction?" Sexuality, an unspoken motivational force but not the only one in a poem concerned with ontological quest, is painfully restrained: "Why a little curtain of flesh on the bed of our desire?" (6: 11, 20). Though the threatening voice seems to come from without, it emanates from Thel's grave as her own projected fear.

Since the hindering of act is here internal, hers is a crisis of will. Blake takes note of Lavater's distinction between wishing and willing. Lavater writes, "Whose will is bent with energy on *one*, *must* renounce the wishes for *many* things." "Thel" is Greek for either "wish" or "will." Her wish for change exceeds her willing of it. Blake's activism

168

exceeds Lavater's; he is "uneasy" with Lavater's assertion that "Calm-ness of will is a sign of grandeur" (AL 584).

Visions of the Daughters of Albion is politically to the left of *The Book of Thel*. For all her own strong willing and readiness for experience, Oothoon, the poem's heroine, is repressed by the company she keeps; the hindering is external. Celebration of the personal will, in the belief that what happens to us is necessarily our own doing, is often an argument of the political right; it dispenses with the idea of class victim. As the "soft soul of America" emblematic of slavery, Oothoon is a victim, brutalized by Bromion, sadistic slave-owner and puritanical rapist, and by her intended lover, Theotormon, a jealous fragment who thinks Bromion's rape has forever polluted her. Bound back to back with Bromion because a self-hindering Theotormon will not forgive her for having been raped, Oothoon is thus victimized both by Bromion's brutality (which she is ready to rise above) and by Theotor-mon's whining and paralysis, his powerlessness before history and consequence, his hatred in the roots of love. Blake does not imply that Oothoon has brought all this on herself or that she can simply imagine happier circumstances. The result of her great oration on love, desire, individuality, and repression (5:3–8:10) implies a gap between percep-tion and power, between language and performance, since she fails to convert the two men, whatever her power over a particular reader. The fundamental "act" of rape – which on Blake's terms is the negation of act – is narrated in one-half a line of verse, beyond which the possibility of genuine acts and events, and of narrative as the told sequence of them, is diminished to talk and a vividly rendered failure of true dialogic exchange.

Early in his career, then, Blake has confronted the sentimentality that where there is a will, there is a way. We should not press too literally on the statement in *The Marriage of Heaven and Hell* that a "firm perswasion that a thing is so, make[s] it so," even to the point of removing mountains. The will can be thwarted, and strong individuals victimized. Resistance from without and within to "Individual propen-sity" is the precondition of a moral situation, since without the possibility of fault one could not speak of obligation. It is only from the highest Edenic perspective that the merely moral is eclipsed. Romantic optimist in his estimate of what a human being can become, Blake laments the rarity of triumphs of willing in virtuous, complete acts.

In the later prophecies – *The Four Zoas, Milton, Jerusalem* – his mythic figures challenge narrative conventions in ways that illustrate the problematics of action. We find few causally linked sequences of scene, situation, cognition, deliberation, decision, and volition leading to act.

Such sequences become evident only in the larger psychological allegory, in which a particular mythic figure has the status of a mental component instead of total mind. Most events in these prophecies are of warring faculties, none of which wholly embodies mind. Los, Urizen, Luvah, and Tharmas are not represented as human beings. Each is a mental component of the sleeping Albion, who is exemplar when awake of what a human being might become. As in Freud's allegory of the psyche with its threefold id, ego, and superego, the Zoas are more agencies than agents; they are the mental means by which an act might be accomplished. There is a redundancy in psychological faculties themselves undergoing a psychological process leading to an act. The Zoas *are* the process.[4] A moral agent, who would embody this process within a single mental theatre, is nowhere and everywhere in the larger narrative of *The Four Zoas*, finally coming into focus as Albion on the Rock of Ages.

What the Zoas and their emanations perform is strangely fugitive, abortive, unreflective, repetitive, and partial. A complete act would be achieved only if the four powers were to work psychodynamically together. The awakening of Albion is precisely this fourfold act. If we consider them also as giant forms shaping cosmic history, they seem of greater magnitude than persons but strangely without a human face. The point is debated in Blake criticism, but it seems to me they do not – even when one observes their lineaments in Blake's illustrations – accumulate sufficient identity or solidity or causal continuity to be considered representations of persons acting as moral agents. (I use "identity" and "character" in familiar senses here.) Whatever else they are, they are not quite that. They have no larger reservoir of self or reflexive consciousness that exists independently of their functioning. Whether as psychological events, or as reimagined mythic figures who were originally persons, or as perennial powers in cosmic history, they

---

[4] Locke makes this point in complaining about how people speak of faculties as if they were "so many distinct agents." "For if it be reasonable to suppose and talk of *Faculties*, as distinct Beings, that can act, (as we do, when we say the *Will* orders, and the *Will* is free,) 'tis fit that we should make a speaking *Faculty*, and a walking *Faculty*, and a dancing *Faculty*, by which these Actions are produced, which are but several Modes of Motion; as well as we make the *Will* and *Understanding* to be *Faculties*, by which the Actions of Chusing and Perceiving are produced, which are but several Modes of Thinking: And we may as properly say, that 'tis the singing *Faculty* sings, and the dancing *Faculty* dances, as that the *Will* chuses, or that the Understanding conceives . . . But in all these, it is not one *power* that operates on another: But it is the Mind that operates, and exerts these Powers; it is the Man that does the action; it is the Agent that has power, or is able to do. For *Powers* are Relations, not Agents: And *that which has the power, or not the power to operate, is that alone, which is, or is not free*, and not the Power itself" (*An Essay Concerning Human Understanding*, Bk. II, 242–3).

170

thus correlate awkwardly with the questions one asks concerning human beings engaged in moral action. Though lacking also the resolute definition of most allegorical figures, they refer us to multiple structures of meaning – psychological, moral, historical, and mythic – and necessarily invite allegorical readings, without which Blakean narrative would be incomprehensible on *any* level.[5]

The four psychological faculties can be distinguished from figures such as Thel, Oothoon, Milton, and Albion, who are represented as persons, whether or not we could comfortably extrapolate them from their texts to life as we know it. Only they can attempt acts in the Blakean sense, and only Milton and Albion ever succeed. *Milton* begins by asking "what mov'd Milton" to plunge from Eden back into the Ulro, Blake's one-dimensional hell of chaos and darkness. The "cause" was a "Bard's prophetic Song!" Taking up several engraved plates, the Bard's Song gives accounts of the mythic Los/Urizen conflict, of modern European history, of Blake's own struggle with his patron, Hayley, and of the dominion of sexual shame – all of which tell Milton that the "Nations still / Follow after the detestable Gods of Priam; in pomp / Of warlike selfhood" (*M* 14:14–15). Milton's vision of a paradise regained has been premature. He utters what by Blakean standards counts as an explanation as to why he will "go to Eternal Death!" – to the world most of us inhabit most of the time. The occasion of the act and Milton's volitional process are narrated beforehand. He seeks an ideal form of himself purged of the imperfection that has dogged him even to Eden. His previous acts have been imperfect and hindered, spawned by a dark conscience that capitulated to moral virtue and selfhood. "I in my Selfhood am that Satan: I am that Evil One!" (*M* 14: 30). Separated from his emanation, Ololon, divided and partial, he seeks to be whole and unhindered.

The events that follow are components of a single free act of purification, empowerment, and regeneration. There are two major descents: in Book the First, Milton's from Eden into the Ulro to join his emanation, paralleled by Ololon's own descent in Book the Second to join him. And there is a complex series of mergings in the comic–grotesque mode: the Bard takes "refuge in Miltons bosom" (*M* 14: 9); Milton descends onto Blake's left foot and "enterd there" (*M* 15: 47–

---

[5] Psychological and/or moral allegory necessarily has it both ways on this point. John Bunyan's characters – Faithful, Giant Despair, Hopeful, and Mr. Worldly Wiseman – are particular mental or moral characteristics which act in a limited way like persons. Such allegory is grounded in synecdoche, whereby one part of the psyche comes to represent the whole. Blake's Zoas do not take on the determinate identity of Bunyan's allegorical figures, however, and less readily create the illusion of persons.

50); Milton falls through Albion's heart (*M* 20: 41); Blake becomes "One Man" with Los (*M* 22: 12; 36: 21); and finally Ololon flees into Milton's shadow (*M* 42: 5–6). These events are temporally separate only along the horizontal axis of narration; as components of a single whole act, extraordinary in its complexity, they are demonstrably simultaneous on a vertical axis of non-temporal vision.[6] The reader is asked, in effect, to transcend narrative. The descents are cathartic and revolutionary; the mergings are energizing and self-defining, as the various powers of imagination, reason, emotion, and sense, embodied in Milton, are transubstantiated into the poet-narrator himself. It is Blake, not Milton, who will write the poem we are reading. He calls on Milton's power, divested of Milton's limitations, when he undertakes to write, unhindered, the poem as free act.

The awakening of Albion – the other "whole" act – is constituted by nine nights of epic mental fight, the entire nightmarish panorama of *The Four Zoas*. This extraordinary epic tells the story of a falling away from perfection, which occasions the imperative of restoration issued to Los by Tharmas, the parent power:

> Deformed I see these lineaments of ungratified Desire
> The all powerful curse of an honest man be upon Urizen & Luvah
> But thou My Son Glorious in brightness comforter of Tharmas
> Go forth Rebuild this Universe beneath my indignant power
> A universe of Death & Decay. Let Enitharmons hands
> Weave soft delusive forms of Man above my watry world
> Renew these ruind souls of Men thro Earth Sea Air & Fire
> To waste in endless corruption . . .   (*FZ* 48: 1–8)

Restoration of the four major powers or staminal virtues to original perfection is identical with the awakening of Albion. The moral imperative is to awaken to a new state of being.[7]

---

[6] See Susan Fox, *Poetic Form in Blake's Milton*, especially pp. 14–22, 166–9.

[7] This self-realizationist perspective is structurally paralleled in Blake's cosmology and theodicy. Eno, the "Aged Mother" who tells the tale of the Zoas, remembers a time of original plenitude, innocence, and harmony from which there was a fall into division and negation. The metaphor of awakening coalesces with the metaphor of building, as mental powers struggle to repair their fallen and disorganized condition. Urizen builds the Mundane Shell, the world of materiality that prevents the Fall from extending into nonentity. Los subsequently builds the city of Golgonooza, or human culture.

Precisely, these are acts of *re*-building. If human beings recapitulate on an individual basis the terms of this cosmic fall, each must be said to have enjoyed an original perfection. This inference conflicts, however, with the dialectic of *The Book of Thel*, *Songs of Innocence and of Experience*, and *Visions of the Daughters of Albion*, which express a more recognizable pattern of development. In these works, original inno-

An awakening is less suggestive of moral dialectic than Milton's decision to descend to the Ulro. It seems much less a willed act. Literal extension of the metaphor prompts the question of what kinds of moral reform are possible in sleep or in unconscious mental activity generally. Prior to his awakening, Albion's most emphatic single gesture is to sneeze seven times, which, despite the allusion to 2 Kings 4: 35, is somewhat deficient in moral resonance. These very limitations of the metaphor remind us of weaknesses in self-realizationist theories, which often center around the progressive development of preexistent but dormant powers. We have heard Nietzsche say that we should become what we are – an imperative at odds with textbook existentialism. The organic metaphor informing self-realizationism suggests that growth of faculties comes about not so much through active moral willing – choosing what it is we will become – as in placing the self in those circumstances that permit latent powers to emerge spontaneously in accordance with their inbred character. "Growing" is not the same as "willing."

Even so, we can conclude from these two acts – Milton's descent and Albion's awakening – that Blake, for all his "optimism," treats the free act as a complex and rare one, requiring the exercise of many human powers. Edenic wholeness is a far remove from simplicity. The transition from potentiality to actuality – from dormancy to the waking state – is arduous and violent. Albion's is a tormented sleep.

Blake does attest to "miracles" in his life and poetry, but these are interventions, not acts, reflecting a condition of grace beyond

cence, associated with childhood, is a limited state of mind, expressing an as yet non-culpable ignorance. It is not perfection. The fall into experience – which, as the visitor to London can see, is a fall into division, chaos, and brutality – is necessary in order that the self grow ontologically. Before we can act freely from "Individual propensity," we must suffer a state of hindering. *Visions* seems to point beyond its conclusion to a new state of being, where Oothoon and Theotormon would be unhindered in their love. Some critics call this "organized innocence" (albeit Blake never so terms it). This is a superior innocence that has weathered experience and grown through suffering: "Sweetest the fruit that the worm feeds on. & the soul prey'd on by woe / The new wash'd lamb ting'd with the village smoke & the bright swan / By the red earth of our immortal river" (*VDA* 3: 17–19).

The Four Zoas in its cosmic narrative appears to revise this dialectic, because what it urges and prophesies is not strictly a new emergent but a repetition, dialectic yielding to cyclical time before the presumed abolition of time in Eden. Preparatory to their return to Eden, Tharmas and Enion, in Night the Ninth, resume the prelapsarian condition of pastoral innocence in Beulah, similar to the very landscape from which Thel attempts to escape. Albion awakened is never said to be ontologically or morally superior to the original Albion. All this makes uncertain the parallelism between moral development and the larger myth of Albion.

individual willing. He may seem to exempt us from long-term teleological struggle if only we can find that moment in each day that Satan cannot find, or that pulse of the artery in which the poet's work is done, or that eternity in a grain of sand. Can we not enter Eden repeatedly on a daily basis in a kind of domesticating of apocalypse? I grant an element of this in Blake but regard it as a lyrical parenthesis within an overriding narratological struggle. (There is a similar split between lyric and narrative in Wordsworth.) The major prophecies could otherwise have concluded before they began. Can eight nights of struggle be dispensed with for the ninth night of apocalyptic fulfillment? Can that arc of development be simply circumnavigated for a more direct confrontation? Even if the answer to these questions is yes, it does not negate the recognition that the larger portion of Blake's poetry narrates the violent mental labors leading up to and preparing for true act and vision.

This complex struggle puts Blake's endorsement of energy into perspective. The hyperbole of "Annotations to Lavater" is echoed in *The Marriage of Heaven and Hell*, which has a refreshing subversive energy. One feels Urizenic to say that only limited concepts of "Moral Virtue," "Moral Law," and "Right & Duty" are transvalued in Blake. It seems a cheap shot to say of the immoralist that he has only substituted one concept of morality for another. Perhaps Blakean energies would generate a surplus to subvert even the envisioned order toward which they tend. But the standard is never energy alone. Free acts from "Individual propensity," in keeping with their complexity, require something beyond energy to lend them form, as Blake makes clear in works prior to *The Marriage*. The energy of Edward the Third and the Black Prince in his early drama, *King Edward the Third* (1783), is eternally *un*delightful because immoderate and self-indulgent (iii 231–8). In *Poetical Sketches* (1783), the miniature political allegory "Blind-Man's Buff" warns that exuberant violation of rules of the game is unfair, as when one playmate tricks another into taking a bad spill. It ends with a seemingly unBlakean pronouncement that nations should be governed by law.

These early works are not altogether misleading. What Blake prophesies is the coming of new *order*. To Lavater's assertion that "Sin and destruction of order are the same," he comments "a golden sentence." The original discord that brings about the fall is the usurpation of Urizen's place by Luvah, of reason by energy or passion.

More than the other Romantic poets, Blake portrays energy in figures of both sexuality and revolution. Their common origin in energy sets up structural parallels: Orc is to Urizen as energy is to repression as libido is to neurosis as the people are to government. It does not follow that governments fall if people make love, but Blake's eroticism extends far beyond specifically sexual contexts. Duty and inclination are merged in such a way as to produce a new rigorism, contrary to the intent of Schiller and Coleridge. For Blake it is our duty (not only our right) to act on our inclinations: "He who desires but acts not, breeds pestilence." His inclinations are more combustible than Coleridge's, his celebration of pleasure and eroticism more open, and his hostility to psychological, moral, political, and religious oppression less equivocal. He is also a far remove from liberal indulgence, instead issuing fierce imperatives that we should desire and act in such and such a way.

Energy is a dialectical contrary, necessary but insufficient in itself to bring about a new order. Release of energy alone does not constitute an act. At the pre-apocalyptic moment described in *The Marriage of Heaven and Hell*, much "rubbish from a caves mouth" must be cleared away forcibly, and hence the dialectic will be imbalanced in favor of energy. But even in this work, Blake gives evidence of the more comprehensive vision of later works. Indeterminate energy must be taken up into human form and new structures of "Right & Duty." This dialectic broadly informs the period. "Kubla Khan" is a great embodiment of it: sexual energy of the woman wailing for her demon lover is transformed into the symphony and song of the Abyssinian maid. Blake's *Marriage* is more explicit in defining the dialectic of desire and form. The principle, "Without Contraries is no progression. Attraction and Repulsion, Reason and Energy, Love and Hate, are necessary to Human existence" (*MHH* 3), prepares for the fundamental conflict between "two classes of men," the "Devouring" and the "Prolific." In this adumbration of the warfare between the order of Urizen and the energy of Orc, Blake clearly asserts that without order there could be no energy: "the Prolific would cease to be Prolific unless the Devourer as a sea rec[ei]ved the excess of his delights" (*MHH* 16).

The dialectic of *The Marriage of Heaven and Hell* points to a transvaluation of conventional notions of good and evil, then, but not to a repudiation of morals. This work may seem, to a new student of Blake, to say that everything negative in human existence – death, hypocrisy, envy, pestilence, and tyranny – constitutes one necessary pole in an indefinitely extensible process. If such negatives are necessary forces in the dialectic, there is no reason for condemning them, hence there are no moral standards. One would then speak of a morally neutralized process of negatives and positives, or worse, some version of commonplace adolescent relativism.

There are two closely related reasons why this inference is mistaken. First, "A Song of Liberty," which concludes the work, makes clear a telos that moralizes the entire dialectical process. True dialectic is not neutral but favors the positive pole, the augmentation of life: "for everything that *lives* is Holy" (my emphasis), not everything that merely exists in some degree. Given the superiority of liberty to repression and hate at whatever moment in the cycles of history, one should attempt to express at all times those energies, sexual and political, that lead to liberation. Blake does not propose a time when it would be better to be repressive. In the later prophecies, dialectical movement points to a time when negativity will disappear. Eden has ideally no tyranny, no lies, no unacted desires. (I say "ideally" because Blake admits imperfection into Eden, as Milton's own presence there has shown.) Vice "is a negative" that would vanish if we acted freely according to "the Staminal Virtues of Humanity."

The second reason is that we can discern, even before he makes it somewhat clearer in later works, the distinction between creative and destructive opposition. Regressive negatives such as jealousy, hate, hypocrisy, and envy can be distinguished from progressive contraries and are ideally *not* necessary to human existence; they should be done away with altogether in free acts.

> There is a Negation, & there is a Contrary
> The Negation must be destroyed to redeem the Contraries[.]
> (*M* II 40: 32–3)

Imagination and even reason, if rehabilitated, can function as progressive contraries of energy, giving it living form. They need not function as madness or hate. To say that imagination is a contrary of energy is simply to confirm a fundamental assumption of Romantic psychodynamics, already seen in Schelling and Coleridge, that imagination is a shaping power which disciplines, contains, and gives permanent living form or "outline" to life's energies. In *The Marriage of Heaven and Hell* imagination is not so prominent a power as energy and reason, but it is implicit in passages dealing with perception and perspective: "How do you know but ev'ry Bird that cuts the airy way, / Is an immense world of delight, clos'd by your senses five?"; "A fool sees not the same tree that a wise man sees"; "What is now proved was once, only imagin'd"; "Where man is not nature is barren"; "If the doors of perception were cleansed every thing would appear to man as it is, infinite." In the all-too-condensed allegory of the printing house in hell, we read of eagles, lions, and "Unnam'd forms" building palaces, "melting the metals into living fluids" in the manner of artists, who give form to chaos after a "Dragon-Man," the future Orc, has cleared away rubbish. Less frequently, reason itself appears in a benign role: "Energy is the only life and is from the Body and Reason is the bound or outward circumference of Energy"; "Truth can never be told so as to be understood, and not be believ'd." There are positive forces in this work not identifiable with energy alone, forces that suggest a richer system of values and that also complicate the nature of the act, which requires more than spontaneous expression of desire.

The Marriage of Heaven and Hell is largely taken up with the conflict of energy and repression. Certainly this work is on the side of those energized devils who attack convention and respectability. This element of Blake's ethic is its most accessible, and requires little critical exegesis. It accounts for his popularity among the unscrubbed, and leads to facile parallels between Blake and sundry modern trends. Most of the Proverbs of Hell and other memorable sayings prefigure the warfare of Orc and Urizen: "The road of excess leads to the palace of wisdom"; "Exuberance is Beauty"; "Sooner murder an infant in its cradle than nurse unacted desires"; "One Law for the Lion & Ox is oppression." We can make allowance for hyperbole and still recognize the strong moral urging here, quite unlike what a morally neutral celebration of process would be. The antinomianism of such statements is qualified by suggestions of visionary order – the propriety of the devouring function, or of true circumference and form. Dialectical imbalance at all moments of human history generates strenuous moral imperatives.

The morally positive nature of dialectic in *The Marriage of Heaven and Hell* does not, however, resolve all questions we have concerning the quality of those acts which it is right to perform. For one thing, it is frequently difficult to distinguish in a Blake text between negative and creative opposition, between "Negations" and "Contraries." Urizen may often seem to be acting as a negative "Idiot questioner," yet his opposition remains instrumental to Los in the struggle toward true human form. Another issue is more troubling. Even where we can distinguish between acts of negation or wrong acts (the worm's destruction of the sick rose) and acts of contrariety or right acts (the ravishment of the nameless shadowy female by Orc), we may be disturbed by the nature of these right acts. This side of paradise all our acts are necessarily partial – even those invested with energy and imagination – and to a degree hindered and hindering. Otherwise we would already inhabit a mental Eden.[8] It must remain "right" to do

[8] Without referring specifically to Blake, Kenneth Burke has made this point: "In reality, we are capable of but partial acts, acts that but partially represent us and that

them, because such interim acts make up the arc of development from innocence to experience to the distant prospect of an awakened four-fold humanity. The distinction between "negation" and "contrary" saves Blake from the charge that he subscribes to the "good of evil." But contrary acts have their own unlovely violence. The major prophecies make plain that the regenerative process requires violent acts. Because Blake does not crudely distinguish between the mental and the physical, such acts are manifested as both. Even if they do not ultimately hinder in the way that acts of negation hinder – even if they lead to the augmentation of life – they inflict pain and anguish and, as I will argue, are qualitatively in opposition to the ends they seek.

Values in Eden and elsewhere

Blake's poetry is the most violent in the English language. *The Four Zoas* (1797) reads as if John Milton's wars in heaven of *Paradise Lost*, Book VI, usurped the rest of the epic panorama. Regeneration in Night the Ninth comes only after eight nights of mental strife imaged as physical violence. The atmosphere is one of abstracted terror. In Blake's corpus as a whole, there exists a pattern of deferring the end: a new order is repeatedly prophesied and approached, but not until Night the Ninth does the narrator break through violence to an account of it. The conclusions of the later prophecies *Milton* and *Jerusalem* do not give the sense of arrival *The Four Zoas* gives. Earlier works yield partial vision and partial development of the mythic narrative: from *The Book of Thel* that ends in failure and regression, to a work that ends in vision frustrated, *Visions of the Daughters of Albion*, to one that ends with apocalyptic urgency and energy, *The Marriage of Heaven and Hell*, to one that ends with the greater promise of Los, *Europe a Prophecy*. These two distinctive traits – Blake's violence and his constant deferring of the end to which his mythic narrative moves – have implications for the moral interpretation of his poetry.

Transformative violence in Blake owes much to the Biblical prophetic books and apocalyptic tradition. The blood, fire, and brimstone of Isaiah 34 make possible the blossoms and springs of fertile water in the New Zion of Isaiah 35. His use of traditional apocalyptic tropes does not make Blakean violence "merely metaphorical," however. As a "literalist of the imagination," he would not understand this phrase.

produce but partial transformations. Indeed, if all the ratios [that is, mutual relationships of the components of acts] were adjusted to one another with perfect Edenic symmetry, they would be immutable in one unending 'moment' " (*A Grammar of Motives*, 19).

178

And one finds in him a surplus of violence beyond what can be assigned to even traditional apocalyptics.

The larger conclusion of my reading of Blake is that his view of "right" and his view of "good" are asymmetric. Simply put, what we are obliged to do is qualitatively incongruous with the values we seek. Though we value love, we are obliged to act in wrath; though we value peace, we must act as insurrectionaries. We have seen the rare, arduous, and complex nature of the whole and free act in Blake – the act that frees both self and others from all hindering. The consequence of the free or "right" act is the actualization of some value or "good." Because the right act is so rarely achieved, the good that is its end – whether a healthy state of consciousness or just socio-political environment or apocalyptic renewal – is repeatedly deferred. Although the free act would not hinder others, performing it requires a lengthy repetitive series of partial acts that do indeed hinder. These partial acts are often violent in their energies and brutal, whether we consider them as the exchange of one form of consciousness for another (mental components struggling for ascendency) or as acts among persons (the rape of Oothoon by Bromion) or as the immersion in experience generally.

Blake's larger mythic narrative implies that this series of partial, hindering acts is necessary and to a degree right. Alteration of vision is not won by merely blinking one's eyes or suddenly tuning into a different psychic channel. The entire personality and the weight of its own history are implied in the acts that would overcome personality and history. Struggling toward Eden – attempting the moral life while in a radically "disorganiz'd" and imperfect condition – requires partial acts not easily distinguished from Hobbesian warfare. Once in Eden there would be no qualitative disparity between right and good. Our acts would be spontaneously imaginative, loving, and whole. But Blake's optimism becomes merely ideal in view of the fact that his mythic narrative is so demonstrably imbalanced toward sub-Edenic strife.

The practical disparity between right and good is more than a static paradox; for better or worse, it empowers the moral progress of the mythic narrative. It helps account for what some critics think is a change of mind in the transition from *The Marriage of Heaven and Hell* to *Jerusalem*, the earlier work urging acts of will that are fierce and threatening, the later praising attitudes of forgiveness, pity, and charity. This larger transformation recapitulates the many local instances when violent acts are means to good.

As one who writes that all deities reside in the human breast and that

179

God exists and acts only through persons, Blake is usually taken to be a humanist with a secular approach to values. This view, though largely true, needs qualification in view of what has just been advanced. If values in Eden were forever more radiant than those within our own purview, if vision outstripped possibility, "good" would forever elude us and human values would have a status structurally analogous to the supramundane. Schiller's humanism is predicated on the gap between desire and fulfillment. In the late prophecies Blake will close that gap (except insofar as these visions of eternity are themselves but a testimony to desire, fulfilled only in the literality of a text). Schiller's humanism seems a gentle affair next to Blake's, however. The extreme difficulty of achieving the good – the horrendously contentious labors of redemption – gives Blake pronounced affinities with an ethic of fault. Formally, he is the optimist who sees powers of humanity working toward their perfect realization in this world. But materially, as seen in the remarkable deferral of ends that characterizes his work, he is a rigorist who foregrounds the dire psychomachia of fallen humanity. Structural parallels with a Christian scheme of fall and redemption, and the rarity with which his mythic figures attain it, make his a most forbidding humanism.

In the previous section I described the nature of a "right" act in Blake; I turn now to his equally complex vision of "good," his patterns of valuation. What values ought be the objects of acts? The briefest glance at the Blake Concordance reveals that much of his vocabulary is made up of the terminology of moral value.[9] Blake is the most plural of value pluralists. This profusion of values is witness to the ethical character of Romanticism, which I have described in Chapter 2 as the conscious and tormented will to value in an era confronting the impoverishment and imminent collapse of collective value structures. Blakean values are neither random nor lacking in implicit structure. They are scaled in their relatedness one to another in ways that define the Romantic revolution in values and that reveal its internal contradictions.

Three broad categories of value can be discerned in Blake: (1) Values correlative to the "Staminal Virtues" of the "Individual." The enabling virtues are love (Luvah), imagination (Los–Urthona), wisdom (Urizen), and what I term experiential readiness (Tharmas). The Zoas are simultaneously mental agencies and the values sought by these agencies. (2) Social values. These include friendship, benevolence (with such related Christian virtues as sympathy, forgiveness,

[9] A Concordance to the Writings of William Blake, ed. David Erdman, 2 vols. (Ithaca, N. Y.: Cornell University Press, 1967), an indispensable tool for any study of Blake.

generosity, pity), distributive justice (often expressed as wrath), culture (Golgonooza, the city of arts and manufacture), and liberty (Jerusalem). (3) Hedonic values. These are psychological experiences occasioned by exercise of the four staminal virtues. These are the rewards of virtue. Not meritorious in themselves, they are occasioned by merit. These are the values of pleasure (including sex and play), happiness, and joy.

This schema comprehends most values given conspicuous treatment in Blake. They all contribute to the good life characterized, as I have said, by the distinctive Romantic emphasis on self-empowerment and enhanced meaning. One might object that just about anybody subscribes to such values. What distinguishes Blake from anybody else? Who does not approve of culture and love and liberty? But a principal way we come to know an author's sensibility is through the kinds and degrees of commitment made to a range of values in their interrelatedness – or, more simply, through what an author would seek or shun. Or, if authors are to be dismissed, then the patterns of valuing within texts. Chaucer, Shakespeare, Goethe, and Blake give us the sense of a rich plurality of values, even though they controvert them on occasion (as in *The Parsons's Tale, Troilus and Cressida, The Sorrows of Young Werther*, and *The Book of Urizen*). Since a writer as great as Swift can work from an opposing sensibility of exclusion and negation, we cannot tie literary value judgments to such limited criteria as that the author "affirms life" or gives us "God's plenty." (Second-rate writers attempt both.) Still, it is Swift's fierce commitment to some values (clarity, sanity, honesty, self-knowledge) and repudiation of others (the body, speculative intellect, pleasure, imagination, pride in self) that give us the quality of his sensibility, that make us know what is meant by "Swiftean."

There are historical differentia to keep in mind as well. In Blake's day it was no commonplace to affirm the values of imagination, distributive justice, liberty, sex, and joy, not to mention "experiential readiness." Values are as historicized as literary fashion. I think *The Marriage of Heaven and Hell* announces a shift in the history of ethics – not in the sense that it has no antecedents (which would be silly to propose) but in that it announces a synthetic reordering as demarcated in its own ethical and literary spheres as Copernican or Newtonian or Einsteinian reorderings were in the history of science. Blake's manifesto of a new morality lacks the influence of *Philosophiae Naturalis Principia Mathematica* and remains its own universe – his method of production and his irony guaranteeing that it would lack the efficacy also of Thomas Paine's *Common Sense* – but it is echoed independently in varying degrees by others in the visionary company.[10] We come to these writers from the other side of the Romantic revolution in values and may miss its audacity.

Relationships among the three categories of values in Blake confirm one reading of Romantic sensibility. He stresses the "Staminal Virtues" of "Individuality" over all others in making them the giant forms of his mythic narrative. All moral process emanates from and returns to the mental theatre of the individual. Staminal virtues make up one's individuality and militate against another family of virtues, the so-called "herd morality" of Christianity that Nietzsche derides. Though Blake does embrace many Christian virtues, he scorns self-denial – especially in the forms of humility, chastity, and (after childhood) innocence as ignorance. "Pride may love" he writes (AL 586).

Blake's social values confront those of the individual, performing a certain "devouring" function in limiting the self through the neighborhood of other selves. His most concise statement of this comes near the end of *Jerusalem*: "Every kindness to another is a little Death / In the Divine Image nor can Man exist but by Brotherhood" (*J* 96: 27–8). Otherwise "Individuality" would degenerate into "Selfhood," the encrusted, restricted ego in its isolation. The relationship between individual and social values is a changing one in his poetry, but I will be arguing that the former ultimately exert greater force, and that Blakean psychology inhibits full acknowledgment of other lives.

All the major British Romantics value pleasure and happiness, but Blake is most resolute in his celebration of hedonic values. Neither Coleridge nor Wordsworth nor Byron divests himself of a scrupulous reflex regarding them, the fear that we must pay for them, that a negative economy is insidiously at work. Coleridge has laid out a qualitative gradation of pleasures, from the physical to the circumstantial to the intellectual to the spiritual, a gradation that makes *hedone* the sensual sloughbed of pleasure – pleasure for pigs and for people like Hazlitt. Shelley and Byron both express something like this negative valuation of *hedone*, Shelley through insistence on a compensatory spirituality, Byron through the labors of indulgence. Only Keats approaches Blake's esteem of physical pleasure. Both poets see pleasure as coexisting with its contrary, pain, however. And Keats,

---

[10] David Erdman writes that "Blake puts Paine in a class with Jesus as 'worker of miracles,' for he had been able to 'overthrow all the armies of Europe with a small pamphlet,' presumably *Common Sense*. Then why should not Blake try the effect of a small pamphlet – or seize his furious harp? The question reverberates endlessly through *The Four Zoas*" (*Blake: Prophet Against Empire*, 302).

while he does not see a moralistic taint in pleasure to the extent Coleridge and Shelley do, senses a more lamentable problem: its impermanence. Keatsian pleasure has a poignancy missing in Blake, who assures us that nothing in the fabric of time need be lost.

Let us examine these three sets of values more closely, with a view to giving a systematic account of what we normally mean by "Blakean" and how the internal pressures and oppositions within his revolutionary value structure make it something more and other than a blanket affirmation of the manifold of life's opportunities.

Values of the "Individual" are pursued by the Zoas, who form a mental structure in which sensing, feeling, thinking, and imagining are psychodynamically interrelated. In the condition of psychological health, this mental structure is called Eden – a visionary abode which one might describe as homeostatic except that the word implies too great a degree of calm. Eden is a highly activated state of mind, the four mental powers still engaged in the progressive strife of contraries but without the negation of inferior mental states. From the Edenic condition all must occasionally rest: hence the state of mind called Beulah, which is an easing of will in the world of dreams and gentle sexuality. Blake's ethics is self-realizationist in its emphasis on unity. Though some passages in *Jerusalem* and elsewhere seem to reinstate it, Blake objects to mind/body dualism, whether Christian or Cartesian, and he makes Tharmas, as the sensate body, the parent Zoa of the other three. Likewise, Coleridge has objected to Cartesian dualism, proposing in its stead a "Psycho-somatic Ology."

In reductive paraphrases of Blake, there is a tendency to speak of this "Perfect Unity" as an egalitarian roundtable of peaceful beatific Zoas passing bread and wine. But the Immortals are engaged, even in Eden, in "Mental Fight" and "thunderous majesty." Peace is a moral value, but it is found in Beulah, not Eden. If there is equality of value, along with differentiation of function, among the four powers – and many critics assume there is – Blake never makes that clear. What is clear is that narrative movement in the prophecies results from radical imbalance among these powers. Imperatives to seek equality and peace among the Zoas are rare, imperatives to gain power over adversaries are common. In fact, Blake's moral prescriptions favor some powers over others in ways that help illuminate the ethics of Romanticism. I will describe the four primary mental powers – feeling, reason, the senses, and imagination – in terms of their cooperative function in the psyche and of Blake's moral valuation of them, one relative to another.

Though the New Humanists think the Romantics indiscriminately value feeling over reason, the myth of *The Four Zoas* begins with the premise that feeling can put us in moral jeopardy, confirming Coleridge's view that there are "wrong feelings." I have mentioned that the original Fall is portrayed as the usurpation by Luvah (feeling) of the horses of Urizen. Urizen cooperates in his own deposition by getting drunk on Luvah's wine. He has his own ambition of supplanting Los-Urthona and sees emotional chaos as the means of subverting imagination. This version of the reason/energy warfare instructively blocks the conclusion, derived from cursory readings of *The Marriage of Heaven and Hell*, that energy's subversion of reason is intrinsically meritorious. In the larger myth reason and energy are related through what Schiller calls mutual subordination, and this subversion becomes the source of the Fall. Enacting the entire emotional spectrum from love to hate, Luvah is potentially the "mildest of the Zoas," but he causes the greatest torment if he is mispositioned in the psyche.

Luvah's complex entanglement with the other Zoas shows that emotion takes on determinate value only in its relatedness to other mental powers. When cast by Urizen into his own furnaces, where he howls in pain and rage, Luvah is improperly subordinated, and expresses himself in prurience, torment, and ill health, smiting Albion with boils. Blake thus portrays the psychology of repression. But in Night the Ninth we learn that Luvah should literally learn his place. Awakened and frowning, Albion says:

> Luvah & Vala henceforth you are Servants obey & live
> You shall forget your former state return O love in peace
> Into your place the place of seed not in the brain or heart
> If Gods combine against Man Setting their Dominion above
> The Human form Divine. Thrown down from their high Station
> In the Eternal heavens of Human Imagination: buried beneath
> In dark oblivion with incessant pangs ages on ages
> In Enmity & war first weakend then in stern repentance
> They must renew their brightness & their disorganizd functions
> Again reorganize till they resume the image of the human
> Cooperating in the bliss of Man obeying his Will
> Servants to the infinite & Eternal of the Human form[.]
> (*FZ* 126: 6–17).

The "Gods" are the "Mighty Ones" or Zoas, and this is the story of Blake's visionary epic. It is Luvah who subsequently announces in response to this diagnosis the closest to the moral of the piece: "Attempting to be more than Man We become less" (*FZ* 135: 21). Applied to the Zoas as components of the psyche, this statement invokes the model of structural propriety; cooperative powers know

184

their place and function, but for the sake of increased power of the whole.

The word "love" occurs with such frequency in Blake that we might suppose it envelops all other values. But he knows, just as Oothoon discovers, that love is not enough, and that it can be even "Enough, or Too Much." In contrast to Shelley and Coleridge, Blake sees love as an expression more of feeling than of imagination. As the highest manifestation of Luvah, love converts easily into a variety of opposites. The word "love" is found in conjunction with "envy," "excrementitious," "fear," "jealousy," "pride," "sadness," "rage," "war," "wrath," not to mention "despair," "deceit," and especially "hate." There exists a "love that kills its beloved" (*J* 48: 16).

In short, love is merely the greatest of the emotions. As the most volatile of the Zoas, Luvah is the most vulnerable, least reliable, but also least guilty. Because his nature is instability, the discriminating Albion thinks him less guilty than Urizen, to whom he cries: "My anger against thee is greater than against this Luvah" (*FZ* 120: 41); and earlier, "Thy brother Luvah hath smitten me but pity thou his youth" (*FZ* 23: 7). The Romantics are hardly alone in thinking the crimes of passion less blameworthy than those of calculation.

Love's place in the ideal human form is the loins, where Orc, its fallen representative, exercises sexual power. Luvah's close association with nature – the world of generation and its vegetative cycles – explains his instability. His emanation is Vala, who in her fallen condition is the shadowy female, inarticulate and imprisoning yet seductive also, voraciously receptive of Orc's impregnating rape. As the fallen natural world, Vala embodies the natural biological process which makes human beings prisoners of their passions. She is the female aspect of Luvah's overthrow of Albionic order, who in seducing Albion begins the process of self-division. Luvah's "Reasoning from the loins" (*FZ* 28: 2) is under the sway of materiality, vegetative growth, and impersonal sexual energy. He is most susceptible to nature's "dishumanizing" power.

Because his roots are fixed in passion and inarticulate natural process, love must take on understanding and cease to be blind. Coleridge and Shelley conceive a union of love with understanding, Coleridge saying that love makes one "think," Shelley that "Love is like understanding, that grows bright, / Gazing on many truths." In Blake's myth, Luvah must unite with Urizen, though ultimately both yield to Los-Urthona.

Wisdom, the highest manifestation of understanding, is the virtue of the unfallen Urizen, who upon ascending to an Edenic condition is no longer the aged Nobodaddy, the repressive deity of bad conscience: "Then glorious bright Exulting in his joy / He sounding rose into the heavens in naked majesty / In radiant Youth" (FZ 121: 30–2). In arguing against a reading of Blake as anti-intellectual, critics tend to argue backwards from this Edenic perspective. It must imply something, however, that Urizen is, in most of his appearances, the villain. In his fallen condition he represents, among other things, the overvaluation of discursive or scientific reason. Hostility to this mental power reveals a reactive component within the Romantic revolution of values. With a degree of prophetic insight, Blake connects discursive reason with the Satanic mills of the new industrialism, with the treatment of persons as if they were things and commodities, and with the debilitating assumption that mind is only matter in motion. But it is a limit to his modernity that, short of its Edenic rehabilitation, Blake disesteems this power.

In his fallen condition, Urizen represents the moral negatives of guilt, prudence, doubt, hypocrisy, temperance, pride, selfishness, and tyranny. He practices what is worst in Hebraic ethics, the prohibitions of the Decalogue, and in Classical ethics, the four Greek virtues, "Temperance, Prudence, Justice, Fortitude, the four pillars of tyranny" (M 29: 49). This is such a compendium of negation that the correlative virtue, wisdom, must be powerful indeed if it is to reverse it all.

Blake does not, however, portray wisdom in persons or acts. He finds it difficult, perhaps, to conceive what form beyond "radiant Youth" the unfallen Urizen would assume, so imbalanced has the mythic narrative been toward his negative form. Most talk of wisdom is in the ironic mode. The Devil's "Proverbs of Hell" "shew the nature of Infernal wisdom better than any description of buildings or garments." Such proverbs as "The road of excess leads to the palace of wisdom," "The wrath of the lion is the wisdom of God," and "The tygers of wrath are wiser than the horses of instruction" reverse conventional wisdom through paradox, linking wisdom with passionate commitment and imprudence. These paradoxes do not tell us what wisdom is, beyond its oppositional function. When Urizen attempts to tell us, he speaks unwisdom: "Here alone I in books formd of metals / Have written the secrets of wisdom." But secrecy is a negative for Blake, and this infernal wisdom is merely the opposite of the Devil's in that it urges the very "one Law" which is oppression (BU 4: 24–5). Similarly, Urizen's address to his daughters in Night the Seventh, "Listen to the Words of Wisdom," is the precise reverse of the Blakean ethic:

So shall [ye] govern over all let Moral Duty tune your tongue
But be your hearts harder than the nether millstone
. . .
Compell the poor to live upon a Crust of bread by soft mild arts
Smile when they frown frown when they smile & when a man looks pale
With labour & abstinence say he looks healthy & happy
And when his children sicken let them die there are enough
Born even too many & our Earth will be overrun
Without these arts.   (*FZ* 80: 2–4, 9–14)

This is the "wisdom" of Malthus, who, as Shelley and Hazlitt agree, is unmatched in his folly.

Enion's lament at the end of Night the Second tells us more directly about the nature of wisdom:

What is the price of Experience do men buy it for a song
Or wisdom for a dance in the street? No it is bought with the price
Of all that a man hath his house his wife his children
Wisdom is sold in the desolate market where none come to buy
And in the witherd field where the farmer plows for bread in vain
                                             (*FZ* 35: 11–15)

Wisdom is gained through suffering and injustice. Unlike the intuitional power of imagination or the immediate powers of the senses and feelings, it is acquired over time and through experience. "Understanding or Thought is not natural to Man it is acquired by means of Suffering & Distress i.e. Experience. Will, Desire, Love, Rage, Envy, & all other Affections are Natural. but Understanding is Acquired" (*PWB* 602). Urizen's emanation, Ahania, seems to represent intellectual pleasure, the eunoia of Coleridge's hedonic schema, and not wisdom more generally, as is sometimes claimed. When Urizen is transformed to radiant youth in Night the Ninth, Ahania falls down dead (temporarily!), still unable to join in living harmony with Urizen. The import of this anti-climactic moment is the great difficulty Blake has in conceiving reason united with pleasure. This is yet more evidence that, relative to other human powers, Blake devalues this King of the Zoas. Like Luvah, Urizen is all the more threatening to Los-Urthona when he is approaching Edenic rehabilitation, error consolidating before its final purge.

Variously identified by critics as the senses, the body, instinct, the will, and life itself, Tharmas in his moral dimension is what I have called experiential readiness. Whereas Urizen is the bitter result of experience, Tharmas is the precondition of it, the initial willingness to immerse in the dangerous element. He is, I will argue, the Byronic Zoa.

In *The Four Zoas* he is literally the parent power, which tells us that for Blake the body is the precondition of consciousness. Since Jungians argue the discontinuous nature of the sensate personality, or at least of the "extroverted sensation type," they might express surprise that Blake links the sensate component of the psyche with will. He implies that the senses, if "enlarged" and renovated, sustain individual will, the power of self-continuity. Tharmas in effect clarifies the logic of Oothoon, who intelligently points out that the senses do not define us as human: all creatures – chickens, pigeons, bees, mice, and frogs – have "Eyes and ears and sense of touch," but "their habitations. / And their pursuits" are "as different as their forms and their joys" (*VDA* 3: 5–6). The senses do not suffice to make us human, but they are a necessary condition of it. To be placed in the human body is already to be placed in a moral situation, for each of the senses is a power that can be used or abused, narrowed or enlarged. Contrary to Wordsworth's famous line, the eye *can* choose to see: "The fool sees not the same tree that a wise man sees." These "Five windows" that "light the cavern'd Man" permit us to "pass out" of ourselves, to see in nature a benevolent friend. They become petrified against the infinite if the will is weak. Of touch, identified with sex, Blake writes that through it one may "himself pass out what time he please, but he will not; / For stolen joys are sweet, & bread eaten in secret pleasant" (*EP* iii: 1–6). If the senses narrow to reflexive nerve endings, their transitive power is lost and human will unstrung. When the eye looks "outward to self," individuality has dissolved into impotent selfhood. The fallen Tharmas is chaos, the sea. Partially regenerated in Night the Ninth, his state is Beulah, the pre-experiential landscape from which Thel wishes, but does not will, to escape.

Tharmas is the prime mover of the four Zoas, issuing imperatives to rebuild and choose life. The alliance of Tharmas with Los-Urthona to repair the damage done by the "ambition" or "pride" of Urizen and Luvah defines the moral contours of *The Four Zoas*. The reason/passion conflict is superseded by a principle of regeneration that is both higher and more fundamental – imagination working through the power of the sensate body. It is largely these two powers that lead the way to a new order in the self. In allying himself with Tharmas and in fulfilling his imperative to choose life, Los-Urthona supersedes both Orc-Luvah as the regenerative power (Orc becomes at this point merely generative) and Urizen as the ordering power.

Blake conceives not an egalitarian society of psychological powers but an organized interdependency of functions, wherein some exert greater force on the totality than others, differences in kind predicating differences in degree. In making the body the parent power and prime mover, he follows out the denial of mind/body dualism. "Man has no Body distinct from his Soul for that calld Body is a portion of Soul discernd by the five Senses," he had written in *The Marriage of Heaven and Hell*. In *The Four Zoas* there is a more radical urging of the body's centrality. His sea mackerel-crowded, Tharmas embodies the life force even when Urizen's black bile infects him. "The body of Man is given to me I seek in vain to destroy / For still it surges forth in fish & monsters of the deeps" (*FZ* 69: 11–12). Tharmas is a clearer analogue of Schopenhauer's will, an unconscious life force expressed through the body, than is the Coleridgean will, which is an unconscious force deeper than the body and the source of individuality and evil. Blake's linkage of primal power with the body has a biological modernity lacking in the Coleridgean will, which has its roots in a theological notion of self ontologically prior to the body. Much of Coleridge's inability to go as far as Blake in renovation of the body is attitudinal, for he otherwise knows too well the profound interconnection of physical and mental functions. He knows it more sorrowfully than Blake, whose addiction is, after all, to cleansing work rather than to opium.

It is curious and disappointing that Tharmas, one of Blake's most original figures, is lost sight of in *Milton* and *Jerusalem*. Whatever the cause, his disappearance is symptomatic of the increasing degree of mentalism in these prophecies. The Zoa of sense and body follows Urizen and Luvah in yielding to Los-Urthona, as Blake veers more and more toward an imperialism of the imagination.

Just as Urizen is usually the villain, so Los-Urthona is usually Blake's hero. It is he who initiates apocalypse in Night the Ninth:

> Los his vegetable hands
> Outstretched his right hand branching out in fibrous Strength
> Siezd the Sun. His left hand like dark roots coverd the Moon
> And tore them down cracking the heavens across from immense to
>   immense
> Then fell the fires of Eternity with loud & shrill
> Sound of Loud Trumpet thundering along from heaven to heaven
> A mighty sound articulate Awake ye dead & come
> To judgment from the four winds Awake & Come away[.]
>
> (*FZ* 117: 6–13)

Los is no aesthete. Tharmas may be the parent power, but Los or imagination functions synecdochically here as fully realized humanity. Though he is often infected by Urizen and other mighty opposites, he is a perdurable force. "Imagination," unlike "love," dominates its opposition. "Jesus considerd Imagination to be the Real Man" (*PWB*

189

663); "For All Things Exist in the Human Imagination" (*J* 69: 25); "The Imagination is not a State: it is the Human Existence itself" (*M* 32: 32); "The Eternal Body of Man is The IMAGINATION" (*PWB* 273). As a moral value, imagination has ascendency over love. *The Marriage of Heaven and Hell* anticipates the coalescence of Tharmas and Los-Urthona: "If the doors of perception were cleansed every thing would appear to man as it is, infinite." By means of the senses and renovated body, Los draws the line of permanent "Individuality," the human form, uniting art and ethics. If Urizen is the consequence of experience, Tharmas the precondition of it, and Luvah the feeling attachment (cathexis) to experience, Los-Urthona is its organization and the arbiter of human purpose. Northrop Frye suggests he might be "called work, or constructive activity."[11] He will be, therefore, the Keatsian Zoa. As Coleridge would say, this "esemplastic" and "coadunating" power can do for the self what it does for art, bringing disparate parts and contraries into living form and unity.

By means of the four Zoas in their interrelatedness, Blake structures a scale of value corresponding to a scale of power within the psyche. The alignment of imagination and the sensate body supersedes the conflict of reason and energy, seen most clearly in the contrast between *America A Prophecy* (1795) and *The Four Zoas*. The earlier work pits Orc (the American colonies, George Washington) against Urizen (England, George III), as well-defined polarities of insurrection and repression, with Washington the somewhat improbable incarnation of Orc, whose fires leave "the females naked and glowing with the lusts of youth." The more complex myth of *The Four Zoas* internalizes this opposition as a dynamic of psychological integration but expands the mental theatre. The imagination is the mental capacity that lends our life narrative its shape and purpose; as the defining line of our individuality and unique "lineaments," it is our "integrity," or what in common parlance is called our "sense of self." That it builds on the power of the sensate body is Blake's advance over discussion of identity in his day. He anticipates the modern view that personal identity (Blake's "Individuality") must include the continuity of the body as well as of consciousness.[12]

Blake's ultimate privileging of imagination and the sensate body is revolutionary in itself. A contrast between him and Mary Wollstonecraft – of particular interest because they share radical politics and

---

[11] "Blake's Treatment of the Archetype," *English Institute Essays 1950*, ed. Alan S. Downer (New York: Columbia University Press, 1951), 171.

[12] See Terence Penelhum's interesting synoptic essay, "Personal Identity," in *The Encyclopedia of Philosophy*, ed. Paul Edwards, 8 vols. (New York: Macmillan, 1967).

because of Wollstonecraft's probable influence on *Visions of the Daughters of Albion* – shows the reordering he effects relative to late Enlightenment thought. In *A Vindication of the Rights of Woman* (1792) Wollstonecraft urges extension of Enlightenment values to the one-half of the human race overlooked by proponents of the "universal" rights of man. She attacks Rousseau, especially his *Emile*, on the grounds that most of what he regards as "natural" in women – quick sensibility, delicacy, fondness for dress, compliance, heated imagination, and a lesser donation of reason – is artificially imposed by the male-dominated social structure. There is no natural "sex in souls," or virtue apportioned by gender. Stylized feminine behavior such as coquetry issues from the need to establish a degree of power within a lesser sphere, achieved through cunning. At best, women are today possessed of the "negative virtues only" – "patience, docility, good-humour, and flexibility"[13] – which resembles Blake's contempt of hypocritical pity, humility, and mildness. In an adumbration of Marxist methodology, she will attack "not the superstructure, but the foundation" of the character of oppressed women – seeking the cause, not condemning the symptoms (p. 24). In finding a parallel between the social oppression of soldiers and that of women – even down to behavioral similarities such as attentiveness "to their persons," and fondness "of dancing, crowded rooms, adventures, and ridicule" – Wollstonecraft works on the principle that "character," comprising both manners and morals, is determined by norms of the collective. Socio-political structures determine consciousness, and not, as the Romantics from Blake to Keats believe, the other way around.

Human beings are placed on earth, she says, to "unfold their faculties," which is similar to Blake's comment about rousing "the faculties to act," but Wollstonecraft has a qualitatively different conception of the ideal ordering of these faculties. For her the ideal psyche is an Enlightenment construct. It is governed by "Reason," which establishes our "pre-eminence over the brute creation" and from which "knowledge and virtue naturally flow . . . if mankind be viewed collectively" (p. 12). In discussing the cult of sensibility, she attacks some assumptions that carry over, modified, to Romanticism. The "passions" are, she thinks, implanted in order that "man by struggling with them might attain a degree of knowledge." She grants them little intrinsic value, and holds the Enlightenment virtue of friendship over that of love: "to restrain this tumultuous passion, and to prove that it should not be allowed to dethrone superior powers, or to usurp the

---

[13] *A Vindication of the Rights of Woman*, ed. Carol H. Poston (New York: W. W. Norton, 1975), 58.

sceptre which the understanding should ever cooly wield," does not offend against "common sense" (p. 27). Her allusions to "imagination" are mostly in the context of phantom-chasing: "I own it frequently happens that women who have fostered a romantic unnatural delicacy of feeling, waste their lives in *imagining* how happy they should have been with a husband who could love them with a fervid increasing affection every day, and all day" (p. 33). One passage sounds like an indictment of what the New Humanists take to be the core of Romanticism:

The lively heated imagination . . . draws the picture of love, as it draws every other picture, with those glowing colours, which the daring hand will steal from the rainbow that is directed by a mind, condemned in a world like this, to prove its noble origin by panting after unattainable perfection; ever pursuing what it acknowledges to be a fleeting dream. An imagination of this vigorous cast can give existence to insubstantial forms, and stability to the shadowy reveries which the mind naturally falls into when realities are found vapid (p. 74).

It follows that Wollstonecraft is wary of "novels, poetry, and gallantry," all which "tend to make women the creatures of sensation" (p. 61).

Blake has preserved the notion of unfolding faculties but has radically readjusted the mental hierarchy, has complicated the psychology of sex and gender, and has by implication raised the question, endemic to Romanticism, of whether a philosophy of augmented individual consciousness can substantiate an activist, socially oriented ethics. As if taking on Wollstonecraft's rather staid dance of faculties, he chastens "reason" by "imagination," now the ordering principle of the psyche. Although he too would qualify the entitlements of love, he thinks the passions and energy that give birth to them ought not be "cooled," but heightened, refined, and used. And as for "sensation," he anchors our very being in it as the precondition of consciousness and life. Both the Enlightenment and the Romantic conception of mind can predicate a feminism, but Wollstonecraft's feminism is based on class analysis and a belief in social progress through practical reason. Blake's feminism in *Visions* is a momentarily despairing one occasioned by private vision of a high order that tragically confronts those who are unteachable. Blake has dramatized the problem of socializing vision, of conveying a private illumination to others. In breaking down the Enlightenment mental hierarchy and reordering the self in organic self-containment – wherein individual consciousness is said to shape its own internal order and its own

visionary world – Blake makes unavailable to himself the Enlightenment's particular insights into social institutions, class, and the relationship of collective to private consciousness. More sympathetic to
Enlightenment values, Shelley will attempt a joining of private imaginative vision with Enlightenment social awareness.

Turning now to consideration of social values in Blake, we see how
his mythology of the self, even because of its profundity, makes
problematic the extension of self to social world. We find, first, the
seeming paradox of Romantic authors: Blake favors individuality,
liberty, and even a certain ruthlessness about obtaining them, but
unlike "Individuality," the word "self" is often a negative. "The Clod
and the Pebble" states the dilemma: both the love that "seeketh not
Itself to please" and the love that "seeketh only Self to please" are
partial. The first in its passivity allows one to be stomped on, the
second, in binding "another to its delight," violates individuality and
takes inappropriate joy in it. When Milton descends from Eden, he
cries, "I in my Selfhood am that Satan: I am that Evil One!" (*M* 14: 30).
In his grand summation in Book the Second, he calls the Selfhood a
"false Body," the "spectre," the "reasoning Power," which is "an
Incrustation over my Immortal / Spirit" (*M* 40: 34–6). It must be
cleansed by "Self-examination":

> To bathe in the Waters of Life; to wash off the Not Human
> I come in Self-annihilation & the grandeur of Inspiration[.]

> (*M* 41: 1–2)

"Self-annihilation" is always positive, "Selfhood" always negative.
"Self" can be used, though, in a positive sense: while Milton is casting
off Selfhood in the Ulro, "His real and immortal Self: was as appeard to
those / Who dwell in immortality, as One sleeping on a couch / Of
gold" (*M* 15: 11–12).

To the point of numbness, a perennial problem in ethics is how self-
love can join with friendship and love, with social and political
commitment. We have seen that eighteenth-century moralists such as
Butler, setting about their obligatory task of refuting Hobbes, assure
that self-love and benevolence need not be in conflict, as long as self-
love is "cool" and within bounds. But their reconciliation is too
notional and non-dialectical for the Romantics, whose concept of self is
greatly augmented at the same time that their experience of love and
revolution seems genuinely more turbulent.

Blake's mythic grammar provides a means of uniting interests of self
and other: the "emanation." Morally considered, the emanation is the
social component of the psyche. "Man is adjoind to Man by his

193

Emanative portion: / Who is Jerusalem in every Individual Man: and her / Shadow is Vala" (*J* 39: 38–40). The emanations of the Zoas are dangerous and willful when separate, but in order fully to exist as emanations they must by definition *be* separate. Blake's vision of how they behave in Eden has a comic domesticity. Observes Los:

> When in Eternity Man converses with Man they enter
> Into each others Bosom (which are Universes of delight)
> In mutual interchange. and first their Emanations meet
> Surrounded by their Children. if they embrace & comingle
> The Human Four-fold Forms mingle also in thunders of Intellect
> But if the Emanations mingle not; with storms & agitations
> Of earthquakes & consuming fires they roll apart in fear
> For Man cannot unite with Man but by their Emanations
> Which stand both Male & Female at the Gates of each Humanity[.]
>
> (*J* 88: 3–11)

This family portrait provides a rare moment of domestic harmony, for much more frequently, in fallen reality, the emanations deceive, lure, reject, berate, disappear, and create those earthquakes and consuming fires among people. They are in keeping with a bitter edge in Blake's view of human relationships. Like Coleridge and Wollstonecraft, he greatly admires the idea of friendship, valuing it over love in some respects. Yet in his most directly autobiographical passage we hear: "O God, protect me from my friends, that they have not power over me / Thou hast giv'n me power to protect myself from my bitterest enemies" (*M* 9: 5–6).

Friendship has allure for Blake because it promises companionship without the "binding" that love threatens. Whereas love is the province of Luvah, friendship is the province of the qualitatively higher Zoa, Los-Urthona. Someone of Edenic vision sees the world as "a human form, a friend with whom he livd benevolent" (*M* 15: 27). The moral progress of individuals depends on friends: "for a Man Can only Reject Error by the Advice of a Friend or by the Immediate Inspiration of God" (*VLJ* 563). Friendship is the human being's most characteristic emanation, his or her protective environment: "The bird a nest, the spider a web, man friendship" (*MHH* 18). But Blake, his mind dominated by contraries, sees friendship in terms of betrayal. His patron Hayley's friendship, which had promised mutual benefits, is a deceit, an exploitative binding. In one of Blake's more extended linear narratives, the Bard in *Milton* mythologizes Hayley's (Satan's) insensitive exploitation, Blake's accusation, and Hayley's counter-accusation (*M* 7–10). Because friendship immediately calls up the spectre of betrayal, forgiveness is its coefficient. Though it is more difficult to forgive friends than enemies, the "severe contentions of friendship" require forgiveness. "Rousseau thought Men Good by Nature; he found them Evil & found no friend. Friendship cannot exist without Forgiveness of Sins continually" (*J* 52). Blake implies everywhere that there is a cloud of unknowing separating persons. Enemies assume the cloak of "mildness," seeming to be friends. The test of friendship is the willingness to die for it, hence few friends are to be found, and "Half Friendship is the bitterest Enmity said Los / As he entered the Door of Death" (*J* 1).

Implicit in his treatment of friendship and other social values is questioning of a power Coleridge, Hazlitt, Shelley, and Keats bring into new prominence: the sympathetic imagination. Despite the sentiments of the early "On Another's Sorrow," in Blake this power tends to act either as weak acquiescence or as violent usurpation. In the first case, we lose individuality through false and condescending pity, or through submission to a stronger or more attractive being. One of the common refrains of the prophecies is, "They become what they behold": an enervating enslavement to alien powers, quite unlike Keats's experience with the Nightingale. "Strucken with Albions disease they become what they behold; / They assimilate with Albion in pity & compassion" (*J* 39: 32–3). "Pity divides the Soul," he warns time and again. Pity is another of those values that can be either positive or negative. (When reading Blake we are called on to distinguish between true pity and false, true reason and false, and even good evil and bad evil.) Vicariousness, so strong an impulse in Coleridge, threatens self-division and heteronomy in Blake.

The Zoa-emanation structure in fact implies that full individuality is achieved only when the emanations have returned home and been absorbed. An egocentrism, or, with an eye to the influence of Boehme, a centripetalism is structurally embedded in Blake's key metaphor. It militates against the Coleridgean view that we know ourselves only by way of knowing another. To be sure, Blake writes that

> Man subsists by Brotherhood & Universal Love
> We fall on one anothers necks more closely we embrace
> Not for ourselves but for the Eternal family we live
> Man liveth not by Self alone but in his brothers face.
>
> (*FZ* 133: 22–5).

But the mechanism of communality – the ego/emanation structure – obstructs that direct, gentle, and enriching extension of self to another manifested in "This Lime-tree Bower My Prison" and "Frost at Midnight."

When the self is extended outward in strength, it often works violence on the object of its "sympathy." Most transforming conjunctions in Blake's works are violent, and if his mythic figures do not recognize and prepare for violence, they may be, like Thel, overwhelmed and deflected by it. The paradigmatic act of sympathetic engagement is violent sexuality. The invisible worm's "dark secret love" in "The Sick Rose" (a nightmare in eight lines) destroys the rose on her bed of crimson joy; this is an act of negation. But violent sexuality also initiates positive transformation and has the power of productive contrariety. Bromion's rape of Oothoon transfigures her into higher vision; Orc's ravishment of the nameless shadowy female – "Round the terrific loins he seiz'd the panting struggling womb" – gives her language.

Tharmas, the stud among the four Zoas, takes a willing Enion violently, conceiving Los and Enitharmon in the beginning of Blake's epic:

Opening his rifted rocks mingling together they join in burning anguish
Mingling his horrible darkness with her tender limbs then high she soared
Shrieking above the ocean: a bright wonder that nature shuddered at
Half Woman & half beast all his darkly waving colours mix
With her fair crystal clearness in her lips & cheeks his metals rose
In blushes like the morning & his rocky features softning
A wonder lovely in the heavens or wandring on the earth
With female voice warbling upon the hollow vales
Beauty all blushing with desire a self enjoying wonder.[14]   (FZ 143: 1–9)

This mutual transformation, in which Tharmas is impregnated with Enion's softness as she is literally impregnated by him, comes as an act of violence originating in death, "trembling fear," and Tharmas's repressed rage at finding his signal organ, the tongue, shut off in inarticulateness. He is more abrupt when without ceremony; he abducts Enitharmon, his daughter, after Los has challenged his authority in this small matter of rebuilding the universe:

my will shall be my Law
So Saying in a Wave he rap'd bright Enitharmon far
Apart from Los. but coverd her with softest brooding care
On a broad wave in the warm west. balming her bleeding wound[.]
(FZ 49: 3–6)

[14] I follow here the text of p. 143 in the manuscript of *The Four Zoas*, which, prior to the latest edition of Blake's poetry, was assumed to represent a revision of p. 6 of that manuscript. Even if, as the editor David Erdman now believes, this passage does not have the status of Blake's final revision, it is poetically superior to the version printed in the 1982 edition.

Though "rap'd" here probably means "abducted" and though the separation of any emanation from a Zoa may result in a bleeding psychic wound, the image remains one of sexual violence.

Sympathetic imagination is implicit too in Los's violent engagement with Urizen in *The Book of Urizen* and Milton's with Urizen in *Milton*. Each antagonist to a degree becomes the other, in a desperate struggle that is, in the strict sense, sympathetic:

> Silent they met, and silent strove among the streams, of Arnon
> Even to Mahanaim, when with cold hand Urizen stoop'd down
> And took up water from the river Jordan: pouring on
> To Miltons brain the icy fluid from his broad cold palm.
> But Milton took of the red clay of Succoth, moulding it with care
> Between his palms; and filling up the furrows of many years
> Beginning at the feet of Urizen, and on the bones
> Creating new flesh on the Demon cold, and building him,
> As with new clay a Human form in the Valley of Beth Peor.
>
> (*M* 19: 6–14).

In this great passage, Milton fashions the human form, doing a somewhat better job of it than Los had when he created a grotesque, "petrific" Urizen. Milton becomes what he beholds, too, though in this case what he beholds, a rehumanized Urizen, is worth becoming.

More than any other Romantic author – and none is basically sentimental about human relationships – Blake sees in the sympathetic merging of individuals an imperialistic conflict of will that agitates nerves and spills blood, but that may also yield new flesh and increased humanity. "Opposition is true Friendship," he writes in *The Marriage of Heaven and Hell*, well before he learns the bitterness this entails. The companionable is rarely portrayed by this poet "who is very much delighted with being in good Company."

Social and political injustice for Blake has roots in the moral relationships of individuals: "Those who are cast out [of heaven] Are All Those who having no Passions of their own because No Intellect. Have spent their lives in Curbing & Governing other Peoples by the Various arts of Poverty & Cruelty of all kinds" (*VLJ* 564). Injustice must first be redressed in individual morality. Benevolence and distributive justice – for Shelley the cardinal virtues – are represented in the mythic figures Palamabron and Rintrah respectively. Benevolence as a virtue often takes the form of pity, and as the embodiment of pity Palamabron exhibits refinement and mildness directly proportionate to his weakness in defending his case. Rintrah responds to injustice with wrath, which is cleansing and righteous but which does not result in a program of political revolution or reform.

The values of both benevolence and distributive justice are expressed in a subgenre, the lament, the finest examples of which are found in *Songs of Innocence and of Experience* and *The Four Zoas*. Pity, wrath, and lamentation all strongly register injustice but do not broach strategies of social and political change. There is such lucidity and power in Blake's poetry dealing with poverty and oppression, that one wonders whether he may not be the greater poet when direct moral comment takes precedence over mythic narration. "Holy Thursday" and "The Chimney Sweeper" in both innocence and experience, "The Little Black Boy," "The Garden of Love," "London," and "The Human Abstract" express pity and wrath, contained within the artifice and puzzlements of irony. How can things be this way? these poems ask, pointing out manifest contradictions of wealth and poverty, power and impotence. "London" and "The Human Abstract" find in human psychology – its "mind-forg'd manacles" – the genetic explanation of social injustice. The poison tree that grows in the human brain bears fruit in chimney sweepers, prostitutes, soldiers, priests, and kings. Like Wollstonecraft before them, Marx and Engels will reverse this diagnosis, arguing that the larger socio-economic system creates the debased psychology. It is characteristic of the Romantics to think psychological and moral factors give rise to institutional and political malaise; this is, many would say, a limitation to their politics.

Whatever the relative sophistication of Blake's political thought, it is clear he acknowledges the priority of ethics to politics as well as their continuity. Political reform begins with moral recognition. The strongest moral testimony in *The Four Zoas* is given by Enion, who as the emanation of sensate body (Tharmas) has her eye on the fine bitter detail of human suffering. Her laments at the close of Nights the First and Second register natural injustice and social injustice respectively:

Why does the Raven cry aloud and no eye pities her?
Why fall the Sparrow & the Robin in the foodless winter?
Faint! shivering they sit on leafless bush, or frozen stone

Wearied with seeking food across the snowy waste; the little
Heart cold; and the little tongue consum'd, that once in thoughtless joy
Gave songs of gratitude to waving corn fields round their nest.
(*FZ* 17: 2–7; quoted in part)

The second lament is a gain in irony and analysis:

It is an easy thing to talk of patience to the afflicted
To speak the laws of prudence to the houseless wanderer

198

To listen to the hungry ravens cry in wintry season
When the red blood is filld with wine & with the marrow of lambs.

It is an easy thing, cries Enion,

To hear sounds of love in the thunder storm that destroys
    our enemies house
To rejoice in the blight that covers his field, & the sickness that
    cuts off his children
While our olive & vine sing & laugh round our door & our children
    bring fruits & flowers[.]   (*FZ* 35: 18–19; 36: 1–2, 6–8; quoted in part)

Pity and wrath are mediated by an irony powerful as literature but impotent as politics in that it registers injustice as unalterable fact. Enion's perspective is limited – as are all perspectives outside Eden – and the epic thereafter moves beyond lament toward a new order. Beyond moral recognition there is need of revolutionary action.

The very priority of moral to political transformation in Blake's Lambeth poems underscores the uncertain status that politics has in his larger mythic structure. I think politics offers no sanctions of its own for Blake. Rather, it gains its authority from other value structures, principally ethical: to put it baldly, ethical in *The Four Zoas*, ethico-artistic in *Milton*, and ethico-religious in *Jerusalem*. This is tantamount to saying that Blake does not formulate a political *structure* as such. (It is only in a poet of Blake's scope that we might even look for such a formulation.)

In the early prophecies an ethics of individualism and energy leads to an insurrectional politics: the state must yield to the self's anarchistic drive for freedom. The power of ethics to dictate politics culminates in *The Four Zoas*. The priority of ethics to politics, and their continuity – whether or not it takes the form of anarchism – is, we saw in Chapter 2, the keynote of Romantic politics of the left. *The Four Zoas* is an epic of the self in which moral awakening resounds outwardly in the abolition of slavery, humanization of commerce, freedom of the press, and punishment of oppressors. An ethics of individualism empowers and sanctions an insurrectional politics.

The place of politics in *Milton* is much debated. The question tends to be misconstrued as an either/or – as whether art or politics is paramount in Milton's descent to complete the work he has left undone. But art *is* both moral and political for Blake. It does not promise a retreat into ideal structures or a merely "private apocalypse." The prophecy that Milton will fulfill is to "set free / Orc from his Chain of Jealousy" (*M* 20: 60–1), which means to initiate political revolution. Even if we acknowledge this essential link between art and politics in Blake, we find his politics empowered and sanctioned by another value system, here the values of poetry or art.

In *Jerusalem* many passages are indebted to a Christian ethics that undercuts the belligerence of the early prophecies: "The Spirit of Jesus is continual forgiveness of sin . . . I am perhaps the most sinful of men!" "We who dwell on Earth can do nothing of ourselves, every thing is conducted by Spirits, no less than Digestion or Sleep" (*J* 3); "O Saviour pour upon me thy Spirit of meekness & love (*J* 5: 21); "O point of mutual forgiveness between Enemies!" (*J* 7: 66); "But Vengeance is the destroyer of Grace & Repentance in the bosom / Of the Injurer: in which the Divine Lamb is cruelly slain: / Descend O Lamb of God & take away the imputation of Sin" (*J* 25: 10–12) – all these from Chapter I alone. In a reversal of earlier works, "pity" in a majority of cases now has a positive valuation, "wrath" a negative. More than the two earlier prophecies, *Jerusalem* emphasizes social values: the values of benevolence, friendship, self-sacrifice. These prevail over both the individualistic values of the earlier prophecies and the political values originating in individualism. (Hazlitt's development, by the way, takes precisely the reverse order.) Individualism, which finds in insurrectionism the most clearcut of political actions, generates the most uncertain of political structures. But a set of social values, as in *Jerusalem*, does not in itself specify a particular political structure and means of effecting it. Blake never makes clear what political structure, if any, he envisions on the other side of a revolutionary situation.

This view oversimplifies Blake's political development. There are many passages in *Jerusalem* that are survivors of the days of wrath, and Erin, the new figure of political revolution, representing Ireland's struggle for independence, emerges as the vanguard of a new period of wars of liberation. But the larger contours of Blake's prophecies still suggest that the ethics of individualism generates the insurrectional and anarchistic politics of *The Four Zoas*; the mingling of art and ethics in *Milton* prepares for such an insurrection, although not yet achieved; and the quasi-Christian ethics of *Jerusalem* leads to a millennialism that largely bypasses the need for political action per se. In all cases, the character of Blake's politics is determined by value systems independent of and prior to it – art, religion, and especially ethics.

The omission of a post-revolutionary political structure is consistent with the absence in Blake's prophetic books of a strong sense of a plurality of persons. A strangely non-dramatic quality attends his perspectivism and dialectical vision, despite the social values of *Jerusalem*. As a poet creating a myth of psychological process – portraying agencies more than agents, and perceiving friendship, love, culture, and poetry as emanations from a central ego – he is not strictly in the position to image a collective enterprise of persons, each with his or her center in a larger socio-political structure. In different ways, Coleridge, Shelley, and Hazlitt will attempt to describe such a structure.

As Blake's expectation of imminent world-wide revolution apparently fades, he puts more emphasis on sub-Edenic cultural values. The status of culture, represented by the city of Golgonooza, alters significantly in the three major prophecies. In *The Four Zoas* the city is Los's rudimentary construction made to arrest the effects of the Fall. To ward off "Eternal Death & uttermost Extinction," he builds its pillars on a foundation laid by Tharmas – imagination and sense working together. In *Milton* culture assumes a larger role as a Garden of Adonis where spectres receive new flesh but also where agriculture, law, commerce, and architecture civilize the human race. Stretching from Ulro with its hideous "Polypus" of unregenerate error all the way to Eden, Golgonooza now represents the regeneration of humankind through cultural evolution. We approach it only through the experience of mortality:

> For Golgonooza cannot be seen till having passd the Polypus
> It is viewed on all sides round by a Four-fold Vision
> Or till you become Mortal & Vegetable in Sexuality
> Then you behold its mighty Spires & Domes of ivory & gold.
>
> (M 35: 22–5)

In *Jerusalem* Golgonooza is transformed into the City of God. Blake's treatment of it imitates Ezekiel's in its precise but suprarational numerical inventory and geometricity. As we have seen, it is built by means of the moral virtues: pity, compassion, affection, forgiveness, honesty, devotion, thanksgiving, and even humility.

In raising Golgonooza from Ulro and Generation to his version of the City of God – a development that parallels the retreat from insurrectional politics in the three major prophecies – Blake is in effect substituting cultural evolution for political revolution. It is a culture fashioned by those very virtues for which he appeared to have little sympathy in *The Marriage of Heaven and Hell*. The Golgonooza of *Jerusalem*, which cannot be visualized as a society or a state, is difficult to distinguish from Edenic reality and from Jerusalem, the emanation of the fully realized human being, Albion. Jerusalem is "liberty," so termed by Blake several times. She is, mysteriously, the realization of all human acts of imagination and the ultimate triumph of the ethical.

201

Jerusalem does not represent a political structure but a culture so enriched by moral value and imagination that no such structure is needed. Blake implies instead a utopian anarchism without specific determinants. In this fully realized culture, the ·need for violent transformations would disappear.

Having outlined individual and social values in Blake, I turn now to the third set: hedonic values. Within the free culture of Golgonooza, when it has approached an Edenic state of being, there would be no contradiction between the reality principle and the pleasure principle. A civilization of "Visionary forms dramatic" conversing in thunderous majesty and with no disabling discontents would not repress pleasure. With regard to pleasure, Urizen, representing repression on many levels, makes two errors. The first is in seeking "for a joy without pain" (*BU* 4: 10). This is a literal act of abstraction, because pleasure and pain, as contraries, are inextricable: "O trembling joy excess of joy is like Excess of grief" (*FZ* 136: 3). "Ah! I am drown'd in shady woe, and visionary joy" (*EP* 2: 12). The second, even more fundamental error is to *seek* pleasure at all. Repenting in Night the Ninth, Urizen recognizes that he has erred in "Seeking for pleasure which *unsought* falls round the infants path" (*FZ* 121: 11; my emphasis). With Coleridge, Blake thinks the psychology of pleasure-seeking is self-contradictory, because to seek a joy is to bind and murder it. Psychological hedonism is experientally untrue. Pleasure, happiness, and joy, if they come, come unsought, as accompaniments of experience undertaken for some other end. His sense of contrariety in pleasure and its separation from the sphere of moral recommendation – for how can one recommend as an end what cannot consistently be sought as an end? – makes Blake's celebration of pleasure a sophisticated one.

Bentham thinks even the pleasures of sadism valuable to the degree the sadist is pleasured. Unlike Bentham, Blake makes qualitative distinctions among pleasures, but sadism is a prevalent mental state in his work, one that sometimes has instrumental value. When Oothoon, after being raped by Bromion, calls on her lover Theotormon's eagles "to prey upon her flesh," Theotormon "severely smiles" while they do their brutal work. His is a debased and barren pleasure. More horrifying are the delights taken by the sons and daughters of Luvah when they torture "Human grapes" in winepresses:

The cruel joys of Luvahs Daughters lacerating with knives
And whips their Victims & the deadly sport of Luvahs Sons.

They dance around the dying, & they drink they howl & groan
They catch the shrieks in cups of gold, they hand them to one another:

These are the sports of love, & these the sweet delights of amorous play
Tears of the grape, the death sweat of the cluster the last sigh
Of the mild youth who listens to the lureing songs of Luvah. (*M* 27: 35–41)

Here sadism is ironically a component of "the sweet delights of amorous play" and must be endured for the sake of a full immersion in sexual experience, with its redemptive power.

Visions of the Daughters of Albion is the work most dominated by the relationship of value to pleasure. The hedonic term that appears most frequently in this poem and throughout the corpus is "joy." It is Blake's basic quantum of intense pleasure. Oothoon the individualist asks Bromion–Urizen: "How can one joy absorb another? are not different joys / Holy, eternal, infinite! and each joy is a Love" (*VDA* 5: 5–6). Is she not in fact asking, "Why *should* one joy absorb another"? Joys *are* everywhere vulnerable to hindering, jealousy, and violence, as this poem shows so painfully. But joy as the fulfillment of desire is, for Blake, the opposite of the Freudian reading of pleasure as a release from a painful excess of mental energy to a momentary neutrality. However vulnerable, joy is an intrinsically positive feeling that accompanies transcendence. Over the worm's porch to the "hungry grave" is written, "Take thy bliss O Man! / And sweet shall be thy taste & sweet thy infant joys renew!" (*VDA* 6: 2–3). Oothoon's vision of joy is occasioned by sexuality, which, opposing a repressive morality, expresses a higher innocence. Her "virgin joy" is conveniently one with the "enormous joys" of "happy copulation." These are contrasted with "secret joys" and the "self enjoyings of self denial," spawned by the pornographic imagination. Joy in itself is thus non-moral and takes on moral value only by its association with other qualities, ranging from the Edenic to the perverse. Hedonic terms such as "pleasure" and "happy" are similarly moralized by larger mental contexts.

Coleridgean joy in "Dejection: An Ode" also has a basis in libido, as a "sweet and potent voice" that yokes nature's energies to intellect. Like Oothoon's joy, it promises "A new Earth and new Heaven" and seems for a time impervious to "distress" and "misfortunes." But for Coleridge, weighed down by "afflictions," joy seems non-renewable. He has spent his fund of it.

Oothoon's vision emerges in the context of repression. She conceives of joys she cannot experience, which (contrary to Isaiah in *The Marriage of Heaven and Hell*) argues experiential limits on imagination. Blake's ethic would lead to an end of repression and the conversion of wish into fact. But far from urging us simply to maximize pleasure, he too urges a degree of discipline and restraint as prerequisite to a time when eros and civilization will be one. To laborers preparing for the great harvest of the apocalypse, Los says:

> [Y]ou sowed in tears
> But the time of your refreshing cometh, only a little moment
> Still abstain from pleasure & rest in the labours of eternity
> And you shall Reap the whole Earth, from Pole to Pole! from Sea to Sea[.]
>
> (M 25: 45–7)

The road to apocalypse takes patience, but the promise of unfallen "intellectual pleasures & energies" (J 68: 65) makes good these trials.

When the Bard ends his Song in *Milton*, many of those in Eden condemn it, "Saying Pity and Love are too venerable for the imputation / Of Guilt" (M 13: 48–9). What we have seen in the major prophecies is that values which make up the good exist in states of radical imperfection, throughout the pre-apocalyptic existence of individuals and the human race, and even beyond. Each Zoa is only partially itself, and the value it pursues is imperfectly embodied in the larger framing consciousness, Albion. Perfect friendship is rare, and imperfect friendship treacherous; pleasure is occasioned by another's pain. The Bard is right: pity and love are *not* too venerable for the imputation of guilt. Both are imperfect and their imperfection extends into Eden itself, where Milton recognizes his own incompleteness. These forms of partial good make up a state of being that would stubbornly perpetuate itself in its own imperfection – the Urizenic principle working as the "great opposer of change" (FZ 120: 21). The values of individuality, society, and pleasure constitute the kingdom of ends Blake calls Jerusalem. We have seen that these values are mutually disciplining: reason disciplining feeling, but imagination and the senses disciplining these in turn. Social values in turn discipline these potentially solipsistic "Staminal Virtues." And pleasure, which should function as accompaniment to the exercise of these virtues rather than as an end in itself, can prove a stern moralist, if abused. The impossibility of realizing all such values simultaneously will merge as the central torment of Byronic morality, where love and wisdom prove incompatible. The distance between Blakean optimism, admitting the extreme difficulty of such a reconciliation, and Byronic pessimism, confessing its impossibility, is narrower than a reductive contrast of the two poets might assert; and yet one must insist on that defining distance.

For a new order to arise, states of being in their imperfection must be altered by acts, whether lovely or unlovely; doing must disrupt being. Transformations in Blake come as acts of violence, and to the extent that these transformations make up a teleological chain of events leading to regeneration, the acts that induce them are "right." Rather than reaching a plateau of extended calm on the other side of violence, the new state of being itself often becomes the target of a disrupting act, in a persistent deferring of ends. The larger pattern of change this side of Eden pits doing continuously against being, act against value, right against good – but for the sake of an ultimate gain in things that are good. *The Marriage of Heaven and Hell* promotes the energies of doing in acts of wrath and violence. But these acts point to a new state of being, still largely beyond the horizon, of love, benevolence, and mutuality. Thus, as the doctrine of contraries might dictate, one must renounce pity in order to feel it, one must be wrathful before one can be loving, one must practice severity of judgment in order to forgive, one must suffer in order to inherit joy, one must break the Ten Commandments in order to become merciful, one must promote a revolution however violent in order to create a society of benevolence and justice.

Most of the things that it is "right" to do at any moment in fallen history are contrary to the spirit of things that are "good," a view in radical contrast to Shelley's. This is tantamount to saying that on a deep level the ends justify the means in Blake. We confront this conclusion uncomfortably, though we know he excludes from such means the acts of negation that murder or defraud or permanently repress. His *Jerusalem*, more than the earlier prophecies, puts forward the moral values of forgiveness, mildness, mercy, friendship, and self-sacrifice – values that he could very well say have lurked in the mythic narrative all along. But it is only in the final moments that they are clearly perceived and practiced by "travellers to Eternity."

4

The tragic Wordsworth

We have seen that Blake and Coleridge, despite some radical differences, share concepts of the moral life. Both emphasize the relationship of certain mental powers within the agent. A psychodynamic
unity of these powers is normative and empowering, even though
Blake favors some powers over others, and Coleridge thinks one must
arduously negotiate the evil personal will. Human feeling is but one
component, positioned and even disciplined, within this larger structure. Despite the importance of psychological health to moral functioning, Blake and Coleridge are "non-naturalists" with respect to moral
judgment and truth: ethics cannot be translated into non-moral,
factual categories derived from natural observation, science,
psychology, or sociology. They dislike the moral implications of
empirical psychology – especially its compromise of human freedom –
and they elevate some powers – imagination, will, higher reason – to
suprapsychological status. The potential for radical freedom, however
thwarted from without and within, makes theirs a voluntaristic ethics
in the sense that human beings can and should originate their own acts
and gain power over nature and social environment.

Wordsworth does not conform to very much of this. Not so preoccupied with unity and structure (and in this he is joined by the other
major figures in this study), he gives the affective life greater prominence as both norm and fact, and hesitates to treat the conative life as
its equal. Hardly peripheral, willing and acting are still secondary to
feeling in both the critical writings and the poetry of Wordsworth.
Feeling is first in his scale of values. He and De Quincey after him, in
weakening the voluntarism of Blake and Coleridge, see the force of
circumstance – both natural and social – as exerting greater power over
the moral agent. In this they are more indebted to the empirical and
associationist model of mind, with the reduction of human freedom
that vulnerability to environment usually implies. For Wordsworth the

206

landscape often takes on the role of a moral agent more powerful than human beings within it. Recovery after reversals of fortune is more the result of nature's grace than of human acts and willing. For De Quincey the force of circumstance acts quixotically and human beings must blunder on in the comic impotence of their gestures and the absurd disproportion of acts to consequences. For him the "world of strife" is a preposterously contingent affair that lacks the tragic dimension of Wordsworthian necessity. He and Wordsworth, in making greater concessions to circumstance, natural process, and loss, challenge the high estimate of potential power the self-originating moral agent is granted within the ideology of Romantic humanism. The will to value, as strong in Wordsworth as it is in Blake and Coleridge, is subjected to a delimiting force more persuasive and final.

The poet of feeling

In his "Advertisement" to the 1798 edition of *Lyrical Ballads*, Wordsworth writes that his poem "Expostulation and Reply" "arose out of conversation with a friend who was somewhat unreasonably attached to modern books of moral philosophy" (*PRW* I 117). The friend was probably Hazlitt, who had been working on his *Essay on the Principles of Human Action*, which he completed and published in 1805. While Hazlitt's early academic excursion into moral philosophy happily gives way to spirited familiar essays, Wordsworth's own career ironically sinks from the celebrated early lyrics to *The Excursion* (1814), with its sober moralism.

Hazlitt says of *The Excursion* that "it affects a system without having any intelligible clue to one . . . Mr. Wordsworth's mind is obtuse, except as it is the organ and the receptacle of accumulated feelings: it is not analytic, but synthetic; it is reflecting, rather than theoretical" (XI 91). Wordsworth has renounced his own strength as poet, which resides in feeling. Attempting to be a moral philosopher in verse, he can only pretend to a system, and the result is neither philosophy nor poetry.

The fragmentary "Essay on Morals," probably written in late 1798 or early 1799, is a concise statement of Wordsworth's thinking about the place of feeling in ethics. Formal systems of ethics such as Godwin's or Paley's are in one sense impotent, in another pernicious. "Now, I know no book or system of moral philosophy written with sufficient power to melt into our affections, to incorporate itself with the blood & vital juices of our minds, & thence to have any influence worth our notice in forming those habits of which I am speaking" (*PRW* I 104).

207

Such works have no "power" because they overvalue "that faculty we call reason." Opposed to discursive reason are the "habits" that emanate from "feelings," "sensations," and "affections," the real sources of our conduct. Wordsworth echoes the morality of the sentiments – as propounded by Hutcheson, Adam Smith, Hartley, and Hume – in denying the relevance of discursive reason to morality. A "series of propositions" never made anyone get rid of a nasty habit and may be deployed in bad faith "to lay asleep the spirit of self-accusation."

Not all habits are nasty. "In a strict sense all our actions are the result of our habits." Observed from without, acts are unreliable signs of inner states of mind. His illustration: vain, proud, avaricious, and benevolent persons could all, but acting from different motives, give alms to some hapless person. The acts would be identical (or so he assumes), but surely their worth would not be. If giving alms requires premeditation, the act is "accidental" or "indefinite." The truly benevolent person gives alms as a matter of habit and could not do otherwise. The Old Cumberland Beggar in making his rounds breeds good habits in the populace by providing regular occasion for small acts of charity: "The mild necessity of use compels / To acts of love; and habit does the work / Of reason." Social custom and personal habit are potentially gentle forms of compulsion that permit us to be ourselves without calculation. Wordsworth thus rejects Godwin's contention that habit is necessarily prejudice in action. More inclined to agree with Edmund Burke's traditionalism and some implications of Hartley's associationism, he thinks a confirmed habit is the best testimony of our essential nature.

In his writings on education, Coleridge too sees the importance of habit, but grants propositional wisdom greater power than Wordsworth does. From a Coleridgean standpoint, Wordsworth gives over too much to the empirical self, from which we can separate ourselves in moments of self-transcendence, whether in dynamic acts or heightened states of awareness. Habit may guarantee a daily decency in our conduct, but a true act requires a leap beyond habit; it requires a self-originated act of will.

Implicit in the "Essay on Morals" is a contrast between the language of moral philosophy and the language of poetry. The former in "presenting no image to the [?mind] can convey no feeling which has any connection with the supposed archetype or fountain of the proposition existing in human life." Even though a philosophical proposition may be true, it is a lifeless affair if not joined with practical feeling. The moral philosopher is as useless as he is pompous:

The whole secret of this juggler's trick[s] lies not in fitting words to things (which would be a noble employment) but in fitting things to words—I have said that these bald & naked reasonings are impotent over our habits, they cannot form them; from the same cause they are equally powerless in regulating our judgments concerning the value of men & things. They contain no picture of human life; these *describe* nothing.   (*PRW* I 103)

Philosophical propositions, containing no images that would convey feeling, have no influence on either habits or value judgments – that is, on either of the two major ethical categories, obligation (as it relates to behavior) and value. The philosopher's linguistic impotence ironically correlates with his overestimation of "words," which should be subservient to "things," to the world without. The moral philosopher therefore fails to tell us how "to be practically useful by informing us how men placed in such or such situations will necessarily act, & thence enabling us to apply ourselves to the means of turning them into a more beneficial course, if necessary, or of giving them new ardour & new knowledge when they are proceeding as they ought" (*PRW* I 104).

Note Wordsworth's emphasis on necessity: a wise interpreter should be able to predict how "men placed in such or such situations will necessarily act"; "habit" or "use" is a "mild necessity" that "compels" to beneficent gestures, etc. Though he makes no Shelleyan case for "Necessity" as the order of the universe, Wordsworth does see the world and human mind alike in terms of strong causal linkages.

Mild beneficent compulsion is the underlying assumption in his view of reader pragmatics. The poet is a more powerful moral force than the moral philosopher, as "A Poet's Epitaph" (1799) makes plain. The "Moralist" is "One to whose smooth-rubbed soul can cling / Nor form, nor feeling, great or small; / A reasoning, self-sufficing thing, / An intellectual All-in-all!" The Moralist is unworthy, he says, of approaching the Poet's grave. The "Essay on Morals," in conjunction with the Prefaces to *Lyrical Ballads* of 1800 and 1815 and a few other texts, suggests a line of transmission that is fairly consistent within a Wordsworthian poetics, despite some changes of view in other respects. The poet transmits feeling to the reader through a linguistic transaction that originates in feeling and that is characterized by necessitated linkages at every stage.

The line of transmission runs from feeling in the poet to the development of habits and moral understanding in the reader. The overflow of powerful feelings, mediated by memory, prompts acts of imagination. Overflow is "spontaneous" in the sense of originating from within the poet's own mental processes; feeling is thus the closest to an originating event. But we see throughout Wordsworth's poetry that feeling is itself triggered by scene, circumstance, and memory; it is never a wholly voluntary process. By means of imagination, the poet "incarnates" the felt experience of "things" in the world into the linguistic "image." The image prompts feeling in the reader that exerts causative force in two ways: the development of "habits" and the development of "judgments concerning the value of men & things."

In my construction of it, this line of transmission does not exempt imagination from the causal chain originating in feeling. In the 1815 Preface Wordsworth gives the imagination its due as an active power that "shapes and *creates*," that confers "additional properties upon an object," that abstracts others away, that "regulates the composition of characters, and determines the course of actions," and that qualitatively rises above the workings of the more object-bound fancy (*PRW* III 30–9). Well before 1815, in Book Thirteenth of the 1805 *Prelude*, he speaks of imagination as a "domination" exerted "upon the outward face of things" that "moulds," "endues," "abstracts," and "combines" these things. But a close look at the Mt. Snowdon passage and other texts will show that imagination is not exempt from the strong causality that characterizes Wordsworthian nature and psychology. Imagination must be anchored in the "language of the sense" if it is not to drift toward frightening vaporous nonentity; it is ultimately governed and *placed* by nature. The imagination does not contradict the "soft determinism" that I think underlies Wordsworthian ethics, in which motives and acts of the moral agent contribute to causal chains in nature but do not stand independently of these chains. (We will see in *The Prelude* that the poet does not always feel his imagination is thus determined and empowered, and that in poetic composition he must confront the underdetermined blank page with hesitancy and self-doubt.)

Wordsworth assumes an alert reader who is vulnerable to what the poet transmits, and who cannot step aside from the causal chain of transmission; he or she has entered into a "contract" with the poet. This vulnerability can work both weal and woe. If poets maintain an habitual association of feeling with "important subjects," the "understanding of the being to whom we address ourselves, if he be in a healthful state of association, must *necessarily* be in some degree enlightened, his taste exalted, and his affections ameliorated" (*PRW* I 126; emphasis added). But not all poets are first-rate, and reading involves moral jeopardy: "moral notions and disposition must either be purified and strengthened, or corrupted and impaired" by what we read (*PRW* II 97–8). We have seen that moral philosophy with its

210

"lifeless words" is a linguistic beast that corrupts higher mental faculties, irrespective of the particular ideas advanced. A melodramatic statement of how language can be not simply lifeless but actively poisonous is found in his *Essays on Epitaphs* (1810):

Words are too awful an instrument for good and evil to be trifled with: they hold above all other external powers a dominion over thoughts. If words be not (recurring to a metaphor before used) an incarnation of the thought but only a clothing for it, then surely will they prove an ill gift; such a one of those poisoned vestments, read of in the stories of superstitious times, which had power to consume and to alienate from his right mind the victim who put them on. Language, if it do not uphold, and feed, and leave in quiet, like the power of gravitation or the air we breathe, is a counter-spirit, unremittingly and noiselessly at work to derange, to subvert, to lay waste, to vitiate, and to dissolve.

(*PRW* II 84–5)

As one treads through the later books of *The Excursion*, so devoid of image and feeling and to most readers so dispiriting, one remembers his own warning and wonders why he does not heed it.[1] *The Excursion* may not poison but it leaves us numb with its "lifeless words." And self-numbing may be a deep motive in its composition. As Hazlitt hints, Wordsworth seems in this poem to desiccate the roots of feeling that nourish language. What has happened, I believe, is that feeling for him has become so linked with loss and grief that to continue writing the poetry of feeling would be necessarily to reanimate a wealth of painful feelings, from grief to guilt to inappropriate desire. To retreat from living, incarnational language seems protective of his sanity, even as it is destructive of his poetry.

Hazlitt's reading of Wordsworth as the poet of "accumulated feelings" can help us situate the ethical in his poetry and the fate of the ethical in modern criticism. We have seen how modern critics – Fredric Jameson, Paul de Man, J. Hillis Miller – have tended to treat ethical themes as "diversionary" or as "displacements." Similarly, in *Wordsworth's Poetry 1787–1814*, the most influential study of Wordsworth this past quarter-century, Geoffrey Hartman tends to treat ethical as well as naturalistic categories as "displacements" of a poet who cannot fully yield to his own religious sense. Relative to the visionary or "apocalyptic" imagination's transcendent longings, the ethical in Wordsworth is, strictly speaking, an overvaluation of persons. Hartman wonders whether, in Wordsworth's scheme of things, the imagination can be naturalized and humanized, and still *be* imagination. "Only at the

---

[1] All negative judgments of *The Excursion* are chastened by Keats's remark that it is one of "three things to rejoice at in this Age" – the others being Haydon's paintings and Hazlitt's "depth of taste."

depth of his crisis does Wordsworth adequately recognize the imagination as a power satisfied by neither nature nor man."[2]

My reading of Wordsworth parallels Hartman's in certain respects, but with a different set of terms. Rather than a fear of apocalyptic consciousness (evidence of which is indeed to be found), I think the pervasive fear – and one that eventually deadens the poetic faculty – is of the ethical, which for him means particularly the sphere of the feelings and affections.[3] Rather than seeing the ethical as a displacement in Wordsworth, I argue that it is the ethical that is eventually displaced. The older Wordsworth is governed by a fear – of feelings more than of imagination – which freezes imagination in its roots. Instead of the term "displacement," I speak of "retreat" and of "numbing." It is an irony that the great poet of the human heart retreats from "accumulated feelings" in tactics of personal and poetic evasion. But a certain wariness of feeling has paradoxically empowered his greatest poetry from the beginning, which emerges from a precarious balance of fear and desire.

Situating the ethical within the dialogue of mind and nature requires, again, a revision of Hartman's seminal argument. For him, Wordsworthian nature is a merciful intervention between mind and its own apocalyptic self-consciousness in the eye of God. Nature draws mind to itself, binding its affections and perceptions which are then transferred to human beings, to prepare it gradually for transcendence and unmediated vision, "the naked self and God." The poet misreads the question of dominance: his imagination has actually dominated nature in its very acquiescence to being naturalized and then humanized.

I reverse this ratio in taking the poet more at his own word. As is articulated directly in the Mt. Snowdon episode, imagination's proper "lodging" remains within nature and within the ethical relatedness of self and others. Far from being insufficient to the demands of imagination, nature inevitably overcomes imagination. Its sublimity overpowers imagination's capacity to contain and order, in keeping with Kant's concept of the sublime. And nature's cosmic authority to strip away and kill eventually turns Wordsworth from "worshipper" to nature's melancholy son. I agree that nature *binds* mind, and would place even greater emphasis on that binding: it extends from the way

---

[2] *Wordsworth's Poetry 1787–1814* (New Haven: Yale University Press, 1964), 234.

[3] Among recent studies emphasizing the place of feelings in Wordsworth are James Averill, *Wordsworth and the Poetry of Human Suffering*; John Beer, *Wordsworth and the Human Heart* (New York: Columbia University Press, 1978); and Jonathan Wordsworth, *William Wordsworth: The Borders of Vision* (Oxford: Clarendon Press, 1982).

nature in its ministries of beauty and fear leads the boy toward greater self-awareness, to the mental theatre of associative linkages, to imagination's domination of landscape, to the tragic necessity of death. I am not reinstating sentimental pantheism, rather tragic naturalism, combining the readings given Wordsworth by Hazlitt and Keats. Hartman's emphasis on the supernaturalism of the imagination is not *easily* reconcilable with a reading of Wordsworth as a tragic poet, for the traditional reason that apocalyptics militate against tragic terminations. It is precisely when Wordsworth yields to supernaturalism, as in *The Excursion*, and retreats from the ethical, that he has lost his distinctive poetic voice. Rather than speak of the inherent antagonism of imagination and nature (conceived of not merely as landscape, which is the "outward face of things," but as the cosmic principle of things), I would speak of a struggle of coordination which finds in *The Prelude* its most profound dramatization. My reading may seem domestic after the dark sublimity of apocalypse and daemonization, but it may account for more about this baffling, extraordinary poet.

The heart of loss

Wordsworth is the most prolific of graveyard poets.[4] We sense an elegiac undercurrent even in such ostensibly celebratory poems as "Tintern Abbey" and *Home at Grasmere*; "Ode: Intimations of Immortality" more directly incorporates elegy into its willed affirmations. In these works suffering and loss occur in the context of a larger life that offers "recompense" of one kind or another, whether it be "philosophic mind," the return of spring and loved ones, or the strengths that memory provides. Here, experience of loss nourishes mind, and trauma can eventually exert a "vivifying Virtue" that increases strength of feeling and promotes a healing "calm." So long as the poet converts loss to gain, trauma to strength, he is "worthy of himself."

This temporalized pattern of conversion from loss to gain through the agencies of memory and imagination is the great Wordsworthian

---

[4] *The Brothers* (1800) and Books VI, VII, and VIII of *The Excursion* adopt the format of an *explication de tombeau*. Grave sites are prominent in such works as the Matthew poems (1799), *The Prelude* (1805), and such later works as *The River Duddon* sonnets (1820), *Ecclesiastical Sketches* (1822), and *Yarrow Revisited* (1835). Memorials abound, and function much like tombstones, in the Lucy poems (1799), *Michael* (1800), and "Yewtrees" (1803). Elegies, or extended epitaphs, can be grouped here: the "Elegiac Stanzas" for his brother John (1806), for Charles Lamb (1835), and for James Hogg (1835); and *Essays on Epitaphs* (1810).

hope. But the poet tests it repeatedly and implies that it is a personal ethic of time and loss incapable of being universalized. Time and nature are not so merciful in their dealings with others, nor do others, he knows, share his special sensibility.

In poems of peasant hardships, such as "The Two April Mornings," *The Ruined Cottage*, "The Thorn," "Resolution and Independence," and *Michael*, no such recompense is available. Matthew will accept no substitutes for his lost children; unable to accept the fact of loss, Margaret disintegrates inwardly and dies, just as her garden goes to pieces; loss combines with guilt to drive Martha Ray mad; the Leech-gatherer must continue to gather leeches in an ever more depressed economy; and Michael's best efforts to finish the sheepfold despite his son's departure and ruin prove futile.

But in the many poems narrating dialogic encounters with suffering country folk, the emphasis is as much on the quality of the observer's response as it is on the suffering per se. These unfortunates impinge on the poet, forcing him to ask questions of them and himself. They put him for the moment out of humor. The pattern of conversion applies here as it does to the poet's own suffering: loss is converted to gain. But these solitaries, deserted women, discharged soldiers, blind beggars, and leechgatherers, who have been unaccommodated by circum-stance, will continue to be so; it is the observing poet who stands to gain something by the encounter. Whatever moral lesson he might derive, the ultimate yield is literature. As James Averill has demon-strated, Wordsworth knowingly converts the observed suffering of others into literary pleasure.[5] The process seems homeopathic: suffer-ing momentarily felt as such by the observing poet converts into tragic pleasure and is purged in writing it up. The Pedlar, as poet-surrogate, is said to be so happy that he can "afford to suffer / With them whom he saw suffering" (*PD* 328–9), and the poet, home again in Grasmere, says that "Here may the heart / Breathe in the air of fellow-suffering / Dreadless" (*HG*, MS B 448–50).

Wordsworth does not heed Moneta's injunction in Keats's *The Fall of Hyperion* that the poet must feel the suffering of others qualitatively *as* his own suffering. Barron Field, a lawyer and would-be biographer of the poet, reports that Wordsworth said to him (probably sometime in the period from 1824–8):

No great poem has been written by a young man or by an unhappy one. It was poor dear Coleridge's constant infelicity that prevented him from being the

---

[5] *Wordsworth and the Poetry of Human Suffering*, especially Chapter Four, "The Pleasures of Tragedy," 116–46.

poet that Nature had given him the power to be. He had always too much personal and domestic discontent to paint the sorrows of mankind. He could not "afford to suffer / With those who he saw suffer."[6]

The comment to Field suggests that after 1805 Wordsworth loses the power of converting suffering and personal loss into the tragic pleasure that has accompanied poetic composition. Rather than give up composition, he then aligns it more with duty than with pleasure.

In the stronger poetry it seems, therefore, that recompense for loss is available to someone with the complex repossessive sensibility not cultivated by peasants. It is particularly available to a poet who can speak of loss and convert it to gain, both in the thematics and in the fact of verse. But Wordsworth often implies that someone like Matthew, who sees that loss is loss, has the greater wisdom. The resolution of the Leechgatherer to persist in a livelihood and not go mad brings the poet up short, as he confronts his own self-indulgence. The Leechgatherer's calm does not derive from recompense, gain, a sense of plenitude, let alone a tragic purgative pleasure. His is instead the stoical calm of discipline, renunciation, and acceptance. The narrator gains from this encounter and will thereafter "think of" the Leechgatherer, but he does not necessarily convert to the Leechgatherer's brand of dignified stoicism. The poem remains dialogic, not dialectical.[7]

Throughout his early career Wordsworth admires stoical sensibility and gives us several portraits of it, but he rejects it explicitly in *The Excursion*. Nor are his own responses to loss stoical. The death of his brother, John, in 1805 forces loss on him so enormously that no complex series of mental adjustments, no memorials, and not even poetic composition bring forth recompense. His letters from this period reveal that for several weeks he was inconsolable and incapable of the fortitude displayed by his own solitaries. This loss cannot be converted into tragic pleasure, and "Elegaic Stanzas" (1805), which describes it, is ironically a farewell to tragic composition and the characteristic and strong Wordsworthian voice.[8] Other losses follow, and his response to all may be tied up in some way with the death of his

---

[6] *Memoirs of Wordsworth* (1839), ed. Geoffrey Little (Sydney, Australia: Sydney University Press, 1975), 100.

[7] For the dialogic element in Wordsworth's poetry, see Don H. Bialostosky, *Making Tales: The Poetics of Wordsworth's Narrative Experiments* (Chicago: University of Chicago Press, 1984).

[8] Though he resumed composition of *The Prelude* in April, 1805, after hearing news on February 11th of the death of John, it was not, he said, "in the regular way," and the best portions of Books Eleventh, Twelfth, and Thirteenth were incorporated from earlier drafts. See *The Prelude: 1799, 1805, 1850*, ed. Jonathan Wordsworth, M. H. Abrams, and Stephen Gill (New York: W. W. Norton, 1979), 520.

mother when he was still seven, an event that receives scant mention in *The Prelude*.[9] I do not wish to suggest that the death of relatives is a sufficient biographical explanation of poetic decline, but I do think that the death of John aggravates a pre-existent melancholia and death-consciousness with which Wordsworth has grappled in different ways previously – ways productive of his greatest poetry. The conversion of suffering into tragic pleasure and poetic composition was chief among these. When the "set" of siblings is broken, he loses confidence in the restorative power of memory and in the idea that "feeling comes in aid / Of feeling, and diversity of strength / Attends us, if but once we have been strong" (*P* XI 326–8).

After 1805 (with some exceptions, such as "The Solitary Reaper," composed November, 1805), Wordsworth's poetic response to loss shows neither lyrical repossession, nor tragic pleasure, nor disciplined stoical recognition. Rather, another pattern of response begins to emerge: a securing of the self against the shock of loss. He trades the volatile sources of his own best art for conventional piety, reactionary politics, and moralistic austerity. He is confirmed in a tendency seen much earlier to retreat or "retire" from forms of social participation and commitment. Instead of feeding the heart, language now wards off whatever might feed.

Before this eventuality in his career, one can chart in several great poems of his maturity a scale of responses to loss. In *Home at Grasmere* (1800, 1806) we find the high point of Wordsworthian optimism in an extended lyric of repossession as William and Dorothy find "a home / Within a home." They must, however, confront the fact of loss in other inhabitants of Grasmere; and whenever the poem shifts to the narrative mode, we hear of missing swans, of adulterous shepherds, and of widowers. In "Tintern Abbey" brother and sister in their shared landscape confront the human mortality implied in the perplexing double image of past and present. Their bond can exist in memory, desire, and the speaking of the poem, but it will not persist in time and the landscape. The covert genre is self-elegy, which surfaces in the lines, "If I should be where I no more can hear / Thy voice . . ." In the Matthew poems we find a check on Romantic myths of transcendence, sympathetic imagination, and repossession. Matthew has lost his children, and the poet in a generous but ultimately sentimental gesture says, "I'll be a son to thee." Conscience rejoins that persons are not

[9] See Richard Onorato, *The Character of the Poet: Wordsworth in The Prelude* (Princeton: Princeton University Press, 1971), on the relationship of Wordsworth and his mother as it relates to *The Prelude*; also Michael H. Friedman, *The Making of a Tory Humanist: Wordsworth and the Idea of Community* (New York: Columbia University Press, 1979).

interchangeable, and Matthew declines the offer as temptation and illusion; he will persist in his own being. On down the ladder of loss, we find Margaret of *The Ruined Cottage* (1797–8), whose husband has not returned from the Continental wars and who in desperation continues to hope for his return. The warm pulse of the eighteenth-century Man of Feeling differs from the Wordsworthian affections, which are enduring attachments that structure one's life in a relational network of other selves. When these attachments persist without an object, they may bring on "heart-wasting" (l. 449). Not all feeling melts into and nourishes "the blood & vital juices of our minds." In Margaret, grief and hope conjoined turn pathological, and nature, elsewhere said never to desert the heart that loves it, becomes a grim reality principle in its indifference to human affairs. Margaret's garden – overrun by weeds, thus upsetting the balance between human artifice and nature with which "Tintern Abbey" begins – is both symptomatic and emblematic of her disintegration.

These illustrative works register different responses to gain and loss, but in each of them, the force of circumstance is the controlling arc within which lyrical poet or beleaguered peasant must make do. It is "scene" in the largest sense – the landscape, the things that happen to one, time, socio-economic conditions – that determines the balance of happiness and unhappiness. If scene exerts this controlling pressure, in what sense can we speak of ethical sanctions, imperatives, and opportunities? I think an ethics of feeling obtains in all cases – the good consists of certain feeling states in the minds of human beings – but with different ways of assigning value, depending on the inner disposition of the agent relative to circumstance. Characteristically, the circumstance for Wordsworth is the depletion of objects of the affections. These objects can be persons, animals, land, or the means of one's livelihood. The affections directed inward, one can mourn the loss of one's own powers – "visionary gleam" or "natural piety," or the projected death of the self altogether. In all instances the self confronts the fact of loss, which gives the ethical the character of challenge – the trial of the feelings.

I propose that the challenge of loss results in three distinct kinds of ethical imperative that govern the value structure of Wordsworth's poetry. The first two structure value as it relates to the self, the third as it relates to others.

(1) Continuance in one's own being. This is the minimal imperative for Wordsworth, and therefore the closest to being "categorical." He is deeply preoccupied with exempla: as we have seen, Michael, Matthew, the Leechgatherer, the Female Vagrant, and the Old Cum-

berland Beggar all persist admirably, despite the loss of persons or the depletion of the landscape (nature has become stingy with its leeches), or economic circumstances that drive some to become beggars. It is to these figures that one is most likely to apply the term "stoical": circumstantial limitation does not break them, and they may be said to be free insofar as they refuse to be altogether defeated by it. They contrast with those for whom the permanence of the affections proves a curse and whose plight results in pathology. Margaret's heart-wasting must be considered cautionary. The shepherd in "Last of the Flock," the sailor in *Adventures on Salisbury Plain*, Martha of "The Thorn," similarly broken, find their attachments turning pathological even to criminality. I have suggested that Wordsworth discovers in a new way the difficulty of continuance in one's own being after his brother's death, when he is no longer witness but himself the suffering survivor.

(2) Conversion of loss to gain. This is a challenge for the poet himself, not for peasants or others from whose inner psychologies he is distanced. As such it is what Kant considers a "lax" or "meritorious" imperative, the obeying of which is not absolutely commanded. Keats calls this process "Soul-making" – the gradual fashioning of identity in the face of loss. The uses of loss take one beyond continuance to augmentation of self, or at least the conversion, often through memory, of what is lost into a compensation. Wordsworth is hardly an optimist, and, with Keats, knows that the loss of primal sympathies and splendour in the grass must be exchanged for "embers," "wisdom," the "philosophic mind," "satisfaction," "calm," or vocation: not a sordid boon but certainly an attentuation of the pleasure principle. So conspicuous a value in Wordsworth's poetry and poetics, pleasure is most vulnerable to attenuation in this process of conversion. Here the question of freedom as empowerment arises: simply to continue in one's own being, challenging the coercion of nature and persons, does not imply the ability to *augment* the fund of the self, to wrest objects of the will from restraints of circumstance, and thereby gain power over circumstance. Empowerment for Wordsworth and Keats is directed, at last, to the means by which they tell of their moral struggle – writing. If Wordsworth is to gain power "rivalling" that of nature, it must be through the act of writing. On Snowdon he understands that this ultimate self-empowerment ironically comes from nature also. Self-empowerment in Wordsworth and Keats submits to tragic limitation.

(3) Receptivity of the witness. Many of Wordsworth's poems are dialogic encounters, one of whose speakers is the poet or poet-

surrogate. The life narrated, in part or whole, is usually that of the solitary, peasant, old huntsman, deserted woman, child who has lost siblings. The poem's center of interest subsequently returns to the interlocutor. In "Simon Lee," the poet is participant in the single "episode" of the encounter, helping the old huntsman, "lone survivor" of the Halls of Ivor, dislodge a stump; in the Matthew poems the poet's speech assumes the nature of an act when he offers himself as substitute for Matthew's children; in *The Ruined Cottage* the narrated life has ended, and all that remains is witnessing.

In these instances we see contexts for the sympathetic imagination, enobled over the lachrymose sentiment of the late eighteenth century to a more substantial acknowledgment of the reality, worth, and suffering of other persons. What is needed is the virtue of receptivity, an ability to monitor another without egoistic distortion. The imperative it ordinarily leads to is distributive justice: pain should be eradicated and the fruits of the earth spread about equally. Wordsworth's poems of dialogic encounter stop short of any such imperative, however. It is in *The Prelude*, Book IX, that he records having felt the force of this imperative.

With the return of focus to the response of the poet, Wordsworth reminds us of the moral jeopardy poets, novelists, and dramatists assume in the act of witnessing. Poems or other belletristic texts have value that reverts to the witness. Their intrinsic poetic value enhances authorial worth. In bearing witness, writers may find their careers promoted, their oeuvres augmented, their own moral sensibilities praised. The sufferings of others offer the good material that is the writer's capital. I recall the resentment – felt by some who marched on the Pentagon in 1967 – toward Norman Mailer, who converted his own experience of this public act of witness to the evils of the Vietnam War into a celebrated book, *The Armies of the Night* (1968), collective suffering and witnessing converted into personal triumph. But do not writers usually stand in an exploitative relationship to the matter of their observation? If they lose all controlling distance from it, they may become participants and cease to be writers, as with Byron in Greece. The imperative of distributive justice in the aftermath of the French Revolution strikes Wordsworth with such force that he risks sacrificing the career of poet, which career, in his case, does more for distributive justice in the long run than would have been achieved by writing propaganda, analyzing social and political structures, or personally manning the barricades.

The chastening of intellect

Wordsworth discovers virtue in calm acknowledgment of tragic limitation, as the glad animal movements of youth give way to more sober ecstasies. Willfully to exceed the limits of natural process is the more positive Wordsworthian conception of evil; it differs qualitatively from the banal evil of negation that characterizes "what man has made of man," the vulgarization of spirit so prominent in modern middle-class life. *The Borderers*, written in 1796–7, explores evil as a positivity associated with aggressive intellect. This play is hardly at the center of the canon. None of its characters captures Wordsworth's characteristic voice. Instead we have only melodramatic voices, with intonations of the same Jacobean rhetoric found in Coleridge's *Osorio* (1797). But there is much about it of first interest, both with regard to Wordsworth's development of the quasi-Faustian theme transposed into the heroics of "Romantic will," and to its place in the corpus. It proves to be interestingly complementary to the Wordsworth we prefer to read.

I have been arguing for a "soft" determinism in Wordsworth. The various coercions of landscape, time, social circumstance, and language govern human life in good part; human psychology itself is governed by associative chains, habits, the passions, and the particular circumstance that impresses itself on individual mind. Yet Wordsworth thinks we have the power to persist in our own being, and not be stripped away internally in proportion to the stripping away of circumstance. Heart-wasting is not legislated for us all. We even have the freedom to augment the self, as we have seen, not by contradicting natural process but by converting it, whatever its character, to psychic nourishment. *The Prelude* develops this theme as it relates to the uses of memory, imagination, and the affections. But no freedom worthy of the name exceeds nature in its largest conception, to which even acts of imagination are ultimately subject.

The villain Rivers deliberately attempts to subjugate natural law to human intellect. He is punished for it in the end, and his chastisement brings to mind other Wordsworthian figures somewhat less grandiose. The boy who sneaks a boat at night from the shores of Patterdale and who indulges in a little bird-poaching may seem an all too distant nephew of this pretentious *Übermensch*, but he too intrudes upon the prevailing powers.

The plot of *The Borderers*, structured on the principle of repetition, contrasts a crime brought on by circumstance with one actively willed. Rivers (Oswald in the revised version) has been duped by mutinous shipmates into stranding the innocent captain of a ship. As the play begins he sets out to recapitulate the crime, but this time in full awareness of what he is doing. Through false witness, he incites Mortimer, his immediate superior in the ranks of the Borderers (the thirteenth-century Scottish barons who revolted against Henry III), to kill an innocent old man. Having had the bad luck to have been duped into crime, Rivers chooses to become in essence a criminal. The progress is from unwitting to intellectual crime. Rivers has been described as a Satan, an Iago, a Faust, an Ancient Mariner, and an existentialist. As for the latter, he does not exactly push self beyond its own essence; he is a somewhat unusual existentialist in making himself more consciously the murderer he has already become, actively confirming his earlier acquiescence.

An essay affixed to *The Borderers*, written probably in late spring or early summer of 1797 and predating the "Essay on Morals," gives us Wordsworth's own reading of his villain and expounds interrelation-ships of act, guilt, imagination, and reason. "On the Character of Rivers" is Wordsworth's single most advanced moral disquisition. Rebuked by the world and feeling a guilt that has destroyed his pride, Rivers recovers self-esteem by "dallying with moral calculations" and "assuming the character of a speculator in morals," to the extent that he affirms crime's potential for a transcendence of values, not merely a repudiation of them. He becomes a "moral sceptic" who uses "meditation" as a prelude to "action." Reason can be used after the fact, as Wordsworth says in the "Essay on Morals," to rationalize just about any crime. Rivers's "Imagination," in turn, is "powerful, being strengthened by the habit of picturing possible forms of society where his crimes would be no longer crimes . . . and he would enjoy that estimation to which, from his intellectual attainments, he deems himself entitled" (*PRW* I 76–7). The increase in personal power brought about through evil acts blunts feelings of guilt. Evil acts seem more gratifying than good acts because "the effects are more frequently immediate, palpable, and extensive. Power is much more easily manifested in destroying than in creating," whereas good acts, says Wordsworth, are "for the most part in their nature silent & regularly progressive" (*PRW* I 76). Rivers is not precisely motiveless, because "the non-existence of a common motive itself [is] a motive to action." Wordsworth explains repetition compulsion:

in a course of criminal conduct every fresh step that we make appears a justification of the one that preceded it, it seems to bring back again the moment of liberty and choice; it banishes the idea of repentance and seems to set remorse at defiance. Every time we plan a fresh accumulation of our guilt, we have restored to us something like that original state of mind, that perturbed pleasure, which first made the crime attractive. (*PRW* I 79)

Rivers's assertions of total liberty are illusory. He is governed internally by a compulsion, instigated by the circumstance of the originating criminal act, to repeat the crime for the bogus sensation of having once again "the moment of liberty and choice."

Wordsworth implies here that there *is* a moment of liberty. In this play it is found not in the original crime, but in its aftermath, when Rivers turns to "meditation." Whatever the original victimization of Rivers, the play holds him responsible for his demented way of coming to terms with it. The evil that befalls us is not wholly exculpatory, because we are the arbiters of our own motives and value judgments.

Rivers lives up to his billing as a man of intellect void of benevolence. His Faustian pride of intellect is in league with his debased, fiercely individualistic imagination. Any power over him is insulting and banal. Having been duped by shipmates into committing murder, he meditates for a time and escapes feelings of guilt in seeing that "every possible shape of action / Might lead to good – I saw it and burst forth / Thirsting for some exploit of power and terror" (IV ii 108–10). His rhetoric far outstrips his acts, which in their meanness parody transcendent willing. Can leaving a blind old man in the wilderness be taken for the route to apocalyptic futurity? In the play's most familiar lines, Rivers attempts to downgrade all action, not merely this one, to "the motion of a muscle," whereas the suffering consciousness attending an act is of transcendent sublimity:

> Action is transitory, a step, a blow—
> The motion of a muscle—this way or that—
> 'Tis done—and in the after vacancy
> We wonder at ourselves like men betray'd.
> Suffering is permanent, obscure and dark,
> And has the nature of infinity. (*B* III v 60–5)

In context Rivers tries to convince Mortimer that the latter's guiltiness must now yield to "thought," by which he means a dialectically higher state of consciousness. "Enough is done to save you from the curse / Of living without knowledge that you live" (IV iii 204–5).

At first glance, this seems to conform to a familiar heroic pattern in Romantic literature: consciousness attempts to free itself *from* conscience and *for* imagination. But as Coleridge argues, true growth of consciousness comes about only through awareness of others – only through conscience. If one feels no guilt for a guilty act, one is numbed, not conscious. Wordsworth seems to agree. Rivers escapes feelings of guilt by abolishing the past in a willed truncation of consciousness, which focuses only on "things to come." His victim Mortimer will live on cursed with his guilt, a figure, as Hartman says, of the Wandering Jew (p. 126).

Wordsworth has created in Rivers a character with many strengths associated with Romantic humanism: an active intellect and imagination, with the will to act out his imaginings; an ontological drive to give himself more abundantly the impression that he exists; an individualism that challenges institutional morality, custom, and social taboo. He looks beyond bourgeois Christian herd-morality to a principle of human freedom. All these qualities are converted into magnificent vices, however, because this peevish connoisseur of consciousness lacks the sympathy that tempers egoism, the humane consciousness that Coleridge believes must transform the evil will. Living on pride and visionary energy alone, he fails to recognize the equality in worth of "Thou" and "I" that Coleridge says is the formal ground of conscience. In *Osorio* the character Ordonio, despite a life of villainy, is moved to contrition at the end through the love of his much-abused brother: conscience can survive its long-term repression, Coleridge implies. But Wordsworth creates a more thorough-going villain in Rivers, who can live beyond conscience. He will be defeated not by the self-chastisement of remorse but by the strength of his adversaries and, more so, by Mortimer's power to forgive him in the end.

The Borderers is written in the aftermath of the poet's disenchantment with Godwinism, but Rivers is not a fair satire on Godwinian rationalism. As we have seen, Godwin thinks both intellect and "benevolent intention" necessary for virtue; Rivers lacks benevolence.[10] Nor is he exactly a satire on the revolutionary, since he seeks power for its own sake as answering to a threatened loss of potency – "the torpid acquiescence / Of our emasculated souls" in "the tyranny / Of moralists and saints and lawgivers" (III v 27–9). He contrasts with the true revolutionary Mortimer, who seeks power for ends beyond power. Indeed Rivers acknowledges no laws as yet adopted by the generality of humankind; he honors only that "immediate law / Flashed from the light of circumstances / Upon an independent intellect" (III v 31–3). He is what I would term an egoistic intuitionist: rational moral laws can be objectively discerned, and they privilege the single intellect (or small group of the fully conscious that Rivers purports to establish) capable

[10] But as Basil Willey suggests, Wordsworth may have in mind the ready degeneration of lofty Godwinian principles into heartless rationalism (*The Eighteenth-Century Background*, London: Chatto & Windus, 1940), 255.

of perceiving them. By implication, Rivers assaults the pretense ethical rationalism makes to universality, as in the theories of Godwin and Kant. The very act of abstracting the self away from the communality of nature and humankind, the act of intellectual transcendence, is a supreme egoism, a sin of intellect. The play indirectly underwrites an ethics of sympathetic benevolism based on social ties and duties – the ethics of Edmund Burke in contrast to that of Godwin – and sees in intellect unbound by the warming prejudices of human culture a mutinous betrayal of human nature. Wordsworth explores the relationship of solitude and pride elsewhere, in an early work such as "Lines Left upon a Seat in a Yew-Tree" (1795), and in a deeper way throughout *The Prelude*. The moral dubiety of willful solitude haunts Wordsworth himself – and Rivers may be an attempt to purge an element of his own being.

It is highly improbable that Wordsworth was of the Devil's party without knowing it. The bulk of his greater poetry confirms a negative judgment of Rivers. The sin of intellect is all the more a fraud because it cannot achieve the independent abstraction it pretends to: it carries the passional self with it, sympathy converted to hate. Wordsworth says of Rivers that, like Iago, "his malevolent feelings are excited, & he hates the more deeply because he feels he ought not to hate" (*PRW* I 79). We see once again the pivotal status of feelings, even in this supposed rationalist.

The Borderers is complementary to *The Prelude*. In Book Tenth the independent intellect that attempts to separate itself from nature, the passions, and human culture will be found wanting, when Wordsworth narrates his own hapless immersion in rationalism (or what he takes to be such). But Rivers sets the problem for *The Prelude* in a more fundamental way still. He is a failed visionary, who alternately privileges the wrong faculty (intellect) or the right faculty in the wrong way (visionary imagination deprived of moral imagination). The poet in *The Prelude* will narrate his struggle to unite moral with visionary imagination and his own nearly tragic fall into the sin of intellect. The rather formulaic and improbable theatricality of *The Borderers* as a tragedy is exchanged for the more plausible, more intimately voiced tragic overtones of *The Prelude*.

Being and doing

Wordsworth's sense of peril in moral engagement, whether in commitments of the affections or exertions of personal will, deeply informs *The Prelude*. This autobiographical poem may seem to portray the happy continuity between absorption in landscape and moral growth, as if to explain the causal link "Tintern Abbey" assumes between response to landscape and "little, nameless, unremembered, acts / Of kindness and of love." I will be arguing a complex linkage here, but not the commonly assumed continuity.

Though participation in natural scene does foster growth of personality on many levels, it is only preparatory to strictly moral growth. At some point the "ministry" of landscape leaves off, and the ethical must be sought out and engaged – not least because the ethical is by definition that which enjoins with its insistent "ought," urging individual consciousness toward a range of ethical recognitions. For the poet these include the reality and worth of other persons, the felt obligation to act according to the dictates of distributive justice, the values of vocational purpose and identity, and the necessity of choice – all of which mean the loss of innocence. For these recognitions the youth must "eloign" himself from the landscape that has nurtured him. His engagement with the ethical is frustrated and debilitating, however. The landscape then offers a retreat that restores imagination and the affections and calms the striving will. In terms of Schiller's explicit and his own implicit dialectic, this outcome is regressive to the degree the poet backs away from becoming the "moral agent" he thought he must strive to become. Reviewing this process, he narrates how he was eventually reabsorbed into natural scene, entering the last phase of the arc of development that prepared for poetic composition. The question raised in *Home at Grasmere* haunts him even to the compositional present of *The Prelude*: how can the deeply self-reflexive poet, knowingly defeated on his own terms by the world's ethical pressure, presume to speak to the generality of humankind on "Man, Nature, and Society"?[11]

---

[11] In *Home at Grasmere* Wordsworth writes that he and Dorothy "do not tend a lamp / Whose lustre we alone participate, / Which is dependent upon us alone, / Mortal though bright, a dying, dying flame" (*HG* 655–8). But he is well aware that a doubt arises as to whether this society of "untutored shepherds," from whom he feels his socio-economic and cultural difference (they are more subservient to "every day's demand for daily bread"), does in fact provide a context adequate for speaking on the larger moral, social, and political dimensions of human life. Such a context he thinks necessary for his continued poetic development and for fulfilling the contract he has made with Coleridge to write *The Recluse*. In the 1806 portions of *Home at Grasmere* he attempts to answer the question of how a poet living in Grasmere could presume to speak for the human race. As Kenneth Johnston has shown (*Wordsworth and 'The Recluse'*, New Haven: Yale University Press, 1984, 217–34), his clumsy reasoning inadvertently affirms the likelihood of continued alienation in an isolated imaginative universe.

Writing is, of course, the writer's action, and not fairly to be confused with retreat or retirement. After absorbing some wisdom in the way of the world, what else is the writer *to do* but close the door and write? Is not this ultimately how a writer best becomes a "moral agent"? *We* do not ask Wordsworth to do anything other than write, or to be anything other than a poet – and surely not a polemicist, politician, or social worker. But *The Prelude* – which is anything but a failed poem – highlights what the poet asks of himself in addition to the life of writing that would empower that very life. It is his own judgmental narration of failure that concerns us here.

The poem narrates the eclipse of its own ethical imperatives and prophesies the exhaustion of its author beyond its own ending. The poet, who is preparing to write a philosophical poem largely ethical in character, has in effect disqualified himself by the poem's end for those large pronouncements on man and society, and has already treated of the only ethical dynamic that he could convert to a strong poetry: the confrontation of his personal imagination with ethical pressure from without and within. This confrontation is rendered both in the account he gives of his life and in what I call the ethics of composition. In either case it is not a sufficiently grandiose, categorical, and public ethical confrontation to fuel pronouncements on "Man, Nature, and Society." In the later books of *The Excursion* Wordsworth will indeed desert the haunting questions he raises in *The Prelude* for ex cathedra pronouncements on all that ails us.

Turning first to the ethics of composition, we see that in foregrounding the act of writing Wordsworth moralizes the whole poem, irrespective of the moral qualities in the life he narrates. He makes us aware that the poem records a series of compositional choices and acts undertaken for an end beyond itself. He claims his poem is merely instrumental in "building up" that more worthy work that should endure. It is the means to a greater good, not the good itself. This "review of his own mind" is thus more an étude than a prelude (the title given the posthumous work by his wife, Mary). It is a spiritual exercise to increase his worth as agent/author. He asks whether he is worthy of the task, not as poetic craftsman but as poet-moralist who understands, feels and imagines the possibilities of nature and human life.

In substituting autobiography for epic narration, he is aware of an inherent egoism and hopes that hereafter he might "accomplish aught of worth / Sufficient to excuse me in men's sight / For having given this Record of myself" (*P* XIII 387–9). Egoism hardly bothers us in an age when strong poets are expected to nurture a will to power. It is qualified in any event by the low status of autobiography, in which the author may be the hero but in a narrative that is not yet worthy of rank within a hierarchy of genres. Beyond this, Wordsworth grants his poem instrumental, not intrinsic, value; it exists to make possible a work beyond itself. As Coleridge said of "Kubla Khan," so might Wordsworth say of *The Prelude*: that it is more a "psychological curiosity" than a work to be read or published "on the ground of any supposed *poetic* merits." He further distances himself from his own work in allowing it to be published only posthumously.

The poet attempts from the beginning to purge himself of the "subtle selfishness, that now / Doth lock my functions up in blank reserve" (*P* I 247–8). It is precisely because he is thrown back on the self in impotent "vague longing" that he will address it. Moreover, his poem originates in a need to discharge his indebtedness to nature for gifts given: he feels like "a false steward, who hath much received / And renders nothing back" (*P* I 271–2). And toward this end of balancing a ledger, he needs self-empowerment as poet, for which this spiritual exercise in autobiography will be the means. (Ironically, it empowers him to write only itself, depleting him for the principal task.) And finally, the entire poem, addressed to Coleridge, is described as a "gift, / Which I for Thee design" and an "Offering" of his love (*P* XIII 411–12, 425); it closes with a prayer for Coleridge's recovery.

Various speech acts ethical in character are thus performed: the promise (the entire poem is a promissory note), the prayer or blessing, the indictment (for instance, of England's betrayal of the revolutionary cause in 1793), the self-accusation, the exorcism (he purges through poetry everything that stands in the way of writing it), the analysis (in something like its modern sense, but with the poet putting himself on the couch), and of course the confession (Rousseau's *Confessions* underwrites this text, as it does most Romantic autobiography). Composed of speech acts as various as these, as well as of manifest ethical thematics, *The Prelude* shows that the poet's will to poetic self-empowerment is one with his will to value.

We can account for some of the poem's contradictory qualities by considering the issue of freedom and necessity, this time as it relates to narrative and the ethics of composition. I will be arguing that scene is the controlling force in the poet's life as narrated, whether the expansive nurturing of landscape or the alienating coercion of city, university, and the revolutionary situation in France; his life seems to him to have been a largely necessitated or determined one. With respect to his special sense of purpose and vocation, he hopes that it *has* been necessitated – that necessity takes the form of a purposeful immanent

227

destiny in which he participates, and that he is destined to write the poem worthy to endure. But with respect to the poem he is now writing, the compositional choices are undetermined, and the liberty he has to write as he chooses is initially and fitfully burdensome. The first 304 lines are an extended act of choosing a subject matter, before the poet backs into the subject of himself and stays there *faute de mieux*. In what is now a hackneyed scenario for would-be writers, he sets out from the city for the countryside to write the great work. He has little trouble choosing an agreeable "vale," braces himself "to some determined aim," thinks himself possessed of the requisite sensibility and knowledge of the world, but suffers writer's block upon confronting a vacancy of theme and matter of observation. He finds nothing that might "be singled out with steady choice" (*P* I 171). He is free to write, in the sense that there are no external restraints of nature or persons, but he lacks empowerment – the ability to choose a course of action (a subject matter) and act on it (actually write the poem). The absurd epic catalogue of heroes, as he searches for "some old / Romantic tale, by Milton left unsung" (say, Mithridates, Odin, Sertorius, Dominique de Gourges, Gustavus, or Wallace?), is good evidence the poet knows he is desperate.

He omits any reference to the act of finally singling out himself, perhaps because it seems less like an act than a default. He asks, "Was it for this" – his present failure to get on with his task – that as a boy he had been nurtured so gloriously in the Lake District near the Derwent River, which tempered "human waywardness" and which, by implication, had directed him purposefully, whether with or against his will? He has felt destined by landscape and early upbringing to put his life to some account. His present quandary is a hiatus in what he has felt since late youth is the destined narrative of his life – to be a poet "else sinning greatly." To tell the story of his life is therefore to find the thread that links early promise with the compositional present. The selection of a story – his own – by the close of Book First does not, however, put an end to irresolution. One could multiply passages throughout to suggest that Wordsworth is never wholly convinced either of his election or of his next move as narrator. *The Prelude* remains, on the level of narration, underdetermined. It is dogged by irresolution, reversals, and alternating highs and lows of mood often correlative to the quality of the verse that expresses them. Aggressive speech acts are countered by moments when the poet "plays the loiterer," when he describes episodes that do not go beyond the "suburbs of the mind," when he becomes a mere observer of scene, when he knows his verse is flat, when he is – most culpable of all for a Wordsworth – killing time.

The Prelude is underdetermined and yet highly mediated, with the poet circling back on himself unpredictably and sometimes almost casually – or, as Coleridge would say, desultorily – in the play of the "two consciousnesses," past and present. He attests to the limits of autobiography and the impossibility of perceiving absolute origins for his attitudes and ideas (*P* II 208–15). Chronological sequence is violated, notably with the great "spots of time" passages of Book Eleventh. The Russian Formalist distinction between story (the unmediated events in what is presumed to be their sequential continuity apart from narration) and plot (or the way the narrator has chosen to order and interpret events) is accentuated in *The Prelude*, which makes no pretense to strictly sequential, matter-of-fact recovery. At the close of Book First he does say that "the story of my life" is "a theme / Single and of determined bounds" – perhaps in the sense that everything in his life has occurred as it has occurred, and autobiography is not therefore a great challenge to invention. But he is soon disabused. The recent argument of Paul Ricoeur is suggestive here: the human need for the "emplotment" of narrative can be accounted for in the fact that narrative gives us an orderly Aristotelian structuring of events answering to our Augustinian bafflement at the meaning of time. "The Augustinian analysis [in the *Confessions*] gives a representation of time in which discordance never ceases to belie the desire for that concordance that forms the very essence of the *animus*. The Aristotelian analysis [in the *Poetics*], on the other hand, establishes the dominance of concordance over discordance in the configuration of the plot."[12]

I think, however, that bafflement at time and the search for its human meaning are incorporated directly into the plotting of *The Prelude*. Thus this poem *does not answer to* our need for narrative. It is an Augustinian text. Without indulging the critical hyperbole that it is instead *about* narrative, I do think Wordsworth forces upon us and himself a bafflement as to the meaning of time, and a doubt that the story of his life can be told without heavy mediation, interpretation, revision, and surmise, all of which work against resolute "emplotment." The tendency toward lyricism – it is often asked whether *The Prelude* is not lyric masquerading as narrative – is another disruption of resolute narrative ordering.

These observations converge in the ethics of composition. A com-

[12] *Time and Narrative*, I, 21–2, and *passim*.

mon motive for autobiography is to see disparate events as conforming to a meaningful narrative pattern, and to vindicate the life by proving it worthy of having been written up. Wordsworth complicates this motive. As he confronts a life that seems to have a special destiny – one in which even pivotal dedicatory vows have been made *for* him, but also a life that has reached yet another crisis at the very moment when he would begin writing – he attempts to gain poetic empowerment. In reviewing the history of his life, he seeks evidence of his election, of his destiny. To be empowered by a sense of destiny is to merge freedom and necessity, and this is what he seeks in writing his autobiography – for the sake, he believes, of writing a later work intrinsically great. The act of writing is in itself his challenge to the power of scene to have dictated his life to the point of unfreedom: writing is the writer's freedom. Never fond of "too much liberty," as he says in "Ode to Duty," he wishes to feel that what he writes is *grandly* necessitated.

But the poetic voice of the compositional present is not always thus empowered, and registers the burden of too much liberty. The life does not write itself and often baffles his best skill at ordering and interpretation. This contrast of what one might call an overdetermined life and an underdetermined narrative accounts for much of the modernity of *The Prelude*. How is the writer to close the gap between story and plot, between the chronicler's sequence of events in its nakedness and the narrator's will to find meaning and value? For all the profundity of his acts of retrieval, Wordsworth remains a skeptical narrator who keeps the good faith of his audience by asking that we join him in watching the act of narration itself, in its hesitancy, slipperiness, and alternating cycles of mood. His is a reading of his own life to be taken on trial, privileged insofar as he is its only speaking witness, his egoism an act more of attention than of self-promotion. His purpose is to gain the writer's self-empowerment, and our estimate of *The Prelude* is that he has grandly succeeded. But he has throughout left traces of the hesitancy with which his project began.

Turning now to thematic structuring, I propose that the relationship of moral development and landscape[13] is best seen in the poet's way of construing the broad categories of being and doing. Wordsworthian landscape is humanized in the sense that it manifests the properties of intentional consciousness, becoming by turns hospitable or inhospitable, gay or solemn, nurturing or abstemious. Wordsworth goes well beyond this "softening mirror of the moral world," however, to

[13] I generally speak of "landscape" or "natural scene" when the poet is describing a localized pastoral scene, and of "nature" whenever he seems to be speaking of a more encompassing cosmic power; the two are, of course, inseparable.

claim for landscape many of the functions of an active moral participant; it is more than humanized, it is sometimes forbiddingly
moralized. It can assume the role of agent as well as of scene, and as
such it prepares the young poet to become a moral agent also. But the
bounty of landscape can accentuate the crisis of moral participation by
seeming to offer an alternative to it. At this point it becomes reduced to
a version of pastoral. Wordsworth vigorously challenges literary
pastoralism (P VIII 183–221), but its seductions are never, in my
reading, fully resisted.

Being and doing are vivid organizational categories for our study of
Wordsworth. The key phrase "sentiment of Being" (P II 420) applies to
a spectrum of related responses the poet registers toward natural
scene, from the Schilleresque calm of "naive" acquiescence in process,
to an oceanic sense of participation, to a meditative state wherein
nature is read as a language, to mystical trance. The literary form that
expresses these responses is lyric, the prevailing trope is metaphor.
Such ontologically heightened states of mind are often achieved on the
other side of moments disrupting or alienating. The "sentiment of
Being" is thus associated with consolation and convalescence, and
with metaphors of nourishment and assimilation. In this state of mind,
one sees the world as pure value, free of the burden of act and
obligation.

Within the category of being, landscape conducts a "ministry of
beauty." Its maternal aspect empowers the renewal of life; as the
season of spring, it gives again what has been taken away. Fostering
the self physically, it "feeds" the senses as well as the body, and it has a
magnetic power that aligns the human being with its own essence,
lending a strong sense of organic kinship, or "the one Life within us
and abroad" whereby natural scene becomes an object of "love."

Within the category of "doing," one can perceive in The Prelude all
human responses of desire and fear that result in movement, gesture,
and act. The early episodes take the forms of excursions into scenes
that respond as if they have been violated. Alienation, not harmony, is
the state of mind here, whether felt as fear, awe, guilt, hostility, terror,
or, in its highest form, the sublime. These episodes are formative, and
in fact only these experiences are episodes, as distinguished from states
of consciousness associated with the "sentiment of Being." The literary form that expresses the category of doing is narrative, and the trope
is metonymy. It is in such moments that a majority of the "spots of
time" are imprinted for the conversions that memory will perform. In
Wordsworth, doing is more aligned with the empirical than with the
organic view of experience. During excursions into scene, one is

vulnerable to multiple sensate impingements, many of them disorienting. Excursion into scene entails a fall into experience, and the disturbing of an original innocence; the poet departs the Schilleresque "naive"
for the "sentimental." To the emotions of fear and disorientation he
adds yearning and desire for an earlier state of being now forever
disturbed and for a reintegration on some new level of consciousness.
Doing belongs more to the sphere of obligation than of value.
Although the interchange of agent and scene is pre-moral in Books
First and Second, the sense of obligation operates even so. The young
boy feels guilty for merely having sneaked out on a lake one evening.

With respect to powers that obtain to natural scene itself as doer, the
poet describes the "ministry of fear," which fosters in its own way.
Fear is a heightening of self more directly moral than ontological.
Instead of maternal beauty, it works through the paternal sublime,
which often appears as a principle of mystery, miracle, and authority,
and which reappears as death. The young boy on the lake has a fear of
extinction, and of course he is right in a premonitory way; nature will
reclaim its own. The boy is "guided" and "led" by the "spirits" of
landscape to do what he does, and these same spirits then pursue,
judge, and punish him for the acts of stealth they have themselves
inspired (*TPP* I 67–129).

The Two-Part *Prelude* of 1798–9 emphasizes somewhat more than
later versions the active role that a quasi-conscious landscape takes, as
if it were a moral agent. *The Prelude* of 1805 will move well beyond the
pre-moral experience of this earlier draft, however, and will
demonstrate that a fall into experience occasioned by excursions into
landscape is different in kind from a genuine moral fall into the world
of human culture, history, and politics. The larger poem will show that
the ministry of landscape, whether of beauty or fear, proves
inadequate.[14]

Landscape is not human, and the boy does not engage in acts for
which he is an unqualified moral debtor. His is but the simulacrum of
culpability. The context landscape provides is one of play, in which
true moral negotiation cannot take place. Pre-moral growth of identity
comes about through metonymic linkages in early life among images

---

[14] *The Prelude* was composed over the years 1798 to 1839, and first published posthumously in 1850. The so-called Two-Part *Prelude* was first published by Jonathan
Wordsworth and Stephen Gill in *The Norton Anthology of Literature* (3rd edition, 1974),
and by Stephen Parrish in the Cornell Wordsworth series in 1977. See the Norton
edition of *The Prelude* cited above for the complex relationship of the three principal
versions, and the de Selincourt edition of the 1805 *Prelude*, cited in this study, on the
relationship of the 1805 and 1850 versions.

and feelings that persist "collaterally" in memory. These linkages originate in episodes: narrative fragments during which a constellation of images impinges on and fastens permanently to the boy's consciousness. The most luminous of these Wordsworth will call "spots of time." These episodes are immediate, non-conceptual, non-metaphoric, and un-literary. Often they work through strong contrasts or unlikely juxtapositions, as when the suicide "bolt upright / Rose with his ghastly face" in Esthwaite's beautiful lake, or when the boy sees a girl bearing a pitcher at the summit of a hill just after he has emerged from a valley where the body of an executed murderer had years before been placed in a gibbet. Such scenes, "by the impressive discipline of fear" and other feelings, have become "habitually dear, and all / Their hues and forms were by invisible links / Allied to the affections" (*TPP* I 440–2). The boy's mind functions by means of empirical associations "impressed" upon him from without. The impressing is the more vivid for being unprecedented, disorienting, and often terrifying.

Despite the many instances of metaphoric reading of scene, Wordsworth is more preoccupied with metonymic impingement and attachment, the juxtaposition, the non-logical association, the confrontation, the crossed boundary, the intersection of the human and the natural.

In the larger *Prelude*, Wordsworth entitles Book Eighth "Retrospect. – Love of Nature Leading to Love of Mankind." Since this book does not fully bear out its title, the question has arisen frequently in criticism as to what love of nature has to do with love of man (are they not often mutually exclusive?), or indeed whether the poet ever loved either in the first place.[15] That one might have "love" for physical objects in any other than a colloquial sense would be morally repellent to the older Coleridge, who follows Kant in distinguishing between persons and things. But Wordsworth knows that cathexes are routinely directed to objects as well as to persons. With reference to Locke, Alan Grob has demonstrated the empirical basis of Wordsworth's poetry of the years 1797–1800, and its use of the Hartleian notion that moral awareness is not innate but trained up through association. In *The Prelude* the child is at best amoral, at worst egoistic, and is motivated in the main by pleasure. Nature gradually leads him away from egoism to value nature for itself, and this habit of externally directed affection for nature is subsequently transferred to humans. To associationist

---

[15] In modern Wordsworth criticism, these questions were raised by John Jones, *The Egotistical Sublime: A History of Wordsworth's Imagination* (London: Chatto & Windus, 1954) and by David Ferry, *The Limits of Mortality* (Middletown, Conn.: Wesleyan University Press, 1959).

psychology, Wordsworth adds his own belief in a landscape of intrinsic value and moral purpose. Grob suggests that as youthful feeling wanes, a "rational benevolence" or generalized "love of mankind," with its precedents in the British rationalist school of ethics from Richard Price to Godwin, supersedes the more visceral, immediate, and limited forms of sympathy for particular persons. Thus, love of nature leads to love of mankind. In the poetry of 1802 a more organic, Coleridgean notion of mind takes over in Wordsworth's poetry; mind is lord and master of natural scene, not the reverse. Given its complex compositional history and the narrative interplay of past and present, *The Prelude* switches back and forth between these conceptions.[16]

I am in sympathy with this view insofar as it elucidates the receptive quality of mind in Wordsworth and the power of scene over it. But I would argue that even in many passages and poems of 1802 to 1805 where mind seems to assume a more organic, voluntaristic character – leading to transcendence of mind over scene – Wordsworth qualifies its power and subtly reasserts the greater power of scene. One thrust of this view is therefore that, at least with regard to the ethical dimension, Wordsworth staves off the influence of Coleridge more than is often thought. Another related qualification of the argument for a Hartleian perspective in Wordsworth is his much darker view of our immersion in sensate experience. Wordsworth has a tragic awareness of our vulnerability to "extrinsic" forces and is always within sight of nature's power to reclaim us in death. By contrast, Hartley adopts an optimistic psychology in a cheerful Christian context; sensation is converted into virtue by natural progression. The developmental aspect of Wordsworth's education in virtue is far from continuous and inevitable. It is fraught with fear of corruption and regression. And the "transfer" of feeling from nature to humankind is problematic in the extreme. If it occurs at all, it seems to require of him a sudden epiphany and renunciation of a former point of view, in addition to progression from lower to higher complexes of feelings and moral ideas. Far from a Hartleian or other kind of gradualism, the evolution of moral consciousness and purpose is characterized by reversals, sudden insights, strides into new states of being, gaps, surprises, and centers of indifference.

Discontinuity in moral development is a function of changing scene and circumstance. The way the young poet confronts this discontinuity confirms that his life as narrated is largely controlled by forces greater than himself. When he finds himself "begirt" with the folly of

[16] Alan Grob, *The Philosophic Mind: A Study of Wordsworth's Poetry and Thought, 1797–1805* (Columbus, Ohio: Ohio State University Press, 1973).

Cambridge "thrust upon [his] view," he confronts, for the first time, the moral pressures of an exposed life. The "uproar and misrule / Disquiet, danger, and obscurity" of human communities are threats to psychic security that provoke something beyond insularity or retreat:

> It might be told (but wherefore speak of things
> Common to all?) that seeing, I essay'd
> To give relief, began to deem myself
> A moral agent, judging between good
> And evil, not as for the mind's delight
> But for her safety, one who was to *act*,
> As sometimes, to the best of my weak means,
> I did, by human sympathy impell'd;
> And through dislike and most offensive pain
> Was to the truth conducted; of this faith
> Never forsaken, that by acting well
> And understanding, I should learn to love
> The end of life and every thing we know.   (*P* VIII 667–77)

Consistent with the central position of feeling in the moral life, action is said to be the result of "human sympathy." The dual positive consequences of feeling are invoked: "acting well" and "understanding." Even here where the poet speaks most explicitly of the "moral agent" acting, he has described a strict causal sequence. "Begirt" with the circumstances of Cambridge life, he is forced to respond. Instead of the agent acting, he speaks of an act "impell'd" by a feeling within the agent. Rather than leading himself to truth, he "was to the truth conducted."

Note, too, that the poet, in acting, makes judgments between right and wrong "not as for the mind's delight / But for her safety." "Safety" is a word so full of implication that Wordsworth, perhaps for that reason, changes it to "guidance" in the 1850 version. "Safety" suggests the egoism that persists in sympathetically impelled acts. The poet is engaged in protective reaction against the uproar, misrule, disquietude, danger, and obscurity that threaten from without and that have begun to take up residence within his mind. Moral choosing becomes for him a guard against mental disequilibrium and insanity. He does not, like Shelley, set out to transform the world, or even Cambridge. Rather he shores up his own identity. This reading is all the more likely because of the otherwise curious omission of what he *acts at*. He invokes a nameless, intransitive kind of act undertaken by "weak means."

In Book Eighth – and more so in Books Ninth and Tenth on his experience in France – he reluctantly accedes to the imperative that the "sentiment of Being" must be supplemented, even supplanted, by the rigors of doing – though object and means will remain obscure. The scene of doing must shift from landscape to human society.

Wordsworth makes clear the contrast between his own qualified resolve to act and true dedication to action in someone like Michel Beaupuy, the revolutionary French officer of noble family who gives him a political education. It is pleasant enough to discuss "rational liberty" in the confines of academe or the pastoral landscape of the Lake District, but in moments of historical crisis, more is called for. Wordsworth admires someone who does not settle for "understanding" alone, someone

> whom circumstance
> Hath call'd upon to embody his deep sense
> In action, give it outwardly a shape,
> And that of benediction to the world.   (*P* XI 406–9)

Yet even this dynamic resolve to act is the calling of "circumstance."

To the recognition that he must become an active moral agent he does not add strong sympathy for mankind until he connects the fact of human suffering with political exploitation. The "hunger-bitten Girl" beside the Loire who fits "her languid self / Unto a Heifer's motion" (*P* IX 511–13) is, like the idealized shepherd, a solitary in a pastoral setting, but she disturbs any bourgeois complacency about the pleasures of poverty, and she does not occasion consoling proverbs on human endurance. Beaupuy points to her and cries: " 'Tis against *that* / Which we are fighting" (*P* IX 518–19). The abstract idea of distributive justice suddenly becomes stubborn and concrete, forcing the poet to question his own complacent moral understanding. It is not rational benevolence but immediate sympathetic feeling that turns him around. The natural egalitarianism of Lake District society had made him read the French Revolution as an outgrowth of the nature of things, instead of as a radical moral and political upheaval:

> unto me the events
> Seemed nothing out of nature's certain course,
> A gift that rather was come late than soon.   (*P* IX 251–3)

Now he recognizes that the course of human affairs depends in part on interventions of human will, even so that natural law may prevail. This is the fulfillment of soft determinism, which includes human agency as cause. Wordsworth is not entitled to watch the course of nature as a spectator. And this means forsaking an insulated theatre of the mind and tracking the world's pain to its source.

236

To human indifference, exploitation, and cruelty is added the even greater shock of betrayal, when Great Britain sides with counter-revolutionary forces against the French Republic in 1793:

> No shock
> Given to my moral nature had I known
> Down to that very moment; neither lapse
> Nor turn of sentiment that might be nam'd
> A revolution, save at this one time,
> All else was progress on the self-same path
> On which with a diversity of pace
> I had been travelling; this a stride at once
> Into another region.
>
> (*P* X 234–42)

The landscape of the Lake District has left his "moral nature" unprepared for a truly moral situation, one requiring something more by way of response than shocks of mild surprise, accommodation, and psychological growth. When prelusory morality in Cumberland yields to real, the poet suffers a *moral* apocalypse, where he looks not into the eye of God but into the heart of man. There are many reversals in *The Prelude*, but none that comes this close to a tragic peripeteia. Human beings are focused as objects of value and affection only at those moments when the poet recognizes their capacity for evil and betrayal.[17] What he calls his generalized "Love of Mankind" has come not by means of a non-specific transfer of a "Love of Nature" or by a Godwinian rational benevolence. Rather, it has come about through pointed moral outrage. His feeling for landscape is inadequate and even inhibitory when moral acts and sympathy are called for. What directly leads to love of mankind – to the extent the poet achieves it – is ironically man's inhumanity, which shocks him out of ease and moral quiescence, the dubious offshoots of excessive confidence in natural process. Far from evolving beyond the state of feeling toward rational benevolence, this rapid progress in moral development is a consolidation of strong feeling.

England's betrayal of the revolutionary cause and France's own subsequent terror and tyranny lead him, in the years 1794–6, to investigate what evil must lurk in institutions and how it might be eradicated. A good portion of Book Tenth shows how the young poet is unable to contend with the enormity of human betrayal. For reasons

---

[17] Wordsworth would have lived for precisely "three and twenty summers" when the British declared war on France, 11 February 1793, which correlates with his account in Book Eighth of when he began to feel "love of man." Thus, I think *P* X 234–42 gives the context for *P* VIII 481–5.

that he chooses to leave obscure, he is helpless to act on his hard-won intuitions concerning distributive justice. Adopting a Godwinian distrust of the Burkean "prejudices" that inform national traditions and institutions, he comes close to denying the legitimacy of feeling in his quest for understanding, forgetting that the original increase in sociopolitical understanding came from a feeling – of outrage. His application of discursive reason to social institutions and ethics leads to a vague ethical relativism:

> Thus I fared,
> Dragging all passions, notions, shapes of faith,
> Like culprits to the bar, suspiciously
> Calling the mind to establish in plain day
> Her titles and her honours, now believing,
> Now disbelieving, endlessly perplex'd
> With impulse, motive, right and wrong, the ground
> Of moral obligation, what the rule
> And what the sanction, till, demanding *proof*,
> And seeking it in everything, I lost
> All feeling of conviction, and, in fine,
> Sick, wearied out with contrarieties,
> Yielded up moral questions in despair,
> And for my future studies, as the sole
> Employment of the enquiring faculty,
> Turn'd towards mathematics, and their clear
> And solid evidence—.
>
> (*P* X 893–905)

His philosophical error is to demand total moral proof, and failing this to conclude, in a non sequitur, that total ethical relativism must follow. But the personal error – to forsake the testimony of feeling for the speculations of intellect – is more germane. The therapy of mathematics as a response to moral uncertainty and the pressures of performance is not jejune – it is simply not the appropriate therapy for Wordsworth.[18]

Why he should seek absolute certainty in moral questions is unclear. Aristotle cautions against this, famously, in *Nicomachean Ethics*. For a time Wordsworth is bereft of negative capability. It sounds as if he is looking for the kind of moral treatise Samuel Clarke, not Godwin,

---

[18] Coleridge is similarly tempted. In a notebook entry of 1801 he projects a poem in which the "best advice" for a man disappointed in love would be "that he should as much as possible withdraw himself from pursuits of morals &c—& devote himself to abstract sciences—" (*N* I 1065).

provides in *A Discourse of Natural Religion* (1706), where ethics is likened to geometry. I think Wordsworth's severe ethical questioning is more symptom than cause in a larger drift toward breakdown. The quest for certainty is symptomatic of a larger anxiety as to the course his life will take, the precise cause and nature of which he leaves to speculation. Mathematics fails to answer this anxiety, and thereafter he retreats more radically from the moral imperatives of action, social participation, and distributive justice.

He is rescued by "Nature's Self." Taking the role once again of active agent, nature "conducted me again to open day / Revived the feelings of my earlier life . . ." (*P* X 924–5). In Books Eleventh, Twelfth, and Thirteenth he dwells on the redemptive power of nature that sustains him after his depression of spring, 1796. Significantly, he speaks of this recovery not as earned through moral effort or even perseverance, but as bestowed by natural process. Throughout these late books landscape once again is a controlling force, but one less possessed of the darker qualities of the ministry of fear. It is now more the bountiful maternal principle; the paternal sublime is evoked in memory, in the "spots of time" passages and elsewhere. The signal truth she offers is that "Spring returns" (*P* XI 23). As a suffering man, the poet has endured until time and natural process have given again what they had appeared to take away:

> What then remained in such eclipse? what light
> To guide or chear? *The laws of things which lie*
> *Beyond the reach of human will or power* . . .
>
> (*P* XI 96–8; emphasis added)

He is schematic about what he calls the two "gifts" of nature: the contrary gifts of "emotion" or "energy" and of "calmness" or "happy stillness" (*P* XII 1–14). Nature ministers to him with a "temperate shew / Of objects that endure," and induces the "wise mood" that eschews "power and action" in favor of "those unassuming things, that hold / A silent station in this beauteous world" (*P* XII 35–52). The poet is "moderated" and "composed" by this ministry. On the other side of suffering, he is being reeducated into the "sentiment of Being," the state of mind that senses a plenitude of value in the world. Discomforts of act and obligation are left behind.

This is but a finer tone of "wise passiveness," a formula usually seen as inadequate to the more mature, less deliberately "simple" Wordsworth. But passages from the late books of *The Prelude* could be multiplied that treat nature as giver, the poet as receiver. Restoration comes as a gift of nature, and what is required is survival, a state of receptivity, and grace, not active willing and moral effort. Coleridge describes love as an act of will (*N* III 3562), but for Wordsworth it is more a state of grace. It is a providential and unearned gift. His unexpected reunion with Dorothy in 1794, whom he had seen only rarely since the age of seven, is such a gift. (Her very name means "gift of God.") And the "spots of time" do not require active willing. They work with or without our will; by means of them "our minds / Are nourished and invisibly repair'd" (*P* XI 260, 264–5). Such moments are "worthy of all gratitude" because they too are gifts.

The Mt. Snowdon passage (*P* XIII 1–119) that begins the final book of *The Prelude* confirms this pattern. Imagination does not become so aligned with strenuous moral willing as it does in Blake, Coleridge, and Shelley. Its full empowerment comes when it arrests any drift toward autonomy ("false imagination, placed beyond / The limits of experience and of truth") and aligns itself with nature in its largest sense, exceeding landscape. Just as nature, in a "domination which she often times / Exerts upon the outward face of things," transforms them in such a way that "even the grossest minds must see and hear / And cannot chuse but feel," so human imagination becomes a transforming and creative power exerting its own domination. Wordsworth makes an analogy between human creativity and nature's power, which is an "express / Resemblance, in the fulness of its strength / Made visible, a genuine Counterpart / And Brother of the glorious faculty [imagination] / Which higher minds bear with them as their own." He hopes

> that a work of mine
> Proceeding from the depth of untaught things,
> Enduring and creative, might become
> A power like one of Nature's. (*P* XII 309–12)

Nature and products of human imagination are "like" one another, but Wordsworth does not grant human imagination power independent of nature – nature conceived of as "the law of things" and not only as a particular scene or landscape that confronts us, or even the entire planet on which we live. The poet grants nature such priority that it orchestrates the terms by which it will be interpreted; he discovers more than interprets the emblem nature has shaped. He finds himself in an engulfing panorama, nature's most sublime show of force in the entire poem. "The universal spectacle throughout / Was shaped for admiration and delight" – shaped by nature, which situates the generic human imagination:

> in that breach
> Through which the homeless voice of waters rose,
> That dark deep thoroughfare, had Nature lodged
> The soul, the imagination of the whole.   (*P* XIII 62–5)

The larger Mt. Snowdon passage describes the dynamic activism of scene: light "fell like a flash," "the moon stood naked" and "looked down" upon a sea "usurped upon" by mist, the waters "roar." Amidst this, the astonished young man lacked the "time to ask" about causes. He "looked about" and "found [him]self" on the shore of a "huge sea of mist," wholly circum-stanced. It is only later that night that he can meditate and understand that the scene was emblematic of the human imagination's own power to usurp.

This meditation, too, emphasizes the power of scene to impress itself on the sensate mind, which "cannot chuse but feel." If human imagination exerts its own usurpations "upon the outward face of things" – through processes of molding, enduing, abstracting, and combining – it has learned to do so through imitation of natural power. This is close to Schelling's reinterpretation of mimesis in *On the Relation of the Plastic Arts to Nature*; imagination is a productive, not reproductive, power in its active imitation of nature's creative process, not simply of nature's face. In his own way, Wordsworth accepts Polixenes's wisdom that human art may "mend" great creating nature: "change it rather, but / The art itself is Nature." The panoramic, imposing, and pedagogical scene that confronts the poet on Mt. Snowdon is a display of nature as great parental power, the source and sanction of his own poetic gift. He has been all along "chosen" by nature to be a "higher mind," a poet.

Wordsworth ends the Mt. Snowdon passage with a non-metaphysical meditation on the moral products of imagination, which promotes "sovereignty within and peace at will," and "Emotion which best foresight need not fear." Imagination fosters "chearfulness in every act of life" (later revised to "cheerfulness for acts of daily life"), and "truth in moral judgments." The moral thrust of quasi-apocalyptic experience on Mt. Snowdon is ironically toward a domesticating of imagination to the varieties of daily human life, just as the artist builds up "greatest things / From least suggestions, ever on the watch." This spirit of accommodation is a far remove from the will to power of an *Übermensch*, whether Zarathustra or Rivers. Unlike Zarathustra, Wordsworth's "higher mind" comes down from the mountain as a gentle spirit, more prone to observation, pondering, quiet sympathy, and a will to value, than to dynamic resolve, action, urging, or

241

confronting in one's naked self the eye of God. Wordsworth has not, as Hartman argues, "displaced" the role of imagination, but has likened imagination to the highest manifestation of nature's own creative force, and has anchored imagination in the lowest forms of daily human life. Thus, imagination assumes its rightful place as "mediatrix," transforming the sublimities of the cosmic "law of things" into the forms of human life.[19]

The ethics of gentleness expressed in the final three books of *The Prelude* – which strikingly contrasts with Blake's more vigorous imperatives – discloses the wisdom toward which the poem has labored. It is a temporary landing-place for the future author of *Sonnets on the Punishment of Death* (1839–40), who will speak, in "Ode: 1815" on Waterloo, of carnage as God's daughter. *The Prelude* concludes with an ethics based still on feeling, not Christian duty, but it urges only one of two major ethical criteria. It urges that we increase our felt sense of value in the world (the "sentiment of Being") – through calm participation in natural process and kind gestures of the intimate domesticated imagination. It does not urge that other emanation of feeling – purposeful act based on the sense of obligation, social and political, and directed toward distributive justice and the eradication of evil.

After his crisis in Book Tenth, the poet is slowly restored, by Dorothy, Coleridge, and the landscape, to himself. He has gained greatly in understanding – he has been a "meditative, oft a suffering man" – but he is back home in the landscape, and with his earliest human companion. He will now participate in a society, but it will be different in kind from that larger society of humankind he has tried to love. It will be a society of intimates. His sister's presence cannot but suggest a degree of narcissism in his love, however gentle and de-eroticized. His return to landscape is not without the enhancements of intervening experience, from hope to despair to renewal, but it signifies also the beginning of a retreat from the ethical. Remembrance of

---

[19] Hartman writes in *Wordsworth's Poetry*: "A true though rather simple view of the structure of *The Prelude* would be gained by showing how the poet continually displaces or interprets apocalypse as akedah" – that is, imagination's drive toward autonomy is (mis)taken for nature's binding. Hence the Mt. Snowdon episode is a displacement: "In it the poet comes face to face with his Imagination yet calls it Nature. It is *The Prelude's* supreme instance of the avoidance of apocalypse" (p. 225). The evidence for Hartman's argument at key moments thus comes perilously close to being identical with its own counter-evidence (cf. pp. 124, 184, 232–3, 238, 251, 254, 257). I have used *Wordsworth's Poetry* heuristically to situate my own argument. See Hartman's new book, *The Unremarkable Wordsworth* (Minneapolis: University of Minnesota Press, 1987), especially Chapter 11, "The Poetics of Prophecy," for additional commentary on the Mt. Snowdon episode.

development and crisis has provided the narrative structure and sustained the compositional energies of *The Prelude*. Beyond the telling of this tale, he will preside, in retirement, over the conversion of these energies to a "dying, dying flame."

The dominance of scene over agent in Wordsworth has reversed Blake's dialectic, in which the agent can "obliterate" scene by dint of will and imagination. When Wordsworth leaves the Lake District for Cambridge or London, he reduces the circumference of scene, as Kenneth Burke might say, to scene-as-society, and as agent he is reduced accordingly. To return to a wider circumference of scene-as-nature (wider in the sense of more encompassing of this poet's sense of values) is to experience an augmentation of his power as agent, but this power remains dependent on scene. His own will is active mainly in seeking a context. And he acknowledges, sensibly enough, limits on our ability even to select our own context. It is a figure for the period that those Pantisocrats Coleridge and Southey dream of a radical change of scene but never arrive at the Susquehanna.

To say that one must leave the landscape (moral innocence) to engage the ethical is not, finally, to imply a fundamental antagonism between nature and morality. "Nature" for Wordsworth is the manifestation of vital order in the universe, not restricted to landscape. We violate nature by "false imagination," misplaced intellect, imbalances of the senses, repressive culture, and political exploitation. Evil is whatever violates nature in this larger sense. We have seen that one shock to the young poet's complacency is his recognition that the pre-moral values of landscape are inadequate to politics. A just revolution to correct social abuse does not occur by a casual extension of the values of the peasantry to the larger society. Human beings must attempt to will it, however little confidence Wordsworth maintains in our power as individuals to alter the course of history, time, and circumstance.

His retreat from ethical engagement is not sanctioned by nature in this larger sense, even though the landscape performs its saving ministry on its defeated returning son. The literal fact of Wordsworth's residence in Racedown, Alfoxden and the Lake District is not the issue. Rather, this retirement is emblematic of the retreat from types of ethical engagement that have become associated with deep psychic pain: the commitment of affection to persons who die, the commitment to social and political movements that betray themselves, the commitment to becoming a moral agent when intellect cannot decide on ends or means. The gentle, domesticated ethic that emerges in the end is inadequate to these larger questions. The final books of *The Prelude* reconfirm cardinal features of Wordsworth's personality: his constitutional social reluctance, his reticence (paradoxical in the speaking mouth that is a poet), his sense of peril, his acting for the mind's safety and sanity, his melancholia and death-consciousness. All these are temporarily answered to by the landscape as maternal gift-giver and by a small society of intimates. Vitality of feeling having been restored after the crisis of 1796, he can embark on the life of writing, and will write in full consciousness of these themes in the great poetry of 1797–1805. But the temptation to drift toward a more total mental retirement – one no longer productive of poetry – is felt throughout *The Prelude* and will prevail beyond its ending.

In the closing books Wordsworth has made fewer claims than critics have tended to assume for the power of imagination to create self and circumstance anew. We have seen something more profound: an acknowledgment of nature as that which gives and takes away and gives again, in a humanly meaningful way. Nature has "restored" imagination more than imagination has restored itself. Nature's power to give again is consoling well beyond the repossessive memory and the creative imagination.

There are obvious limits to renewal. Matthew's children, Lucy, and the boy of Winander cannot be revived; Michael will never finish the sheepfold. It is sobering to recall that *The Prelude* is described as a "Gift" for Coleridge, who had left in 1804 for Sicily and Malta, hoping for a release from opium addiction. The poem is an extended blessing of him, just as his conversation poems end with blessings; it is a prayer for his recovery. But in Malta Coleridge is confirmed in addiction, and his reappearance shocks the Wordsworth household, so mentally and physically ruined does he appear to be. Wordsworth suffers so much in the deaths of his brother John in 1805, and of two young children in 1812, that he does not need an additional lesson in Dorothy's mental disintegration. Gifts freely given are soon taken back, and one feels a sad irony in reading the 1805 *Prelude* while reflecting on the stripping away that begins from that year on.

Retreat from the ethical

The span of Wordsworth's great productivity lies, therefore, between two moments of intense suffering. The first is seen in his total retreat from ethical engagement, in 1795–6 by most accounts, following disillusionment with the French Revolution and the failure of rationalism or other commitments to fill the void. The second is the death of his brother John in 1805. These poles suggest in broad terms the changing relationship of composition to suffering. In the earlier period, suffering eventually proves enabling. The nadir of his life narrative proves to be a rite of passage into full creative potency; he writes *The Prelude* to fill the void. In it and other great poems, we find a death-consciousness that memory and imagination have converted to a poetry of hope and beauty. Suffering lends itself to a personal myth of restoration. But the death of John destroys this precarious, paradoxical myth. As Wordsworth writes in "Elegiac Stanzas" in response to his brother's death, "A power is gone, which nothing can restore; / A deep distress hath humanized my Soul." Humanization here means diminishment, the merely human that has lost its sustaining myth of a nourishing, caring nature. The drowning at sea of his brother seems a betrayal beyond the betrayals of history. By coincidence it occurs as he nears completion of the 1805 *Prelude* – which also signals the *de*pletion of his best material. Perhaps the period of great accomplishment was nearing its end, anyway. But the death of John still seems to have influenced the direction his verse was to take thereafter, in confirming a death-consciousness in ways no longer susceptible of a personal myth of restoration.

Though it contradicts the spirit of his great poetry, *The Excursion* (1814) is an extension of isolable elements in his earlier work. It has the effect of making one doubt, retrospectively, the profundity of the earlier work and should probably be read, beyond Book One and a few other passages of great power, only for diagnostic purposes.[20] Its fundamental motive is containment – of every emotion, idea, or event that might raise an overwhelming question about providential justice and the ability of human beings to stay sane and happy. Nothing ruffles the Wanderer and the Pastor. Containment has several strategies, foremost a bourgeois complacency about the adaptability of human mind to circumstance. An inherent fitness makes everything tend toward accommodation and comfort. Calamities are fortunate in that they promote the exercise of virtue. These strategies of containment emerge from the poet's anxiety that truly threatening forces are afoot: the force of circumstance without, the passional self within. But the sense of peril that invests the psychomachia of *The Prelude* is dismissed summarily by the ideology of *The Excursion*.

We have seen the stoical element in such narrative works as *Michael* and "Resolution and Independence," where calamity is met with quiet suffering and endurance, without hope of material recompense. *The Excursion* is not precisely stoical. The disenchanted Solitary – the

[20] See Hartman, *Wordsworth's Poetry*, 292.

philosophical malcontent whom the Wanderer and Pastor attempt, book after book, to cheer up – finds something to admire in the *"ends"* but not the *"means"* of the stoic, for whom wisdom is found in "Security from shock of accident, / Release from fear." Stoical disengagement from the world would mean freedom from "the persecuting sword," "defeated pride," "friendship betrayed," "love with despair, or grief with agony." Positively, it would mean seeking the "universal instinct of repose, / The longing for confirmed tranquillity, / Inward and outward; humble, yet sublime" (*EX* III 397–9). This qualified admiration is as close as any speaker comes to endorsing stoicism.

The Solitary has good reason to be sympathetic to the ends of stoicism, if not the means. Among other calamities he has lost his wife and two children. Having been raised happily as a youth on nature's bounty, he has had everything taken from him and implies that it would be better never to have made a passionate commitment to human values.

He is temporarily rescued from despondency not by stoicism but by the millennial prospects of the French Revolution. He is "reconverted to the world; / Society became my glittering bride" (*EX* III 734–5). When the Revolution fails, he turns to a self-serving individualism based on "rights" and the "Nature of the dissolute," instead of "fostering Nature." When individualism proves risky in the repressive Great Britain of the early nineties, he embarks for the New World where he hopes to roam at large,

> to observe, and not to feel,
> And, therefore, not to act—convinced that all
> Which bears the name of action, howsoe'er
> Beginning, ends in servitude—still painful,
> And mostly profitless. (*EX* III 892–6)

Here we see once again the link between feeling and act, and the withdrawal from both because of their exacerbation of loss, futility, and danger. The Americans prove a vulgar lot, however, with "big passions strutting on a petty stage." He sets out for the territory in search of a Rousseauistic paradise, only to find that the noble savage is a "creature, squalid, vengeful, and impure; / Remorseless, and submissive to no law / But superstitious fear, and abject sloth" (*EX* III 953–5).

The Solitary does not lose all vestiges of a Wordsworthian sensibility: to nature as a dynamic power he remains responsive, and he finds in it a foil for his reflections on the futility of human hopes. But in many ways he is the disappointed Romantic: he has failed in love, in revolution, in vocation, and in a quest for the primitive and innocent. His embittered withdrawal from the world is correlative to the poet's retirement in the closing books of *The Prelude*. Wordsworth has thus worked himself into a corner, eschewing both act and solitude, both the world and the self.

To the Solitary's narration of calamity and thwarted will, the Wanderer has but one response, which in effect forecloses any argument on behalf of stoicism. And although *The Excursion* continues for five more books, he intones here the final wisdom:

> One adequate support
> For the calamities of mortal life
> Exists – one only; an assured belief
> That the procession of our fate, howe'er
> Sad or disturbed, is ordered by a Being
> Of infinite benevolence and power;
> Whose everlasting purposes embrace
> All accidents, converting them to good.   (*EX* IV 10–17).

With this speech, the tragic sensibility that implicitly questioned aspects of Romantic humanism for its overconfidence in human powers has been overridden by doctrinal overconfidence. Moral dialectic has given way to supernaturalism. What follows is an elephantine extension of the epitaphic mode, in which language is not much more vital than the corpses it memorializes in the country churchyard.

This dismaying conclusion need not surprise us. It is another way of negotiating the same sense of peril we see in his great poetry. Stoicism, with which Wordsworth is often associated in later years, implies a balance of forces and resistance to circumstance that he admires in the days of his poetic faith, as he tests those sturdy solitaries against calamity. Later he discovers in his own real calamity how sturdy these figures must have been. Like his own disillusioned Solitary in *The Excursion*, he is unable to continue in his own being when confronted by loss: stoicism requires strength beyond his means. The traditional social commitments of stoicism are out of the question for the Solitary; nor is he able, in the manner of the poet of memory and imagination, to convert loss to gain. In his later work, Wordsworth negotiates the Solitary's doubt as to the value of human life. Christian incarnation and redemption promise an absolute recompense for loss and evil. Neither stoicism nor Romantic humanism survives the piety of this later work. Wordsworth's is a non-activist type of Christian ethic, based on suffering, consolation, patience, and other-worldly compensation. It is quite unlike what might be termed the residual Christian element in Shelley, who expresses an activist ethic based on human sympathy and equality. (Shelley hates the Christian Church and dogma but admires many aspects of Jesus's ethical teachings.)

It is ironic that *The Excursion*, which is so stifled by moralistic sentiment, represents Wordsworth's mental retreat from the ethical, a retreat that began in the final books of *The Prelude* in a disengagement from act and social participation. The disengagement here is more radical: from act, feeling, image, and even from that "sentiment of Being" so nourishing of the will to value. Duty no longer finds its primary sanction in human conscience – as in "Ode to Duty" – but in the revealed word of God.

Even in his earlier poetry Wordsworth has been critical of the overconfidence of human powers that Blake and Coleridge manifest in their concepts of imagination, love, and will. His great creating nature, with its donations of lakes, trees, and sky, is also an inexorable force that takes away what it has given. Pathos is found in the self's resistance to the stripping away that nature inflicts: the affections strive for permanence, language attempts to incarnate meaning for all time, memory to gain a sense of presence in the past. The Leech-gatherer, whose supply of leeches has dwindled, strives to maintain his sanity and make do with those leeches he can find. Things turn over, and the poet holds out for the return of spring, when his depression will be lifted. Nature brings other gifts. Yet the sadness of natural process and his disillusionment in social regeneration prompt him to seek compensation beyond either humanity or nature. The cycles of nature are broken and transcended not by Blakean humanistic imagination but by supernaturalism, by ideas of order that repress, in the moral and political sphere, the feelings and energies he had valued in his youth.

These capitulations occur, though, only after he has wrought the most complex poetic vision of self and circumstance in the period. Greatly influenced by him, De Quincey explores the plight of the moral agent confronted by the force of circumstance and tempers the human-ist's overconfidence in his own way.

5

De Quincey and Romantic decadence

When Thomas De Quincey escaped Manchester Grammar School in 1802, he felt the "deep, deep magnet" of William Wordsworth pulling him toward the Lake District. But the "principle of veneration" itself paralyzed him: Dove Cottage would have been "vulgarised" had he rushed in excited, truant, and impecunious. He went instead to Wales. In 1805 and again in 1806, he approached the Vale of Grasmere only to retreat "like a guilty thing, for fear I might be surprised by Wordsworth," whom he encased in the rhetoric of religious hyperbole. "The very image of Wordsworth as I prefigured it to my own planet-struck eye, crushed my faculties as before Elijah or St. Paul" (II 231). He indulged his most characteristic act: he fled. The five-foot tall De Quincey, who had in 1803 written an unctuous fan letter saying he was literally willing to die for Wordsworth, took confidence only when the opportunity arose in 1807 of escorting Coleridge's wife, Sarah, and three children from Bridgewater to Grasmere. His approach to Coleridge a few months earlier, once he had found the elusive poet and metaphysician, had not been such a trial. The image of Coleridge had not crushed his faculties.

De Quincey's arrival in Grasmere as a Coleridge-surrogate prefigured the larger structure of his life. He became in many respects like Coleridge. Both were opium-eaters, both were linguists and encyclopedists, both were plagiarists and procrastinators, both wrote apologiae, both looked to seventeenth-century British writers for prose models, both were famed for accounts of dream visions, and both had a cooling of friendship with their mutual idol. But De Quincey was an inexact *Doppelgänger*, as is seen in his different approach to such moral concerns as act and consequence, conscience and guilt, love and grief. Like Wordsworth, De Quincey qualified the Blakean/Coleridgean reading of the self's powers, but where Wordsworth had dwelt on tragic necessity, De Quincey saw human life engulfed in contingency, sometimes comic, sometimes sad. He magnified and made grotesque many Wordsworthian intuitions: their darker implications were exploited, their affirmative components subverted or attenuated. De Quincey practiced the extravagant revisionism of a decadent. Though much of his life and work echoed Coleridge, his more significant literary debt was to the poet he worshipped. ·

In the labyrinth

De Quincey fashions three elaborate metaphors to illustrate his leading moral concepts: the palimpsest, the Dark Interpreter, both in *Suspiria de Profundis* (1845), and the Whispering Gallery, in the 1856 revision of *Confessions of an English Opium-eater* (1822). The first is a metaphor of how mind stores and uses memory, the second of how mind acquaints itself with its own evil potential, and the third of how the world augments the significance of our slightest gestures. The palimpsest is a revision of Wordsworthian memory, the Dark Interpreter of the Blakean Idiot Questioner, and the Whispering Gallery of Coleridgean dread. De Quincey engages the ethical mostly on the level of moral psychology.

One of the most bookish of literary figures, De Quincey habitually speaks of "reading" or "deciphering" human character and events. The mind as palimpsest is the mind as literature:

What else than a natural and mighty palimpsest is the human brain? Such a palimpsest is my brain; such a palimpsest, O reader, is yours. Everlasting layers of ideas, images, feelings, have fallen upon your brain softly as light. Each succession has seemed to bury all that went before. And yet, in reality, not one has been extinguished. (*SP* 169)

To begin to know ourselves, we must read the stored imagery and associations of the brain, a process less likely to be initiated by willed introspection than by dreams and sudden trauma. The prospect of sudden death can flood us with all layers of memory in blinding simultaneity.

De Quincey assures us that although "grotesque collisions of . . . successive themes, having no natural connection," will be impressed upon the palimpsest, still all mental phenomena will be somehow fused so that "the grandeur of human unity" is affirmed (*SP* 169–70). From one stage of development to another, however, a human being does not manifest unity:

Man is doubtless *one* by some subtle nexus that we cannot perceive, extending from the new born infant to the superannuated dotard; but as regards many affections and passions incident to his nature at different stages, he is *not* one;

250

the unity of man in this respect is coextensive only with the particular stage to which the passion belongs. (*SP* 133)

The metaphor of palimpsest, implying accidental juxtapositions, miscellaneous accretion, and dim traces, expresses the De Quinceyan predicament. Like Wordsworth, he invokes unity as a notion – by his time it is even a tenet of Romantic ideology – but it is often overridden by fresh, concrete ironic observation or by the implications of his disquieting metaphors.

An account of his anxiety at the prospect of entering the "unfathomed abyss" of London for the first time – an anxiety reinforced en route by the high-ceilinged hollow rooms of a hotel in Shrewsbury – recalls the opening scene of Poe's "Fall of the House of Usher." De Quincey writes:

More than ever I stood upon the brink of a precipice; and the local circumstances around me deepened and intensified these reflections, impressed upon them solemnity and terror, sometimes even horror. It is all but inconceivable to men of unyielding and callous sensibilities how profoundly others find their reveries modified and overruled by the external characters of the immediate scene around them. Many a suicide that hung dubiously in the balances has been ratified, and carried into summary effect, through the forlorn, soul-revolting aspect of a crazy, dilapidated home. (*CEO* 346)

The force of circumstance is De Quincey's recurring theme, as it is Wordsworth's, but it is differently conceived. Instead of the vital interpenetration of self and surroundings – the precarious Wordsworthian commonplace of the great lyrics – we find the self in De Quincey deserted and alone, fearful but without any confidence in a "ministry of fear." And instead of the tragic necessity that runs through Wordsworthian narrative, we find in De Quincey only an absurd contingency in the nature of things. The mind as palimpsest has no say as to what is to be inscribed, yet what is inscribed dictates its volitional character.

Mental associations making up the labyrinth of memory reveal that "far more of our deepest thoughts and feelings pass to us through perplexed combinations of *concrete* objects, pass to us as *involutes* (if I may coin that word) in compound experiences incapable of being disentangled, than ever reach us directly and in their own abstract shapes" (*SP* 130). These compound associations often work through contrariety or paradox. De Quincey remembers the death of his older sister Elizabeth – which, as J. Hillis Miller says, "colors all his existence thereafter"[1] – as the more poignant for having occurred in summer. Seasonal incongruity is an involute that enhances grief. As a boy he

---

[1] *The Disappearance of God: Five Nineteenth-Century Writers* (Cambridge, Mass.: Harvard University Press, 1963), 19.

approached his sister's dead body in her bedchamber and heard through an open window the summer wind that "had swept the fields of mortality for a hundred centuries . . . [T]hree times in my life I have happened to hear the same sound in the same circumstances, namely, when standing between an open window and a dead body on a summer day" (*SP* 131). The complex oxymoronic image of summer wind and death is inscribed permanently. He explains Coleridge's departure from the Lake District in 1810 as a retreat from the pain of recollection that nature has forced upon him. Nature – a beautiful and living presence but associated with decay and solitude – is a "negative torment" reminding Coleridge, by ironic contrast with its fecundity, of the "blank annihilation" of his former strength. It is in a natural setting that "such evanescent hauntings of our past and forgotten selves are most apt to startle and to waylay us" (II 205).

De Quincey probes the darker implications of Wordsworthian memory. "Shadowy restorations" of the past are not necessarily luminous and restorative. They can be simply the renewal of trauma, or they may remind us of loss and failed promise. The traces of memory on the palimpsest of mind make up a ghostly miscellany of all that no longer exists for us. To remember – quite the opposite of repossession – is to aggravate the sense of loss.

If Wordsworth is cheered that the child is father of the man, De Quincey is appalled. We cannot escape the consequences of how we were treated as children. Unable to choose an environment, the child is wholly vulnerable to it: "the deep, deep tragedies of infancy, as when the child's hands were unlinked forever from his mother's neck, or his lips forever from his sister's kisses, these remain lurking below all, and these lurk to the last" (*SP* 171). His brother Pink's ruin at the hand of pirates was the inevitable result of his having been coddled, when young, by women and then thrashed by a schoolmaster. As a young boy, De Quincey heard a rumor of the harsh treatment given his sister Jane by a woman servant, which was sufficient to have "had a lasting revolutionary power in colouring my estimate of life," and which contributed, along with the deaths of father and siblings, to a premature loss of innocence (*A* I 35). Such chapter headings in his *Autobiography* as "The Afflictions of Childhood" and "Introduction to the World of Strife," tell the quality of his own experience. His early relationship with Elizabeth is a rare exception that proves the rule, because it is a lost happiness for which he yearns his entire life. His last words are a cry for his sister. Whether early experience is traumatic or wondrous, memory of it is a curse.

Throughout the autobiographical writings, De Quincey shows that the story of a life is a matter of luck and accident within the contingencies of scene, but that the human mind thus victimized is itself woefully determined. I think this unjust incongruity of mind to scene structures his absurdist vision of things. We have seen that for Wordsworth the act of composition promises to return a degree of freedom and power to the moral agent; it is a way of challenging the compulsions of scene without and the causality of mind within. But whereas Wordsworth in *The Prelude* confronts the burden of too much compositional liberty and converts a menacing indeterminacy into resolute acts of writing, De Quincey gives the impression of being content to follow his humors, whether they dictate impassioned prose or idle chatter. Diverging also from the Freud he in some ways anticipates, he sees psychological determinism canceling any therapeutic advantage in self-exploration. The purpose of autobiography is not self-empowerment, as it is for Wordsworth. De Quincey writes for no expressed purpose, his commentary accreting at random on his own commentary in the revised *Confessions of an English Opium-eater*.

Self-knowledge forever eludes the inquisitor, who must settle for interpretation. De Quincey assumes an inexpiable and incomprehensible guilt as the foundation of human personality, an awareness of which is pressed upon us by a perverse alter ego, the Dark Interpreter. This figure is the self beyond the self who judges, cajoles, and reminds. It is a "self-projection" who acts as a Greek chorus, "not to tell you anything absolutely new . . . but to recall you to your own lurking thoughts . . . pointing the moral or deciphering the mystery" (*SP* 183). As a projection of one's shadow self, not unlike the Jungian figure, it is the haunting representation of evil potential in oneself and others, "the abysses which a human will can open," the "pain and agony and woe possible to man" (*SP* 191). Like Blake's Idiot Questioner, it reminds us of dark potential. He notes Coleridge's encounter with the Spectre of the Brocken – our own image so projected in mountain mists that it is often mistaken for a phantom, which phenomenon Coleridge uses as a metaphor for pursuit of an illusory ideal ("Constancy to an Ideal Object," 1826). De Quincey claims the image as a dark presence, not the "glory" of Coleridge's poem. The opium-eaters agree, however, that there is an abyss in the self which consciousness can probe only in a limited way, from which come perversity and evil but from which also comes creative energy. A fiend incarnate

would be a poor trivial bagatelle compared to the shadowy projections, *umbras* and *penumbras*, which the unsearchable depths of man's nature is capable, under adequate excitement, of throwing off, and even into stationary forms . . .

253

There are creative agencies in every part of human nature, of which the thousandth part could never be revealed in one life.   (*SP* 188–9)

Since the Dark Interpreter is a source more of mystery than of knowledge – its deciphering yields only the fact but not the nature of a deep truth – it enhances the sense of the sublime. Images of shadows, veils, mist, darkness, the indefinite, the unfathomable, and the infinite abound in De Quincey. He is drawn to the "abyss of idealism" that Wordsworth fears. Unlike Coleridge – an inquiring spirit seeking answers to mysteries while acknowledging that *omnia exeunt in mysterium* – De Quincey seeks out mystery and prefers not to dispel it. As reader of hieroglyphs without and within, he does not seek a complete decoding and confesses that his mind "demands mysteries" (II 154). Among the British Romantics he is the most ardent and willful practitioner of the sublime for its own sake, and contrasts in this respect most pointedly with Shelley. The Dark Interpreter puts us in mind of what De Quincey calls the "dark sublime" (*A* I 130).

Language is itself hieroglyphic and mysterious, as well as inefficient, misleading, and perverse. This operative concept of language under-writes De Quincey's moral view. In an essay on style, he alludes to Wordsworth's statement in *Essays on Epitaphs* that language is not the dress of thought but its "incarnation," and thus inseparable from it. The union of thought and language, writes De Quincey, "is too subtle, the intertexture too ineffable, each co-existing not merely with the other, but each *in* and *through* the other" (X 229–30). His practice contradicts this high estimate, however; neither the sign nor its augmentation in the symbol donates so much reality. Both authors are aware of the limits of language – that hackneyed theme of modern criticism – but De Quincey more than Wordsworth and other Romantic writers exploits the comic irony in the disproportion between our strong need to communicate and our inability to do so.

Many episodes in *Confessions of an English Opium-eater*, especially in its revised version of 1856, portray language's comic unreliability. These episodes suggest that we are indecipherable one to another. One of young De Quincey's guardians had been a preacher vain enough to require his ward to use his 330 sermons "as a textual basis upon which I was to raise a mimic duplicate – sometimes a pure miniature abstract – sometimes a rhetorical expansion – but preserving as much as possible of the original language, and also (which puzzled me painfully) preserving the exact succession of the thoughts," a difficult feat since there was no logical succession at all (*CEO* 239). The preacher's idolatry of his own utterance was in direct proportion to its emptiness. Shortly before running away from Manchester Grammar

School, De Quincey receives a letter addressed to "Monsieur Monsieur De Quincey," with a draft for about forty guineas. Certainly not a "Monsieur" to the second power, he knows he is not the intended recipient. The enclosed letter, written by a servant because a gentleman does not demean himself with calligraphy, is illegible: "I could not make out two consecutive sentences." It typifies De Quincey's sense of accidentality in language that an illegible letter, written not by the sender himself but by an intermediary, bearing, however, obviously important information, finds it way to the wrong receiver.

Shortly thereafter, he and an unfamiliar woman narrowly escape drowning in a flash flood of the River Bore. Audaciously breaching the first law of English manners, he speaks to her even though "*I had never been introduced to her.*' He would propose an exception to the code: "In the midst of any great natural convulsion – earthquake, suppose, waterspout, tornado, or eruption of Vesuvius – it shall and may be lawful in all time coming (any usage or tradition to the contrary notwithstanding), for two English people to communicate with each other" (*CEO* 307). Later, however, he holds his tongue: upon being suspected by a bishop of being a swindler, he is tempted to let him

know my mind in Greek; which, at the same time that it would furnish some presumption in behalf of my respectability, might also . . . compel the bishop to answer in the same language; and in that case I doubted not to make good my superiority as a versatile wielder of arms rarely managed with effect, against all the terrors of his lordship's wig.
(*CEO* 323)

But he refrains from this act of verbal aggression, sensing an unfair advantage in his linguistic competence itself. When a Malaysian on mysterious business in the Lake District is met at the door by De Quincey's servant, "*his* knowledge of English was exactly commensurate with *hers* of Malay . . ." Since De Quincey's knowledge of "Oriental" languages is limited to the Arabic word for barley and the Turkish for opium, he addresses the Malaysian "in some lines from the *Iliad*" (*CEO* 403).

These instances imply an absurdist view of language and communication. When his mother, who is "predisposed to think ill of all causes that required many words," is stupefied by her son's departure from Manchester Grammar School, De Quincey senses the hopelessness of speech. "She and I were contemplating the very same act; but she from one centre, I from another." "If in this world there is one misery having no relief, it is the pressure on the heart from the Incommunicable" (*CEO* 315). Whereas Wordsworth says language is ideally the incarnation of thought, De Quincey declares it incapable of incarnating for one's own mother the most elementary truth about oneself. Those who are most voluble only confirm the void behind language, and here the paradigm is Coleridge, whose famed conversation is not conversation at all. His "eternal stream of talk which never for one instant intermitted, and allowed no momentary opportunity of reaction to the persecuted and baited listener," left one "in the exhausted condition of one that has been drawn up just before death from the bottom of a well occupied by foul gases" (*CEO* 331–2). But De Quincey himself confesses to doing much the same: "my way of writing is rather to think aloud, and follow my own humours, than much to inquire who is listening to me (*CEO* 413–14). His writing has the syntactical character of a labyrinth in which contingency reigns, the writer following his humors with no assurance they are taking him anywhere. The revised *Confessions* is notoriously garrulous, symptomatic of his anxiety at a void behind language that he covers with still more language, insert after insert, digression upon digression, and irksome gestures of false intimacy toward "dear reader." And sometimes his chatter seems an evasion of the Dark Interpreter, who would remind him of evil and nightmare.

These observations suggest a correlation between the absurd and the sublime: both issue from caprices of interpretation. The absurd decrees that the greater our wish to communicate, the more we will be subjected to reductive and deflating misinterpretation. The result is comic pathos. De Quincey has an affinity here with "Jean Paul" Richter, whom he reads extensively and translates. With respect to language, he more precisely recapitulates the dilemma of Sterne: great inner need for communication and great inefficiency in the agency of communication. The moment of deepest communication in *Confessions* is accordingly non-verbal: Ann of Oxford Street's gesture of kindness in bringing him a glass of port-wine and spices when he is close to expiring on the street. De Quincey terms this a "noble act," but absurdly he fails in all their time together to ask her surname and is unable, after separation, to trace her.

The sublime, as turn of the coin, is a way of inflating the import of signs. We sense that there is an overwhelming meaning in signifiers – whether they be words, acts and gestures, landscape, or dreams – but what it is, is unknown. The psychic impact of experience is all the greater when it is, as De Quincey says of dreams, "incommunicable by words," and when it outstrips our cognitive apparatus generally. The sublime bespeaks the inadequacy of language to incarnate experience, but for this reason language yields the promise of enhanced meaning. The Dark Interpreter reads the daily, familiar, cautious self as the cypher of an abyss of evil potential and dark sublimity. The sublime is, in this sense, an inflation and overvaluation of signs based on their very inadequacy, while the absurd is their comic undervaluation. De Quincey oscillates between the sublime and the absurd, the apocalyptic and the trivial, in a non-dialectical fracture of vision. These oppositions are joined only insofar as they are all interpretive readings of confessedly problematic status, undertaken by the solitary mind – the mind of De Quincey talking to himself in print. (A larger fracture, I will argue, exists between all these disorienting oppositions in his best writing and the unquestioning commitment to orthodoxy in his worst.)

The figure of the Whispering Gallery at St. Paul's Cathedral, both sublime and absurd, sets forth the enigmas of moral decision-making, act, and consequences. It illustrates the incommensurateness of act and consequences, culpability and guilt, and thus the uncertainties of moral judgment. Just as a "word or a question, uttered at one end of the gallery in the gentlest of whispers, is reverberated at the other end in peals of thunder," so an act, seemingly inconsequential at the time, may have ruinous consequences that can be neither predicted nor thwarted. This "fact" wraps him up in a "sort of trance, a frost as of some deathlike revelation." (One hesitates to disabuse him – the Whispering Gallery does not in fact augment sound – for fear of spoiling a fine figure.) Just as he prepares to escape Manchester Grammar School, the figure (so he says) comes to mind, and thereafter becomes a leitmotif that accompanies perilous decisions.

For De Quincey the future is a void waiting to be filled with catastrophe. "Death we can face; but knowing, as some of us do, what is human life, which of us is it that without shuddering could (if consciously we were summoned) face the hour of birth?" (*SP* 221). An act's value alters as time carries it forward in its consequences. One's life is itself an accumulation of unforeseen consequences that attend blind acts:

In fact, every intricate and untried path in life, where it was from the first a matter of arbitrary choice to enter upon it or avoid it, is effectually a path through a vast Hercynian forest, unexplored and unmapped, where each several turn in your advance leaves you open to new anticipations of what is next to be expected, and consequently open to altered valuations of all that has been already traversed. (*CEO* 314).

Since the value of all acts is "conditioned and contingent upon what is yet to come," there is no way of knowing, at any moment, what one ought to do. Judgment of past actions is biased by perpetual revisionism. A life of moral intelligence is impossible. De Quincey contracted

257

his opium habit, for instance, the fatal day he innocently entered an apothecary's shop hoping for relief from toothache.

In a world of rank contingency, why do we deserve the burden of bad conscience? De Quincey experiences a Coleridgean perplexity: he feels judged guilty, and he feels guilty, even though he knows he is not culpable. Like Coleridge, he thinks William Paley errs in making consequences or utility the ground of morality. All acts "expand themselves through a series of alternate undulations, expressing successively good and evil," none of which can be judged practically in advance, as the aftermath of the French Revolution demonstrates on a large scale (VIII 138–40; V 192–4). If consequences can be used as a test of an act's rightness or wrongness, De Quincey stands incriminated in his addiction. But what is a practical guide, before the fact, to the moral life? The conscience seems inefficient; it may merely whisper against some questionable act at the moment of commission, "but at the other end of thy long life-gallery that same conscience will speak to thee in volleying thunders" (CEO 297). Upon his mother's suggestion that his own bad example in absconding from school might injure his brothers, his conscience "smote" him, and once again the Whispering Gallery emerges. Though these dreadful consequences did not come to pass, "the fear that they *might* take effect thrilled me with remorse" (CEO 313).

In a Borgesian tale of the mathematical grotesque, De Quincey recounts his "earliest trespass" (SP 155–63). Having at about age ten run up a debt of three guineas to a bookseller, he begins to feel "remorse and deadly anxiety," not so much because of the three guineas as because of his conviction that having purchased one volume of a history of Great Britain and one of naval exploration, he is committed to buying all subsequent volumes in the set – which, in the case of a subject so immense as the sea, must be thousands of volumes. Surely the bookseller will show up at his door followed by immense carriages filled with books for which he will be unable to pay. De Quincey now sees the absurdity and pathos of this, and also the "fearful caprice of lunacy" in a child's imagination as in an adult's dreams. But the tale expresses a lunacy close to reality: in a world of perilous contingency, a minor indiscretion can exact a mighty debt of suffering and guilt. One approaches the Hercynian forest with dread.

De Quincey's evaluation of his own guilt or innocence is ambiguous. In the original preface to his *Confessions*, he says that opium-eating was only an anodyne, not an indulgence: "guilt, therefore, I do not acknowledge" (CEO 211). He and Coleridge exchange charges that opium is a self-indulgence, each claiming the drug was originally, for himself alone, doctor's orders. But De Quincey does highlight the pleasures of opium and admits that he has taken it for pleasure and experimentation. His making light of what his audience would find opprobrious rings of nervous, hollow jocularity. He even makes moral claims for the drug, noting that it produces "exquisite order, legislation, and harmony" among the mental faculties; and "with respect to the temper and moral feelings in general, it gives simply that sort of vital warmth which is approved by the judgment . . . Thus, for instance, opium, like wine, gives an expansion to the heart and the benevolent affections . . ." (*CEO* 383). In dichotomizing the "pleasures" and the "pains" of opium, he evades a final judgment of its moral value.

Only once in *Confessions* does he describe the mental state of the addict in horrific terms, with echoes of Coleridge:

The opium-eater loses none of his moral sensibilities or aspirations; he wishes and longs as earnestly as ever to realise what he believes possible, and feels to be exacted by duty; but his intellectual apprehension of what is possible infinitely outruns his power, not of execution only, but even of proposing or willing. He lies under a world's weight of incubus and nightmare; he lies in sight of all that he would fain perform, just as a man forcibly confined to his bed by the mortal languor of paralysis . . . is compelled to witness injury or outrage offered to some object of his tenderest love . . .   (*CEO* 433)

This last image of an inability to rescue others from harm recurs in De Quincey's writings. As a boy he may have felt somehow responsible for the deaths of father and siblings, thus suffering a neurotic fear of repeating the crime.

The English Mail Coach (1849) explores the theme of helplessness and non-performance. Even when he can foresee a calamitous chain of events, he lacks the "presence of mind" to act, as if in submission to the inevitable:

The palsy of doubt and distraction hangs like some guilty weight of dark unfathomed remembrances upon my energies when the signal is flying for *action*. But, on the other hand, this accursed gift I have, as regards *thought*, that in the first step towards the possibility of a misfortune I see its total evolution; in the radix of the series I see too certainly and too instantly its entire expansion; in the first syllable of the dreadful sentence I read already the last.
(*EM* 311–12)

Like Coleridge, he suffers a separation of consciousness and will. De Quincey can foresee the calamity, as the mail coach he is riding is on the verge of colliding with a small carriage. He feels helpless to prevent it, though only he can prevent it and the death of a young couple. In a criminal acquiescence, he will permit it to happen. The episode, which does not turn out calamitously, is nonetheless swept into his dreams forever.

Not wishing to brand it idiosyncratic, De Quincey reads this willlessness before a threat to be a repetition of man's original fall from grace and innocence. It "exposes a dreadful ulcer, lurking far down in the depths of human nature." The childhood dream of lying down before the menacing lion "publishes the secret frailty of human nature – reveals its deep-seated falsehood to itself – records its abysmal treachery." Each of us would take the bait "offered to the infirm places of [our] own individual will" (*EM* 304). The mere thought of it fills him with a remorse of the imagination, remorse for an event that has never occurred.

Shame is, he confesses, a stronger motive in him than guilt; if he could save someone's life "only by facing a vast company of critical or sneering faces, I might perhaps shrink basely from the duty" (*SP* 136) – a reflection that in itself prompts feelings of guilt. In his autobiographical writings, all permutations of guilt, shame, and pride occur. He feels guilty because of the prominence of shame where guilt would be more appropriate; he feels shame as he confronts a reader who will perhaps not be talked into granting indulgence for his guilt; and in confessing it all publicly, he seems proud of both his shame and guilt.

As if to confess that feelings of guilt have lurked there all along, De Quincey closes his *Confessions* with two dreams. The first, of resurrection on Easter Sunday, shifts from a vision of a child's grave (Wordsworth's daughter, Kate) to a vision of Ann, walking with him down Oxford Street just as she had eighteen years earlier. The second dream is the contrary of the first, a dream of loss just as the first is a dream of recovery. Set in a morning of crisis but of "ultimate hope for human nature," it ends in disaster for which the dreamer himself feels responsible. In this "undecipherable issue," he feels he had the power to decide it "if I could raise myself to will it; and yet again [I] had not the power, for the weight of twenty Atlantics was upon me, or the oppression of inexpiable guilt" (*CEO* 446). Apocalyptic urgency yields to "the sense that all was lost, female forms, and the features that were worth all the world to me." The vision ends when the "incestuous mother," Sin, utters the "abhorred name of Death," with "everlasting farewells" reverberating as if through the caves of hell. This dream connects De Quincey's obsessive sense of loss with guilt, which has its origin in the happenstance of his own life. It is notable for its combination of moral absolutes – ultimate hope, inexpiable guilt, catastrophic battle, power, hell, sin, death, loss – with total moral indeterminacy.

Any context that would locate or define the source of guilt, the purpose of the warfare, the distribution of good and evil, and the nature of the power that might decide the issue, is missing. "Somewhere, but I knew not where—somehow, but I knew not how—by some beings, but I knew not by whom—," he cries. Moral accountability survives, but all the contexts that would help "decipher" its meaning have dissolved. The weighty bad conscience that does not speak the nature of his guilt also paralyzes his will to act for the good. This is conscience detached from origins and purpose; it is omnipresent and oppressive. It is a surrealistic heightening of the moral pressure that scene exerts in Wordsworth.

The signal feature of De Quincey's moral view is revealed in this tormenting dream (whether or not he actually had it): a lack of control over the contingent circumstances that perversely hold him accountable. The dream's dreadful revelation glosses the waking state.

To be sure, he takes up the expected Romantic quest for freedom from authority. Up to age eighteen, "I was engaged in duels of fierce continual struggle with some person or body of persons that sought, like the Roman *retiarius,* to throw a net of deadly coercion or constraint over the undoubted rights of my natural freedom" (*SP* 202). It was not only a right but "the noblest of duties to resist." A lengthy chapter in the *Autobiography* chronicles the torture of being forced to play a minor lieutenant in his oldest brother's military games. These were quite imaginative, rivaling Uncle Toby's, but they were impositions. His brother's superiority in "decision of purpose, and in energy of will" thwarted "the free spontaneous movements of a contemplative dreamer like myself" (*A* I 115). When his brother finally leaves home, it is for young De Quincey a "revolutionary experience," the beginning of a new epoch. The later escape from Manchester Grammar School is also described as "revolutionary," and has, he says, something of the same impact on him that the French Revolution had on Wordsworth.

The account of his decision to escape the Grammar School discloses more of De Quincey's attitude toward freedom, which, from all he has said about mind and circumstance, ought to be inconceivable. But he does see brief opportunities for mental and physical release from "strife," the conflict between personal will and authority or circumstance. This conflict can be creative: "Either the human being must suffer and struggle as the price of a more searching vision, or his gaze must be shallow and without intellectual revelation" (*SP* 201–2). What one notes first about this episode, however, is that the decision itself, which "transformed my whole being," is not "intellectual" but blind. The resolution to abscond comes "in the twinkling of an eye . . . not as

261

if issuing from any act or any choice of my own, but as if passively received from some dark oracular legislation external to myself" (*CEO* 278). In the next breath he says that the "fulminating word—*Let there be freedom*" is "spoken from some hidden recess in my own will." He is thus ambivalent on the issue of whether the impulse to freedom comes from within or without. If it comes from without, then individual freedom is the "soft determinism" we have seen in Wordsworth, which includes the agent as cause within a larger causal chain. Even if the decision is from within, freedom is a far remove from humanistic alignment of intelligence with choosing. The word "freedom" is spoken *for* him by the unconscious, the "hidden recess in my own will." An earlier revolutionary upheaval, the departure of his oldest brother, had been for him a "deliverance, so sudden and so *unlooked for*" (*A* I 119–20). An element of the fortuitous, even of grace, is implicated in acts of freedom. De Quincey likens the feeling accompanying his escape to Wordsworth's description of the "festal state of France during the happy morning-tide of her First Revolution" as "*the senselessness of joy*" that was all the more sublime for being "irreflective" (*CEO* 279).

There had been some comforts in submission. In suffering the tyranny of his brother William, he had felt disburdened of a certain anxiety:

By temperament and through natural dedication to despondency, I felt resting upon me also too deep and gloomy a sense of obscure duties attached to life, that I never *should* be able to fulfil; a burden which I could not carry, and which yet I did not know how to throw off. Glad, therefore, I was to find the whole tremendous weight of obligations—the law and the prophets—all crowded into this one pocket command, 'Thou shalt obey thy brother as God's vicar on earth'. (*A* I 71)

The passage hints at a deeper psychology of submission and pleasure in orthodoxy.

Meanwhile, to what use is freedom to be put? It is for young De Quincey at first a vision of "sweet pastoral hills," an "earthly heaven, a perpetual spring." And later, on the road and sleeping among cows, he feels like the Wandering Jew "liberated from the persecution which compelled him to move . . . Happier life I cannot imagine than this vagrancy" (*CEO* 329). Pastoral innocence in the Romantic period has the status of a wish, not a project of the will. The way back to Eden, if at all, is through experience. This brief interlude must give way to a larger loss of innocence in the streets of London.

Though these early episodes suggest the happy vagrancy of a

picaresque narrative, De Quincey is unsuited to write one. The typical picaresque hero has little memory and goes through experience without absorbing it. Episodes accumulate in the narrative, not in the protagonist. But De Quincey's concepts of memory and environment so permeate his tale that cheerful discarding is out of the question. What events there are, especially in the 1856 version, are so encased in the narrator's chatter that they seem a pretext for commentary.

The young De Quincey has no idea where he is going. The impulse to escape banal authority is greater than any particular goal. The future for him is without content. Being on the road is always a misleading metaphor of freedom; it gives one the giddy feeling of "indifferentism" – the ability to choose among options free of a strict causality of motives – and it seems to give the option of escaping whatever set of circumstances comes one's way. But it does not offer freedom in the larger sense described in Chapter 2: freedom from the coercion of other people and of nature, and also empowerment, or the ability to obtain objects of the will. De Quincey depicts the life of the truant as a series of entrapments leading to a loss of innocence and near-death. Each new set of circumstances is more threatening than the last. Keats's idea that circumstance and suffering result in greater "identity" is not operative in this narrative, although De Quincey has nominally subscribed to it. He is caught in a contradiction we have seen in self-realizationist perspectives. The cry, "Let there be freedom," is diminished by indeterminate ethical desire. He does not know what he wishes to do or become – and a deeper psychological necessity will assert itself as corrective. The narrative ends abruptly and anti-climactically when without explanation De Quincey is reconciled with his guardians. The vagrant leaves off the down-and-out life in London and prepares to enter Oxford. Any existential impulse to freedom has been diminished to truancy, and if the youth ever had a destiny it appears to have been with the deep deep magnetic pull back to legitimacy.

The lure of orthodoxy

Since the unrepentant opium-eater is also a Tory and an Anglican, we might well ask whether De Quincey ever integrates his views. The answer is no. He continues to oscillate between the absurdist sublime and various orthodoxies. In turning from Blake to Wordsworth to De Quincey, we have seen a movement from the revolutionary to the political apostate to the inveterate Tory, which mirrors their differing estimates of human power relative to social and natural circumstances. In making our way down the scale of power, we have moved from strong to problematic to weak humanism. As an absurdist, De Quincey has interestingly weakened, even subverted many tenets of Romantic humanism: the moral agent is too much a pawn of scene to have the power of self-determination; the child is father of the man in an oppressive way; the mind is the product of random accumulation in a contingent universe; love and imagination prove weak forces. This weak humanism is incapable of displacing the orthodoxies to which De Quincey has perfunctorily granted a life-long lease. His writings expressly dealing with moral topics, to which I turn now, might seem to reclaim humanistic values – and De Quincey does participate, haltingly, in the Romantic will to value – but reclamation is half-hearted when it is not illusory.

He, like Coleridge, expounds a moral liberalism with regard to human infirmities. Rejecting stoicism because he is "too much of an Eudaemonist," he seeks a morality that would "condescend more to the infirm condition of an opium eater . . . An inhuman moralist I can no more endure, in my nervous state, than opium that has not been boiled." He would decline spending any of his remaining energies "upon desperate adventures of morality" (*CEO* 400). He and Coleridge independently criticize Wordsworth and Southey for their moral severity. And like Coleridge, De Quincey finds Kant's ethics too inflexible and austere, especially his belief that lying, no matter what the context, is never justified:

So sacred, in his estimate, was the obligation to unconditional veracity that he declared it to be a duty, in case a murderer should apply to you for information as to the route taken by a man who had just escaped from his murderous fangs, to tell him the truth, the whole truth, and nothing but the truth. Not to save a poor innocent fellow-creature from instant and bloody death, not even to save the assassin from the guilt and misery of so hideous a crime, would it be lawful, in Kant's judgment, to practise any the slightest evasion or disguise.

(VIII 104; cf. XIII 13)

Most people would, he thinks, "pronounce monstrous" Kant's rigidity on the question of veracity. But the general moral rule against lying remains just. Kant's error lies in single-minded imposition of the general rule. "Not truth individual or personal, not truth of mere facts, but truth doctrinal – the truth which teaches, the truth which changes men and nations – this is the truth concerned in Kant's meaning, had he explained his own meaning to himself more distinctly" (VIII 365).

"Perhaps it is not very important how a man theorises upon morality," he writes, since moral concepts in themselves have little bearing on life. Even so, he considers applying in 1830 for the Chair of

Moral Philosophy at London University. We may place him, like Wordsworth, in line with the moral school of the sentiments, deriving from Shaftesbury, Hutcheson, Hume, and Adam Smith, but the debt is non-specific. Occasionally he refers to "moral sense," more frequently to "the heart" or "sensibility." In a diary kept during 1803, he rejects "the idea of judging of a person's *character* from his *outward actions* . . . which so many circumstances might make incongruous with his *character*," a Wordsworthian sentiment. And in discussing Addison's depiction of Cato, he remarks to a neighbor that Cato

> had no one trait in his character but that of being dead to all human feelings . . . "which indeed," said I, "is a necessary prelude and accompaniment of the Stoic philosophy"; — C[ragg] affirmed that the Stoic philosophy went to *regulate* . . . not to *annihilate* the feelings. "However," rejoined I, "though I do not admit that, yet, admitting it, it is not likely that a man, who had ever tasted the pleasures of sensibility, would embrace a doctrine which professed even to *regulate* the feelings," — he must have a sympathetic coldness.[2]

Elsewhere, he continues to downgrade "outward action": a particular act may originate, messily, in a "large variety of motives," and motives, in turn, are nothing "when compared with the absolutely infinite influxes of feeling or combinations of feeling that vary the thoughts of man; and the true internal *acts* of moral man are his thoughts, his yearnings, his aspirations, his sympathies or repulsions of heart" (XI 80).

This internalization of the concept of action contains some wishful thinking when it comes from procrastinating, paralytic opium-eaters like De Quincey and Coleridge, or even from an upright procrastinator like Wordsworth. Coleridge's occasional elevation of "being" over "doing" never answers to his guilt over non-performance, and he accedes to the Socratic truth that "perfect Well-*being* is one and the same with well-*doing* . . . A spirit made perfect is a self-ponent act, in which (or whom) the Difference of Being and Doing ceases" (*PL* 409 n34).

De Quincey believes that our feelings provide an ample intuitional grasp of first principles, which are Christian in character. First principles are blandly notional, however, and do not take us that far in the conduct of life, nor do they redress moral indeterminacy. One must attempt to judge particular moral acts or situations in their falling away from these self-evident principles, which is the purpose of casuistry. His extended essay entitled "Casuistry" (1839–40) is his most direct

[2] *A Diary of Thomas De Quincey*, ed. Horace A. Eaton (New York: Payson & Clarke, 1927), 178–9.

engagement with the subject of ethics. Casuistry has been unjustly scorned, he thinks, because of its association with the Catholic confessional. It has been used opportunistically to evade moral rules in tough cases and has been too much concerned, as Coleridge also notes, with prurient inquisition – into the weighty matter, for instance, of whether or not digital sacrifice of the hymen constitutes loss of virginity. But De Quincey argues for the respectability and necessity of this moral discipline. Defined as the study of "oblique deflexions from the universal rule," casuistry is "absolutely indispensable to the *practical* treatment of morals":

After morality has done its very utmost in clearing up the grounds upon which it rests its decisions—after it has multiplied its rules to any possible point of circumstantiality—there will always continue to arise cases without end, in the shifting combinations of human action, about which a question will remain whether they do or do not fall under any of these rules.　　　(VIII 313)

The Scottish Common-Sense School errs in thinking moral intuition easily decides practical issues of right and wrong. Thomas Reid committed a "ludicrous blunder" in declaring Aristotelian logic a superfluous "elaborate machinery" for "bringing out the merest self-evident truths" (VIII 312n). In the practical affairs of the moral life, close syllogistic reasoning is often needed to see, for example, if a particular act of suicide is or is not subsumed, as a minor proposition, under the major proposition that killing someone is unjustified, "except under the palliations x, y, z."

The essay on casuistry is in keeping with De Quincey's sense of human life as a Hercynian forest of moral confusion. Life is too slippery an affair to submit gracefully to our moral categories. Ethics properly gives way to casuistry, since all our acts are a "falling away" (*casus*) from those certainly true but only obliquely applicable imperatives and rules to which we cling in the "desperate adventures of morality." Each act has its own personal character, its variation on the rule, and the "tendency of such variations is, in all states of complex civilisation, to absolute infinity" (VIII 314). He gathers together a hodge-podge of "cases," amusingly inapposite – from Napoleon's slaughter of prisoners at Jaffa and Charles the First's execution of Lord Strafford, to more general questions of suicide, usury, dueling, health, and veracity, to those persistent knotty issues, "Giving Characters to Servants Who Have Misconducted Themselves" and "Criminal Prosecution of Fraudulent Servants." Some of these he presses to firm conclusions, others not, but in each case he attempts to fill out the context, whether on historical, personal, or logical grounds. With reference to suicide, he cites Donne's essay, *Biathanatos* (?1609, 1646), for its plausible argument that just as killing can be scaled – from murder to manslaughter to justifiable homicide – so suicide can be scaled from "self-murder" to "culpable self-homicide" to "justifiable self-homicide" (VIII 336).

The most interesting, or at least "De Quinceyan," of these discussions concerns "Health," which he thinks has been incorrectly excluded from the matter of obligation. It is, after all, a duty "which a man owes to himself," the lack of which deprives one of "free agency." The Quakers are morally culpable in discouraging the free expression of emotion, which results in "anomalous forms of nervous derangement,"

the secret principle of which turns not . . . upon feelings too much called out by preternatural stimulation, but upon feelings too much repelled and driven in. Morbid suppression of deep sensibilities must lead to states of disease equally terrific, and possibly even less tractable; not so sudden and critical it may be, but more settled and gloomy. I speak not of any physical sensibilities, but of those which are purely moral – sensibilities to poetic emotions, to ambition, to social gaiety, or to impassioned and exalted love. Quaker philosophy takes notice of no possible emotions, however modified or ennobled, as more or other than as morbid symptoms of a morbid derangement. Accordingly, it is amongst the young men and women of this body that the most afflicting cases under this eccentric type occur.   (VIII 349)

Whatever the justice of this comment as it applies to Quakers, De Quincey, like Coleridge, adumbrates modern notions of the physical and moral consequences of psychological repression.

The implicit ethic is, of course, that one should be permitted to express such feelings freely, but although De Quincey admits a sympathy for "Eudaimonism," he is never so bold as to proclaim the pleasure principle as doctrine. The "pleasures of opium" have covertly linked pleasure with indulgence and ruin. The duty of health, lamentably, entails discipline as well, and just as the Whispering Gallery supposedly augments the volume of our speech, so acts of intemperance may yield woe in excess of their intrinsic demerits:

Many men fancy that the slight injuries done by each single act of intemperance are like the glomeration of moonbeams upon moonbeams—myriads will not amount to a positive value. Perhaps they are wrong; possibly every act—nay, every separate pulse or throb of intemperate sensation—is numbered in our own after-actions; reproduces itself in some future perplexity; comes back in some reversionary shape that injures the freedom or action for all men, and makes good men afflicted.   (VIII 354)

De Quincey is ambivalent regarding the degree of ethical liberalism he will permit himself. The stance of his *Confessions* is to ask our indulgence: his entire life is a special *case*, an obliquity from moral absolutism. Everything should be excused insofar as he has meant well, he seems to say. The harsh rules against self-indulgence – whether Pauline, Moslem, or Kantian – must be eased, taking into account the palliations of accidentality, good intentions, humor, and the fact that indulgence has already been its own punishment. But his own view of act and consequences suggests the wisdom of the Biblical injunction quoted by Coleridge in the context of opium-eating: "Whosoever shall keep the whole law, and yet offend in one point, he is guilty of all" (James 2: 10). De Quincey's chatty, familiar, anecdotal, compulsive, repetitious, grandiloquent, impassioned prose does not mask the dread he feels of the nightmare world of guilt and ruin, and the dread of repercussions of all acts springing from personal inclination. His *Confessions* itself ironically became an extended speech act that talked innocent readers into opium addiction throughout the nineteenth century.

The message is thus ambivalent as to whether, given these lurking dangers, we should be more resolute in watching out, or whether we should go ahead and act, as Blake says, on our impulses. In either case, De Quincey implies a low estimate of human freedom, and his brand of ethical liberalism suggests only a weak humanism. Acting on individual impulses is likely to come to nothing in the end, as the escapee from a grammar school discovers.

A weak humanism is found also in De Quincey's critical theorizing. His well-known distinction, indebted to Wordsworth and found as well in Hazlitt, between the "literature of knowledge" and the "literature of power" expresses a strong pragmatics: "the function of the first is to *teach*; the function of the second is to *move*." "It is in relation to these great *moral* capacities of man that the literature of power, as contradistinguished from that of knowledge, lives and has its field of action" (XI 56). "The commonest novel, by moving in alliance with human fears and hopes, with human instincts of wrong and right, sustains and quickens those affections. Calling them into action, it rescues them from torpor" (XI 57). De Quincey sees an alliance of aesthetics and ethics in great works of literature, which address not the "discursive understanding" but the "heart, i.e. the great intuitive (or nondiscursive) organ." His essays *On Murder Considered as One of the Fine Arts* (1827, 1839, 1854) are best understood, I think, as a reductio ad absurdum of the position that ethics and aesthetics can or ought to be disjoined. Since a murder cannot be undone, we might as well make the best of a bad situation: "Enough has been given to morality; now comes the turn of Taste and the Fine Arts . . . [L]et us treat it aesthetically, and see if it will turn to account in that way. Such is the logic of a sensible man" (XIII 16). Judged aesthetically, a murder done with flair, finesse, and good taste has great charm.

That ethical categories could be so neatly supplanted by aesthetic is the source of the satire here, which has as its target the sleazy tendency of human mind to clear its conscience by whatever means. De Quincey senses the emergent aestheticism in discussions of taste from Shaftesbury to Burke to Kant, which will attain full development later in the nineteenth century.

Moral and aesthetic categories ideally implicate one another. Pope is a bad moralist, says De Quincey, because he lacks the imagination of a poet. Disagreeing with Byron's droll disparagement of poets in preference for moralists (*DJ* III 64), he asks, in a vein reminiscent of Shelley's *A Defence of Poetry*:

How, or in what sense that would satisfy even a lampooner, are moralists as a class the "betters" in a collation with poets as a class? It is pretty clear at starting that, *in order* to be a moralist of the first rank,—that is, to carry a great moral truth with heart-shaking force into the mind,—a moralist must begin by becoming a poet. (XI 114).

These texts combined do not, however, make De Quincey anything more than a half-hearted partisan of Romantic humanism. His essays *On Murder Considered as One of the Fine Arts* indulge the satiric conceit in so gourmandizing a manner that we begin to feel De Quincey actually does enjoy murder on some level. His own literary texts express quite the opposite of any confidence that they will morally impel ("move") their readership. The dream visions, for which he is best known, separate imagination from personal and authorial responsibility. And the ethical liberalism of the autobiographical writings is unintegrated into his larger ideological commitments, political and religious, and lacks, in any event, a confidence in the means and ends of human freedom.

Consider the moral status of dreams in De Quincey. We have seen that the second great dream vision at the end of *Confessions of an English Opium-eater* registers guilt that has been denied and repressed throughout the narrative. Such a dream is hardly escapist or wishfulfilling, and shows that dreams can act as dark interpreters of our moral evasions. We do not so much interpret them as they us. But he acknowledges no imperatives that they might issue for the waking state. And within the dream of "inexpiable guilt," he cannot raise

269

himself to will the nameless act he feels is required of him. Bad dreams are a recurring torment without any therapeutic advantage. Good dreams in turn tend to be merely substitutive of moral willing. The "Dream-Fugue" that ends *The English Mail Coach* resolves in a mental way the guilt of having acquiesced in harm to others, of lying down before the lion. In his dream (as he purports to have had it), De Quincey transforms the real-life situation of two approaching carriages into an epic canvas of international, even mythopoeic scope and import. The carriages become large ships, and the threatened young woman is transformed by turns into a female child and the beautiful "lady of the pinnace." The dream-fugue, weaving together such transpositions, moves toward an apocalyptic resolution in which the victory of the British at Waterloo fulfills millennial hopes. (This resolution is ironic in view of the fact that these hopes for Blake, Wordsworth, and Coleridge had hung on the French Revolution, quite the opposite of "Recovered Christendom" and the restoration of monarchies.) De Quincey's guilty, conflictual state of mind is writ large and resolved in this glorious epic warfare with its sudden reversal of fate. Just as the child-woman is about to die, God relents and suffers his angel "to turn aside His arm," snatching her from ruin.

The dream's narrative logic is thus to reverse an act of acquiescence by means of an act of grace, neither of which has required active willing, whether within the dream or without. Concerning his "Dream-Fugue," De Quincey writes, only partly in jest, "If there be anything amiss—let the Dream be responsible. The Dream is a law to itself; and as well quarrel with a rainbow for showing, or for *not* showing, a secondary arch . . . But the Dream knows best; and the Dream, I say again, is the responsible party" (*EM* 329–30).

Whether good or bad, dreams unhinge the dreamer-agent from a strict causal relationship with his or her own will, even while they impose an unnegotiable sense of moral urgency. Since De Quincey regards dreams as heightened, not diminished, reality, this breakdown of moral intelligibility applies in some degree also to the waking state. His absurdist view of will, act, and consequences has already confirmed this breakdown. The import of his dream visions for the waking state is that the moral agent is a kind of somnambulist, lacking control within a world of radical contingency.

De Quincey ends his *Confessions* with a dismissal of its implication: "The moral of the narrative is addressed to the opium-eater; and therefore, of necessity, limited in its application" (*CEO* 448). Despite a *prima facie* resemblance to Coleridge, he speaks from out a sensibility basically different. In preaching a sermon at Shrewsbury, Coleridge gives Hazlitt the "language" without which he would have remained

270

"dumb and brutish." It is difficult to imagine De Quincey in the pulpit; he lacks even the pretense to moral gumption. He is more an ironist than Coleridge, and any tendency to moral recommendation (at least in his best writing) is dissipated in obliquity. Coleridge anxiously hopes to gain a solid ground where he might say, "He hath stood." The sense of duty contends with the inclinations of the "natural man." His paralysis, mental verging on physical, checks a will of great energy and purpose. De Quincey does not give us a comparable sense of struggle with the passional self – it is rather with the circumstantial world of "strife," which seeks to repress that "deep sensibility" he nourishes within. He lacks also the moralist's sense of purpose. Unlike Coleridge, he does not dream of bequeathing some grand statement on the Logos that might set the human race straight for all time. Even lesser ambitions – addressing a misdemeanor in a reader here and there – go unmentioned.

The Romantic humanist concept of love as an expression of sympathetic imagination is metamorphosed in De Quincey. He has less to say expressly on love and friendship than the other major British Romantics. From early in life, love is known to him by means of loss. Grevel Lindop, his most recent biographer, writes that De Quincey's witnessing of his sister's suffering and death by meningitis, combined with his mother's and older brother's admonitions not to show tears, resulted in withdrawal and day-dreaming. "It was not so much the shock of Elizabeth's death as Thomas's inability to complete his mourning and resolve his grief that conferred on the event a lasting significance."[3] The death of Wordsworth's daughter Kate in 1812 provoked a lengthy period of inconsolable grief and may have led to the opium addiction. Female figures – Kate, Ann of Oxford Street, his wife Margaret – haunt De Quincey's writings, and they are fully recognized by him only in their vanishings. Others – the lady of the pinnace, Levana and her attendant Ladies of Sorrow, the Daughter of Lebanon – manifest his habitual mythologizing of the feminine. The real and the mythic coalesce in his writings, and neither is conceived as fully present to him in the waking state. There is a gap between him and the objects of his affection and interest; his perspective as writer is of one severed from early bliss.[4] De Quincey does not dwell on love as union – the full presence of one human being to another – because he does not believe in presence.

The breaking of his friendship with Wordsworth reinforces his sense

---

[3] *The Opium-Eater: A Life of Thomas De Quincey* (New York: Taplinger Publishing, 1981), 11–12.

[4] See V. A. De Luca, *Thomas De Quincey: The Prose of Vision* (Toronto: University of Toronto Press, 1980), 5.

of being an outcast, as it does Coleridge's. Both regard Wordsworth as someone whose "unity of interest" (Coleridge) or "*Einseitigkeit*" (De Quincey) is the cause of his greater achievement and more resolute identity. But one corollary of this sturdy nucleus of self is pride and an inability to reciprocate friendship. De Quincey notes Wordsworth's assumption that only he and blood relatives are able to take in the "picturesque beauty" of nature with sufficient "depth of organic sensibility to the effects of form and colour" (III 198). Irked by the "fending and proving" of "all attempts at reciprocal explanations," Wordsworth shuns interrogation and intimacy. "If you have occasion to write a life of Lucifer, set down that by possibility, in respect to pride, he might be some type of Wordsworth" (III 204). Since his relationship with Wordsworth is – Elizabeth excepted – the pre-eminent one of his life, failure here has implications for him beyond the anecdotal.

There are more blatant contraries to Romantic humanism, however, than moral somnambulism and pessimism concerning human love and friendship. These at least foster pathos for the human predicament. But De Quincey writes as apologist for religious orthodoxy and a reactionary politics in a way that dispels pathos. As a Tory, he opposes the emancipation of slaves and greater rights for Irish Catholics; as editor of the Tory journal, the *Gazette*, he opposes reform in Kendal; he opposes the Reform Bill of 1832 and supports British imperialism in China and everywhere else; he likes dueling and war, thinks English morality superior to all morality anywhere, thinks all the working poor are Jacobins, and detests the French. Whereas Wordsworth, Southey, and Coleridge change in political perspective from radical liberalism to conservatism, De Quincey is constant in his politics. Contrasting himself with these figures, he says that as late as 1807 he

had no opinions at all upon politics, nor any interest in public affairs, further than that I had a keen sympathy with the national honour, gloried in the name of Englishman, and had been bred up in a frenzied horror of jacobinism. Not having been old enough, at the first outbreak of the French Revolution, to participate (as else, undoubtedly, I should have done) in the golden hopes of its early dawn, my first youthful introduction to foreign politics had been in seasons and circumstances that taught me to approve of all I heard in abhorrence of French excesses, and to worship the name of Pitt.   (II 322)

Perhaps the genesis of this conservatism is to be found in his hoity-toity mother, who restored the "De" before "Quincey." Though the hero of *Confessions of an English Opium-eater* resists the authority of Manchester Grammar School, he cheers at the attentions of Lord Westport.

De Quincey argues that just as individuals may duel to uphold their sense of honor, so nations may go to war for honor's sake. Here is his plain-spoken opinion:

It is interesting to observe the steps by which (were it only through impulses of self-defence, and with a view to more effectual destructiveness) war exalted itself from a horrid trade of butchery into a magnificent and enlightened science. Starting from no higher impulse or question than how to cut throats most rapidly, most safely, and on the largest scale, it has issued even at our own state of advance into a science, magnificent, oftentimes ennobling, and cleansed from all horrors except those which (not being within man's power utterly to divorce from it) no longer stand out as reproaches to his humanity.

(VIII 390)

There is an obvious lack of integration between the reactionary Tory and the escapee from a grammar school or the opium-eater asking for our indulgence. There is a lack of integration between the apologist for poverty and the down-and-outer in London. It is not that De Quincey changes his mind in these matters as he gets older. Rather, it is that he never permits the moral sensibility of the autobiographical writings to pervade the opinions of the public essayist. It is difficult to say why, but we have seen that this liberal sensibility lacks a sturdy moral ground in him. Its only imperative is to treat with indulgence all creatures who are thrown into this world of strife. This is a weak imperative with which to undermine the superstructure of the right-wing ideology De Quincey inherits. More important, he regards himself as a kind of walking parenthesis, who in his own voice does not presume to speak for others and who cannot speak with legislative force. In the non-autobiographical writings he is a bigger plagiarist than Coleridge and willingly adopts other, more respectable voices. These voices, too, must be considered De Quincey's, and they remain impervious to the voice of the impassioned outsider.

We might expect that his religious convictions would be colored by his fascination with the sublime and tempered by moral liberalism. But they remain settled and doctrinaire. In his essay "On Christianity as an Organ of Political Movement" (1846), he argues that – unlike the Greek and Roman religions, which do not contain an ethics except in the negative sense that their gods are barbarous – Christianity contains an ethics in its "doctrinality" from which "we derive arms for all moral questions." The moral problematics of his other writings are forgotten here. Christian doctrine has so far infiltrated English consciousness that scripture informs behavior even when it is not cited. His unimpeachable illustration is "our sense of the deep responsibility to India with which our Indian supremacy has invested us" (VIII 241–2).

A pagan religion would not imbue imperialists with so deep a respect for their colonies as Christianity has imbued England with for hers.

Rejecting the idea that ethics can be divorced from right religion, he claims that the treacherous human psyche – in which feelings and thoughts of a distressingly "tainted" nature flit through the minds of even the most virtuous – requires some "governing" or "predominant element . . . which gives the character and tendency to the thought." This governing element must come through "the quality of the ideas deposited in the heart by the quality of the religious faith" (XI 81–2). Though he finds the ground of human virtue in "feelings" of the "heart," he also advocates, therefore, an ethic of "self-conquest," in which wayward impulses are regulated or suppressed. In his ambivalence he is not unlike Adam Smith, who, despite an ethics based on sentiment, admires stoicism where De Quincey admires Christianity. As one of the "Constituents of Happiness," De Quincey lists "consciousness of a supreme mastery over all unworthy passions (anger, contempt, and fear), and over all appetites; together with a highly cherished benevolence; or, to generalize this canon, a sense of moral elevation and purity."[5] A young De Quincey answers Wordsworth's fears that he might be "seduced into unworthy pleasures" at Oxford (the Lake poet has in mind his own mild dissoluteness at Cambridge) with the assurance that "I have been through life so much restrained from dissolute conduct by the ever-waking love of my mother."[6]

To be sure, this Anglican's attraction to infidels indicates a split in his sympathies. V. A. De Luca argues convincingly that in De Quincey's apocalyptic writings there is a homologous relationship of God and death, "a fear that goes to the bottom of De Quincey's dark imaginings" (p. 90). But he suppresses any "wicked whisper" that would express hatred of God. In his *Autobiography* he devotes an entire chapter to the story of "The Female Infidel," Antonina Dashwood Lee,

---

[5] H. A. Page (pseudonym for A. H. Japp), *Thomas De Quincey: His Life and Writings* (London: John Hogg, 1877), I, 107–8. Written in 1805, shortly after De Quincey's twentieth birthday, this list of twelve "Constituents of Happiness" is highly idiosyncratic. In addition to the right degree of solitude and society, health, intellectual stimulation, and so forth, he lists "a personal appearance tolerably respectable" (in contrast to his own) and financial security: "To this end one's fortune should be concentrated in one secure depositary, so as that the interest may be most easily collected." More curiously (if the text has not been corrupted), he lists "a vast predominance of contempt, varied with only so much of action as the feelings may prompt by way of relief and invigoration to the faculty of contempt."

[6] John E. Jordan, *De Quincey to Wordsworth: A Biography of a Relationship, with the Letters of Thomas De Quincey to the Wordsworth Family* (Berkeley: University of California Press, 1962), 40.

an illegitimate daughter of Lord le Despenser and in possession of a modest fortune. She had been in De Quincey's household long enough to have had the better of a guardian and a rector in passionate arguments against Christianity. De Quincey likens her to Coleridge's Lady Geraldine, "a traitress couchant . . . armed with incomparable pretensions" (*A* I 138), and to Shelley, since "she looked upon her principles, not only as conferring rights, but also as imposing duties of active proselytism" (*A* I 141). She had scandalized his mother, concerned about the family reputation, and she eventually scandalized much of England when she brought suit against two Oxonians for abduction and rape. De Quincey at age nineteen attended the trial and gives an account. The case was thrown out of court when she was asked whether she believed in the Christian religion: "Her answer was brief and peremptory, without distinction or circumlocution—*No*. Or, perhaps, not in God? Again she replied, *No*; and again her answer was prompt and *sans phrase*. Upon this the judge declared that he could not permit the trial to proceed" (*A* I 147). Afterwards, De Quincey tried to call on her and, upon being told she was too agitated to see anyone, repeated his call later in the evening, about the time a mob was forming, presumably to lynch her. "Fortunately, a body of gownsmen formed round her, so as to secure her from personal assault."

De Quincey sympathizes with this person but does not permit himself to enunciate the grounds of his sympathy. He closes his account by mentioning that the only modern work Wordsworth ever read "very nearly the end" was a book by Antonina Dashwood Lee, probably *An Essay on Government* (1808), which "he spoke of . . . repeatedly as distinguished for vigour and originality of thought" (*A* I 148). Having been forced to memorize his guardian's inane sermons as a boy, De Quincey might have included Christianity among those institutions from which he would "abscond." "Let there be freedom!" But the opium-eater has no acknowledged appetite for heresy, only a kindly regard for some heretics.

In his essay "Levana and Our Ladies of Sorrow," in *Suspiria de Profundis*, he describes the most dreadful of these ladies as "*Mater Tenebrarum*,—Our Lady of Darkness," who is "the defier of God. She also is the mother of lunacies, and the suggestress of suicides" (*SP* 177). But as J. Hillis Miller notes, Levana intervenes and raises the human sufferer before he dies. In a world from which God has seemed to disappear – a world in which his sister can die – there is a last-minute reprieve, a vision of a restored Eden that comes as an act of grace only to one who has profoundly known suffering.[7] In this way De Quincey,

[7] See J. Hillis Miller, *The Disappearance of God*, 72–80.

the defier of God, affirms God's existence in the end, and even God's continuing presence through his suffering. The Lady of Darkness "can approach only those in whom a profound nature has been upheaved by central convulsions, in whom the heart trembles and the brain rocks under conspiracies of tempest from without and tempest from within" (SP 177). The "commission" that Levana and the Ladies of Sorrow have received from God is an educative one: "to plague [a human being's] heart until we had unfolded the capacities of his spirit" (SP 178). De Quincey has been in his modest and apologetic way a defier of God, but in this brief allegory he clings to a theodicy of sorts, and affirms the presence of God on the very grounds that human beings suffer as directionless beings in a moral wilderness, guilty for acts over which they have had no control, unable to divest themselves of their own pasts, and condemned to lose the objects of their love.

The contrast of De Quincey with Wordsworth with which we began can now be extended. As he ponders Wordsworth's central themes, he warps them interestingly or extends some of their more disquieting implications. Instead of the gift of luminous moments and a sense of personal continuity, memory gives us renewed trauma and tells us that we can never project ourselves freely beyond our past. The child is indeed the father of the man, but if our childhood is unfortunate, the remainder of life in this "world of strife" recapitulates this original lack of accommodation. Where Wordsworth views scene as an all-powerful force that is often a benevolent "ministry," De Quincey, much less the student of nature, views scene as a circumstantial stranglehold that imprints, without rhyme or reason, on our vulnerable palimpsestic brains. Where Wordsworth speaks of language as incarnation or as simple communication, of "man speaking to man," De Quincey sees it miscarrying when we are most in need of communication. It is a comic instrument of miscommunication that confirms human solitude. Where Wordsworth seeks refuge from the abyss of idealism and terrors of the sublime, De Quincey willfully pursues the sublime, hoping to engage mysteries that give him the impression of a grandeur not actually possessed; the cost of this pursuit is to be reminded of his evil potential. Where Wordsworth sees human acts and their consequences – whether the prideful exploits of Rivers or little unremembered acts of kindness and love – as morally interpretable, De Quincey questions whether such judgments can ever be fair. If we are benevolent, we may wish to do our best by others, but there is an absurd disproportion between act and consequences, the act taking on reverberations the way a whisper does in St. Paul's. It is a cosmic bad joke that we are accountable for an infinity of implication from a single, simple act. The consequences will grossly, impertinently miscarry;

there is no accounting for what happens. Wordsworth's hesitancy about acting becomes justifiable paralysis in De Quincey. The moral agent who is inclined to "retirement" in Wordsworth heads alone to the fields of sleep in De Quincey.

Remembering his interest in casuistry, whose etymological root is *casus* (from *cadere*, to fall), I would invoke a word stemming from the same root and in a non-pejorative sense pronounce De Quincey a "decadent." He falls away from the Wordsworthian ideas – and many others – that he by turns reveres, revises, and downgrades. He thinks human power and freedom minimal, sees the self as a randomly collected layering of memory and association without a substantial ground, sees obligation and guilt as problematic, and does not impose a moral sensibility on his readership. His envisaged retreat from action to the purely mental drama of dreams and chatter is a falling away from the will to value. Since we cannot coordinate act and value through moral intelligence – the things we value elude our best-laid plans for obtaining them – values exist in a dissociated limbo of structureless, ungratified desire. Instead of a moral will to value, desire then perpetrates, as he knows, its hyperbolic, compensatory frauds – in worship and self-deprecation, in the pursuit of bogus sublimity, in sentimentality, in futile acts of repossession through dreams and revisionary memory.

Frequently he betrays sources of guilt deeper than those he intends to acknowledge as self-conscious narrator and raconteur. Carlyle writes of him: "One of the smallest figures I ever saw; shaped like a pair of tongs, and hardly above five feet in all. When he sate, you would have taken him, by candlelight, for the beautifullest little child; blue-eyed, sparkling face, had there not been a something, too, which said '*Eccovi* – this child has been in hell!' "[8] But he does not force upon us anything like Coleridge's awareness of guilt, shame, and despair; he rivals him only in dread. It is not simply that he tries to deny guilt or that he is more eloquent on the pleasures than on the pains of opium. He also has a prominent vestige of the Age of Sensibility in a sentimentality of the kind with which Coleridge has little sympathy. He anticipates Poe's and Baudelaire's *esthétique du mal*, whereby grief and terror become, in the nineteenth-century sense, "exquisite" and "thrilling." Despite their satiric intent, his essays *On Murder Considered as One of the Fine Arts* are linked with this tradition and exert considerable influence, especially on Baudelaire.

Sensing the unmanageable contingency of things, yet feeling

---

[8] *Reminiscences*, ed. James Anthony Froude (London: Longmans, Green, 1881), I, 257. See Aileen Ward's Foreword to *Confessions of an English Opium-Eater and Other Writings* (New York: New American Library, 1966).

strongly fated even so, whatever purpose the inscrutable powers may have in mind, De Quincey not surprisingly suffers a fracture of vision; he opposes an ironic, questioning, surprised, touching sensibility with a set of political and religious principles wholly doctrinaire. He does not propose a common ground between the sensibility of the opium-eater and the apologist of convention. To a lesser degree, similar fractures exist in Coleridge and Wordsworth. It is Shelley who affirms the ideal continuity of moral sensibility with larger social, political, and religious values, although his own life and personality manifest some fractures of their own.

PART THREE

The Pressure of Reality

6
Shelley and the poetry of life

Coleridge and Shelley invite the easy censure that they contradict, in the patterns of their lives, the moral ideas they espouse, Coleridge in acts of omission that imperil mostly himself, and Shelley in callous, willful acts that scandalize and kill. In *Alastor* the Poet rejects a loving Arab maiden, "wildered, and wan, and panting," to pursue a "veiled maid," whose "voice was like the voice of his own soul," and who eludes him to the end. Similarly, Harriet Shelley, Elizabeth Hitchener, and Mary Shelley are deserted by a poet crazed by other lights, whether other women, like Claire Clairmont, Teresa Viviani, and Jane Williams, or whether some nameless, relentlessly beckoning horizon of possibility. His self-absorption, projected outward in an undefined and ceaseless pursuit, ostensibly destroys his wife Harriet, his children, Clara and William, and later his two shipmates, Edward Williams and Charles Vivian, in that final suicidal attempt to run out a gale in the Gulf of Spezia.

This easily propounded paradox, in which there is a measure of truth, can obscure those gestures of gentleness and passionate resolve where Shelley acts coherently. It can also reduce this complex vision itself to what I term moral bombast, adapting a phrase from Coleridge. Shelley speaks of "beautiful idealisms of moral excellence" with suspect high-mindedness, as in his letters to Elizabeth Hitchener. One could fill a volume with peevish illustration that he does not reck his own rede. But I will be arguing that next to Coleridge he is the major moralist of the age.

Pervading Shelley's poems are images of masks falling, vapors condensing, veils being removed, light filling voids. His is a mind drawn toward clarity in a world fraught with obscurity, and his task is first to give a precise rendering of obscurity itself: to describe the mind's confrontation with those masks, vapors, veils, and voids. The world is obscure; his rendering of it is difficult but not intrinsically obscure. I will be focusing on the moral implications of his passion for clarity, which is ultimately one with his "passion for reforming the world." The telos of the imagination is a reordering of social world in a victory over obscurity and darkness. If other writers respond with greater inwardness to resistant circumstance and failed revolution, Shelley is eloquent on the dangers of such a retreat. Though himself tempted (as he dramatizes in many of his works), he resists the Wordsworthian ideal of "individual Mind that keeps her own / Inviolate retirement." Instead, he would correct imagination's drift toward either retirement or autonomy by strengthening its participation in the ethical life.

Much of what I say is directed against the de-politicizing of Shelley that persists in the wake of modern consciousness criticism. The complex consciousness is there, but in Shelley's view it is ill-defined and pathological to the extent it does not achieve clarifying linkage with world through action, whether literal revolutionary acts or the speech acts of a legislating poet.

Shelley and first-generation Romantics

Often paired with Blake as the corresponding visionary and revolutionary in the second generation of Romantic poets, Shelley would find major components of Blake's vision uncongenial. As means of moral and political reform, Shelley urges mildness and gentleness, even passive resistance to the tyrant's sword, quite unlike Blake, whose Orc rages and whose Los calls his sons to the strife of blood. Blake's myth does eventually incorporate mildness, and depending on one's reading of *Jerusalem* even a certain pacifism. Then too, Shelley's *Laon and Cythna* (1817–18) has violent energies reminiscent of *The Four Zoas*; and Shelley lives a life of such energies just barely defused. But the distinction holds as a significant generalization: unlike Blake, Shelley thinks the ends of peace, benevolence, and justice are gained by acts themselves qualitatively peaceful, benevolent, and just. Violence in his poetry is portrayed as regressive and non-transformative. "In no case employ violence; the way to liberty and happiness is never to transgress the rules of virtue and justice" (*SPR* 46). He tries to resolve the conflict I see in Blake between "right" and "good' with a more peaceful vision of apocalyptic change, or, if this must be deferred, of social reform.

Shelley's revision of Coleridgean ethics is equally emphatic. For Coleridge, the conscience as tribunal returns its verdict that whatever our alibis, we are guilty; to be human is to be at fault. Though he seeks a gentler monitor in conscience as humane consciousness, his paradigmatic emotion is remorse. Bad conscience and remorse are inconspicuous in Shelley's poetry and personality. Even those who must justify his character sense something amiss in the avoidance of a ritual of conscience upon the suicide of his first wife, Harriet Westbrook. However indirect his part in this tragedy, it might have occasioned a degree of hesitancy and self-examination, if not sorrow and remorse. (His friend Thomas Love Peacock relates an episode several months thereafter in which Shelley confesses seeking to "deaden [his] feelings" about Harriet.) Just as disquieting is his unreflective banishment of Elizabeth Hitchener. Shelley creates the conditions of her near-ruin when in July, 1812 he lures her away from a position as schoolteacher to enlarge his circle of women in Lynmouth, Devon. By November he has demoted her from "soul of my soul" to "brown demon," and sent her packing. He portrays confrontations with conscience infrequently. When Beatrice Cenci does consult conscience in the matter of whether to kill her father, she comes up with what Shelley regards as the wrong answer.

In lieu of a strong reflexive conscience, Shelley urges confrontational moral witnessing of the world's injustice. Eschewing scrupulosity and what he calls "self-anatomizing" (self-analysis for the sake of power over others), he would free the self through "self-knowledge." Inwardness for Shelley, as for Hegel, is only a fraction of the moral life and can be dangerously overvalued.

In the autobiographical *Epipsychidion*, we find little of the inwardness of a Rousseau or Wordsworth. Imagery is already transmuted to symbol, the miscellanea of his own life taking on the forms of artifice, his women represented by moon, sun, and comet. Wordsworth's politics have a way of redounding to the sensibility of the poet: the pathetic gratitude of Simon Lee leaves the *poet* mourning, the Old Cumberland Beggar reminds the poet of his and others' generosity, the Leechgatherer triggers a doubletake that sends the poet briefly into an interior haze. But Shelley rarely narrates a personal epiphany.

A related difference between Wordsworthian and Shelleyan sensibility is the weak function of memory in the latter. Shelley tends not to make memory thematic; like Blake, he is prospective in vision. When personal and political hopes are dimmed – in the Jane poems, for example – memory gives evidence that a possible future has been cut off, the serpent shut out of paradise. Wordsworth works with the disturbing double image of past and present, as he struggles to overcome elegy; Shelley's double image is a radiant unrealized future that legislates against the doleful imagery of the present – and he must struggle to overcome hatred. The triumph over hatred begins the process of renovation in *Prometheus Unbound*, which is Shelley's answer to the tragic naturalism of Wordsworth.

Writing in what he calls an "age of despair," yet finding patterns of resistance in some parts of the world that might fulfill the prophecies of the earlier revolutionary period, Shelley, like Byron and Hazlitt, views with dismay the political apostasy of Coleridge and Wordsworth, and would consider Blake's drift (if there is one) toward private apocalyptics to be regressive. Whereas the older Coleridge sees a separability and even contrariety of ethics and politics (the former based on principles, the latter on the cautionary light of prudence), the young Shelley insists on their coherence: "Expediency is inadmissible in morals. Politics are only sound when conducted on principles of morality. They are, in fact, the morals of the nation" (*SPR* 71). To grasp his politics, one must begin and end with this predicating ethics. It has been correctly observed that Shelley himself – especially in *The Triumph of Life* (1822), but also in earlier poems such as *Lines Written Among the Euganean Hills* (1818) and *Julian and Maddalo* (1819) – doubts there can ever be a total continuity of ethics and politics, of vision and history. His "meliorism" is qualified by doubt, impatience, and a sadness that the "serious folly" of human affairs goes on unabated. The gradualist program of reform he proposes for England makes its compromise with prudential politics. But whatever the depressed tone of some poems or the circumstances of their composition, he does not urge a retreat into the interior self, let alone a "quest" in that direction. Quest should be outward, directed toward reforming the world, or beyond, toward some vista or isle of the imagination where the process of human regeneration might begin – Euganean Hills or Greece or India. He resists the felt threat of a subjective idealism that would declare no difference between the world as perceived and the world as object and that would render political action illusory.

Holding to those values in light of which the spectacle of human history is so bewildering and disappointing, Shelley confronts in *The Triumph of Life* the possibility that his vision may be merely ideal. But we cannot conclude from disappointment alone that he has given up his "passion for reforming the world."

Skepticism, sublimity, and language

In proposing skepticism as the exegetical key to Shelley, modern critics from C. E. Pulos and Earl Wasserman to Harold Bloom, Donald Reiman, and Lloyd Abbey have relocated the poet in a tradition more in line with modern sensibility than that suggested by radiant Platon-ism.[1] Whatever its validity, the argument for skepticism lends Shelley a certain intellectual respectability at the same time that it quells any embarrassment we might feel about Shelley's sometimes overwrought affirmations. What better way to rescue *Alastor* from the charge of adolescence? The more recent shift from skepticism to nihilism – which has conveniently directed its deconstructive ambitions at *The Triumph of Life* – is another such relocation.[2] Those arguing skepticism emphasize Shelley's estimate of cognitive powers with respect to metaphysics. The conclusion that he thinks one cannot have direct knowledge of metaphysical absolutes is convincing, and I suppose important, though I wonder just how many poets *have* presumed such knowledge.

This school of criticism has overlooked the fact that Shelley does believe in cognitive power as it relates to moral intuition. And this exception is of such force that it demolishes the case for skepticism as the key to Shelley. I propose that moral intuition grounded in imagina-tion overrides for Shelley both skepticism and nihilism, sustaining knowledge and value, and that far from being a vacuous notional affirmation in the face of denial, this overriding is the motive ground of Shelleyan narrative and drama, inscribed in the language and struc-ture of his major writings.

Skepticism and moral commitment, it should first be noted, are not necessarily contraries, just as skepticism and religious commitment have in fideism a long history of cohabitation. The union of epistemo-logical uncertainty and moral certainty recurs throughout literature and philosophy of the period. In the *Essay Concerning Human Under-standing*, Locke denies we have certain knowledge of the substance of real things in nature. But morality consists of a human-made combina-tion of ideas, and as such is accessible to the mind that produces it. He is "bold to think, that *Morality is capable of Demonstration*, as well as Mathematicks: Since the precise real Essence of the Things moral

---

[1] C. E. Pulos, *The Deep Truth: A Study of Shelley's Scepticism* (Lincoln: University of Nebraska Press, 1954); Earl R. Wasserman, *Shelley: A Critical Reading* (Baltimore: The Johns Hopkins University Press, 1971); Harold Bloom, Introduction to *The Selected Poetry and Prose of Shelley* (New York: New American Library, 1966); Donald H. Reiman, *Shelley's "The Triumph of Life": A Critical Study* (Urbana: University of Illinois Press, 1965); Lloyd Abbey, *Destroyer and Preserver: Shelley's Poetic Skepticism* (Lincoln: University of Nebraska Press, 1979).

[2] *Deconstruction and Criticism*, ed. Geoffrey Hartman (New York: Continuum Publish-ing, 1979); see especially the essays by Paul de Man, Jacques Derrida, and J. Hillis Miller. See also Tilottama Rajan, *Dark Interpreter: The Discourse of Romanticism*, 58–96, for a qualification of such an approach.

Words stand for, may be perfectly known; and so the Congruity, or Incongruity of the Things themselves, be certainly discovered, in which consists perfect Knowledge" (Bk. III 516). In his *Confessions*, Rousseau says that he might err in details and chronology but that his recall of states of feeling is infallible. Hume's probabilism, argued in *Enquiry Concerning Human Understanding* (1748, 1758), undermines naive inferences about causal relationships, but Hume embraces an ethics of feeling in *An Inquiry Concerning the Principles of Morals* (1751), in which a strict dissociation of reason from ethics permits the certainties of affective testimony. Broadly speaking, Kant formulates limits to knowing in his first critique, and moral absolutes in his second. The first explains a specially defined skepticism about ultimate reality, or things-in-themselves, but the second defines the grounds of moral commitment, despite the hypothetical nature of moral assertions.

But Shelley makes claims for imagination as a cognitive and moral power that places ethics on a broader epistemological ground than would a Lockean conventionalism or a Humean ethics of feeling or a Kantian rationalism, in which practical reason yields only hypothetical truths. Shelley's ethics is conceived as a fierce contrary of metaphysical skepticism, not a complacent bedfellow; it challenges the dominion of skepticism. In calling imagination "the basis of all knowledge" (*DP* 503), he prepares the ground for this challenge. In matters ethical, he is, like Blake, an intuitionist, claiming direct knowledge of moral truth. In his fragmentary "Speculations on Morals" (1817, 1821), he writes that "metaphysical science will be treated merely so far as a source of negative truth; while morality will be considered as a science respecting which we can arrive at positive conclusions" (SM 182). This is a pointed statement in the matter. Metaphysical skepticism need not frustrate direct cognition of moral truth.

Shelley is less interested than Coleridge, for whom no knowledge is academic, in metaethical questions of the nature and justification of moral judgments and the meaning of moral terms. But what writings he devotes to these questions show that he, like most of the Romantics, is an intuitionist or "cognitivist non-definist": we can have direct knowledge of moral rightness and wrongness, good and bad, and morality is a legitimate form of knowledge with its own criteria of truth. If after hearing all that can be said on behalf of benevolence and justice, someone still

persists to inquire why he ought to promote the happiness of mankind, he demands a mathematical or metaphyscial reason for a moral action. The absurdity of this scepticism is more apparent, but not less real than the exacting a moral reason for a mathematical or metaphysical fact. (SM 190)

Proponents of Shelley as skeptic shirk quoting a passage that speaks of skepticism as an "absurdity," but Shelley conforms to this view throughout his career. Earl Wasserman begins his book, *Shelley: A Critical Reading* (1971), with the assertion that "at the center of the mind in Shelley's collective works [is] a denial of any self-evident truths that may serve as constructive first principles" (p. ix). Yet the young Shelley writes to Hitchener in 1811, "Virtue is self evident, consequently I act in unison with it's dictates, *where* the doctrines of Christ do not differ from virtue, *there* I follow *them*—" (*LPS* I 109).

The system of thought that most compromises the autonomy of ethics is not skepticism but religion. While ethics should sanction politics, it should not itself be sanctioned by religion. Shelley usually argues its independence of religion. An absolute proof of God "or even the divine mission of Christ, would in no manner alter one idea on the subject of morality" (*LPS* I 109). In *A Defence of Poetry* he writes that discursive reason and the skepticism it promotes are appropriate challenges to religious superstition but not to products of the imagination: "But whilst the sceptic destroys gross superstitions, let him spare to deface, as some of the French writers have defaced, the eternal truths charactered upon the imaginations of men" (*DP* 501). Note again his relegation of skepticism to a prophylactic or disestablishing function, and imagination's positive link to "truth." An ethics grounded in imagination can be challenged, then, by a skeptical left or a dogmatic right. Shelley has sympathies with the former, but sees its legitimate function to be its attack on the latter, not on "the eternal truths charactered upon the imaginations of men." That skepticism does threaten imagination is a major thematic of the poetry, but skepticism in this role is a pathology.

Shelley's exemption of ethics from the skeptical temper is defended not merely in isolated moments but in the larger tendency of his writings. Whatever the degree of optimism or pessimism expressed regarding our ability to realize objects of moral knowing, he thinks we all have at hand these self-evident intuitions of the imagination. His passion for reforming the world originates in the cognitive certainty of moral intuitions.[3]

The modern school of Shelley criticism has erred in not following out the implications of imagination as a cognitive faculty. Pulos recognizes that even in Hume the "sceptic is rescued from total scepticism by means of imagination" (p. 21), and that "Shelley's hostility toward

[3] See Kenneth Neill Cameron, *Shelley: The Golden Years* (Cambridge, Mass.: Harvard University Press, 1974), 157–8, for another repudiation of the view that Shelley is foremost a skeptic.

Christianity was primarily based not on metaphysical but moral grounds, upon which his acquisition of a sceptical point of view was not necessarily bound to exercise any influence" (p. 94). But this exclusion of ethics from metaphysical skepticism does not lead Pulos or others to consider that ethics, based on imagination's cognitive powers, supplants skepticism as Shelley's dominant tendency. After Pulos, other critics have been more aggressive in their claims, making informal and philosophically dubious extensions of skepticism into areas where it has little or no relevance, or where it is patently overridden by ethics. We should not conflate a skepticism about ultimate reality with moral or political uncertainty, or with caution and brooding. Shelley is not at all "skeptical" about the necessity for political reform or the value of benevolence. When Lloyd Abbey asserts that "skepticism is not an undertone in the poetry; it is the major theme" (p. 3) and that Shelley as skeptic "is ultimately concerned more with [the severe limits placed on imaginative vision] than with the defeat of socially destructive dogma" (p. 146), he not only takes skepticism to be the master-key but also sees it mitigating Shelley's social and political commitments. Classical skepticism as propounded by Pyrrho was indeed a politically acquiescent view. If we cannot know what the *summum bonum* is, why make an effort to obtain it? Why not acquiesce in social and political convention? Thus, the temptation to extend Shelley's metaphysical skepticism to all areas of his thought may lead to the view that he did not fully believe his own ethics and politics. The next step would be to recast him as a closet right-winger.

Shelley's skepticism of received systems should not be conflated with metaphysical skepticism, even though, as in his case, the same mind can adopt both. The former is indeed focused by the confidence that we do have moral knowledge. This is a polemical skepticism based on cognitive certainties: here the state is wrong, there the church is wrong. In such arguments Shelley's passionate commitments and this form of skepticism are mutually reinforcing. We sense the passion in polemical writings such as "The Necessity of Atheism" (1811), *An Address to the Irish People* (1812), the Notes to *Queen Mab* (1813), and "Essay on the Punishment of Death" (1820). With an impatient pedagogical fervor occasioned by logic confronting absurdity and injustice, he questions false assumptions and invalid arguments of religion and politics, subjecting to reductio ad absurdum the virgin birth and divinity of Christ. He does not share Blake's hostility to discursive reason (Coleridge's "understanding"), albeit *A Defence of Poetry* subordinates it to imagination. Discursive reason has the need-

288

ful task of clearing away all dogmatism, obsolete mythologies, prejudices, and absurdities; Enlightenment figures like Hume and Holbach have left much still to do. Far from a denigration of the mind's powers, this healthy skepticism affirms the mind's ability to ward off assumptions that enervate intellect. In its clearing function, discursive reason achieves in Shelley something of what energy achieves in Blake.

Shelley restricts the authority of discursive reason to this clearing function; it is unable to propose constructions of its own. Employing reason as a primary tool, philosophy "destroys error, and the roots of error. It leaves, what it is too often the duty of the reformer in political and ethical questions to leave, a vacancy" (*SPR* 173). The imagination – so frequently imaged in Shelley's poetry and prose as a radiating, filling power – renovates and creates values that fill vacancy. Since he has such sympathies with the Enlightenment attack on dogmatic value structures, while at the same time acknowledging vacancy, Shelley becomes the most programmatic of Romantic authors with respect to the will to value. The historical climate necessitates an agenda directing the uses of the imagination. Texts from *Queen Mab* to *The Mask of Anarchy* to *Prometheus Unbound* to *A Philosophical View of Reform* present the various scenarios of imagination filling the vacancies of modern life with renewed value. He hopes in poems and disquisitions to give a self-fulfilling prophecy of a reversal in the depressed moral economy of late European history.

Shelley's belief in direct moral intuition does not alter from early writings to late. What does alter is his estimate of the importance of moral philosophy, which declines in his writings as we approach *A Defence of Poetry*, where it is judged to be of little use. This declining estimate in no way suggests a growing distrust of moral intuition and even confirms its preeminence. In his early essay, "On the Vegetable System of Diet" (1814), he writes, "The speculative truths of moral sciences when perceived never fail perhaps [sic] to acquire an empire over the conduct; the difficulty consists in impressing them durably on the conviction of men," which can be done only if men are in good health, i.e. if they are vegetarians (*SPR* 91). And he writes Peacock in January, 1819, apropos of his finishing Act I of *Prometheus Unbound*, "I consider Poetry very subordinate to moral & political science, & if I were well, certainly I should aspire to the latter; for I can conceive a great work, embodying the discoveries of all ages, & harmonizing the contending creeds by which mankind have been ruled" (*LPS* II 71). (Contrast Wordsworth on the efficacy of moral philosophy in his "Essay on Morals." Shelley may ironically encourage Peacock here in his subsequent attack on poetry, *The Four Ages of Man* [1820], which in turn provokes Shelley's *Defence*.) In *A Philosophical View of Reform* (late 1819), he writes that "poets and philosophers are the unacknowledged legislators of the world" (*PVR* 240). But in *A Defence of Poetry* (1821) he drops "philosophers" from the famous formula and denigrates their influence on history relative to poets:

Ethical science arranges the elements which poetry has created, and pro-pounds schemes and proposes examples of civil and domestic life: nor is it for want of admirable doctrines that men hate, and despise, and censure, and deceive, and subjugate one another. But Poetry acts in another and diviner manner. (*DP* 487)

Moral philosophy does not in itself increase our powers of moral intuition, but poetry "compels us to feel that which we perceive, and to imagine that which we know" (*DP* 505). Poetry combats the broad conspiracy of modern life to blunt our apprehension of self-evident truths – from tyrannies of church and state to the weight of custom to the corruptive powers of language to a misplaced skepticism that infects our confidence in these truths.

Even those works usually cited in discussions of Shelley's skepticism – "Mont Blanc," *Prometheus Unbound*, *Epipsychidion*, and *The Triumph of Life* – express moral certainties in the midst of anxious questioning. To cite one example: "Mont Blanc" (1816) invokes moral categories that subvert the poem's seeming phenomenological neutrality. The mountain has "a voice . . . to repeal / Large codes of fraud and woe." The "wise, and great, and good" can only "interpret," not understand, that voice emanating from the motive ground of ultimate reality. But they can recognize the fraud and woe of human tyranny unambiguously. These "large codes" – the rigid forms of social and political repression – do not require any oblique hermeneutical decoding. We can know them as evil directly and we can know their vulnerability to the power imaged in the Ravine.

Shelley does, of course, admit limits to imagination. But arguments concerning such "limits" usually employ a disqualifying absolutist criterion: if imagination cannot move mountains or bring back the dead or perceive powers beyond the phenomenal, it is said to be "limited" or "self-subversive," and the poet is skeptical or downright defeated. But who besides Blake's Isaiah in the history of Western literature does *not* admit limits to imagination? Has not the hue and cry about limits been overblown in modern criticism? Why do we think a poet the more mature and modern for acknowledging what most of us learn before puberty – that beyond a point the world successfully resists our imaginings and desires? Shelley is no absolutist of the imagination, but the alternative is not wholesale skepticism or despair, which he resists with moral certainties and hope, and an imagination possessed of a fair degree of empowerment. After great exertions, imagination implodes at the end of *Epipsychidion*, when the poet perceives his own vision as baseless willed rhetoric of no legislative force. In *Alastor* and *The Triumph of Life*, imagination turns to dark vision, becomes the dark interpreter, and in lieu of light and plenitude admits darkness and void that eclipse consciousness. And imagination turns to madness in *Julian and Maddalo*. But these instances do not imply that Shelley extends skepticism to operations of the imagination, only that imagination is of course vulnerable to skepticism, among other mentalities. The first principle in Shelley, as in Blake, is imagination, which denies the ultimacy of the skeptical temper.

This conclusion has bearing on Shelley's relationship to the tradition of the sublime. I have mentioned that Kant speaks of the sublime (*das Erhabene*) as hostile to imagination; in its grandeur and limitlessness it defeats the imagination's power to gather together the data of sensibility. Shelley reverses this: imagination, as a faculty of broader function than Kant allows, works to overpower the sublime and on occasion succeeds.

It may seem surprising that Shelley, whose imagery is rife with mists, veils, chasms, mountains, and diaphanous light, is a proponent of the anti-sublime. The seeming contradiction is simply resolved: in a world of inscrutable and awesome powers, the imagination seeks clarity of form beyond obscurity, the radiance behind the veil. The sublime of the Burkean tradition (not the Longinian) is the aesthetic correlate of metaphysical skepticism, telling us *that* there is a grandeur in reality but denying we can ascertain *what* it is. Skepticism and sublimity are for Shelley complementary forms of the larger category of human unknowing. Neither one is a value in itself. If we assume, to the contrary, that the sublime is for him an "aesthetic that idealizes the immaterial and numinous properties of the landscape,"[4] we might conclude that sublimity has positive intrinsic value in compensating for unknowing. But despite his occasional use of the word "sublime" in the conventional sense of elevated and noble, Shelley manifests a hostility toward the properties of the sublime and conceives of imagination as a clarifying faculty that works to dissipate them.

His imagery is sublime in a special way: it is a poetically precise, not vague or amorphous, rendering of a manifold of experience as yet itself obscure. The tendency of his imagery, in terms of narrative causality, is

[4] Angela Leighton, *Shelley and the Sublime* (Cambridge: Cambridge University Press, 1984), 40.

toward greater clarity as the objects of mental experience themselves gain greater definition in the poet's mind. While Donald Davie certainly testifies to the experience of many readers in speaking of how Shelley's "sublimity is peculiarly indefinite and impalpable,"[5] it is precisely this indefiniteness against which Shelleyan narration militates.

The dialectic of *Prometheus Unbound* (1818–19) answers the perplexities of "Mont Blanc": it seeks to convert the sublime, with its emotions of awe and terror, into form, beauty, and love. These have no place in "Mont Blanc," where landscape is by turns awesome, terrifying, hideous, unfathomable, dark, deathly, ghostly, and veiled. The mountain's forbidding power resists humanization, perhaps even to the poem's ambiguous conclusion, which leaves us with the conundrum of whether or not the mind's "imaginings" at least prevent the mountain's silence and solitude from falling still further into the total negation of "vacancy" – and, if so, whether we are left with any true power of our own. "Mont Blanc" confirms Kant's reading of the sublime; human mind is overpowered by such a scene. (Perhaps the poem "as poem" can be said to testify to the mind's power over landscape.) The landscapes of *Prometheus Unbound*, most of them as ghastly as that of Mont Blanc, embody the dialectical interplay of nature-refusing-form and clarifying light, this time with an advance beyond the sublime. The new emergents are altered states of being in the main characters and a new clarity in the world that surrounds them.

Panthea dreams prophetically of Prometheus's transformation:

> his pale, wound-worn limbs
> Fell from Promethus, and the azure night
> Grew radiant with the glory of that form
> Which lives unchanged within.   (*PU* II i 62–5)

Transformation of ill-defined into true form is accompanied by internally generated and widely projected light. Their love-making is a mutual absorption:

> I saw not—heard not—moved not—only felt
> His presence flow and mingle through my blood
> Till it became his life and his grew mine
> And I was thus absorbed—until it past
> And like the vapours when the sun sinks down,
> Gathering again in drops upon the pines
> And tremulous as they, in the deep night

[5] *Purity of Diction in English Verse* (London: Routledge & Kegan Paul, 1967), 133.

> My being was condensed, and as the rays
> Of thought were slowly gathered, I could hear
> His voice, whose accents lingered ere they died
> Like footsteps of far melody.   (*PU* II i 79–89)

This ontological focusing – "My being was condensed" – coincides with discovery of form; vapors are "gathered" just as "rays / Of thought" are gathered, losing their amorphous and dark character.

Similar imagery occurs when Prometheus prophesies the life of fully realized art and power in a cave analogous to "the cave of the witch Poesie" of "Mont Blanc":

> And lovely apparitions dim at first
> Then radiant—as the mind, arising bright
> From the embrace of beauty (whence the forms
> Of which these are the phantoms) casts on them
> The gathered rays which are reality—
> Shall visit us, the progeny immortal
> Of Painting, Sculpture and rapt Poesy
> And arts, though unimagined, yet to be.   (*PU* III iii 49–56)

The phrase, "the gathered rays which are reality," best describes the final cause of Shelley's imagery. Whereas the meditative, questioning poet of "Mont Blanc" had not presumed beyond "Ghosts of all things that are," had not penetrated the veil of phenomena, the poet's presumption is now greater: ghosts and shadows are supplanted by radiant creatures, veils and masks are removed, in an imaginative gathering of all sensation. This process is anti-sublime because it seeks clarity, unity, beauty, and radiance as ends. Shelley grants the imagination greater gathering power than does Kant. And his habit of mind is the opposite of De Quincey's: as we have seen, the opium-eater deliberately seeks a greater sense of mystery.

Shelley's anti-sublimity should not be confused with the "egotistical sublime," which Thomas Weiskel has termed a "positive" sublime, in contrast to the negative, alienating sublime of Kant.[6] The egotistical sublime – the term Keats applies to Wordsworth – finds the imagination triumphing over Kantian dualism and alienation by subsuming what Hegel calls "all otherness, all possibility of negation," whether through the immanence of pantheism or through projection of an ego in love with itself. But successful or not, Shelley spends a career fighting projective narcissism. The tendency of this struggle is to

---

[6] *The Romantic Sublime: Studies in the Structure and Psychology of Transcendence* (Baltimore: The Johns Hopkins University Press, 1976), 48–62.

supplant the alienating otherness of sublimity with a humanizing recognition of beauty in a world of social renovation.

The same imagination that overpowers dim, vaporous scene in a radiant "gathering" works as a morally self-defining power; brought into focus, Prometheus becomes a moral agent able to love and act. Love, too, is spoken of as a gathering. In Act II we learn that Prometheus has given mankind love

> to bind
> The disunited tendrils of that vine
> Which bears the wine of life, the human heart.   (*PU* II ii 63–5)

By contrast, a key image of Act I had united disease and tearing, the two kinds of dissolution that inform the entire act:

> Heaven's winged hound, polluting from thy lips
> His beak in poison not his own, tears up
> My heart,   (*PU* I 34–6)

cries Prometheus to Jupiter. But love gathers what has been torn asunder; Act II is rife with imagery of purification, clarification, and restoration.

Shelley's assault on obscurity, seen in his treatment of skepticism and the sublime, extends to his scattered comments on language and its corruptions. Language can be a primary means of obscuring self-evident moral truths. The "misuse of words and signs" insures that "our whole life is . . . an education in error" (*SPR* 173–4). Arguing in 1812 against Godwin's advocacy of learning classical languages when young, the Romantic period's finest classicist writes:

You say that words will neither debauch our understandings, nor distort our moral feelings.—You say that the time of youth could not be better employed than in the acquisition of classical learning. But *words* are the very things that so eminently contribute to the growth & establishment of prejudice: the learning of *words* before the mind is capable of attaching correspondent ideas to them, is like pos[s]essing machinery with the use of which we are so unacquainted as to be in danger of misusing it. But words are merely signs of ideas, how many evils, & how great spring from the annexing inadequate & improper ideas to words. The words honor, virtue, duty, goodness, are examples of this remark.[7]   (*LPS* I 317)

Learning Latin, even though it is "a key to European languages," is still "an affair of minor importance, inasmuch as the science of things is

---

[7] Shelley derives these notions from Locke's *Essay Concerning Human Understanding*, Bk. III, 10, "On the Abuse of Words." For a good discussion of Shelley and Locke on language, see William Keach, *Shelley's Style* (New York: Methuen, 1984), 37–8, 47–50.

superior to the science of words" (*LPS* I 318). And some five years later he writes, "Words are the instruments of mind whose capacities it becomes the metaphysician accurately to know, but they are not mind, nor are they portions of mind" (*SPR* 185).

Poetic language, too, is referential and instrumental. The poet's "vitally metaphorical" language "marks the before unapprehended relations of things" through "pictures of integral thoughts" (*DP* 482). This is metaphor in the service of understanding. Poetic language is more cognitively charged than ordinary discourse and should oppose obscurity. Shelley's primary interest is in semantics and the relationship of meaning to "things." He objects to overvaluation of the signifier. In the Preface to *Laon and Cythna*, he writes that he has not permitted

any system relating to mere words to divert the attention of the reader, from whatever interest I may have succeeded in creating, to my own ingenuity in contriving to disgust him according to the rules of criticism. I have simply clothed my thoughts in what appeared to me the most obvious and appropriate language.

Signifiers that draw attention to themselves and away from signifieds are dangerous. In *A Defence of Poetry* he describes not the way poetic language draws attention to itself as language but the way it becomes meaningful and refers us to world. Even its phonetic properties echo a rhythm out there, in the nature of things. There exists a potential correspondence of mind and nature that language can express. Only in its referential and instrumental functions is language of value; otherwise, it is what he calls "mere words" or "marks." Poets like philosophers should strive to overcome the problematics of language, instead of wielding it in such a way as to confound our ideas of things.

Poetic language, then, is a metaphorically enriched, deeply cognitive, and phonetically imitative use of language that serves the utilitarian ends of aesthetic pleasure and moral reform. Whatever we make of his poetic practice – his overt comments on language hardly exhaust the question of Shelley and language – he would have little patience with talk of a "play of signifiers," of semantic "indeterminacy," of poems written only in terms of other poems. Nor would he think talk of "poems as poems" or the "poem itself" anything other than effete academicism. Poetry takes on larger tasks: it lifts "the veil from the hidden beauty of the world," it lifts the reader "out of the dull vapours of self," it makes clear a thousand hitherto "unapprehended combinations of thought," it reveals the "inmost naked beauty" of meaning, and it embraces "at once the centre and

295

circumference of knowledge" – all leading us from obscurity to greater clarity. The enormous semantic burden he feels poetic language must accept helps account for the highly charged texture of his verse, from *Alastor* to *Prometheus Unbound* to *Epipsychidion*. Shelley struggles to find signifiers ("marks") adequate to signifieds, and linguistic signs adequate to "things" of the world – and to what must be done in it.

Figures of love and imagination

I have said that the Romantics dramatize the dangers of both the egoistic and the sympathetic functions of imagination. Visionaries may be regarded as supreme egoists, fashioning the world according to their idea of it, occasionally on the grand scale of a Milton or a Blake. Visionaries risk disengagement and solipsism, trapped in a self-created private universe, as can be seen in the tormented history of Blake's Los. Wordsworth narrates a moment when, walking through the woods, he suddenly confronts the "abyss of idealism" and is so unhinged that he must literally grasp for trees to connect once again with terra firma. Coleridge's and De Quincey's visionary landscapes convert readily to nightmare. On the other hand, imagination in its sympathetic linkage with the world of objects and other persons can capitulate to a narrow, coercive reality principle; the world then becomes too much with us. Blake sees "pity" as a potentially self-divisive emotion that enslaves and incapacitates Los. Coleridge thinks we can become so "circum-stanced," our sense of responsibility to the world may become so burdensome, that we deplete the personal self. His "hauntings of conscience" and "sense of Duty" paradoxically *de*crease his willingness to engage in beneficent action: he suffers the "effect of Selfness in a mind incapable of gross Self-interest—" (*N* II 2531). His sympathetic identification with Wordsworth has, he fears, depleted his own poetic strength. The imagination, functioning between poles of egoism and sympathy, puts us at risk at either pole, fostering a vital egoism that can lead to unreal, prideful separateness, or a sympathy with the world that can lead to loss of power.

Romantic literature suggests the rarity of a dialectical resolution of these contrary tendencies. The age-old problem – how adjust the claims of self to the claims of others? – is cast in extremist terms. Such works as Blake's "The Clod & the Pebble" and *Visions of the Daughters of Albion*, Wordsworth's *The Borderers* and even *The Prelude*, Coleridge's "Dejection: An Ode," and De Quincey's *Confessions* problematize rather than resolve the question. It takes works of the willful magnitude of Blake's *Milton* and Shelley's *Prometheus Unbound* to engage these contraries and work beyond them. In this visionary drama Shelley will show how sympathy can be empowerment, not depletion; but the journey of the self toward love and empowerment is a perilous one, as we see in many texts that, in a non-chronological sense, prepare for his largest exercise in visionary dialectics.

In *A Defence of Poetry* he describes the relationship of love and imagination. The well-known passage is a locus classicus of the ethics of Romanticism:

> The great secret of morals is Love; or a going out of our own nature, and an identification of ourselves with the beautiful which exists in thought, action, or person, not our own. A man, to be greatly good, must imagine intensely and comprehensively; he must put himself in the place of another and of many others; the pains and pleasures of his species must become his own. The great instrument of moral good is the imagination. (*DP* 487–8)

In context, he is arguing that all exertions of imagination, whether toward persons or works of art and culture, heighten moral sensibility. They are not useless, as the satiric Peacock claims. Shelley finds a genetic link between ethics and "poetry" (in the broad sense of all artistic, cultural, and philosophical products of the imagination). Periods of moral gain have demonstrably coincided with periods of great literature, or so Shelley's wishful reading of history goes. More pointedly than Coleridge, and in opposition to Kant, he describes imagination as the genetic ground of both poetry and the moral life, which co-exist therefore in a homologous relationship. Since both morals and poetry exercise the imagination that originates both, each is linked genetically to the other. The experience of poetry strengthens morality, just as the morally aware person is the more sensitive to poetry. Despite Spenser's having been a poet laureate – his politics offend Shelley – poets tend to be moral folk. In this treatise and *A Philosophical View of Reform* (1819), Shelley does not argue that great poetry directly *causes* moral progress in history or vice versa. True to his genetic model, he speaks instead of linkage or co-existence: "The presence or absence of poetry in its most perfect and universal form has been found *to be connected with* good and evil in conduct and habit" (*DP* 490; emphasis added). In a world now dominated by discursive reason and greed, Shelley thinks we lack "the poetry of life," by which he means not a school of verse invested with reality (though he certainly favors one) but a moral life invested with the "creative faculty." Only by means of this faculty can we "imagine that which we know" or "act that which we imagine" (*DP* 502).

Shelley calls for a replenishment of value and specifically designates imagination as the valuing faculty. "Reason is the enumeration of quantities already known; imagination is the perception of the value of those quantities, both separately and as a whole" (*DP* 480). This is a large claim, because he ascribes to imagination the function earlier said to be performed by "moral sense," yet with an increase of cognitive power. The phrase "perception of the value" implies that values are discovered by a faculty empowered with a special kind of knowing; imagination tells us what is good in the world. But elsewhere it is clear that imagination creates as well as perceives value, and that in Shelleyan dialectic the distinction between projection and intuition breaks down.

Within this broad association of imagination with morality, Shelley develops the dual concept of imagination – organic, self-fashioning, on the one hand, and sympathetic on the other – characteristic of the period. The former has been implicit in what we have already seen in the imagery of *Prometheus Unbound*. Imagination functions as a gathering, condensing, shaping, and clarifying power that focuses energy and light purposefully, whether in human personality or in works of art and culture. Upon uniting with Asia, Prometheus gathers within himself the powers he has dissipated. Shelley has also seen imagination functioning as sympathy, in a "going out of our own nature," metaphorically if not essentially the reverse of the primary action of *Prometheus Unbound*. In "Speculations on Morals" he observes that "familiarity with the finest specimens of poetry and philosophy" develops our sympathy beyond our own "immediate sphere of sensations."

Imagination or mind employed in prophetically [imaging forth] its objects is that faculty of human nature on which every gradation of its progress, nay, every, the minutest, change depends . . . The only distinction between the selfish man and the virtuous man is that the imagination of the former is confined within a narrow limit, while that of the latter embraces a comprehensive circumference. (SM 188–9)

As the chief moral manifestation of imagination, love would reconcile the contraries of self and other – which is simple to say. But for Shelley such a reconciliation requires an extended spiritual and compositional struggle. On the level of language, reconciliation is attempted through his ponderous use of synecdoche. In the essay "On Love" (1818), he speaks of love variously as a power of attraction between persons or even natural objects, as mutually vibrating lyres, and as a sense of "correspondence" between self and other. Love begins as a perception of the potential value of our own self:

We dimly see within our intellectual nature a miniature as it were of our entire self, yet deprived of all that we condemn or despise, the ideal prototype of every thing excellent or lovely that we are capable of conceiving as belonging to the nature of man. Not only the portrait of our external being but an assemblage of the minutest particles of which our nature is composed, a mirror whose surface reflects only the forms of purity and brightness; a soul within our soul that describes a circle around its proper paradise which pain, and sorrow, and evil dare not overleap.

(SPR 170)

The "soul within our soul" – our inviolate core of worth and integrity – exists in synecdochic relationship to the larger self. It is a condensation of being and of value. Its protective circle wards off intrusions. Since the trope seems therefore to seal the self off, how convert it into a trope of correspondence? Shelley answers that the "soul within the soul" is a "prototype" that "thirsts after its likeness" or "anti-type." The type "demands" the

discovery of its anti-type; the meeting with an understanding capable of clearly estimating our own; an imagination which should enter into and seize upon the subtle and delicate peculiarities which we have delighted to cherish and unfold in secret.

(SPR 170)

But he must still chart the process by which this thirst for the anti-type can transcend the "dimly" perceived circle of self-love, and unite with the more dimly perceived circle of another.

In *Epipsychidion* (1821) Shelley employs synecdoche legislatively, as if a rhetorical figure could bring objects of desire into full being. He eventually confronts the ontological fallacy in this. After thirty-two extravagant lines addressed to Emilia, he laments his "dim words" and then corrects the suggestion that he is hers. "I am not thine: I am part of *thee*" (52). Synecdoche assumes the grammatical case of partitive instead of possessive genitive. Neither person belongs to the other but each is part of the other, and therefore *is* the other. "Not mine but me, henceforth be thou united / Even as a bride" (392-3). "Twin Spheres of light who rule this passage Earth, / This world of love, this *me*" (345–6). Like Blake, Shelley expresses abhorrence at the possessive element in love. Emilia's and the poet's magic circles of self will, ideally, participate one in the other, so that each becomes the other, not the other's. The image of the self's miniature circle, which would otherwise express self-centeredness, is transmuted by synecdoche into an image for an ultimate kind of sympathetic identification. (Donne works with similar figures.)

Pushing figuration to extremes is what Coleridge calls "mental bombast." It is symptomatic of an impatience with the way things are,

299

as if rhetoric could supplement or alter this. Shelley asks how it is that we can love more than one person at a time:

> True Love in this differs from gold and clay
> That to divide is not to take away.
>
> . . .
>
> If you divide suffering and dross, you may
> Diminish till it is consumed away;
> If you divide pleasure and love and thought,
> Each part exceeds the whole; and we know not
> How much, while any yet remains unshared,
> Of pleasure may be gained, of sorrow spared.
>
> (E 160–1, 178–83)

When he writes that the "part *exceeds* the whole," he cannot precisely mean anything; rather, he urgently compounds the trope's inherent hyperbole that the part equals the whole, as if to say that love can spill beyond all containment, whether in figure or fact.

Love impinges on environment, filling, expanding, and clarifying it:

> Love is like understanding, that grows bright,
> Gazing on many truths; 'tis like thy light,
> Imagination! which from earth and sky,
> And from the depths of human phantasy,
> As from a thousand prisms and mirrors, fills
> The Universe with glorious beams, and kills
> Error, the worm, with many a sun-like arrow
> Of its reverberated lightning.
>
> (E 162–9)

In its visionary anti-sublimity, love destroys illusion and dispels the "dull vapours of self." Just as imagination invades the domains of truth and morality in Shelley, so love grants, beyond an affective state of being, an enlarged consciousness that is like "understanding" and that "kills error."

But in *Epipsychidion* the speaker makes even greater professions. With the audacity of a prophet, he will legislate new reality. His quest in the past for an appropriate woman has failed because each woman has offered only a portion of that sense of reality he thinks is his due in this "world of love, this *me*." Emilia seems now to answer to this ontological thirst, but he is not yet united with her. The latter part of the poem (383–591) shifts from past to future tense, in a compendium of Shelleyan desire. The movement is from the restraints of a "vacant prison" to a "far Eden of the purple East," an Hellenic Eden. Getting there requires the "invisible violence" of love that accepts no limits to its movement outward toward the other. Left behind is the Dantesque "obscure forest"; love militates against sublimity, removing veil after veil until this green and golden island of the imagination is "like a naked bride" (474). Here the synecdochic expansion of self into the other creates a "calm circumference of bliss" where "to love and live / Be one" (550–2). Under the radiant Aegean sun, the poet attempts through language to unite two selves sexually and metaphysically. But as if assenting to his own comparison of love with death (401–4), he watches this rhetorical expansionism finally implode into vacancy:

> The winged words on which my soul would pierce
> Into the height of love's rare Universe,
> Are chains of lead around its flight of fire—
> I pant, I sink, I tremble, I expire!
>
> (E 588–91)

Prophetic vision is what the poet would "call reality" (512), if he could. The plaintive wish of *Lines Written Among the Euganean Hills* (1818) that the world become young again would be fulfilled not only in the poem but in reality. The poet panics upon recognizing that he has not escaped the vacant prison of his own poem. This concession to the "cold hill side" is a moral correction, for the speaker has not heeded the wisdom of *Prometheus Unbound* that we can never be exempt from "chance and death and mutability." In *Epipsychidion* the poet "oversoars" and confronts an "intense inane" on earth instead of in the empyrean. By contrast, the Poet of *Alastor* fails to socialize his vision, to recognize that the world he imagines must be shared and attested to by others. Sublimity here becomes a phantasmagoric nightmare. In *Epipsychidion* the speaker as another persona of Shelley advances morally: "understanding" and "light" invest the imagery of the anti-sublime, and the use of synecdoche rhetorically unites self and other. Visionary landscape is no longer the terrifying chasms of the Hindu Kush but the beautiful clear Ionian isles. When the poet attempts to place extreme burdens on this trope – in effect literalizing it – when he seeks total transformation of scene through prophetic urging, and when he pushes love's violence to an extreme pitch, he is corrected by that reality beyond the poem to which the strongest imagination must eventually concede. Unlike Blake, Shelley portrays love's violence in the cautionary mode.

This poem has dramatized what Shelley might have learned earlier from his epistolary courtship of Elizabeth Hitchener, where the language of moral hyperbole attempts frantic acts of legislation. The forty-six extant letters to Hitchener of 5 June 1811 to 18 June 1812 are a display of impassioned moralism and the world's most high-minded seduction talk. Is Hitchener to be blamed for thinking Shelley wants something more than friendship of her?

> My dearest friend, for I will call you so, *you* who understand my motives to action which I flatter myself unisonize with your own, you who can contemn the worlds prejudices, whose views are mine, I will dare to say I *love*, nor do I risk the possibility of that degrading & contemptible interpretation of this sacred word, nor do I risk the supposition that the lump of organised matter which enshrines *thy* soul excites the love which that soul alone *dare* claim.
>
> (*LPS* I 149)

Alluding to her physical person as a "lump of organised matter" is a not so flattering way of concealing his sexual motive from them both. After her disastrous stay with the Shelleys, he tells his friend, Thomas Jefferson Hogg: "She is an artful, superficial, ugly, hermaphroditical beast of a woman, and my astonishment at my fatuity, inconsistency, and bad taste was never so great, as after living four months with her as an inmate. What would Hell be, were such a woman in Heaven?" (*LPS* I 336).

With the language of moral hyperbole working as a preemptive strike, Shelley has attempted to bully away real doubts about moral purity. Hitchener protests in her letters that she is not the celestial spirit he makes her out to be: "My dearest friend you deceive yourself, see me more such as I *really am*." (*LPS* I 160.) There is unconscious aggression in the letters to Hitchener, as if in covert protest of her own sexual nature. There is also a notable lack of introspection and quiet in them. Shelley looks strenuously outward, or forward into the future, scheming his version of a small utopian community. To live always in the state of moral desire is to risk mental dislocation. Absolutist projects of the imagination are properly disciplined, as Shelley and many of his friends and lovers discover the hard way.

Epipsychidion, *Prometheus Unbound*, and many other works make clear that in Shelley we find the most pointed effort among the Romantics to deny the separation of aesthetic categories from epistemology and ethics. As I have said, this is the Romantics' implicit revision of Kant's *Critique of Judgment*. The imagination is for Shelley a higher form of understanding that kills error. And contrary to Kant's view that aesthetic experience is disinterested and but contingently or analogically linked to desire and the good, Shelley links imagination genetically with the highest moral experience, love. The poet is for him a moral force who helps legislate the very conduct of human history.

Rather than a regression to pre-Kantian blurring of distinctions among these three categories, Shelley is engaged in an ultimately disciplined imperialism of the imagination. The counter-examples of *Epipsychidion* and the Hitchener correspondence underscore the need for discipline. Shelley's would be a benign imperialism that induced the ethical to become more urgently ethical, the cognitive more radiantly cognitive. His concessions to limits do not signify that skepticism or nihilism has consumed him at last. Rather, they signify that the creative faculty must, for the sake of moral sanity, both contend with and acknowledge the pressure of reality. Wallace Stevens has written that the imagination exerts "a violence from within that protects us from the violence without." Shelley moralizes the imagination's role, seeing that love's violence and visionary desire may attempt too grand a usurpation, and make us doubly vulnerable to violence without. This check on visionary presumption chastizes but does not obliterate it. Poets can continue to imagine and their poems will survive as the history of imagination and desire. Prometheus and Asia will continue to love. The ultimate check on Shelley's presumption is the rotting corpse that washed ashore between Massa and Via Reggio ten days after his drowning. This is a final concession to violence without, but there is a saving resistance suggested by the tale passed down that upon the funeral pyre Shelley's heart refused to burn.

The tempered heart

Shelley never dispenses with an early distrust of passion. "What is *Passion*? The very word implies an incapacity for action," he says to Hogg, upon learning that his friend (with some unconscious encouragement from Shelley) has attempted to seduce Harriet Shelley. "Is constitutional temperament the criterion of morals?" he asks, expecting a "no." Admitting some truth in the charge that he is himself "cold, phlegmatic, unfeeling," he exculpates Hogg for his irrational behavior because neither passion nor its absence is a sufficient moral criterion (*LPS* I 179). Affective states of being – passion, feeling, emotion – have value, but unlike Wordsworth Shelley does not think them the radical of larger mind.

Affective moral psychology (as distinguished from conative moral psychology, which deals with questions of willing, volition, and action, to be discussed in the next section) circles around the "heart" for Shelley. The extent to which he conceives of heart literally or only metaphorically is debatable. The word "heart" occurs in his poetry and prose with a frequency rivaling Wordsworth's. From what has already been said, it is clear that healthy feeling for Shelley is social in nature.

Unsocialized feeling is manifested as claustrophobic self-enclosure; its symptom is the bad mood.

A poet commonly known for passionate excess, Shelley reveals himself on closer look to be an advocate of patience and control. The heart must be "tempered," he implies well before his final poem. The Madman of *Julian and Maddalo* (1819), for instance, has loved passionately, impatiently, and futilely. Shelley's ideal self masters those processes Kant calls "pathological": instinct, passion, feeling. But instead of being mastered by forms of reason, as in stoic formulations, they are mastered by imagination, which in its own way negotiates psychological process and counsels patience.

The structure resembles stoicism insofar as emotion is regulated, as Earl Wasserman has noted, but it is a structure more in keeping with the Romantic reordering of values, echoing, for instance, Blake's repositioning of Luvah in the "place of seed" where he no longer dominates Urizen or Los.

Left incomplete at his death, *The Triumph of Life* (1822) is Shelley's last word on the instability of the natural human heart and the role that imagination plays as regulator of feeling. This visionary work has a heavily moralistic format. The poet seeks an explanation for all the "serious folly" he observes in a frenzied pageant, where the ruinous Chariot of Life unceremoniously smears desperate people with dust. Addressing the question to Rousseau is doubly appropriate: he is seen to be progenitor of the revolutionary era Shelley hopes to reinvigorate, and his novel *Julie: ou La Nouvelle Héloîse* portrays the holiness of the heart's affections. Rousseau as Virgilian guide sadly confesses that the heart must be "tempered" to its object, since it has become corrupt and mutinous.

The moral crux of the poem is found in the contrast between "tempering" and "conquering." The renowned "conquerors" of history – priests, kings, and even philosophers – have discovered too late that their lore "Taught them not this – to know themselves; their might / Could not repress the mutiny within" (211–13). Exercising power over others has made them powerless with respect to their own mutinous hearts. "Life" – here, the implacable course of human events – has the more handily conquered them. Napoleon has been defeated, Voltaire forgotten, and Rousseau has failed to discipline the mutiny within:

> I was overcome
> By my own heart alone, which neither age
> Nor tears nor infamy nor now the tomb
> Could temper to its object. (TL 240)

Anticipating Babbitt's denunciation of naive Romantic morality, Shelley has had Rousseau offer a self-critique along similar lines, but one that would prepare for a more compelling structure rather than leave a vacancy. Three inferences can be made about Rousseau's predicament. The first is that if we do not temper feeling, we may well be conquered by it. Though not denying the heart's affections, Shelley sees in Rousseau the disastrous results of benighted feeling. As a grotesque parody of human form, Rousseau is mistaken for an old distorted root growing out of a hillside, his hair for weeds, his eyes for holes in the ground. The natural man of feeling has come to this, an excrescence on the face of nature, a corrupted organism. The varieties of human feeling deriving from nature – the source of energy, emotion, and sexuality – are said by Rousseau to have been corrupted by nature itself:

> I feared, loved, hated, suffered, did, and died,
> And if the spark with which Heaven lit my spirit
> Earth had with purer nutriment supplied,
>
> Corruption would not now thus much inherit
> Of what was once Rousseau—.   (*TL* 200–4)

The Triumph of Life caps a tendency throughout Shelley's work to mediate feeling, in itself insufficient and potentially noxious, with other mental activity.

The second inference is that reason has proved its inadequacy also, as is shown by Shelley's inclusion, in his parade of death, of such Enlightenment figures as Voltaire, Kant, and Frederick the Great. It has failed even in its clearing function, for orthodoxies and super-stitions prevail. These notables in life's dismal pageant have not converted a merely instrumental reason into a substantial wisdom.

The third inference, also pertaining to "faculties," is that imagina-tion – a source of nightmare and madness – retains its redemptive power. As I read this much-debated poem, imagination enters figuratively as the "shape all light" (352), which Donald Reiman and Sharon Powers have termed the "Ideal creativity reflected by an earthly medium (the human imagination)" (*SPP* 465n).[8] Later in the poem, as charmed seductress and radiant vision, the "shape all light" offers Rousseau a cup, one sip from which turns his brain to sand. The radiant vision is supplanted by nightmarish visions of humans in a dance of death, encased in the imagery of vampires, apes, vultures, gnats, and flies. But significantly the "shape all light" first appears to

---

[8] On the problematics of the "shape all light," see Rajan, *Dark Interpreter*, 62–5.

Rousseau as a figure of dance and music, of harmony in nature. She induces "invisible rain . . . to sing / A silver music." Her feet kiss the "dancing foam" and "ever to the ceaseless song / Of leaves and winds and waves and birds and bees / And falling drops moved in a measure new / Yet sweet" (375–8). This harmony of dance and music will metamorphose to "savage music, stunning music," the Apollonian to the Dionysian, the redemptive imagination to the dark. Multiple transformations of unstable light imagery give the poem its manic character. But Shelley has not *canceled* the redemptive imagination, deconstructive readings notwithstanding.[9] He has, more profoundly, indicated the range of its functions for good or ill.

Imagination functions for the good in tempering the mutinous heart through harmony and synaesthesia. The process echoes Blake's alignment of Los-Urthona (imagination) with Tharmas (the senses and bodily instincts) and the higher discipline they impose on Luvah (feeling) and Urizen (reason). Passions are not "quelled" but converted into harmonies of music and dance. Amidst the ensuing nightmare vision, Rousseau prophesies the imagination's triumph somewhere beyond the termination of this poem, whose subtext is Dante's *Divina Commedia*. The very hellishness of the vision puts him in mind of Dante,

> who from the lowest depths of Hell
> Through every Paradise and through all glory
> Love led serene, and who returned to tell

> In words of hate and awe the wondrous story
> How all things are transfigured, except Love. (*TL* 472–6)

This passage is sufficiently direct: it exempts love from transfiguration. Instability of figuration, the fodder of deconstruction, need not penetrate the protective circle of love. Eventually the dark irony of the poem's title, which Hazlitt thought should more appropriately read *The Triumph of Death*, would be resolved: this would be a triumph of life even as the *Divina Commedia* is. Compare Demogorgon's assertion in *Prometheus Unbound* that to "Fate, Time, Occasion, Chance and Change . . . All things are subject but eternal Love" (II iv 119–20). Whether Shelley fully believes this is a matter for the biographer or psychologist. The poem he wrote resists its own entropic movement toward darkness and disintegration. And once again the powers of resistance are imagination and love. Perhaps a despairing Shelley

---

[9] The contributors to *Deconstruction and Criticism* were asked to take *The Triumph of Life* as their illustrative text.

would not have completed his own divine comedy, but *The Triumph of Life* points to something beyond its margins other than his drowned corpse.

Anticipated, therefore, in Shelley's own critique of "Rousseau and Romanticism" are the very objections Babbitt makes to naive Romantic morality. The affective life has in this late stage European history been deeply corrupted, but love, the ultimate shape the light of imagination can produce, is less a feeling than a knowing, and need not submit to history. Shelley has never been a *callow* meliorist, not even in the days of *Queen Mab*. In his last, dark poem, he has not altogether forsaken his claim that "the great instrument of moral good is the imagination."

Against this final critique of the heart and its passions, we can observe in earlier texts Shelley's anatomy of self-incarceration, a pathology that afflicts many of his fictive surrogates. "Self" is a term of approbrium for him from the early letters on. To Hogg, apropos of Shelley's effort in 1811 to marry off his sister to his best friend, he writes: "But adieu to egotism; I am sick to Death at the name of self," the antithesis of love, though he fears there may be some residual "selfishness in the passion of Love" (*LPS* I 34–6). With implications for his narrative, *Alastor*, he writes, again to Hogg,

I cannot endure the horror the evil which comes to *self* in solitude . . . What a strange being I am, how inconsistent, in spite of all my boasted hatred of self—this moment thinking I could so far overcome Natures law as to exist in complete seclusion, the next shrinking from a moment of solitude, starting from my own company as if it were that of a fiend, seeking any thing rather than a continued communion with *self*—Unravel this mystery—but no. I tell you to find the clue which even the bewildered explorer of the cavern cannot reach.

(*LPS* I 77–8)

Years later, in connection with publishing *Julian and Maddalo* anonymously, he writes: "So much for self—*self*, that burr that will stick to one. I can't get it off yet" (*LPS* II 108–9). And in *Laon and Cythna*, he writes, echoing Wordsworth, that "we have one human heart," which is empowered to override 'the dark idolatry of self' (3361, 3390).

Yet Shelley speaks of the evils of "self-contempt," and elsewhere of the value of "individuality." In the same letter to Elizabeth Hitchener in which he declaims against selfishness, he urges, "Preserve your individuality" (*LPS* I 189). A section of "Speculations on Morals" is entitled, "Moral Science Consists in Considering the Difference, not the Resemblance, of Persons" (*SM* 191–3). He repeats a figure from his early letter: investigating the moral basis of "individual man" is like visiting the "deepest abyss of [a] vast and multitudinous cavern." In this fragment, he attacks categorical moral judgments of human acts. Persons and their acts are infinitely variable, notwithstanding a superficial resemblance in the "habitual conduct" of social life in occupation, marriage, and education:

In truth no one action has, when considered in its whole extent, an essential resemblance with any other. Each individual who composes the vast multitude which we have been contemplating has a peculiar frame of mind, which, while the features of the great mass of his actions remain uniform, impresses the minuter lineaments with its peculiar hues. Thus while his life, as a whole, is like the lives of other men, in detail it is most unlike.   (SM 192)

The extreme nominalism of this passage cannot be wholly reconciled with Shelley's own brands of utilitarianism and cosmic love (in which we are said to thirst after our own likeness), but this grounding of the self in "difference" certainly informs his anarchistic politics, in which society is to be based not on uniformity but on equality, fostered by distributive justice and benevolence. Within this society each individual has an inviolate core of self – the "profounder source" of actions – that can be only dimly perceived but that must be granted free agency. Individualism is not, in any event, the ethical standard for Shelley. One preserves one's "Individuality" by means of social commitments. (He thinks Elizabeth Hitchener will preserve hers by joining his entourage at Lynmouth.) This will become clear in the contrast between him and the emphatic individualist, Hazlitt.

Such terms as "individuality," "peculiar frame of mind," "individual man," and "self-knowledge" are positive for Shelley and mutually implicating. Negative terms include "self-anatomizing," "self-contempt," and "selfishness." What he objects to is not "individual man," rather to self-preoccupation in all its forms, or what Blake has termed the "selfhood" and Coleridge "selfness." There are psychological disabilities to consider here: narcissism (the Poet in *Alastor*), affective disorder (Maddalo), and paranoia (the poet-surrogate in *Adonais*). Merely psychological states of mind are portrayed as obsessional and delimiting. They inhibit the impulse toward moral and ontological discovery and growth.

The Poet in *Alastor* has this impulse in the extreme and would seem well equipped to carry out the will to value on an epic scale. He appears empowered by the requisite moral virtues – generosity, kindliness (like Shelley he is a vegetarian, respectful of the "one life" the Ancient Mariner violates in killing a bird), "uncorrupted feeling," "adventurous genius," etc. His search for his own anti-type is part of a larger search for enhanced *meaning*. He seeks "strange truths in undiscovered lands," he pores over the ruins of history for the origins of things, "and gazed, till meaning on his vacant mind / Flashed like strong inspiration, and he saw / The thrilling secrets of the birth of time" (126–9). But his imagination, which leads him forth, is tragically flawed and unable to master passion, which, as Shelley has said, "implies an incapacity for action." More than *Epipsychidion* – in which the speaker reaches beyond passion to a self-created landscape generated by imagination and emotion, a more active stage of mind if frustrated on other grounds in the end – *Alastor* is the supreme Shelleyan poem of passion. What appears as pursuit is actually a willlessness in the face of compulsion. The fated poet cannot create his own humanized landscape but is driven through a totally alien one, haunting and debilitating in its sublimity – and driven by "ministers" that are the projected "genii" of his own "vacant" self. The Plotinian search for a divinity without that would resonate with the "divinity within" is noble, as Stevens might say, but the noble Poet, in fixing his imagination on one whose "voice was like the voice of his own soul" and who was "herself a poet," experiences love as sickness (181–2), its passionate excess not spilling outward to the other but self-absorbed as a poison.

In his Preface to *Julian and Maddalo*, Shelley writes: "I say that Maddalo is proud, because I can find no other word to express the concentered and impatient feelings which consume him." His brilliance relative to common folk gives him "an intense apprehension of the nothingness of human life," and he is consumed by melancholia. Repression of the affective life has infected the conative: "His ambition preys on himself, for want of objects which it can consider worthy of exertion," and fails to be directed outward, as it should be, in political action. A partial portrait of Lord Byron, Maddalo has a different affliction from the Poet in *Alastor*. Whereas the Poet covers Eurasia in a frenzied pursuit of a phantom, Maddalo is incapacitated for the larger action his destiny cries out for, and he contents himself with smaller gestures, such as fixing up some living quarters for a madman. His feelings are too "concentered" to undertake anything grander. Julian interprets this failure as unnecessary acquiescence in circumstance:

> We are assured
> Much may be conquered, much may be endured
> Of what degrades and crushes us. We know
> That we have power over ourselves to do
> And suffer – what, we know not till we try,
> But something nobler than to live and die—.　　(*JM* 182–7)

This statement is something more than a blind optimism undercut by the fate of the Madman, whose rantings take up the middle portion of *Julian and Maddalo*. Julian's trust in the instrumental value of trial and suffering, as well as in self-empowerment, comes close to Shelley's own position. The Madman represents the complete loss of patience brought about by an untempered sympathetic extension of the heart's affections to an uncertain object. He too is a cautionary figure, not a walking, raving repudiation of Shelleyan hope. Maddalo and the Poet in *Alastor* exhibit truncated imaginations; the moral commitment of imagination to world is absent. The Poet is blind to what the world in fact offers in beauty and love; he is at once narcissistic, projective, and myopic. Maddalo lacks the will to alter that world where it fails in its offerings.

Shelley's self-representation in *Adonais* (271–306) combines elements of these two figures. Like the Poet in *Alastor*, he has been engaged in a quest after an indefinite object "O'er the world's wilderness," but is now a "frail Form." He is a "pardlike Spirit beautiful and swift," who is for that reason "neglected and apart." Like Maddalo, he negates his inherent power with despondency: "A Love in desolation masked;—a Power / Girt round with weakness." The pardlike Spirit has committed the sin of gazing on "Nature's naked loveliness" (245), for which he is pursued by hunters, those agents of the same hostility to beauty that slew Adonais. The view of the poet as someone who sacrifices himself for his art – who takes on the wrath of the unlovely for his very visionary excellence – has obvious appeal to Shelley, but in the larger context of his work the pardlike Spirit, too, is judged weak and insufficient. The external threat is mimicked in paranoiac self-haunting, as "his own thoughts, along that rugged way, / Pursued, like raging hounds, their father and their prey." The poet must be not an invalid but a legislator: he must in effect speak to those hunters and convert them to vision.

These frustrated and crippled figures – the Poet, Maddalo, and the pardlike Spirit – are thus all cautionary. Each participates in a romance of the self, now part of our collective mythology, that values self-sufficiency, passion, the nerve to say "non serviam," and a depth of agonized consciousness resistant to analysis. Self-love, melancholia, and invalidism are vices in an ordinary handbook of morality, but in such figures they verge on becoming magnificent vices. Shelley, who argues the continuity of ethics and politics, sees the danger of glamorizing a voyage into the interior. These figures signify a frustrated dialectic: as haters of bourgeois sensibility and of the "selfish, blind, and torpid," they are arrested in antithesis, unable to move beyond opposition to power.

Shelley questions the romance of self found in the first generation of Romantic poets. He opposes the tendency to align ethics too closely with psychology; Coleridgean conscience and Wordsworthian memory, I have said, are forms of self-preoccupation. The projective nature of Blake's ego-emanation structure of the psyche implies a potential self-sufficiency; it does not grant full being to the world beyond individual mind, an error *Alastor* warns against. The temptation to which Coleridge sometimes succumbs – of accepting the priority of being over doing – must be resisted; it makes a romance of the invalid. And any Wordsworthian evasion of the ethical life through a turn toward nature, let alone "individual retirement," must be declined. The Poet, Maddalo, and the pardlike Spirit all find compensation for the nothingness of human life in nature's loveliness. But this is a delusory temptation, an idolatry of a non-moral force that drains off moral energy. Instead, Shelley assumes the primacy of doing over being, and urges that passions of the heart be directed to responsibilities in the world.

Reforming the world

The poet with "a passion for reforming the world" adopts early in his career some philosophical notions that might seem to rule out even lifting one's finger. Materialism and the doctrine of necessity carry with them, on first glance, the corollaries that human beings do not freely originate acts and that the grander scheme of things carries on its business whatever we do or say. In *Queen Mab* Necessity promises to bring about a new age, no matter what the moral resolves of individuals. In *Prometheus Unbound*, the amoral Demogorgon, who dethrones the tyrant Jupiter, may appear to work independently of Prometheus, the moral force in the drama. There is much moral talk in both works, but it appears to many readers to be an amoral dynamic that brings about the new age. In poetry and prose, Shelley addresses the issue with some sophistication. If he does not ultimately solve it, we can surely excuse a poet for failing where all the philosophers have failed also. And what may be uncertain as philosophy proves convincing as literature: the paradox of freedom and necessity generates some of his finest verse.

The paradox is at work in the great lyric, "Ode to the West Wind" (1819–20). The wind's freedom is its power to operate in conformity with its own law. Not a desultory breeze, it renders the distinction between freedom and necessity meaningless. The poet wishes to be empowered with the wind's strength, "only less free / Than thou, O Uncontrollable!" (emphasis on "thou," not on "free"). Freedom is empowerment in the sense of persisting in our being more fully; it is an augmented version of Spinoza's *conatus suo esse perseverandi*. The poet is by nature "tameless, and swift, and proud" like the West Wind, and his wish, as one whose power has been made void by a circumstantial "heavy weight of hours," is to be restored to the necessary law of his own being in a heightened way, his power supplemented by the wind's. The wind is transformed, by dint of the poet's large rhetoric, from an external to an internal power, as he moves stanza by stanza toward the imperative, "Be thou me!"

The criteria of freedom discussed in Chapter 2 – absence of constraints from other people, absence of constraints from nature, and empowerment or the ability to obtain objects of desire – work interestingly in the poem. "Mankind," evidenced in stanza III as ruined civilization beneath the sea, enters the poem overtly only in the concluding stanza, where the poet foresees his poetry having an incantatory power over it. His prophetic utterance will liberate mankind from self-imposed constraints. The other criteria are fused: nature instead of constraining would empower, taking the poet up into its own ineluctable process without effacing him. "Mont Blanc" and "Ode to the West Wind" thus represent opposing responses to nature's power. In "Mont Blanc" the response is awe and sublimity in the meditative mode, the poet not presuming (with allowance for ambiguity in the final lines) that he is any match for the mountain's power. Graduating from meditative to active mode, the poet in "Ode to the West Wind" places himself in line with nature's power, which he converts to language, the "leaves" of his writings. For Spinoza, self-empowerment within a necessitarian scheme requires the freedom from passion or confused emotion gained through adequate ideas of nature as substance, not contingency. This rational understanding of our place in nature is an end in itself. But Shelley foresees a crescendo of enlightened emotion as he issues a series of imperatives to the West Wind and seeks to make nature's power his own. The end is not this intensity in itself but social regeneration, his words "the trumpet of a prophecy." Unlike the introjected feeling of Maddalo and the Poet of *Alastor*, his is purposeful feeling directed outwardly. The poet would be a conduit for the conversion of natural to human power, with all mere brooding purged. Moral freedom does not mean one engages in random or indifferent acts; it means harnessing those causative powers that most perfectly fulfill the human function. The poem has succinctly portrayed the union of freedom and necessity.

We recall the ethics of composition in *The Prelude*, where Wordsworth, reviewing a life in great measure determined by natural scene, confronts the task of composition as itself underdetermined and problematic. "Ode to the West Wind" – an overdetermined formal structure consisting of five *terza rima* sonnets interrelated in theme and image in an intricately schematic way – conceives a poetic self-empowerment in which the strong prophet's voice would be absolutely "determined," in both strict and colloquial senses. The personal predicament of having fallen on the thorns of life would give way to a public voice presumptuous enough to pronounce on what the retired, chastened, suffering Wordsworth has in effect disqualified himself for by the end of *The Prelude*.

But "Ode to the West Wind" is itself only a lyrical prelude to vision, a prefiguring of a time when the problematics of writing and voice would be resolved by a visionary clarity of purpose. In Blakean terms, the Orc cycle is broken by Los's hammer, but the visionary renovation of Night the Ninth is yet to be narrated. The earlier *Queen Mab* (1813) is more blatantly futuristic. The power of Necessity, described as amoral (VI 197–238), will promote human happiness, for whatever reason. The Fairy Queen, who looks into secrets of the future, tells us that mankind "perceives the change, his being notes / The gradual renovation, and defines / Each movement of its progress on his mind" (VIII 142–4), but this renovation is the result of "blindly working" cosmic will (IX 5). Though she urges us to pursue virtue, the role of virtue is uncertain in a world where all human activity "tend[s] to perfect happiness" anyway (IX 151). Her vision of renovated earth mingles imagery from various Biblical and Classical utopias, adding Shelley's own emphasis on the death of religion and overthrow of tyranny. But the closest the poem comes to a specific moral recommendation that might help bring all this about is vegetarianism. The difference between "Ode to the West Wind" and this earlier work is thus the Ode's centering on self-empowerment. An older Shelley has come to believe that human will and intelligence are needed to give purpose to natural process. On a grander scale, *Prometheus Unbound* will address this issue.

Much of Shelley's lengthy note on Necessity in *Queen Mab* is taken up with conative moral psychology, which barely enters the poem proper. (By "conative" I refer to the conscious drive or volition to perform certain acts, which is classically distinguished from affective moral psychology, discussed in the last section, and from cognitive psychology.) Patching together Spinoza, Hume, and Holbach, Shelley maintains without qualification that "motive is to voluntary action in the human mind what cause is to effect in the material universe. The word *liberty* as applied to mind is analogous to the word chance as applied to matter: they spring from the ignorance of the certainty of the conjunction of antecedents and consequents" (*SPR* 109). It is surprising to encounter a strict psychological determinism in the family of Romantic poets, and the idea is with difficulty reconciled with Shelley's later writings on love, imagination, and intelligent choice.[10] He makes a frightening claim for the moral philosopher, who sounds more like a cyberneticist:

The precise character and motives of any man on any occasion being given, the moral philosopher could predict his actions with as much certainty as the natural philosopher could predict the effects of the mixture of any particular chemical substances.　　　　　　　　　　　　　　　　　　　　　(*SPR* 110)

This premise revises conventional notions of free will: "The advocates of free-will assert that the will has the power of refusing to be determined by the strongest motive," which, Shelley points out (following Hobbes, Spinoza, Locke, Hume, and Holbach), is a self-contradiction because "the strongest motive is that which, overcoming all others, ultimately prevails" (*SPR* 111). Besides destroying religion, these notions "introduce a great change into the established notions of morality," but like Godwin and others he does not believe that necessity does away with morality. It "does not in the least diminish our disapprobation of vice." We would continue to avoid a tiger despite the fact that he "is constrained by the inevitable condition of his existence to devour men" (*SPR* 111).

Shelley's necessitarianism becomes in fact the first premise of an activist ethics of social change, in which an enhanced understanding of the causality underlying social evils permits us to enter into and influence causal chains more effectively. He denies "free-will" as indeterminacy, indifferentism, and as Blakean–Coleridgean free origination, but thinks necessity alone makes rational behavior possible, since without it we could not engage in diagnosis and prediction. With Godwin he says that instead of punishing criminals for their necessitated acts, we should treat them with the compassion that might change their behavior. The ability initially to elect such an enlightened course of action is probably incompatible with strict psychological

---

[10] There is some evidence that Shelley never wholly relinquished psychological determinism. Well after *Queen Mab*, he claims that we are not responsible for our own beliefs since belief is not a matter of free choice.

determinism. Rather, Shelley adheres more consistently to a variety of "soft determinism," in which human beings can freely enter into causal chains and influence them. Shelley's is qualitatively different from the soft determinism I have described in Wordsworth. Instead of tragic naturalism, we find in the Shelley of *Prometheus Unbound* a strongly teleological necessity in which human agency plays a large role and which is directed to global renovation.

The other major philosophical doctrine that might seem to contradict morality – materialism – proves simply irrelevant: "I cannot see how they interfere with each other, or why the two doctrines of materialism & disinterestedness cannot be held in one mind, as independently of each other, as the two truths that a cricket ball is round, and a box square" (*LPS* I 316). Materialism, unlike necessity, Shelley later gives up unambiguously, but when he does adhere to it he still defends the privileged position of morality, always his central philosophical commitment.[11]

Questions of conative moral psychology, freedom, and justice are most deeply explored by Shelley in his five-act play, *The Cenci* (1819), his dramatization of Count Cenci's murderous hatred of his children, his incest with his daughter Beatrice, her plotting with her stepmother Lucretia and brother Bernardo to have the Count murdered by two hired assassins, and their subsequent arrest, torture and execution by order of Pope Clement VIII in 1599. The drama is a severe testing of a principle Shelley urges elsewhere: of returning hate with love or of resisting injustice non-violently. Here he draws our sympathies to a heroine who violates this principle. He portrays the extreme circumstances that appear to compel Beatrice to retaliation, and yet he does not in his Preface excuse her. In the Preface he says he has "sought to avoid the error of making [my characters] actuated by my own conceptions of right or wrong, false or true, thus under a thin veil converting names and actions of the sixteenth century into cold impersonations of my own mind." Beatrice does violate one of Shelley's moral conceptions, but *The Cenci* is no less vivid for that in portraying the fate of his conceptions in action, and it is a good example of how, in Ricoeur's phrase, the "ethical laboratory" of literature permits writers to experiment with values, to revise preconceptions, and even to contradict themselves.

To pose most precisely the questions raised by Beatrice's predicament, we can first turn to Shelley's ethical writings elsewhere, especially "Speculations on Morals" and *Essay on Christianity*, where a

---

[11] The subject index to the Clark edition of Shelley's prose has its largest entry under "Morals."

predominantly utilitarian view is merged with some deontological criteria. He argues, with Godwin, for a universal act-utilitarianism: the worth of a particular act is calculated by the extent to which it provides the greatest good for the greatest number of people. "To consider whether any particular action of any human being is really right or wrong we must estimate that action by a standard strictly universal. We must consider the degree of substantial advantage which the greatest number of the worthiest beings are intended to derive from that action" (*SPR* 215).[12] The principle of utility is generated by "benevolence," our wish to "seek the happiness of others" in accordance with a hedonistic concept of value: that is "called good which produces pleasure; that is called evil which produces pain" (SM 187). (Shelley eventually gives up this hedonistic value monism.)

Shelley, like Godwin and Hazlitt, thinks that the principle of benevolence or utility is insufficient: one could within its terms promote the pleasure of the majority and yet wreak pain and indignity on some minority group. Hence he adds that

> there is a sentiment in the human mind that regulates benevolence in its application as a principle of action. This is the sense of justice. It is through this principle that men are impelled to distribute any means of pleasure which benevolence may suggest the communication of to others, in equal portions among an equal number of applicants. (SM 190)

He draws an example of ten men shipwrecked on a desert island who must distribute subsistence equally.

Shelley's act-utilitarianism is modified further by his attraction to some features of formalist theories and his dislike of weighing moral cases by consequences alone, or sometimes by consequences at all. Some acts are just despite their consequences; some acts are to be valued on the basis of their motive alone, their intrinsic merit, and not on pain or pleasure that might result. Inducements to virtue, such as the heaven and hell of William Paley's theological utilitarianism, are degrading. Like Godwin, Shelley thinks "purity of virtue" consists in the motive rather than the consequences:

> A person who should labor for the happiness of mankind lest he should be tormented eternally in Hell would with reference to that motive possess as

---

[12] Shelley's definition is compromised by his use of "worthiest," which technically makes this *limited* act-utilitarianism, in which the happiness of only a certain group is considered. I take this to be a flaw in exposition overridden by his emphasis on a "standard strictly universal" and by his comments on justice, below; but it could indicate vestigial elitism even so.

316

little claim to the epithet of virtuous as he who should torture, imprison, and burn them alive, a more usual and natural consequence of such principles, for the sake of the enjoyments of heaven.

(SM 191)

He praises the ethics of Jesus for the principle "that virtue is its own reward" (*SPR* 201–2). Though he leans toward a utilitarianism based on consequential maximizing of happiness for the largest number of people, his sense of justice is informed by a conviction that some acts are intrinsically right or wrong, irrespective of consequences.[13]

Shelley speaks of three principles of human action to keep in mind: benevolence, which impels to beneficent acts and which he calls the principle of utility; distributive justice, which "regulates benevolence" by spreading its effects equally; and retributive justice, which he considers intrinsically wrong and which he refuses to distinguish from revenge: "The distinction between justice and mercy was first imagined in the courts of tyrants" (*SPR* 203).[14] In *The Cenci* he fashions a conflict between the claims of benevolence and the claims of retributive justice in a historical situation where the possibility of distributive justice is nil.

Benevolence is said to have been part of Beatrice Cenci's basic nature. Her brother Giacomo speaks of Beatrice,

> Who in the gentleness of thy sweet youth
> Hast never trodden on a worm, or bruised
> A living flower, but thou hast pitied it
> With needless tears!
>
> (C III i 366–9)

In his Preface, speaking of the famous portrait falsely presumed to have been by Guido and which is not even of Beatrice Cenci, Shelley describes her as "one of those rare persons in whom energy and gentleness dwell together without destroying one another," and he emphasizes her "patience," "imagination," and "sensibility." What causes her to plot her murderous father's death? and what would Shelley have her do otherwise? To this latter question he provides a

---

[13] As I have noted in Chapter 2, this kind of seeming contradiction can be resolved by act-deontological theories that accept consequences as one of the criteria of right, or by theories that mingle deontological and teleological perspectives.

[14] In this scheme Shelley is probably influenced by Hume, who in *An Inquiry Concerning the Principles of Morals* (1751) calls benevolence and justice the principal "social virtues." But Hume, a conservative, regards justice as an "artificial" utilitarian virtue based on social convention, while benevolence is a "natural" virtue. Shelley alters Hume with a Godwinian passion for equality and distributive justice as intrinsic values; he repudiates retributive justice and unjust conventions. The classical discussion of distributive and retributive justice is found in Aristotle, *Nicomachean Ethics*, Bk. V.

direct answer in his Preface, but its implementation is, to say the least, difficult to conceive:

Undoubtedly, no person can be truly dishonoured by the act of another; and the fit return to make to the most enormous injuries is kindness and for-bearance, and a resolution to convert the injurer from his dark passions by peace and love. Revenge, retaliation, atonement, are pernicious mistakes. If Beatrice had thought in this manner she would have been wiser and better; but she would never have been a tragic character.   (*SPP* 240)

We might recall in this context Julian's assurance to Maddalo that

> Much may be conquered, much may be endured
> Of what degrades and crushes us. We know
> That we have power over ourselves to do
> And suffer—what, we know not till we try,
> But something nobler than to live and die—.

But Count Cenci, who rejoices publicly over the deaths of two of his sons, is degrading and crushing in the extreme. Perversely analogous to Necessity, he is an external power that literally becomes internal. Nature in the form of the West Wind enters and heightens the self in its freedom and power. But Count Cenci enters his daughter incestuously and corrupts her nature, depriving her of all power, freedom, and identity, in an extreme Blakean "hindering." In all this he appears to have God on his side: his prayers for the deaths of his sons are swiftly answered, one of them dying when a church falls on top of him. Shelley never suggests that the Count is capable of redemption, that he *could* warm to his daughter's love or refrain from raping her. He lacks the potential shame that Shelley credits to British soldiers, who could be won over by passive resistance in the populace (*The Mask of Anarchy*, 1819). Significantly, Beatrice has in the past futilely "sought by patience, love and tears / To soften him" (I ii 115–16). What is Shelley implying that Beatrice ought to do or not to do beyond this? Earl Wasserman writes that she "should have defeated the tyrant with patient, stoic endurance and pity."[15] But does not "should" imply "could"? And she has already tried this tactic.

Rather than create a character as a blunt ideological tool in the resolution of such a question, Shelley has given Beatrice a complex characterization that shows how psychological dislocation infects ethical perception and will. Much of the play dwells on her response to the incest and on her vocalized decision-making. She weighs commit-ting patricide like a well-intentioned moralist, but comes to the wrong

---

[15] *Shelley: A Critical Reading*, 100.

conclusion from the standpoint of the playwright who writes the Preface. "I have prayed / To God, and I have talked with my own heart, / And have unravelled my entangled will, / And have at length determined what is right" (III i 218–21). Shelley has said in his Preface that no human being can be dishonored by the act of another. Beatrice's response to incestuous rape, however, is one of a profound sense of contamination, so profound that her mental imagery compounds incest with necrophilia, herself the corpse. She complains of

> a clinging, black, contaminating mist
> About me . . 'tis substantial, heavy, thick,
> I cannot pluck it from me, for it glues
> My flesh to a pollution, poisoning
> The subtle, pure, and inmost spirit of life!   (C III i 17–23)

She is not "mad" but "dead," her limbs putrefied. A good actor playing Count Cenci can convince any audience that her response is not overblown.

Is hers not the special case limiting the general rule that one should respond to hate with love? Does not the play's logic insist that circumstances can so collude as to make retribution both necessary and to that degree right? To the claims of retributive justice are added those of self-defense: the Count is eager to repeat the rape. "What have I done? / Am I not innocent?" she cries, and most of us agree.

But following the rape she begins to speak in a way that reveals her own moral contamination. She has absorbed her oppressor's poison. To her stepmother Lucretia she says:

> Aye, something must be done;
> What, yet I know not . . . something which shall make
> The thing that I have suffered but a shadow
> In the dread lightning which avenges it;
> Brief, rapid, irreversible, destroying
> The consequence of what it cannot cure.
> Some such thing is to be endured or done:
> When I know what, I shall be still and calm,
> And never any thing will move me more.   (C III i 86–94)

Throughout the play, she stops short of naming the deed, whether patricide or incest. Terming the incest "expressionless," she can "feign no image in my mind / Of that which has transformed me" (III i 108–9); "there are deeds / Which have no form, sufferings which have no tongue" (III i 141–2). She asks her stepmother not to "speak" a simple matter of fact – that Lucretia is indeed Lucretia – for if this were true, then the world would be real, and it would follow "that the other [the incest] too / Must be a truth, a firm enduring truth, / Linked with each lasting circumstance of life, / Never to change, never to pass away" (III i 59–63).

These speeches imply her deep evasiveness about the nature of "deeds." The incest and the patricide do and do not exist in fact. Beatrice's unhinging has its psychological component in the breaking of an incest taboo, compounded with the horror of rape. It also has a more conceptual component in her assuming false alternatives as to the nature of the act: either that the incest has somehow never taken place, or that it has become for all time part of her essence.

In this error we find the key to the Beatrice who is horrendously injured, the Beatrice who orders the murder of the Count, and the Beatrice who unheroically denies that she has participated in the murder plot. In not naming the incest, she tries to lend it an unreality, but the attempt results only in a psychically dislocating dread, the deed taking on the overpowering indefiniteness of dark sublimity. In saying that "something must be done" without naming the deed of patricide, she betrays the same kind of evasion.

The signal phrase here is "destroying / The consequence of what it cannot cure." Unlike Blake's Oothoon, she regards the sexual contamination as permanent, yet in retaliation she will contradictorily attempt to deny the consequence that has already seized upon her. Later speeches bear out that she wishes to contain the event almost mathematically. Revenge or "atonement" implies an equivalency that would result in erasure, leaving her "calm and still." When Lucretia fears the consequences of the murder, Beatrice replies: "O fear not / What may be done, but what is left undone: / The act seals all" (IV iii 5–7). Thus she would bracket the patricide, regard it as a self-sealing act without consequence, the incest and the patricide canceling one another out. After the Count is dead, she says to Lucretia:

> The deed is done,
> And what may follow now regards not me,
> I am as universal as the light;
> Free as the earth-surrounding air; as firm
> As the world's centre. Consequence, to me,
> Is as the wind which strikes the solid rock
> But shakes it not.   (C IV iv 46–52)

She errs: acts do have consequences and there is no such thing as complete erasure of the past. Retributive justice, instead of balancing and canceling, is inefficient; it compounds the original crime, and makes the avenger vulnerable to the powers she challenges.

Her subsequent unheroic denial of patricide in court is a continuation of the effort to cancel both incest and patricide. It is not out of cunning that she self-righteously forces Marzio, the assassin she hired, to lie about her involvement, even though this sends Marzio back to the torture chamber and to his death. She has almost convinced herself, through these evasions, of her own non-involvement. There is a split in her consciousness between being and doing: her being disclaims the doing as a desperate means of protecting what remains of her ego. Perhaps Shelley has Coleridge's play *Remorse* (1812; revision of *Osorio*, 1797) in mind, for *The Cenci* is written as if in qualifying refinement of Coleridge's conviction that acts necessarily stick to us because of conscience, no matter what our tactics of evasion or repression. Only Count Cenci's son, Giacomo, feels the stylized remorse of Jacobean tragedy (V i 2–4). Beatrice feels no remorse, but not because she defiantly knows retaliation to have been just. Rather, she has dissociated herself mentally from the act. To confess the patricide would be to admit to herself, as Coleridge puts it, the "abiding *presentness*" of both the patricide and, worse, the incestuous rape that provoked it. Thus, she voices explicitly the doubleness, not duplicity, that has been characteristic of her throughout. When the judge asks if she is guilty of her father's death, she refuses to decide. Her father's death

> is or is not what men call a crime
> Which either I have done, or have not done. (C V iii 84–5)

How, then, do we see the role of Beatrice in relation to Shelleyan ethics? She demonstrates in the first place that her natural benevolence is not enough to soften tyrants or even to prevent its own conversion into hate. Her own heart becomes "cold," just as Count Cenci's is "hardened." Some other virtue or power is necessary, as complement of benevolence. She does have a fair degree of prudential wisdom: she is said by Orsino to have an "anatomizing" power, whereby she can read hidden motives of other characters; she has coped wisely with the Count before the incest, and has provided refuge from him for other members of the family; she is wary of the ambitious Orsino's motives in seeking her hand in marriage. But all this proves insufficient. We must ask whether there is any personal virtue or power she might have practiced that would have prevented her victimization.

I think the answer is no. She is wholly coerced into moral compromise despite her many strengths. Shelley acknowledges that there are victims in the world. Wasserman has argued that she can decide whether in the first place to permit the motive of revenge to enter her will, and is therefore culpable. Once she has freely given admission to the motive, she becomes part of a causal chain of evil; motive is to act as cause is to effect, as the Count is to Beatrice. Humans always have the choice as to whether they will break the causal chain of evil and deny it entrance into their own will.[16] Wasserman's reading has the strength of making the play consistent with the Preface, where Shelley says that no person can be truly dishonored by the act of another and that Beatrice has erred in taking revenge. But this is one instance, in my view, where we should trust the play, not the playwright. Beatrice's prior power of choice is in no way dramatized or alluded to. What we do know is that she *has* attempted by love and patience to convert the Count prior to the rape. The revenge motive is indeed *implanted* against her will by her father's act of rape; about this she has no choice. Shelley has used the strongest possible images of violation and contamination to make vivid the fact of evil having been forced upon her from without. Like Christabel, Beatrice becomes evil without having been culpable. His statement in the Preface that no person can be dishonored by another's act must be regarded as a wishful misreading of his own play.[17] The Cenci portrays a world so evil that it can tragically infect the innocent. Shelley is more cogent when he says in the Preface that Beatrice is "violently thwarted from her nature by the necessity of circumstance and opinion." Evil is a power that overrides the question of culpability. Ours is a world so evil that retribution can seem attractive to the most hardened pacifist.

If the moral force of an individual – here, Beatrice's benevolence – is insufficient to extreme situations, the other tactic, retribution, proves self-defeating for reasons beyond the self-corruption of the agent. The Count is part of a larger network of depravity and power, a network so canny it is prepared to dispense with him when his grotesquerie

---

[16] *Shelley: A Critical Reading*, 101–15.

[17] Parallels between *The Cenci* and Shelley's life are suggestive, as Donald Reiman has pointed out to me. Shelley acknowledges no guilt in the deaths of Harriet and two of his children. Count Cenci feels no remorse at the death of his two sons and indirectly causes the death of Beatrice. Beatrice's own lack of remorse recapitulates the Count's. In both Beatrice and Shelley there is a strong sense of duty at the same time that there is, relative to their own actions, a curious repression of a sense of violation. Another unflattering parallel exists between Count Cenci and Shelley's obtuse and tyrannical father, Timothy, toward whom Shelley must have felt aggressions of a magnitude he never fully acknowledged. One compositional motive might be to express the aggression against his father that he otherwise repressed.

endangers it. Shelley is not indulging a cheap irony when he has it disclosed that the Count was to be executed by the church anyway. This turn of events in no way exonerates the church from its collusion with power; it simply reaffirms its commitment to power at whatever cost. The moral force of an individual, working as an assassin seeking retribution, does not stamp out evil in the state and, as it turns out, only makes Beatrice more vulnerable to the powers that be. She exchanges the condition of rape for that of death. Shelley has written a play in which no act totally right can be undertaken by the heroine; only the "wild justice" of revenge is available to her.

Since neither benevolence nor retributive punishment redresses tyranny, how can hope persist? The covert answer is a reordering of power within the state that would make Count Cencis and corrupt cardinals unthinkable. This reordering would be under the dictates of distributive justice. Beatrice and the rest of us could be free only in a state free of the authoritarian collusion with which *The Cenci* begins. The Count's parental tyranny is a figure of tyranny in general; to redress it would require a socio-political, not domestic, solution. At this point, however, Shelley's vacillation between a revolutionary and a reformist politics makes itself felt. He wants the ends of revolution, but unlike Blake he cannot stomach violent means. Beatrice's act of assassination proves futile, but what means are available? To be sure, none in late-Renaissance Rome. Shelley is writing in a post-revolutionary period that does have paradigms for collective action against tyranny. He proposes a reformist program for England in *A Philosophical View of Reform*; America, France, Spain, Italy and Greece set forth, in his eyes, the revolutionary posture, whether successful or abortive. It would have been anachronistic, however, to suggest these options in *The Cenci*. What Shelley says of the persecuted Tasso applies well to Beatrice: "Tasso's situation was widely different from that of any persecuted being of the present day, for from the depth of dungeons public opinion might now at length be awakened to an echo that would startle the oppressor. But then there was no hope" (*LPS* II 47).

The Cenci implies that authority can truly dishonor the innocent and powerless, and that there may be, at certain times in history, no salvation for individuals. Salvation must come through a larger socio-political movement seeking distributive justice. Short of this, individuals can only band together for local and temporary retaliation. Beatrice has been forced, for all her inherent benevolence, into the role of an assassin; a truly revolutionary role is unavailable to her. *The Cenci* has demonstrated that the moral life of individuals must in extreme circumstances be supplemented by a larger politics. The Poet in *The*

Triumph of Life laments that "God made irreconcilable / Good and the means of good" (230–2) – a lament suitable to a moment in the historical continuum but not with reference to the larger dialectics of history. The complete vindication of Shelleyan ethics can come only by way of historical accommodation, and the historical moment for it is necessarily closer now than it was in Beatrice's day.

The play contains still more of Shelley's ethical questioning. Count Cenci's comic–grotesque sadism says not a little about the insufficiency of hedonism. The Count outdoes Hobbes in his conception of human nature as brutal and predatory: "All men delight in sensual luxury, / All men enjoy revenge; and most exult / Over the tortures they can never feel— / Flattering their secret peace with others' pain" (I i 77–80). Shelley values pleasure as one component of the happiness that is the utilitarian end. Yet the pursuit of pleasure corrupts. There is a pronounced ascetic note in him, observable in his vegetarianism, his views on "tempering" the heart's affections, and even in his views of sexuality. The Count is the reverse of all this: "When I was young I thought of nothing else / But pleasure." Pursuit of pleasure, if divorced from collateral moral values, can turn to sadism: "till I killed a foe, / And heard his groans, and heard his children's groans, / Knew I not what delight was else on earth, / Which now delights me little" (I i 103–4, 106–9). To judge by these fine sentiments, hedonism in itself does not quite provide a sufficient moral criterion. The Count has a hedonic calculus of his own and is the only character in the play to have a good time. The pain of others is directly proportional to his own pleasure. Benthamite principles alone could not condemn him. He is admirably skilled in maximizing pleasures within the Benthamite categories of "intensity," "fecundity," and especially "propinquity." The additional principle of distributive justice is needed to see to it that pleasures are spread around and that one person's ecstasy is not another's stab in the heart.

Shelley's view of pleasure, expressed in this play and elsewhere, is far removed from the hedonistic utilitarian's value monism he has occasionally spouted. Pleasure is not the only good, and there are qualitative distinctions to be made among pleasures:

There are two kinds of pleasure, one durable, universal, and permanent; the other transitory and particular. Utility may either express the means of producing the former or the latter. In the former sense, whatever strengthens and purifies the affections, enlarges the imagination, and adds spirit to sense, is useful. (*DP* 500)

Like Godwin, Coleridge, Hazlitt, and Aristotle for that matter, he anticipates John Stuart Mill's better-known objection to Bentham's quantitative hedonism in distinguishing qualitatively among pleasures. Though nominally an act-utilitarian with a hedonist concept of value, Shelley is a value pluralist. Whenever notions of qualitatively higher versus lower forms of pleasure enter in, we begin to have a plurality of values – pleasure *accompanied by* knowledge or art or love. The hyperbole with which he speaks of these other values is uncharacteristic of the utilitarian temper.[18]

Count Cenci is the best argument against a view of pleasure not integrated into a larger scheme of values. He is so depraved that one wonders to what extent he is human. But Shelley is no sentimentalist about human nature. In "Speculations on Morals" he asks, "Wherefore should a man be benevolent and just? The immediate emotions of his nature, especially in its more inartificial state, prompt him to inflict pain and to arrogate dominion." As infants, "the tendencies of our original sensations, indeed, all have for their object the preservation of our individual being. But these are passive and unconscious. In proportion as the mind acquires an active power, the empire of these tendencies becomes limited" (SM 187–8). Human nature in its higher, benevolent sense is given us only *in potentia*; it must be developed in time as unconscious forces become conscious. Shelley corrects the sentimental belief, often associated with Romanticism, in childhood innocence. True innocence is something acquired through self-know-

---

[18] Like Keats in his "Ode on Melancholy," Shelley sees the ironic interrelatedness of pleasure and pain, attributed to "an inexplicable defect of harmony in the constitution of human nature":

> It is difficult to define pleasure in its highest sense; the definition involving a number of apparent paradoxes. For, from an inexplicable defect of harmony in the constitution of human nature, the pain of the inferior is frequently connected with the pleasures of the superior portions of our being. Sorrow, terror, anguish, despair itself are often the chosen expressions of an approximation to the highest good. Our sympathy in tragic fiction depends on this principle; tragedy delights by affording a shadow of the pleasure which exists in pain. This is the source also of the melancholy which is inseparable from the sweetest melody. The pleasure that is in sorrow is sweeter than the pleasure of pleasure itself.
> (DP 500)

When falling in love with Teresa Viviani ("Emilia"), he writes to Claire Clairmont that his health is improved,

> & the *relapse* which I now suffer into a state of ease from one of pain, is attended with such an excessive susceptibility of nature – that I suffer equally from pleasure & from pain – You will ask me naturally enough *where* I find any pleasure? The wind the light the air, the smell of a flower affects me with violent emotions. There needs no catalogue of the causes of pain. – I see Emily sometimes: & whether her presence is a source of pain or pleasure to me, I am equally ill-fated in both.
> (LPS II 256)

ledge when emotion is gradually, ideally directed away from self. United are the contraries of Hobbes and Rousseau: whereas human nature is initially selfish and brutal, it is capable of enlightenment – and is "good" to the extent it has so risen. The Count, who never grows beyond his youthful fixation on pleasure, is an improbably obnoxious case of arrested development.

If Count Cenci is the degraded hedonist, Orsini, the suitor of Beatrice, is the egoist, indeed the Romantic individualist of *The Cenci*. He attempts to manipulate the revenge plot to his own advantage. In him we see the corrupted Romantic will in action. Seeking power, not pleasure, and yet possessed of a rudimentary conscience and suscept-ible to Beatrice's charms, he is a subtly drawn opportunist who, despite his intelligence and irony, lacks self-knowledge. He does not know what it is he actually needs. He too has not graduated from unconsciousness to enlightenment, for all his cunning. Giving up love for prospects of wealth and power, he hopes in the process to do "as little mischief as I can; that thought / Shall fee the accuser conscience" (II ii 19–20). Throughout, he pretends to moral complacency. He thinks Beatrice exaggerates her father's loathsomeness the way daughters with testy fathers traditionally do (I ii 73–9); he encourages the plotters to think of the Count's murder as just; and when his scheme fails, he judges it a "plot of mingled good and ill" (V i 80). Yet he exits fearful that, though he may dodge the law, he will have to contend with his own reproaches (V i 97–104). Thinking he can elude moral categories, this egoist is finally caught up in them. Egoistic self-realization and the pretense to a transvaluation of good and evil are not legitimate responses to a world of tyranny. The will is inclined to evil, to pride and separateness, and must be directed by love and imagination, benevolence and justice. "Self-anatomy" – the egoistic evaluation of the self's powers relative to circumstances – must yield to true self-knowledge and power.

The Cenci, then, is a dark play, a tragedy, but this is not to say that it represents a "negative" view of humankind in contradistinction to the "positive" of *Prometheus Unbound*, with which it shares many themes as well as proximity of composition. Rather, it is an analysis of human action that explores the limits of benevolence and personal ethics, and the dangers of retribution, pleasure, and egoism. Within its historical setting, the "dark spirit" is certainly in control. Even the benevolent Beatrice is corrupted by circumstances and by what seems to many of us – if not to the rather pious Shelley of the Preface – the only response she can make to barbarism. But Shelley is hardly legislating total nihilism here. The principle of human action only implied in the play –

distributive justice – can be engaged in contemporary England and other countries, if it could not have been in late-Renaissance Rome. He gives the tyrannies of church and state the worst possible face, as if to say to his audience that they must be resisted now in England and elsewhere. And even within the historical moment of this play, we do not find total nihilism but the corruption of unambiguous virtue into a morally ambiguous condition. Beatrice's dignified closing speeches, though revealing still her inner confusion about her moral status, counsel her brother: "Err not in harsh despair, / But tears and patience" (V iv 144–5).

The play has described the continuity of bad morality and bad politics; the implied remedy is continuity of good morality and good politics. Shelley began to develop this view long before he wrote *The Cenci*. In 1812 the young Godwinian writes:

Southey says Expediency ought to [be] made the ground of politics but not of morals. I urged that the most fatal error that ever happened in the world was the separation of political and ethical science, that the former ought to be entirely regulated by the latter, as whatever was a right criterion of action for an individual must be so for a society which was but an assemblage of individuals, "that politics were morals more comprehensively enforced." (*LPS* I 223)

Coleridge had argued Southey's position extensively in *The Friend* (1809–10), ascribing to Rousseau what later becomes Shelley's position concerning the continuity of morality and politics. Since politics should be the morality of the nation, and since Shelley advocates benevolence and mildness in dealing with injustice, we can see why many of his political writings tend more toward reform than revolution, in line with Godwin instead of Paine. *The Mask of Anarchy* urges passive resistance, with revolutionary energy channeled into the pedagogy of moral demonstration. Equality of property is a moral ideal toward which "it is our duty to tend," but it would be "mischief" to attempt to secure it immediately (*PVR* 253). Likewise, universal suffrage. The harmony of morality and politics is a political ideal that must be applied with some elasticity. I said in Chapter 2 that Romantic authors tend to have dual perspectives on social change: the one is visionary and often anarchistic, the other, as a fall-back of sorts, is reformist and organicist.

Shelley's vision remains revolutionary and anarchistic, but his list of practical reforms in *A Philosophical View of Reform* is not. Possibilities of change through parliamentary procedures exist in Great Britain, if not elsewhere. The continuity of morality and politics requires a gradual evolutionary process, despite the fact that moral inequities must be tolerated over a longer period of time than the revolutionary would wish. With regard to equality of property, Shelley writes that "when we have drawn inspiration from the great object of our hopes it becomes us with patience and resolution to apply ourselves to accommodating our theories to immediate practice":

Morals and politics can only be considered as portions of the same science, with relation to a system of such absolute perfection as Christ and Plato and Rousseau and other reasoners have asserted, and as Godwin has, with irresistible eloquence, systematized and developed. Equality in possessions must be the last result of the utmost refinements of civilization; it is one of the conditions of that system of society towards which with whatever hope of ultimate success, it is our duty to tend.   (*PVR* 253–4)

The consistency of ethics and politics is the goal toward which our actions must tend, but Shelley disavows any hope for an immediate millennium. Once again, vision must make its accommodation with history.

Shelley's longest poem, the epic *Laon and Cythna* (*The Revolt of Islam*), has two plots – the love of brother and sister, and the struggle of Greece against Islam – that are actually one. Moral enlightenment of the couple in spiritual and carnal love is the precondition of revolution. The antecedence of ethics to politics is evident throughout Shelley's works: "You ought to love all mankind, nay, every individual of mankind; you ought not to love the individuals of your domestic circle less, but to love those who exist beyond it more. Once make the feelings of confidence and affection universal and the distinctions of property and power will vanish" (*SPR* 208). The French Revolution failed of immediate success because the moral development of the masses lagged behind the clear prophetic insights of the intelligentsia. Shelley's humanism may therefore be contrasted with Marx's in the *Economic and Philosophic Manuscripts of 1844*, where the elimination of self-estrangement comes about through a new socio-economic system, communism making humanism possible. In hoping that reform might come through the efforts of a sufficient number of previously enlightened exemplary people and through the kindly leadership of a few with egalitarian ideals (egalitarianism in the Godwinian sense of an equality of private property), Shelley represents an historically interesting position in the spectrum of ideas from Romantic individualism to Marxist socialism. His is the politics of a moralist, who begins with outrage at others' pain and who proposes means to a new world – means that would not give pain even to the oppressors. Many would say that Shelleyan mildness and the priority of the moral center are

inadequate to a world of Count Cencis and Castlereaghs and Met-
ternichs, a world where even the absence of tyrants would not
reestablish the priority of ethics over larger socio-economic forces.
Shelley admits his own doubts in making Count Cenci impervious to
Beatrice's initial love and patience, and in taking the morally
enlightened Laon and Cythna to their deaths in a failed revolution.
Holding to a continuity of ethics and politics, he still acknowledges the
historical gap between them, as well as the insufficiency of an
individual's moral resolve to counter tyranny.

Shelley does, of course, portray a successful revolution in *Prometheus
Unbound*, and in so doing makes the historical leap of the prophet. The
play for all its affirmations does not say that this climactic moment is
necessarily at hand, the hungry clouds swagging on the deep. But
through a kind of cosmic contagion, Prometheus assures the triumph
of benevolence and distributive justice, and the eclipse of all vindictiveness. Several Shelleyan preoccupations are given their consummate expression in the play and can be rapidly summarized.

The broadest diagnosis of corruption is that there exists – generally
among humankind and not in Prometheus alone – a breach between
ethics and politics: "The good want [lack] power," and "the powerful
goodness want" (I 625–6). The means of establishing continuity comes
from the ethical end of the spectrum. When Prometheus supplants
hate for his oppressor with pity, he inaugurates a chain of mental and
physical events that leads toward the triumph of rational, egalitarian,
mutualistic anarchy. To "recall" his curse of Jupiter is to alter the mode
of his sense of justice from retribution to distribution. As the Fury says,
"Many are strong and rich, – and would be just, – / But live among their
suffering fellow men / As if none felt" (I 629–32). Prometheus's pity
begins the reign of benevolent fellow-feeling and a just distribution of
products of human labor and culture. Shelley believes that at this late
date in European history a scarcity economics is no longer necessary,
Malthus's arguments notwithstanding.

The alleviations of man's dark estate that Prometheus will per-
petually donate consist of a plurality of values. In a visionary way,
Prometheus Unbound is consistent with ideal utilitarianism. Asia's narration of the drama's prehistory (II iv 32–109) gives an inventory of
values not collapsible into a unitary value such as pleasure or happiness: knowledge, power, science, self-empire, love, wisdom,
freedom, speech, art, transportation, and culture. She does not mention pleasure, as if in final repudiation of hedonistic utilitarianism. The
manifest joy of Act IV is a consequential by-product of a broader
pursuit of the good. The Spirit of the Hour and Demogorgon, who

have the last word of Acts III and IV respectively, speak not of happiness but of patience, endurance, gentleness, justice, hope, and wisdom.

The single imperative Prometheus utters is, "Let man be free" (II iv 45). In Shelley's necessitarian view of things, the imperative means freedom from restrictions that groups or individuals impose on others, plus the self-empowerment gained by harnessing natural power to human will. In terms of the implied dramatic causality, Prometheus's moral regeneration prompts Demogorgon (necessity) to dethrone Jupiter (false authority). Moral regeneration radiates so powerfully that it revitalizes natural process. Earth feels her geological sap flowing once again after Prometheus and Asia unite. This potential revitalization is an article of faith in Shelley and underscores his radical commitment to the priority of the ethical in all matters. As in "Ode to the West Wind," he does not precisely show us how human will gains power by means of necessity, only that it can. The process remains mysterious. We know, however, that freedom and necessity can become one and the same only when the historical moment arrives that permits it, and when human beings incorporate necessity into their moral nature as "self-empire," the power to "imagine that which we know" and "to act that which we imagine." Full control over our own inner causality comes in the union of wisdom and love represented by the union of Prometheus and Asia.

The type of ideal socio-political arrangement Shelley has in mind is notoriously described in terms of negatives: humankind will be "unclassed, tribeless and nationless, / Exempt from awe, worship, degree" (III iv 195–6); it will be "free from guilt or pain." To be sure, the true anarchist might properly resist reification of the ideal on the grounds that this thwarts the anarchistic tendency by premature imaging of Utopia. Shelley admires aspects of the city-state pluralism of Renaissance Italy, but he does not extrapolate from this or other models to propound the precise character of an anarchistic society.[19] (We noted a similar limitation in Blake.) Certainly the role of Asia as love tempers the individualistic dimension of anarchism. Egalitarian

[19] See Michael Henry Scrivener, *Radical Shelley: The Philosophical Anarchism and Utopian Thought of Percy Bysshe Shelley* (Princeton: Princeton University Press, 1982), and P. M. S. Dawson, *The Unacknowledged Legislator: Shelley and Politics* (Oxford: Clarendon Press, 1980), for a fuller exposition of Shelley as anarchist. My own view of his politics conforms largely with Scrivener's in emphasizing its radical-revolutionary character despite its undeniable reformist elements. These studies build on Kenneth Neill Cameron's indispensable *The Young Shelley: Genesis of a Radical* (New York: Macmillan, 1950).

anarchy is based on a mutualism of moral interest. (Mutualism was to be developed in economic terms later in the century by Pierre-Joseph Proudhon.) The practical terms of the new society must be inferred from Shelley's various prose writings, and have been variously inter- preted according to libertarian, anarchistic, and Marxist points of view. Any reading of his politics must acknowledge Shelley's conviction of the priority of the ethical in all matters.

The triumph of love cures the merely psychological states of mind that signal Beatrice's ruin and that inhibit Prometheus, especially his "self-contempt." Asia is more than a Blakean "emanation"; she is an equal of Prometheus, even as she represents an oppositional warming of his mental life. Shelley escapes the mentalism implicit in the structure of Blake's myth. *Prometheus Unbound* affirms the reality and worth of other selves. In learning love, Prometheus reverses the inwardness portrayed as psychic-physical torture in the opening scene. The "self-empire" that results is an overriding of the psycho- logical by the ethical. He will be no longer possessed of negativity of mood and tortured self-expression but will direct energies outward in the productivity and sharing of imagination and love. To be sure, he and Asia decide to trot off to a cave following their reunion – a surprising metaphor – but Shelley returns, in effect, to his recurring image of the small community of imaginative spirits from which redemptive light radiates. Prometheus and Asia form an anarchistic cell preparatory to a socialization of their vision. The geographical imagery of *Prometheus Unbound* has tended to identify mountains with tyranny, and subterranean spaces, as in Demogorgon's cave, with release. The cave may also represent the dark, unconscious psychic power on which the artist draws in producing those "gathered rays which are reality." Prometheus becomes the prototype of the legis- lative artist whose imagination (contrary to Hazlitt's assertion that imagination is attracted to the glamorous trappings of authority) is a levelling, egalitarian force.

Without suggesting that Shelley's revisions are necessarily "correc- tions," I would extend the contrasts initially made between him and Blake, Coleridge, and Wordsworth. Prometheus has achieved a blood- less, non-violent revolution, despite Jupiter's evident displeasure in being toppled. The transition from tyranny to new heaven and earth has not required apocalyptic violence. Blake gives prophetic cursing the very initiating function in revolutionary progress that Shelley gives its retraction. Prometheus's "pity" has also proved a form of self- empowerment instead of the self-divison and heteronomy Blake often ascribes to it. Through pity Prometheus frees himself of Jupiter. The quality of a "right" act (the retraction of a curse) is in keeping with the quality of the "good" state of being Prometheus seeks. The opposition in Blake between right and good is healed. In Prometheus, Shelley challenges the Coleridgean concept of the ineradicably evil will that forms the basis of human identity. Just as evil comes into the world through a failure of human imagination projected into human institutions, so evil can be eradicated through will and imagination. Finally, Shelley in granting will greater empowerment – whatever the degree of personal torment or disappointment with revolutionary progress – opposes both Wordsworthian tragic acquiescence and Byronic fatalism. "Chance and death and mutability" still obtain for him, but they need not thwart human will in its struggle to "be all / We dream of happy, high, majestical." Shelley is not such an absolutist of the imagination that he cannot be consoled by approximations to the ideal.

Profoundly aware of the lure of Romantic egoism, he offers the most persistent attack on it in the period, and he urges that imagination be directed outward in socio-political reform. In neither his life nor work does he sanction an internalization of quest. A drift to the interior is the great temptation for many in an era of failed millennialism and faded collective mythologies. But the epic of the self that Wordsworth had intended to write must be superseded by a true *ex*cursion, the poet not living in retirement but accepting the historic role as legislator. Uniting pity for the world as it is with vision of what it might become, the poet initiates change with a "perpetual Orphic song." If we tend to admire the Shelley who doubts and whose vision darkens at the "eclipsing Curse / Of birth," we must nevertheless acknowledge his own greater valuation of the gentle, radiant form he thinks can invest human personality.

7

Hazlitt: common sense of a dissenter

Of the great nineteenth-century essayists, Hazlitt leaves the largest body of writings specifically directed to moral questions. From his first publication, *An Essay on the Principles of Human Action* (1805), to such late essays as "On Disagreeable People" (1827), "The Main Chance" (1828), and "The Sick Chamber" (1830), he develops a moral commentary that rivals Samuel Johnson's in its comprehensiveness. Complaining of Johnson that his "reflections present themselves like reminiscences; do not disturb the ordinary march of our thoughts," and that Johnson is "a complete balance-master in the topics of morality" (VI 100–2), he himself writes to disturb us, even though he entertains little hope that he will change us. Hazlitt has a resoluteness, clarity, and pointed irony that are winning after the laborious problematics of visionaries, opium-eaters, and infidels. He is the best *writer* of the period.

Hazlitt is more a moral dissenter than a socio-political reformer like Shelley, whatever the progressive character of many of his political views. He does not cast his eye on futurity with the passion or hope of the poet. But he shares with Shelley and others a dismay at the slippage to orthodoxy of the period's larger minds – Burke, Coleridge, and Wordsworth. This seems to Hazlitt a desertion of the ethical center he finds in the human being's sphere of free agency – free of coercive orthodoxies of church and state, and free of social pressure and prejudice. In a few respects he is closer to Blake than to Shelley: Blake's ethics is anchored in individualism and rights, while Shelley urges duties more than rights and is critical, if not dismissive, of individualism. Still, all three figures are in the tradition of philosophical anarchism, whose progenitor is Godwin.

Though Hazlitt dissents from many views we call Romantic (he uses the word "romantic" in the sense of utopian, insubstantial, skittish, or fanatic), he accedes to others with enough conviction that we must

333

group him with these writers over his protest. With Coleridge he attacks the mechanico-corpuscular tradition going back to Hobbes: mind is not reducible to matter in motion, mental activity is not wholly the result of association, psychological egoism is not the only motive spring of human behavior, pleasure and pain are not the only values. Like Blake, Shelley, and Keats, Hazlitt bases the moral life on the imagination and begins his career with a treatise on it.

He claims to have "no theory to maintain," no prophetic vision of what the human race might become, or even what a human individual might become. He is no self-realizationist, except insofar as natural rights would permit the individual to become whatever he or she sees fit. (The power to do so is another matter.) Despite his early *Essay* on the disinterestedness of human mind, he takes an increasingly dyspeptic view of human affairs, and sees the passional self as a reservoir of envy, egotism, hypocrisy, and vindictiveness. I will argue that for all his resoluteness and praise of consistency, he undergoes what is best termed self-controversion. He eventually loses what confidence he had in the practical worth of the imagination, because of its attraction to displays of power, its goading of desire toward unattainable objects, and its idealizing. Human nature is at best an unstable merging of the noble and the base. Idealists lack the mental tact of common sense, and, worse, they are helpless when their ideals get trounced by the reality principle.

Passionate common sense

Hazlitt's animadversions on Shelley constitute a misreading that tells us not a little about the essayist himself. "The author of Prometheus Unbound . . . has a fire in his eye, a fever in his blood, a maggot in his brain, a hectic flutter in his speech, which mark out the philosophic fanatic." Shelley is an unhinged visionary who creates nothing out of nothing. "Bubbles are to him the only realities:—touch them, and they vanish" (VIII 148–9). Hazlitt's critical and moral judgments of Shelley converge: in creating poems with the substance of bubbles, the poet does us no good. "No one (that I know of) is the happier, better, or wiser, for reading Mr. Shelley's Prometheus Unbound" (XII 245–6). Shelley's first error is to be enamored of systems and abstractions for which there is no experiential grounding. Instead of the vanity he is usually accused of, Hazlitt accuses him of "extreme levity." "It would seem that he wished not so much to convince or inform as to shock the public by the tenor of his productions, but I suspect he is more intent upon startling himself with his electrical experiments in morals and philosophy" – even though they may "scorch" other people. As an extreme visionary, Shelley has not given the culture and wisdom of the ages their due: "If a thing was old and established, this was with him a certain proof of its having no solid foundation to rest upon; if it was new, it was good and right." Hazlitt thinks the "principles of sound morality, liberty and humanity, are not to be found only in a few recent writers, who have discovered the secret of the greatest happiness to the greatest numbers, but are truths as old as the creation" (XVI 268).

He gives a character sketch that shows how contemptuous the commonsensical dissenter can be of the visionary reformer:

A man to be a Reformer must be more influenced by imagination and reason than by received opinions or sensible impressions. With him ideas bear sway over things; the possible is of more value than the real; that which is not, is better than that which is. He is by the supposition a speculative (and somewhat fantastical) character; but there is no end of possible speculations, of imaginary questions, and nice distinctions; or if there were, he would not willingly come to it; he would still prefer living in the world of his own ideas, be for raising some new objection, and starting some new chimera, and never be satisfied with any plan that he found he could realise. (VII 15)

Shelley is the poet as reformer who cannot be relied upon even to sustain his opposition to authority. Hazlitt agrees with Shenstone that poets end up as Tories.

Hazlitt thus depreciates the poet and thinker with whom he has not a little in common. Both conceive of imagination as (ideally) a disinterested power of moral sympathy; both believe in the doctrine of necessity as the condition of human freedom; both think the Lockean/ Hartleian model of mind insufficient; belonging to no party or church, both are misfits in the society they radically criticize; both despise authoritarianism, whether political or psychological; and both find the political apostasy of first-generation Romantic poets disturbing, especially since both owe so much to them.

But Hazlitt's knowledge of Shelley is too slight for him to feel any kinship, and on the surface the poet contradicts some of the essayist's fundamental convictions.

First among these is Hazlitt's passion for the concrete, the particular, the factual, the sensate. To the extent Shelley is susceptible of abstractions, theories, and systems unhinged from particulars, he is a "philosophic fanatic." In his "Prospectus of a History of English Philosophy" (1811), Hazlitt makes clear that he is not urging some nominalistic retreat from abstraction: "The power of abstraction is a necessary consequence of the limitation of the comprehending power of the mind: since if it were a previous condition of our having the ideas of things that we should comprehend distinctly *all* the particulars of which they are composed, we could have no ideas at all" (II 117). Though abstraction oversimplifies experience, it is a necessary function *because* the mind is inadequate to the multiplicity of experience.[1] Abstraction is practical or impractical to the extent it embodies experience, as Godwin argues also. Elsewhere he writes that "there is no language, no description that can strictly come up to the truth and force of reality . . ." (XII 45). Erring greatly in degree, Shelley with his bubbles only compounds language's inherent inadequacy.

In moral questions Hazlitt thinks there should be no conflict between theory and practice: "if a theory does not answer in practice, it is proof positive that the theory is good for nothing; and no practice can be good that is at variance with sound theory. Theory, indeed, is nothing but assigning the reasons or principles according to which causes and effects are connected together in fact" (XIX 220). Robert Owen, like Shelley, is an impractical visionary; his institution for the formation of character and social reform, New Lanark, confirms Hazlitt's suspicion that Owen is "a little romantic, both as to matters of fact and reasoning." Owen is "so blinded by his zeal for a theory" that he invents "facts" to support it (XIX 159). Such moralists promote the dangers of idealism, since they "treat of things as *they ought to be* and not *as they are*." It is better not to learn the hard way that "good and evil, folly and discretion [are] more mingled, and the shades of character running more into each other than they do in the ethical charts" (*LWH* 226).

Hazlitt considers himself a practitioner of "common sense" who stands in opposition to the community of prejudice. He begins his *Notes of a Journey through Italy and France* (1826): "The rule for travelling abroad is to take our common sense with us, and leave our prejudices behind us" (X 89). There is, of course, an entire philosophical school devoted to this notion. The empiricism of Locke, Berkeley, and Hume breeds its own contrary in the Scottish School of Common Sense. Thomas Reid and Dugald Stewart reject the empiricist view that we have no unmediated experience of the world but only "ideas" of it. Objecting to any "metaphysics" that contradicts "common sense" – defined as the common cognitive inheritance of humankind – they believe in a few unanalyzable first principles: the power to originate our own acts, the substantive continuity of human identity, the objectivity of moral values and our ability to perceive them, and the reality of the external world. These directly intuited principles are left

[1] See David Bromwich, *Hazlitt: The Mind of a Critic* (New York: Oxford University Press, 1983), 75–7.

unrelated one to another so as to avoid philosophical system-building, which seduces us from this common cognitive inheritance. Social conventions and prejudices also seduce; what the majority in a society happens to believe does not constitute common sense.

Hazlitt alludes infrequently to Stewart, and only once to Reid, and is not directly influenced by them. But he is a proponent of his own brand of common sense and, with Byron, a hater of system-building and metaphysical presumption. Good and evil are objective properties of things that can be perceived by the unprejudiced mind. And common sense often urges a dissenting opinion. It is what he calls "tacit reason": a tact in the practical affairs of life, a sense of what is real and what is not. "It is a kind of mental instinct, that feels the air of truth and propriety as the fingers feel objects of touch" (XX 289). Goldsmith has what Dr. Johnson lacks: "The fine tact, the airy, intuitive faculty with which he skimmed the surfaces of things, and unconsciously formed his opinions. Common sense is the just result of the sum-total of such unconscious impressions in the ordinary occurrences of life, as they are treasured up in the memory, and called out by the occasion" (VIII 32). It develops experientially, instead of being, as Stewart and Reid would have it, our cognitive inheritance. Contrary to these thinkers, Hazlitt is sufficiently indebted to "the intellectual philosophy" that he believes we act in terms of "ideas" of things, not from unmediated experience of the objective world.

The mind is a more efficient computer than the empiricist Hartley had imagined, because it learns shortcuts to common sense through its own associative chains:

By the law of association, as laid down by physiologists, any impression in a series can recal[l] any other impression in that series without going through the whole in order: so that the mind drops the intermediate links, and passes on rapidly and by stealth to the more striking effects of pleasure or pain which have naturally taken the strongest hold of it. By doing this habitually and skilfully with respect to the various impressions and circumstances with which our experience makes us acquainted, it forms a series of unpremeditated conclusions on almost all subjects that can be brought before it, as just as they are of ready application to human life; and common sense is the name of this body of unassuming but practical wisdom. (VIII 35)

Just as common sense is tacit reason, so "conscience is the same tacit sense of right and wrong, or the impression of our moral experience and moral apprehensiveness on the mind" (VIII 33–4).

Unlike Reid and Stewart, Hazlitt thinks common sense in good part a matter of feeling. Echoing Coleridge, he says feeling cuts through associational chains and overrides empirical skepticism:

It is the fashion at present among the philosophical vulgar to decry *feeling*, both the name and the thing. It would be difficult, however, to do without it: for this embraces all that mass of knowledge and of common sense which lies between the extremes of positive proof or demonstration and downright ignorance.

(XX 289)

He is uniting aspects of opposing traditions – the Scottish School of Common Sense and British empiricism – in this matter of common sense as it relates to cognition. But these two schools conceive the issue too narrowly, and he complements them with an emphasis on feeling, suggestive of the school of natural passions and sentiments, Shaftesbury and Hutcheson. In a word, common sense is for Hazlitt the feeling that puts us reliably in touch with the objective world. (Compare Coleridge's more linguistic, conventionalist view: common sense is found when "the language itself does as it were *think* for us" [*BL* I 86n; cf. *N* III 3549]; common sense is historically determined, relativistic, and in need of refinements such as Coleridge proposes in his desynonymizations.) Eschewing metaphysics, Hazlitt leaves this notion of what I call passionate common sense at the commonsensical level. But it is the motive ground of his discourse on a multitude of subjects.

If his critique of Shelley and reformers is taming Romantic sensibility with a strong dose of common sense, Hazlitt's critique of Godwin, Shelley's mentor, is a Romantic's correction of a too confident rationalism. It is important to see that his commitment to passionate common sense launches this double-edged attack. He echoes aspects of Coleridge's assault on Godwin, which has a Hartleian tenor and which, as we saw in Chapter 2, oversimplifies Godwin's views on the emotions, at least as presented in the second and third editions of *Enquiry Concerning Political Justice*. Godwin's error, writes Hazlitt, is to have "conceived too nobly of his fellows" when he takes "abstract reason for the rule of conduct, and abstract good for its end." He "absolves man from the gross and narrow ties of sense, custom, authority, private and local attachment, in order that he may devote himself to the boundless pursuit of universal benevolence." But it is dangerous to raise "the standard of morality above the reach of humanity" (XI 18–19), because it reminds us of our worthlessness and makes all acts futile and desperate. "If custom, will, imagination, example, opinion, were nothing, and reason were *all in all*," then one could not dispute Godwin's conclusion that we should act entirely from "moral arithmetic." It would follow that we sympathize as much with a stranger as with a friend, that we promptly perform whatever we see is best to be done, that we "take an interest in the people in the moon, or in ages yet unborn, as if they were our own flesh and blood" (XVI 405). But because human beings act according to "habit, sense, sympathy," it is self-contradictory to expect them to respond to local suffering with no more or less feeling than to distant or future suffering.

Instead of reason or moral arithmetic, passion is "the essence, the chief ingredient in moral truth; and the warmth of passion is sure to kindle the light of imagination in the objects around it. The 'words that glow' are almost inseparable from the 'thoughts that burn.' Hence logical reason and practical truth are *disparates*." The brutality of the slave trade should not be greeted dispassionately; invective is more in keeping because "there are enormities to which no words can do adequate justice." Discussion of slavery should be as graphic as possible "so that what they suffered in reality was brought home to you in imagination . . . Those evils that inflame the imagination and make the heart sick, ought not to leave the head cool" (XII 46–7). Like Hartley, Hazlitt thinks "partial and personal attachments are 'the scale by which we ascend' to sentiments of general philanthropy," an argument Coleridge employs also (*CL* I 86).

This line of reasoning brings us to a philosophical problem that has broad consequences in Hazlitt's writings. He is less than clear as to how he is making a transition from "is" to "ought." From the premise that people are guided by passion instead of by reason, it does not necessarily follow that they *should* be so guided. Hazlitt himself is hardly an enthusiast for all natural passions. Those of self-love frequently have ascendency over those of benevolence. How can he propose as "the chief ingredient in moral truth" the very passional self that indulges envy, egotism, hypocrisy, cant, vulgarity, perversity, cruelty, frugality, and respectability? This is a more than formal question and one not settled by passionate common sense. It underlies a prominent qualitative shift in his work. He begins his career with an essay on the inherent quality of disinterested sympathy in the human mind, and yet writes a book of maxims, *Characteristics* (1823), in La Rochefoucauld's mode of embittered irony, anatomizing the crooked human heart. The young Hazlitt is at least ambivalent about the worth of the natural passions, and by 1815 or so ambivalence has converted to a more thorough-going hostility.

Sympathies and antipathies

Hazlitt ingratiates by his contempt for his own work. "What abortions are these Essays!" (VIII 79). They are so detestable that he cannot bring himself to revise or reread them. The single exception he makes, as the logic of perversity would have it, is the single work many readers find most abortive, *An Essay on the Principles of Human Action* (1805), his first published work and one he labored on the better part of a decade. Though he calls it "a dry, tough metaphysical *choke-pear*," he alludes frequently to the "discovery" made there, quotes from it at length, and insists that it is the one work that could vindicate him as author. This is rather puzzling. Why is he obsessed with this matter of self-love versus benevolence, by his time reduced to a rather moldy issue in logomachy? Why is the not very benevolent Hazlitt so murderously intent on proving we have the capacity of disinterested behavior? The obsessive character of the work is seen in its extreme repetitiveness; he makes the argument what seems like scores of times. If he were confident of its truth, could he not let it rest? He writes, "I do not see how ideas are the better for being often repeated," and we agree.

Biographical explanations of his obsession are speculative, and of course irrelevant to his argument's validity, but worth bringing in here. The letters of the young Hazlitt, even more so than those of Coleridge and at an earlier age, reveal a knack for moralizing that would alarm most parents. At age twelve he writes home that

the man who is a well-wisher to slavery, is always a slave himself. The King, who wishes to enslave all mankind, is a slave to ambition; The man who wishes to enslave all mankind, for his King, is himself a slave to his King . . . The man who is a well-wisher to liberty, wishes to have men good, and himself to be one of them, and knows that men are not good unless they are so willingly, and does [not] attempt to force them to it, but tries to put them in such a situation as will induce them to be good. Slavery is not a state for men to improve in, therefore he does not wish them to be in that condition. In a state of liberty men improve. He therefore wishes them to be in such a state. . . The RICH take their fill in a few years, are cut short in the midst of their career, and fall into ruin; Never to rise again. But the good shall have joy for evermore.—Be sure to tell me if I may sell my old Buckles. (LWH 48)

And to his father in the same year, "How ineffectual are all pleasures, except those which arise from a knowledge of having done, as far as one knew, that which was right, to make their possessors happy" (LWH 53). In 1791 (aged 13) he writes a letter to the *Shrewsbury Chronicle* protesting a Birmingham mob's treatment of Joseph Priestley on the occasion of the second anniversary of the fall of the Bastille: "Universal benevolence," he complains, has been defeated by "prejudice and bigotry" (LWH 57). At about the age of 14 he undertakes an essay on law, eventually completed and published posthumously as "Project for a New Theory of Civil and Criminal Legislation" (1836), on which he works so arduously that he has a mild nervous breakdown. During this period he reads Richard Price, Priestley, and Hartley. When his father worries that he is overdoing it, Hazlitt replies magisterially, "By having a particular system of politics I shall be better able to judge of the truth or falsehood of any prevarication which I hear, or read, and of the justice, or the contrary, of any political transactions" (*LWH* 67).

With kids the rhetoric of moral fervor is likely to be acquired for the sake of pleasing elders, and there is an element of this in the young Hazlitt. My surmise is that his theory of natural disinterestedness, whatever its merits, is offered by way of compensation to his father for having failed (and Hazlitt felt it as a failure) to become a Unitarian minister. He never fully believes his own theory and spends much of his career undermining it or finding darker implications that belie its manifest optimism. William Hazlitt, Senior, was a militant Unitarian minister well read in Cambridge Platonists, Shaftesbury, and Hutcheson. He rejected his own father's Scottish Calvinism and became, in a ministry that ranged from Bandon in County Cork to Philadelphia and Boston to Wem, an important father of the Unitarian Church in America. His antipathy to kings and support of the American Revolution provided a telling example for his son, who continued the spirit of dissent, if by other means and in the secular sphere.

In a letter to his father, probably written in 1796 shortly after leaving Hackney College and deciding against the ministry, Hazlitt speaks of the "repeated disappointment" and "long dejection" that have characterized his brief life, and then of an essay he is writing:

I have proceeded some way in a delineation of the system, which founds the propriety of virtue on it's coincidence with the pursuit of private interest . . . I know not whether I can augur certainly of ultimate success. I write more easily than I did. I hope for good. I have ventured to look at high things. (*LWH* 70)

What better way of showing that he has not forsaken the ends of moral enlightenment than to publish such a theory, thus not denying his father's plans for him altogether? He will still concern himself with "high things." In part written to please his father and soothe his own conscience, then, the *Essay* does not catch the intonation or embody the attitudes of the later public essayist. At the same time, as John Kinnaird has argued, Hazlitt's restating of "the Unitarian ethic in terms of Godwinian freedom" is a departure from his father's belief in the interest we should take in our own immortality; it is a rejection of any supernatural sanctions of the ethical.[2]

[2] *William Hazlitt: Critic of Power* (New York: Columbia University Press, 1978), 28–30.

Hazlitt's "discovery" in his *Essay*, begun in 1795–6, is made by linking the concept of sympathy – developed in the moral sense theories of Shaftesbury and Hutcheson, in Butler's system of human nature, and thereafter in the moral psychology of Hume and Adam Smith – to a temporal schema. He neatly cleaves mind into three faculties, of which memory pertains to the past, sense to the present, and imagination to the future. Our "identity" must consist of the first two of these alone; the imagination is directed to a future and therefore not yet existent self. As we ponder future action, this imaginary future self is no more ours than other selves are ours, and what we do on its behalf is equally "disinterested":

> The imagination, by means of which alone I can anticipate future objects, or be interested in them, must carry me out of myself into the feelings of others by one and the same process by which I am thrown forward as it were into my future being, and interested in it. I could not love myself, if I were not capable of loving others. Self-love, used in this sense, is in it's fundamental principle the same with disinterested benevolence. *(Essay* 3)

No one else in the history of moral philosophy had advanced quite this argument, which Hazlitt brands a "discovery," not a theory, in keeping with his announcement elsewhere that he has "no theory to maintain." The discovery seems silly until we attempt to refute it – perhaps on the grounds of its presumptive categorizing of mental functions – and then we might see some justice in David Bromwich's comment that it "is sufficiently plain and sufficiently profound to attract and retain the allegiance of a subtle mind" (p. 101).

My own mind finds some ambivalences in the *Essay* that make it difficult to say exactly what my allegiance would be *to* – ambivalences that prove useful, however, in charting the *Essay*'s continuity with Hazlitt's later work. They pertain to its treatment of key issues: the status of imagination, the nature of identity, the relationship between disinterestedness and benevolence, and the causes of moral decline. In some of these matters the choke-pear seems unswallowable by Hazlitt himself and, in any event, does not work so efficiently that it suffocates all protesting shrieks of tortured readers.

Taking up first the status of imagination, we should be aware that, in keeping with commonsensical notions, Hazlitt takes value to be an intrinsic property of things in the world and not something bestowed by the mind's projections. This is the basic assumption of the *Essay*:

> It is plain there must be something in the nature of the objects themselves which of itself determines the mind to consider them as desirable or the contrary previously to any reference of them to ourselves. They are not

342

converted into good and evil by being impressed on our minds, but they affect our minds in a certain manner because they are essentially good or evil.

(*Essay* 52)

"Good" in turn cannot be "resolved into one simple principle, or essence," but is multiple and distinguishable both in degree and in kind (39–40n). As a value pluralist and intuitionist (cognitivist non-definist), Hazlitt joins with Coleridge, Shelley, and others, but is more insistent that value is independent of our valuing acts. I have said that the Romantics tend to merge the productive and perceptual functions of imagination, but in his *Essay* Hazlitt implies that no productive component is required to give substance to value. If it has not exceeded its proper function, the imagination is less visionary than what he calls "reasoning" (p. 61).

So conceived, imagination proposes objects to the will, indeed dictates to it, and is thus the "immediate spring and guide of action" (p. 66). As the faculty that images objects of value or "ends" not yet possessed, it deals with the future – in which these objects will be pursued and, if we are lucky, possessed. Hazlitt does "not use the word *imagination* as contradistinguished from or opposed to reason" (p. 55n); the "reasoning imagination" is the sole faculty that adapts previous experience to possible eventualities. (Both Kinnaird and Bromwich find in Hazlitt an anticipation of Jamesian pragmatism. It should be said, however, that Hazlitt in no way discards the idea of intrinsic value for instrumental, which is characteristic of pragmatism, especially of Dewey.) Without the imagination, we would not know enough to avoid running into a fire, even though previous experience had taught us the hard way that fire causes pain. Why? because the self that is lurching toward the fire is not the "same" self that, moments in the future, will find itself engulfed in flames. To make the connection between present self and future pain requires an ability to imagine an "ideal" future self that would be thus incommoded (pp. 59–61).

But Hazlitt just as frequently speaks of this ideality of the imagination as if it were a negotiation with unreality, whatever its pragmatic successes. The daily assumption that our future self is part of our identity is an illusion perpetrated by imagination:

We take the tablets of memory, reverse them, and stamp the image of self on that, which as yet possesses nothing but the name. It is no wonder then that the imagination constantly outstripping the progress of time, when it's course is marked out along the strait unbroken line of individuality, should confound the necessary differences of things, and confer on my future interests a reality, and a connection with my present feelings which they can never have.

(*Essay* 118–19)

343

The disquieting implications of this view are developed years later in a discussion of his *Essay* in 1819. He now describes the predicament in his mature idiom:

The next year, the next hour, the next moment is but a creation of the mind; in all that we hope or fear, love or hate, in all that is nearest and dearest to us, we but mistake the strength of illusion for certainty, and follow the mimic shews of things and catch at a shadow and live in a waking dream. Everything before us exists in an ideal world. The future is a blank and dreary void, like sleep or death, till the imagination brooding over it with wings outspread, impregnates it with life and motion. The forms and colours it assumes are but the pictures reflected on the eye of fancy, the unreal mockeries of future events. The solid fabric of time and nature moves on, but the future always flies before it. The present moment stands on the brink of nothing. We cannot pass the dread abyss, or make a broad and beaten way over it, or construct a real interest in it, or identify ourselves with what is not, or have a being, sense, and motion, where there are none. Our interest in the future, our identity with it, cannot be substantial; that self which we project before us into it is like a shadow in the water, a bubble of the brain.   (IX 58)

The passage expresses Hazlitt's mixed feelings about his discovery. Imagination may "impregnate," but it is still directed toward non-entity. Human action is illusory. The self projects itself moment by moment into the abyss of the future. Imagination has been deflated by the very temporality Hazlitt thought substantiated its own province and lent it credibility. His phrase, "a bubble of the brain," reminds us of his indictment of Shelley. By 1819 at the latest, he has directly confronted the threatening ideality of the faculty that had promised to redeem human nature from egoism.

One function of the imagination, then, is to give us the illusion that our "identity" is continuous with our future selves. It gives the illusion that there is a unity of self when in fact there is what Hazlitt calls an "aggregate." The imagination perpetrates a "pretended unity of consciousness." The *Essay* makes claims for the imagination yet begins the process of unmasking it. Like De Quincey, Hazlitt undoes the Blakean/Coleridgean unity of self, with temporal discontinuity instead of with palimpsestic layering. He does ascribe to the body a "real connection" among its various parts, such that a pinprick in one part of the nervous system affects and "has an equal interest in the whole sentient system." Our present sensations, which at one point he terms "consciousness" (p. 110), and our memory of our past selves are linked and constitute a "real individuality of person." But he does not conceive of this as an organic unity:

Till some such diffusive conscious principle [as we see in our sensate con-

344

sciousness of a pinprick] can be shewn to exist, producing a real connection between my future sensations and present impulses, collecting, and uniting the different successive moments of my being in one general representative feeling of self-interest as the impressions made on different parts of my body are all conveyed to one common principle of thought, it is in vain to tell me that I have the same interest in my future sensations as if they were present, because I am the same individual. However nearly allied, however similar I may be to my future self, whatever other relation I may bear to that self, so long as there is not this intercommunity of thoughts and feelings, so long as there is an absolute separation, an insurmountable barrier fixed between the present, and the future, so that I neither am, nor can possibly be affected at present by what I am to feel hereafter, I am not to any moral or practical purpose the *same* being.

(*Essay* 29–30)

Note that imagination does not rate as a total unifying principle of consciousness or self: it is not a "diffusive conscious principle," which Hazlitt thinks either non-existent or not yet discovered. The self is cumulative and ever-changing: "In this sense the individual is never the same for two moments together. What is true of him at one time is never (that we know of) exactly and particularly true of him at any other time" (p. 85). He concludes that individuals "are aggregates, and aggregates of dissimilar things" (p. 97).

I think, therefore, that there is some wishful reading in Kinnaird's statement that Hazlitt's *Essay* transforms "the meaning of 'sympathy' from the function of a benevolent 'faculty' into a primary activity of *consciousness* itself, which is here made nearly synonymous with 'imagination' " (p. 56). Hazlitt has linked the word "consciousness" more with sensate bodily presence and says that he will not embark on a discussion of consciousness in general (p. 110n). More important, his strict demarcation of the various faculties – memory, sensation, imagination – militates against the model of organic unity Kinnaird sees as fundamental to the *Essay*. There *is* no single unifying principle of self that unites these three faculties. The "true notion of personal identity" is said to depend "entirely on the continued connection which subsists between a man's past and present feelings" – i.e. between memory and sensation (p. 92). Imagination is entirely excluded from personal identity, whatever other claims Hazlitt makes for it. He does not go so far as Locke and Hume in arguing against unity: his is not exactly the "serial" or "bundle" self of these thinkers, who nonetheless have considerable influence on the *Essay*.[3] He grants

---

[3] See John Locke, *Essay Concerning Human Understanding*, Bk. II, 328–48, "Of Identity and Diversity"; David Hume, *A Treatise of Human Nature*, I iv 6, "Of Personal Identity."

a solidity to the self as regards memory and sensation – past and present – and more than they, for whom the question of identity is restricted to mental phenomena, Hazlitt, like Blake, anticipates modern discussion of personal identity in emphasizing the body's central role (pp. 106–7).

Of equal consequence for our understanding of Hazlitt's development is the relationship between "disinterestedness" and "benevolence." As both Kinnaird and Bromwich have pointed out, the first does not entail the second. One could in theory place the interests of self and others on an *a priori* equal footing and still feel and behave murderously toward both, or treat both with indifference. The mature Hazlitt likes a good hater; if a disinterested judgment of someone proves that person odious, then he or she is properly hated. Benevolence would be out of keeping. The developmental issue is whether Hazlitt in his early *Essay* does link natural disinterestedness and natural benevolence, thus producing a rosy view of human nature; and whether he breaks this linkage later on. Do we move from an optimistic young to a pessimistic middle-aged Hazlitt?

With some important qualifications, I believe the answer is yes.[4] Bromwich, who understands the issues involved very well, underestimates in my view the degree to which Hazlitt makes this linkage of disinterestedness and benevolence in the *Essay*. Bromwich writes that the "leap from the principle of natural disinterestedness to that of natural benevolence" is "disabling": "Were our interest in a thing the simple consequence of its being 'really and truly interesting' in itself, then there could be no virtue in unselfishness: our course of action would be entailed by the meaning of 'interest' "(p. 53). *Any* theory of natural benevolence could similarly be termed "disabling" in the sense that we can hardly be praised for doing what we do by nature. In any event, the linkage of disinterestedness and benevolence is consistent with other premises in Hazlitt's *Essay* and is not, as Bromwich says, "a misplaced fragment of an altogether different argument." I have mentioned that for Hazlitt good and evil are essential properties of things in the world. He further argues that "there is something in the very idea of good, or evil, which naturally excites desire or aversion, which is in itself the proper motive of action, which impels the mind to pursue the one and to avoid the other by a true moral necessity" (p. 33). A child pursues his own good "not because it is *his*, but because it is good" (p. 34; cf. pp. 50–2, 89). He goes on to say that we "are not

---

[4] In this reading of Hazlitt – which attests to some basic changes in point of view from his early writings to later ones – I am largely in agreement with Herschel Baker, *William Hazlitt* (Cambridge: Harvard University Press, 1962).

born benevolent" in the sense that we automatically act with a generalized love of humankind. Rather, benevolence is an "inherent" disposition awakened situationally by the immediate presence of other people (pp. 35–6); a "general benevolence can only arise from an habitual cultivation of the natural disposition of the mind to sympathize with the feelings of others" (p. 41). Thus, he can speak of "natural benevolence" (pp. 35, 45). If another person is intrinsically worthy of our benevolent interest, then the mind is naturally inclined to bestow it. Though the *Essay* does not express confidence in human behavior, which is corruptible, it does in human nature: people naturally pursue the good.

Bromwich argues for the consistency of the younger with the older Hazlitt even to the extent of finding two ostensibly polar texts – the *Essay* and *Characteristics* – to be compatible. Indeed the "findings of the *Essay* might even be supposed to gain a new authority in *Characteristics*, by the detection of sympathy in what appear to be our most selfish or vicious actions" (p. 97). I think, to the contrary, that a transformation has taken place in Hazlitt's views and that the natural benevolence principle of the *Essay* has been reduced in the grouchy *Characteristics* to a merely notional reminder of a human being's mixed nature *in potentia*.

On somewhat different grounds, however, I would agree that there is a fundamental consistency in the early and later Hazlitt. I am not convinced he ever fully believed the more optimistic tenets of his own discovery. The reiterative text of the *Essay* suggests that he protests too much. Perhaps he bullies himself into this belief in natural benevolence. Moreover, the agency of both disinterestedness and benevolence – the so-called "reasoning imagination" – has already been seen to deal in unreality. Is it not therefore a frail reed on which to place the burden of moral vindication? Ostensibly complacent in its view of human nature, the *Essay* does not set forth a strong defense against a later pessimism. Hazlitt never renounces his *Essay* but does overtly turn against the imagination; during the Regency period he implicates it more and more frequently in power play and treachery. He ceases to believe in natural benevolence as a dominant predisposition; people do not by nature pursue the good. He can continue to reject Hobbesian psychological egoism, however, by holding merely to the possibility of a disinterested and/or benevolent act, even if there were only one such act every two thousand years.[5]

[5] Although Hazlitt may not have read Hobbes's *Leviathan* until after 1805, it is Hobbesian thought against which the *Essay* is directed. Subscribing to natural disinterestedness and benevolence, he must still explain the fact of human evil. In the *Essay* he

The various ambivalences of the *Essay* in charting the relationship of self, time, and the affections are resolved in favor of pathos in several later essays, "On Antiquity" (1821), "Why Distant Objects Please" (1825), "On the Past and Future" (1825), "On the Feeling of Immortality in Youth" (1827), "On a Sun-Dial" (1827), "The Sick Chamber" (1830), and "The Letter-Bell" (1831). The discontinuity of self in time is felt strongly in youth, when all experience is unprecedented. In youth,

> our continuity of consciousness is broken, crumbles, and falls in pieces. We go on, learning and forgetting every hour. Our feelings are chaotic, confused, strange to each other and to ourselves. Our life does not hang together,—but straggling, disjointed, winds its slow length along, stretching out to the endless future—unmindful of the ignorant past. We seem many beings in one, and cast the slough of our existence daily. (XII 258)

But as we grow older, we repeat ourselves, and "rehearse our parts by rote." Trying to shore up our self by memory of things past, we find only dim traces. The sensate present deceives: objects in our line of vision have a "singleness and integrity of impression" that make it seem "as if nothing could destroy or obliterate them," so firmly are they stamped on the brain. "We take out a new lease of existence from the objects on which we set our affections, and become abstracted, impassive, immortal in them." But time obliterates both objects and our memory of them. When we feel the future to be cut off, we turn to the past, retrieving fragments to construct an identity. "It is thus that when we find our personal and substantial identity vanishing from us,

> attempts to account for moral decline in two ways, one of which undercuts the "discovery" he has just advanced. The first is by means of "habit," "association," and "abstraction"; in effect, he blames that portion of mind where Lockean psychology still obtains. Hazlitt's exposition is here at its most imprecise, but the gist seems to be that after childhood we overvalue our own limited experience in "a long narrowing of the mind to our own particular feelings and interests" (p. 41), and we blunt disinterestedness of imagination through habit – the loss of free unbiased options in judging and acting. He later acknowledges the Wordsworthian view that our natural sympathies are developed and expressed precisely through habitual attachments and the associative transfer of feeling from immediate personal contexts to larger social ones.
>
> The second reason for moral decline is said to arise "out of the necessary constitution of the human mind, and not [to be] founded like the former in a mere arbitrary association of ideas" (p. 121). We are prompted to judge and act on the basis of what we can image vividly, and the image of our own mind and body is naturally more vivid than that of others; we therefore take a greater degree of interest in our own future feelings and pleasures. The difference in degree, if not kind, between the way we regard ourselves and others seems decisive, and unintentionally debilitating to the argument Hazlitt has advanced. In an essay that legitimizes social affections we can see him edging toward the often petulant individualism of his later work.

348

we strive to gain a reflected and substituted one in our thoughts" (XVII 195–7). Time strips away what it has seemed to give. *"That things should be that are now no more*, creates in my mind the most unfeigned astonishment" (XVII 242).

In these later essays Hazlitt forgets the "disinterestedness" of the imagination as he treats future prospects as objects of a very personal will. The argument of the *Essay* has become all too notional. We long for futures just as we do for pasts, and we want them for ourselves. The future engrosses entirely "the principle of action or will." It is the "importunity of desire, the irritation of the will" that make us "regret the pleasures we have lost, and eagerly anticipate those which are to come . . . The good we expect is like a store yet untouched, and in the enjoyment of which we promise ourselves infinite gratification" (VIII 25–6).

This pattern of self-controversion is found in Hazlitt's broader treatment of philosophical tenets associated with the Romantic humanist tradition. In his "Prospectus of a History of English Philosophy" he handily lists ten, all of which have bearing on moral issues. With some overlapping, these are: that the mind is not material, that its intellectual power is distinct from perception or sensation, that abstraction is symptomatic of limits to comprehension, that reason gives knowledge "over and above *experience*," that "the principle of association does not account for all our ideas, feelings, and actions," that there is a "principle of natural benevolence in the human mind," that "the love of pleasure or happiness is not the only principle of action," that moral obligation is not determined by the "strongest motive," that "the mind is not a mechanical, but a rational and voluntary agent," and finally that "the idea of power is inseparable from activity" (II 118–19). These he opposes to "modern philosophy," in which "all thought is to be resolved into *sensation*, all morality into the *love of pleasure*, and all action into *mechanical impulse*" (II 113–14). These tenets echo the Coleridgean attack on mechanico-corpuscular philosophy, and with Coleridge and others of the period Hazlitt rejects the various premises of associationism, psychological egoism, and hedonistic utilitarianism. He adopts the high estimate of human possibility that props up the Blakean/Coleridgean self.

But Hazlitt's greater familiar essays cripple this manifesto. Some of the crippling may result from the different conventions and expressive opportunities that obtain when an essayist instead of a philosopher is at the writing desk. The less dignified compositional mode is more Hazlitt's linguistic medium and more likely, one feels, to embody his

349

closer readings of things. And what the essayist doubts is that human beings are so capable of running their own lives, of resisting the lure of pleasure as a ruling motive, of putting off envy, and of being "rational and voluntary agents."

One humanist assumption he challenges is that we have the power to create ourselves according to our own lights. Personal character, he says, does not change over a lifetime; it is something we are born with, an "internal, original bias." This observation may seem to contradict not only humanist notions but also his own concept of the discontinuous self of the *Essay*. But there he was speaking of "identity" (the sum total of mental and physical experience, past and present), whereas now he is speaking of "character," those personality traits that distinguish us as this or that kind of person. Personal character is a function not of memory or sensation or imagination but of will. If the hypocritical Blifil and the virtuous Tom Jones were to have exchanged circumstances, they would not have exchanged character. "The accession of knowledge, the pressure of circumstances, favourable or unfavourable, does little more than minister occasion to the first predisposing bias—." This is, Hazlitt intones, his concept of original sin: "indeed, the colour of our lives is woven into the fatal thread at our births: our original sins and our redeeming graces are infused into us; nor is the bond, that confirms our destiny, ever cancelled" (XII 230–3).

He writes dozens of vivid character portraits: of historical persons, of characters in drama and other literary texts, and of personality types. They often begin with a paradoxical definition or thesis: "By a *respectable* man is generally meant a person whom there is no reason for respecting" (XII 360–1); "He who is not in some measure a pedant, though he may be a wise, cannot be a very happy man" (IV 80). Then follows a marshaling of related traits. But however copious these may be, Hazlitt portrays the fundamental character as fixed in predisposition or humor. This fixity he melodramatically calls our original sin, but it in fact lends his vision a comic structure: people will go on being themselves with a sorry predictability. This is in keeping with a curious fact about this often vehement moralist: he rarely indulges a rhetoric that implies the possibility of change. When defending an historical figure like Napoleon, accusing one like Pitt, or mixing defense and accusation in the case of Burke, Hazlitt employs a strong forensic rhetoric; in portraying contemporaries or announcing "the spirit of the age," he bestows praise or blame, always with a sense of occasion, by means of a rich epideictic rhetoric; but I think that, unlike the reformer Shelley, he inflicts little on us by way of hortatory rhetoric. He has small confidence that this kind of talk will work, since we are basically unteachable.

Whatever their predispositions, most people are neither wholly good nor wholly evil, Hazlitt acknowledges, and he also senses that this is a boring conclusion. No "balance master in the topics of morality," he will write with his own compelling bias, with what Keats terms his "demon." La Rochefoucauld practices a logical error in his maxims of human character but is the more powerful a writer for it:

> The whole artifice of the author consists in availing himself of the *mixed* nature of motives, so as to detect some indirect or sinister bias even in the best, and he then proceeds to argue as if they were *simple*, that is, had but one principle, and that principle the worst.
>
> (XX 36–7)

Hazlitt cleverly notes that we could just as easily argue that vice does not exist because it has a residual virtuous motive behind it. "Or is it to be taken for granted that our vices are sincere, and our virtues only hypocrisy and affectation?" He quotes from *All's Well that Ends Well*: "The web of our life is of a mingled yarn, good and ill together." This latitudinarian approach to human personality is antipathetic to Hazlitt's temper, however. The appeal for him of La Rochefoucauld's method is clear in that *Characteristics* is directly imitative; and the method is employed elsewhere. Hazlitt does not wish to defuse the salutary effect of antipathy with liberal good will: "Nature seems . . . made up of antipathies: without something to hate, we should lose the very spring of thought and action" (XII 128). As a writer he eschews the trimming mentality, and we take delight in the bias, the enthymeme, the falling away from a strict standard of logic. The general estimate he gives is that human beings are driven and obsessional creatures, impelled by their original ruling biases; and he recapitulates something of this in his own life of writing.

The two powers he has valued most – imagination and passion – are readily coopted into stupidity and evil. Hazlitt's method here as in all matters is to deluge us in the copia of evidence. The same imagination said to be disinterested and benevolent engenders illusive hope, love of perversity, and susceptibility to tyranny. Merciless in the dream world, imagination imposes dreams ruinously in the waking state (XII 21). Many of his later writings refute the *Essay's* view that imagination inclines toward benevolence. If someone is repeatedly accused of crimes he has not committed, for example, his best friends will drop him though they know him to be innocent: "We involuntarily associate words with things: and the imagination retains an unfavourable impression long after the understanding is disabused" (XX 277). Imagination outstrips performance in hatred; we learn not to kill in fact all the people we kill every day in our imagination (XII 127).

Phantoms of the imagination become destructive objects of the will. The miser, driven by "romantic" impulses, accumulates wealth for wealth's sake, not to be better off in the world. This is a Johnsonian reflection – the hunger of the imagination drives us after chimeras – but a closer parallel is Balzac, who portrays the imagination as obsessional. The psychology of gambling, writes Hazlitt, illustrates the madness that results "merely because that is possible to the imagination which is impossible in fact." Imagination's quarrel with necessity points up its own absurdity. If we pick the wrong straw, we do not immediately concede the fact: "It was so easy to have fixed upon the other, nay, at one time we were going to do it – if we had – the mind thus runs back to what was so possible and feasible at one time." "We still try to have it our own way, and fret, torment, and harrow ourselves up with vain imaginations to effect impossibilities." It is the "involuntary power exerted by the imagination over the feelings" that impels us to leap over cliffs, to clasp a corpse, to murder someone we love. Imagination is a "*power of fascination*" that sends us in pursuit of nightmares, if only to satisfy a perverse craving to know (XX 43–7). The imagination, which he had declared in his first publication to be disinterested and benevolent, thwarts both self-interest and benevolence, both pleasure and the reality principle. To be a great philosopher is to resist the imagination and adopt the maxim, "*That if a thing is, it is*" (VIII 231–2).

Hazlitt's analysis of the passions of self-love is, in turn, reminiscent of Coleridge's. A spirit of perversity invests human encounters, whether expressed in tone of voice, facial expression, acts of omission or outright aggression. "It is easy to judge right, or at least to come to a mutual understanding in matters of history and abstract morality. Why then is it so difficult to arrive at the same calm certainty in actual life? Because the passions and interests are concerned" (XVII 296). Again he gives copious evidence. Friends take their opinion of us from the world's opinion, and are reluctant to defend us for fear of being implicated (XVII 303); they acknowledge our errors "out of candour," and fail to mention our good qualities "out of envy" (XII 79); they withhold good news to torture us with suspense, and so forth. Genuine good will is rare because of an inveterate "hardness and severity in our judgements of one another" (XII 85). Such judgments are often based on envy, which Hazlitt – who earlier touted bene-volence – terms "the most universal passion" (IX 169). He echoes Coleridge's rumination that envy is in part a response to incongruity;

we hate to attribute excellence to someone who is in other respects repellent. Hazlitt thinks he may be envious of Sir Walter Scott because someone with such gruesome politics ought not to have been capable of writing the Waverley novels. Scott represents a painful *"misalliance* between first-rate intellect and want of principle" (XII 99). Confronted by merit in another, we hope to accommodate it comfortably by saying, *"It is his trade!"* But we demand praise from others for any merit, whether inside or outside our own trade: "It is *a feather in our cap*, a new conquest, an extension of our sense of power" (IX 171).

Hazlitt's writings are a treasury of such observations on the various vices of egotism, envy, hypocrisy, and frugality. Since his petulance is in part stylized, he gives us something more and less than literal statements of belief, but the literal differs here only in degree from the rhetorical. In his Preface to *Characteristics*, he writes: "There is only one point in which I dare even to allude to a comparison with Rochefou-cauld – *I have had no theory to maintain*; and have endeavoured to set down each thought as it occurred to me, without bias or prejudice of any sort" (IX 165). We do not believe that he or Rochefoucauld works without bias, but we do believe that his is a mind that can be disturbed and even changed by the copiousness of evidence that fires his own rhetoric. What this text and others do is to assault Hazlitt's own theory of human benevolence by setting forth the counter-examples that dismantle theories. "I believe in the theoretical benevolence, and practical malignity of man" (XX 343).

From ethics to politics

Hazlitt's writings on major issues of human action – freedom and necessity, mind and act, utilitarianism, ethics and politics – will take us beyond the relationship of self and other to broader questions of social and political participation. He contrasts interestingly with Shelley on these issues, often in ways that manifest his more aggressive individualism.

Like Shelley, Hazlitt gamely takes up the issue of liberty and necessity and displays a respectable gift for philosophical disputation. In two essays, "On Liberty and Necessity" (1812) and "On the Doctrine of Philosophical Necessity" (1815), he explains how he can be both a necessitarian and a libertarian. Where Shelley leans on Spinoza, Hume, Holbach, and Godwin, Hazlitt leans on Spinoza, Hobbes, Locke, Priestley, and Jonathan Edwards. He attacks the "scholastic" notion that a free act is "self-caused," "independent of motives," the "fantastical" result of "absolute self-will." Coleridge and Blake assume a power of self-origination, but Shelley and Hazlitt deny that the will wills itself. Rather, all mental acts, like all physical ones, are caused by previous acts. There is no such thing as an absolute "beginner of action," says Hazlitt, but there is such a thing as an agent who "contributes to an effect." Liberty is

the power in any agent in given circumstances to operate in a certain manner, if left to itself; or perhaps more unequivocally, opportunity given to any agent to exert certain powers to produce an effect, when nothing but those powers and the absence of impediments is wanting to produce it. To be free is to possess all the requisites for acting in one's-self, and in the circumstances, and not to be counteracted. (II 266–7)

As in Shelley, liberty is absence of restraints from persons and from circumstances. And, as I noted in Chapter 2, Hazlitt, like other Romantic authors, has added the criterion of empowerment, the ability to obtain objects of the will. These criteria, he thinks, co-exist with and even depend on the doctrine of necessity – once again, as a "soft" determinism – because without strict causal succession we would live in a chaotic world unnegotiable by human mind. This rather dry statement concerning empowerment implicates the passionate core of Hazlitt's thinking about the self as existing fully only in the felt sense of its own power.

Unlike Shelley in some of his writings, Hazlitt does not assent to psychological determinism. Shelley says that the strongest motive is by definition the one yielded to, but Hazlitt agrees with Coleridge in this matter, giving the larger entity of mind the power to choose among motives. Once again we find the philosopher speaking more hopefully than the essayist:

Motives do not act upon [mind] simply or absolutely; but according to the dictates of the understanding or the bias of the will. At one time we yield to any idle inclination that happens to prevail, and at others resist to the utmost the strongest motives. That is, *the mind is itself an agent, one chief determining cause of our volitions.* (II 296; emphasis added)

The mind as agent need not be impelled or compelled wholly by "motives," which means for him any emotion, need, or bodily appetite that influences volition. Hazlitt invokes a larger arbitrating mind that can overrule even the strongest motive as merely parochial, in favor of some course of action deemed more consistent with its larger purpose. He is not reinstating man as a rational creature. Note his statement that motives can be arbitrated "according to the dictates of the understanding or the bias of the will." We have heard him speak of the constitutional "ruling bias" that keeps us fixed in our ways, that makes us this or that person or "character." Here this bias is equated with "will," a faculty which can be directed to a degree by the understanding or, more persuasively, by the quasi-cognitive imagination – but which is the ultimate spring of human action. Hazlitt does not give us a disquisition on the will as such, leaving it ambiguous as to whether it is a conscious or an unconscious power. But he does say that it can assert its own purposiveness over stubborn external circumstance (the physical world and other people) and over lesser psychological functions. Our reflexive awareness of will in action – whether it registers success in loving, statesmanship, painting, or writing – is a vital factor in mental health and is close to what for Hazlitt it means to be human. Self-empowerment is a daily human need that can be fulfilled for some in going to the apothecary and for others only in the conquest of Egypt. It is not for Hazlitt a dialectical or self-realizationist matter, which would tacitly assume a narrative trope of incremental, evolutionary, and purposeful growth. Rather it is a need for pragmatic success in our daily functions, from the trivial to the grand. Hazlitt feels it in talking his way into closed art galleries; if he wishes to see a Titian, nothing can stop him, "neither the surliness of porters, nor the impertinence of footmen" (VIII 101n).

Shelley the social critic sees moral repercussions in the doctrine of necessity – it forces us to reassess matters of praise and blame – but Hazlitt the individualist thinks its moral import negligible with regard to the question of whether moral value and judgment still obtain:

The doctrine of necessity leaves morality just where it found it. It does not destroy goodness or disposition or energy of character, any more than it destroys beauty or strength of person. It does not take away the power of the mind any more than the use of the limbs. That every thing is by necessity, no more proves that there is no such thing as good and evil, virtue and vice, right or wrong, in the moral world, than it proves that there is no such thing as day or night, heat or cold, sweet or sour, food or poison, in the physical. (XX 60–1)

Rejecting the idea that mind is reducible to matter, he defines a difference in kind between a physical and a moral cause. "A man differs from a stone in that he has feeling and understanding," and "human mind differs from an inanimate substance or an automaton, inasmuch as it is actuated by sympathy as well as by necessity." Praise and blame are moral causes in themselves: "The lever, the screw, and the wedge, are the great instruments of the mechanical world: opinion, sympathy, praise and blame, reward and punishment, are the lever, the screw, and the wedge, of the moral world" (XX 61, 63). In such passages, Hazlitt like Byron invokes a dualism that distinguishes him from Coleridge, Wordsworth, and Shelley. He begins the essay from which I have been quoting, "On the Doctrine of Philosophical Necessity," with lines from "Tintern Abbey" that speak of "a sense sublime / Of something far more deeply interfused" that "impels / All thinking things." He comments that the "vast fabric of the universe is held together in one mighty chain" (XX 60). But he does not assent to a Wordsworthian interpenetration of mind and matter, of the moral and the physical. In this essay he has argued quite the reverse: moral causes are independent of physical ones. The case for a Wordsworthian organicism in Hazlitt has been somewhat overstated. The fact that so comparatively little of the corpus is devoted to natural description makes one wary of such a view.[6]

Independence of mind from matter is the main premise of Hazlitt's attack on associationism. Human action cannot be reduced to workings of vibrations and, worse, vibratiuncles. Hartley's mechanistic model has it that all human action is a response to stimuli in fixed patterns depending on arbitrary associations imprinted in memory. If Hartley's model were correct, we would have no control over our movements:

There could be no such thing as reasonable action among men, our actions would be more ridiculous than those of a monkey, or of a man possessed with St. Vitus's dance; they would resemble the diseased starts and fits of a madman, not the actions of a reasonable being . . . The *momentum* of the will is necessary to give direction and constancy to any of our actions; and this again can only be determined by the ideas of future good and evil, and the connection which the mind perceives between certain actions, and the attainment of the one or the prevention of the other. (I 81)

Hazlitt's argument, which has parallels in Coleridge's Opus Maximum, is engendered by "a common-sense feeling against the refinements of a false philosophy" (I 67). Though it turns out to be more tortured than commonsensical, the argument is basically that because not everybody appears to have St. Vitus's dance, Hartley must be

---

[6] Here I am resisting one aspect of John Kinnaird's often compelling *William Hazlitt: Critic of Power*. Kinnaird sees Hazlitt as an organistic, dialectical, vitalistic thinker (at least the more interesting half of him), who "does not let the dualism of body and mind develop into a contradistinction of opposed tendencies" and who sees mind "co-extended" with matter to a degree greater than Coleridge does. To my mind, the passages Kinnaird cites – some of them persuasive (e.g. pp. 66–7) – simply do not suffice to undercut Hazlitt's basic tendency to reinstate dualisms and irreconcilable contraries. An exception to Hazlitt's relative indifference to natural description is *Notes of a Journey through Italy and France* (1826), in which he tries his own hand, like Wordsworth, the Shelleys, and Lord Byron before him, at getting into language the sublimity of the Alps.

wrong. The counter-evidence is human adaptability and conscious selection of means toward ends. If a child had to rely on previously formed associations of ideas alone, he would lose all power of adaptation and could never learn to make his way around a new house.

Hazlitt admires the ability to make one's way – and those who have it are few. Usually an "imbecile" in action, he thinks he gets what he deeply wants. "Where there is a will," he says in an upbeat moment, "there is a way." A rejected lover has only himself to blame – probably his "fear, his pride, his vanity was greater" than his love, or so he thinks until he meets Sarah Walker.

One of his best essays, "The Fight" (1822), demonstrates the ways of strong willing, and has as its motto the above adage. This jaunty autobiographical narrative tells of his dogged efforts to see a boxing match in Hungerford, Berkshire, in December of 1821. Getting there is a series of obstacles: finding out where the match is to be held, missing the mail coach ("The Bath mail I had set my mind upon, and I had missed it, as I missed every thing else, by my own absurdity, in putting the will for the deed, and aiming at ends without employing means" [XVII 74]), getting a bed and supper upon arrival in Newbury, a sleepless night, and finally a nine-mile hike to Hungerford the next morning. The match itself recapitulates such trials of the will in a higher key. By the twelfth round Tom Hickman, the gas-man, is close to death at the hands of Bill Neate: "All traces of life, of natural expression, were gone from him. His face like a human skull, a death's head, spouting blood." Yet he fights on for another five or six rounds. "Ye who despise the FANCY [the sport of boxing], do something to shew as much *pluck*, or as much self-possession as this, before you assume a superiority which you have never given a single proof of by any one action in the whole of your lives!" (XVII 83). One can imagine what Shelley would have thought of this brutal match. For him as for Coleridge, such acts of will for will's sake are prideful. But for Hazlitt our "character" is confirmed in resisting obstacles.

Winning private battles compensates somewhat for losing public ones. In "On the Feeling of Immortality in Youth," he writes that he "set out in life with the French Revolution" and never dreamt that that "dawn would be overcast, and set once more in the night of despotism – 'total eclipse!' Happy that I did not. I felt for years, and during the best part of my existence *heart-whole* in that cause, and triumphed in the triumphs over the enemies of man!" (XVII 197). In a period when revolutionary hopes are thwarted, the need to shore up that last stronghold of freedom, the individual, supplants a larger social vision. Hazlitt's increasing attention to individual rights and acts of strong willing is correlative to disappointment in revolutionary progress. The early stress in his *Essay* on disinterestedness and benevolence, which might have led to a predominantly social orientation, gives way in later essays to individualism and rights. The more the author of a treatise on natural disinterestedness discovers that the vices of self-love hold sway in this world over the virtues of benevolence, and that they are magnified in larger historical events and social institutions, the more he thinks protective rights necessary.

As a principled individualist, Hazlitt hates many contemporary social philosophies. Hedonistic utilitarianism, the ethic to which Shelley alone among major Romantic figures at times claims adherence, is attacked by Hazlitt – notably in "The Utilitarian Controversy" (1829), "The New School of Reform" (1826), "On People of Sense" (1821), and in essays on Bentham and Godwin – on grounds somewhat different from Coleridge's. Where Coleridge notes the impracticality of weighing long-range consequences and argues that rightness or wrongness of acts derives from their intrinsic character, Hazlitt more broadly attacks the utilitarians' indifference or hostility to individual rights, culture, and art. The quality of life in a utilitarian culture is shabby. Utilitarians use "the cant-phrase of the *good of the whole*" as justification for depriving individuals of pleasure and freedom (XX 257). The argument for the greatest happiness of the greatest number of people can be used to justify the slave trade. That "the actual and intolerable sufferings inflicted on the individuals were compensated by certain advantages in a commercial and political point of view" may be a sound utilitarian argument but it offends the "moral sense." Even entertaining the argument proves us hideous. "An infinite number of lumps of sugar [produced in the slave trade] put into Mr. Bentham's artificial ethical scales would never weigh against the pounds of human flesh, or drops of human blood, that are sacrificed to produce them" (XII 49–50). The exercise of governmental power should be chastened by natural sympathy:

A calculation of the mere ultimate advantages, without regard to natural feelings and affections, may improve the external face and physical comforts of society, but will leave it heartless and worthless in itself. In a word, the sympathy of the individual with the consequences of his own act is to be attended to (no less than the consequences themselves) in every sound system of morality; and this must be determined by certain natural laws of the human mind, and not by rules of logic or arithmetic. (XII 50)

Hazlitt can see no circumstance where the good of all is promoted by performing outrage on individuals or minorities. The theory of utility ironically "first reduces everything to pleasure and pain, and then tramples upon and crushes these by its own sovereign will" (XII 189).

Even if utilitarianism did not have a built-in principle of tyranny of the majority (which Godwin and Shelley have corrected by the supplementary, principle of distributive justice), its very concept of pleasure is limited and fraudulent. A vegetable garden is "useful" with regard to consequences; a flower garden is merely "agreeable." The utilitarians, because they are incapable of receiving real pleasure from anything, exclude the agreeable flower garden because it is useless, and by the same reason are hostile to "polite literature and the arts" (X 256–8). There is a pronounced austerity in utilitarianism that sits oddly with Bentham's assurance that all pleasures are good.

Pleasures should instead be assessed qualitatively. "There are some tastes that are sweet in the mouth and bitter in the belly" (XI 9). The utilitarians' concept of the ideal commonwealth, "where each member performs his part in the machine," leaves little room for the higher pleasures of beauty and culture. Against the Benthamite utilitarian (called the "Rationalist" in Hazlitt's dialogue, "The New School of Reform"), he pits his spokesman, the "Sentimentalist," who argues obnoxiously on behalf of beauty, culture, passion, imagination, and individualism. Bentham leaves all this out in propounding the human being as felicific calculator. "They hate all grace, ornament, elegance. They are addicted to abstruse science, but sworn enemies to the fine arts. They are a kind of puritans in morals" (XII 248).

Like Godwin and Shelley, Hazlitt thinks there should be a continuity between ethics and politics, the latter deriving from the former. Each has its own sphere of action, but they must be consistent. We have seen his distrust of "visionary" proposals such as Godwin's or Owen's, which are based on too high an estimate of human reason. There is no progress in the arts and, as we have seen, little change or improvement in individuals. Hazlitt does not go quite this far with regard to human history: the Glorious Revolution of 1688–9, which stripped away the divine right of kings in England, and the French Revolution, which for a time got rid of the Bourbon monarchy, testify to the possibility of limited progress. But "visionary schemes of ideal perfection" have never fostered progress and even discourage what limited reform there can be, by feeding the self-interested illogic of reactionaries. It is rather

the knowledge of the past, the actual infliction of the present, that has produced all changes, all innovations, and all improvements—not (as is pretended) the chimerical anticipation of possible advantages, but the intoler-

able pressure of long-established, notorious, aggravated, and growing abuses.
(VIII 155)

The future-oriented imagination is thus as untrustworthy in politics as it is in morality. Papal corruption, not visionary schemes, brought on the Reformation; King John's tyranny provoked the Magna Carta; the "abuses, licentiousness, and innumerable oppressions" of the monarchy produced the French Revolution. Hazlitt does not ordinarily favor revolution. Rather, one must work, in response to abuses, for as much reform as is possible – and it is not much – at any one moment in history. All governmental acts that offend our sense of justice, such as capital punishment for bread-stealing, must be resisted.

The most repellent socio-economic doctrine of the day – an extreme utilitarianism – is propounded by Malthus, whose first *Essay on the Principle of Population* (1798), published the same year as *Lyrical Ballads*, attacks reform on the grounds that – given the ratio of food production to population growth – poverty and vice among the lower classes are necessary as a population curb. Since a just distribution of goods and property would only equalize the human race in poverty, the principle of utility counsels that at least some of us should remain happy and rich. In several replies, brief and lengthy, Hazlitt makes the case for distributive justice and attempts point by point to demolish Malthus's reasoning as unscientific, invalid, untrue, and immoral. Malthus commits a non sequitur in concluding that because the population will *eventually* outstrip food production, the haves are entitled *at the present moment* to ignore the claims of distributive justice. He errs also in not seeing that economic amelioration in underdeveloped countries results in a decrease of population growth. His greatest error is in not seeing how such views, in their lack of sympathy, degrade the sensibilities of those who hold them. To his dismay, Malthusian doctrine became the reigning economics in the years after Waterloo, with even the liberal *Edinburgh Review* adopting it.

In his incomplete "Project for a New Theory of Civil and Criminal Legislation," Hazlitt gives his most extensive theoretical treatment of the relationship of ethics and politics. He makes a case for individual rights that reduces political jurisdiction to a minimum, or even toward the vanishing point. The first premise is that individuals have complete sovereignty over the conduct of their own lives insofar as this conduct pertains to them alone. The inviolable "circle of individuality" is a right "inseparable from the order of the universe," a natural right (XIX 310). A person may peruse his own desires according to what is "good in his own eyes, and according to his will," even if it is not in his

best interests. We have the right to commit suicide so long as we do not
jeopardize the lives of others by jumping from a building on top of
them. Government has the role of arbitrator among conflicting wills,
but it can in no way dictate personal morality. It can also not make
demands of its own. Hazlitt acknowledges virtually no duties that the
individual has toward the state. "The good of society is not a sufficient
plea [for making such demands on individuals], for individuals are
only bound (on compulsion) not to do it harm, or to be barely just:
benevolence and virtue are voluntary qualities" (XIX 306). Government should restrict itself to arbitration and occasional enforcement,
and should permit free expression of individual will in all other
respects. This libertarian concept guarantees equality, says Hazlitt, or
at least equality of rights. In a society with equality of rights, a principle
of "give and take" or "balance" is possible. He dismisses the threat
that rights of individuals would be so fundamentally in conflict that
one party would almost inevitably seek domination over another.
Cases of conflicting rights could be arbitrated justly, without handing
undue power over to the arbitrator. In cases of outright aggression,
what he calls the "general voice" of an enlightened people, instead of a
coercive government, would somehow arbitrate.

One doubts that this political theory is commensurate with the view
of the self Hazlitt has developed elsewhere. In his portraiture of
human types, most of us – whether pedants, egotists, Tories, or
Methodists – seek more than is our due. Would there not have to be a
greater degree of prior legislation as to what individuals may or may
not do? Then too, Hazlitt, though he is as condescending to peasants
and working-class people as he is hostile to ruling classes, is outraged
by poverty. Does he not deny government the legislative might that
could address it? He speaks of a right to property and is at the same
time disgusted by gross inequality of property distribution. Since
laissez-faire economics prompts inequality, how can he advocate a
minimal "hands off" government, as he puts it? What is to be the agent
of amelioration, if not the government acting as popular sovereign?
His answer, like Godwin's, would appear to be individuals acting
morally in small aggregates or alone.

One omission from his "New Theory" is a perspective on the uses
and abuses of capital. Witness his justification of trade unions and the
workers' right to "strike" (his term):

A man's labour is his own, at least as much as another's goods; and he may
starve if he pleases, but he may refuse to work except on his own terms. The
right of property is reducible to this simple principle, that one man has not a

right to the produce of another's labour, but each man has a right to the benefit of his own exertions and the use of his natural and inalienable powers, unless for a supposed equivalent and by mutual consent.   (XIX 309)

The "equivalent" is indeed "supposed." Marx argues that a person's labor in a capitalist economy is necessarily undersold, which creates the surplus value appropriated by the ruling classes. Hazlitt understands that the conditions for a revolution exist in that the wages of workers have not risen in forty years, but he does not acknowledge the complicity in this of minimal governmental regulation. Could he hope for economic equality in a republic preserving so stubbornly the right to property, without presupposing a government that exercises, through popular sovereignty itself, strong powers of distribution?

These and similar questions arise ultimately because of Hazlitt's commitment to both the theoretical benevolence and the practical malignity of man. A treatise such as the "New Theory of Civil and Criminal Legislation" implies a high estimate of human nature that he elsewhere undermines. This treatise covertly argues an anarchistic program: leave human beings to their own will, let them bargain as much as possible among themselves for conflicting objects of desire, and trust in an inner sense of balance and justice to promote the general good. But Hazlitt does not see that this program conflicts with the bulk of his observations on man's practical malignity.

The right-wing imagination

Why does Hazlitt think poets end up Tories? In a post-Waterloo essay on *Coriolanus* in *Characters of Shakespeare's Plays* (1817, the essay first published 15 December 1816) and in *Letter to William Gifford* (1819), he once again indicts the imagination. Reversing Shelley's argument in *A Defence of Poetry*, Hazlitt sets forth, for the first time in the history of criticism, an appalling aspect of the psychology of imagination and power:

The cause of the people is indeed but little calculated as a subject for poetry . . . The language of poetry naturally falls in with the language of power. The imagination is an exaggerating and exclusive faculty: it takes from one thing to add to another: it accumulates circumstances together to give the greatest possible effect to a favourite object. The understanding is a dividing and measuring faculty: it judges of things not according to their immediate impression on the mind, but according to their relations to one another. The one is a monopolising faculty, which seeks the greatest quantity of present excitement by inequality and disproportion; the other is a distributive faculty, which seeks the greatest quantity of ultimate good, by justice and proportion.

The one is an aristocratical, the other a republican faculty. The principle of poetry is a very anti-levelling principle . . . It has its altars and its victims, sacrifices, human sacrifices. Kings, priests, nobles, are its trainbearers, tyrants and slaves its executioners. – "Carnage is its daughter." (IV 214)

Hazlitt's is a resigned indignation, because, as he repeatedly says, the attraction of imagination to the spectacle of power is inherent. He cannot urge that we behave differently. Poets have what is but a worse case of a universal human malady:

We had rather be the oppressor than the oppressed. The love of power in ourselves and the admiration of it in others are both natural to man: the one makes him a tyrant, the other a slave. Wrong dressed out in pride, pomp, and circumstance, has more attraction than abstract right. . .

  The whole dramatic moral of *Coriolanus* is that those who have little shall have less, and that those who have much shall take all that others have left . . . This is the logic of the imagination and the passions; which seek to aggrandize what excites admiration and to heap contempt on misery, to raise power into tyranny, and to make tyranny absolute . . . The history of mankind is a romance, a mask, a tragedy, constructed upon the principles of *poetical justice*; it is a noble or royal hunt, in which what is sport to the few is death to the many, and in which the spectators halloo and encourage the strong to set upon the weak, and cry havoc in the chase though they do not share in the spoil. We may depend upon it that what men delight to read in books, they will put in practice in reality. (IV 215–16)

In his *Letter to William Gifford* he continues this unmasking of the imagination, with its presumed sympathy and knowingness. Gifford, the first editor of the conservative *Quarterly Review*, had attacked Hazlitt unremittingly in his journal. The political treachery of the imagination is what Hazlitt, in a telling phrase, calls the "original sin in poetry." It is a sorry fact "that poetry, that the imagination, generally speaking, delights in power, in strong excitement, as well as in truth, in good, in right, whereas pure reason and the moral sense approve only of the true and good." This love of excitement or intensity "gives a bias to the imagination often inconsistent with the greatest good," in both life and art. We may "read with pleasure of the ravages of a beast of prey . . . from the sense of power abstracted from the sense of good; and it is the same principle that makes us read with admiration and reconciles us in fact to the triumphant progress of the conquerors and mighty hunters of mankind . . ." (IX 37). Arrested as it is by pomp and majesty, imagination leads us to regard a tyrant as a hero *because* he has murdered thousands of people. Imagination has a tendency to side with evil in a "sacrifice of common humanity." Far from working as the subversive freedom that Schiller takes to be its essential function, imagination aligns itself with slavery and tyranny. As Hazlitt writes elsewhere, "Man is naturally a worshipper of idols and a lover of kings. It is the excess of individual power, that strikes and gains over his imagination" (VI 149). Keats will transcribe large portions of the *Letter to William Gifford* and thereafter confront its threatening arguments in *The Fall of Hyperion*.

The implications of this argument for our reading of Hazlitt and other Romantics are many. It repudiates the idea that the sympathetic imagination is the agency of disinterestedness. Imagination is now said to propose objects to the will in an interested way, even though our sense of our own real interest is so dim that we sympathize with those who abuse us. Hazlitt has gone well beyond the explanation, proposed in his *Essay*, of moral decline in terms of a gradual narrowing of vision. Something more, he thinks, is needed to explain the large-scale movement away from the libertarian thrust of the French Revolution to the post-Waterloo restoration of monarchy and, worse, the accommodation of the best minds to that restoration. Now he sees the ground of apostasy in a natural attraction of imagination to power. It is not exactly a will to power in either a Hobbesian or a Nietzschean sense that he ascribes to us all. Rather, it is our natural *sympathy with* power, our vicarious participation in it, as the supplement to our own unrealized aspirations.[7] The kinetic spectacle of power arrests the imagination, with its inherently bad taste. Imagination becomes a particular appetite of the self, the sating of which ironically renders us less powerful in the political sphere.

Hazlitt agrees with the conservative Whig Edmund Burke that moral and political decisions should not be made on the basis of abstract reason: he "was so far right in saying that it is no objection to an institution, that it is founded in *prejudice*, but the contrary, if that prejudice is natural and right" (VII 306). In his 1807 character study of Burke, he attempts to see what there is to admire in an enemy, and concludes that Burke, in arguing the human need for tradition, honor, hierarchy, and monarchy, has correctly seen a diversity of human truths based on feeling, whereas a standard of reason alone would impose uniformity. "It is said, I know, that truth is *one*; but to this I cannot subscribe, for it appears to me that truth is *many*" (VII 308). Kinnaird goes so far as to say that by 1807 Hazlitt in his practical politics is a "constitutional Whig"– that although he regards monarchy and aristocracy as neither inevitable nor just they do lamentably answer to the human need for the covert flattery of a vicarious sense of power

[7] John Kinnaird argues persuasively that Hazlitt's view of power is the master key to his multitudinous writings.

(pp. 107–8). Although I think Kinnaird thereby risks knocking too many of the antinomian stuffings out of Hazlitt, I agree that his view of the inherent instability of human feelings and the need for a supplementary image of power does push him toward an accommodation of his own with power – if more with Napoleonic empire than with constitutional monarchy. Burke is such a problem for Hazlitt because they begin with many of the same assumptions. Burke could have little objection to Hazlitt's assertion that passion "is the essence, the chief ingredient in moral truth," and in political reality as well. They share a hostility to theory and an acknowledgment that the retention of political power requires the reciprocal imagination of leader and people, and the incarnation of power in skilled rhetoric. Such shared assumptions make Burke a formidable counter-spirit.

Hazlitt later attributes the generosity of his 1807 portrait of Burke to a "fit of extravagant candour." Burke's weakness is that he does not know when a "prejudice is natural and right," and when it is not. He lacks the common sense that would correct the alignment of imagination with power. In his support of the American Revolution and subsequent condemnation of the French, he becomes the prototype of the nineteenth-century apostate. "In the American war, he constantly spoke of the rights of the people as inherent, and inalienable: after the French Revolution, he began by treating them with the chicanery of a sophist, and ended by raving at them with the fury of a maniac" (XVI 130). Hazlitt thinks that passion and imagination have missed the mark this time. A deluded Burke forsook a position based on respect of tradition and "prejudice" for a reactionary hyper-romantic dream:

A crazy, obsolete government was metamorphosed into an object of fancied awe and veneration, like a mouldering Gothic ruin, which, however delightful to look at or read of, is not at all pleasant to live under. Thus the poetry and imagination of the thing were thrown into the scale of old-fashioned barbarism and musty tradition, and turned the balance [against the Revolution] . . . The *good old times* are good only because they are gone, or because they afford a picturesque contrast to modern ones; and to wish to bring them back, is neither to appreciate the old or the new.
(XIII 51)

The "poetry and imagination of the thing" run against all common sense.

Hazlitt's problem is that without recourse to a political *theory* that can properly situate passion, imagination, prejudice, and tradition within a larger judgmental scheme, he cannot refute Burke and is caught up in some question-begging. How do we know when to trust imagination and prejudice? His notion of passionate common sense is hardly raised to the level of theory and entails question-begging also, as the historical shifts in common sense readily show. Hazlitt was himself attracted to displays of power: he would travel miles, as we have seen, for a boxing match, he was a mental pugilist of the first order, and he admired Napoleon to the end. Some would say that boxing and polemics and Napoleon offend *their* common sense. The various manifestations of power must somehow be discriminated, Hazlitt knows, before value can be assigned. To sympathize with Napoleonic power is to encourage the attack on tyranny; to sympathize with Pitt is to acquiesce in banality. Napoleon's deliberate mystification by means of regal props is a necessary concession to the popular imagination that this thorn in the side of kings must make in order to direct power toward ultimately libertarian ends. But how do we make this discrimination? As we have seen, Hazlitt's "Project for a New Theory of Civil and Criminal Legislation" attempts a sophisticated political theory but creates problems of its own.

A mixture of admiration and contempt similar to his view of Burke informs Hazlitt's writings on the Lake poets, in whom instability of feeling and excess of imagination lead to a reactionary politics. Apostasy is for him the most pointed moral contradiction, which he subjects to satire and ridicule often enough, as when the reactionary Southey's early radical tract, *Wat Tyler* (1794) surfaces in 1817. It is a contradiction that troubles him deeply as it does Byron and Shelley. He is dismayed that larger minds yield to so much that is obtuse.

As the largest mind of the age, Coleridge is the most disquieting of the political apostates. His eloquence as Unitarian preacher in a small church in Shrewsbury had for Hazlitt the power of a divine afflatus:

> My soul has indeed remained in its original bondage, dark, obscure, with longings infinite and unsatisfied; my heart, shut up in the prison-house of this rude clay, has never found, nor will it ever find, a heart to speak to; but that my understanding also did not remain dumb and brutish, or at length found a language to express itself, I owe to Coleridge. (XVII 107)

And elsewhere, after pronouncing Coleridge's prose works to be "dreary trash," he tells us that Coleridge is the "only person from whom I ever learnt any thing" (V 167). Only Shakespeare and Napoleon occupy more of his thoughts. Yet Coleridge is the genius as charlatan, sophist, and turncoat. The famous portrait in "My First Acquaintance with Poets" (1823) treats him as demi-god and prodigal force of nature. He seems possessed of demiurgical power, and Hazlitt is mesmerized. But Coleridge may all along have had a constitutional impairment, emblematized in his nose: "The rudder of the face, the index of the will, was small, feeble, nothing – like what he has done."

And there is his wobbly walk, suggesting "instability of purpose or involuntary change of principle" (XVII 109, 113). In Coleridge he comes to see incapacity of will, intellectual promiscuity, and emotional dependency. "Two things are indispensable to him – to set out from no premises, and to arrive at no conclusion" (VII 116). The poet/preacher who had impregnated Hazlitt with language now employs a language that is "swelling and turgid" and that brings forth "only *still births*" (XII 15). There is a lack of tenacity in Coleridge, which the poet himself complains of, dictating, as usual, the harsh terms others pick up in judging him. Hazlitt notes that "no subject can come amiss to him, and he is alike attracted and alike indifferent to all – he is not tied down to any one in particular – but floats from one to another, his mind every where finding its level, and feeling no limit but that of thought—" (XII 199). Coleridge's habit of mind is "tangential."

In an essay, "On Consistency of Opinion" (1821), Hazlitt contrasts his own tenacity with Coleridge's lack of it. He had told Hazlitt that not changing one's ideas over a period of years is symptomatic of a "want of sympathy with others." But Hazlitt thinks that what Coleridge "calls *sympathising with others* is their admiring him" (XVII 23), and that this need for admiration is one cause of his intellectual and moral inconstancy. He finds it difficult even to call Coleridge a "deserter from the cause he first espoused," because it is difficult to determine what cause that was. "He lived in a round of contradictions, and never came to a settled point. His fancy gave the cue to his judgment, and his vanity set his invention afloat in whatever direction he could find most scope for it, or most *sympathy*, that is, admiration" (XVII 29). Hazlitt admires consistency: "By adhering to the same principles you do not become stationary. You enlarge, correct, and consolidate your reasonings, without contradicting and shuffling about in your conclusions" (VII 33). Adhering to the same principles means retaining the locus of power within the self, instead of vacating personal power, whether through excess of sympathy or need of admiration.

Coleridge's inconstancy would not be so alarming were it not political and evidenced in condemning those who adopt positions similar to those he and Wordsworth adopted in their youth. The apostasy of the Lake poets governs Hazlitt's judgments of their poetry and moral character. Coleridge's "philosophical skepticism" is exercised "with a regular leaning to the side of power" (XVI 102–3) that undermines all claim to catholicity and liberality. Indeed, "the worst sort of illiberality is that which, with broad unblushing effrontery, imputes to the worst motives those very principles which the revilers, before their new illumination, themselves professed and propagated"

(XIX 196–7). Byron denounces Southey on identical grounds (*LJ* V 220–1). Southey and Coleridge, as brothers "in the same cause of righteous apostacy," praise church and king, says Hazlitt, and would persecute dissenters. Coleridge praised the French Revolution when it was succeeding, "and now that it is fallen, this man of mighty mind,—of gigantic genius, and superiority to interested motives and mob-sycophancy, insults over it,—tramples on the carcase,—kicks it with his asinine hoofs,—and brays a long, loud, dreary, doleful, bravura over it" (XIX 208).

Coleridge is thus the most blatant contemporary instance of a poet whose sense of weakness and promiscuous imagination attract him to the powers that be and their supplementary image of power. When government censors during the Pitt repression of the early nineties began subjecting dissenters to ridicule and imprisonment, "the poets, and creatures of sympathy, could not stand the frowns both of king and people. They did not like to be shut out when places and pensions, when the critic's praises, and the laurel-wreath were about to be distributed" (XI 37). And Coleridge, weakest among them despite his mighty voice, led the retreat back to orthodoxy. The transformation is so appalling that Hazlitt decides there has been, in one sense, no transformation at all. Poets are inherently fickle and subject to the pull of authority. An indignant Hazlitt once again proposes no remedy or alternative.[8]

In his essay on *Coriolanus* he had quoted an infamous portion of Wordsworth's "Ode: 1815" (1816) in celebration of the defeat of Napoleon at Waterloo. The poet exclaims to God:

> But Thy most dreaded instrument
> In working out a pure intent,
> Is Man—arrayed for mutual slaughter—
> —Yea, Carnage is Thy Daughter!

Shelley in *Peter Bell the Third* (1819, first published 1839), fiercely parodies the unlovely idea that carnage is God's daughter (634–40). Wordsworth removed the line in 1845. The allusion to it early in Hazlitt's 1816 essay on *Coriolanus* suggests that Wordsworth is in the back of his mind as he speaks of imagination and power. But Hazlitt here and elsewhere fails to provide a convincing and consistent

---

[8] I have challenged the reading that Hazlitt is himself consistent. In moving from a belief in benevolence and disinterestedness to a belief in "original sin" (whether in poetry or the "original bias" of character), Hazlitt recapitulates something of Coleridge's arc of development. Sin is for Hazlitt exclusively a secular matter, however, an inherent susceptibility to the "sense of power abstracted from the sense of good."

analysis of ethico-political change in Wordsworth, and the reason is clear. Perhaps more than any previous poet, as Hazlitt knows, Wordsworth *does* keep the locus of power within the self. Why should someone with such powerful reserves of self be swayed by the flattery of aristocrats to renounce the very sources – those "primal sympathies" with nature and humankind – of his own poetic power? Hazlitt has spoken of the "vanity" and inner sense of weakness that attend poets such as Coleridge, but Wordsworth, however comically vain in some respects, has something beyond vanity that is a measure of personal and poetic strength. It is what Hazlitt calls his "egotism," the sort of egotism that Coleridge, speaking of Milton, praises as a "revelation of spirit." Egotism is a power that attracts Hazlitt, even as he finds it irksome. In a particularly cranky moment, he writes that Wordsworth

tolerates only what he himself creates; he sympathizes only with what can enter into no competition with him, with "the bare trees and mountains bare, and grass in the green field." He sees nothing but himself and the universe. He hates all greatness and all pretensions to it, whether well- or ill-founded. His egotism is in some respects a madness; for he scorns even the admiration of himself, thinking it a presumption in any one to suppose that he has taste or sense enough to understand him.

(V 163)

And of *The Excursion* he complains that an "intense intellectual egotism swallows up every thing"; the characters are all different versions of Wordsworth himself, whose mind "is the reverse of the dramatic" (IV 113). But Hazlitt, with his leanings toward individualism, also thinks Wordsworth is "the greatest, that is, the most original poet of the present day, only because he is the greatest egotist" (VIII 44). To get rid of the egotist in him would be, he fears, to get rid of the poet. "We might get rid of the cynic and the egotist, and find in his stead a commonplace man" (XI 94). Wordsworth's egotism enables him to be the most original poet of the day. Far from a Coleridgean reliance on admiration, Wordsworth has, as Hazlitt describes him, the strength of vision that comes from a resistant isolationism, which paradoxically enables him to speak the poetry of a common humanity. Hence the generic analysis of imagination and power does not fit Hazlitt's own reading of Wordsworth, who ought to have been the poet most resistant to the lure of orthodoxy.

The other point at which his reading of Wordsworth blatantly contradicts his own analysis of power and imagination relates to the politics of form and content in the poetry. Hazlitt has said that "the principle of poetry is a very anti-levelling principle," but he nonethe-

369

less thinks Wordsworth's muse is "a levelling one" that partakes of "the revolutionary movement of our age . . . It proceeds on a principle of equality, and strives to reduce all things to the same standard. It is distinguished by a proud humility" (XI 87). In his essay on Wordsworth in *The Spirit of the Age* (1825), he paints an ironic portrait of an egotist about whom it can still be said that "no one has displayed the same pathos in treating of the simplest feelings of the heart." It is his poetic egotism – the fact that he is a strong poet – that enables him to describe the world of nature "in a way and with an intensity of feeling that no one else had done before him, and [he] has given a new view or aspect of nature. He is in this sense the most original poet now living, and the one whose writings could the least be spared, for they have no substitute elsewhere" (XI 89). Since his poetry, more than any other, undercuts the intrinsic anti-levelling propensities of verse, is he not a poet who, in terms of Hazlitt's own reading, should have resisted the spurious sense of power which results from acquiescence in repressive socio-political structures?

In fact, Hazlitt cannot explain Wordsworth's "apostasy," and only laments the contradiction. This same champion of the "common people in country places," with a stroke of the pen, "disfranchises the whole rustic population of Westmoreland and Cumberland from voting at elections, and says there is not a man among them that is not a knave in grain." Wordsworth "has hardly, I should think, so much as a single particle of feeling left in his whole composition, the same that he had twenty years ago" (XVII 25–6). Hazlitt, by the way, does not base his own radical politics on love of the people. In his critique of *The Excursion*, he takes an inventory of country barbarisms: country folk are creatures of passion, hardened, vulgar, vain, selfish, and full of hate (IV 122–4). It is Wordsworth's radical inconsistency that is finally so baffling, not that the poet is contemptuous of peasants.

There has been an obvious contradiction in Hazlitt's own thinking: he never attempts to reconcile the disinterested with the right-wing imagination. He might have argued, in keeping with his early *Essay*, that the imagination is formally non-aligned with any particular politics, but that it is prone to strong commitments materially when poets engage the politics of their day – commitments that have historically tended toward alliances with the powers that be. Such an argument might have provided the grounds for a nominal explanation of political apostasy. The formal non-alignment of imagination could also persist as a check on the lure of power, perhaps explaining why a few poets do *not* end up Tories. This argument is not made, but Hazlitt's analysis of the imagination's disquieting tendency to identify with power remains the period's most vigorous and ominous questioning of its idol, a questioning that Byron continues by different means.

Love's nightmares

From 1820 to 1823 Hazlitt, unhinged by a passion that differed in intensity from any he had previously known, engaged in calamitous pursuit of a young woman at his lodging-house. The bizarre literary product of this frenzied wooing, an autobiographical epistolary narrative, may seem an aberration, but in fact it implicates much of his life and thought. The tragical farce, *Liber Amoris: or, The New Pygmalion* (1823), is a severe testing of his concepts of imagination and sympathy.[9]

Separated from his first wife, Hazlitt was forty-two when he met Sarah Walker, half his age. She obliged him during her morning rounds of the lodging-house, spending an hour in his room each day fondling and kissing him and granting him certain liberties among her petticoats – liberties apparently granted other lodgers as well. Greatly infatuated with her, Hazlitt returned to Scotland to obtain a divorce, writing letters while there to Patmore, who counseled him and did some dutiful spying on Sarah back in London. The essayist was suspicious that she might be a teasing "lodging-house decoy" cynically manipulating lodgers, under instructions from her mother, for the sake of getting gifts. Modern readers are more apt to see in her behavior the strategies of sexual powerplay that, given Hazlitt's witless misogyny, are justly deployed. After extremes of worship and sex nausea, Hazlitt returned to London freshly divorced, only to find that Sarah with dignity refused to continue the flirtation, let alone marry the graceless middle-aged fool. *Liber Amoris* is a series of petitions and rejections, the author of *Essay on the Principles of Human Action* incapable of taking no for an answer. He went so far as to dispatch a decoy to see if she was seducible, declaring that if he knew she was a whore, he might rid himself of his obsession. Despite his prurient, hopeful reading of this minutely recorded trial by proxy, it is clear that Sarah permitted the decoy fewer liberties than she once granted Hazlitt.

[9] This text is flanked by others with bearing on it and is enriched if opened up to them. These other texts include the original letters to his friends P. G. Patmore and James Sheridan Knowles, from which a good portion of *Liber Amoris* is taken; "Advice to a Schoolboy," which is a letter written to his ten-year-old son in February or early March, 1822; and Hazlitt's diary notes of 4–16 March 1823, on the testing by proxy of his beloved's virtue.

Liber Amoris and its related texts describe several acts of sympathetic identification that betray Hazlitt's depleted ego. In "Advice to a Schoolboy," he identifies wistfully with his son as one who will make none of his father's mistakes, who will learn to dance and dress well and enter a room without making everyone uncomfortable, and who will court a woman who loves him. Much of the letter encourages a tolerance of human stupidity that would have destroyed the Hazlitt we admire. "Do not begin to quarrel with the world too soon: for, bad as it may be, it is the best we have to live in—here. If railing would have made it better, it would have been reformed long ago; but as this is not to be hoped for at present, the best way is to slide through it as contentedly and innocently as we may." This is Hazlitt? Turning to specifics, he writes: "The best antidote I can recommend to you hereafter against the disheartening effect of such writings as those of Rochefoucauld, Mandeville, and others, will be to look at the pictures of Raphael and Correggio" (*LWH* 219–20). Hazlitt echoes his indictment of Shelley: he has himself suffered from an overabundance of imagination. "By indulging our imaginations on fictions and chimeras, where we have it all our own way and are led on only by the pleasure of the prospect, we grow fastidious, effeminate, lapped in idle luxury, impatient of contradiction, and unable to sustain the shock of real adversity, when it comes" (*LWH* 255).

Made in the midst of the Sarah Walker affair, this self-diagnosis of a pathology of the imagination reveals a capacity for analysis concealed in *Liber Amoris*. The contrast between letter and narrative demonstrates the deliberate artifice of the narrative, the "wisdom" Hazlitt actually possesses withheld from the text. With his first wife in mind, he cautions his son never to marry someone he does not immediately like, and with Sarah's stubbornness in mind he observes: "There is no forcing liking. It is as little to be fostered by reason and good-nature, as it can be controlled by prudence or propriety. It is a mere blind, headstrong impulse." Romantic notions spent on an unloving woman make "no more impression" than on a piece of marble. None of this did he learn soon enough: he has imagined wildly, he has attempted to will someone else to love him. And now, "as my frail bark sails down the stream of time, the God of Love stands on the shore, and as I stretch out my hands to him in vain, claps his wings, and mocks me as I pass" (*LWH* 231–5). In this letter, father identifies with son as a potential supplement, who might inherit a world lost to the father. The letter is also an aggressive act, as most advice contains an element of aggression, made more intense here by the hint that these are the wishes of a dying man.

In *Liber Amoris* acts of sympathetic imagination are mediated by a talismanic prop – the small bronze figure of Napoleon, Hazlitt's life-long idol in a country where almost everybody thinks the emperor a devil. His four-volume *Life of Napoleon Buonaparte* (1828–30) treats the emperor as a *"thorn in the side of kings,"* who had hoped to interpose an "arm of steel" between them and the people, who fights off a hypo-critical England and the powers seeking restoration of Continental sovereigns, which powers force him into acts of militarism. Napoleon's tyrannical aspect answers, Hazlitt has said, to the people's need for a manifest display of power with which they can identify. The small figure of Napoleon in *Liber Amoris* is the object of three distinct acts of sympathetic identification. Hazlitt identifies himself with it as the figure of his own resistance to powers that be, in a way loosely analogous to Julien Sorel's Napoleon complex in *Le Rouge et Le Noir* (1830). Sarah sees a resemblance between the Napoleon figure and a former suitor, to whom she proclaims her steadfast love. And in forcing her to accept the Napoleon figure as a gift (one given ludicrous phallic significance), Hazlitt identifies himself with her former suitor as well as with Napoleon. "How odd it was that the God of my idolatry should turn out to be like her Idol," he tells her, adding that *"it was no wonder that the same face which awed the world should conquer the sweetest creature in it!"* (*LA* 37–8). Napoleon, Sarah, her former suitor, and he will all commingle in the figure. Taking on its talismanic powers, he will be her lover, with the force of Napoleon.

And these intricacies are not Hazlitt's rococo artifice; they are, he says, a factual record of a relationship. The *Liber Amoris* texts assault the formalist insularity of art from life.

In his greatest outburst, the spurned suitor stomps on the figure, breaking it to pieces. He learns that where there's a will, there may not be a way. His will to power over Sarah is frustrated, just as Napoleon's over Europe had been. In courting her symbolically through the figure of Napoleon, he commits an act of symbolic aggression, even though he initially announces himself as disinterested, seeking fulfillment in her happiness alone. In his imagination, working through the figure, he wishes to become the other suitor. It is a sympathy with power that demonstrates his own lack of it, the author disappearing into the idol. Sympathetic identification is cause and symptom of a depleted ego.

The original letters to Patmore, more than the published text, reveal that he felt sexually supplanted. A record of a bawdy conversation indistinctly overheard in the kitchen among members of Sarah's family reads like a Joycean epiphany. This banter proves that Sarah wants a stallion, that "the girl runs mad for size," that she prefers a certain

373

Griffiths who "tumbled over Mr. Hazlitt one night." "Death, death, death," he cries, but he cannot help but seek to know more about his rivals, even at the risk of insanity (*LWH* 220). Hiring the decoy to try Sarah is an extreme act of identification, simultaneously self-effacing and aggressive. Hazlitt thinks his motive is therapeutic; to know she is a whore (on his terms) would be to make her so abject that he could not conceive of an attachment. He has in mind too the psychology of dread: as he says elsewhere, we sometimes seek out the object of dread to rid ourselves of dread, as we might embrace a corpse. But one suspects a stronger motive: ravishment by proxy. It is evident throughout that he is the more slavishly committed to Sarah the more whorish he fears her to be. It is a love exasperated and confirmed by jealousy.

The character toward whom he can direct *no* act of direct identification is, revealingly, Sarah herself. She is everything and nothing, and his imagination is crazed by a hyperbole that makes Shelley look restrained and chaste. The untalkative woman is in the same breadth angel and demon. As Hazlitt tells his son, the problem is in the nature of idealization. If an angel seems anything less than angelic, the imagination will transform her into a serpent. Sarah is a "scorpion" who has mortally poisoned him. She has "an itch for being slabbered and felt" (*LWH* 263). "The cockatrice, I said, mocks me: so she has always done . . . She was divine! I felt that she was a witch, and had bewitched me. Fate had enclosed me round about. I was transformed too, no longer human (any more than she, to whom I had knit myself) my feelings were marble; my blood was of molten lead; my thoughts on fire" (*LWH* 308–9). "I had embraced the false Florimel instead of the true; or was like the man in the Arabian Nights who had married a g[h]oul . . . Still I seemed to clasp this piece of witchcraft to my bosom" (*LWH* 317). Shelley has made us aware of the moral problem in idealization, when imagination brutalizes its objects with expectation. Through excess of idealizing imagination, Hazlitt brutalizes Sarah Walker, as Shelley does Elizabeth Hitchener.

At other times Sarah appears to have the non-human intractability of marble, unyielding before Pygmalion's prayer to Aphrodite. His imaginings do everything except humanize her. She is an actress: "It is one faultless, undeviating, consistent, consummate piece of acting" (*LWH* 319) that shields what is behind her hazy, indifferent eyes. All his acts of identification with other suitors, with statuary, and with professional seducers are assaults of the imagination on what he takes to be her impenetrable and unfeeling nature. By re-imaging her through others, perhaps he can reverse the power she has over him.

But Sarah comes to represent a stubborn resistance to all assaults of the imagination, a corrective to the narrator's presumption.

What does he say of himself in this predicament? What on earth does he think he is doing? Has he any objectivity? His state of mind is "a sort of spectre-ship, moving on through an infernal lake, without wind or tide, by some necromantic power" (*LWH* 260). Like the Ancient Mariner, Hazlitt feels taunted, out of control, punished by something that had first seemed "some especial dispensation of a favouring Providence to make me amends for all" (*LWH* 275). But he has the objectivity to say, significantly, that "I am in some sense proud that I can feel this dreadful passion" (*LWH* 275), and that a "more complete experiment on character was never made" (*LWH* 318).

An authorial objectivity, if certainly not wisdom, is shown in the complexities of rhetorical stance that distinguish the *Liber Amoris* texts. We have seen how the central action hinges on multiple acts of sympathetic identification. There are analogous acts informing the relationships of author and correspondent, author and reader – evidence of a controlling intelligence that perceives analogies among different components of a complex act and its telling. Writing to his friends gives him a sense of reciprocity that balances the lack of it with Sarah. They should identify with him in his madness and perceive that it is not *uncaused*. Tailoring these letters to the requirements of fiction objectifies the experience further, and enlists the reading public to identify with him, however foolish or loathsome his presentation of self. His concluding letter shows an artist's sense of an ending:

My seeing her in the street has gone a good way to satisfy me. Her manner there explains her manner in-doors to be conscious and overdone; and besides, she looks but indifferently. She is diminutive in stature, and her measured step and timid air do not suit these public airings. I am afraid she will soon grow common to my imagination, as well as worthless in herself. Her image seems fast 'going into the wastes of time,' like a weed that the wave bears farther and farther from me. Alas! thou poor hapless weed, when I entirely lose sight of thee, and forever, no flower will ever bloom on earth to glad my heart again!

(*LWH* 321; *LA* 191–2)

The *Liber Amoris* texts are thus a dramatization of the complexities of Hazlitt's ethics. Some of his premises are tested the hard way and found to be true in unforeseen ways. To say the least, passion does have greater influence than reason, which fails to get the upper hand even in retrospect. Hazlitt's perception remains both distorted and dangerous; if Sarah is not a slut, as seems clear enough, he has done all he could to turn her into one. The darker powers of imagination take over, leading passions into a frenzy of love expressed as aggression, obtuseness, voyeurism, sex nausea, and necrophilia. Imagination's hankering for power is seen in these fallen modes of sexual politics. They are acts of the moral imagination, but in forms not broached in the *Essay on the Principles of Human Action*. There Hazlitt had finessed the issue of the "reasoning" imagination's reliability in matters beyond whether one should run headfirst into fires. He did not fully acknowledge that imagination on his own terms necessarily works through idealization, a mental process he later finds so suspect. In failing to project any plausible image for Sarah as a potential object of sympathetic identification, the imagination proves in this case to be both ideal and solipsistic, the opposite of "reasoning."

In his reply to Malthus, Hazlitt had argued, on behalf of "moral restraint" as a means of population control, that Malthus overestimated the power of the passions. His anecdotal evidence was his one previous experience of love, which had been a "temperate" emotion. "It was not a raging heat, a fever in the veins: but it was like a vision, a dream, like thoughts of childhood, an everlasting hope, a distant joy, a heaven, a world that might be" (I 283). Malthus eventually wins on this point: love *is* a raging heat. Hazlitt does not for that reason give up the idea that there is something good in the nature of passion, whatever form it takes. In the midst of agony, he is proud to be able to feel dreadful passion.

With respect to issues of freedom, *Liber Amoris* unceremoniously deflates the Romantic will. Like the Ancient Mariner, Hazlitt acts out a repetition compulsion both in wooing the resolute Sarah and thereafter in telling the tale – indeed telling "the whole story" five times in a single day to various people throughout London. Acting out an inner compulsion is only a simulacrum of strong willing. A young servinggirl can thwart his will to power. He acknowledges that even his idol Napoleon, symbol of Romantic striving, "was not strictly a free agent" (XIII x), and did not get what he wanted. Where there is a will there may not be, even for Napoleon, a way. The "empowerment" that informs Hazlitt's concept of freedom is granted us stingily.

Hazlitt prides himself on his consistency – claiming never to have altered his ideas after the age of sixteen – but we have seen in him perhaps the most blatant self-controversion among the major British Romantics. Imagination, on which his argument for the inherent disinterestedness of human mind has turned, unhinges and crazes us if it is misdirected. Passion, the "essence, the chief ingredient in moral truth," takes the form of an antinomy in his work as a whole: it is the source of both our worth and our loathsomeness.

There are hints in Hazlitt's writings of a resolution of the latter antinomy – and perhaps the former – in the concept and psychological fact of catharsis. As purgation, catharsis manifests a doubleness with respect to the imbalance of passion it ultimately eases or cures.[10] One takes on the dis-ease of passion in order to experience it fully and be purged of it. The process as a whole is healthy and good precisely because corruption has been for a time incorporated and felt. A passion's normal progress would be to come into being, reach a certain level of intensity, be answered to, and cease for a time to importune us. If this progress is somehow arrested, the passions can degenerate into obsession, inflexibility, fanaticism, melancholy, and other neurotic patterns described in Hazlitt's character portraits. A passion seeks relief of itself or we become ill. Catharsis as purgation leads to equilibrium and self-mastery.

Such in general terms is the function of catharsis in the healthy mind, with a view to psychological categories available to Hazlitt. When he says that he is proud to be able to feel dreadful passion, he affirms that to be human is to attain a degree of passionate intensity, despite the intrinsic danger. *Liber Amoris* has portrayed a series of efforts to gratify and then to purge passion. As we have seen, he attempts to purge his worst fear – that Sarah is a whore – by confirming it. He attempts to purge jealousy by seducing Sarah with a proxy. His therapy is homeopathic: he will attempt to cure passion by injecting himself with the source of it. The therapy's success is, to be sure, dubious. To add passion to passion does not necessarily work toward a purging crescendo, and Hazlitt seems to be cured rather by attenuation.

But perhaps also by the act of writing, which is throughout his career a continuous purgation. It is a venting, a ridding. The flood of language gives momentary relief to a tormented sensibility. The status of his writings is in his own eyes correspondingly low: they are the waste product of passion and purgation, his "abortions." The cathartic therapy of writing proves partial. One is reminded of Byron's amiable comment: Hazlitt *"talks pimples—a red and white corruption rising up (in little imitation of mountains upon maps), but containing nothing, and discharging nothing, except their own humours"* (*LJ* VIII 38). Hazlitt's pain outlasts the composition of *Liber Amoris*. He never quite gets what he wants.

The great literature that he can only presume to comment on, not to write, ministers more successfully through the therapy of catharsis. It engenders in us a liberating "storm of passion" (V 6). In *King Lear*, for

---

[10] Catharsis as purification or clarification is not a significant concept in Hazlitt.

example, "our sympathy with actual suffering is lost in the strong impulse given to our natural affections, and carried with the swelling tide of passion, that gushes from and relieves the heart" (V 271–2). We sympathize with stage action not through moral analogies between self and fictional representation but through direct kinaesthetic participation that activates and purges feeling. Catharsis also answers to the dangerous alignment of imagination with power. Literary experience defuses our sympathy with power by gratifying it textually. We are attracted to "objects of terror and pity" in literature because these are part of the reality we know, and to witness them in literature is to gain power over what normally exercises "despotic control" over us. "The imagination, by thus embodying and turning [such objects] to shape, gives an obvious relief to the indistinct and importunate cravings of the will" (V 5–6). Catharsis leads to a sense of mastery over what is fearful and strange: we control in our imagination what cannot be controlled in life, and this control is therapeutic. Although poets themselves may turn Tory at the last, their poetry excites, purges, and calms the audience by a substitute gratification of its identification with power.

Hazlitt does not fully recognize the import of catharsis for his own vision. Fully to have explored it might have enabled him to go beyond the self-controversion that characterizes his work. Catharsis, as a potential resolution of the antinomy of passion, does not attain to the level of theory in his writings. Seeing the passional self as engaged in a process of intensification and purgation might have resolved the ambivalent moral value of the passions. It might have resolved the contradiction of the imagination as both disinterested and murderous. But he only hints at such resolutions.

As Hazlitt has said, "*I have had no theory to maintain*" (IX 165). Though not acknowledged as a major figure in the history of moral philosophy, he remains a major British moralist, whose cogency derives in part from this very lack of system. The early attempt at it in the *Essay* is tacitly repudiated by his later adoption of the familiar essay, with its merely testimonial format. After weighing extremes of human nature, from the angelic to the depraved, he declares himself "common-sensical" in rejecting both too high an estimate of human powers, which he terms "romantic," and one too low: "Man is neither a God nor a brute; but there is a prosaic and a poetical side to everything concerning him, and it is as impossible absolutely and for a constancy to exclude either one or the other from the mind, as to make him live without air or food" (XVII 350). We have seen that in praising or blaming particular persons or factions Hazlitt is no trimmer, no balance-master. But in assessing the generic human being he does reach a balanced view:

The mind of man is like a clock that is always running down, and requires to be as constantly wound up. The *ideal* principle is the master-key that winds it up, and without which it would come to a stand: the sensual and selfish feelings are the dead weights that pull it down to the gross and grovelling . . . There must be a mixture of the two, as long as man is compounded of opposite materials, a contradiction and an eternal competition for mastery. (XVII 350)

Such contradictions remain simply that and do not tend toward dialectical resolutions. Cynics may deride the various ideals of "friend-ship, genius, freedom," but Hazlitt argues that "it is no small consideration that the mind is capable even of feigning such things" (XVII 352). To his son he writes: "The abstract hatred and scorn of vice implies the capacity for virtue: the impatience expressed at the most striking instances of deformity proves the innate idea and love of beauty in the human mind" (*LWH* 220). His passionate common sense does not yield altogether to the spirit of negation. We could not recognize ourselves as perverse if we had no sense of what it means to act well. To echo Auden, we are still empowered to love our crooked neighbors with our crooked hearts.

8

Keats and the ethics of immanence

Poetic onanism

Keats and Byron, ostensibly at odds as people and poets, share some tendencies significant in the context of Romantic ethics. Neither is much given to moral urging, unlike many of the visionary company. Each has a moral view of things but not one that yields precepts, or even more generalized recommendations as to the conduct of life. I have said something similar of Hazlitt, whose vigorous normative stance co-exists with recognition that people will go on being their sorry selves, whatever he might say. Keats and Byron share with him a habit of moral demystification, seen, for instance, in their restraint in prophecy. Unlike Blake's Bard, "Who Present, Past & Future sees / Whose ears have heard, / The Holy Word, / That walk'd among the ancient trees," Keats does not presume imagination is possessed of prophetic power, and sees the doors of prophetic perception darkened by mist.[1] In his rhetoric of denial, Byron pronounces all pages of human history the same. *The Prophecy of Dante*, an exception, soon proves a false prophecy. The dialectical view of history and personality found in Blake, Coleridge, and Shelley can be found in Keats's letters, but in the poetry he often constructs antinomies to arrest dialectical movement. Byron disallows dialectics altogether. Like Hazlitt, Byron and Keats might better be considered dialogic than dialectic.

Keats and Byron share a skeptical bent more pronounced – if not necessarily more profound – than that of the other Romantics. Keats's skepticism is more comprehensive than Shelley's because directed

[1] Here I differ with the view that imagination for Keats "does not merely foreshow to the poet the blissful sequel of mortal existence; it actually *creates* this sequel or appears to." Newell Ford, *The Prefigurative Imagination of John Keats* (Stanford: Stanford University Press, 1951), 31n.

toward ethical as well as metaphysical truths. And when Byron embarks on philosophical discourse in his *Journals* and *Don Juan*, he suspects the excursion will only confirm the futility of seeking. They share an attitudinal resistance to alliances with one or another philosopher or moral thinker. Unlike Coleridge, who over a space of a few years commits himself, serially, to such figures as Hartley, Berkeley (he plans "a bold avowal of Berkeley's System!!!!"), Kant, and Schelling; unlike Wordsworth and Shelley who boldly avow, for a time at least, Godwinism, Keats is relatively indifferent and Byron hostile to philosophical affiliation. (Literary affiliation is another matter.) Keats's admiration of Hazlitt is more for the "demon" in his writing – the "manner in which [his argument] is managed: the force and innate power with which it yeasts and works up itself" – than for some body of ideas the poet appropriates. Byron cites Epicurus frequently as someone with a sensible view of the good life, but he is a far remove from discipleship.

It is perhaps surprising – given portraits of Keats that emphasize his talk of "the march of passion and endeavour" and "intensity" – that the two poets share a *tedium vitae*. Early in his brief career, Keats equated a "sense of real things" with "nothingness," an equation he never completely disavowed and one brutally confirmed for him on his deathbed. Whereas Byron voices theatrical disdain of the world through his various personae with their saving play of perspective, Keats supplements disdain with visions of another world in which the first in beauty would be first in might. But Keats is at no time an aesthete: this other world exists only in relation to the experiential world of desire and suffering. Byron's response to a world which he has not loved and which has not loved him (or so Childe Harold snorts) is more willful and less poignant but shares Keats's sense of a basic lack of accommodation.

Viewing the world in terms of circumstantial limitation, the poets voice an ambivalent estimate of action. Each complains of doing nothing (in the midst of a life rather busier than average), and hopes to engage in some act that goes beyond the condition of wishing to will and display. On occasion each expresses exasperation at the merely symbolic action of a life of writing – Keats toying with a career in political journalism as a more pragmatic form of writing than verse, Byron in fact giving up versifying to don a general's helmet. But Byron sees a futility in our most headstrong acts, and Keats is able to conceive only in *The Eve of St. Agnes* of action that fully attains objects of the will.

These affinities are all sober in character, yet one turns to Keats and Byron not for sobriety of vision but for their manifest delight in life and writing. To resolve this paradox – to show how, as Byron puts it, the world is after all a *"glorious* blunder" – is one goal of the next two chapters.

Despite their affinities, the two poets are hostile to each other, and in ways that reveal their commitment to a moral component in poetic vocation. Following Keats's death, Byron restrains his abuse, since he shares Shelley's dim view of unkind reviewers and thinks *Hyperion* an admirable work. But earlier, irked as he is by Keats's attack on the School of Pope in *Sleep and Poetry* (1816) (and, he might have noticed, on his own poetry as well), he complains to his publisher John Murray of "Johnny Keats's p—ss a bed poetry" (*LJ* VII 200); Keats's poetry "is a sort of mental masturbation—he is always f—gg—g his *Imagination*.—I don't mean that he is *indecent* but viciously soliciting his own ideas into a state which is neither poetry nor any thing else but a Bedlam vision produced by raw pork and opium" (*LJ* VII 225). "[W]hy his is the *Onanism* of Poetry," and Keats is "this miserable Self-polluter of the human Mind" (*LJ* VIII 217). These warm tributes are offered around the time Byron issues his defense of ethical poetry and of Pope. After Keats's death he is more temperate: "I think he took the wrong line as a poet—and was spoilt by Cockneyfying and Suburbing—and versifying Tooke's Pantheon and Lempriere's Dictionary" (*LJ* VIII 102).

For his part Keats probably has Byron in mind when, in *Sleep and Poetry*, he writes that

> in truth we've had
> Strange thunders from the potency of song;
> Mingled indeed with what is sweet and strong,
> From majesty: but in clear truth the themes
> Are ugly clubs, the poets Polyphemes
> Disturbing the grand sea. (230–5)

Byron, like Napoleon, manifests the "worldly, theatrical and pantomimical" temper of mind (*L* I 395), the kind of willfulness Coleridge finds in some ways fiendish. In *The Fall of Hyperion* (1819) Keats targets Byron when he declaims against "mock lyrists, large self-worshippers / And careless hectorers in proud bad verse" (I 207–8).

Neither poet, then, is perspicacious in his criticism of the other, but one can infer something more than myopic poetic rivalry here, and more than Keats's inadequate appreciation of Pope. Some of the hostility derives from station, reflecting Keats's resentment of aristocracy and Byron's condescension toward "Cockneys." But more to the point, their hostility relates to the ethics of poetry. In *Sleep and Poetry* Keats writes, probably with Byron in mind, that poetry need not indulge brute muscularity, feeding on "the burrs / And thorns of life" (244–5). If it tempers such willfulness, poetry is more likely to "charm / A thousand willing agents to obey" (238–9). His notion of literary pragmatics culminates in *The Fall of Hyperion*, where the poet is said to be a "humanist, physician to all men," who "pours out a balm upon the world." Keats thinks Byron guilty of self-worship, his "pantomimi-cal" inventiveness not exculpating the famed poet. His jaundiced self-promotion merely compounds the poet's problems with our own. It lacks the disinterestedness and healing properties of great poetry. Keats objects to a stanza in *Don Juan* "against literary ambition." Byron's narrator asks, "What is the end of Fame?" and answers that it is to have "a name, a wretched picture and worse bust" (*DJ* 1 218). "Some liken it to climbing up a hill," he says, and Keats might recall that he too made such a comparison in describing his own zealous and unabashed pursuit of literary fame (*L* I 139). In his eyes, Byron demeans, with his posturing, cynicism, and celebrity status, the idea of noble fame. He ridicules the strong sense of vocation that is virtually Keats's raison d'être.[2] Byron gives us back the nothingness of the world again, painfully compounded with self. He too is guilty of poetic onanism.

Each poet accuses the other, then, of a self-incarceration that corrupts the moral nature and ends of poetry. Their mutual hostility is ironically incited by an affinity in poetics and confirmed by a misreading of one another's poetic practice. Keats's revisionary perspective offers a critique of the Romantic will displayed in the dialectic of transcendence and the "ugly clubs" of the "large self-worshippers." He conceives of what I call an ethics of immanence, in which human will is eventually calmed and sensate intelligence garners a world of immanent value. In Byron we find the ethics of predicament, which is its own correction of an overconfidence in will, imagination, and dialectics. Any poetic onanism in his "proud bad verse" is purged in the epic perspectives and comic cleansing of *Don Juan*. Keats's deepest affinity will prove to be with Wordsworth, while an unlikely precursor of Byronic sensibility will be found in Blake's Tharmas, chastened somewhat by a different concept of time and history.[3]

---

[2] See Aileen Ward, " 'That Last Infirmity of Noble Mind': Keats and the Idea of Fame," in *The Evidence of the Imagination: Studies in Interactions between Life and Art in English Romantic Literature*, ed. Donald Reiman, Michael Jaye, and Betty Bennett (New York: New York University Press, 1978), 312–33.

[3] My treatment of Keats builds on the work of several critics and biographers, especially Walter Jackson Bate, *John Keats* (Cambridge, Mass.: Harvard University Press, 1963), Robert Gittings, *John Keats* (Boston: Little, Brown and Company, 1968), Aileen

Act and activity

If with some Romantic narratives we have pondered the meaning and consequences of an act, whether killing an albatross or escaping Manchester Grammar School, with many others, such as *Alastor* and *The Prelude*, we have wondered whether anything like an agent acting is ever portrayed. *The Four Zoas* takes us through nine dark nights of partial acts before arriving at what is on Blake's own terms the only complete act, the awakening of Albion. But it requires special contexts to consider an awakening as anything more than a preliminary to action. Wordsworth tells us in "Simon Lee" to make a tale, if we can, of an "incident," and in *The Prelude* he narrates incidents, happenings, and events brought on more by landscape and circumstance than by an agent acting, whatever the poet's occasional resolve to act in a dynamic and conspicuous way.

We have associated action with the ethical category of "right" and "obligation." Certainly there is no lack of an expressed sense of obligation in Romantic literature, which is dogged by conscience and a sense that something ought to be done or that something else ought not to have been done. If this literature is not quite "Hebraic," in Arnold's sense, it is hardly "Hellenic" either. Blake, Coleridge, and Shelley have showered us with imperatives – to drive our cart over the bones of the dead, to be loving toward the creatures, to rise like lions in resistance to our oppressors – even as they have declaimed against restrictive notions of duty. Whatever their censures of plodding didacticism, theirs has been a literature with a palpable design on us.

In some important respects Keats modifies these tendencies. "Ode on Melancholy" is a poem exceptional in the Keats oeuvre which ultimately proves the rule: this is a poet who normally shuns the imperative mood. The first two stanzas *are* cast as imperatives: do not give way to Melancholy but know and master her through her contrary, Joy; glut your sorrow on a morning rose; feed on your mistress's eyes whenever the melancholy fit falls upon you. But the third stanza shifts abruptly from the imperative to the indicative, with the quiet, dread declaration that beauty "must die," which overpowers the inflated imperatives of the preceding stanzas. There is a melancholy so

Ward, *John Keats: The Making of a Poet* (New York: Viking Press, 1963; rev. edn. Farrar, Straus, and Giroux, 1986), Stuart M. Sperry, *Keats the Poet* (Princeton: Princeton University Press, 1973), John Middleton Murry, *Keats* (New York: Noonday Press, 1955), Helen Vendler, *The Odes of John Keats* (Cambridge, Mass.: Harvard University Press, 1983), and Morris Dickstein, *Keats and His Poetry: A Study in Development* (Chicago: University of Chicago Press, 1971).

deeply embedded in the nature of things that nothing we do or say will make a difference. The first two stanzas have an element of the theatrical extravagance Keats deplores in Byron. The image of a man imprisoning the hand of his angry mistress while absorbing her ravings conveys an improbable athleticism. Is "Mister John Keats five foot hight," as he describes himself, imaging this scene in the spirit of overcompensatory bluster? Are we not reminded of how infrequently Keats tells us what to do? and has he not implicitly corrected himself in the third stanza?

My larger reading of Keats takes its cue from what has happened in "Ode on Melancholy." Central to his idiom, with its master trope of apostrophe, is the impulse to value. As Helen Vendler has noted, the Odes are attempts to situate and define objects of veneration.[4] They are explorations of what is good. In Keats's life, letters, and poetry, we sense this valuing impulse, directed to what are often regarded as non-moral values (beauty, art, health, nature) and even more to moral values (love, friendship, honesty, generosity, disinterestedness, benevolence, freedom). Like other Romantic writers, Keats tends to moralize non-moral values. "Gusto" – his verbal excess, generosity, and spirited identification with persons, animals, and objects – is one component of the valuing impulse.

I have said that any complete ethical articulation of things must have a concept of value or the good and a concept of obligation and action. Concerning the latter, Keats is considerably less resolute. His Endymion is, as he knows, "led on" by circumstance, hardly acting at all; and Keats implies that only a god such as Apollo is capable of shaping actions to overcome circumstance.

What is to be done? The Hyperion myth as Keats recreates it urges by turns an activist challenge to usurping powers and a resignation to the naked truth that the old order must give way – and no imperative emerges. His poetic world contains a rich plurality of values – preferred objects of desire – without clear or pronounced moral imperatives as to how they might be obtained. To pick up on Yeats's description of Keats in "Ego Dominus Tuus," how are we to stop pressing face and nose to the sweet-shop window and obtain the sweets within? This asymmetry contrasts with Blake, who is urgent in his imperatives even when they qualitatively contradict the values sought, as when he urges insurrection as a means to peace. It contrasts with Byron, who will lament the incommensurability of values one with another and who will praise action for its own sake – ethics merging with an aesthetics of performance even when it does not

[4] *The Odes of John Keats*, 13.

increase the fund of value. The various problematics of action in other Romantic writers do not lead to an easing of such imperatives.

Instead of action thought of as a function of obligation, strong willing, resistance and choice – action that reveals or betrays human character in difficult or pivotal moments – Keats tends to conceive of it anew as what I would term life *activity*. What is the kind of work he will meaningfully pursue, and what kind of daily life will he lead in this pursuit? This theme is prominent in the letters but is to be found in the poetry as well, from *Sleep and Poetry* to *Endymion* to "Ode on Indolence" to *The Fall of Hyperion*. The "ought" regulates daily acts of self-fulfillment and vocation. This is rather like a working man's version of self-realizationism, stripped of Teutonic sublimity. Keats writes, "I feel I must again begin with my poetry – for if I am not in action mind or Body I am in pain"; by "action" he means the activity that constitutes his vocation. He must write poetry and shun social gatherings, where he is "obliged to smother [his] Spirit and look like an Idiot—" (*L* II 12).

Keats's concern with pragmatic and vocational life activity contributes to the demystifying tendency of his writings. Human virtue is tested not in grandiose or transcendent or disembodied contexts requiring expansive, pivotal acts, but in daily experience amidst stubborn circumstance, at last the circumstance that life and beauty must die. He questions several period conceits: that various moral dualisms resolve themselves dialectically, that a firm persuasion a thing is so makes it so, that where there's a will there's a way, that visionary imagination is redemptive, that we can find happiness in a world of circumstantial limitation. For visionary expectation Keats substitutes a pragmatic humanism. He declines both the expectant apocalyptics of Blake and (sometimes) Shelley and the wisdom of Hazlitt and Byron that if a thing is, it is. He will accept limits to vision yet will see some hope in the "advance of intellect." He seeks a balance that seems very like sanity. Yet even he will take on, in *The Fall of Hyperion*, the burden of "curious conscience" beyond what normal human functioning can tolerate.

With these perspectives in mind, I will examine some sets of oppositions or "contraries" that help define Keats's engagement with the ethical. Never an aesthete, he confronts ethical questions directly throughout his brief career. His corrective to others of the visionary company is hardly to escape from the ethical dimension that haunts Mariners and Cains, but to focus it through the perspectives of immanent value and life activity.

The principal oppositions I am considering are: (1) act and activity;

(2) nihilism ("nothingness") and immanent value; (3) happiness and the growth of identity; and (4) aesthetic disinterestedness and moral disinterestedness. Interpreters of Keats characteristically proceed in terms of oppositional constructs, so vigorously does he fore-ground them in poetry and letters. His career can be read, I propose, as a deeply considered shifting of emphasis from one set of moral possibilities – act, transcendence, happiness, and aesthetic disin-terestedness – to another – activity, immanent value, identity, and moral disinterestedness. So read, the tendency is away from an optimistic voluntaristic ethics based on a high estimate of human power, in which happiness is directly proportional to virtue, in which ends answer to human desire, and in which the poet is privileged by the freedom and power of imagination. This set of possibilities is one formulation of the optimistic Romantic humanism sometimes associ-ated with Blake and Shelley (but which, as we have seen, is severely qualified in them as well). The tendency in Keats is instead toward a pragmatic ethical humanism that still retains something of the Roman-tic humanist perspective. The paradigm of the moral agent is nothing so grandiose as Blake's Milton or Albion or Hazlitt's Napoleon or Keats's own Greek gods; it becomes instead the worker, whether personified Autumn in the granary or the poet drafting poems at his desk. Work is the productive introduction of value into the world. The compensation for circumstantial limitation, suffering, and the loss of happiness is the increased sense of identity. And as one who works for others, not himself, the poet is one whose powers are a duty, not a privilege.

More symmetrically than other Romantic authors, Keats fleshes out two sets of ethical possibility, and sees renunciation of one for the other as requiring a slow series of tragic recognitions – recognitions that build on Wordsworth in ways unforeseen by the poet of human suffering.[5]

Immanent value and the nihilism of transcendence

The cheat of transcendent experience is a pervasive, oft-noted theme in Keats's poetry. A grim justice is implied insofar as he treats the will to transcendence as ethical violation. Endymion's evanescent vision of Cynthia leaves him grief-stricken, and though in the end he is

---

[5] This shift is not strictly sequential, since Keats can entertain two or more possibilities simultaneously. Nor is it strictly chronological, since many of his insights are hinted as early as *Sleep and Poetry* and *Endymion*. But in general the shift occurs later into Keats's brief career.

rewarded by a *deus ex machina* for his heart-ache, the poem cautions
against visionary yearnings. Reluctantly deciding to settle for a mere
Indian maid, Endymion senses he has previously "loved a nothing," a
"dream." He has been "presumptuous against love, against the sky, /
Against all elements, against the tie / Of mortals each to each" (IV 638–
41). Then he utters what we might have thought would be the final
moral of the piece:

> There never lived a mortal man, who bent
> His appetite beyond his natural sphere,
> But starv'd and died.   (ED IV 646–8)

Keats wishes Endymion to have it both ways, however. The Indian
maid turns out to be an incarnation of Cynthia, who whisks him
happily off.

We should approach spiritual love through earthly love, one might
blandly conclude from this benevolent deception, except that a problem remains for those of us with little hope of being transfigured into
the empyrean. I am reminded of E. T. A. Hoffmann's "The Golden
Pot" ("Der goldne Topf," 1814), in which the bungling, sensitive
Anselmus wins the fabulous Serpentina and is removed to the exalted
spiritual freehold of Atlantis. This residence is so removed from our
own "paltriness of existence" that the tale implies happiness cannot be
integrated into human life. The moral of Hoffmann's tale, like Keats's,
is a disquieting one. Having been "spiritualized," Endymion and
Cynthia vanish, leaving Endymion's sister walking home alone
"through the gloomy wood in wonderment," condemned to terra
firma. We must ask whether Endymion's new status has anything in
common with "human life," earlier described as

> the war, the deeds,
> The disappointment, the anxiety,
> Imagination's struggles, far and nigh,
> All human; bearing in themselves this good,
> That they are still the air, the subtile food,
> To make us feel existence, and to shew
> How quiet death is.   (ED II 153–9)

Transcendent vision, upon fading, makes human life all the more
unbearable and ironically merges with nihilism. This recognition
informs the structure of Keats's greater poetry, though it is not a
preoccupation of the generally more optimistic early letters. Hazlitt
cautions against the visionary groping of a Shelley or Robert Owen,
which sets one up for a grand disappointment. And in *Sleep and Poetry*
Keats writes that when the "visions all are fled," a "sense of real things

comes doubly strong, / And, like a muddy stream, would bear along / My soul to nothingness" (155–9). Visionary experience proves calamitous and devaluing. At the opening of *Endymion* the poet says, in what may be his single most important line, that true beauty instead "bind[s] us to the earth," prompting us to value earth as earth, not devalue it as mud. Beauty and transcendence are thus importantly differentiated in Keats, the former promoting value, the latter, as a bogus form of the sublime, undercutting it. His major corrective to the Romantic will to value is to image value normatively in figures of healthy immanence, not debilitating transcendence. His career from *Endymion* to the ode "To Autumn" is a perilous quest for a rejuvenated immanence of values.

A desultory verse epistle to J. H. Reynolds (25 March 1818), which in its early lines expresses the wish to render in language an "Enchanted Castle" for his ailing friend, ends in confrontation with the ways of dark imagination. Transcendent vision converts dream romance to nightmare. Imagining the horrors of predatory sea creatures, the poet sees "too distinct into the core / Of an eternal fierce destruction" (96–7), when he could have been enjoying himself at the beach:

> is it that imagination brought
> Beyond its proper bound, yet still confined,—
> Lost in a sort of purgatory blind,
> Cannot refer to any standard law
> Of either earth or heaven?—It is a flaw
> In happiness to see beyond our bourne—
> It forces us in summer skies to mourn:
> It spoils the singing of the nightingale. (78–85)

Imagination brought beyond its proper bounds imposes on and devalues the world at hand.

Keats repeatedly dramatizes in binary form the threat of transcendent vision: vision indicts reality with confinement and "leaden-eyed despairs," reality indicts vision with cheat and illusion. There is no easy way out of this mutual indictment; vision and reality both make a strong claim, and Keatsian narrative often portrays the failure of the speaker or protagonist to resolve it. As is well known, many of his great poems – "La Belle Dame Sans Merci," "Ode to a Nightingale," *Lamia*, and "Bright Star" – share this binary form. *The Fall of Hyperion* will resolve it – urging the immanence of value on earth – but only by increasing the moral responsibility of the poet, as minister of value, beyond his powers of performance. Not until "To Autumn" does Keats portray a resolution that would temper the unquiet heart.

Beyond the Pleasure Thermometer

Keats's most overt and sustained efforts at ethical formulation before *The Fall of Hyperion* are to be found in three well-known texts: the "Pleasure Thermometer" lines of *Endymion* (I 777–842), the "Chamber of Maiden-Thought" letter to J. H. Reynolds of 3 May 1818, and the "Vale of Soul-making" letter to George and Georgiana Keats of 21 April 1819. In all three texts he contrives a programmatic dialectical structure that might answer to the binary form and frustrated dialectic of several of his major poems. That these three texts *are* pointedly ethical is significant in itself and insufficiently noted. Keats the sensate poet keeps always in mind the imponderables, and they are for him less cosmological, religious, epistemological, or even aesthetic than they are ethical. These three key texts address, respectively, the questions of moral value, of moral knowledge, and of human identity – and the relationship of all three to happiness.

"Wherein lies happiness?" asks young Endymion, who without mulling it over very much answers his own question. Keats thought Endymion's answer a "regular stepping of the Imagination towards a Truth," because it "set before me at once the gradations of Happiness even like a kind of Pleasure Thermometer—" (*L* I 218). Endymion sets forth a hierarchy of values, beginning with a compressed account of the origins of music, poetry and myth in human responses to the natural world. In a canceled line, Keats writes that pleasure is felt in the very act of "blending": "that delight is the most treasureable / That makes the richest Alchymy." The lines he substitutes are less clear but make much the same point. Human beings are altered or "alchemiz'd" when they blend with nature and other human beings, in experiences of nature, art, myth, friendship, and love. All five of these entail "a sort of oneness" and thus a heightening of pleasure – a "blending pleasure-able." Keats's optimism here – and it will be qualified greatly – is that any heightening of the sense of being is a transmutation experienced as pleasure, a notion with analogues in Spinoza.

The Pleasure Thermometer metaphor suggests that happiness is correlative to these other values as a symptomatic index. Pleasure and happiness are resultants of the pursuit of other values; they are hardly the only values, and they are qualitatively differentiated, unlike their fate in Bentham's felicific calculus. Keats is no hedonist.

Of special interest in the passage is the poet's hierarchical discrimination of values. There are "richer entanglements, enthralments far / More self-destroying" (destructive of selfhood in a positive way), richer indeed than those of nature, art, and myth. These enthrallments

390

lead "by degrees / To the chief intensity," which is a moral state of being – friendship and, more so, love. As the ultimate "blending," love preempts lesser values of politics and "this poor endeavour after fame" – lines self-directed. The point I would emphasize is that even for the younger Keats moral values have ascendency over values of nature, myth, religion, statesmanship, music, and poetry. They represent the "chief intensities." Through Endymion, Keats voices neither hedonism nor a religion of beauty but an ethical humanism based on the idea that nourishment of the self through virtuous activity evolves into a pleasurable "self-destroying" that somehow spreads "the world with benefits." Hereafter, Keats remains the humanist, but a greatly chastened one who doubts that virtue is so happily served by pleasure or that it is necessarily so beneficent.

The Eve of St. Agnes (1819) also affirms moral values over others and anchors them more than *Endymion* in the world of sense. One antithetical category, religious values, is associated with cold, denial, penance, and death. Another, political values, produces the obstacle of two warring families that love must overcome. Love also supersedes other moral values themselves, such as fair play. Jack Stillinger's observation is that Porphyro is not a little cunning in his seduction of Madeline.[6] But in view of the "gradations of Happiness" and their precise correlations with virtue, I think he acts morally on Keats's terms despite the cunning. Love's beneficence is guaranteed; as Endymion might say, love overrides whatever "human serpentry" Porphyro has employed. The "slime / Left by men-slugs" is purified into the "solution sweet" of the lovers' carnal embrace; they are "alchemiz'd" by love in a "blending pleasureable." Hierarchy obtains within the scale of moral values itself as well as with respect to other systems of value.

Keats's belief in the ascendency of the ethical persists after *Endymion*, but his inquiry into the grounds of moral knowledge proves sobering. In April of 1818 he announces his intention to John Taylor, the publisher, of retiring from the world to engage in a disciplined pursuit of "knowledge." "I have been hovering for some time between an exquisite sense of the luxurious and a love for Philosophy," and now he will choose philosophy. Probably he means by "philosophy" a general search for wisdom not restricted to philosophy per se as developed by Plato, Locke, and Hume; but he wishes to undertake some heavy reading even so and thinks of asking Hazlitt "the best metaphysical road I can take" (*L* I 273–4). Hazlitt's *Essay on the Principles*

---

[6] "The Hoodwinking of Madeline: Scepticism in *The Eve of St. Agnes*," in *Keats: A Collection of Critical Essays*, ed. Walter Jackson Bate (Englewood Cliffs, N. J.: Prentice-Hall, 1964), 71–90.

of Human Action (1805) is listed by Charles Brown in 1821 as among Keats's books, and Hazlitt with his suspicion of metaphysics would be consulted as a moral philosopher.[7] Keats thus conforms to the pattern among Romantic authors from Coleridge to Hazlitt to Shelley of wishing early on to explore philosophical questions, especially moral ones, as preparation for a literary career. Like Coleridge, who retired in 1797 to a cottage in Somersetshire to devote his thoughts to the "foundations of religion and morals," Keats has in mind the somewhat moldy idea of anchoritic apprenticeship in wisdom. It is only a week after his letter to Taylor that he writes to Reynolds the "Chamber of Maiden-Thought" letter, the first fruit of this new resolve to give "thought" its due, in contravention of the antinomy he had cheerfully set forth in a letter of 22 November 1817 to Benjamin Bailey, favoring a life of "Sensations" over a life of Thoughts."

Blake and Shelley have denied the place of skepticism in ethical inquiry. Blake writes, "The truth & certainty of Virtue & Honesty i.e Inspiration needs no one to prove it it is Evident as the Sun & Moon He who stands doubting of what he intends whether it is Virtuous or Vicious knows not what Virtue means" (*PWB* 613–14); Shelley writes that "metaphysical science will be treated merely so far as a source of negative truth; while morality will be considered as a science respecting which we can arrive at positive conclusions" (*SPR* 182). But Keats holds to a skeptical view. While affirming the desirability of moral knowledge, he fears it is difficult to come by. In his verse epistle to Reynolds, he had dared not "philosophize":

> Oh never will the prize,
> High reason, and the lore of good and ill,
> Be my award. Things cannot to the will
> Be settled, but they tease us out of thought.   (74–7)

In the Chamber of Maiden-Thought letter, he still affirms, in effect, that "Things cannot to the will / Be settled."

The three stages of human life he outlines in the familiar letter have a resemblance to Blake's Lambeth dialectic of innocence, experience, and higher innocence, but some notable differences make Keats closer to Wordsworth, whom he is interpreting, than to Blake. Human life he likens to "a large Mansion of Many Apartments," only two of which can be described. The first, the state of innocence, is the "infant or thoughtless Chamber," which we leave reluctantly, even though the next chamber, "Maiden-Thought," has an invitingly "bright

---

[7] *The Keats Circle: Letters and Papers, 1816–1878*, ed. Hyder Rollins (Cambridge, Mass.; Harvard University Press, 1965), I, 254.

appearance." This alters the rite of passage in Blake's *The Book of Thel* (1789), where the experiential world has so horrifying an appearance that Thel is too timid to enter. In Keats the world of experience seems to beckon brightly. We leave childhood in adolescent eagerness, with the risk more of disappointment than psychic wounding.

In the Chamber of Maiden-Thought, we experience for a time the pleasure of transmutation described by Endymion. Keats's "blending pleasureable" is the precise reverse of Blake's violent, even rapacious blending. The more knowledge we take on, however, the more we know "the World is full of Misery and Heartbreak, Pain, Sickness and Oppression." As in Endymion's progressive alchemy, Keats describes stages of development but no longer assumes that ontological heightening is felt as pleasure. He confirms the reading of Wordsworth as a tragic sensibility, "Tintern Abbey" as covert self-elegy. The Chamber of Maiden-Thought has doors leading out, but they all lead to dark passages:

We see not the ballance of good and evil. We are in a Mist—*We* are now in that state—We feel the 'burden of the Mystery,' To this point was Wordsworth come, as far as I can conceive when he wrote 'Tintern Abbey' and it seems to me that his Genius is explorative of those dark passages. (*L* I 281)

Wordsworth's sad perplexity contrasts with Milton's philosophical and religious certainty and his "apparently less anxiety for Humanity." Wordsworth, who "martyrs himself to the human heart," is more the humanist than Milton is. Keats argues as an historicist: even the "mightiest minds" are subdued by Providence "to the service of the time being." The author of *Paradise Lost* lived at a time when Protestantism was liberating Great Britain from the vulgar superstition of Catholicism but when Christian dogma still prevailed, without its source and sanction in the human heart – in an independent, humanly sanctioned ethic.

The "general and gregarious advance of intellect" that Keats affirms is thus ironically marked by a passage from intellectual and moral certainty to uncertainty. His moral skepticism is yet another check on transcendence. We cannot know which dark passage would lead us beyond the world of suffering and limitation. Our ethical recognitions are as time-bound as Milton's, but we know how little we know. The allegory is consistent with the value/act dichotomy we see in Keats elsewhere. The "bright appearance" and "pleasant wonders" we first register in the Chamber of Maiden-Thought are analogous to the value-rich world that answers for a time to imagination and desire. But our growing awareness of suffering begins to dim our sense of those values, and the means of pursuing them turn to dark passages, leaving us puzzled as to what is to be done. Like Wordsworth, Keats expresses a chastened humanism here. Value remains human-centered, but there are checks on our moral power and our ability to settle things for the will. Intensity is now linked more with suffering than with happiness. Keats's response to this entrapment will not be to argue a leap to a world elsewhere but to find within the chamber of suffering itself a principle of compensation – the growth of identity.[8]

In the letter to the George Keats's describing the "Vale of Soul-making," written 21 April 1819, just before the May in which he wrote the great Odes, Keats goes beyond the question of moral knowledge to the question of identity. Rather than dwell on the baffling fact of human suffering, he now speculates as to its uses, in an overt attempt to exculpate the way things are. As in Endymion's speech to Poena, he begins with reflections on happiness, this time not its nature relative to a scale of value but the degree to which anyone can hope to obtain it. He can "imagine" that through the improvement of man's estate, with the applied intelligence "of a seldom appearing Socrates," humankind might approach an ultimate happiness resembling Paradise, to be thwarted with the approach of death, which would then loom as an all the more unhappy prospect. But he immediately pronounces this optimism an imagining only: "in truth I do not at all believe in this sort of perfectibility," because at whatever stage of ascent up such a felicific ladder we would confront "a fresh set of annoyances" (L II 101). Like Wordsworth, Keats knows nature can assume the inhospitable force of circumstance, and we can no more achieve "earthly Happiness" than we can do away with "the sands of Africa, Whirlpools and volcanoes." Just as a rose cannot escape "a cold wind, a hot sun," so we cannot escape the circumstances or "worldly elements" that limit our happiness.

Keats then outlines a quasi-secular theodicy. As in the meditation on the Chamber of Maiden-Thought, he propounds a triadic structure.

---

[8] Finishing the letter to Reynolds abruptly, Keats writes, "Your third Chamber of Life shall be a lucky and a gentle one—stored with the wine of love—and the bread of Friendship—" (L I 282–3). He has already said that we cannot prophesy beyond our own moment in history; the future is unspecified and contentless. Keats rarely assumes prophetic knowledge. The prospect of a third chamber of friendship and love is a rhetorical blessing he hurriedly bestows on Reynolds in bringing the letter to a close. Although the blessing echoes Endymion's hierarchy of moral value culminating in friendship and love, the third chamber is not given serious mental furniture and does not qualify as a dialectical upgrading of the previous two. Keats never presumes on his own happiness and can speak of it only in the abstract as the possession of a friend.

Instead of describing stages of moral knowledge, he now describes the structural components of the process that results in identity:

> This is effected by three grand materials acting the one upon the other for a series of years—These three Materials are the *Intelligence*—the *human heart* (as distinguished from intelligence or Mind) and the *World* or *Elemental space* suited for the proper action of *Mind and Heart* on each other for the purpose of forming the *Soul* or *Intelligence destined to possess the sense of Identity*.   (*L* II 102)

Each person enters the world with a faculty of intelligence devoid of the personal identity which it must acquire as its entelechy. The intelligence gains its full realization as identity by interacting with the "Heart," which is the "seat of human Passions" and the faculty that suffers the world's circumstances. The intelligence, in a metaphor of feeding so common in Keats, "sucks its identity" from the suffering human heart, which is its "medium" linking it to the world. Keats compounds these tropes with a pedagogical metaphor, in which the world is likened to a school, the heart to a hornbook, and human identity to a child who has learned to read.

The moral skepticism induced by the Chamber of Maiden-Thought, wherein we do not see "the ballance of good and evil" and wherein we no longer find a correlation between virtue and happiness, is answered to now with a postulate of purpose: the burden of the mystery and of human suffering is instrumental to a further good, the evolution of human identity.[9]

Keats's formulation is obviously dialectical: identity is the new emergent from an interplay of two forces, intelligence and heart. It

---

[9] Keats's letter on Soul-making is quoted at length (after a transcription in A. C. Bradley's *Oxford Lectures*) by the English neo-Hegelian, Bernard Bosanquet (1848–1923), in *The Value and Destiny of the Individual* (1913; London: Macmillan, 1923), 63–6. Bosanquet adopts Keats's phrase, "Soul-making," in his discussion of the development of individuality through adaptation to circumstances. "Soul-making . . . is the leading function of the finite universe. Souls are cast and moulded by the externality of nature, and of other finite souls" (p. 16); "the troubles and adventures of the finite creature have the same root as its value, for both are inherent in the spirit that seeks the whole. And, moreover, these very troubles and adventures are instrumental, through shattering the given, to that very awareness of self-recognition in which the nature of the self-transcendence stands revealed" (p. 19). Bosanquet's use of Keats is grudging, probably because of polar opposition in their concepts of identity and individuality. For Keats identity as product of Soul-making is what makes each finite intelligence unique; Soul-making works toward greater and greater differentiation of individuals. But in Bosanquet's Hegelian scheme, individuality is achieved only when the finite intelligence is fully absorbed into the Absolute, in a denial of mere subjectivity and the personal self. The state is a fuller realization of individuality than finite persons are. Bosanquet is accordingly hostile to the liberalism implicit in Keats's account.

supplants pleasure or happiness as the validating consequence of moral engagement. Keats has in effect declared the Pleasure Thermometer obsolete. I think his conception of personal identity, as gleaned from this letter and others, as well as from depiction of persons in the poetry, is the most sophisticated of the Romantic authors. It is a measure of his modernity that for him the concept of identity must accommodate both permanence and change, and that it has a physical as well as mental basis. Permanence is seen in the initial "spark" of undifferentiated "intelligence" that is ours at birth, as well as in what Keats calls "an unchangeable attribute" (L II 387) that immediately defines a person or object as that particular entity and not another. But he also sees identity as developmental: intelligence converts into identity gradually through experience of the world. This more empirical emphasis can lead to the serial or bundle self of Hume, and Keats probably does have in mind Hazlitt's assertion in the 1805 *Essay* that "the individual is never the same for two moments together." Keats insists therefore that personal identity is a matter of continuity amid change:

We are like the relict garments of a Saint: the same and not the same: for the careful Monks patch it and patch it: till there's not a thread of the original garment left, and still they show it for St Anthony's shirt. This is the reason why men who had been bosom friends, on being separated for any number of years, afterwards meet coldly, neither of them knowing why—The Fact is they are both altered—Men who live together have a silent moulding and influencing power over each other—They interassimulate. 'T is an uneasy thought that in seven years the same hands cannot greet each other again. All this may be obviated by a wilful and dramatic exercise of our Minds towards each other.

(L II 208–9)

This jocoserious passage suggests both the tenuousness of identity and the fact that one can will to hold on to it, to intensify it. Keats thinks that he has perhaps lost one aspect of his identity ("poetic ardour and fire") but that he will "substitute a more thoughtful and quiet power," and in this sense, one infers, continue with his own "Soul-making."

The physical basis of identity, in addition to the mental, is explicitly voiced by Keats. (Until the present century, theoreticians tended to limit personal identity to mental criteria, especially memory.) To his brother and sister-in-law, George and Georgiana Keats, now living in America, he writes:

From the time you left me, our friends say I have altered completely—am not the same person—perhaps in this letter I am for in a letter one takes up one's

396

existence from the time we last met— I dare say you have altered also—eve[r]y man does—Our bodies every seven years are completely fresh-materiald—.

(*L* II 208)

He had earlier emphasized the extent to which one's sense of another's identity depends on physical attributes. Those whom he does not know well would seem less present to him than his brother and sister-in-law; these others "would be so much the farth[er] from me in proportion as their identity was less impressed upon me," but his relatives have impressed themselves upon him more lastingly, both by their manner of thinking and feeling and by their physical manner of "walking, standing, sauntering, sitting down, laughing" (*L* II 5). This image of identities "pressing" on him recurs frequently in the letters, often in contexts that suggest a fear of engulfment and loss of his own identity through the physical proximity of others.

Perhaps it goes without saying that identity in Keats's poetry is manifested in highly physical imagery. Whether he is portraying a human being such as Madeline or gods and demi-gods such as Saturn, Moneta, and Lamia, he incarnates the identity of his characters. The theme of metamorphosis, seen in Cynthia's incarnation in an Indian maid or Lamia's change of form from serpent to seductress, poses identity as a puzzle, and suggests that continuity of consciousness is its *sine qua non*. But unlike Coleridge, whose Geraldine can espy "the bodiless dead," Keats cannot imagine a disembodied consciousness; identity must include some bodily form or other. A qualitative difference between humans and gods in Keats's poetry is that the latter are better able to maintain identity freed of continuity of the body.

Experientially acquired, personal identity is in large part made up of our idiosyncrasies, our particular "manner" of doing this or that, our accidental properties and props, our "Ways and Manners and actions" (*L* II 5). Keats does not insist on some Blakean–Coleridgean idea of unity as the key to identity, which is not so transcendental an entity. He also makes a strong linkage between identity and something as non-metaphysical as vocation. His dying brother Tom's "identity presses upon me so all day" that he wishes to escape the sickroom and take up composition in order to purge himself of his brother's image: "If I think of fame or poetry it seems a crime to me, and yet I must do so or suffer—" (*L* I 369). At social gatherings he feels himself "surrounded with unpleasant human identities; who press upon one just enough to prevent one getting into a lazy position; and not enough to interest or rouse one . . . I do not know what I did on monday—nothing—nothing—nothing—" (*L* II 77). The fear that engulfment by the identities of others will interfere with his own vocational identity as poet extends also to love. Committed to the life of writing, he resists for a time the encroachment of love in the person of Fanny Brawne. "Blending" is not always a "pleasureable" prospect, and at the very least Keats discovers he is no Endymion, Fanny Brawne no Cynthia.

In sum, identity is a *process*, not a fixed entity, for Keats. Its primary criterion is growth and retention of consciousness ("Intelligence") in a world resistant to desire ("Heart"). It is also double-edged: a reflexive consciousness that registers one's difference and vulnerability, and a consciousness of world (other selves, human society, nature, and circumstance). Identity emerges from the difference between self and world that is experienced as suffering or "proving." The physical component of identity – its secondary criterion – is, I suggest, the concretized Keatsian "Heart" as body. The body desires, suffers, and disintegrates, but it thereby teaches us (as a Hornbook) the human meaning of time. The body is instrumental to growth of identity – as efficient to final cause – at the same time as it announces its own temporality and therefore the precariousness of the identity it feeds. Our physical manifold of characteristics – our way of sauntering and sitting down, our face, our hands – is that portion of identity perceived by the five senses and is accordingly the social principle, the means by which we can become aware of other identities. It is what we make love to or shun, often perceived as the pressure of otherness. Although time is entropic, the human experience of it can – for a time – lead to the higher degree of organization that Keats calls identity. One can will identity through "dramatic exercise" of mind, but the body – the cells of which are replaced every seven years – is a constant reminder that all hearts stop. Identity is thus a human challenge to time. At best it is the willed continuity and increased organization of the human in the face of discontinuity and death. Keats sees vocational activity – work – as the efficient organization of human time; it directs the growth of identity, instead of letting identity occur as it occurs through passive, patient suffering, or through "indolence." So conceived, identity is for Keats an intrinsic moral value of the first order, and one that we can in fact achieve over the years through purposeful activity, without necessarily engaging in dynamic moral acts and decisions. It is not some transcendent ideal always beyond our grasp.

In the letter on Soul-making, Keats makes no moral pleas and does not take on the role of prophet (which would not have been out of keeping in a letter to a younger brother). He invests the letter with no "ought" at all. He describes the way things are, not what ought to be done about them. Nowhere does he say we have a *duty* to increase the sense of identity or strive against circumstance. There is a sophistication in this, since most self-realizationist theories flounder on an is/ought conflation in urging that we become what in a sense we already are. And, as Kant points out, what is only meritorious cannot be morally commanded. Soul-making happens to us as we live our daily suffering lives in a state of watchfulness and vocational purpose. It is anchored more in activity than acts. Keats assumes that identity, as the result of "provings and alterations and perfectionings," is its own reward. If he implies a nominal theism in the letter, his redemptive scheme should not "affront our reason and humanity" with talk of some ultimate reward, he hopes (*L* II 103). His perspective on suffering and evil is this-worldly and ethical.

What we have seen in these three texts is Keats's declining to think of dialectic as leading to transcendence of humanly possible ethical categories, the comings and goings of daily human life. Instead, dialectic leads to an immanence of value, ethical and aesthetic. The implicit model is Aristotelian entelechy, not Platonic transcendence. We can confirm now that *Endymion* is a poem that loses sight of its own wisdom, announced in Book I, in ultimately perpetuating the false dualism of transcendence and earth.

Keats is better able to speak of these developmental schemes in an expository format (Endymion's Pleasure Thermometer speech shares something of this format with the two letters) than he is able to realize them in either the greater poetry or the conduct of his own life. In the former the agony of irreconcilables is apt to prevail, and in the latter the values of love, vocation, and identity prove torments, as if he were being punished for the very generosity of his will to value.

Buffeting with circumstance

The letter on Soul-making resonates with Keats's commentary on the circumstances of his own life. A few months earlier, apropos of a quarrel between Benjamin Haydon and Leigh Hunt, he had written that "the best of Men have but a portion of good in them – a kind of spiritual yeast in their frames which creates the ferment of existence – by which a Man is propell'd to act and strive and buffet with Circumstance" (*L* I 120). Keats's poems and letters up to his final illness manifest a generous portion of that spiritual yeast; we feel the ferment of existence there. His is never a mindless exuberance, and he can be by turns sarcastic, bitter, frustrated, grief-stricken, jealous. Several months before his death he knows he has already been defeated by circumstance. It is a tale more poignant than Shelley's, because Shelley seems, in his own extraordinary ferment, to pursue a dark fate, even creating the circumstances by means of which he can submit to it the sooner. But Keats is a victim.

He tends to speak of the conduct of his own life in terms of whether he is active or passive, energetic or indolent, in the face of circumstance. The difference between Endymion and Apollo is so defined:

> In Endymion I think you may have many bits of the deep and sentimental cast—the nature of *Hyperion* will lead me to treat it in a more naked and grecian Manner—and the march of passion and endeavour will be undeviating—and one great contrast between them will be—that the Hero of the written tale being mortal is led on, like Buonaparte, by circumstance; whereas the Apollo in Hyperion being a fore-seeing God will shape his actions like one.   (*L* I 207)

This remark points up the restraints Keats sees on human freedom: if even Buonaparte is led on by circumstance and if one must be a fore-seeing god to shape actions, what freedom of movement can be won by an infirm young poet or the rest of us? Keats worries that the spiritual yeast enabling him to strive and buffet with circumstance, and the fever compelling him to write poems, are squandered to little purpose. He does not shape his actions or even get on with his life activity of writing. At the end of his annus mirabilis he laments that another year has passed with no accomplishment. Yet among the Romantics he has the clearest notion of what he wishes to be: an English poet of noble fame. This resolute sense of vocation, combined with a low estimate of poems actually written, makes him feel sometimes like a "dead lump" (*L* II 179). His is a skilled workman's bad conscience at non-performance of a craft, to be distinguished from Coleridgean bad conscience, which results from a more generalized non-performance of the whole range of life's obligations.

Keats is tormented by his own brand of work ethic, whose roots are not in Adam's sin or in some notion that we should pay our way as we go. It has none of Carlyle's apocalyptic urgency or Fichte's austerity. Keats pursues excellence in a particular craft for love of that craft. Derelict professionalism gives him the feeling of being nothing at all, of having lost his identity. (The pleasurable loss of identity in the actual practice of poetry is another matter, to be discussed shortly.) Unlike Wordsworth, who in *The Prelude* mingles pursuit of poetic vocation with almost every other aspect of self-development – to the point of rarely mentioning his special ambition after the first 304 lines – Keats more single-mindedly addresses the question of "why I should be a Poet more than other Men,—seeing how great a thing it is,—how great things are to be gained by it—" (*L* I 139). To be sure, poetry requires powers other than what carpentry and bricklaying require—it requires both "Sensation" and "Thought" and much more—but it is a determinate vocation that answers to the indeterminate ethical desire that plagues Romantic sensibility. Once again the moral realist, Keats knows what he would be: the particular content of his own identity is in large part that of poet. But this gain in clarity is scuttled by what he takes to be so little evidence of accomplishment.

Since he perceives the life of poetry as a trial requiring the greatest diligence and ambition, strategies of evasion prove tempting. He entertains in September 1819 the idea of a career in political journalism (*L* II 176–8). "Now an act has three parts—to act, to do, and to perform—," he writes. At last he will set out to do something. But the sardonic lifting from *Hamlet's* gravedigger hints he might be digging his own grave. He never rids himself of the fear that, having failed to climb Mount Parnassus, he has been fusting wholly unused.

"Ode on Indolence" (May or early June, 1819), paradoxically a poem of active renunciation, finds the poet attempting to withdraw from vocational pressure through a different tactic. In a languorous mood he banishes love, ambition, and poetry. The poem reverses "Ode on Melancholy" in shifting from the indicative to the imperative mood. But the imperative is directed against the same experiential seeking that "Ode on Melancholy" urges in its second stanza. He now agrees with Byron on the futility of the will's exertions and of ambition: "it springs / From a man's little heart's short fever-fit." In a letter of 9 June 1819, he writes, "I have been very idle lately, very averse to writing; both from the overpowering idea of our dead poets and from abatement of my own love of fame" (*L* II 116). And in a letter the after-perusal of which may have prompted "Ode on Indolence," he describes the indifference to pain or pleasure as the "only happiness." This state of mind results when "the fibres of the brain are relaxed in common with the rest of the body" (*L* II 78–9). In one of the few instances where Keats invokes the idea of harmony of functions, therefore, it is at a reduced energy level, quite unBlakean in character. "Ode on Indolence" represents a withdrawal from all pressures on the ego, all annoyances from without, all pressings on his own identity by the identities of others.[10] His only wish is that the shadowy vestiges of earlier wishes would disappear, leaving him in a state of "nothingness."

We have seen that Endymion's Pleasure Thermometer speech, the letter on the Chamber of Maiden-Thought, and the letter on Soul-making constitute a realist check on any flight from ethical categories

[10] See *L* I 173–4 on Wordsworth's poem "Gipsies" (1807) and on Hazlitt's critique (IV 45–6n); also *L* I 231–2.

into visionary unreality. But whatever optimism they retain about the progressive march of intellect and endeavor is itself checked by Keats's commentary on his own life. For him, happiness proves illusory, identity gained through suffering proves tenuous where it is not repellent, his vocation seems to languish, and love is a torment, made all the more so when the problem becomes not love's interference with vocation but its probable eclipse by early death. Having said what he could on behalf of providential justice, Keats still smarts at the injustice of it all.

These struggles certainly argue the insufficiency of the ethical. But we do not find Keats assenting to political, metaphysical, or doctrinal extenuations. He embraces no utopian or millennial or apocalyptic views that might transcend moral categories. And poetry or art remains immersed for him in the ethical. In the sad last year and a half of his short life, Keats did not turn to religion, whatever his religious sense of things. His friend, the young painter Joseph Severn, gives an account of Keats's nightmarish final days, when the force of circumstance did its brutal work, and he fell into resentment, despair, and terror. Severn writes, "This noble fellow lying on the bed—is dying in horror—no kind hope smoothing down his suffering—no philosophy—no religion to support him—." There is no alternative value system, philosophical or religious, to support this moral realist in his final days. He cries, "—this last cheap comfort—which every rogue and fool have—is deny'd me in my last moments—why is this—O! I have serv'd every one with my utmost good—yet why is this—I cannot understand this" (L II 368). In the end his integrity of mind resists any hope of a deus ex machina and any false consolation for the infamous way he has been served.

The original sin in poetry

In view of Keats's skeptical treatment of many leading ideas of the period, what moral powers does he grant poetry and what is the responsibility of the poet? In *Hyperion* Oceanus tells the defeated Titans they should take consolation that " 'tis the eternal law/ That first in beauty should be first in might" (II 228–9). The image of Keats wasting from tuberculosis in Rome obtrudes as if to give the lie to Oceanus. But Keats has never maintained that beauty-making poets attain power over circumstance more than the rest of us. The instance of Chatterton ("a Poet's death") early on corrected such an illusion. The "eternal law," of rather parochial application, seems to privilege only the most beautiful of the gods. Otherwise, Keats holds a more skeptical view of the correlation of beauty with power. Shelley's notion that poets are unacknowledged legislators is by his standards vainglorious. Only in one of his earliest poems does he come close to Shelley's view of the influence poetry has on culture and politics. These lines, written in August of 1816 to his brother George, are uncharacteristic, in more ways than one, of the later Keats:

> The patriot shall feel
> My stern alarum, and unsheathe his steel;
> Or, in the senate thunder out my numbers
> To startle princes from their easy slumbers.
> The sage will mingle with each moral theme
> My happy thoughts sententious; he will teem
> With lofty periods when my verses fire him,
> And then I'll stoop from heaven to inspire him.

We catch him writing these stentorian absurdities late into his "Leigh Hunt period," when he is otherwise inclined to an effete "poesie of luxuries." The poetry of luxuries and the poetry of grit turn out to be false alternatives in literary pragmatics. From *Sleep and Poetry* to *The Fall of Hyperion* Keats speaks of poetry's gentler role – of "balm," of "friend," of "physician to all men." Poetry has moral power, but not the kind that shapes history or even changes the course of individual lives. Instead the poet administers the balm of immanent value.

The opening lines of *Endymion* anticipate *The Fall of Hyperion's* concept of poet as physician, an especially telling metaphor in Keats, who gave up a career in medicine to become a poet.[11] The main pragmatic function of poetry is not in moving us to a course of action or refining our sensibilities; rather, it is in healing: poetry has the power to dispel gloom, to give us "health, and quiet breathing." The therapy of beauty, whether natural or created, is non-mystical. Beauty, we have seen,

> bind[s] us to the earth,
> Spite of despondence, of the inhuman dearth
> Of noble natures, of the gloomy days,
> Of all the unhealthy and o'er-darkened ways
> Made for our searching: yes, in spite of all,
> Some shape of beauty moves away the pall
> From our dark spirits. (*ED* I 7–13)

---

[11] An entire volume has recently been devoted to this subject: Donald C. Goellnicht, *The Poet-Physician: Keats and Medical Science* (Pittsburgh: University of Pittsburgh Press, 1984).

A therapy presumes a pathology. As in so many of Keats's poems, bright vision implicates disease, deprivation, and gloom.

"Ode on a Grecian Urn" (1819) struggles, stanza by stanza, toward this view of the uses of art. In what way is the Urn a "friend to man"? How does it answer to time's destructiveness ("unravish'd" implies its contrary of ravished, *our* trees lose their leaves, *our* generation shall be wasted in old age), the impermanence of the passions (*our* love does not stay forever warm), the exhaustion of the imagination (*our* melodists eventually weary), the agony of the desiring state ("breathing *human* passion" leaves "a heart high-sorrowful and cloy'd, / A burning forehead, and a parching tongue")? The Urn, instead of standing there in monumental mockery of our own fallen condition, consoles by putting us in mind of the sameness of beauty and truth. Somehow we respond to these words as consolation before we take upon us to probe their possible meaning.

To speculate on what Keats's Urn means by her riddle and how it relates to art's therapeutic function, I would invoke Kant's *Critique of Judgment*. To the Romantics Kant's distinguishing of taste (the apprehension of beauty) from both truth (cognition) and the good (ethics) would limit the range and power of art, depriving it of a more than analogous participation in truth and goodness. Keats's Urn asserts the sameness of beauty and truth. The third category, the ethical or desire of the good, is hardly omitted in the poem; it is implicated in human suffering and our consequent yearning toward the condition of art. The sameness of beauty and truth is a proposition answering to this suffering and yearning; it answers pragmatically to what we are said in the final line to "need." That it is not an unconditional or unambiguous truth has been prepared for: the Urn, just prior to her speaking, is said to be a "silent form" that "dost tease us out of thought." This line, we recall, appeared in the verse epistle to Reynolds, where the context was specifically moral: "Oh never will the prize, / High reason, and the lore of good and ill, / Be my award. Things cannot to the will / Be settled, but they tease us out of thought." Just as the nature of good and ill cannot be decided, neither can the nature of art. But its pragmatic value – its intrinsic relationship to truth and our moral predicament – can still be felt.

Keats's comments elsewhere are helpful in grasping the pragmatic import of the final two lines. Frequently he speaks of beauty as the "essence" of things. The venerable distinction between essence and existence applies here precisely. Essence does not guarantee existence, even if we allow for the special meaning Keats attaches to "essence" as the quality of beauty in real things. The Urn and her paintings are a real

404

thing, a *thing* of beauty, that is not held to a standard of literal representation of existence, or referred reality. The essential truths of poetry need not be existentially true. Adam awakes to find, with God's assistance, that his dream of Eve is true: there is a correspondence of essence, or the idea of her, with existence, or the fact of her out there. The same does not hold *in the same way* for those of us who must pursue our Eves or Adams without divine assistance. But objects of human desire can be true somewhere: they can be essentially true, if not existentially true, *in art*. Products of the imagination can give us in essence what we lack in existence, imaging essence on the basis of our fragmentary lives. The artist images essence not by immersion in some Neoplatonic deep but by "think[ing] into the human heart." The essence that beauty offers is "real" as essence and is "truth" in the sense of heightened reality. Keats writes to his brothers on 21 December 1817, that the "excellence of every Art is its intensity, capable of making all disagreeables evaporate, from their being in close relationship with Beauty & Truth" (*L* I 192), which, I think, is a clearer gloss on the poem than the "Adam's dream" letter to Bailey of 22 November 1817. Intensity is felt as a "swelling into reality," which is what Keats considers the "truth" of art. This is beauty that binds us to the earth. It is contradistinguished by its necessarily positive value from the reality he has sometimes associated with mud and nothingness – the existential or referential world. Thus he can reverse the formula: not only is all beauty truth, or heightened reality, but all *heightened* reality as value is beauty.[12]

The consolation the Urn offers in equating beauty with truth is a pragmatic and moral one. As a "friend to man," art enables us to experience in essence what we lack in existence. Contrary to Kant's belief, art answers to the ethical faculty of desire of the good. Its intensity makes images seem to swell into reality, making for a time all the disagreeables of human life evaporate, and supplementing our own "dull, uninspired, snail-pacèd lives" with a heightened sense of reality and value. Instead of transcendent, disembodied beauty that leaves us desolate upon its passing, with the world we inhabit correspondingly devalued, this is beauty that binds us to the earth, telling us what we need to know, as the Urn says, "on earth." Our "need" to know does not extend past the limited information of the Urn's riddle

---

[12] In the letter to Bailey, Keats speculates that somewhere or other the products of imagination *will* prove existentially the case. But even here he does not say that art will be existentially confirmed in human life. Rather, our present incomplete happiness will perhaps be repeated in a "finer tone" hereafter, in a sensuous heaven of pure delight (*L* I 185).

because we cannot on earth transcend the moral situation – of desiring, valuing, and acting in a world resistant to human will, a world that makes us seek out art as therapy and ethical supplement. It is the better part of wisdom and health not to need (require) what we cannot have. In a word, art is a therapy because it temporarily calms the desiring that turns neurotic for not having. Through art we have what we need, for a time.

The Urn does not therefore claim that the truth/beauty formula is the answer to all that ails us, let alone that the pursuit of knowledge can be let go once we have mastered this single equation. It claims that within the limits of our knowledge and terrestrial context, we can still attain a heightened sense of reality that is no sweet cheat; we can find a momentary redemption from the ravages of time. I say "momentary" because the poet makes clear that time will lay waste to him and everybody else:

> Cold Pastoral!
> When old age shall this generation waste,
> Thou shalt remain, in midst of other woe
> Than ours, a friend to man.

The Urn as friend offers a palliative, not a cure, for what ails us. What ails us is time, and from that only the Urn (if not the Elgin Marbles) is exempt. Besides being non-living and "cold," the Urn in her continuing historical presence will not bring about some large-scale redemption from woe. The efforts of all the world's artists throughout time will never make all disagreeables evaporate. There will always be "other woe." In the heart of this climactic stanza on the triumph of art, Keats has also acknowledged the limitations of his Urn.

Neither the Urn nor the poet has taken a prophetic stance. The Urn is "historian," not prophet, and the poet has taken the still humbler role of interrogator. His vision of the future as a continuation in kind of past woe is non-prophetic because he simply interchanges past and future without further specifying a content and without a sense of futurity as something that responds to human will. Shelley argues by turns that imagination has a valuing function – it discovers value through the kind of light it casts – and a prophetic, obliging function. By imposing an ideal image on the present, it issues an imperative to realize that image existentially in the future. Keats has once again retained imagination's valuing function – the Urn has imaged a heightened reality of truth and beauty as permanent values – but he has abjured its prophetic, obliging function. We cannot, and therefore should not, attempt to emulate the condition of the Urn's image: we can only apprehend it in the moment of aesthetic attention, wherein its therapy resides. Art does not tell us what we must become or what we must do. Beauty consoles us for a time with a heightened sense of value, but does not permanently alter our condition.[13]

I have mentioned that as Keats becomes more disgruntled with his career as poet – composition of the great Odes having done nothing for his self-esteem – he thinks of at last "doing" something. Note how his praise of poetry is qualified: "I am convinced more and more day by day that fine writing is next to fine doing the top thing in the world" (*L* II 146, 24 August 1819). The concern with "fine doing" becomes a pronounced theme of the late poems. In 1817 he had written in the margin of *Paradise Lost*, "There is always a great charm in the openings of great Poems, more particularly where the action begins—."[14] We have heard him complain that Endymion never acts but is simply "led on" by circumstance. He implies that poetic value is undercut by the moral flaccidity of this heroic representation. The one fully conceived act narrated in the major poetry is the successful copulation of the lovers in *The Eve of St. Agnes*. This is hardly negligible, but in *Hyperion* Keats seeks to carry narrative possibility beyond erotics.

Here he sets out to represent fine doing on the Miltonic scale, with a hero who will "shape his actions" in a way that Matthew Arnold would presumably have approved of. But the story he intends to tell – the fall of the Titans and the superseding of Hyperion by Apollo – revealingly comes to a halt when Keats confronts this active agent, Apollo. He has already lent his interest and sympathy to the fallen Titans, who like Milton's fallen angels have embarked on a futile effort at restoration and who will of necessity lose the name of action. This parallel points up the problem: Milton's Satan has much to do, he has many perverse triumphs to savor, from Adam's expulsion to the consolidation of error that afflicts Milton's time and our own. But what are the Titans to do? It is a foregone conclusion that they can do nothing; only Apollo has the power and placement in mythological history to act. The Titan Oceanus sees this all too clearly:

> on our heels a fresh perfection treads,
> A power more strong in beauty, born of us
> And fated to excel us . . .
>
> (*H* II 212–14)

---

[13] My reading has assumed that both final lines are spoken by the Urn (" 'Beauty is truth, truth beauty, – that is all / Ye know on earth, and all ye need to know' "), but I think the major strands of my argument would hold even if the lines are punctuated this way: " 'Beauty is truth, truth beauty,'—that is all / Ye know on earth, and all ye need to know."

[14] *John Keats: The Complete Poems*, ed. John Barnard (New York: Penguin, 1977), 517.

For the Titans the appropriate response is resignation, not Byronic heroics:

> for to bear all naked truths
> And to envisage circumstance, all calm,
> That is the top of sovereignty. (H II 203–5)

The march of endeavor and intellect is here a tragic circumstance with respect to individuals. What might otherwise seem to be a rosy meliorism in Keats is the basis of tragic vision. Progress assumes the role that fate assumes in Greek tragedy. But tragic consciousness in Keats inhibits the representation of action, whereas action is, as Aristotle says, the heart of Greek tragedy. Keats cuts off the action precisely at the point where it begins – with Apollo shrieking as he dies into life, destined to become the fresh perfection that tramples an anxious Hyperion underfoot.

Why? I think the shape of this action must repel Keats: its ruthlessness, its inevitability, and its empty pretension to optimism, because who will, in turn, tread on Apollo? And since his sympathies remain with Hyperion – who, rather than Apollo, is the poet-surrogate – one surmises that Keats may halt his narration in advance of representing an act of self-murder. In this case, it is not that he loses interest in the story; rather, he takes too much personal interest and fails to attain to the "disinterestedness" he takes as the mark of the great poet, who does not let local, lyrical attachments inhibit the ends of art.

This observation takes us to Keats's comments on the "poetical character" in a letter of 27 October 1818, to his friend Richard Woodhouse, lawyer for Taylor & Hessey, Keats's publisher. These comments, in my view, are antithetical to the moralism of The Fall of Hyperion, but they serve as a bridge in charting the relationship of this fragment to the earlier Hyperion. Just as Coleridge undertakes in Biographia Literaria to disprove the "supposed irritability of men of genius" (Genus irritabile vatum), of which Horace speaks in the Epistles, so Keats begins his letter with an allusion to the "genus irritabile," as he sets out to define its character more precisely than the conventional wisdom.[15] Keats speaks in deliberate, playful paradox, while making a serious point. The poetical character

---

[15] Although Hazlitt is usually cited as the primary source, I think these famous comments may owe more to Coleridge, whose Biographia Literaria was published in July 1817. There is no external evidence that Keats read this work, but in November of 1817 we find him writing to Bailey that "Men of Genius are great as certain ethereal Chemicals operating on the Mass of neutral intellect—[but] they have not any individuality, any determined Character. I would call the top and head of those who have a proper self Men of Power—" (L I 184). This is similar to the distinction

has no character—it enjoys light and shade; it lives in gusto, be it foul or fair, high or low, rich or poor, mean or elevated—It has as much delight in conceiving an Iago as an Imogen. What shocks the virtuous philosopher, delights the camelion Poet. It does no harm from its relish of the dark side of things any more than from its taste for the bright one; because they both end in speculation. A Poet is the most unpoetical of any thing in existence; because he has no Identity—he is continually [informing?] and filling some other Body—The Sun, the Moon, the sea and Men and Women who are creatures of impulse are poetical and have about them an unchangeable attribute—the poet has none; no identity—he is certainly the most unpoetical of all God's creatures.

(*L* I 386–7)

Since Keats is speaking paradoxically, we must sort out what he does and does not mean. There is an implicit devaluing of the poetry of self-expression here. He applies what Coleridge conceives of as the motive structure of Shakespearean drama to the poetical character generally. Though it is evident, at least from such an ill-conceived collaborative abortion as *Otho the Great* (1819), that Keats would not in any event have become a dramatist, he describes his own creative process as the dramatic one of identifying with other persons and objects, and canceling his own identity. This is disinterestedness; poets do not let self-interest inhibit the interest they take in others, dramatis personae as objects of sympathetic identification.

Two clarifications need be made. First, this conception of poetic

Coleridge makes between "absolute Genius" and "commanding Genius." Though not arguing that the absolute genius is without "individuality," Coleridge does argue his "creative, and self-sufficing power" and his "calm and tranquil temper," which is contrasted with the commanding genius, who "must impress [his] pre-conceptions on the world without, in order to present them back to [his] own view with the satisfying degree of clearness, distinctness, and individuality" (*BL* I 31–3). Commanding geniuses convert their conceptions into existential constructs, often on a large scale in the case of revolutionaries, tyrants, and statesmen. In addition, the closeness of Keats's definition of negative capability (*L* I 193–4) to Coleridge's comment on artistic illusion has been noted before: "That *illusion*, contra-distinguished from *delusion*, that *negative* faith, which simply permits the images presented to work by their own force, without either denial or affirmation of their real existence by the judgement, is rendered impossible by their immediate neighbourhood to words and facts of known and absolute truth" (*BL* II 134). But the passage in *Biographia Literaria* most likely to have influenced Keats's comments on the poetical character occurs in a contrast of Shakespeare and Milton: "While the former darts himself forth, and passes into all the forms of human character and passion, the one Proteus of the fire and the flood; the other attracts all forms and things to himself, into the unity of his own IDEAL. All things and modes of action shape themselves anew in the being of MILTON; while SHAKSPEARE becomes all things, yet for ever remaining himself" (*BL* II 27–8). The "wordsworthian or egotistical sublime" I take to be an echo of Coleridge's comment on Milton, appropriated by Keats to Wordsworth (cf. *L* I 223–4).

function does not conflict with Keats's notion of Soul-making. The poet as one who has suffered slings and arrows like anybody else has an "identity." In creating a work of art he simply divests himself of it for the moment. Woodhouse makes this distinction in his interpretation of the letter: "He may well say that a poet has no identity—as a man he must have Ident^y" (L I 390). By implication, Keats distinguishes more than Wordsworth between the generic growth of human identity and the specific development and exercise of the poetic faculty. We could go further and say that the poet's identity *qua* poet is paradoxically confirmed in the temporary relinquishing of personal identity.

The second clarification is that in this letter Keats speaks of dramatic or sympathetic identification in non-moral terms. Aesthetic disinterestedness is distinguished from ethical. The poet differs from the moral agent or judge by declaring the irrelevance of moral judgment to sympathetic identification. He takes "as much delight in conceiving an Iago as an Imogen. What shocks the virtuous philosopher, delights the camelion Poet."

This may strike one as a liberating poetics, but Keats himself is unable to live with it. Can sympathetic identification in the poetic act declare itself so blissfully free of "curious conscience, that still hoards / Its strength for darkness, burrowing like the mole"? In a moral identification of self with poetic representation, the poet would be debtor to the feeling he creates in another, the misery of Desdemona experienced *in some way* as his misery. Identity would not be so easily cast aside, because the metaphor of "filling some other body" would be countered by the fact that the poet remains aware of his own as reciprocally filled, his identity imposed upon in the creative act by the identities of others. I have suggested that Keats may have given up *Hyperion* through too much *self*-interest when he recognized in Hyperion an uncomfortable mirroring of his own sense of poetic powerlessness. Whether or not this was the case, it is quite unlike the state of moral disinterestedness I am describing now in the abstract but which Keats describes precisely in *The Fall of Hyperion*. In moral disinterestedness, the poet would feel another's pain even without this mirroring of self.

The Fall of Hyperion is, I think, a repudiation of Keats's own letter on the poetical character and of Hazlitt's more disturbing argument that imagination sides with power, not with good. (Its relationship to the earlier *Hyperion* I will take up in a moment.) In one of his marathon letters to George and Georgiana, Keats copies out a lengthy passage from Hazlitt's *Letter to William Gifford* (1819) – in itself a notable act of homage since his relatives would surely have preferred more *news* (L II

410

74–6, 13 March 1819). The amorality of the imagination, even its promiscuity (similar to Keats's metaphor of the poet's filling other bodies independently of moral worth), is the main point of Hazlitt's *Letter*. He goes further, however, in describing the moral and political implications of such a view, especially imagination's tendency to side with the glamorous trappings of authoritarian power. Its amorality and attraction to power are the "original sin in poetry," a phrase Keats copies out with many other passages. Some four months later – near the end of July 1819, by best estimate – Keats is reworking his *Hyperion* in first person, with the new introductory lines that make *The Fall of Hyperion* his most agonized piece of self-analysis. Here he contends with the original sin in poetry.[16] It is not that he denies imagination's tendency to liberate itself from moral freight; it is that the great poet must, for art's sake, resist such a liberation as temptation. *The Fall of Hyperion* imposes still greater sacrifices on the poet than Keats had imagined years before when he spoke of a difficult uphill climb to join the English poets. Moneta – high priestess of the temple of what I take to be all that has been worthy of veneration, poetic, moral, and religious, in human history – issues the challenge to all would-be poets:

> "None can usurp this height," return'd that shade.
> "But those to whom the miseries of the world
> Are misery, and will not let them rest.
> All else who find a haven in the world,
> Where they may thoughtless sleep away their days,
> If by a chance into this fane they come,
> Rot on the pavement where thou rotted'st half. (FH I 147–53)

This pronouncement undercuts all amoral privileging of the poetical character.

Keats has spoken of how few people "have ever arrived at a complete disinterestedness of Mind: very few have been influenced by a pure desire of the benefit of others—" (*L* II 79–80), and indeed he can think of only two, Socrates and Jesus. (Perhaps it seemed inapposite to add to this list his sister-in-law Georgiana, whom he had earlier declared to be "disinterrested," *L* I 293.) Keats picks up the word "disinterested" from Hazlitt – who does a better job of spelling it – and like Hazlitt he has assumed the linkage of moral disinterestedness with benevolence or sympathy. Early in the letters he notes with some

---

[16] For a discussion of some other implications of this phrase for our reading of Keats, see Stuart Sperry, *Keats the Poet*, 310–35. For the consummate account of Keats's progress toward tragic recognition, see Walter Jackson Bate, *John Keats*, 525–699.

anxiety that his own capacity for *moral* disinterestedness is limited by the same *aesthetic* disinterestedness he will later describe as the poetical character. The latter can function as an evasion of responsibility. In the letter to Bailey on the "authenticity of the Imagination" and "holiness of the Heart's affections," he speaks of his inability to respond deeply to the calamities of others. The passage is sometimes misread as Keats's tribute to his powers of sympathetic identification. In the face of a calamity, his own or another's, the setting sun

will always set me to rights—or if a Sparrow come before my Window I take part in its existence and pick about the Gravel. The first thing that strikes me on hearing a Misfortune having befalled another is this. 'Well it cannot be helped.—he will have the pleasure of trying the resourses of his spirit, and I beg now my dear Bailey that hereafter should you observe any thing cold in me not to [p]ut it to the account of heartlessness but abstraction—for I assure you I sometimes feel not the influence of a Passion or Affection during a whole week—and so long this sometimes continues I begin to suspect myself and the genuiness of my feelings at other times–thinking them a few barren Tragedy-tears—. (L I 186)

Keats often associates the power of "abstraction" with beauty and poetry. It entails self-distancing from suffering, here illustrated by the very act of aesthetic (non-moral) identification – his taking part in the existence of a sparrow. In a type of home therapy, he casually identifies with the sparrow as a way of projecting himself beyond the moral suffering which the immediate context would otherwise impose. He is confessing a weakness.

Doubts about his depth of feeling arise again when he hears a friend's father is dying. The news prompts some reflections on how "Circumstances are like Clouds continually gathering and bursting —While we are laughing the seed of some trouble is put into the wide arable land of events—while we are laughing it sprouts i[t] grows and suddenly bears a poison fruit which we must pluck—." But even giving himself the "leisure to reason on the misfortunes" of his friend gives him pause: "From the manner in which I feel Haslam's misfortune I perceive how far I am from any humble standard of [moral] disinterestedness—" (L I 79). Near the end of his letter on the poetical character, he remarks, "All I hope is that I may not lose all interest in human affairs" in the very attempt "to reach to as high a summit in Poetry as the nerve bestowed upon me will suffer" (L I 387–8). And to George and Georgiana, upon their urging that he get married, he observes that an active identification with imaginative constructs – of world literature and his own poems – makes him "content

412

to be alone." He sees that literary pleasure can substitute for human attachments.

Keats is haunted therefore by this other pair of contraries, insufficiently perceived as such in modern criticism: moral disinterestedness and aesthetic disinterestedness. For him the latter militates against the former; ironically his very power of disinterested sympathy threatens to disengage him from the moral sphere. Aesthetic identification and the loss of identity free us from feeling the misery of others as misery. This is an original sin in poetry for which Keats has expressed a degree of guilt, at the same time that he has wished to indulge it. Moneta's challenge – which is both admonition and self-revision – is that the great poet is not entitled to put aside the pain of moral identification. Aesthetic and moral identification must combine. Creative acts, instead of emanating from pleasurable impulses alone, find their origins also in a deep pain. The contraries of pleasure and pain, of the aesthetic and the moral, are at the heart of creation. Since both modes of identification are disinterested, the poet is ideally a disinterested sufferer. Only through sacrificial suffering is the original sin in poetry expiated.

Keats gave up verse too soon, and died too soon, to follow out and teach to us the full implications of this evolution in his vision of the poetical character. But we can learn much from the texts we have. Hazlitt's disturbing observations on the promiscuity of the imagination – its attraction to strong stimulus irrespective of moral worth – find an answer in this coalescence of aesthetic and moral, the moral imagination. The hard conclusion would follow that Shakespeare has nodded *poetically* to the extent that his real sympathies tilt toward power; even he, at least in *Coriolanus*, does not fully temper aesthetic vision with moral suffering, and Keats would make a value judgment of the play accordingly, where Hazlitt would not.

As for the balance of pain and pleasure in the creative act, I think it fair to say that Keats finally exceeds Wordsworth in emphasizing tragic consciousness as the mark of the great poet. Moneta enjoins a sacrifice of visionary pleasure – the pleasure of the "dreamer" or "visionary," the aesthete, the seeker after sensation – far in excess of anything Wordsworth thinks necessary. In his Preface to *Lyrical Ballads*, Wordsworth says the poet is susceptible of "an infinite complexity of pain and pleasure," but that the "sympathies" he feels "are accompanied by an overbalance of enjoyment." But Moneta clearly places the balance with pain. She is the figure of human memory, tragic consciousness, and admonition, who is said to have an "immortal sickness" from which, of course, there is neither recovery nor termination. Part of her

413

hospitable reception of the staggering poet is to infect him with this same loss of ultimate hope for humankind, as well as profound sympathy for it. The poet's ascent up the steps of the temple is an agony of suffocation approaching death. (Here and elsewhere Keats makes conspicuous use of the imagery of suffocation, induced perhaps by his mother's and brother's deaths, and anticipating his own.) To be a sage, a humanist, a physician to all humankind, and to give others the momentary redemption of beauty, the poet must himself suffer, taking on the pain of the world.

This high seriousness is a considerable remove from the "poetic onanism" of which Byron accuses Keats. It is fair to ask what the poet as sacrificial sufferer – who suffers to give others the healing powers of art – has to do with Keats's emphasis on vocation, craft, and the poet's proper fame. I propose that the relationship of *Hyperion* to *The Fall of Hyperion* reflects his struggle with the dual claims of action and life activity. Having failed to give us the "charm" of action in *Hyperion*, he conceives anew the question of action as that of life activity, and in *The Fall of Hyperion* switches to first-person narration and addresses the problem of poetic vocation. The lengthy new introductory episode (19–310) is, I think, by way of compensation for the earlier failure to represent action. He now asks what it means to pursue the vocation of poetry, and what good can come of it.

We have seen that he is hard on himself. The poet must become a sacrificial figure – in itself an unhappy prospect – and Keats berates himself for having in the past indulged his propensity for non-moral dreaming. One reads the poem with a frustrating wish to intervene, to tell Keats that with only twenty-four years spent he has hardly been remiss, that if he requires a sign of poetic promise he might re-read his own Odes, and, more important, that no poet can take on the Christ-like burden Moneta assigns and hope to retain that sense of play without which a poet becomes paralyzed.

The Fall of Hyperion is indeed *over*-compensation for his earlier retreat from moral imperatives and action, whether in life or poetry. Keats's hugely inappropriate guilt prompts him to transfer the weight of obligation – which ordinarily pertains to single pivotal acts the moral agent must sometimes perform – to the entire career, from beginning to end, of the poet. He moralizes vocation beyond the possible performance of it. How can one lead such a life? how stay in touch with those fundamentals of sensation and pleasure that make creativity a "deep delight"? Once again Keats leaves off composition, and *The Fall of Hyperion* remains a fragment. We do not know how he would have pursued his vocation in light of this moralization of goals, or even if he could have. Moneta's injunction inhibits completion of the very poem in which she utters it. Poets are surely not required to be Christ. If Keats gave up *Hyperion* because of a too intimately extended self-interest, he may have given up *The Fall of Hyperion* because he *has* extended sympathy beyond what a poet can do and remain a practicing poet. Adjusting for his inordinate degree of self-accusation, one can still say that Keats has confronted, as nakedly as anyone in the period, the fact that the poet cannot and should not evade the ethical dimension of art – for the sake of art. And he has also demonstrated the perils of too great a commitment to the ethical.

Keats did, of course, write one more great poem, "To Autumn," composed on 19 September 1819, only two days before the last probable day by which he would have abandoned work on *The Fall of Hyperion*.[17] This poem overcomes the bar to composition Moneta has set up, even if it does not quite chart the career that would have been.

In the kind of casual disburdening that occurs only at the end of a long struggle, Keats writes in "To Autumn" a poem notable for what it omits. There is no personal pronoun now, no merely personal perspective on scene, no agonized self-consciousness or conscience, no moral imperatives being issued, no personal will that must overcome obstacles. There is no invocation of the gods, Keats having at last put his pretty paganisms to rest. (One could chart his career, ironically, as the gradual escape from classical myth.) There are no riddles or philosophical statements from which to hang an interpretation, or on which to hang trying. There is no wish for transcendence and no wrenching of binary oppositions. In place of frustrated dialectical movement, we have cyclical time. But tragic consciousness remains, registering the daily and seasonal passage of time and lending elegiac intonation to the final stanza. The warm days will cease, the harvest will be done, the "soft-dying day" will ease into night. This is hardly a pure, non-moral naturalism: moral values remain, fully infiltrating non-moral ones. The beautiful scene is invested with the human virtues of benevolence, patience, generosity, mercy, the willingness to work, and the ability to mourn.

In its totality the poem is a valuing act that merges moral and non-moral value in sketching the continuum between human mind and nature. The poet attains a disinterestedness here, both moral and aesthetic, because projection of consciousness onto scene negates the very distance between self and object that would create the possibility of merely personal interest. In "To Autumn" interest is coextensive

[17] Concerning the date of these two works, see Jack Stillinger, *The Texts of Keats's Poems* (Cambridge, Mass.: Harvard University Press, 1974), 258–9.

with totality of perspective. Keats has not had to resort to drama to attain disinterestedness; he has done so within the sensuous lyric, wherein beauty is once again a binding to the earth.

The poem perfectly captures some tendencies we have seen in Keats. While the element of obligation is nil, there is a plenitude of value. In place of moral action, Keats envisages activity – here, the activity of humanized nature leading its own life, the personified Autumn engaged in the daily productive work of harvest. The non-localized human consciousness of the poem, registering the tragic implications of time and natural process, feels neither resentment nor guilt nor fear. A significant difference between fate in *Hyperion* and natural process in "To Autumn" is found in the quality of acquiescence. In *Hyperion* individuals are *in the way of* an impersonal, quasi-evolutionary process so ruthless that moral qualities of fairness and mercy are suspended. But "To Autumn" implies a human con-sciousness that *becomes a part of* the very process that will eventually eclipse it. And that process entails a large initial donation of life in a benevolent "conspiracy" of sun and seasons. The initial donation of life and the promise of still more in seasonal time ease the seeming ruthlessness of time in its eclipse of individuals. Blake had said that time is the mercy of eternity, and Keats accepts this here. With these intuitions he has ceased to fret about the enormous moral burden on the vocation of poetry; he simply writes a poem.

The premonitory tone of "To Autumn," perfectly blended with a spirit of acceptance, is heightened in our own ears, since we know that this was to be Keats's last great poem. The final year and a half of his life witnessed dual struggles with love and death. His response to neither was "disinterested," and both made impossible—doctor's orders or no—the composition of verse. "There are impossibilities in the world," he wrote to Fanny Brawne. The creation of beauty out of suffering became one of these.

416

9
Byron: *The world as* glorious *blunder*

The authenticity of performance

Byron has often seemed anomalous in the family of British Romantics. Both Weltschmerz and satire seem incompatible with Wordsworthian remembrance and Keatsian appetite. But Byron is hardly alone in notable darkness and negativity – or satirical play. Keats sees more painfully than he the incommensurateness of desire to having; Coleridge expresses a profounder sense of evil; Blake's psychological warfare rivals the siege of Ismail in violence; Shelley's Mont Blanc exerts an even more forbidding necessity than Byron's ocean; Wordsworth voices a deeper sadness at loss and heart-wasting. A spirit of negation is found in them all and is not Byron's special counter to some euphoric romance of the imagination. And they all try their hand at satire.

Byron's distinctive character, ethically considered, is found elsewhere, and can be seen in his relationship to structures of Romantic thought and in his authorial stance and voice. Neither relativist nor nihilist, he has a resolute commitment to the values of energy, honesty, affection, courage, pleasure, and cash. At the same time he subverts a prevalent structure in Romanticism: dialectical movement, with its promise of dynamic change in persons and history. This subversion is a corollary to an ethically precise recognition that I find surprisingly consistent in his work: values exist in patterns of mutual exclusion. We do not simultaneously have both love and knowledge, both power and goodness, both pleasure and happiness – or to extend the list, both carnality and spirituality, innocence and experience, love and friendship, passion and reason, nature and civilization. Byronic narrative, whether grandiose or satiric, is grounded in this recognition. Like other Romantic authors, Byron emerges as an aggressive value pluralist, but one who perceives severe existential limits on the incorporation of value. No ideal of harmonious human faculties is

417

proposed, no hope in a progressive play of contraries. Mind/body dualism is reluctantly reinstated. He follows out negatively some of the hesitant affirmations we have seen in Keats – for example, that suffering produces a compensatory new emergent, human identity. No metaphysics, no theodicy, no concept of human personality or history, justifies suffering, as *Cain* tells us. But Byron grasps that suffering would be no moral problem if human life were not in itself a value of the first order

These recognitions lead to an ethics of predicament. Rather than issue glum imperatives of restraint and careful choice, however, Byron creates heroes who display a reckless bravura in dynamic acts of will – or at least of speech – undertaken in full awareness of futility. Unlike Shelley's, Byron's tales are not morally cautionary, nor do their isolated heroes suggest universalizable courses of action or imperatives for the readership. Like Keats, Byron urges nothing on us, but he displays ways and means of dealing with predicament. Some are blatantly desperate, as in *Childe Harold's Pilgrimage* and *Manfred*, but others permit inferences as to how sanity might be preserved. In *Don Juan* we find a hero who has that underrated virtue, pluck, and a narrator who has the power of intellectual negotiation, both of which encourage the continuance of life and sanity.

The critical school of deconstruction appends an ontology of denial as well as a non-moral concept of play to its characteristic methodology. Ontological assumptions give this critical orientation an overlay of the dark sublime, compelling to critics in search of new ways of engaging the abyss. In practical criticism, deconstruction often seeks a textual aporia, a subversive contradiction of the text's manifest tendency. Thus, Shelley's *A Defence of Poetry*, which we might have thought consistent with its own title, becomes "a sentimental text [in the Schilleresque sense], which engages in strategies of self-avoidance to escape being consumed by its own contradictions."[1] Contradiction cuts two ways, of course: that which contradicts is itself contradicted. The same critical ploy, directed instead toward an ostensibly negative or nihilistic text, might as plausibly discover a fissure through which an affirmation issues.

Such a critical tack would accord with our common experience in reading Byron. He is a poet who denies that human history goes anywhere, that human beings are noble or honest, that imagination is a particularly worthy faculty, that human energy can be preserved or augmented, that happiness is real. *Yet* he supports revolutionary

---

[1] Rajan, *Dark Interpreter*, 74–5. Rajan finds both deconstructive and idealist strategies in Romantic texts.

causes and creates some characters (Haidee, Leila, Don Juan) quite worth saving in the literal extra-textual sense; he creates in the narrator of *Don Juan* someone whose energies are such that cantos can be spun out indefinitely; and in the midst of great suffering and disaster, he admits of happiness: Manfred's experience of Kalon, Childe Harold's pleasure taken in nature, and Don Juan's bliss in the Cyclades. Reading Byron, we sense an intellectual pleasure taken in negation itself. Spotting such contradictions does not require critical subtlety, let alone a view of language as trace, echo, or void, because with Byronic display it is all there on view.

The positive–negative polarity with regard to the balance of values in the world is the most fundamental of Byronic contradictions, or to use his word, "antipodes." Which pole prevails depends in large part on literary genre. The comic vision of *Don Juan* is axiomatically brighter than the gloom of the lyrical tragedy, *Manfred*. Especially in Byron's case, electing a genre must have more to do with a writer's appetite than with a will to impart a preconceived set of ideological convictions, moral or otherwise. We can be wary of branding Byron a pessimist because *Manfred* happens to be pessimistic, just as optimism would be its own ideological constraint on the writer's freedom. "Poetry is in itself passion, and does not systematize. It assails, but does not argue; it may be wrong, but it does not assume pretensions to Optimism" (*LJP* V 582). Although many Byronic texts seem to labor under a pretension to pessimism, Byron is sufficiently free of this ideology to question it also. As Michael Cooke has argued, his skepticism facilitates many affirmative energies.[2]

No poet is free of assumptions, but Byronic skepticism of larger belief systems – which he says absurdly eat one another up from era to era in an intellectual cannibalism – feeds his compositional energies. The intellectual patterns which emerge in the larger Byronic oeuvre – and which I will be tracing – do not contradict this freeing skepticism, since they do not arise from or descend to the systematization he disparages.

This skeptical play of mind informs the ethics of composition in *Don Juan*. Against the conventions of both life and literature, the narrator pits his own experience and observation of the world, at the same time that he reminds us, in violation of narrative decorum, that his poem is written, invented. The double blade of his satiric method cuts through Canto the First, where as evidence of his narrative's literal truth – in contradistinction to works of his "epic brethren" – he testifies that he

[2] *The Blind Man Traces the Circle: On the Patterns and Philosophy of Byron's Poetry* (Princeton: Princeton University Press, 1969), 175–213.

himself, "and several now in Seville / *Saw* Juan's last elopement with the Devil" (CCIII). In "baring the devices" of his own compositional process, even to confessing use of a rhyming dictionary as he makes his way from stanza to stanza, the narrator as persona of Byron creates the conditions of his own authenticity. Telling us how his poem comes into being – the tricks of the trade, rather than the sublimities of creative mind – is its own subversive testimonial, a debunking of the Romantic myth of inspiration. Byronic authenticity is discovered in his mock-serious display of skeptical, experiential mind as the validating or invalidating source of its own observations and judgments. What is said attaches to the persona, whether we find him trustworthy or flip or deliberately deceitful. Instead of merely announcing the fictionality of all narrative discourse (that trite ploy of modern criticism), Byron manages to have it both ways, but ultimately to rescue fictional discourse for reality as he perceives it: at least the reality of a mind disclosing and inventing itself as it goes, at most the conduct of human life and history. He tells his publisher that *Don Juan* is authenticated by his own experiential observation of the world. After all the involuted play with fact and fiction, he means what he says. His poem satisfies the conditions of what he terms "ethical poetry," a poetry that eschews Platonic lies and old wives' tales for the truth of things.

I have said something similar of Wordsworth, who writes the process of composition into his narrative *The Prelude*. But Wordsworth, addressing his poem to Coleridge, is engaged in self-exploration rather than display, is not creating and manipulating a public persona, is not writing his poem as an attack on the institutions of literature, and is apologetic about the provisional nature of the enterprise. Authenticity for Wordsworth means baring the process of composition as one component of a larger spiritual exercise. The poetic lens through which the life and mind are examined must be simultaneously examined, and any suggestion of persona cleared away in what attempts to be an *un*masking. Byron's is more a display of self than an exploration of it, and authenticity is one with a theatricality directed to the satiric end of showing us a "reflection of the world."

This drive toward display takes us to the modern reading of Byron as master performer.[3] The sense of mastery he gives us in his greatest

---

[3] For this reading of Byron, see Paul West, *Byron and the Spoiler's Art* (New York: St. Martin's Press, 1960); Jerome J. McGann, *Fiery Dust: Byron's Poetic Development* (Chicago: University of Chicago Press, 1968); Peter J. Manning, *Byron and His Fictions* (Detroit: Wayne State University Press, 1978); John Bayley, "Byron and the 'Lively Life,' " *New York Review of Books*, 30 (2 June 1983), 25–32; and Frederick L. Beaty, *Byron the Satirist* (DeKalb: Northern Illinois University Press, 1985).

work derives from what Michael Goldman has called, relative to drama, the "actor's freedom": a performative, thrusting energy that creates a protective circle around the actor and that is the source of his or her mesmerizing power.[4] The performance analogy is more apt for Byron than for Wordsworth, Coleridge, and Keats. More than they – and poets in general – Byron arrogantly announces his own free, mesmerizing power, takes delight in improvisation, changes costumes while we watch, and sets about holding the attention of the very audience toward which he expresses hostility. *Don Juan*, which holds us today, is the paradigm of Byronic composition. *Childe Harold's Pilgrimage* held a nineteenth-century audience on somewhat different grounds but with its own unrepentant theatricality.

Byron is a master performer who, through aggressive acts of the writer's freedom, reads human nature, behavior, and history in terms predominantly negative but whose compositional energies and metaphysical skepticism allow for a partial conversion from dark to bright; whose commitment to values – ultimately the value of human life, in accord with Blake's wisdom that "Everything that *lives* is holy" – is found in his darkest lament and satire; and whose restorative power is communicated to us in the comic mastery of one who has seen an oppressive panorama of human history and yet finds the pluck to go on writing.

Ethical poetry

In a dispute of 1821 with William Lisle Bowles (the minor versifier whom Coleridge claims as a strong influence in his own poetic career), Byron casts himself as defender of the high moral content of Pope's poetry and the propriety of his life. The Reverend Mr. Bowles had complained of Pope's indecencies in poetry and life. Undercutting both Bowles and Byron, Hazlitt congratulates Byron for "laughing outright at Mr. Bowles's hysterical horrors at poor Pope's platonic peccadillos," but he complains that Byron "gets up in the reading desk himself, without the proper canonical credentials, when he makes such a fuss as he does about didactic or moral poetry as the highest of all others." Merely because "moral truth" and "moral conduct" are "good things in themselves, does it follow," asks Hazlitt, "that they are the better for being put into rhyme? We see no connection between the 'ends of verse, and the sayings of philosophers' " (XIX 65–9).

It is rather amusing to watch the author of *Beppo* and *Don Juan*

---

[4] *The Actor's Freedom: Toward a Theory of Drama* (New York: Viking, 1975).

outflank Bowles on the preacherly right. One motive for his epistle may be to perplex those back home who brand him satanic seducer. But he seems proud of it. He finds time to write it during his participation in the Carbonari uprising and is more than usually interested in the response back home in England. Here is what he says:

In my mind, the highest of all poetry is ethical poetry, as the highest of all earthly objects must be moral truth. Religion does not make a part of my subject; it is something beyond human powers, and has failed in all human hands except Milton's and Dante's, and even Dante's powers are involved in his delineation of human passions, though in supernatural circumstances. What made Socrates the greatest of men? His moral truth—his ethics. What proved Jesus Christ the Son of God hardly less than his miracles? His moral precepts. And if ethics have made a philosopher the first of men, and have not been disdained as an adjunct to his Gospel by the Deity himself, are we to be told that ethical poetry, or didactic poetry, or by whatever name you term it, whose object is to make men better and wiser, is not the *very first order* of poetry; and are we to be told this too by one of the priesthood [Bowles]?

(*LJP* V 554)

Concerning Pope, "the purest of our moralists," he writes:

Of his power in the *passions*, in description, in the mock heroic, I leave others to descant. I take him on his strong ground as an *ethical* poet: in the former, none excel; in the mock heroic and the ethical, none equal him; and, in my mind, the latter is the highest of all poetry, because it does that in *verse*, which the greatest of men have wished to accomplish in prose. If the essence of poetry must be a *lie*, throw it to the dogs, or banish it from your republic, as Plato would have done. He who can reconcile poetry with truth and wisdom, is the only true '*poet*' in its real sense, 'the *maker*,' 'the *creator*,'—why must this mean the 'liar,' the 'feigner,' the 'tale-teller'? (LJP V 559–60)

Byron's various statements on the nature and purpose of poetry are maddeningly contradictory, but these passages from the epistle to Bowles point the way to a Byronic poetics even so. "Ethical" is employed in a variety of ways here. It has, first, the meaning of "didactic." In his letters Byron sometimes derides the pragmatic function; he defends *Cain* and *Don Juan* on the grounds of their harmlessness: "*Who* was ever altered by a poem?" (*LJ* IX 53); "No Girl will ever be seduced by reading D[on] J[uan]" (*LJ* X 68). And he says it is hardly worthwhile defining what a poet should be, "for what are *they* worth? What have they done?" (*LJ* VIII 41). But now he writes that the highest "object" of poetry is to "make men better and wiser." Lest we protest that grimly to pose such an object might be self-defeating, he announces that ethical poetry "*does*" in verse what the greatest of men have only "wished" to accomplish in prose. "Ethical" also refers to the

422

poem's isolable "wisdom," "moral truth," or "precepts." The implication is that the better the precepts, the better the poem. Finally,
"ethical" stands in opposition to lying or feigning or what Byron
elsewhere calls "pure invention," and as such it assumes the corollary
of "real." Poetry tells us what the case is. The true poet is thus someone
who, reconciling invention with fact, communicates moral wisdom.

This sober formula underlies pronouncements elsewhere possessed
of greater Byronic flair. He makes the degree of reality a qualitative
gauge: "—there should always be some foundation of fact for the most
airy fabric—and pure invention is but the talent of a liar" (*LJ* V 203). It is
"the fashion of the day to lay great stress upon what they call
'imagination' and 'invention,' the two commonest of qualities: an Irish
peasant with a little whiskey in his head will imagine and invent more
than would furnish forth a modern poem" (*LJP* V 554). The original sin
in poetry is the Platonic one of lying, to be expiated through mimetic
correlation of language with fact – fact authenticated by the poet's
personal observation and experience. He defends *Don Juan* to his
publisher, John Murray, whose moral qualms would force him to make
"canticles" of his "cantos":

—confess—confess—you dog—and be candid—that it is the sublime of *that
there* sort of writing—it may be bawdy—but is it not good English?—it may be
profligate—but is it not *life*, is it not *the thing*?—Could any man have written
it—who has not lived in the world?—and tooled in a post-chaise? In a hackney
coach? in a Gondola? against a wall? in a court carriage? in a vis a vis?—on a
table?—and under it?   (*LJ* VI 232)

Later he brags to Murray that "almost all Don Juan is *real* life—either
my own—or from people I knew" (*LJ* VIII 186). One of his complaints
of the Lakers is that they "know nothing of the world; and what is
poetry, but the reflection of the world? What sympathy have this
people with the spirit of this stirring age? . . . They are mere old wives"
(*LJ* IV 85). Like Shelley, he speaks of "the poetry of life," a phrase he
uses to describe the relationship of "poetical temperament" and
human experience (*LJ* VII 170). The ethical poet is one who most
vigorously gives us *"the thing."* In his multitudinous tooling, Byron has
earned the credentials of the ethical poet.

Validation of poetry by the life experience of the poet and by the
mental experience that attends the act of composition distinguishes
Byron from Augustan critics. It is not enough to be a wise observer of
nature, human or otherwise. Byron writes, "per dipingere le passioni
forti bisogna averle provato" ("in order to depict strong passions, it is
necessary to have experienced them") (*LJ* VI 158). To be sure, this is in

keeping with Horace's dictum, "Si vis me flere, dolendum est / Primum ipsi tibi" ("If you wish to make me weep, you must first feel sorrow yourself"). But even Samuel Johnson, who enlists an experiential standard, speaks mainly, as does Pope, of the common or representative experience of humankind as the proper subject of poetry. The experience Byron enlists is his own, or at least that of his personae, whether representative or idiosyncratic.

Byron functionally desynonymizes "moral" and "ethical." Throughout *Don Juan* he delights in irreverent use of "moral," forcing on us the recognition that its standard usage implies an unsavory judgmental hypocrisy. He calls Lady Byron his "moral Clytemnestra," which we might take for an oxymoron until we see that "moral" can mean cruel and murderous. Donna Inez, modeled on Lady Byron, sees to it that her son Don Juan's "breeding should be strictly moral," which means keeping out of his reach anything that hints at the "continuation of the species" (*DJ* I 39–40). Morality or "morals" is the wet blanket of hypocrisy that would stifle the natural passions of the heart, particularly sex. An obvious source of comedy is how fire finds fuel and outlet anyway. So used, "moral" expresses opposition to Byron's most fundamental value – life, or what I will call, after Blake, the complex of values associated with Tharmas. "Moral" takes on connotations quite the opposite of "ethical," which Byron has used in conjunction with "truth" and "wisdom." Sultry, sexy Spain is contrasted with England: "Happy the nations of the moral North! / Where all is virtue" (*DJ* I 64); man and wife are termed a "moral centaur," and his own poem has a "moral end":

> For like an agéd aunt, or tiresome friend,
> A rigid guardian, or a zealous priest,
>   My Muse by exhortation means to mend
> All people, at all times, and in most places,
> Which puts my Pegasus to these grave paces.   (*DJ* XII 39)

Don Juan undermines the bigotry of virtue, which makes the poet an immoralist: "But now I'm going to be immoral; now / I mean to show things really as they are, / Not as they ought to be" (*DJ* XII 40). In their political apostasy, the Lake poets "cut a convict figure, / The very Botany Bay in moral geography." Their "loyal treason" makes them "moralists" in the conventional hypocritical sense (*DJ* III 93–4).

But Byron drops the inversion to say of the English, "You are *not* a moral people, and you know it" (*DJ* XI 87). One passage sums up, I think, his intent as satirist:

> 'Tis strange,—but true; for Truth is always strange—
>   Stranger than fiction: if it could be told,
> How much would novels gain by the exchange!
>   How differently the World would men behold!
> How oft would Vice and Virtue places change!
>   The new world would be nothing to the old,
> If some Columbus of the moral seas
> Would show mankind their Souls' antipodes.   (*DJ* XIV 101)

Though Byron is often cynical about the moral efficacy of poetry – and is thus more in line with the modern temper than Plato, Blake, and Shelley are – he still has a moral purpose, in which he may fail where Pope succeeded. Expressed in the vein of the comic–grandiose, the intent is to "*show* mankind their Souls' antipodes," whether or not he can do anything about their sorry contradictions and failings. His use of "show" implies both the demonstrative stance of the moralist who confronts us with a judgmental mirror, and the display of the writer-as-actor who keeps our attention. Encyclopedic ambition in *Don Juan* is in keeping with the grandiose metaphor, "Columbus of the moral seas," which I consider self-descriptive. The metaphor confirms the playfulness of all Byronic disclaimers of moral purpose. In this satire, the serious and the comic are not antipodes at all.

Antipodes and restless action

The phrase "Soul's antipodes" defines Byron's sense of the contradictions that prevail in the moral life. The most pointed statement of the stubborn irreconcilability of values is found in *Cain* (1821). Adah has distinguished between the Seraphim, who "*love most*," and the Cherubim, who "*know most*." Lucifer says to her and Cain:

> And if the higher knowledge quenches love,
> What must *he be* you cannot love when known?
> Since the all-knowing Cherubim love least,
> The Seraphs' love can be but ignorance:
> That they are not compatible, the doom
> Of thy fond parents, for their daring, proves.
> Choose betwixt Love and Knowledge – since there is
> No other choice . . .   (*CN* I 423–30)

Throughout the play, Lucifer's is the humanist's wisdom, which Cain adopts, unlike Abel who relies on supernatural sanctions. Love and knowledge are both indisputably values, but they do not well cohabit.

Shelley expresses the problem with greater resonance in *Prometheus Unbound*:

> The wise want love, and those who love want wisdom;
> And all best things are thus confused to ill.   (*PU* I 627–8)

For Byron the problem is not that there are no moral values; there *are*, and like other Romantics he is a value pluralist. Lucifer acknowledges intrinsic value: "Evil and Good are things in their own essence, / And not made good or evil by the Giver" (II ii 452–3). Lucifer, Cain, and Byron cannot be termed nihilists or relativists. But whereas Shelley's drama unfolds the dialectical reconciliation of love and knowledge – Asia joining Prometheus in wedlock – Byron's drama bears out the dreaded prognosis. In choosing knowledge, Cain cannot live with his brother, whose callow and complacent assumptions about God's justice make Cain's ill-tempered homicide seem in context downright pardonable.

Cain witnesses as well the incompatibility of power and goodness, indicting God much in the manner of Hume in his *Dialogues Concerning Natural Religion*. If an omnipotent God were good, why would he permit evil? Cain has received one answer from Adam, also found in the various theodicies of Blake, Shelley, and Keats:

>   I asked
> This question of my father; and he said,
> Because this Evil only was the path
> To Good. Strange Good, that must arise from out
> Its deadly opposite.   (*CN* II ii 285–9)

Sensibly enough, Cain thinks it better "never to be *stung at all*" by a reptile than to be stung and agonizingly nursed back to health. Thus Cain, and Byron with him, would scorn Keats's talk of Soul-making – the saving enlargement of identity through suffering – and he would lack Blake's confidence that the contraries of good and evil are progressive. Shelley points to the problem:

> The good want power, but to weep barren tears.
> The powerful goodness want: worse need for them.
>
> (*PU* I 625–6)

Prometheus Unbound prophesies a reconciliation of power and goodness, in which love will spring "from its awful throne of patient power / In the wise heart" (IV 557–8). But the permanent punishment of Cain and his offspring ensures that no such reconciliation will occur in human history, throughout which all pages are the same.

The irreconcilables of *Cain* – knowledge and love, power and goodness, gentleness and rage, supernaturalism and humanism – are characteristic of the larger oeuvre. Byron gives no theology or metaphysics to account for this predicament; he simply testifies to it in context after context. The dramatic and narratological structuring of ideas in Byron is blatantly anti-dialectical. The famous Haidee episode of *Don Juan*, for instance, argues the incompatibility of love and knowledge. Haidee, who "was all which pure Ignorance allows," could not have "dreamt of falsehood" (*DJ* II 190). The only love that does not torture is an idyllic love grounded in innocence and ignorance. Blakean dialectic treats loss of innocence as a prelude to recovery of innocence in a higher form. But Byron's narrative sacrifices Haidee, who cannot endure witnessing her father's brutal treatment of Don Juan.

Innocence and experience are irreconcilable time and again in Byron. Once innocence is lost, it is lost. The condition of Adam, who mourns for paradise, is permanent. Byron expresses more nostalgia for paradise lost than the other British Romantics, who tend to disparage primitivism. In addition to Haidee's paradisical life in the Cyclades, he wistfully evokes life in America, where "General Boon" (Daniel Boone) lives a life of hunting, "Simple, serene, the *antipodes* of Shame / Which Hatred nor Envy e'er could tinge with wrong; / An active hermit, even in age the child / Of nature—" (*DJ* VIII 63). Antipodes of civilization and nature reappear in Byron's final narrative, *The Island* (1823), where two innocent lovers differ from Haidee and Don Juan in that they expel destructive civilized forces. No reconciliation of nature and civilization takes place.

Central among the antipodes that define the human predicament are those of mind and body. Byron reinstates this dualism. For Blake, body is the portion of soul perceived by the five senses; for Coleridge with his "Psycho-somatic Ology," the passions unite body and mind. But dualism underlies both Manfred's suffering and Don Juan's comic predicament. To the spirits of nature, Manfred exclaims that his "Promethean spark, / The lightning of my being" will not yield to them, even though it is "cooped in clay!" (I i 154–7). We human beings,

> Half dust, half deity, alike unfit
> To sink or soar, with our mixed essence make
> A conflict of its elements, and breathe
> The breath of degradation and of pride,
> Contending with low wants and lofty will,
> Till our Mortality predominates.   (*MF* I ii 40–5)

Clay "clogs the ethereal essence," and assures that "knowledge is not happiness, and science / But an exchange of ignorance for that / Which is another kind of ignorance" (I iv 57, 61–3). In his journal *Detached Thoughts* (15 October 1821 to 18 May 1822), Byron's commitment to dualism leads him to question an earlier repudiation of immortality. Mind, he observes, acts

> so very independent of body—in dreams for instance incoherently and madly—I grant you;—but still it is *Mind & much more Mind*—than when we are awake. — —Now—that *this* should not act *separately*—as well as jointly—who can pronounce?—The Stoics Epictetus & Marcus Aurelius call the present state 'a soul which drags a Carcase'—a heavy chain to be sure, but all chains being material may be shaken off.   (*LJ* IX 45)

This reflection leads to his familiar conclusion: "Man is born *passionate* of body—but with an innate though secret tendency to the love of Good in his Main-spring of Mind.— —But God help us all!—It is at present a sad jar of atoms.— —" (*LJ* IX 46).

Dialectical progression is thwarted by a stubborn lack of accommodation in the nature of things. Hazlitt, we recall, says that the greatest wisdom is to acknowledge that if a thing is, it is. Eschewing metaphysics, Byron writes, "If I agree that what is, is—then this I call / Being quite perspicuous and extremely fair" (*DJ* XI 5). And one thing that decidedly is, is our permanent lack of luck. Reflecting on Johnson's *The Vanity of Human Wishes* (1747), Byron observes that the "lapse of ages *changes* all things . . . *except man himself*, who has always been, and always will be, an unlucky rascal. The infinite variety of lives conduct but to death, and the infinity of wishes lead but to disappointment" (*LJ* VIII 19–20). Hazlitt finds it absurd that a wealthy lord, who possesses what the rest of us can only want, should complain of his hard luck. But the Byron of *Childe Harold's Pilgrimage* sees us all as victims of the same intransigent circumstances: time, contingency, the forces of nature, the negative economy of human desire, and death. Just as Wordsworth is the epitaphic poet, Byron is the poet of ruins, of human artifacts and human beings themselves overpowered and degenerate. He is a "ruin amidst ruins," he is not what he has been, he too mourns for a lost paradise.[5]

The ruins of empires and the decay of Venice bespeak national power now lost, a wholeness now fragmented, but ruins are imperfectly analogous to the fallen human personality. Childe Harold does not describe any prior state of power and wholeness from which he has

---

[5] See Robert F. Gleckner, *Byron and the Ruins of Paradise* (Baltimore: The Johns Hopkins University Press, 1967) and Thomas McFarland, *Romanticism and the Forms of Ruin* (1981).

fallen. Making no extravagant claims for childhood, Byron gives us no conception of an unfallen human personality who has joined power and goodness, knowledge and love, body and mind, desire and fulfillment. Childe Harold's is an objectless nostalgia for a personal wholeness and power never possessed. The *ubi sunt* theme and the decay of empire, which Volney had made fashionable in *Les Ruines, ou Méditations sur les révolutions des empires* (1791), tell Childe Harold that nothing human is exempt from time. Lacking a myth of human integration, such as we find in Blake, Coleridge, and Shelley, Byron cannot prophesy reintegration as a challenge to time and ruin. In short, he can give us no answer to the problems he has set forth in *Childe Harold's Pilgrimage.*

Byron's anti-dialectical vision could have led to a single-minded lament on the futility of action and the wisdom of resignation. But he is always urging himself and his heroes to act. In response to Cain's understandably plaintive remarks over their eviction from paradise, Eve says, "Content thee with what is." "Behold thy father cheerful and resigned— / And do as he doth" (I i 45, 50–1). But Cain does not resign himself to God's arbitrary and unjust will, and commits a murderous act, the moral nature of which is profoundly ambiguous. My reading – one that accords with contemporary readings of the play as blasphemous – is that Cain, in murdering Abel, heroically resists fatuous resignation. He asserts human will against an infinitely greater power and becomes the more human for doing so. Coleridge thinks an act of will for the will's sake is satanic; yet with Schelling he feels the resigned will is not fully human. Whatever else it is, Cain's is an act of will that exhibits the impulse to freedom in a fallen world. If murdering one's brother is not particularly humanistic, it is at least all too human. Once again, Byron is neither cautionary nor legislative; in *Cain* we find no answer to what is to be done.

Doing rather too much, like Cain, is inversely correlative to doing too little – and Byronic heroes tend to swing from one pole to the other in self-concept, rhetoric, and behavior. Byron adds some shadings to the Coleridgean–Keatsian anatomy of "indolence" or "idleness." All three poets complain of it, often in connection with vocation. Coleridge, whose ambitions point in so many directions at once, never decides what his vocation is. Coleridgean indolence approaches paralysis in a radical dissociation of consciousness from will. We have seen that Keats, who decides single-mindedly that his vocation is poetry, has doubts later on, and longs for real acts. To the writer, complaining of idleness is an enabling rhetorical act. The writer's idleness is necessarily reversed in writing of it, or simply in writing.

Johnson's inability to rise in the morning and his ability to write a dictionary make up a causal continuum. Perhaps someday we will have edited and published all of Coleridge's voluminous writings. Not writing is a necessary condition for writing, a fact confirmed even by the Balzacs and Trollopes, for whom continuous writing is a counter-thrust to not writing, which haunts them as an intolerable negation and which serves all the more as a goad. Similarly, not acting is an enabling condition of acting. One cannot always be acting; for a time, Yeats tells us, Caesar must stay in his tent, "His eyes fixed upon nothing, / A hand under his head," his mind moving upon silence. Writing is, as I have said in connection with *The Prelude*, the writer's action.

Byron is of interest in this matter because he purports to separate writing from action and declares it an idle trade that in no way answers to his own need for action. His comment to Annabella Milbanke, the future Lady Byron, expresses more than aristocratic indifference to scribbling. To poetry and poets he prefers

the talents of *action*—of war—or the Senate—or even of Science—to all the speculations of these mere dreams of another existence (I don't mean *religiously* but *fancifully*) and spectators of this.——Apathy—disgust—& perhaps incapacity have rendered me now a mere spectator—but I have occasionally mixed in the active & tumultuous departments of existence—& on these alone my *recollection* rests with any satisfaction—though not the *best* parts of it.

(*LJ* III 179–80)

And to Murray he writes:

If I live ten years longer, you will see . . . that it is not over with me—I don't mean in literature, for that is nothing; and it may seem odd enough to say, I do not think it my vocation. But you will see that I will do something or other—the times and fortune permitting—that, 'like the cosmogony, or creation of the world, will puzzle the philosophers of all ages.' But I doubt whether my constitution will hold out. I have, at intervals, exorcised it most devilishly.

(*LJ* V 177)

There is one piece of evidence that he means what he says; he follows this script in leaving off *Don Juan* for the Greek War of Independence. But this comment also fits a pattern in his life and work, wherein a sense of idleness or futility proves an enabling condition of productive acts or grandiose gestures. If Byron had not nourished a suspicion that writing is an idle trade, he might not have written so much.

We can sort out the varieties of idleness in Byron and see how each is correlative to an extraordinary productivity. First there is Byron the writer who says that writing is not his vocation, that poets as a class have "done" nothing, and that he will "do something or other" by way of compensation. Yet the Byronic corpus, as a large and many-sided totality of writerly acts, insists that writing was his vocation after all. Next there is the Byron who performs acts other than writerly ones and who declares that these too, whether of love or war, are futile; one forces objects of attainment on oneself only to avoid rusting in the scabbard. Yet Byron leaves the record of a monumental life, which his biographers read as a purposeful narrative sufficient for at least three volumes, ending in death for a good cause. Finally, there is the representation of action and value in his poems and plays themselves, with which I am chiefly concerned here. We see his protagonists engaged in acts of exclusion and denial. Childe Harold is strictly a do-nothing, Manfred a suicide, and Cain a murderer. Yet they exhibit a saving bravura both in following out the experiential imperative for its own sake and in rejecting life only on the other side of a glut of it; and they make way for the productive energies of *Don Juan* and its inexhaustible narrator.

In the same entry of the *Ravenna Journal* in which Byron observes that man "has always been, and always will be, an unlucky rascal," he reflects on the forthcoming Carbonari uprising. Though he doubts its success, he exclaims: "But, onward!—it is now the time to act, and what signifies *self*, if a single spark of that which would be worthy of the past can be bequeathed unquenchedly to the future? It is not one man, nor a million, but the *spirit* of liberty which must be spread" (*LJ* VIII 20). The larger journal entry, in its obvious contradiction, defines the Byronic dilemma: though history insists that there can be no permanent change in our bad luck, it is necessary to act as if there could be.

There is as much theatrical bravura as existential angst in this text. A commitment to action-as-performance despite an overriding sense of futility is pronounced in Byron's heroes, whose compensation for a dark fate must be limited to our applause. Within the dramatic and narrative worlds they inhabit, they exhibit a recklessness in response to the nonnegotiable contradiction between the impulse to freedom and the tyranny of history and fate. When Childe Harold sets off, at the beginning of Canto the Third, he exclaims:

> Once more upon the waters! yet once more!
> And the waves bound beneath me as a steed
> That knows his rider. Welcome to their roar!
> Swift be their guidance, wheresoe'er it lead!

> Though the strained mast should quiver as a reed,
> And the rent canvass fluttering strew the gale,
> Still must I on; for I am as a weed,
> Flung from the rock, on Ocean's foam, to sail
> Where'er the surge may sweep, the tempest's breath prevail.
>
> (CH III 2)

Childe Harold is "self-exiled," and his embarkation seems his own initiative. But the stanza points up the contradiction in this free and reckless submission to forces beyond one's control. He makes a reckless contract with fate, in which he will be both noble rider and a weed demeaningly flung about by waves. It is an attempt at self-abandonment, or as Childe Harold says (with Manfred), of "forgetfulness." In the free surrender of personal will to larger forces of nature, circumstance, and fate, Childe Harold hopes – as Byron says of himself in a journal kept for his half-sister Augusta – "to lose my own wretched identity in the majesty & the power and the Glory—around—above— & beneath me" (LJ V 105). The Coleridgean distinction obtains here: Childe Harold hopes to lose "conscience" and gain a heightened non-reflexive "consciousness" in identifying with larger cosmic forces. But the very act of parading the search for forgetfulness subverts it. Childe Harold remains shackled by conscience, and all of London's readership applauds him for it.

The figuration of personal will, sensation, and water (natural power) suggests that Childe Harold has stepped into the domain of the Blakean Zoa, Tharmas. Much of Byron's work from Childe Harold's Pilgrimage to Don Juan is, in effect, an investigation of this Zoa, which represents variously the body, the senses, instinct, sexuality, will, and life, and whose domain is water, the chaotic element out of which emerge new life and power. I have called him the Zoa of experiential readiness, and think his disappearance in the prophetic books after The Four Zoas is symptomatic of the older Blake's drift toward mentalism. Byron's reinvigoration of this Zoa is in keeping with his own militant anti-mentalism. But unlike Blake, who speaks of life as forever renewable, the Byron of Childe Harold's Pilgrimage would conceive of Tharmas as limited in his power of renewal. Given a human being's continuous slow decay ending in ruin, a last-ditch imperative one can give oneself is to fight off entropy through sensation, desire, and act, not directed toward goals but for the sake of life's intensity. To Annabella, he writes, undoubtedly to disturb her with a weary bravura, that the "great object of life is Sensation—to feel that we exist—even though in pain—it is this 'craving void' which drives us to Gaming—to Battle—to Travel—to intemperate but keenly felt pursuits of every description whose principal attraction is the agitation inseparable from their accomplishment" (*LJ* III 109). Heightening sensation to give ourselves the impression we exist is one way of avoiding the characterless state of being most of us occupy most of the time. "When one subtracts from life infancy (which is vegetation),—sleep, eating, and swilling—buttoning and unbuttoning—how much remains of downright existence? The summer of a dormouse"(*LJ* III 235).

Four non-satiric heroes – Childe Harold, Prometheus, Cain, and Manfred – depict the powers of the Blakean Tharmas.[6] They lack what Byron calls the "insipid virtues." His friend, John Claridge, is "a good man, a handsome man, an honourable man, a most inoffensive man, a well informed man and a *dull* man, & this damned epithet undoes all the rest" (*LJ* II 102–3). Byron observes that "the worst of civilization & refinement is that we are reduced to a most insipid medium between good and harm and must get very much out of the beaten path to do either" (*LJ* IV 162). These four heroes drift wide of the beaten path, and are severely punished for it.

All are accused by other parties of overvaluing some human bond. Manfred has presumably destroyed his sister through incestuous love; Prometheus has stolen fire from Zeus in order to be "kind" to the sorry human race; Cain has slain his brother because he thinks human conscience should take precedence over brutal divine will. Childe Harold's transgression in Cantos the Third and Fourth is less tangible, but Byron presumes public awareness of his rumored affair with Augusta and separation from Lady Byron. More generally, Childe Harold has given offense by his prideful renunciation of insipid bourgeois virtues. In all four, the ethical dimension is defined by acts of resistance, often speech acts, that assert the right to experience more, to eschew either supernatural or conventional human sanctions for the more compelling sanction of personal will.

These heroes are of interest in that each represents a different brand of dead-end humanism. The larger Byronic oeuvre – especially *Don Juan* – contextualizes their failures as failures. But within their own contexts, none submits to moral adjudication. In different ways they dramatize the ethics of predicament, to which each adds an aesthetic dimension by dint of bravura and showmanship. Their existential solitude is somewhat qualified by our suspicion that they are playing to an audience. They contrast with Shelley's poet in *Alastor*, Maddalo, and the "pard-like Spirit" of *Adonais*, who, we recall, are crippled in

---

[6] For a discussion of these and other major Byronic protagonists, exclusive of Don Juan, see Peter L. Thorslev, Jnr., *The Byronic Hero: Types and Prototypes* (Minneapolis: University of Minnesota Press, 1962).

their self-preoccupation and are portrayed in the cautionary mode. Byron's heroes more resolutely assert themselves beyond the moral categories they confront. They garner a larger share of authorial admiration. Their master trope is the brag.

As I have said, Childe Harold upon setting forth once again in Canto the Third derives a self-contradictory empowerment from the non-moral force of nature. This initiates an entire set of contradictions. Experiential readiness is directed toward forgetfulness, and pursuit of sensation in his wanderings yields only a sense of emptiness, not the feeding and filling that sensation offers in Keats and Wordsworth. Giant passions prompt him

> to steel
> The heart against itself; and to conceal,
> With a proud caution, love, or hate, or aught,
> Passion or feeling, purpose, grief, or zeal,—
> Which is the tyrant Spirit of our thought.   (CH III 111)

In every respect Childe Harold wishes to have it both ways: to be free and not free, to feed on experience and yet be empty, to feel and not feel, to exhibit and yet conceal, and to have great power in reserve and yet declare himself impotent. The narrator, barely distinct from Childe Harold, wishes he could throw "Soul—heart—mind—passions —feelings—strong or weak—" and all his experience of life into a single word with the power of "lightning." Such Olympian power would transport an audience, as Longinus says, "like a thunderbolt." But he confesses his impotence, and he must "die unheard / With a most voiceless thought, sheathing it as a sword" (CH III 97). The life-affirming functions of Tharmas are both seized on and converted to negatives by Childe Harold's duplicitous moral calculus. The overriding of human power by non-moral powers of ocean at the end of Canto the Fourth is a vision of total purgation, which resolves no problem *within* moral consciousness.

Prometheus, Cain, and Manfred differ from Childe Harold in that the ethical maintains its dominance in their own reckless pursuit of experience. They renounce the consolations of nature and the supernatural. Prometheus acts with clearest moral purpose, the alleviation of man's dark estate, and his self-denial contrasts with Childe Harold's contradictory having and not having. In the 1816 lyric, "Prometheus," the hero's suffering is "silent" and "patient," in contrast to which Childe Harold's is noisy and incontinent. There is no blunting the "sensation" Prometheus feels, and it is pure pain. There is also no limit to his will for more life. Even torture does not engender a

434

wish for death or forgetfulness. Prometheus embodies the powers of Tharmas – sensation and will – without the countervailing weariness, guilt, and death wish of Childe Harold, Manfred, and Cain. To these powers he adds mind and enlightenment: his increase of consciousness includes conscience. Whereas Childe Harold does not love mankind nor mankind him, Prometheus acts from pity and kindness. The result is that while Childe Harold says "the Moral of his Strain" must be left up to the reader, Prometheus bequeaths us a "mighty lesson." It is that human will can be the equal of fate, ignorance, and death.

The poem's conclusion strikes my ear as a crescendo of formulaic heroics and titanic wishful thinking. Prometheus represents, relative to other Byronic heroes, a projection of their own desire for a human will equal to all adversity in this "sad unallied existence." As such he is propped up by gaseous hyperbole. Byron does not leave the impression elsewhere that there is some way of "making Death a Victory," or that in torture there can be any "concentered recompense."

Cain is cast into an existence sad and burdensome, but not yet unallied; it is an existence watched over by a supernatural power whose administration offends Cain's moral sense. In his defiance, he rejects fellowship for alienation and exile, supernaturalism for frustrated humanism. In the play's beginning, the toiling and morally perplexed Cain would die were it not for

> an innate clinging,
> A loathsome, and yet all invincible
> Instinct of life.
>   (CN I i 111–13)

The instinct of life, the Tharmas function, shows itself most profoundly in the murder scene, where Cain refuses to sacrifice animals to Jehovah, thus incurring his displeasure. Abel, who loves "God far more / Than life," obediently murders animals. The censors were right to think *Cain* blasphemous, because Byron goes out of his way to exculpate Cain, who values life and strikes Abel to prevent his carrying out God's murderous arbitrary will. In acting independently of God, Cain confirms himself as moral agent. But unlike "Prometheus," this play does not propose that human will is the equal of larger, malignant forces – God, time, death. Cain and his descendants are permanently accursed and overpowered.

Manfred follows out most systematically Byron's vision of the defiant, reckless humanist who acts according to his own lights despite forebodings of futility and even damnation. Claiming the "Pro-

435

methean spark" and defiant will, he lacks the Promethean "patience," which he scorns like a Nietzschean. The incest he broadly hints at (though like Shelley's Beatrice, he stops short of naming the deed), is the culmination of a life of reckless exploration, in which he has experienced the extremes of violence, pleasure, study, toil, weariness, disease, insanity, and a broken heart, all before the customary onset of midlife crisis (III i 138–53). One passion he has never felt or acted on is cruelty; his greatest sin has been love itself. The incestuous bonding of Manfred and Astarte is a defiant humanism, but unlike the proud and guiltless Prometheus, Manfred is tortured by his transgression, because his was the love that kills. Why it killed, Byron leaves unclear, but the implication is, as in *Cain*, that human beings are punished by obtuse powers for human acts sanctioned by secular conscience alone. Manfred's sense of guilt is not for the incestuous love – he does not display undue pudeur – but for its fatal consequence.

As the play progresses, he performs a series of divestitures, which reduce to nullity the enlargement of being he has previously gained through exercising the powers of Tharmas. He seeks "forgetfulness" in a most general sense. The various encounters with spirits of nature and of hell, the chamois hunter, Astarte, and the Abbot, are defiant and renunciatory. The seven spirits of nature – the four elements, energy, darkness, and necessity – cannot claim him, though he admits that, "cooped in clay," he shares their makeup. In his encounter with the chamois hunter he disclaims the grandiose identification with nature's power that purges Childe Harold of the merely human. More difficult to renounce is the Witch of the Alps, who represents beauty, elsewhere termed a "fatal gift." The phantom of Astarte, his dead love, then fails to answer his questions as to whether he is forgiven or still loved, whereupon he renounces love also. The Abbot, who asks him to repent and be reconciled with the true church, is no obstacle. Manfred's response is humanistic: he stands condemned by his own conscience, not by the external sanction of church. And by the same token he defies the spirit of evil, whose torture would be merely redundant with what he self-inflicts: the mind "makes itself / Requital for its good or evil thoughts, — / Is its own origin of ill and end— / And its own place and time" (III iv 129–32). In a letter Byron says the whole meaning of the play resides in the penultimate line that Murray cut in its first publication: "Old man," Manfred says to the Abbot, " 'tis not so difficult to die." Since Manfred has not had so easy a time of it onstage, the line makes sense only as it applies to the end of the process of renunciation and defiance. Calm is possible after desire has been purged, but purgation of desire is the most difficult task of all.

Manfred therefore pushes to extremes of negation Byron's vision of desire, act, freedom, sensation, energy, and limitation, explored variously in *Childe Harold's Pilgrimage*, "Prometheus," and *Cain*, as well as many other works. It reverses Keats's Soul-making, since suffering results not in increased identity but in a gradual, deliberate self-annihilation. Instead of progressive dialectic, we have a triumphant regression to the null point. Manfred refuses the duplicitous sentimentality of Childe Harold in continuing to have what he professes to be renouncing. He declines the self-righteousness of Prometheus, the strength of good conscience. And he finally declines that innate and instinctive clinging to life that carries a tortured Cain to his wanderings. What Byron must admire here is the strength and autonomy of Manfred's conscience, which is the last power to be divested, with consciousness itself.

But it is of course an unamiable humanism that takes the form of solipsism and death. Manfred acts as if the autonomous conscience offers sufficient sanctions, but his is no answer to the question of how human beings might cope with moral reality. No ethic can be extrapolated from this drama, no imperative for its readership. Manfred's melodramatic exit is his alone, all alone. He demonstrates the Byronic hero's strong commitment to action despite an overriding sense of futility, but he only accelerates the progress of ruin.

Byron's antipodal ordering of values has implied throughout that resolute human acts must be acts of exclusion. "Choose betwixt Love and Knowledge," because you cannot have both. Childe Harold cannot act because he always tries to have it both ways. His anguish is occasioned by his own willful indeterminacy; this is his adolescence. Cain and Prometheus act with great *determination*, Cain losing home and happiness, Prometheus losing everything except his honor and identity. Both gain the condition of permanent pain. Manfred has completed the pattern by acts of exclusion to the point of nullity in a total renunciation of values. But this is not Byron's final say in the matter.

The controlless core

In a soliloquy at the beginning of Act III, Manfred says that an "Inexplicable Stillness" has come over him:

> If that I did not know Philosophy
> To be of all our vanities the motliest,
> The merest word that ever fooled the ear
> From out the schoolman's jargon, I should deem

The golden secret, the sought "Kalon" found,
And seated in my soul. It will not last,
But it is well to have known it, though but once:
It hath enlarged my thoughts with a new sense,
And I within my tablets would note down
That there is such a feeling.

(MF III i 9–18)

Manfred has just renounced the phantom of Astarte. His speech contains a clue to a continuing intellectual interest of Byron's that might provide a path of transit from out the dead-end humanism we have just explored. As I have said, Manfred's recognition of Kalon – the Greek ideal of physical and moral beauty – could subvert the drama's manifest negativity. Manfred himself brackets the feeling by noting it down in his tablets, as if writing his own textual aporia. It contradicts the larger tendency of the drama Manfred has scripted in other ways, and gives us a clue as to how we might go beyond willful egoistic humanism to a fuller ethical ground.

In two early letters, one of 1810 to Robert Charles Dallas and another of 1815 to Annabella Milbanke (both correspondents possessed of the moralistic temperament that would call forth such reflections), Byron brings up the question of the Kalon. He defines it in terms of an Epicurean ethic:

I once thought myself a Philosopher [says he the day before his twentieth birthday] and talked nonsense with great Decorum, I defied pain and preached up equanimity, for some time this did very well, for no one was in *pain* for me but my Friends, and none lost their patience but my hearers, at last a fall from my horse convinced me, bodily suffering was an Evil, and the worst of an argument overset my maxims and my temper at the same moment, so I quitted Zeno for Aristippus [i.e. Stoicism for Epicureanism], and conceive that Pleasure constitutes the "τó Καλον."—In Morality I prefer Confucius to the ten Commandments, and Socrates to St Paul (though the two latter agree in their opinion of marriage) . . . —I hold virtue in general, or the virtues severally, to be only in the Disposition, each *a feeling* not a principle.

(LJ I 148)

This passage, to my knowledge, is the closest we get to an outright statement of an ethic in the entire corpus. Characteristic of the Romantics, it comes near the beginning, not the end, of his career. Subsequent comments suggest that Epicureanism – as taught by Aristippus, Epicurus, and Lucretius – engages Byron and glosses even those many aspects of his art, thought, and life that directly contradict the doctrine. I propose that Epicureanism is the principal heuristic of Byron's life and poetry.

He enjoys informing the proper Annabella that she herself has unwittingly subscribed to the doctrine of Epicurus:

I am much amused with *your* "sovereign good" being placed in *repose*—I need not remind you that this was the very essence of the Epicurean philosophy—and that both the Gods (who concerned themselves with nothing on earth) and the Disciples of the illustrious idler the founder of that once popular sect—defined the "τó Καλον" to consist in literally doing nothing—and that all agitation was incompatible with pleasure.—The truth possibly is that these materialists [Epicurus subscribed to the atomism of Democritus] are so far right—but to enjoy repose we must be weary—and it is to "the heavy laden" that the invitation to "rest" speaks most eloquent music.

(*LJ* IV 168)

This qualified assent to Epicureanism is useful in defining the Byronic attitude towards pleasure and the moral life. He agrees with the Epicurean that pleasure is a primary value, but he rejects the Epicurean ethic of inactivity and control of desire as a means of attaining it. To enjoy repose, one must first be weary from a life of active engagement, and one must have pursued values other than pleasure. This is the value we most seek, yet it is also the most vulnerable to the exclusionary, antipodal pattern that characterizes Byron's view of the economy of values. It maintains a perilous co-existence with any other value in his ethical lexicon.

In 1820 he is still pondering the question. To John Cam Hobhouse, his Cambridge friend and travel companion, he writes of being constitutionally incapable of the Epicurean life, although this has greatest appeal:

The life of an Epicurean—& the philosophy of one are merely prevented by "that rash humour which my Mother gave me" that makes one restless & nervous—& can overthrow all tranquillity with a Sirocco.——Surely you agree with me about the real *vacuum* of human pursuits, but one must force an object of attainment—not to rust in the Scabbard altogether.   (*LJ* VII 115–16)

To force objects of attainment is to violate the Epicurean principle that for the sake of pleasure one should maintain equilibrium and control of desire, which occasions pain and imbalance. Byron knows Epicurus has priority on wisdom here. His alternative to rusting in the scabbard – the willed pursuit of objects of attainment – has led to disappointment, satiety, and bad conscience, the penalties for not heeding the Samian sage.

Aware of Epicurus's qualitative distinctions among pleasures, he assures Leigh Hunt that he has not been engaged in "the frivolous forgetfulness of a mind occupied by what is called pleasure (*not* in the true sense of Epicurus)" (*LJ* III 188).[7] Critics have often spoken of

---

[7] Influenced by Aristotle (who in turn is influenced by Plato's *Philebus*), Epicurus distinguishes between kinetic pleasures, which are short-lived and usually derived

THE PRESSURE OF REALITY

Byron's "Calvinism," a legacy of his Scottish background, but ironically many of his laments on the mental cost of indulgence could be sanctioned as well by Epicureanism. Neither set of principles contains him. The narrator of *Don Juan* speaks of a "rack of pleasures" to which aristocracy must submit, and, reflecting on what "late hours, wine, and love" do to rakes and aldermen, he observes that "There is no sterner moralist than Pleasure" (*DJ* III 65). He sees comic pathos in its negative economy: " 'T is pity though, in this sublime world, that / Pleasure's a sin, and sometimes Sin's a pleasure" (*DJ* I 133). "Oh Pleasure! you're indeed a pleasant thing, / Although one must be damned for you, no doubt" (*DJ* I 119), he complains at the beginning of a catalogue of pleasures – moonlight, rainbows, lark's songs, wine, money, revenge, legacies, quarrels, and "first and passionate Love" (*DJ* I 122–7). Epicureanism as popularly misconceived has a dangerous allure:

> there's Epicurus
> And Aristippus, a material crew!
> Who to immoral courses would allure us
> By theories quite practicable too;
> If only from the Devil they would insure us,
> How pleasant were the maxim (not quite new),
> "Eat, drink, and love, what can the rest avail us?"
> So said the royal sage Sardanapalus.   (*DJ* II 207)

from the satisfaction of some appetite or want, such as hunger or sex; and catastematic pleasures, which if less immediately intense are perdurable and worthier, such as a general sense of physical well-being free of pain and desire. This latter category includes physical sensation, but sensation taken up by mind to produce a calm that is antithetical to physical appetite and the desiring state. Epicurus writes, as if with Byron in mind, "The limit of quantity in pleasure is the removal of all that is painful": one may take pleasure in food to the extent that the pain of hunger is assuaged, but any pleasure beyond this injures the health and harmony of the system.

> When, therefore, we maintain that pleasure's the end, we do not mean the pleasures of profligates and those that consist in sensuality, as is supposed by some who are either ignorant or disagree with us or do not understand, but freedom from pain in the body and trouble in the mind. For it is not continuous drinkings and revellings, nor the satisfaction of lusts, nor the enjoyment of fish and other luxuries of the wealthy table, which produce a pleasant life, but sober reasoning, searching out the motives for all choice and avoidance, and banishing mere opinions, to which are due the greatest disturbances of the spirit.
>
> (*The Stoic and Epicurean Philosophers*, ed. Whitney J. Oates,
> New York: Random House, 1940, 35.)

And he urges, "Live unknown." Although lasting catastematic pleasure is the highest good, he advises us not to seek it corrosively, and could point as evidence to Byron, who writes to Leigh Hunt: "I am about to be married – and am of course in all the misery of a man in pursuit of happiness" (*LJ* IV 209).

Allusions to "Sin" and the Devil are hardly Epicurean, but Byron's humorous eclecticism here and elsewhere results in a satiric deflation of such "Calvinist" melodrama. Damnation for him is found in the aftermath of indulgence. The secular correlate of hell is the hangover.

The first premise of Byron's best-known narrative is the corruptive force of kinetic pleasure. In the moralistic preface to the first two cantos of *Childe Harold*, he disclaims any intention of drawing an "amiable character" in the protagonist, who "never was intended as an example, further than to show, that early perversion of mind and morals leads to satiety of past pleasures and disappointment in new ones, and that even the beauties of nature and the stimulus of travel (except ambition, the most powerful of all excitements) are lost on a soul so constituted, or rather misdirected" (*CH* II pp. 7–8). Had he continued the narrative, he would have portrayed in Childe Harold the figure of a "modern Timon, perhaps a poetical Zeluco," the latter a sadistic scoundrel who rivals Shelley's Count Cenci, similarly ruined by too early an indulgence in kinetic pleasure. If with Peter Brooks we think of the motive force of most narrative to be found in structures of desire, we see that Byron's narrative reverses the pattern, since its first premise is exhaustion.[8]

Severe judgment of his own fictional character (whom I have said he rather admires also) does not inhibit Byron's own indulgence, which culminates in Venice, where, with months remaining before his departure to Ravenna, he claims to have made love to "at least two hundred [women presumably] of one sort or another" (*LJ* VI 66). Shelley and others are shocked at his physical transformation: he has the fatty blurry-eyed demeanor of the stereotypic debauchee. It is as if he is begging for such judgments as Epicurus would bring to bear. From an early indoctrination in the art of kinetic pleasures to an eventual recoiling from them (at one point, he brags, "I have not had a whore this half-year—confining myself to the strictest adultery," (*LJ* VI 232), he enacts a truth he already knows: that pursuing strong sensations of kinetic pleasure ferrets its antipode, pain. It is with special authority that he writes, in agreement with Epicurus, that the "more intellectual our pleasure, the better for the pleasure and for us too" (*LJ* VIII 28). To the Byronic set of antipodes we must add passion (erotics) and pleasure (hedonics). A true Epicurean would moderate passion for the sake of higher pleasure or happiness, but the Byronic personality suffers for its futile coupling of passion and pleasure.

If we flank Byron with Epicurus on one side chronologically, we can

[8] Peter Brooks, *Reading for the Plot: Design and Intention in Narrative* (New York: Knopf, 1984).

flank him with Freud as our own heuristic on the other, and turn to his treatment of desire and pleasure in *Don Juan*. Though all the Romantics have been either compared with Freud, or explicated in Freudian terms, or put on the couch, I think it is Byron who most overtly anticipates Freudian perspectives on pleasure and desire, and the place of these in civilization. The negative economy of pleasure is a frequent theme in them both. Byron has himself "squandered [his] whole summer while 't was May," and Childe Harold's early dissipation has been precisely that – an expenditure of energy that has gone beyond detensioning to devitalization. It is Byron, not Blake, who sees civilization in Freudian way as forever destined to suppress instinct. Don Juan will continue encountering obstacles – prudish mothers, tyrannical fathers, uxorious husbands, slavery, brutality, cant – to gratification of his desires, though he will also have notable moments of triumph. Blake's myth is somewhat brighter than Byron's or Freud's: though we do much to impede our desires, sexual joy is forever renewable, and the great civilization of Golgonooza will fully accommodate the pleasure principle.

Don Juan is well-equipped to embrace the pleasure principle. "A thing of impulse and a child of song; / Now swimming in the sentiment of joy, / Or the sensation (if that phrase seem wrong)"; when called upon to perform as soldier he is delighted to join in, "but always without malice" (*DJ* VIII 24–5). Byron's narrative does not totally frustrate the capacity for pleasure. Comic contingency gives and takes away, and yet gives again, the objects of pleasure. It imposes the reality principle on Don Juan and also rescues him from it. In moving from the dark necessity of *Manfred* and *Cain* to the comic contingency of *Don Juan*, Byron has paralleled in his own career the movement from Wordsworth to De Quincey, but with an increase in the fund of pleasure. Don Juan has pluck in place of grandiose will, appetite in place of consuming passion, and the capacity for joy unspoiled by a weary consciousness of history. As such he becomes a vehicle for a view of pleasure and desire somewhat less funereal than that found in Schopenhauer and Freud, or in other works of Byron.

Like Epicurus, Schopenhauer and Freud see desire as a form of pain, a disequilibrium both mental and somatic. Not a positive value in itself, pleasure is the feeling that attends the transition from a state of deficiency or want (as in Schopenhauer) or a state of surplus energy (as in Freud) to a state of satiety or neutral balance. For both, the recommendation is a certain resignation to the way things are and the restoration of equilibrium. We should desist from desiring what we cannot possess because, says Freud, desiring turns neurotic when

442

forced into surrogate gratifications. And we never can get all that we want. But Byron, in his commentary on Epicurus and in many of his works, heroic and satiric, does not recommend that we adjust our desires and aggressive energies to reality. Rather, he urges resistance even when it seems futile, and he implies that it is the desiring state itself that keeps us actively alive, that gives us the sensation of life. It is in moments only that the sensation of joy overtakes us as an unexpected donation of experience, but such moments suffice to dispel cosmic gloom.

This exemption is consistent with the recognition that Byron is no nihilist. As I have said, he has a clear sense of what has value – beauty, love, pleasure, energy, food – but is glum about our incorporating a plurality of values at any one time. Human beings as a rule do not get what they want; to choose one thing is to lose another. The comic contingency of *Don Juan* continues these patterns of exclusion but with less sulking. Byron tells us that the world is at worst a *"glorious blunder"* (*DJ* XI 3: his emphasis).

Byron's slightly more positive assessment of the human predicament than that found in Schopenhauer and Freud can be seen in his disposition of what the later Freud takes to be the dual instincts of libido (eros) and aggression (thanatos). In *Beyond the Pleasure Principle* (1920) and *Civilization and Its Discontents* (1929), "pleasure" denotes the general object of human motivation – aggression as well as libido – which the instincts seek in attempting to neutralize themselves. We have seen in Byron the vivid presence of what Blake calls Tharmas – the body, the senses, and the instincts. Combining Blake and Freud, we can say that libido (Luvah) and aggression (Urizen) both originate in the somatic predisposition of Tharmas, the "parent power." This formula helps us perceive the relationship of Don Juan to other Byronic heroes. In Manfred, Cain, and Childe Harold, eros – as an instinct of human bonding, whether directed toward individuals or groups – has been frustrated by whatever reality principle is operative (a censorious social community, an authoritarian deity, time, geography, unspeakable events that have befallen the hero). Aggression has gained domination in their lives, with its corollaries of ambition, recklessness, guilt, masochism, and death wish. Don Juan, in turn, is not so passive as he is sometimes said to be, albeit he is a pawn of chance. If forced to it, he will enter into warfare and excel in reckless honor, will slay a bandit and fight off henchmen. But aggression is not his leading trait and must be provoked. He is as frequently thrown into situations that spur his impulse toward community – sexual or social. Expelled from the arms of Donna Julia, he finds himself in a community of shipwrecked sailors. Expelled from Haidee's arms, he falls in with an itinerant opera company. Sexuality is his means of entry into social communities, from Turkish harems to the court of Catherine the Great to Regency society. Eros prevails over aggression in his own character and is the equal of it in the larger narrative.

Examining the function of eros more closely – and thereafter that of aggression – I think it can be said that Byron more than Freud sees the possibility of eros transcending its narcissistic component. If the world were ruled by self-love, how could we account for Don Juan himself, who in the midst of the seige of Ismail, rescues, cares for, and comes to love a Turkish girl? Whereas the Russian commander Suwarrow fails to suffer with the sufferings of his troops, seeing things only "in the gross," Don Juan has an eye for particulars of suffering and can act selflessly, just as he can, to be sure, fall into "that no less imperious passion, / Self-love" (*DJ* IX 68). How do we account for his and Haidee's love if the only motive for human acts is self-love? To be sure, much of what passes for love is actually aggression, as seen in the crossed Sultana Gulbeyaz's murderous treatment of Don Juan. Byron also registers in Don Juan the narcissism of love, which "is vanity, / Selfish in its beginning as its end" (*DJ* IX 73), or so the narrator intones in a sorry mood. But unlike Freud, for whom the libido is an instrument of self-love even when it spills over to another, Byron acknowledges an occasional disinterestedness in love. He entertains a somewhat higher estimate than Freud of the libido's ability to leave the self and fasten, selflessly, onto another through love or friendship. Occasionally this happens.

The Byronic eros extends beyond sex to other forms of human bonding, particularly friendship. Don Juan's love for the ten-year-old Leila is non-sexual, non-authoritarian, protective, and caring:

> Don Juan loved her, and she loved him, as
>   Nor brother, father, sister, daughter love.—
> I cannot tell exactly what it was;
>   He was not yet quite old enough to prove
> Parental feelings, and the other class,
>   Called brotherly affection, could not move
> His bosom,—for he never had a sister:
> Ah! if he had—how much he would have missed her!
>
> (*DJ* X 53)

He is better able to say what this love is not than what it is; it is neither parental nor brotherly nor sensual, and yet there is a tender and companionable bond. Freud treats friendship as "aim-inhibited": it is an attempt to escape the purposiveness and pain of genital love.

Friendship occurs when "people make themselves independent of their object's acquiescence by displacing what they mainly value from being loved on to loving," thus bringing about "a state of evenly suspended, steadfast, affectionate feeling, which has little external resemblance any more to the stormy agitations of genital love, from which it is nevertheless derived."[9] This self-protective and often culturally beneficial form of love is, for Freud, sexual in its roots and, as such, displaced and diminished. It is even fraudulent if it pretends to reach out indiscriminately to "love of humankind."

Byron and the other Romantics verge on declaring friendship a paradigm in its own right, instead of a falling away from some greater intensity. We think of major friendships within the period – Coleridge and Wordsworth, Byron and Shelley, Keats and Haydon – as exerting a larger disturbing, generative force than their overtly erotic engagements. Coleridge calls his periodical *The Friend* and spends much of his life rupturing and patching up friendships. His relationship with Sara Hutchinson, Keats's with Fanny Brawne, Shelley's with Claire Clairmont, Wordsworth's with Mary Hutchinson, and Byron's gigantic erotic labors with woman after woman do not apparently satisfy their hunger for relationship or our hunger for meaning. Passionate friendship fails to satisfy also, but comes somewhat closer. Is it not the passionate non-sexual friendship of Julian and Maddalo, rather than the frenzy of the madman frustrated in love, which holds us in Shelley's narrative?[10]

But the Romantics do not bring this possibility to the level of conscious articulation. They do not admit the possible superiority or distinctiveness of friendship relative to passionate love, despite the fact that Luvah smites them with boils, or at least leaves them with burning foreheads and parching tongues. In a letter to Mary Shelley shortly after the drowning of Percy, Byron admits to qualms about his own underachievement of friendship:

As to friendship, it is a propensity in which my genius is very limited. I do not know the *male* human being, except Lord Clare, the friend of my infancy, for whom I feel any thing that deserves the name. All my others are men-of-the-world friendships. I did not even feel it for Shelley, however much I admired and esteemed him; so that you see not even vanity could bribe me into it, for, of

---

[9] *Civilization and Its Discontents*, trans. James Strachey (New York: W. W. Norton, 1961), 49.

[10] The homoerotic dimension of Romantic friendship does not disqualify my point that the Romantics are attracted to a paradigm of non-genital friendship. Fear of the homoerotic may be one reason, however, that they do not explore the grounds of friendship more than they do.

all men, Shelley thought highest of my talents,—and, perhaps, of my disposition. (*LJ* X 34)

The recently widowed Mary Shelley may have hoped for a more zealous testimonial. Friendship is, I think, the unacknowledged paradigm of human relations – a selfless, non-genital eros – towards which the Romantics are drawn, but which they never permit themselves wholly to engage, either in their lives or art. Their friendships, too, do not quite satisfy our search for significance.

Erotic love in *Don Juan* is suppressed by "moral" codes practiced by mothers, teachers, and society at large, but it triumphs again and again as a subversive force. The same mind/body dualism that takes on tragic properties in *Manfred* and *Detached Thoughts* generates rich comedy in *Don Juan*. Byron's description of Donna Julia's seduction of Don Juan is reminiscent of Sartre's illustration of bad faith, in which a woman submits to early stages of sexual engagement, permitting her hand to be clasped without "noticing" it, while continuing to address her suitor on the higher level of personality.[11] Byron gives a less dyspeptic account: "One hand on Juan's carelessly was thrown, / Quite by mistake—she thought it was her own; / Unconsciously she leaned upon the other / Which played within the tangles of her hair" (*DJ* I 109, 110). The self-deception, which in other contexts could be brutal and immoral, is witness to the triumph of the "controlless core / Of human hearts" over what both Byron and Blake call moral virtue, here incarnated as Plato, who is a "charlatan, a coxcomb," and a "go-between." When Donna Julia and Don Juan make love, they oust Plato, the antipode of passion overpowering that of reason. In the final scene of *Don Juan*, the sexual body triumphs momentarily over death, as the sweet-breathed Lady Fitz-Fulke emerges from out the ghost costume she has worn to the seduction of Don Juan. This is hardly some dialectical Liebstod; it is a momentary triumph of eros over death, the controlless core of the heart prevailing for a time over civilized hypocrisy.

Even the icy Lady Adeline Amundeville has a controlless core of passion that dictates her behavior, whether or not she is aware of it. Byron likens this motive power to the liquid center of a bottle of otherwise frozen champagne. The repressions of a code of respectability or cant have not crunched her libido, but the code is so ingrained that she does not recognize her own motive in getting Don Juan safely married to someone sexually uncompetitive. Byron pretends to "hate a

---

[11] *Existential Psychoanalysis* (from *Being and Nothingness*), trans. Hazel Barnes (Chicago: Henry Regnery, 1962), 72–6.

motive," and says, " 'T is sad to hack into the roots of things, / They are so much intertwisted with the earth" (*DJ* XIV 58, 59). Lady Amundeville's social life is a programmed hypocritical act that makes Don Juan doubt "how much of Adeline was *real*" (*DJ* XVI 96). But part of her remains real: the root motive of passion as the antipode of civilization and its cant. For Byron, a civilization held together by cant looms not as a reality but as an unreality principle. He values the energies of the sensate body, despite the pain they inflict. They are where reality resides, and they occasionally overpower civilized unreality. "I like energy—even animal energy—of all kinds" (*LJ* III 216). The difference between Blake and Byron is one of degree: subversive sexuality for Blake initiates apocalyptic change, personal and social, whereas for Byron it wins out only momentarily and then resumes its subterranean status. This kind of sexuality differs also from the libertinage of the aristocratic rake, which is itself convention-bound. Byron's behavior in Venice merely carries a convention to an unconventional extreme.

I am not implying that Byron has all along been covertly buoyant about human relationships. The momentary triumph of subversive sexuality, although emphasized in *Don Juan*, does not make a relationship. Occasional selflessness in love does not disprove this generalization:

I have always laid it down as a maxim—and found it justified by experience—that a man and a woman—make far better friendships than can exist between two of the same sex—but *then* with the condition—that they never had made—or are to make love with each other.—Lovers may [be]—and indeed generally are—enemies—but they never can be friends—because there must always be a spice of jealousy—and a something of Self in all their speculations.—Indeed I rather look upon Love altogether as a sort of hostile transaction—very necessary to make—or to break—matches and keep the world a-going—but by no means a sinecure to the parties concerned. (*LJ* X 50)

Don Juan journeys from his lost paradise in Greece to modern England where love is vanity, coquetry, aggression, powerplay, and the working of "sensibility," a quality which Byron thinks hypocritical and which he condemns in Rousseau, as Coleridge condemns it in Sterne. Embittered by his marriage ("Love and Marriage rarely can combine"), Byron goes through an extraordinary succession of affairs. The principle of non-incremental repetition makes the series of "Byron's women" merely that – a series. In neither his life nor his art does he give full witness to an erotic love relationship based on a progressive dialectic of love and self-love.

We have already, in effect, investigated aggression in Childe

Harold, Cain, and Manfred, but it remains to sort out on what grounds Byron finds value in it. More than Freud, he does admire aggression, provided that its target is evil or ludicrous. To admire aggression indiscriminately is a dangerous sentimentality, which he, like Blake, sometimes approaches, as when he says that even evil acts are superior to inactivity (*LJ* IV 162). In Childe Harold and Manfred a large degree of aggression is introjected as guilt or remorse, but not to the extent that they cease to resist banal authority; aggression extends both inwards and outwards. But Cain's aggression, after the murder of Abel, is totally introjected as guilt. At that point he is done in, having lost the energies that made him Cain. Aggression if directed outward is not necessarily death-dealing, and it can prevent one's rusting in the scabbard. But in itself it does not announce its moral value, positive or negative. The aggression of a Suwarrow or Castlereagh or Lambro is evil; that of Napoleon is of ambivalent value, sharing the best and the worst of qualities; that of Don Juan, a non-combatant unless provoked, is good. Other ethical modalities – context and the intrinsic qualities of the agent – determine its value. Byron himself, though often a peace-maker, retains a notable degree of lordly honor and is ready to demand "satisfaction" if affronted or betrayed. Rather than challenge Southey to a duel, upon hearing that Southey has spread a false rumor about him, he works his animus off in verse, accusing Southey in the Dedication to *Don Juan* of everything from committing apostasy to having married a whore to being incapable of seminal emission. The vein of satire happily gets the better of his sense of honor; aggression takes a different tack from dueling and grants a qualitatively higher pleasure.

Which brings us, finally, to the narrator of *Don Juan* himself. I emphasize his great sanity, moral and psychological. The transfer of energy from the context of dueling to that of writing might be termed a sublimation – of aggression instead of libido – but I would describe it in somewhat different terms. We have noted Byron's anxiety that in writing poetry he is not actually doing anything; he longs to drop symbolic for literal action. But throughout *Don Juan* we feel the presence of a master performer. There is quite a lot *doing* from stanza to stanza as the narrator tells his tale. And we also feel the great authorial pleasure taken in aggressive compositional energies expended in poetic feat after poetic feat. This pleasure is far from the pleasure Manfred takes in his discovery of Kalon; rather, it springs from great mental activity and writerly aggression and desire. It is an "intellectual pleasure," to use Byron's phrase. It is what Coleridge calls *Eunoia*, the "joyousness" that is "the immediate consequent or accompaniment of the intellectual energies" (OM B₂ f. 79; N III 4422).

Byron as satirist speaks with all the sophistication of the late European civilization that discontents him. The nostalgia he feels at visions of innocence – whether Haidee in the Cyclades or Daniel Boone in Kentucky – is an urban one. The narrator of *Don Juan* ruminates on the vanity of human wishes and the decay of civilization, but he does so with a play of mind that yields pleasure of a kind not so vulnerable as those kinetic pleasures Epicurus and Freud describe. Such pleasure accompanies successful mental negotiation of circumstances that would otherwise outrage or depress.

Byron's narrator, in short, demonstrates in stanza after stanza that, although civilization and pleasure are at odds, there is a potential pleasure of highest value that accompanies our mental confrontation itself with civilization. Although Freud might call this a sublimation too, I prefer to describe it as a direct mastery – through invention, intellect, writing, and talk – of the world which the poet confronts and to which he testifies. As master of the painful content of his own vision, he need not become what he beholds; and he takes pleasure in his resistance to convention, cant, and stupidity. The narrator's resilience – or Byron's resolve that the show will go on, no matter what – bespeaks an intellectual pleasure that renews itself. In addition to the aggression directed against his audience and the targets of his satire, we sense an indefatigable interest in the human fact of things, and even an affectionate bonding of Byron with the human race he disparages. He displays generosity as well as aggression.

Through the rapidly moving text of *Don Juan*, no dialectical progress is discernible, as distinct from a structural progression of the text as text. Antipodes remain antipodes. A new society is not promised when the poem breaks off, only the intermittent subversion of the old. The sanity of comic vision has suggested an alternative to the regressive divestitures of Manfred, however: creative intellect can gather up its energies of love and aggression, and persist in its own being, even when what it confronts is stupid and cruel. We can remain experientially ready for those occasional donations of pleasure and significance that make all the difference in a human history where the pages are otherwise all the same. In *Don Juan* we have watched a strong imagination confronting "*life*," or what Byron has called "*the thing*," and taking its pleasures in the face of all that would deny it.

10

The ethical bearing of literature

In this strenuous excursion through the moral landscapes of Romantic authors from Blake to Byron, we have seen shifting patterns more complex than can be gauged by the single variable of relative brightness or darkness. Famous for his "pessimism," Byron is linked to Blake through his reanimation in *Don Juan* of the instinctive passion for sensate life that may even have begun to dim in the later Blake. And we have noted that Byron, like the others, affirms a plurality of values, if in patterns of mutual exclusion. Byron's non-dialectical ethics does not remove him from this larger effort to re-value a moral landscape that has come to seem ruined and bereft of value.

Like Blake before him, Byron has found it difficult to coordinate the imperatives of action with this reanimation of values. Blake urges acts of "intellectual fight," often imagistically brutal, in pursuit of values themselves both spirited and pacific. For Byron, the antipodal ordering of values that defines the human predicament forces the agent to acts of exclusion, demonstrated in the extreme by Manfred, who affirms himself as agent in the act of permanently excluding all values down to his very life. In *Don Juan* Byron implies that a comically contingent world has a way of giving the agent sufficient opportunities to balance for a time this pattern of loss and self-ruin. Much comes along answering to our energies and appetites. Rather than himself choose or seek out opportunity, however, Don Juan lets the world make choices for him and donate opportunity. He maintains his pluck, the narrator his power of intellectual negotiation, while Lord Henry "preserve[s] his perpendicular." Byron does not tell us what, if anything, is to be done and how we might set about acting to increase the fund of value. A spirited maintenance is the best we can hope for in an entropic world. In *Don Juan* the act of writing – audacious, inventive, prolific – becomes a last-ditch affirmation in itself, subverting closure and censorship as if they were repressions of life and intellect.

But Byron renounces composition – it does not at the last suffice – and sets off for Greece in search of another kind of act. It is Shelley who, for all his torments and contradictions, coordinates obligation and value, whose imperatives to action are usually as pacific and loving as the values toward which they tend, who sees ethical imperatives as continuous with socio-political ones, who would prefer to alter the world than affirm the agent, who holds to redemptive possibility in the midst of the seeming triumph of death, and who until his drowning goes on writing.

Rather than summarize again the larger concerns of this study, however, I would like to position some of them anew within a simple schema that emerges readily from earlier chapters. In my introductory remarks, I suggested that the ethical dimension of literature – the plane of organization of all that pertains to obligation and value – functions as an internal resistance to any reduction, from within or without, of the literary text to purely hypothetical status. It conveys the sense that a literary text has some bearing on our lives, that something beyond but not excluding the pleasures of the text is at stake in the act of reading. I propose now that our sense of a text's bearing on us – its relational force, morally considered – arises in large part from the ways the text makes "reality claims."[1]

I must distinguish, first, between the ethical and another textual dimension that can be called the "naturalistic." This is the plane of organization of all textual phenomena that claim correlation with the world as it is (or was or will be). It too makes reality claims and does so more directly. It is not synonymous with the mimetic, both because the ethical dimension can also function mimetically and because mimesis requires recognition of sameness (the world is represented as it is) and difference (the world is mediated by poetic form). As I define it, the naturalistic is limited to the claim of sameness, and in its purest manifestation (i.e. in the abstract) it is morally neutral. It is what prompts us to say of a poem or play or novel, "Yes, that is the way things are," or "No, that is not the way things are." Its textual matter can include anything assumed to be the case in reality: nature as scene, the world of objects, or transcendental reality. It includes human nature insofar as the text implies, neutrally, "This is the way people behave," or "This is the way people are," and even "This is the way people feel and think." We have seen Byron make such a claim for *Don Juan*, which he calls "*real* life," and which answers to his conviction

---

[1] Elsewhere I expect to describe more closely these "reality claims" and other character-istics of the ethical dimension, in the context of modern criticism. I do not restrict the ethical dimension of literature to these reality claims alone.

that "there should always be some foundation of fact for the most airy fabric—." No literary text can be so naturalistic, however, that it is totally cleansed of moral judgments and values. One could show that the novels of Robbe-Grillet, from which he has attempted to purge "humanistic" categories, are tainted by the ethical, from larger narrative to smaller linguistic structures.[2]

Reality claims of the ethical dimension arise from the linguistic category of "ought," not "is," and if anything they occasion in us a greater sense of bearing than the naturalistic.[3] The Romantics have given vivid illustration of four modes in which such claims are made, in itself evidence of their commitment to the ethical.[4] These modes often overlap in a single text, but their relative emphasis signals a particular writer's approach to the moral nature and purposes of literature. They could be cast and recast in terms of many of the prevailing schools of critical theory.

The first is what I call "legislative," engaged most by Blake and Shelley, least by Byron and Keats. It is the pressure the text exerts on its readership to alter the way things are. Shelley's formula is that poets are the unacknowledged legislators of the world, but we are likely to take a more modest view. In everything from direct authorial recommendation of a course of action (as in Shelley's *The Mask of Anarchy*) to cautionary narration (which, we have seen, is rife in Romantic literature) to prophetic urging (as in Blake's Lambeth books), the literary text imposes on the reader's reality by urging another possible reality. This mode contradicts the Kantian aesthetic of freedom from interest. The prophetic stance of Blake and Shelley is a paradoxical manifestation of the legislative mode whenever it implies the inevitability of what it urges. Among Romantic writers, they entertain the

[2] See Robbe-Grillet's *For a New Novel: Essays on Fiction*, trans. Richard Howard (New York: Grove Press, 1965), especially "Nature, Humanism, Tragedy," 49–75.

[3] Moral philosophers who believe that ethics is itself "naturalistic" – that all "ought" statements can be converted to "is" statements without changing their meaning – would merge the categories of the naturalistic and the ethical as I describe them, but could not for that reason alone argue against my view that the ethical dimension in a literary text often functions as a contrary of fictionality. Indeed they can make that claim more directly, since they believe moral judgments relate to matters of observable fact, instead of to some "non-natural" property difficult to define, locate, or verify.

[4] These four ways of making reality claims are correlative to the four critical orientations – pragmatic, mimetic, expressive, objective – as expounded by M. H. Abrams in *The Mirror and the Lamp: Romantic Theory and the Critical Tradition*, 3–29. My treatment emphasizes that the ethical is not confined to the "pragmatic," the consideration of a literary text as it relates to audience or reader; rather, it pervades all these critical orientations.

grandest redemptive expectations. We have seen that Byron and Keats are least likely to issue imperatives or adopt the mantle of prophesy. Byron does not foresee any ultimate redemption of human history; Keats has a heightened sense of value but, apart from the vocational imperatives he issues to himself, does not exhort his readership to one or another course of action.

The legislative mode is not confined to outright imperatives, however. Even in works of quiet demeanor, the difference implied between fictional world and whatever is constituted as reality by particular readers exerts a force – if only a microvolt or two – on readers to make the world they inhabit conform to the fictional world, or to see to it that this does not happen. Wordsworth's "A slumber did my spirit seal" exerts a suasive force with regard to the states of mind described. As a cautionary tale in miniature, this poem contradictorily implies both the perils of complacency concerning those we love and the wisdom of ultimate acquiescence in death and natural process. The extra-textual reality of a different set of responses to mortality – responses that may differ radically from the eerie ones of the poem's speaker – occasions the reader's vulnerability to the poem's legislative implication.[5] We cannot ignore the fact of impervious readers, but I suggest that a legislative or cautionary force of greatly varying degrees is felt as part of the normal dynamics of reader response, whether or not we regard this as properly *aesthetic* experience.

A second kind of reality claim is made through the "demonstrative" mode, which is a literary text's moral contextualizing of its own representations of human action and value. Instead of a legislative concern with readers, this mode concerns representations of the world and moral understanding. It is more cognitive than conative, and Byron and Hazlitt practice it most vividly. Byron is not one to urge us to a course of action but, as he says, he will "show" us the truth about ourselves, will make his satiric judgment, and we can take it from there. This is distinguished from the morally neutral witnessing of the naturalistic dimension, because it both focuses attention on the moral properties of persons, acts, or states of mind, and makes judgments concerning them. Readers cannot help but silently gauge the plausibility of moral representation – do people in the world think and feel and act this way? – and the terms of judgment brought to bear on it. They may find themselves in or out of sympathy with the writer's "moral sensibility." Moral judgments in literary texts assume referen-

[5] My argument holds for that contemporary phenomenon, the reader who thinks all the world's a text. One could then speak of an implicit incommensurability of texts – the poem versus the world-as-text constituted by the reader.

tial force in the experience of most readers, whose own interpreted world may or may not corroborate the moral premises of the text.

This process is potentially naive and question-begging, but it occurs as it occurs, and is not necessarily non- or extra-literary. Particularly in irony and satire, a demand is made on readers to consult their own conception of moral reality *in order that* textual conventions can be recognized. Jane Austen's *Emma* requires that we recognize, by deciphering the ironic code, an operative moral norm against which its heroine is judged both extraordinary and deficient. We work by means of internal evidence of the text, but we must also bring to bear the larger extra-textual world of moral assumptions. That one should not presume to run other people's lives for them is a moral convention that must be imported by the reader before this text can be grasped as ironic. Here and elsewhere we must be knowledgeable of extra-textual moral conventions in order to recognize textual conventions.

In *Don Juan* Byron's narrator provides overt moral contextualizing of action with his satiric chatter, whereas the ironic narrators of Austen's fictions usually do not. We readers may not have to supply some silent moral premise, as in *Emma*, but we must sort through the mass of self-deprecating, pompous, misleading commentary for what this epic satire is saying about the world as *"glorious* blunder." Subverting his own pretensions to wisdom and truth-telling, Byron expects us, from the fund of our own extra-textual moral awarenesses, to see that such subversions reinstate him as that "Columbus of the moral seas" after all. He implies that reading *Don Juan* requires an already considerable knowledge of a referred world shared by narrator and reader – whatever more he has to show us about it – so that the narrator can retain more authority than a buffoon. The Lakers, by contrast, "know nothing of the world; and what is poetry, but the reflection of the world?"

The familiar essay format adopted by Hazlitt has, as the basis of its contract with the reader, the notion of "common sense" or "tacit reason," which tells us what is what. His moral commentary begs for confirmation by this shared fund of extra-textual moral assumptions. As a practitioner of *passionate* common sense, Hazlitt writes not with the mild, judicial air of an Addison but with the heat and nervousness of someone pleading on behalf of moral intelligence at a time when most have lost touch with it. He is continually asking us to consult whatever stock of common sense we may have left, to look beyond the margins of the essay we are reading to things that are real in the world. He sets out to disabuse us of our prejudices and put us in touch once again with the real, changing our minds even if he entertains no illusions about changing our ways.

Many Romantic writers are either suspicious of bluntly demonstrative literary texts or are less in their element when they attempt them. Shelley tells us "didactic poetry" is his "abhorrence," in contrast to the impertinent Byron, who calls it the highest literary kind. We prefer Wordsworth when he does not have too palpable a moral design on us. Those baffling electric episodes of the early books of *The Prelude* override the commentary that encases them. What fascinates us about the spots of time is that they resist easy moral contextualizing. *The Excursion* – where a moral lurks under every tombstone – is fatiguing. If we happen to hold extra-textual moral assumptions neither pietistic, Christian, nor conservative, we feel like talking back or walking out. Though a conspicuous moralist in many of his prose writings, Coleridge in his greater poetry tends not to firm up propositionally his own moral adjudication. When his Mariner does so at the end of his tale, we sense this is not the last word. In his *Confessions* and elsewhere, De Quincey attempts a narrative in which ready moral packaging – for instance, the opprobrium of opium-eating – is disallowed. He treats praise and blame as inappropriate readerly impositions, preempted by the obliquities of the particular case.

A third mode pertains to the author as agent and may be called "expressivist." Here we see the very production of a literary text as an act as real as other acts in the world, with its own defining properties of agent, agency, purpose, and scene and with its own openness to being judged in part by moral criteria. Although the common notion of the author as a central originating consciousness still somehow joined to the text has come under siege in recent years – in the work of Foucault and Derrida, for instance – one assumes the author will repossess the text in due time, if on less favorable terms. (Some now speak of the author-in-the-text as a principle of intentional coherence, a textual construct that has unceremoniously unseated our quaint biographical author sitting at a writing desk.) The Romantic period is well known for its strengthening of the author function; and Coleridge and Wordsworth are the most important figures to consider here. With the development of expressive theories of poetry comes a larger sense of responsibility for the act of writing. If a literary text is only symbolic action, it is no less "real" as a moral act than many other acts, themselves often negotiated through sign systems, whether of language or gesture. No generic definition of what it means to "act" has been agreed on by ethicists; it suffices here to say that the verbal expression of an author and the production of a literary text make a reality claim on us. We see the coming-into-being of any book as a moral act that has as much status in reality as other moral acts. It might be regarded as an extended speech act for which the author is responsible and which has embedded in it evidence of the intentional consciousness that shaped it.[6] A text so considered is an extension of its author; he or she has certainly intended it and must pay the consequences. Beyond the matter of copyright and royalties, authorship entails ownership in only weak analogy to capitalist ownership of property. To have their property abused by bad reviews, lawsuits, or censorship, or to be imprisoned and tortured, causes authors a qualitatively different anguish from what is endured by a capitalist taking a beating at the stock exchange. A book as an expressive act attaches to and represents the author in ways that stocks and bonds do not attach to the investor. Nor can an author in such a predicament win release by pointing out to his torturers that the concept of "author" is an outmoded fiction anyway, and that they should put a textual construct or a signifier on the rack instead.

If the characteristic feeling attending the legislative mode is urgency, with the expressivist it is anxiety. Coleridge's poetics of organic expressivism culminates in assigning demiurgical powers to the poet, as in "Kubla Khan" and *Biographia Literaria*. Yet his own stance is one of disclaiming responsibility for his own texts, said to be "desultory" or fragmentary or given him in a dream. It is precisely because greater power and responsibility have accrued to the author that Coleridge looks at his own work with dread. In his lectures and published writings he labors embarrassedly to establish his own ethos in such a way as to be acquitted in advance for anything he might say. In *The Prelude* Wordsworth hedges in his own way, undertaking a compositional act which he says is but an exercise in self-examination and empowerment prior to greater writerly acts, and which will not be published in his lifetime. He narrates the development of moral and poetic consciousness commensurate with poetic ambition, so that the role of poet can be performed in good faith. Before this can happen, he must renegotiate the moral demons he has confronted throughout his life – his instinctive childhood guilt, his isolationism, his pastoral and gothic sentimentality, his despair of intellect and of the human race, his secret sin with Annette Vallon. He anxiously hopes that mastering the demons of his circumstantial life as already lived in reality –

[6] Charles Altieri pursues a complex line of argument similar to this in *Act and Quality: A Theory of Literary Meaning and Humanistic Understanding* (Amherst: University of Massachusetts Press, 1981).

456

mastering through writing about them – will metonymically empower him to write beyond the perimeter of the self about those ultimate extra-textual realities, "Man, Nature, and Society."

A biographical text makes the reality claim of any historical narration but is more immediately moralized. To place a human being within a narrative format implicates Burke's relational determinants of an ethical grammar: agent, act, situation or scene, agency, and purpose. Autobiography compounds this moralization: author-agents are accountable for the life they testify to as well as for the quality of their testifying. The recent emphasis on the fictional and figurative properties of all narrative – including "factual" narrative forms such as history, biography, and autobiography – tends to relieve authors of the burden of being "authoritative." If autobiography is but one version of a life – a story pieced together by a necessarily interested party – then some will argue that ordinary moral problems such as lying or revisionism or sins of tactical omission are defused. Carl Woodring writes that *The Prelude* is, as it were, a *Bildungsroman* in verse and that Wordsworth cannot strictly lie about the facts of his own life in such a context. J. Hillis Miller thinks autobiography is inherently figurative, grounded in the master trope of prosopopoeia, or summoning the mask of the dead; as such, autobiography is yet another way of "doing things with words."[7]

I place myself between the schools of fact and fiction in this matter, and offer as evidence the compositional strategies of the Romantics. It is their anxious awareness of their personal responsibility for expressivist acts of writing – their awareness that the text does disclose the moral reality of the author – that leads them to distancing, fictionalizing maneuvers, as in Coleridge and Wordsworth. The others have their own displacements. Byron employs persona, De Quincey tells us that the dream is the responsible party, Hazlitt publishes *Liber Amoris* anonymously (while blabbing his fiasco all over town), Shelley transforms the women he has loved into astronomical bodies, while Blake more drastically mythologizes autobiography, for example portraying his well-meaning patron William Hayley as Satan. Keats's letter on the "poetical character" goes so far as to deny the relevance of extra-textual authorial identity to poetry. The poet as poet is a protean figure with liberty to delight in all moral phenomena equally, from fair to foul. I have argued that Keats renounces this position in *The Fall of Hyperion*, where he owns up to the various realities that obtrude on such distancing: his own real vocational anguish, his sense of responsibility

---

[7] "Shaping Life in *The Prelude*" and "Prosopopoeia and *Praeterita*," in *Nineteenth-Century Lives*, 9–11, 129.

for those who suffer in the world, and his sense that the escape from reality offered by the mere "dreamer" is ironically a vexation of spirit. In various ways, all these writers have *owned up to* the moral implications of the life of writing – implications that redound to them personally as living authors, whether they are writing autobiography or not. And they share a passion for finding out what the case is, eschewing the merely visionary.

A fourth mode, which I call "substitutive," is discovered when we consider the literary text as a formal structure. Two arguments common among formalists support my view that even here the ethical dimension and its reality claims are not evaded. It has been insufficiently recognized that if the formalist says a poem is an ontologically heightened verbal construct, then it follows that any moral element within it must be correspondingly heightened. A dramatic performance of *King Lear* gives us "real" action – not simply a representation of an action that would have greater reality if it were to occur offstage somewhere in "real life." (Chicago Aristotelians interpret mimesis in such a way as to unite formalist, ontological, and ethical criteria in a repudiation of mimesis as naive re-presentation of extra-textual reality.) King Lear's passion may seem ontologically higher than our own. For the few hours that the play usurps the interest we normally pay ourselves, our own moral situation seems less real than Lear's and pales beside it. His passion stands in place of our own, profoundly "substituting" for it. Too frequently an assumption is made that formalism leads logically to aestheticism – as the separation of the aesthetic object from the relational grid of other objects in the world, including objective moral reality. But the enhancements of form logically and experientially enhance the ethical components taken up into form. The burden of proof falls on those who commit a seeming non sequitur in arguing a necessary or desirable separation of the formal and the ethical.

Formalists do not necessarily hyperbolize the ontology of art to this extent. A. C. Bradley states a common position when he says that life and literature are distinct categories, life "having reality, but seldom fully satisfying imagination; while [literature] offers something which satisfies imagination but has not full reality."[8] Life and literature are therefore "analogues" one of the other. To say that a literary text is "like" life still weighs against the strictly hypothetical or fictive character of the text, if to a lesser degree. One poem has sufficient reality to stand in for life, in the same way that a simile substitutes one entity for

[8] "Poetry for Poetry's Sake" (1910), in *Critical Theory Since Plato*, ed. Hazard Adams (New York: Harcourt Brace Jovanovich, 1971), 737–47.

another, while indicating in "like" that the equivalence is only approximate. By virtue of analogical correspondence, if not ontological heightening or full-scale usurpation, a poem that is "like life" is to that extent "real."

With respect to what formalists have called "the poem itself," the ethical is structurally constitutive, whether one considers the moral causality of plot and character in drama and narrative which Aristotle describes in the *Poetics*, the ethos or qualitative self-presentation of the speaker within a lyric poem, or the ethical properties, affective and conative, of language. All these contribute to what William Wimsatt calls "the moral quality of the meaning expressed by the poem itself," which is not to be confused with "the qualities of the author's mind nor the effects of a poem upon a reader's mind."[9] Moral qualities are declared "intrinsic" to the text. Wimsatt argues that in its "concreteness and dramatic presentation of value situations," poetry achieves its value *as poetry*. A purely imagistic and non-moral poetry is, he notes, a rarity; most poetry achieves force only through presentation of moral possibility. *Antony and Cleopatra* in its celebration of illicit love is a play Wimsatt, in line with his acknowledged Christianity, finds immoral. That the play is nonetheless great demonstrates poetic value is not the same as moral value. Yet Wimsatt goes on to affirm the interdependency of the two: poetic values are "strictly dependent" upon the "immoral acts," and thus poetic value in Shakespeare's play is not "autonomously removed from the rest of human experience." Wimsatt cannot but think that "the greatest poetry will be morally right," with the result that in the upper echelons of poetic value we can still rank *King Lear* above *Antony and Cleopatra* – i.e. moral value *is* ultimately determinative of poetic, even if not identical with it.

This last argument will make even non-formalist moral critics nervous, but we might retain the thrust of Wimsatt's essay if we were to see poetic value as in part a function of, say, Aristotelian moral "magnitude" or of a refined Arnoldian "high seriousness," rather than of moral correctness.

The substitutive mode puts us in mind of Keats, who is neither formalist nor aesthete but who explores the ontology of art relative to what he calls the "paltriness of existence." His search for objects of veneration leads him to literature and the arts and to a nightingale's song. In "Ode to a Nightingale" the ecstasy of song is a momentary release from moral suffering, a usurpation of all that concerns him. While hearing the song, the poet almost stands outside a life in which

[9] "Poetry and Morals: A Relation Reargued," in *The Verbal Icon* (with Monroe Beardsley) (Lexington: University of Kentucky Press, 1954), 85–100.

459

youth grows pale, spectre-thin, and dies. The Nightingale herself is said to be in an ecstasy; her song – non-moral, non-human, non-cognitive – rises above onerous moral concerns. As such, it is not the heightened moral ontology of *King Lear* that usurps the listener's attention but a "transcendence" of the moral altogether. The Ode in which this possibility is explored is intensely moral, however; it does not lose sight of the human suffering to which the song stands in antithesis. Ecstasy is never complete for the poet, any more than it is for the sad Moabitess Ruth standing in tears amid the alien corn. He unmasks the Nightingale's cheat in the end; her therapy, so intense for the moment, leaves him "here" once again, skeptical and bewildered. In "Ode on a Grecian Urn" the poet confronts representational art that does have moral content – in the Urn's depiction of striving lovers and human ceremony. Her paintings in one respect assert their ontological superiority over the life situation of the poet because they are permanent and he is not. But Keatsian sanity and wakefulness resist total assent to the superiority of art, which in its immemorial coldness proves no substitute for human life. It is only "like" life, and assumes its more modest status of minister to human suffering, of "friend." It is supplement, not substitute. Seeing a temptation in yielding to the formalist worship of art, Keats affirms instead the fascination of its moral representations, their bearing on human reality, and their potential balm for human suffering.

In *The Fall of Hyperion* Keats affirms that only the poet who has absorbed moral suffering can treat of it in art and become "physician" to humankind. Modern critics, following Harold Bloom, have adopted the Coleridgean I AM, paradigm of authorial power, and grafted onto it the Nietzschean will to power and Freudian aggression against the father – to produce a complex portrait of the poet as patricide and *Übermensch*. Perhaps too little attention has been given the Coleridgean eros, which looks beyond the enclosed world of poetic discourse to "alterity," to the world at large with its suffering humanity.

Many teachers and critics still acquiesce in the now stale wisdom that "realist" or "referential" or "representational" aspects of a literary construct can (and should) be shown to be as "fictive" as anything else. The residue of modernist assumptions, bolstered by analogies from Saussurean linguistics, can convert even contemporary non-fiction novels into *jeux d'esprit* of fictive discourse. To be sure, the reader can resist reality claims, whether naturalistic or ethical. They are only "claims," after all. But it seems reasonable, even in the spirit of modern skepticism, to insist that the question of which has priority – the real or the fictive – should not be begged. These reality claims exert a certain force within the text and without. To regard them as axiomatically overcome by fictionality is to enervate both them and the larger fiction. I think critics of diverse philosophies could consistently hold that the real and the fictive – however these might be defined – are better perceived as engaged in a permanent interplay. The force of reality in art has its claim on us, as Keats knows when he writes of a painting by Benjamin West that it has "nothing to be intense upon; no women one feels mad to kiss; no face swelling into reality."[10]

Of these various ways of negotiating the relationship of poetry and ethics, the Romantics most charactisterically employ the legislative and expressivist, Neoclassical poets the demonstrative, and modern poets the substitutive. But we have seen that the Romantics (as well as other major poets) are more comprehensive in their moral interests than this suggests. And it is to their comprehensiveness that I would like to return in closing.

In Aldous Huxley's *Point Counter Point* (1928), Mark Rampion, modelled on D. H. Lawrence, says:

Blake was civilized . . . *civilized*. Civilization is harmony and completeness. Reason, feeling, instinct, the life of the body – Blake managed to include and harmonize everything. Barbarism is being lop-sided. You can be a barbarian of the intellect as well as of the body. A barbarian of the soul and the feelings as well as of sensuality. Christianity made us barbarians of the soul and now science is making us barbarians of the intellect. Blake was the last civilized man.[11]

We have seen imbalance within the Blakean myth and have questioned its completeness – he is supplemented by others in the visionary company – but Rampion is worth listening to, especially if we take

[10] We have seen that reality claims are not to be confused with simple referentiality, as the one-to-one correspondence of text to a world out there, or with some preexisting, immutable "truth." Through the legislative mode, poets imagine a world that the existing world should emulate. Through the substitutive with its ontological enhancements, they attempt to create a textual reality higher perhaps in intensity and kind than the world we normally inhabit. Through expressive acts, poets may bring into being the unprecedented. The demonstrative mode brings to representations of the way of the world the supplement of judgmental moral consciousness. Nor does my argument imply that the ethical cannot itself be seen as constitutive of fictionality. Act, character, value, desire, motive, and other ethical phenomena are some of the means by which poets make fictions, creating imaginary worlds that may be read as governed by their own internally constituted rules of judgment and moral causality. "Interplay" must give ample scope to the fictive, and the ethical is itself not wholly confined to the real. To pursue its fictionality would yield yet more evidence of the pervasiveness of the ethical dimension in literary texts, even within, say, science fiction novels that attempt to establish "other worlds."

[11] *Point Counter Point* (1928; New York: Harper & Row, 1965), 107.

Blake as an embodiment of the larger Romantic enterprise. I argued, in Chapter Two, that the Romantics' position in the development of European ethics is synthetic – that they are more notable for what they retain of the warring opposites of earlier ethical schools than for what they exclude. The oppositional character of European moral schools, which can be charted in the historically evolving dialogue from the Renaissance and before, is inscribed internally in Romantic moral psychology, in the Romantics' enlarged notion of human personality, value, and act. The writers whom we have considered are notable for the breadth of their moral engagement, seen in the fact that even Keats, often taken to be most inclined toward aestheticism, has confronted the major concerns: pleasure, duty, act, value, love, sympathy, egotism, conscience, identity, suffering, evil, the responsibility of the poet. I do not wish to belittle the wealth of moral engagement we see in poetry thereafter – Victorian, modernist, contemporary – but would simply pose the question of whether any subsequent poems have addressed as much moral reality as *The Four Zoas*, *The Rime of the Ancient Mariner*, *The Prelude*, *Don Juan*, *Prometheus Unbound*, and *The Fall of Hyperion* – those supremely presumptuous works.

The Romantics' conscious struggle toward moral synthesis abated in subsequent literary periods. Matthew Arnold, we recall, complains that the Romantics do not know enough and that only Wordsworth can tell us much about "how to live." In his Preface to the 1853 edition of *Poems*, Arnold insists that the poet "has in the first place to select an excellent action," which criterion disqualifies, as he says, his own morbid, inactive "Empedocles on Etna." The Romantics would not be so severe on Arnold's poem: moral reality and the poetry that mediates it include the morbid as well as the active. These writers who supposedly do not know enough about life could turn tables and accuse Arnold of trying to exclude too much of life from the proper domain of literary art. Victorian moralism, itself an often underrated episode, does seem to reinstate a certain fracturing. One thinks of Carlyle's Fichtean censoriousness in splitting duty from inclination; of John Stuart Mill's uncertain retention of hedonism despite a strong attraction to value pluralism; of Tennyson's early polarizing of art and social participation; of Pater's subjectivism, and so on. Even the extraordinarily broad canvas of human possibility given us by Dickens, Thackeray, and Eliot does not represent an exercise in willed moral synthesis, as the Romantics have undertaken it. (Certainly it can be argued that the Victorian novelists give us something more and other than "synthesis.") But to make this argument would require another book and might prove a thankless task at that.

The Romantics' breadth of engagement with the ethical dimension tells us that far from being inimical to imagination, ethical categories are seized upon by writers to incarnate their imaginings. Take away from literary texts such stock-in-trade as the antagonism of duty and inclination, the problem of choosing among imperfect goods and lesser evils, the "torments of Love & Jealousy," acting well or badly, the psychology of conscience, the moral values implicit in the very language of lyrical poetry, the urge within individuals to discover an identity apart from what is willed by circumstance, parents, or groups, the urge within writers to establish their own authorial identity – take away the entire range of human virtues and vices, and ask what remains. The Romantics have served as a large-scale demonstration that the ethical dimension of literature expresses a writer's denial, internal to the literary text, of the strictly hypothetical status of imaginative literature. Far from being necessarily inhibitions or repressions, a writer's moral persuasions fuel imagination to demonstrate, judge, exhort, and tell us what we might become. Sartre says without embarrassment that Bach's *Well-Tempered Clavier* is telling us "how to live." If music, surely literature. The writer's moral persuasions – whether noble or repellent, humanistic or indeterminate – are deeply implicated in the will to create and our willingness to listen.

Select bibliography

This bibliography is limited to modern studies in Romantics, critical theory, ethics, and intellectual history that have been cited in this study or have some bearing on it.

Abbey, Lloyd. *Destroyer and Preserver: Shelley's Poetic Skepticism*. Lincoln: University of Nebraska Press, 1979

Abrams, M. H., ed. *Literature and Belief*. New York: Columbia University Press, 1958

   The Mirror and the Lamp: Romantic Theory and the Critical Tradition. New York: Oxford University Press, 1953, rpt. New York: W. W. Norton, 1958

   Natural Supernaturalism: Tradition and Revolution in Romantic Literature. New York: W. W. Norton, 1971

Adams, Hazard. *The Interests of Criticism*. New York: Harcourt Brace, 1969

Aers, David, Cook, Jonathan, and Punter, David. *Romanticism and Ideology: Studies in English Writing, 1765–1830*. London: Routledge & Kegan Paul, 1981

Altieri, Charles. *Act and Quality: A Theory of Literary Meaning and Humanistic Understanding*. Amherst: University of Massachusetts Press, 1981

Anderson, Quentin. *The Imperial Self: An Essay on American Literary and Cultural History*. New York: Knopf, 1971

Anscombe, G. E. M. *Intention*. Ithaca, N. Y.: Cornell University Press, 1969

Auerbach, Erich. *Mimesis: The Representation of Reality in Western Literature*. Princeton: Princeton University Press, 1953

Averill, James. *Wordsworth and the Poetry of Human Suffering*. Ithaca, N. Y.: Cornell University Press, 1980

Babbitt, Irving. *Rousseau and Romanticism*. Boston: Houghton Mifflin, 1919

Baier, Kurt. *The Moral Point of View*. Ithaca, N. Y.: Cornell University Press, 1948

Baker, Herschel. *William Hazlitt*. Cambridge, Mass.: Harvard University Press, 1962

Ball, Patricia. *The Central Self: A Study in Romantic and Victorian Imagination*. London: Athlone, 1968

Barfield, Owen. *What Coleridge Thought*. Middletown, Conn.: Wesleyan University Press, 1971

Barth, J. Robert. *Coleridge and Christian Doctrine*. Cambridge, Mass.: Harvard University Press, 1969

Barzun, Jacques. *Classic, Romantic, Modern*. New York: Doubleday, 1961

Bate, Walter Jackson. *From Classic to Romantic: Premises of Taste in Eighteenth-Century England*. Cambridge, Mass.: Harvard University Press, 1946

Coleridge. New York: Macmillan, 1968

John Keats. Cambridge, Mass.: Harvard University Press, 1963

Bayley, John. "Byron and the 'Lively Life,' " *New York Review of Books*, 30 (2 June 1983), 25–32

Beardsley, Monroe. "Intrinsic Value," *Philosophy and Phenomenological Research*, 26 (1965), 1–17

Beaty, Frederick L. *Byron the Satirist*. DeKalb: Northern Illinois University Press, 1985

Light from Heaven: Love in British Romantic Literature. DeKalb: Northern Illinois University Press, 1971

Beer, John. *Blake's Humanism*. Manchester: Manchester University Press, 1968

Blake's Visionary Universe. Manchester: Manchester University Press, 1969

Coleridge's Poetic Intelligence. New York: Barnes & Noble, 1977

Wordsworth and the Human Heart. New York: Columbia University Press, 1978

Bernstein, John A. *Shaftesbury, Rousseau, and Kant: An Introduction to the Conflict between Aesthetic and Moral Values in Modern Thought*. Madison: Fairleigh Dickinson University Press, 1980

Bernstein, Richard. *Praxis and Action*. Philadelphia: University of Pennsylvania Press, 1971

Berthoff, Warner. *Literature and the Continuances of Virtue*. Princeton: Princeton University Press, 1986

Bialostosky, Don H. *Making Tales: The Poetics of Wordsworth's Narrative Experiments*. Chicago: University of Chicago Press, 1984

Bloom, Harold. *The Anxiety of Influence: A Theory of Poetry*. New York: Oxford University Press, 1973

Blake's Apocalypse: A Study in Poetic Argument. Garden City, N.Y.: Doubleday, 1963

Poetry and Repression: Revisionism from Blake to Stevens. New Haven: Yale University Press, 1976

The Ringers in the Tower: Studies in the Romantic Tradition. Chicago: University of Chicago Press, 1971

The Visionary Company: A Reading of English Romantic Poetry. New York: Doubleday, 1961

Bonar, James. *Moral Sense*. London: Allen & Unwin, 1930

Bond, E. J. *Reason and Value*. Cambridge: Cambridge University Press, 1983

Booth, Wayne. "Criticulture: Or, Why We Need at Least Three Criticisms at the Present Time," in *What is Criticism?*, ed. P. Hernandi. Bloomington: Indiana University Press, 1981

Modern Dogma and the Rhetoric of Assent. Notre Dame: University of Notre Dame Press, 1974

Bosanquet, Bernard. *The Value and Destiny of the Individual*. London: Macmillan, 1913

Bostetter, Edward. *The Romantic Ventriloquists: Wordsworth, Coleridge, Keats, Shelley, Byron*. Seattle: University of Washington Press, 1963

Brandt, Richard. *Ethical Theory: The Problems of Normative and Critical Ethics*. Englewood Cliffs, N. J.: Prentice-Hall, 1959

A Theory of the Good and the Right. Oxford: Clarendon Press, 1979

Brinton, Crane. *The Political Ideas of the English Romanticists*. London: Oxford University Press, 1926

Brisman, Leslie. *Romantic Origins*. Ithaca, N. Y.: Cornell University Press, 1978

Broad, C. D. *Ethics and the History of Philosophy*. London: Routledge & Kegan Paul, 1952

Five Types of Ethical Theory. New York: Harcourt, Brace, and World, 1935

Bromwich, David. *Hazlitt: The Mind of a Critic*. New York: Oxford University Press, 1983

Bronowski, Jacob. *William Blake and the Age of Revolution*. New York: Harper & Row, 1965

Brooks, Peter. *Reading for the Plot: Design and Intention in Narrative*. New York: Knopf, 1984

Buckley, Jerome Hamilton. *The Turning Key: Autobiography and the Subjective Impulse since 1800*. Cambridge, Mass.: Harvard University Press, 1984

Buckley, Vincent. *Poetry and Morality*. London: Chatto & Windus, 1968

Burke, Kenneth. *A Grammar of Motives*. 1945; rpt. Cleveland: World Publishing, 1962

Language as Symbolic Action: Essays on Life, Literature, and Method. Berkeley: University of California Press, 1966

Butler, Marilyn. *Romantics, Rebels and Reactionaries: English Literature and its Background, 1760–1830*. New York: Oxford University Press, 1982

Bygrave, Stephen. *Coleridge and the Self: Romantic Egoism*. New York: St. Martin's Press, 1986

Cameron, Kenneth Neill. *Shelley: The Golden Years*. Cambridge, Mass.: Harvard University Press, 1974

The Young Shelley: Genesis of a Radical. New York: Macmillan, 1950

Casey, John. "Emotion and Imagination," *Philosophical Quarterly*, 34 (1984), 1–14

Cassirer, Ernst. *An Essay on Man: An Introduction to a Philosophy of Human Culture*. New Haven: Yale University Press, 1944

The Philosophy of the Enlightenment (1932), trans. Fritz Koeller and James Pettegrove. Princeton: Princeton University Press, 1951

The Platonic Renaissance in England (1932), trans. James Pettegrove. Edinburgh: Nelson, 1953

Cavell, Stanley. *The Claim of Reason: Wittgenstein, Skepticism, Morality, and Tragedy*. New York: Oxford University Press, 1979

Christensen, Jerome. *Coleridge's Blessed Machine of Language*. Ithaca, N. Y.: Cornell University Press, 1981

Clausen, Christopher. *The Moral Imagination: Essays on Literature and Ethics*. Iowa City: University of Iowa Press, 1986

Cohen, Ted and Guyer, Paul, eds. *Essays in Kant's Aesthetics*. Chicago: University of Chicago Press, 1982

Colmer, John. *Coleridge: Critic of Society*. Oxford: Clarendon Press, 1959

Cooke, Michael. *Acts of Inclusion: Studies Bearing on an Elementary Theory of Romanticism*. New Haven: Yale University Press, 1979

The Blind Man Traces the Circle: On the Patterns and Philosophy of Byron's Poetry. Princeton: Princeton University Press, 1969

The Romantic Will. New Haven: Yale University Press, 1976

Copleston, Frederick, S. J. *A History of Philosophy*. Vol. V: *Hobbes to Paley, Berkeley to Hume*; Vol. VI: *The French Enlightenment, Kant*; Vol. VII: *Fichte to Hegel, Schopenhauer to Nietzsche*; Vol. VII: *British Empiricism and the Idealist Movement in Great Britain*. Garden City, N. Y.: Doubleday, 1959–66

Culler, Jonathan. *Structuralist Poetics: Structuralism, Linguistics, and the Study of Literature*. London: Routledge & Kegan Paul, 1975

Curran, Stuart and Wittreich, Joseph Anthony, Jnr., eds. *Blake's Sublime Allegory: Essays on The Four Zoas, Milton, Jerusalem*. Madison: University of Wisconsin Press, 1973

Damon, S. Foster. *A Blake Dictionary: The Ideas and Symbols of William Blake*. Providence: Brown University Press, 1965

Damrosch, Leopold, Jnr. *Symbol and Truth in Blake's Myth*. Princeton: Princeton University Press, 1980

Davidson, Donald. *Essays on Actions and Events*. Oxford: Oxford University Press, 1980

Davie, Donald. *Purity of Diction in English Verse*. London: Routledge & Kegan Paul, 1967

Dawson, P. M. S. *The Unacknowledged Legislator: Shelley and Politics*. Oxford: Clarendon Press, 1980

De Luca, V. A. *Thomas De Quincey: The Prose of Vision*. Toronto: University of Toronto Press, 1980

De Man, Paul. *Allegories of Reading: Figural Language in Rousseau, Nietzsche, Rilke, and Proust*. New Haven: Yale University Press, 1979

Derrida, Jacques. *La Faculté de juger*. Paris: Minuit, 1985

Margins of Philosophy, trans. Alan Bass. Chicago: University of Chicago Press, 1982

Dickstein, Morris. *Keats and His Poetry: A Study in Development*. Chicago: University of Chicago Press, 1971

Donoghue, Denis. *Ferocious Alphabets*. Boston: Little, Brown, 1981

The Sovereign Ghost: Studies in Imagination. Berkeley: University of California Press, 1976

Eaves, Morris and Fischer, Michael, eds. *Romanticism and Contemporary Criticism*. Ithaca, N. Y.: Cornell University Press, 1986

467

Edwards, Paul, ed. *The Encyclopedia of Philosophy*. 8 vols. New York: Macmillan, 1967

Ellis, John. *The Theory of Literary Criticism: A Logical Analysis*. Berkeley: University of California Press, 1974

Engell, James. *The Creative Imagination: Enlightenment to Romanticism*. Cambridge, Mass.: Harvard University Press, 1981

Erdman, David. *Blake: Prophet Against Empire*, 2nd rev. edn. Princeton: Princeton University Press, 1969

Ewing, A. C. *The Definition of Good*. New York: Macmillan, 1947

Ferguson, Frances. *Wordsworth: Language as Counter-Spirit*. New Haven: Yale University Press, 1977

Ferry, David. *The Limits of Mortality: An Essay on Wordsworth's Major Poems*. Middletown, Conn.: Wesleyan University Press, 1959

Findlay, J. R. *Language, Mind, and Values*. London: Allen & Unwin, 1963

Foot, Philippa. *Virtues and Vices*. Berkeley: University of California Press, 1978

Ford, Newell. *The Prefigurative Imagination of John Keats*. Stanford: Stanford University Press, 1951

Foucault, Michel. *The Order of Things: An Archaeology of the Human Sciences*. New York: Pantheon, 1971

  "What is an Author?" in *Language, Counter-Memory, Practice*, trans. Donald Bouchard and Sherry Simon. Ithaca, N. Y.: Cornell University Press, 1977

Fox, Susan. "The Female as Metaphor in William Blake's Poetry," *Critical Inquiry*, 3 (1977), 507–19

  Poetic Form in Blake's Milton. Princeton: Princeton University Press, 1976

Franck, Isaac. "Self-realization as Ethical Norm: A Critique," *The Philosophical Forum*, 9 (1977), 1–25

Frankena, William K. *Ethics*. Englewood Cliffs, N. J.: Prentice-Hall, 1963

  "The Naturalistic Fallacy," *Mind*, 48 (1939), 464–77

Freud, Sigmund. *Civilization and Its Discontents* (1929), trans. James Strachey. New York: W. W. Norton, 1961

  Beyond the Pleasure Principle (1920), trans. James Strachey, New York: Liveright, 1961

Friedman, Michael H. *The Making of a Tory Humanist: Wordsworth and the Idea of Community*. New York: Columbia University Press, 1979

Fromm, Erich. *Man for Himself: An Inquiry into the Psychology of Ethics*. New York: Rinehart, 1947

Frosch, Thomas R. *The Awakening of Albion: The Renovation of the Body in the Poetry of William Blake*. Ithaca, N. Y.: Cornell University Press, 1974

Fruman, Norman. *Coleridge: The Damaged Archangel*. New York: George Braziller, 1971

Frye, Northrop. *Anatomy of Criticism*. Princeton: Princeton University Press, 1957

  "Blake's Treatment of the Archetype," in *English Institute Essays 1950*, ed. Alan S. Downer. New York: Columbia University Press, 1951

  Fearful Symmetry: A Study of William Blake. Princeton: Princeton University Press, 1947

A Study of English Romanticism. New York: Random House, 1968

Frye, Northrop, Hampshire, Stuart, and O'Brien, Conor Cruse. *The Morality of Scholarship*, ed. Max Black. Ithaca, N. Y.: Cornell University Press, 1967

Furst, Lilian R. *Romanticism in Perspective: A Comparative Study of Aspects of the Romantic Movements in England, France and Germany*. New York: St. Martin's Press, 1969

Gans, Eric. "The Victim as Subject: The Esthetico-Ethical System of Rousseau's *Rêveries*," *Studies in Romanticism*, 21 (1982), 3–31

Garber, Frederick. *The Autonomy of the Self from Richardson to Huysmans*. Princeton: Princeton University Press, 1982

William Wordsworth and the Poetry of Encounter. Urbana: University of Illinois Press, 1971

Gardner, John. *On Moral Fiction*. New York: Basic Books, 1978

Garner, Richard and Rosen, Bernard. *Moral Philosophy: A Systematic Introduction to Normative Ethics and Metaethics*. New York: Macmillan, 1967

Gaull, Marilyn. *English Romanticism: The Human Context*. New York: W. W. Norton, 1988

Gay, Peter. *The Enlightenment: An Interpretation*. Vol. I: *The Rise of Modern Paganism*. Vol. II: *The Science of Freedom*. New York: Random House, Knopf, 1966, 1969

Gittings, Robert. *John Keats*. Boston: Little, Brown and Company, 1968

Gleckner, Robert F. *Byron and the Ruins of Paradise*. Baltimore: The Johns Hopkins University Press, 1967

Gleckner, Robert F., and Enscoe, Gerald, eds. *Romanticism: Points of View*, 2nd edn. Englewoods Cliffs, N. J.: Prentice-Hall, 1970

Goellnicht, Donald C. *The Poet-Physician: Keats and Medical Science*. Pittsburgh: University of Pittsburgh Press, 1984

Goldman, Michael. *The Actor's Freedom: Toward a Theory of Drama*. New York: Viking, 1975

Goodheart, Eugene. *The Failure of Criticism*. Cambridge, Mass.: Harvard University Press, 1978

Goodman, Nelson. *Ways of Worldmaking*. Indianapolis: Hockett, 1978

Grave, S. A. *The Scottish Philosophy of Common Sense*. Oxford: Clarendon, 1960

Grob, Alan. *The Philosophic Mind: A Study of Wordsworth's Poetry and Thought, 1797–1805*. Columbus, Ohio: Ohio State University Press, 1973

Guyer, Paul. *Kant and the Claims of Taste*. Cambridge, Mass.: Harvard University Press, 1979

Hagstrum, Jean. *William Blake, Poet and Painter: An Introduction to the Illuminated Verse*. Chicago: University of Chicago Press, 1964, 1978

The Romantic Body: Love and Sexuality in Keats, Wordsworth, and Blake. Knoxville: University of Tennessee Press, 1985

Halévy, Elie. *The Growth of Philosophical Radicalism* (1901–4), trans. Mary Morris. London: Faber & Faber, 1928

Hampshire, Stuart. *Thought and Action*. London: Chatto & Windus, 1959

Handwerk, Gary J. *Irony and Ethics in Narrative: From Schlegel to Lacan*. New Haven: Yale University Press, 1985

Harding, Anthony John. *Coleridge and the Idea of Love*. Cambridge: Cambridge University Press, 1974

Hare, R. M. *The Language of Morals*. Oxford: Oxford University Press, 1952

Hartman, Geoffrey, ed. *Deconstruction and Criticism*. New York: Continuum Publishing, 1979

  Wordsworth's Poetry 1787–1814. New Haven: Yale University Press, 1964

  The Unremarkable Wordsworth. Minneapolis: University of Minnesota Press, 1987

Hauerwas, Stanley and MacIntyre, Alasdair, eds. *Revisions: Changing Perspectives in Moral Philosophy*. Notre Dame, Ind.: University of Notre Dame Press, 1983

Haven, Richard. *Patterns of Consciousness: An Essay on Coleridge*. Amherst: University of Massachusetts Press, 1969

Heidegger, Martin. *Being and Time*. trans. John Macquarrie and Edward Robinson. Oxford: Blackwell, 1967

Heller, Erich. *The Disinherited Mind: Essays in Modern German Literature and Thought*. Cambridge: Bowes & Bowes, 1952

Hirsch, Eric Donald. *Innocence and Experience: An Introduction to Blake*, 2nd edn. Chicago: University of Chicago Press, 1975

  Wordsworth and Schelling: A Typological Study of Romanticism. New Haven: Yale University Press, 1960

Hobsbawm, Eric J. *The Age of Revolution: 1789–1848*. Cleveland: World, 1962

Hudson, W. D. *Modern Moral Philosophy*. New York: Anchor, 1970

  Reason and Right: A Critical Examination of Richard Price's Moral Philosophy. London: Macmillan, 1970

Huxley, Aldous. *Point Counter Point* (1928). New York: Harper & Row, 1965

James, D. G. *The Romantic Comedy: An Essay on English Romanticism*. London: Oxford University Press, 1948

Jameson, Fredric. *The Political Unconscious: Narrative as a Socially Symbolic Act*. Ithaca, N. Y.: Cornell University Press, 1981

Johnston, Kenneth. *Wordsworth and 'The Recluse.'* New Haven: Yale University Press, 1984

Jones, John. *The Egotistical Sublime: A History of Wordsworth's Imagination*. London: Chatto & Windus, 1954

Kaufman, Walter. *From Shakespeare to Existentialism*. New York: Doubleday, 1960

  Nietzsche: Philosopher, Psychologist, Antichrist. New York: Vintage, 1968

Keach, William. *Shelley's Style*. New York: Methuen, 1984

Kenny, Anthony. *Action, Emotion, and Will*. New York: Humanities Press, 1963

Kermode, Frank. *Romantic Image*. New York: Macmillan, 1957

Kinnaird, John. *William Hazlitt: Critic of Power*. New York: Columbia University Press, 1978

Krieger, Murray. "In the Wake of Morality: The Thematic Underside of Recent Theory," *New Literary History*, 15 (1983), 119–36

Kroner, Richard. *Von Kant bis Hegel*. 2 vols. Tübingen: J. C. B. Mohr, 1921

Kuhns, Richard. *Structures of Experience: Essays on the Affinity between Philosophy and Literature.* New York: Basic Books, 1970

LaCapra, Dominick. *Rethinking Intellectual History: Texts, Contexts, Language.* Ithaca, N. Y.: Cornell University Press, 1983

Langbaum, Robert. *The Mysteries of Identity: A Theme in Modern Literature.* New York: Oxford University Press, 1977

  The Poetry of Experience: The Dramatic Monologue in Modern Literary Tradition. New York: W. W. Norton, 1957

Leavis, F. R. *The Common Pursuit.* London: Chatto & Windus, 1952

  Revaluation: Tradition and Development in English Poetry. London: Chatto & Windus, 1936

Leighton, Angela. *Shelley and the Sublime.* Cambridge: Cambridge University Press, 1984

Levi, Albert William. *Literature, Philosophy, and the Imagination.* Bloomington: Indiana University Press, 1962

Levin, David. "The Moral Relativism of Marxism," *The Philosophical Forum,* 15 (1984), 249–79

Lévy-Bruhl, Lucien. *History of Modern Philosophy in France* (1899). New York: Burt Franklin, 1971

Lindop, Grevel. *The Opium Eater: A Life of Thomas De Quincey.* New York: Taplinger Publishing, 1981

Locke, Don. *A Fantasy of Reason: The Life and Thought of William Godwin.* London: Routledge & Kegan Paul, 1980

Lockridge, Laurence S. "Coleridge and the Perils of 'Self-Realization,' " in *Coleridge's Theory of the Imagination Today,* ed. Christine Gallant. New York: AMS Press, 1989

  Coleridge the Moralist. Ithaca, N. Y.: Cornell University Press, 1977

  "Explaining Coleridge's Explanation: Toward a Practical Methodology for Coleridge Studies," in *Reading Coleridge: Approaches and Applications,* ed. Walter Crawford. Ithaca, N. Y.: Cornell University Press, 1979

Lockridge, Laurence S., Maynard, John and Stone, Donald, eds. *Nineteenth-Century Lives.* Cambridge: Cambridge University Press, 1989

Lovejoy, A. O. "Coleridge and Kant's Two Worlds," in *Essays in the History of Ideas.* Baltimore: The Johns Hopkins University Press, 1948

  The Great Chain of Being: A Study in the History of an Idea (1936). New York: Harper, 1960

Lyotard, Jean-François and Thebaud, Jean-Loup. *Just Gaming,* trans. Wlad Godzich. Minneapolis: University of Minnesota Press, 1985

MacIntyre, Alasdair. *After Virtue: A Study in Moral Theory.* Notre Dame, Ind.: University of Notre Dame Press, 1981

  A Short History of Ethics. New York: Macmillan, 1966

Magnuson, Paul. *Coleridge and Wordsworth: A Lyrical Dialogue.* Princeton: Princeton University Press, 1988

Mandelbaum, Maurice. *History, Man, and Reason: A Study in Nineteenth-Century Thought.* Baltimore: The Johns Hopkins University Press, 1971

471

Manning, Peter J. *Byron and His Fictions*. Detroit: Wayne State University Press, 1978

Marcuse, Herbert. *Reason and Revolution: Hegel and the Rise of Social Theory*. London: Oxford University Press, 1941

Marshall, Peter. *William Godwin: Philosopher, Novelist, Revolutionary*. New Haven: Yale University Press, 1984

McCormick, P. "Moral Knowledge and Fiction," *Journal of Aesthetics and Art Criticism*, 41 (1983), 399–410

McFarland, Thomas. *Coleridge and the Pantheist Tradition*. Oxford: Clarendon Press, 1969

　Romanticism and the Forms of Ruin: Wordsworth, Coleridge, and the Modalities of Fragmentation. Princeton: Princeton University Press, 1981

McGann, Jerome J. *Fiery Dust: Byron's Poetic Development*. Chicago: University of Chicago Press, 1968

　The Romantic Ideology: A Critical Investigation. Chicago: University of Chicago Press, 1983

McKean, Keith. *The Moral Measure of Literature*. Denver: Alan Swallow, 1961

McKeon, Richard. *Thought, Action, and Passion*. Chicago: University of Chicago Press, 1954

McKusick, James. *Coleridge's Philosophy of Language*. New Haven: Yale University Press, 1986

Mellor, Anne K. *English Romantic Irony*. Cambridge, Mass.: Harvard University Press, 1980

Mileur, Jean-Pierre. *Vision and Revision: Coleridge's Art of Immanence*. Berkeley: University of California Press, 1982

Miller, J. Hillis. *The Disappearance of God: Five Nineteenth-Century Writers*. Cambridge, Mass.: Harvard University Press, 1963

　The Ethics of Reading: Kant, de Man, Eliot, Trollope, James, and Benjamin. New York: Columbia University Press, 1987

　"Prosopopoeia and *Praeterita*," in *Nineteenth-Century Lives*, ed. Lockridge et al.

Mitchell, W. J. T. *Blake's Composite Art: A Study of the Illuminated Poetry*. Princeton: Princeton University Press, 1978

Moore, G. E. *Ethics*. New York: Holt, 1912

　Principia Ethica. Cambridge: Cambridge University Press, 1903

Mothersill, Mary. "Moral Philosophy and Meta-Ethics," *The Journal of Philosophy*, 49 (1952), 587–94

Muirhead, John. *Coleridge as Philosopher*. London: Allen & Unwin, 1930

Murdoch, Iris. *The Sovereignty of Good*. London: Routledge & Kegan Paul, 1970

Murry, John Middleton. *Keats*. New York: Noonday Press, 1955

Natanson, M. "The Schematism of Moral Agency," *New Literary History*, 15 (1983), 13–23

Nielsen, Kai. "Alienation and Self-realization," *Philosophy*, 48 (1973), 21–33

Norman, Richard. *The Moral Philosophers: An Introduction to Ethics*. Oxford: Clarendon, 1983

Noyes, Russell. *William Wordsworth*. New York: Twayne, 1971

Nozick, Robert. *Philosophical Explanations*. Cambridge, Mass.: Harvard University Press, 1981

Nussbaum, Martha. *The Fragility of Goodness*. New York: Cambridge University Press, 1985

Ohmann, Richard. "Speech Acts and the Definition of Literature," *Philosophy and Rhetoric*, 4 (1971), 1–19

Olafson, Frederick A. *The Dialectic of Action: A Philosophical Theory of History and the Humanities*. Chicago: University of Chicago Press, 1979

Olsen, Stein. *The Structures of Literary Understanding*. Cambridge: Cambridge University Press, 1978

Onorato, Richard. *The Character of the Poet: Wordsworth in The Prelude*. Princeton: Princeton University Press, 1971

Orel, Harold. *English Romantic Poets and the Enlightenment: Nine Essays on a Literary Relationship*. Oxfordshire: Voltaire Foundation, 1973

Orsini, G. N. G. *Coleridge and German Idealism*. Carbondale and Edwardsville, Ill.: Southern Illinois University Press, 1967

Paley, Morton. *Energy and Imagination: A Study of the Development of Blake's Thought*. Oxford: Clarendon Press, 1970

Paton, H. J. *The Categorical Imperative: A Study in Kant's Moral Philosophy*. London: Hutchinson's University Library, 1947

Peckham, Morse. *Beyond the Tragic Vision: The Quest for Identity in the Nineteenth Century*. New York: George Braziller, 1962.

Romanticism and Behavior: Collected Essays II. Columbia: University of South Carolina Press, 1973

Romanticism and Ideology. Greenwood, Fl.: Penkevill, 1985

The Triumph of Romanticism: Collected Essays. Columbia: University of South Carolina Press, 1970

Penelhum, Terence. "Personal Identity," in *The Encyclopedia of Philosophy*, ed. Paul Edwards, 8 vols. New York: Macmillan, 1967

Perkins, David. *Wordsworth and the Poetry of Sincerity*. Cambridge, Mass.: Harvard University Press, 1964

Piaget, Jean. *Structuralism*, trans. Chaninah Maschler. London: Routledge & Kegan Paul, 1971

Plamenatz, John. *The English Utilitarians*, rev. edn. Oxford: Blackwell, 1958

Pulos, C. E. *The Deep Truth: A Study of Shelley's Scepticism*. Lincoln: University of Nebraska Press, 1954

Punter, David. *Blake, Hegel, and Dialectic*. Amsterdam: Rodopi, 1982

Rajan, Tilottama. *Dark Interpreter: The Discourse of Romanticism*. Ithaca, N. Y.: Cornell University Press, 1980

Randall, John Herman, Jnr. *The Career of Philosophy: From the Middle Ages to the Enlightenment*. New York: Columbia University Press, 1962

The Career of Philosophy: From the Enlightenment to the Age of Darwin. New York: Columbia University Press, 1965

Raphael, D. Daiches. "Can Literature be Moral Philosophy?" *New Literary History*, 15 (1983), 1–12

The Moral Sense. London: Oxford University Press, 1947

Rashdall, Hastings. *Theory of Good and Evil* (1907). 2 vols. London: Oxford University Press, 1924

Rawls, John. *A Theory of Justice*. Cambridge, Mass.: Harvard University Press, 1971

Reiman, Donald. *Shelley's "Triumph of Life": A Critical Study*. Urbana: University of Illinois Press, 1965

Reiman, Donald, Jaye, Michael, and Bennett, Betty, eds. *The Evidence of the Imagination: Studies of Interactions between Life and Art in English Romantic Literature*. New York: New York University Press, 1978

Richetti, John. *Philosophical Writing: Locke, Berkeley, Hume*. Cambridge, Mass.: Harvard University Press, 1983

Ricoeur, Paul. *The Symbolism of Evil*, trans. Emerson Buchanan. Boston: Beacon Press, 1967

 Time and Narrative, trans. Kathleen McLaughlin and David Pellauer. 2 vols. Chicago: Chicago University Press, 1984, 1985

Robbe-Grillet, Alain. *For a New Novel: Essays on Fiction*, trans. Richard Howard. New York: Grove Press, 1965

Roberts, Mark. *The Tradition of Romantic Morality*. London: Macmillan, 1973

Robson, W. W. "Byron as Poet," *Proceedings of the British Academy*, 43 (1957), 25–62.

Rorty, Amelie, ed. *The Identity of Persons*. Berkeley: University of California Press, 1976

Ross, Sir David. *The Right and the Good*. Oxford: Clarendon Press, 1930

Russell, Bertrand. *A History of Western Philosophy*. New York: Simon & Schuster, 1945

Sabin, Margery. *English Romanticism and the French Tradition*. Cambridge, Mass.: Harvard University Press, 1976

Said, Edward. *The World, the Text, and the Critic*. Cambridge, Mass.: Harvard University Press, 1983

Sammons, Jeffrey. *Literary Sociology and Practical Criticism: An Inquiry*. Bloomington: Indiana University Press, 1977

Sartre, Jean-Paul. *Being and Nothingness*, trans. Hazel E. Barnes. New York: Citadel, 1971

 Existential Psychoanalysis, trans. Barnes. Chicago: Henry Regnery, 1962

Schorer, Mark. *William Blake: The Politics of Vision*. New York: Henry Holt, 1946

Scrivener, Michael Henry. *Radical Shelley: The Philosophical Anarchism and Utopian Thought of Percy Bysshe Shelley*. Princeton: Princeton University Press, 1982

Searle, John R. *Expression and Meaning: Studies in the Theory of Speech Acts*. Cambridge: Cambridge University Press, 1979

Sheats, Paul. *The Making of Wordsworth's Poetry, 1785–1798*. Cambridge, Mass.: Harvard University Press, 1973

Sidgwick, Henry. *Outlines of the History of Ethics*. London: Macmillan, 1886

Siebers, Tobin. *The Ethics of Criticism*. Ithaca, N. Y.: Cornell University Press, 1988

Smith, Barbara Herrnstein. "Actions, Fictions, and the Ethics of Interpretation," *Centrum*, 3 (1975), 117–24

"Contingencies of Value," *Critical Inquiry*, 10 (1983), 1–35

Stallknecht, Newton P. *Strange Seas of Thought*. Durham, N. C.: Duke University Press, 1945

Sperry, Stuart. *Keats the Poet*. Princeton: Princeton University Press, 1973

Stephen, Leslie. *The English Utilitarians*. 3 vols. London: Duckworth, 1900

A History of English Thought in the Eighteenth Century (1876). London: John Murray, 1902

Stevenson, C. L. *Ethics and Language*. New Haven: Yale University Press, 1944

Stillinger, Jack. "The Hoodwinking of Madeline: Scepticism in *The Eve of St. Agnes*," in *Keats: A Collection of Critical Essays*, ed. Walter Jackson Bate. Englewood Cliffs, N. J.: Prentice-Hall, 1964

The Texts of Keats's Poems. Cambridge, Mass.: Harvard University Press, 1974

Strawson, P. F. *Individuals*. Garden City: Doubleday, 1963

Swabey, W. C. *Ethical Theory from Hobbes to Kant*. New York: Citadel Press, 1961

Taylor, Charles. *The Explanation of Behavior*. New York: Humanities Press, 1964

Hegel. Cambridge: Cambridge University Press, 1975

Thompson, E. P. *The Making of the English Working Class*. New York: Random House, 1963

Thorslev, Peter L., Jnr. *The Byronic Hero: Types and Prototypes*. Minneapolis: University of Minnesota Press, 1962

Romantic Contraries: Freedom versus Destiny. New Haven: Yale University Press, 1984

Trawick, Leonard. "William Blake's German Connection," *Colby Library Quarterly*, 13 (1970), 229–45

Trilling, Lionel. *A Gathering of Fugitives*. New York: Harcourt, Brace, 1977

Sincerity and Authenticity. Cambridge, Mass.: Harvard University Press, 1972

Vendler, Helen. *The Odes of John Keats*. Cambridge, Mass.: Harvard University Press, 1983

Ward, Aileen. *John Keats: The Making of a Poet*. New York: Viking Press, 1963; rev. Farrar, Straus, and Giroux, 1986

" 'That Last Infirmity of Noble Mind': Keats and the Idea of Fame," in *The Evidence of the Imagination*, ed. Reiman *et al.*, 312–33

Warnock, G. E. *Morality and Language*. Oxford: Basil Blackwell, 1983

Wasserman, Earl R. *Shelley: A Critical Study*. Baltimore: The Johns Hopkins University Press, 1971

Weaver, Richard M. *The Ethics of Rhetoric*. Chicago: Henry Regnery, 1953

Weiskel, Thomas. *The Romantic Sublime: Studies in the Structure and Psychology of Transcendence*. Baltimore: The Johns Hopkins University Press, 1976

Wellek, René. *Confrontations: Studies in the Intellectual and Literary Relations between Germany, England, and the United States during the Nineteenth Century*. Princeton: Princeton University Press, 1965

The Romantic Age, in *A History of Modern Criticism, 1750–1950*, Vol. II. New Haven: Yale University Press, 1955

West, Paul. *Byron and the Spoiler's Art*. New York: St. Martin's Press, 1960

White, Hayden. *The Emergence of Liberal Humanism: An Intellectual History of Western Europe*. New York: McGraw-Hill, 1966–70

"The Value of Narrativity in the Representation of Reality," *Critical Inquiry*, 7 (1980), 5–27

Wilkie, Brian and Johnson, Mary Lynn. *Blake's Four Zoas: The Design of a Dream*. Cambridge, Mass.: Harvard University Press, 1978

Willey, Basil. *The Eighteenth-Century Background: Studies on the Idea of Nature in the Thought of the Period*. London: Chatto & Windus, 1940

The English Moralists. London: Chatto & Windus, 1964

Nineteenth-Century Studies: Coleridge to Arnold. New York: Columbia University Press, 1949

Williams, Bernard. *Ethics and the Limits of Philosophy*. Cambridge, Mass.: Harvard University Press, 1985

Williams, Raymond. *The Country and the City*. New York: Oxford University Press, 1973

Culture and Society, 1780–1950. New York: Columbia University Press, 1958

Wimsatt, William K. "Poetry and Morals: A Relation Reargued," in *The Verbal Icon* (with Monroe Beardsley). Lexington: University of Kentucky Press, 1954

Winters, Yvor. *In Defense of Reason*. Denver: University of Denver Press, 1942

Wittgenstein, Ludwig. "Lecture on Ethics," *Philosophical Review*, 74 (1965), 3–12

Philosophical Investigations, trans. G. E. M. Anscombe. Oxford: Blackwell, 1953

Wollheim, Richard. *The Thread of Life*. Cambridge, Mass.: Harvard University Press, 1984

Woodring, Carl. *Politics in English Romantic Poetry*. Cambridge, Mass.: Harvard University Press, 1970

"Shaping Life in *The Prelude*," in *Nineteenth-Century Lives*, ed. Lockridge *et al*.

Wordsworth, Jonathan. *William Wordsworth: The Borders of Vision*. Oxford: Clarendon Press, 1982

Wylie, Ruth. "The Present Status of Self Theory," in *Handbook of Personality Theory and Research*, ed. Edgar Borgatta and William Lambert. New York: Rand McNally, 1968

Index

Abbey, Lloyd, 284–5, 288
Abrams, M. H., 21n, 40n, 58, 452n
absurdism, 4, 255–8
action, 3–4, 8, 33, 148; Blakean, 166–78,
179; in Blake, Fichte, and Lavater, 91;
in *The Borderers*, 222; conflicts with
value, 154; De Quinceyan, 257–9, 265;
distinguished from activity, 121–2;
Keatsian, 407–8, 414; Keats and Byron
compared on, 381; the Romantics on,
51–2, 384; Shelleyan source of, 308;
sympathy as, 76; Wordsworthian,
235–6, 246–7; as writing, 226, 429–30,
455–6
Addison, Joseph (1672–1719), 41, 165,
265, 454
Adler, Alfred, 120
aesthetics, and Kantian ethics, 78–81;
relation to ethics in De Quincey,
268–9
affections, 43, 52, 76, 136; the Romantics
on, *58–63*; Wordsworthian, 217
agent, 4, 18, 33, 48, 148, 154; in
associationist psychology, 63; Blakean
Zoas as agencies, not agents, 170 and
n; contrasted with moral judge, 51; in
De Quincey, 270; in German idealism,
82; mind as, in Hazlitt, 354;
Prometheus as, 294; in Wordsworth,
225, 235–6, 243; as worker in Keats,
387; as writer, 455–6
Albee, Edward, 28
Allport, G. W., 121
Altieri, Charles, 24n, 456n
anarchism, 20; affinity with Romantic
utopianism, *105–8*; in Blake's politics,

167, 168, 202; Godwinian, 138–9;
Shelleyan, 308, 330–1
Anderson, Quentin, 26
Aristippus of Cyrene (4th c. B.C.), 438,
440
Aristotle (384–22 B.C.), 2, 33, 120, 122,
123, 139, 145, 151, 266, 324, 399, 439n;
Poetics, 33, 162, 229, 408, 459;
Nicomachean Ethics, 121, 238, 317n;
Chicago Aristotelians, 458
Arnold, Matthew (1822–88), 133, 145,
384, 407, 459; on the Romantics, 1–2;
"Empedocles on Etna," 462
associationism, Coleridge on, 61–3;
Hazlitt on, 337–8, 349, 356–7;
Wordsworthian, 206, 233–4
Augustine, St., of Hippo (345–430),
Confessions, 229
Austen, Jane (1775–1817), *Emma*, 454
Averill, James, 59n, 212n, 214

Babbitt, Irving (1865–1933), 17, 18, 22,
26, 40, 50, 58, 79, 82, 129; Shelley
and, 305–7; *Rousseau and Romanticism*,
14–16
Bacon, Francis, (1516–1626), 72
Bailey, Benjamin (1791–1853), 392, 405,
412
Baker, Herschel, 346n
Balguy, John (1686–1748), 40, 42, 44, 70
Balzac, Honoré de (1799–1850), 129, 352,
430
Bate, Walter Jackson, 383n, 411n
Baudelaire, Charles (1821–67), 277
Bayley, John, 420n
Beaty, Frederick L., 420n

477